TRANSFERS OF PROPERTY IN ELEVENTH-CENTURY NORMAN LAW

TRANSFERS OF PROPERTY IN ELEVENTH-CENTURY NORMAN LAW

EMILY ZACK TABUTEAU

THE UNIVERSITY OF NORTH CAROLINA PRESS
CHAPEL HILL AND LONDON

The publication
of this work was made possible in part through
a grant from the Division of Research Programs of the
National Endowment for the Humanities, an independent federal
agency whose mission is to award grants to support education,
scholarship, media programming, libraries, and museums,
in order to bring the results of cultural activities
to a broad, general public.

Library of Congress Cataloging-in-Publication Data

Tabuteau, Emily Zack.
Transfers of property in eleventh-century Norman law / by Emily Zack Tabuteau.
p. cm.—(Studies in legal history)
Revision of thesis (Ph.D.)—Harvard University.
Bibliography: p.
Includes index.
ISBN 0-8078-1774-0 (alk. paper)
1. Land titles—Registration and transfer—France—Normandy—History. 2. Feudal law—France—Normandy—History. I. Title. II. Series.
KJW3181.52.T33 1988
346.44'20436—dc19   87-21736
[344.206436]   CIP

The paper in this book meets the guidelines for
permanence and durability of the Committee on
Production Guidelines for Book Longevity of the Council
on Library Resources.

92 91 90 89 88   5 4 3 2 1

TO MY PARENTS

Contents

Preface and Acknowledgments

In a book of this sort, the translation of names poses a problem. For personal names, I have translated first names into modern English or occasionally French equivalents, if such exist. I have rendered toponyms into French whenever possible; place names which are left in the Latin are italicized. I have turned patronymics into "son of . . ." in most instances, though a few conventional fitzes—fitz Osbern, for example—remain. Unless the translation of a nickname seemed incontrovertible, I have kept the Latin form. Most of these choices have no better rhyme or reason than that I am comfortable with the results.

Several steps have been taken to reduce the inordinate length of the notes. First, references to discursive primary sources and to secondary sources use short titles only. The full details will be found in the Bibliography. Second, each document cited has been assigned a number, and the number alone appears in the notes. Full citations, with dates of the documents, indications of the beneficiaries of the acts, and comments on the quality of some individual pieces, are in Appendix B, Documents Cited. Third, the original version of a passage translated in the text is not reproduced in the notes if the passage comes from a document which has been printed and if the exact wording is not an issue. Because of the varying age and quality of both the publications and the manuscript copies of the sources, the notes make no attempt to reproduce orthographical anomalies such as -ę (which is rendered -e) or to follow the medieval system of punctuation in unpublished documents.

This book has been a long time in the making, and in the course of the years I have benefited from the help and encouragement of many institutions and persons whom I am now privileged to thank. First and foremost, I thank Professor Samuel E. Thorne, who suggested the topic and oversaw the original stages of the work. Without him, this book would not have come to be. In its evolution, drafts of the book have been read, in whole or in large part, by Elizabeth A. R. Brown, Charles R. Donahue, Thomas A. Green, and Stephen D. White; and I have also profited from discussion with David Bates. The book is much the better for their suggestions and corrections. I am grateful to David Bates, Jean-Michel Bouvris, Marjorie Chibnall, Warren Hollister, Eleanor Searle, James Ross Sweeney, and Stephen D. White for providing me with offprints and/or prepublication drafts of articles cited in the bibliography. I have thanked in the appropriate places several scholars who provided specific information or saved me from committing mistakes. In matters of style, I am greatly indebted to Harold Marcus. All remaining errors of fact and argument and infelicities of style and organization are, of course, entirely my own.

Much of the research on which the book is based was done in the archives and libraries of Paris and Normandy, specifically, the Bibliothèque Nationale in Paris, the Archives Départementales of the Calvados, the Eure, the Orne, and the Seine-Maritime, the municipal libraries of Avranches and Rouen, the library of the University of Caen, and the Musée de la Bénédictine de Fécamp. I am grateful to the directors and the staffs of all these depositories for providing access to their collections and assistance with the varied problems which arise as one does research in such sources. I have received much financial support over the years: both a Graduate Prize Fellowship and a Frederick W. Sheldon Traveling Fellowship from Harvard University, an Andrew W. Mellon Postdoctoral Fellowship in the Humanities from the Mellon Foundation and Duke University, and a Humanities Research Center summer grant from Michigan State University. Though it was primarily intended for other research, my recent sabbatical, funded in part by a grant from the American Bar Foundation and an All-University Research Initiation Grant from Michigan State, enabled me to clear up a few cloudy points.

Along the way, good friends have provided invaluable services. Milton Dickman, who taught me Latin, helped me with knotty problems of translation and proofread all the original footnotes. I wish that he had lived to see the book. Carol Barker, too, proofread valiantly. Mary Beth Norton helped mightily in a moment of crisis. G. Edward White, who until recently oversaw Studies in Legal History for the American Society for Legal History, and Lewis Bateman of the University of North Carolina Press have, between them, made the production of a first book much less traumatic than I had imagined it might be.

I have dedicated this book to my parents, Jacob Bernard Zack and Marion Millstein Zack, in loving tribute to their help and encouragement, which have ranged from proofreading to chicken soup and are beyond the power of mere words to describe.

1

Introduction

THIS WORK attempts to determine the nature and content of one aspect of the law of Normandy in the eleventh century, the earliest period during which that law can be studied. The material is scarce, which doubtless explains why such a study has not been attempted before now. Modern scholarship concerning Normandy in the tenth and eleventh centuries has concentrated on a few areas, none of them legal: the nature of the Viking settlement in Normandy and the degree of continuity between Normandy after 911 and Viking Scandinavia or the Carolingian kingdom; the development of ducal power and governmental institutions;[1] and the history of the church in Normandy, especially the reestablishment of ecclesiastical institutions after the Viking conquest. The nine hundredth anniversary of the Norman conquest of England produced a deluge of books, relatively few of them of scholarly value. Current research is sometimes indirectly of interest to legal historians: work on the economic development of individual churches has produced information on certain types of alienations, and study of the development and nature of ducal power and government has increased knowledge about various aspects of public and criminal law. Private law in Normandy in the tenth and eleventh centuries, however, is an undeveloped field of investigation.

The advantages of determining the law of Normandy in the eleventh century are considerable. The subject not only is intrinsically interesting but also forms a valuable background to studies of the later development of Norman law. In the past century these studies have been actively pursued by many scholars.[2] Their works, however, usually begin with the first Norman custumal, the *Très Ancien Coutumier* of the end of the twelfth century,[3] taking perhaps a glance back at how in the course of the twelfth century the law recorded in the *Très Ancien Coutumier* developed but hardly making an attempt to extend the inquiry earlier than that. Yet, though the *Très Ancien Coutumier* is especially significant as the earliest custumal to have been written anywhere in France, it records law which had been in the process of formation for nearly three centuries; and reconstruction of the earlier stages, insofar as it is possible, should prove illuminating.

The present study may thus be considered an effort to reconstruct, for one aspect of the law, the custumal—a "très très ancien coutumier"—such as it might have been written in about 1100, even though I will rarely be able to address the subject of the development, as opposed to the contents, of the law by that date. Some developments are certainly perceptible, and it will be one of my principal contentions, perhaps the most important one, that the custom of Normandy was a consciously perceived legal system by the end of the eleventh century.[4] Nonetheless, for the period covered here, extant documents which refer to any one point of the law are few, come mostly from the last half century or less, and can normally be dated only within broad limits rather than to specific years.[5] In consequence, inferences about changes in the law almost always seem dubious if not downright impossible. Although a fairly static picture of Norman law will emerge, these pages, by laying a foundation for study of twelfth-century developments, should help to illuminate the process through which the law of Normandy arrived at the stage recorded in the *Très Ancien Coutumier* and thus contribute to knowledge of the process whereby medieval customary legal systems reached the forms in which they were written down in the thirteenth and later centuries.

Study of the law of Normandy in the eleventh century is also important to the early history of the Common Law of England. If, as Frank Barlow, like many another scholar, has remarked, "When we study the . . . history of English law it is difficult to be sure what contribution, either in substance or in procedure, was made by the Normans,"[6] the reason is as much the insularity of English legal studies as the irrecoverability of knowledge of Norman law.[7] Early Norman law is knowable, at least in part, although it remains largely unknown. This book will attempt to determine the legal baggage which William the Conqueror carried with him across the Channel.[8] As such it ought to cast light on the all too silent century of English legal history between the Conquest and the beginnings of Henry II's remolding of the law in the 1160s.

In some instances, the relevance of my findings to post-Conquest England will be obvious, especially my conclusion that even in the later eleventh century Normans did not live in a predominantly "feudal world," either tenurially or mentally. This contention implicitly contradicts the thesis of S. F. C. Milsom that Henry II's reforms were merely an attempt to force seigneurial courts to conform to the assumptions of an "ancient" feudal mentality, which was shared by the king, his barons, and their tenants, and that the profound changes those reforms worked were unintended consequences of a series of measures which had no such dramatic purposes.[9] It is not my purpose to engage in a debate about the situation in late twelfth-century England, nor would it be appropriate to argue directly from eleventh-century Normandy to conditions a century later in another country. Nevertheless, I wish to emphasize that this study shows that, although Normandy was undoubtedly predominantly tenurial by the late eleventh century, it was by no means predominantly feudal, unless "tenurial" and "feudal" are taken as synonyms, which they should not be.[10]

A study of early Norman law ought to begin at the beginning, with the establishment of Normans in Normandy in 911. In practice, however, this is impossible for lack of documents. Nor does this study end where it perhaps should, in 1066. Instead, I have carried it down to 1106, again for practical reasons. The number of Norman documents from the forty years after the Norman Conquest of England is much greater than the number from the entire century before the Conquest,[11] especially documents in which the lay participants are not from the most exalted levels of society. Because a certain amount of distortion is more or less likely in cases involving the great, it seemed important to base my investigation as much as possible on cases involving persons of lesser importance.[12] This study could not have been done if its only sources had been documents dating from 1066 or earlier. It would, perhaps, have been possible to stop in 1087; but the material would still have been thin. Moreover, the most specific problem with using documents from after 1066 applies at least as much to the reign of William the Conqueror as to the rule of Robert Curthose.[13] There was no reason, therefore, not to continue through 1106.

I have, however, deliberately excluded later records. The paucity of contemporary sources has often encouraged historians to turn for information to the much more numerous documents produced in Normandy in the twelfth and even in the thirteenth century. Two great feudal documents, the Bayeux Inquest of 1133 and the Inquest of 1172, for example, are consistently called upon to illuminate not only their own times but the Normandy of a century earlier.[14] The temptation to use all this material is strong, understandably, but the danger of using it is equally great. I have argued elsewhere that it is anachronistic to use the twelfth-century inquests to study feudal tenure in the eleventh century,[15] and the same argument applies to sources of information about other matters. If one approaches documents as ill-drafted and erratic as the charters of eleventh-century Normandy with preconceived notions, acquired through the study of later documents, one may well find what one seeks even though it is not there.[16] The problem is, indeed, even broader. One of the greatest historians of the law of Normandy accepts as an explicit methodological principle that "the origins of Norman law ought to be studied only on the basis of the better known law of the thirteenth century."[17] Such a method is widely practiced, but it is self-defeating. If, as I am inclined to believe, there was a good deal of development and change in the course of the Middle Ages, even from one century to the next, then sources from one century do not illustrate conditions in an earlier century; if they are used to do so, the resulting picture is misleading. If I am wrong and the pace of change was slow, the absence of change cannot be proved unless each period is studied on the basis only of contemporary documents. Otherwise, one assumes what one is trying to prove, and one's reasoning becomes circular.[18]

To argue thus is not to reify the centuries, which remain mere historians' conventions. In effect, the "eleventh" century studied here begins in the 960s, with the earliest surviving Norman charter,[19] and ends in 1106. Most of the sources come from the latest few decades. Hence one cannot assume that because something is first mentioned in a particular year it began only then or only shortly before then. In addition, a particular problem in using documents from the forty years after the Conquest is that practices adopted or developed by the Normans in England may have influenced the development of law in Normandy. Some Anglo-Norman influence on Normandy in this period is admitted by almost every writer who has raised the issue.[20] Indeed, I agree with recent scholarship which emphasizes the importance of the Normans' new opportunities in England for the form feudal tenure eventually took on both sides of the Channel.[21] The risk that between 1066 and 1106 the purity of legal development in Normandy was contaminated by practices first developed in England is, nonetheless, outweighed by the advantages to be gained from studying the more abundant documents afforded by that period. Until 1106, any contamination by specifically English practices was probably relatively slight.[22] The two areas were united for twenty-five of the forty years, from 1066 to 1087 under William the Conqueror, whose outlook and orientation remained Norman throughout his reign, and from 1096 to 1100 under William Rufus, who held Normandy in mortgage from his brother Duke Robert Curthose. It was only in 1106 that an English king with a somewhat English orientation took permanent control of Normandy.[23] Moreover, the barons of Normandy were the same men as the barons of England throughout this period, and their outlook, too, remained Norman.[24] Also, it is likely that many of the resemblances between post-Conquest England and Normandy derive not from the deliberate introduction of the practices of one area into the other but from pragmatic solutions to similar problems as yet unsolved on either side of the Channel.[25] Finally, whatever contamination may have occurred is a problem only with reference to the influence of Norman law on English law; for the development of Norman law itself, English influence, where it can be demonstrated, is merely a relevant fact.

Many influences on Norman law other than Anglo-Norman practice have been alleged, including the customs of other areas of France, Roman law, and canon law. None was important in a general way before the thirteenth century; certainly, little influence can be traced as far back as the eleventh century.[26] Scholarly discussion has been concerned principally not with influences but with sources: was Norman law an inheritance from the Carolingian Frankish past of the territory or from the traditions of the Scandinavian invaders? The few other alleged sources—pre-Frankish or pre-Norman non-Frankish—have been easily excluded from consideration.[27]

The debate over whether Normandy followed Scandinavian or Carolingian practice, with its ancillary questions, has produced much of the recent literature on early Normandy.[28] Predominant continuity with the Scandinavian past of the invading Normans has had its defenders and still does; but Frankish influence is, at present, generally recognized as more important. Scandinavian influence is seen only in scattered survivals in particular aspects of life, especially criminal offenses and penalties, maritime law and practice, and, perhaps, marriage customs.[29] A few authors suggest other areas of influence,[30] but it is also possible to reject even the ones which are generally recognized.[31] Carolingian influence, in contrast, is now seen in almost every aspect of life in Normandy in the tenth, eleventh, and even twelfth centuries, including the position of the duke, his rights, the duchy's frontiers, its internal subdivisions and its governmental, military, and domainal organization.[32] Much work has been done on the nature of the Viking conquest of and settlement in Normandy and the numbers of invaders who settled there. Some consensus exists that, however heavy or light settlement may have been, it was both heavier and less centrally organized in lower Normandy, especially the Cotentin peninsula, than in upper Normandy; that Scandinavian habits lasted longer in lower Normandy, which resisted the willingness of the dukes—customarily inhabiting the vicinity of Rouen in upper Normandy—to adopt French ways; and that this difference in the pace of assimilation had profound effects on Norman history at least as late as the mid-eleventh century.

The modes of transmission of Frankish institutions and practices need more attention than they have received. The impulse toward rapid assimilation most often cited is intermarriage between invading Vikings and the women of Carolingian Neustria. Aside from the women, the medium of transmission of Carolingian practice usually cited is Frankish clergy who survived the invasions, those who fled and later returned, and non-Normans who became prelates in post-Viking Normandy. Moreover, Normandy was not stripped bare of inhabitants in the course of the invasions, nor were its borders closed to French immigrants after 911.[33] Thus, peasants who stayed and immigrant lay persons of all stations may have played a significant role in ensuring continuity. Finally, Carolingian practices which survived in the areas of Normandy which were added late and were least heavily settled by Scandinavian immigrants may have been reintroduced into other parts of the duchy as late as the early eleventh century.[34]

The evidence presented in this book falls mostly on the Frankish side of the debate, at least by negation: I have found no eleventh-century Norman practice which demands a Scandinavian explanation.[35] The general similarity between eleventh-century Norman legal habits and contemporary practices in the rest of northern France is, in contrast, beyond dispute. Moreover, much in the Norman scribal tradition recalls Carolingian diplomatic practice, especially in the charters of the five great abbeys of Frankish origin which were the first to be refounded after the Norman settlement, namely, Fécamp, Jumièges, Mont-Saint-Michel, Saint-Ouen and Saint-Wandrille.[36] Some evidence of contemporary outside influence on the development of law in Normandy in the eleventh century occurs in the area of temporary and conditional tenures. The rental tenement known as a *métairie* may be an imitation of non-Norman practice, as may the use of the name "farm" for other rental tenements.[37] The use of life estates at Fécamp during the abbacy of John of Ravenna may have had something to do with John's Italian origins, though other explanations are at least equally likely.[38] Norman feudal practices may have achieved the characteristics of definiteness for which they are famous not in Normandy before 1066 but in England after the Conquest; definition may subsequently have been introduced into Normandy.[39] I do not, however, think that this conclusion carries as a corollary an important degree of Anglo-Saxon influence on Anglo-Norman feudal practice: even if the habit of precisely defining feudal obligations developed only after the Conquest and in England, the practices being defined were continental in origin and were introduced by the Normans into England.[40] All in all, in law as in most other areas, eleventh-century Normans were basically French.

2
The Sources

ELEVENTH-CENTURY NORMAN LAW has heretofore been neglected largely because almost the only sources available are charters,[1] documents drawn up for the benefit of ecclesiastical institutions—bishoprics and communities of monks or nuns, mostly the latter. With very rare exceptions, the charters were drawn up by the churches which benefited from the transactions they recorded.[2] Although the Normans established themselves in their new homeland in the early tenth century, no documents survive—probably none was produced—before the last third of the tenth century. The earliest charter in which a Norman participated in any way dates from 965; the first from a Norman alienor comes from 968; the earliest for a Norman church, from 990.[3] Only during the reign of Duke Richard II, between 996 and 1026, did the writing of charters become at all common in Normandy.[4] Toward the end of his reign, probably all at the same time, Richard issued four charters, each summing up for a particular church the gifts of his ancestors Rollo, William Longsword, and Richard I and of their men, as well as his own gifts of the preceding three decades.[5] Two of the charters explicitly recognize that transfers by Normans of earlier generations "were not written down in their own charters at all."[6] The complete absence of charters from the first half-century of the existence of Normandy and their scarcity in the next half-century, therefore, accurately reflect the extent of Norman acquaintance with the art of writing charters.

From the second quarter of the eleventh century on, both the number of extant Norman charters and the percentage originating from someone other than the duke increase steadily. Table 1 shows the increase in numbers.[7] Both changes were largely the result of a wave, which began about 1030, of foundations of monasteries and nunneries sponsored by an aristocracy which itself had just begun to emerge into prominence.[8] Another factor was probably the growing Norman familiarity with written records and their utility.[9] Indeed, in the second half of the eleventh century, assertions that the writing of charters was ancestral custom begin to be found.[10]

Even by the end of the century, however, the Normans had, unfortunately, not begun to record transactions among lay persons. Instead, these appear to have occurred entirely without charters. The only exceptions are two documents describing feudal relationships, in each of which the lord is an ecclesiastic, one account of a legal suit concerning dower which somehow made its way into the cartulary of Saint-Martin de Sées, and records of the dowers granted by Duke Richard II to his wife, Judith, and by Duke Richard III to his wife, Adela.[11] Almost certainly written by ecclesiastical institutions, the first two are invaluable to this study and the third is quite useful. The last two do little more than list the properties which constituted the dowers. Who drew them up is unknown. It may have been Dudo of Saint-Quentin, who drafted two other ducal charters, in one of which he referred to himself as the duke's *cancellarius*.[12] Nevertheless, it is beyond dispute that before 1066 no Norman lay person, not even the duke, had an organized chancery;[13] and even after 1066 almost all surviving documents were drawn up by the churches involved in the transactions recorded. Knowledge of eleventh-century Norman law perforce comes almost exclusively from ecclesiastical charters, a major problem for historians interested in the law relevant to lay persons because what did not interest the clergy rarely, if ever, was recorded.

The vast majority of the extant charters concern pious donations by lay persons to churches. Wholly or even partially unremunerated donations, however, probably occurred rarely if at all among the laity; but it is impossible to know whether they did or not. Whether lay persons used among themselves the protective techniques described at length for gifts to churches is usually a mystery. Existing information indicates that there was little difference,[14] but the information is too slight to permit a generalization. Sales, exchanges, and conditional and temporary alienations must have formed the bulk of transfers among the laity; but even here the data come from brief, rare, and incidental references in ecclesiastical charters. Moreover, it cannot be assumed that such transactions, when they took place between lay persons, were substantially identical to those in which one party was a church, for pious motives irrelevant to transactions among the laity intrude at least potentially into every transfer involving a church. In effect, everything said about the different types of transfers is more or less conditioned by the ecclesiastical nature of the sources—but it is difficult to say how much more or less.

The survival of charters has been subject to all the hazards of history: as recently as 1944 the archives of the department of the Manche, then in Saint-Lô, were almost totally destroyed. As a result of the onslaughts of time, the eleventh-century charters of some institutions are entirely lost,[15] and those which have survived are mostly copies made at different dates and of very different quality. Many of the problems thereby created are obvious. One which may not be is the matter of statistics. I have from time to time resorted to primitive statistics, but these should be regarded as indicative only: they can be regarded as suggestive at best when only an unknown percentage of the documents survives, documents are found sometimes only in abbreviated form, and there were few rules governing what was included in them in the first place.

Not all the blame for the unevenness of the sources can be placed at the door of history. Medieval archivists themselves were almost undoubtedly responsible for the very poor rate of survival of records of temporary alienations. Perhaps there always were more records of permanent alienations to churches than of the conditional gifts, mortgages, and life estates granted to or by churches; but it seems unlikely that the disproportion was as great as the extant charters suggest. Most surviving copies of charters describing such transactions concern transfers to churches, rather than by them, and show that what was initially acquired temporarily eventually became a permanent possession. Churches may often have accepted temporary alienations with the intention of converting them into permanent transfers if they could, but they cannot have been so nearly universally successful as the extant charters imply. Indeed, among the extant originals the proportion concerning temporary transactions which were never more than temporary is significantly higher than among the copies.[16] The obvious conclusion is that, when archives were organized or copies made, the persons in charge felt no need to preserve for posterity records of arrangements which had expired without creating a permanent profit for the institution.[17] The result for a modern historian is, again, to distort the picture of the actual practices of eleventh-century Normans in a way difficult to correct.

Nonetheless, the custodians of ecclesiastical archives had every interest in preserving records of permanent transfers to their institutions. The original charters, loose pieces of parchment, could get lost: "Charters which are many in number are easily either often lost through negligence or secretly subtracted by the deceit of evil men," says the preamble to one document, and it is echoed by others.[18] Eventually the usual method of preserving charters was to copy them all into a book, known as a cartulary, a method coming into use in Normandy by the end of the eleventh century.[19] The late eleventh-century cartulary compiled by La Trinité du Mont is still extant, as is a roll containing forty-nine charters for Saint-Evroul.[20] Fécamp compiled a cartulary in the early twelfth century, and Marmoutier had one before 1087 for its possessions in Normandy—both now lost.[21] Another method of preserving records of transfers, intermediate between the original charters and the cartulary, was the pancart, a charter which sums up the alienations of many persons.[22] Some of these simply transcribe most or all of the texts of individual charters and were apparently drawn up as a primitive form of cartulary. Others take this form but are introduced or followed by a notice that the duke or the church's patron confirmed all the acts copied into the document. Most often, the individual acts were only briefly summarized and the charter's principal purpose was clearly to record their confirmation by the person from whom the pancart emanates.[23] Not every church was in agreement that such measures were necessary or even desirable, for an unusually long preamble on the reasons for recording acquisitions in charters concludes: "Nevertheless, as it is certain that different things were given or bought at different times, we decided to write them down in individual accounts and individual charters, lest if they should all be written down together in the same [document] they should be thought by younger men wholly false or fictitious."[24] In hindsight, the author of this preamble was wrong. The many extant eleventh-century charters of his abbey survive because they were later copied into a cartulary;[25] and though originals are extant from many abbeys, most transfers are known because now lost originals were copied into cartularies or were summarized in pancarts which were themselves copied into cartularies. These modes of transmission of the documents pose certain problems. Cartulary copies are often truncated, especially in those parts which deal with the more common modes of assurance: acts of donation, witnesses, and signatures. In pancarts, descriptions of individual transfers are often very much abbreviated.

The scribes of the original charters also come in for reproach, for they were usually remarkably taciturn. Most charters say, in essence, no more than that so-and-so gives such-and-such property to this-or-that church. Genealogists and geographers may rejoice—many significant conclusions have been drawn from this minimal information[26]—but a legal historian is less happy. Just occasionally, two accounts of a transfer survive, one of the usual laconic sort, the other giving a great deal of supplementary detail and thereby indicating how uninformative, indeed how delusively simple, the usual notices are. The most striking example concerns a gift William the Conqueror's chaplain Rainald made to Jumièges in about 1080. The brief charter recording the gift says little more than that King William conceded the gift.[27] Some time after Rainald entered the abbey as a monk, however, a cleric named Samson claimed part of the possessions which Rainald had given. Rainald therefore drew up a memorandum detailing the very complex, in one respect quite astonishing, history of his possessions. The memorandum is outstanding among eleventh-century Norman documents both in clarity and in explicit legal reasoning; it seems, in effect, to be a brief setting out the abbey's case against the claimant.[28] Such illuminating documents, all too rare, suffice to make clear that the few surface facts reported about most known transfers must not be assumed to be the whole story.[29] Moreover, explicit statements of what the law was in Normandy in the eleventh century are virtually nonexistent, and even inferential information is scattered and thin. Perhaps the most galling silence occurs in charters which refer to disputes over possession. Simple references to disputes are numerous, but they rarely state the grounds of the claims. Records of the settlement of disputes—whether through concession, negotiation, or trial—are considerably less abundant, and only a few rehearse any of the arguments of the parties. The few exceptions—among them the memorandum of Rainald the chaplain—provide much valuable evidence,[30] making the prevalent silence all the more frustrating.

What exists is not, however, so little as to be meaningless. Elaborations on the simple formula "so-and-so gives such-and-such property to this-or-that church" are of three main types. First, references to the spiritual and material considerations in return for which alienations were made provide information on the different types of transfers which could be made. As a result, knowledge of such alienations, especially of permanent ones, is mostly concerned with the narrow subject of what alienors received in return. Charters concerning temporary alienations sometimes present more detail about the terms of transfer; yet, although such terms were of the essence of the transactions, full information is by no means always given. The second type of elaboration occurs when, in describing the property being transferred in order to identify it, a scribe notes how it had been acquired by the alienor and thereby provides knowledge of an earlier transaction, usually between lay persons. Most explicit information on the nature of the different types of transfer comes from such references. The third type of elaboration is the most common: charters usually include at least some information about how an alienation was rendered, in aspiration if not in fact, secure from later challenges; at the least, they list witnesses or signers or refer to them. The cumulative amount of information on this subject is staggering in comparison with the amount available on any other topic, as the structure of this work reflects.

Several qualifications should be made here, however. First, in any charter which survives only in a copy information about modes of assurance is likely to be more or less abbreviated, if not excised entirely. Second, the charters of individual churches display considerably different degrees of interest in the various modes of assurance which were known, and it is often difficult to decide whether these disparities reflect actual differences in practice or merely the vagaries of scribal habit.[31] Indeed, the problem exists on a much broader scale: some churches consistently betray an interest in one particular element which other churches rarely or never mention.[32] Finally—and this point applies to virtually the whole of this work—the taciturnity of the charters as a group raises a fundamental epistemological question: does an interesting detail represent a scribe's sudden fit of loquacity or does it indicate something unusual, worth mentioning in the interests either of specificity, when the detail concerns what was transferred, or of memorability, when the detail concerns how it was transferred? In other words, do charters record nothing but the exceptions to the general rules?[33] For the most part, common sense must be the guide, and it suggests that there is no single answer. Some things which are only sometimes mentioned probably usually or even always happened; others probably appear because they were out of the ordinary. Because the only outside standard on which common sense can operate in deciding whether a practice was the norm or the exception is the frequency with which it is mentioned, I have tried consistently to indicate at least the approximate rarity or frequency of mention, so that the reader may make an independent judgment.

The baffling pattern of normally minimal information interrupted here and there by illuminating, but also possibly misleading, detail is closely related to another feature of the charters, their lack of adequate formulas to convey the legal significance of the transactions they record. Certain stock phrases or clauses, similarly though rarely identically worded, were widely used, especially a clause, of ancient origins, to introduce signature lists and some other modes of assurance.[34] By and large, however, formulas characterize only the charters of individual churches. A few had achieved a more or less standard phraseology for the introductory and concluding portions of their charters.[35] On rare occasions a church uses a nearly set phrase to indicate the nature of a type of alienation.[36] These formulaic elements do not, however, bulk large in the charters as a group. There is, instead, great fluidity of language concerning even the simplest transactions[37] and virtual anarchy when complex ones are involved. From a group of charters each of which records the same sort of alienation it is often possible to put together a composite picture of the nature of the alienation; but few charters individually give the whole picture of any type of transfer, and the same is true of modes of assurance. The lack of formulas means that an inept scribe faced with a complex transaction might be incapable of writing a comprehensible record. Bad drafting, however, often takes the form of inconsistent and erratic recording, rather than of incoherence.

To all this there is a bright side of sorts. The inconsistency of the charters sometimes raises the suspicion that eleventh-century Norman scribes were scatterbrained: instead of giving elementary information about alienations, they describe apparently trivial details of the circumstances, or the like. Later, when rules of drafting were generally recognized, such idiosyncracies would have been eliminated. For a period in which sources are as poor as they are in the eleventh century, however, it is probably fortunate that set patterns and common formulas did not yet exist. The absence of formulas is frustrating; yet their very formlessness means that the charters give more information than they otherwise would. The information is fragmentary, incapable of being subjected to rigorous statistical analysis, and sometimes enigmatic; but it may be presumed that, precisely because of the lack of formulas, it was recorded in an attempt to portray the actual circumstances accurately. Formulas, once they develop, may conceal aspects of a situation, especially new developments.[38]

Sources with which to supplement the information in the charters are scarce. Eleventh- and twelfth-century Norman historians are, with one exception, of little assistance. The earliest, Dudo of Saint-Quentin, who wrote, during the reign of Duke Richard II, about the Viking conquest of Normandy and the first three dukes, is extremely untrustworthy;[39] he was, in any case, interested much more in "international" relations than in mundane matters of law or administration. Neither William of Jumièges, who finished his work in the mid-1070s, nor William of Poitiers, panegyrist of William the Conqueror, who apparently finished writing the surviving portion of his book in 1073 or 1074, has much to say about law or institutions.[40] Robert of Torigny, abbot of Mont-Saint-Michel from 1154 to 1186, wrote a highly esteemed chronicle and made interpolations to William of Jumièges's work, and his approximate contemporary Wace wrote a famous poem on Norman history; but both must be used with caution, for they are too late to be considered direct evidence on the eleventh century.[41] The eleventh-century historians, therefore, are of little help, and the later twelfth-century ones are problematic because of their date.

The exception is Orderic Vitalis, both in his *Ecclesiastical History* and in his interpolations to William of Jumièges.[42] Orderic, born in England in 1075, became a monk at Saint-Evroul in Normandy in 1085 and spent the rest of his life there. His interpolations to William of Jumièges were begun before 1109.[43] His *History* may have been begun at about the same time and was certainly under way by 1114 or 1115, but most was written after 1123 and he was still writing about the late eleventh century in the mid-1130s; he may have introduced concepts of a later time into his account.[44] He is nonetheless closer to the eleventh century than either Robert of Torigny or Wace; and as a boy at Saint-Evroul he knew men whose memories went back at least as far as mid-century, when the abbey was founded. Moreover, although Orderic set out to write a history of his abbey, he was too interested in wider events to do so; instead, he wrote a history of the Normans—in Normandy, in England, in southern Italy, on crusade—with emphasis on those who had close associations, amicable or hostile, with Saint-Evroul.[45] He thus provides incidental but invaluable information on many aspects of law. His interpolations to William of Jumièges have the same character and, therefore, a similar value, which is increased by their earlier date. Orderic also copied a good many charters of the abbey into his *History*, thus preserving them; and he often added comments which further increase their value.[46] In short, though no legal historian, he is by far the most valuable source aside from the charters.

Few others are available. Orderic's English contemporary William of Malmesbury is occasionally useful.[47] Several short historical works are of varying—sometimes disputed—value.[48] The *Consuetudines et Iusticie*, a list of ducal rights composed on the basis of an inquest held in 1091 under the joint aegis of Duke Robert Curthose and his brother King William II of England, is relevant once in a while,[49] as are the canons of the church councils held in Normandy in the eleventh century.[50] Gilbert Crispin's life of Herluin abbot of Bec and Eadmer's life of Anselm contain a little useful information.[51] I have also used a brief list of the rents and services due to the nuns of La Trinité de Caen from certain of their peasant tenants.[52] In sum, however, these miscellaneous additional sources do not substantially increase the available information on the eleventh-century Norman law of property. Most of what can be known must be deduced from the charters.

3

Permanent Alienations

PERMANENT ALIENATIONS were of three types: gifts, sales, and exchanges. In practice, it is not always easy to tell one from another, for the verb *dare* could be used not only in the technical sense of "to give" but also in the wide sense of "to transfer." There were, however, specialized verbs to indicate sales and exchanges; and I have, when possible, described these two types of alienations on the basis only of instances when the specialized verbs are used. Nonetheless, the border between the different types of alienations is, as will become evident, less a line than a no-man's-land.

GIFTS

Most transfers of property recorded in eleventh-century Norman charters were gifts. Right at the outset, therefore, the documents are misleading, for it seems unlikely that transfers among lay persons were normally gratuitous. It is ironic that, despite its preponderance, the gift is the type of transfer about which a legal theory emerges least from the documents, perhaps because everyone apparently knew what a gift was, and no one felt a need to define it. Occasionally, a charter refers to a "legal gift"[1]—but none ever says what made a gift legal. The only explicit statement extant concerning the nature of a gift comes from the memorandum of Rainald the chaplain. Concerning the legitimacy of his gift to Jumièges, Rainald says, "For as long as I was in clerical habit I held all these things undisturbed and without any claim [against them]; and, if it was rightfully conceded to St. Peter's place at Jumièges, it [the abbey] will have undisturbed everything I mentioned which I gave, since I held them undisturbed."[2] In other words, if a donor's possession was legitimate the donee's possession would be too. Several documents imply a corollary of this elementary principle, namely, that a donor could transfer as much control over possessions as he or she had but no more.[3] Both principle and corollary may have been so obvious as normally not to need stating.

Insofar as a legal theory of gifts can be discerned, their principal characteristic seems to have been that they were gratuitous acts on the part of the donors. One source contrasts a sale with a "gratuitous donation,"[4] thus confirming the overriding impression left by the charters. Nonetheless, gifts to churches were not absolutely unrequited. They were made for a reason: the salvation of the donor and sometimes of relatives, lords, and friends as well. To give one's possessions to a church was a good work: many charters begin with long preambles expressing the motive of personal salvation in exactly these terms.[5] Even charters with no such introductory passages almost always say that the motive for the gift was to save the donor's soul. Indeed, motive rather than form seems to have been the characteristic of gifts which distinguished them from sales and exchanges, for which the alienors received adequate compensation in worldly goods.

Although a donor earned merit from his or her gift precisely because it was an act of charity rather than a mercenary transaction, many forms of compensation were available to induce donors to make gifts.[6] The preeminent recompense for a gift, of course, was merit in heaven; but it had an earthly analogue so closely related that the two seem to have been indistinguishable.[7] This was "society." A recipient church often recognized the redemptory purpose of a gift by granting the donor the "society," "fraternity," "benefits," or "prayers" of the church,[8] but few charters state what precise spiritual services society entailed. Two seem especially concerned with the scope of the benefits the donors receive: the "associate" is to benefit from the merit of all the good works done by the monks.[9] Other charters have a more limited outlook: they stress the church's prayers as the source of the benefit; if they specify at all, they are concerned with the assiduity or continuity of the prayer.[10] Still others mention one or two specific practices which might be included among spiritual services, and five give lengthy lists.[11] The most common specific service mentioned is anniversary masses.[12] The others, too, are almost exclusively aspects of masses and prayers: trentals,[13] the writing of the beneficiaries' names in a book,[14] masses while the beneficiary is still alive,[15] masses for the dead,[16] explicit mention in the canon of the mass,[17] special prayers "as if for our founder,"[18] "assiduous" prayer by three monks "for the remedy of the souls of whomever I wish."[19] A few include the support of paupers or other charitable expenditures.[20] From such lists, it would seem that not every grant of society included all possible spiritual services. Perhaps society itself meant simply that when a church prayed for all its benefactors the persons accorded society would be included among the beneficiaries of the prayers; but if one wanted one's name mentioned or wanted a special mass or prayer, and so on, one had to receive that right explicitly.[21]

Churches used spiritual services not only to attract but also to retain donations. Jumièges induced the son of a donor to abandon his claim to what his late father had given the abbey in return for the same spiritual services the father was already receiving, as well as a horse and some money.[22] Many claims may well have been made so that the claimant might extort concessions or gifts from the aggrieved church in return for a quitclaim.[23] In such a situation the prospect of a countergift might incite the claim which it then quieted. Other charters show a different way in which spiritual services granted to donors served to discourage claims. Two state the general principle: "While my alms remain perpetually stable, so also my memory will persist in that monastery."[24] A third demonstrates that the threat to withhold spiritual gifts already granted could coerce recalcitrant relatives of donors to behave: a relative abandons his claim, "conquered by money and by the prayers which they were assiduously doing for my ancestor—of which, if I should do otherwise, I would deprive him."[25]

A good many other ends more particular than salvation could be achieved by a donation to a church. Most common, with regard to religious houses, was the reception of the donor or a relative—in the case of men, as remote as cousins; in the case of women, as remote as nieces—as a monk or nun in the convent to which the gift was made.[26] The extant charters indicate nothing distinctive about such gifts, except for two variants, which apparently applied only to men; no instances occur in charters from nunneries.

A man who wanted to give land to a monastery but was both unready to enter the religious life and unwilling to forego that advantage of making a gift could solve his problem in one of two ways.[27] The less common solution was to establish a place in the convent for a monk who would represent the donor. Sometimes the representative was an individual known to and associated with the donor.[28] Ralph de Montpinçon, says Orderic, asked the abbot of Saint-Evroul "that some clerk fit for the service of God might be received as a monk in the monastery . . . to pray devoutly to God for his salvation and that of his wife"; the prospective monk was presented to Ralph before being admitted to the abbey and "offered his prayers and the labours he might undertake for Christ to the knight," and Ralph's gifts were made explicitly for the support of this monk.[29] In other instances the donor's gift is intended to endow a permanent increase of one in the size of the congregation of monks.[30] Only Orderic states that in cases of this sort the prayers and labors of the new monk were specifically intended to benefit the donor, but that may have been understood. If so, such arrangements provided permanent benefits closely akin to spiritual benefits which included the special prayers of one or more monks.

Such benefits would not, however, be as effective as would becoming a monk oneself and, indeed, deferred entry into the monastery was the second and more frequent solution to the problem of how to take full advantage of the potential benefits of making a gift without becoming a monk at the moment of the gift. Twenty-five charters reserve to the donor, and sometimes to one or more relatives as well, the possibility of entering the monastery at a later date but as the result of the current gift.[31] In one example from Saint-Martin de Sées the donor promises not to enter any other monastery; in another, not only do both the donor and his brother, who confirmed the gift, make the same promise, but the donor's wife promises not to become a nun without consulting the monks of Sées first.[32] These two charters appear to be exceptional in suggesting that it was a monastery's right to claim any donor who might ever wish to become a monk; the other charters which include a reservation of the right to become a monk imply that it was a concession by the monastery to the donor.

Sometimes the current gift alone will suffice to gain later admission as a monk. In other cases, at the time when he becomes a monk the man must make another contribution, always of movable property. The most interesting examples of reservations are those which take into account various contingencies. When, for example, Robert de Tosny granted to the monks of Marmoutier land their possession of which he had been challenging, the abbey granted that either Robert or his brother Berengar could later become a monk as a result of the quitclaim; moreover, if both chose not to do so, Robert's son could become a monk. Robert was to consent to Berenger's admission, probably because once Berengar was admitted Robert would lose his right of admission, and both were to consent to Robert's son's admission, doubtless because the son's admission would cancel the right of the father and the uncle to enter; but the death of neither was to prevent the operation of the arrangement.[33] The agreement seems intended to ensure that at least one member of the family would benefit in this particular way from Robert's concession. Similar though less elaborate provisions for substitution in like circumstances are common.

Two charters of Saint-Martin de Sées, both from 1089, limit the duration of the option to enter the abbey to the ten years after the gift.[34] Why this provision? It may be significant that all the charters from this monastery which refer to the reservation of a right to enter later can be dated to 1091 or before.[35] The monastery was founded about 1056,[36] but few charters survive from its first two decades: only eight to ten are extant from between 1060 and 1079; by contrast, more than twelve times as many survive from between 1080 and 1100.[37] The monastery obviously took good care of the charters it drew up after about 1080; because there is no reason to think that less care was expended on earlier documents, the dearth of charters for the first twenty years probably is not the result of carelessness. Instead, the new foundation may have had difficulty getting started and may, consequently, have been eager to secure gifts by means of promises of future admission.[38] The bright prospect of a larger community in the future may also explain the promises of donors to become monks there if anywhere.[39] Then, as the endowment increased and the number of monks reached a more satisfactory total, the monastery may have become less willing to incur obligations for the future, first limiting the duration of the obligation to ten years, then ceasing to make such arrangements at all.

Another explanation, compatible with the first, of the large number of reservations in the documents of Saint-Martin de Sées is possible. Three monasteries, with Saint-Martin de Sées, account for all but two of the reservations. Troarn, like Saint-Martin de Sées, was founded by Roger de Montgomery, one of William the Conqueror's closest advisers and friends. Saint-Pierre de Préaux was founded by Humphrey de Vieilles, whose son Roger de Beaumont, the abbey's great patron, was another member of William's inner circle. Saint-Etienne de Caen was founded by William himself.[40] All but Préaux were founded in the decade before the conquest of England.[41] Perhaps the right to make such arrangements as deferred entry into a monastery was a special boon, granted only to the duke's most favored institutions or those of his closest companions, intended to obtain for the fortunate foundation an initial endowment larger than might otherwise have been expected. For new convents, conditions may have been somewhat difficult in the second half of the eleventh century: a great many had been created in a short period, and the competition for donors must have been considerable. On the other hand, the reservations may have been a restriction imposed by the duke to prevent these establishments from depriving him and his friends of the fighting abilities of men who might be tempted to enter the abbeys as a consequence of their gifts. Gifts to abbeys follow *mouvances*, that is, a founder's men tend to make their gifts to—and to become monks, if anywhere, at—their lord's foundations. Yet William could ill afford, as much after the conquest of England as before, to lose the military services of his own men and those of Roger de Montgomery and Roger de Beaumont. Moreover, after the Conquest, the landed wealth of his supporters and their men was greatly increased. They may well have felt able, now, to make gifts of Norman land, which, before, they would have needed for their own support; but they would not want to give the land away without securing advantages from the gifts.[42] The events of the Conquest and the years immediately following may even have made them feel that gifts for the salvation of their souls were especially necessary and that eventual entry into a monastery would be especially advisable[43]—all at the very moment when William needed every man he could get so as to hold both England and his continental possessions. This complex of new pressures and new opportunities would have died out toward the end of William's reign—as military necessity eased somewhat,[44] as fathers died and left their Norman lands to one son and their English lands to another, and so on—and with it would have gone the transient custom of giving now and going into the monastery later.

A few fathers gave land to churches for the education of their sons, usually with the express intention that the boy become, when adult, either a monk or a priest.[45] If the father chose to have the boy become a priest, he gave the monastery a church which was reserved for the son. In undertaking such arrangements, some monasteries were careful to protect themselves against the situation in which the boy, when old enough to begin his career, was judged unfit to be a priest: he is to be the abbot's tenant at will; or, if the monks "should find him unworthy, they would concede to him nothing more than to any other stranger."[46] It was similarly foresighted for a father to provide for the situation in which the son whose education was in view died young. Marmoutier accepted a son of Richard de Méré

> under this agreement: that they would have him reared and taught, either at Bohun or in another of their houses, until he should come to that age when he is able and wants to be a monk and be *in riga*. If the child should die in the meanwhile and his father Richard wishes to be a monk, they will receive him; and if he does not wish to be a monk but wants to make a monk of one of his sons, they will receive him [the son] alone on this condition and nothing more: that if he is a child, he [Richard] him-

self, not the monks, will have him reared and educated, until he reaches the age when he can be *in riga*.[47]

Marmoutier, also thinking about eventualities, was not about to risk having to raise two children for the price of one.

Orderic reports that Athelelm de Gaseran gave Saint-Evroul's priory of Maule his son Amaury and a tithe which Amaury later held for many years while he was a priest and gave to the monks when he died, "since they had brought him up and educated him well." Athelelm provided that "if the boy were to die within seven years [of his oblation] the monks should have the tithe in perpetuity in return for seven pounds."[48] Maule was not in Normandy, and the donor, too, was from outside the duchy, which may be why the arrangement points interesting contrasts with Norman provisions in similar circumstances. Here, unless the boy dies, the grant to the priory is only temporary: the tithes pay for Amaury's education, then become his, to support him while he is a priest; as they returned to the priory only because Amaury chose to bequeathe them, it is apparent that, once Amaury had become a priest, the priory had no right to them. Moreover, should the boy die, the abbey must compensate his father if it was to retain the tithes. By contrast, the presumption behind the various alternatives provided by Norman charters seems to be that gifts for the purpose of education were both permanent and final. Indeed, Norman arrangements concerning not only education but also entry into a monastery provide that if the intended beneficiary died the balance between the interests of donor and donee was to be restored not by the termination of the arrangement or by the payment of a price for the alienated property but by the substitution of another person for the deceased.

Two other kinds of spiritual benefits were widely granted in return for gifts: absolution and, especially, burial. Men on the point of death often became monks so they could be buried as monks; and other lay persons, even women, were buried as though they were monks.[49] Saint-Martin de Sées sometimes used burial as an alternative in cases when someone reserved the right to become a monk in future and then either did not choose to exercise his option or died before he could do so.[50] Gifts could be and were made during the burial of a loved one as a *quid pro quo* for the burial. Most references to burial, however, are about the future, with no apparent prospect of the recipient's imminent death. A person granted future burial was usually expected, in addition to the gift for which the right was granted, to leave the abbey all or part of the movable goods in his or her possession at the moment of his or her death.[51] Although some charters make explicit modifications[52] and a few say nothing on the subject, only one explicitly leaves the question of such a contribution up to the future decedent.[53]

The regular association of burial with society and other privileges implies, as one would expect, that the right to be buried in a monastery or a nunnery was regarded as a boon to the donor. There are, however, indications that abbeys actively encouraged donors to be buried in their cemeteries, that, in other words, the abbeys thought they had a right to the bodies of their deceased benefactors. Orderic describes the legal suit which the nuns of Saint-Désir de Lisieux brought in 1077 in their attempt to have one of their founders, Hugh bishop of Lisieux, buried at the nunnery rather than by the canons of his cathedral.[54] A bishop's body might be a special prize, but two charters in which donors promise their bodies to particular abbeys indicate that abbeys may have felt similarly possessive about all their benefactors.[55] One of these donors promised the monks his body "wherever he should die,"[56] but others restricted similar promises in various ways. One, who was to be buried at the abbey only "if his body can be conveniently secured and brought back," apparently intended to spare the monks a troublesome journey.[57] Others, who limit the concession to burial if the benefactor should die on the same side of the Seine as the abbey or in Normandy, were probably also thinking of the monks' convenience, although it is possible that they had granted other churches similar rights if they died outside the areas indicated.[58]

Absolution might be associated very closely with the right or privilege of burial, for the two needs tended to seem pressing at the same moments. In 1060, Richard de Reviers fell gravely ill just after he had become custodian for Duke William of the castle of Thimert, near Chartres, a castle which was then under anathema. Not wishing to die in a cursed place and condition, he made a substantial gift to the abbey of Saint-Père de Chartres, receiving in return not only burial at the abbey but one monk's intercession with the bishop of Chartres for his absolution. One version of the transaction says that the bishop absolved not only Richard but all the Normans who had accompanied him to Thimert and that all the Normans at Thimert were to be buried at Saint-Père.[59] In other cases absolution alone was a sufficient reward. A few charters cite notorious misdeeds as causes of the need for absolution. One common crime against churches was disseisin. Ralph son of Walbert de *Bodriz* had disseised the cathedral of Rouen but gave the land back and was absolved.[60] Another frequent misdeed for which absolution was sometimes acquired by a gift was violence against a church or its lands. William fitz Osbern and Roger de Montgomery had raided the lands of Saint-Pierre de Préaux and had therefore been excommunicated; Ralph de Conches had participated in Arnold d'Echauffour's destruction by fire of the bourg of the abbey of Saint-Evroul; Robert son of Bernard had burned houses and a press belonging to Saint-Etienne de Caen; William de *Claraio*, who thought that he was dying, "had in many ways done grave injury to the church [of Saint-Martin de Sées] . . . and therefore feared to be accused before a strict judge."[61] Others mention only unspecified sins or simply say that absolution is their purpose.[62]

Because burial, absolution of sins, and one's chances of salvation were especially important concerns to those in imminent danger of dying, deathbed gifts and gifts made while a person was lying ill or wounded are numerous. They differ from donations made in less pressing circumstances only in two respects. First, a person in such a state was not usually able to travel to the church. Therefore, it was common to summon a member of the church to come to a deathbed donor. Second, because a dying donor would not be able to supervise the actual transfer of the property to its destined recipient, signs occur in the records of deathbed gifts of an unusual amount of concern with matters such as verification that the gift had actually been made and protection of the gift against possible challengers.[63] There does not seem, however, to have been any prejudice against deathbed gifts, even when a donor had a lord or an heir whose interests might be jeopardized if the donor on the point of death was overly generous with his worldly goods in an attempt to secure a heavenly reward.[64]

Spiritual matters are not the whole of life, as eleventh-century Norman donors were well aware. Several of the spiritual benefits already discussed include a material component, the lifelong maintenance of the donor or someone close to him or her as a monk, nun, or priest. Moreover, instead of—or, more commonly, in addition to—spiritual benefits, donors often received material rewards for their gifts, for it was customary to seal a donation with reciprocal gifts from the recipient church to the donor and to the confirmers of the donation. In charters which state the purpose of such countergifts, the motive cited is assurance; therefore, countergifts will be discussed again when the subject of techniques of assurance arises.[65]

The most common material countergift was a sum of money. Almost any object might also be used, although useful items were preferred. By far the most usual was one or more horses; but other animals, military equipment, articles of clothing and jewelry, useful or decorative objects, even quantities of grain, are also found.[66] Because the most common material countergift was money, the modern student of Norman documents can find it hard to distinguish between a gift in return for which a countergift was given and a sale.[67] Given the redemptory purpose of gifts, the problem must have been a serious one for alienors of the eleventh century as well, when the transfer really was a gift. Probably for this reason, a good many charters stress that a gift was "spontaneous" or that a countergift was given "from the charity" of the recipient church, or both. These phrases suggest that eleventh-century Normans thought that the essence of a gift was that it was made of the donor's free will, unprompted by the thought of material reward. Concomitantly, the material rewards which so often followed had to be regarded as equally unprompted demonstrations of the gratitude of the recipients, given to donors, as one charter puts it, "although they had not requested it in the slightest."[68] A few charters go so far as to say that it was precisely because a gift or concession was made "spontaneously" that a monetary countergift was given[69]—an association of ideas which, however illogical, illustrates the situation nicely.

Various motives might prompt a donor to ask for a specific countergift. Reception of donors and their dependents into monasteries and nunneries and education of boys are examples. Some material countergifts, too, were—at least by inference—specifically requested by their recipients. Countergifts of money or animals corresponded to the needs of donors who were about to go on journeys. A good many monetary countergifts are said to have been used to ransom captives. Others were used to pay off mortgages. The connection between the donor's need and the nature of the countergift is not always made explicit. In one last case, the countergift, a horse, is explicitly said not to have been requested by the brothers who received it, "but they gratefully accepted it since the elder brother . . . was then wishful to train his younger brother as a knight."[70] It certainly was convenient that the countergift should fit in so well with the donors' plans, so convenient that it is hard to imagine that this happened by pure chance, in this instance or any of the others. The first purpose of a gift, whatever else it was intended to achieve, was the salvation of the donor's soul. That effect was thought to depend on the voluntary nature of the gift, its spontaneity. It is probable, therefore, that the drafters of charters avoided, to the best of their ability, giving the impression that any transaction in which a spiritual countergift played a role had any ulterior motive. Nevertheless, the strong implication of coincidences like those cited is that, when they had need, donors managed to drop adequate hints about their preferences for certain countergifts.[71]

Late in the period another sort of countergift appears, the corody, whereby in return for a gift the donor was assured the wherewithal to live in the future.[72] Thirteen or fourteen charters recording corodies are extant from the century, the earliest from between 1070 and 1079.[73] Corodies were most often conferred in return for gifts. There are exceptions: the earliest example was the result of a sale; another was given in return for a gift of land plus the services as a shoemaker of the man receiving the corody; a third was among the alternatives granted a man who had been engaged in a profit-sharing arrangement with the abbey; and a fourth was part of an arrangement to pay off a mortgage.[74] The property involved was nearly always small: a few acres of land or the like.[75] In return, the donor is said to receive his or her *prebenda* or *victus* or a specifically defined quantity of food.[76] Five charters define the amount as per year; another states it as per day.[77] Four say that the recipient of the corody will be clothed as well as fed.[78]

Corodies seem usually to have resulted from need. Lancelin d'Airan had mortgaged his benefice to Troarn to finance a journey to Jerusalem; on his return, he was able to pay off only half the mortgage in the usual way and was forced to resort to unorthodox methods, including giving the abbey permanent possession of part of the profits of his church in return for a corody.[79] Durand son of Fulcheran was also unable to redeem mortgaged land in the normal fashion.[80] William son of Theobald describes himself thus: "his eyes dimming toward the end [of life], his own substance being almost completely lacking to him."[81] After her only son entered the abbey of Saint-Martin de Sées, a woman named Emma was "destitute of the solace both of her husband, who had died earlier, and of her son."[82] Four of the possible fourteen corodies concern women.[83] That in itself may indicate the necessitous nature of the transaction: a much smaller proportion of all extant alienations was made by women; and Emma's charter is not the only one to suggest that in the eleventh century women without husbands were likely to need help.[84] Necessity as a motive is occasionally indicated in connection with sales,[85] mortgages, and other transactions from which the lay party received material profit. Corodies may, however, have been used especially by lay persons such as William son of Theobald —and probably also Emma—who were elderly and possessed only limited resources: they had the advantage of providing not a definite amount in return but a guaranteed annual amount.

Donors sometimes attempted to control the destiny of their property after they had given it away. Five anathema clauses single out for punishment anyone who might alienate the property transferred, two specifically mentioning members of the recipient church as potential culprits.[86] Two other charters, without mentioning anathema, forbid the abbots or monks of recipient monasteries to alienate.[87] If the language of three of these clauses is taken literally, only some types of alienations are excluded: two mention only grants "in benefice" and sales,[88] another forbids only alienation to "secular men."[89] The others are comprehensive, however; and it may be that all seven were intended to exclude every type of alienation, for grants "in benefice" might mean any transfer remunerated by services and sales any transfer remunerated in money or in kind. Certainly, eleventh-century Normans must have been well aware that individual members of the clergy often tried to turn the property of their churches to their own use or profit or that of their relatives or friends—and sometimes succeeded. A good many of the extant references to disputes are to such losses.

Very occasionally a charter explicitly permits alienation by the recipient. Roger de Montgomery made a sweeping concession to Saint-Etienne de Caen; and another donor gave a donee permission to exchange the property just given.[90] These concessions, however, seem to have been truly exceptional: they are the only examples extant of unrestricted rights to alienate. A few additional donors recognized that recipient churches might legitimately alienate gifts in certain circumstances. A charter might stipulate that if ever the recipient church should decide to grant out property comprising the gift the grant should go by preference to the donor's heirs;[91] and a donor or someone designated by a donor sometimes took back as a tenement from a recipient church some or all of the property just given it.[92] Moreover, Odo Stigand made gifts to Saint-Ouen "in such a way that they should be in the demesne of that place, and that no abbot nor any man who may ever exist should give [them] to any man; and if he [any prospective alienor] shall have done [so], the heir of Stigand, who gives these gifts, should come and should receive [what was alienated] without contradiction for such service as he [the prospective alienor] had wished to give [it] to the other."[93] This arrangement is, in form, a reminiscence of an arrangement common under the Carolingians.[94] Whether the reminiscence is purely verbal—the scribe simply copying the clause from a model—or corresponds to an actual agreement between Odo Stigand and the abbey seems impossible to decide. The analogous cases suggest that eleventh-century Normans did regard the heirs of donors as maintaining residual rights in their ascendants' gifts. Family claims, however, had not yet developed into the *retrait lignager*: with one exception,[95] these heirs cannot forestall the initial alienation but only preempt a subsequent subtenement.[96]

POST-OBIT OR OTHERWISE DEFERRED GIFTS

Although most gifts were intended to take effect immediately, it was possible to make a gift which would take effect, instead, at some later time, usually after the death of the donor or of some person designated by the donor. I have counted eighty-four certain examples of such post-obit transfers.[97] This type of alienation had as yet no name, but two abbeys were beginning to standardize their terminology. Five of the six post-obit gifts to La Trinité de Caen say that the donor gave the gift "so that he should hold it in his lifetime and the church should possess it after his death"; one is further said to be destined to come into the church's "own possession" and another to the church "in ownership."[98] Three of the four post-obit gifts to Troarn say that the donor "gives and concedes wholly at [his] death."[99] Such gifts differ from the deathbed gifts discussed earlier[100] in that they were not made while the donor was in imminent expectation of death. Instead, they were gifts whose effects were intentionally delayed: a donor issued a charter or made a statement conferring on a church—very slight evidence exists of such grant to individuals—the eventual possession of certain property but declaring that the property was not to pass to the donee until the death of the donor.[101]

Many variations were possible. One mortgagor arranged that if he died within the term of the mortgage the mortgaged land was to become the property of the mortgagee; if he survived the term, other arrangements were to apply.[102] This is the unique instance of a post-obit gift which takes effect only if the donor dies within a certain period. Most variations concern the persons whose deaths affect the timing of the transfer. A man might make a post-obit gift which was to take effect only when he and his wife were both dead, or he might be joined by his wife in making a post-obit gift which was to take effect after the death of both.[103] Only twice, however, does a man make a gift which is to take effect after his wife's death alone.[104] Because spouses do not usually die at exactly the same time, a few donors who made such post-obit gifts specified how the eventual transfer was to occur. Probably the most common solution was to consider that each spouse had a half-interest in the property: when one died half the property went to the recipient, the survivor keeping the other half until his or her death.[105] In at least one instance, perhaps three, no transfer seems to have been intended to occur until the survivor of the spouses died.[106] In another case, "if the husband should die, without an heir, before his wife, the husband's part of the money will be given to the saint and the land will remain to the woman because it comes from her inheritance"; what would happen if the wife died first is not stated.[107] A man might also specify that his widow could keep her part of their designated post-obit gift only so long as she did not remarry.[108]

A donor might make a post-obit gift conditional on his or her dying without a direct heir, as for example in a case just cited.[109] Others specify that the heir must be legitimate in order to render the post-obit gift void.[110] In such cases, however, if the donor did have children, the donee would get nothing. Therefore, a few donors provided that their gifts were to be divided in particular ways between the donee and the donor's children.[111] Donors also provide for children who were already born, usually by making their gifts take effect not when they died but when the children did.[112] It was possible to modify the gift so that it took effect only if a child had no children: in one of the extant instances the children must be legitimate;[113] in the other, the land will go to the church if the donor's daughter "does not live legally or dies without an heir," which amounts to a requirement that here too the children be legitimate.[114]

Wives and direct descendants were not the only relatives in connection with whom post-obit gifts were made. Gifts are known which were to take effect on the deaths of a mother, an uncle, a sister in two different cases, a brother (if he dies without legitimate children), a step-daughter and her son, and possibly a nephew.[115] Moreover, two gifts made to Saint-Etienne de Caen, by Robert count of Mortain and Roger de Montgomery, were each to take effect after the death not only of the donor and his wife but also of the donor's lord, Duke William.[116]

Lay tenants and ecclesiastics, as tenants both of lay fee and of churches, were often allowed to hold until their deaths property their lords had already given away. Whether the tenure was lay or ecclesiastial in nature, this arrangement solved, to some extent at least, an obvious problem. What appears in a charter as a gift by a lord of his tenant's lands is often explicitly done at the request of the tenant, that is, such "gifts" are really confirmations; presumably the same was true in many of the instances when the nature of the lord's action is not made explicit.[117] At times, however, the initiative was the lord's and tenants were reluctant to go along.[118] Given the redemptory purpose of most transactions and its corollary that whenever possible transactions should appear spontaneous and wholehearted, such reluctance was probably more widespread than the rare indications in the charters suggest. One way of overcoming unwillingness would be to postpone the actual effect of a gift until after the death of the tenant. When a church occupied by canons or by "clerics" was given to an abbey so that it might be made into a priory, it was more usual for the incumbents to be allowed to become monks or to be replaced with monks only when they died than to provide for their expulsion while still living.[119] This pattern was followed occasionally with regard to the incumbents of churches which were given without any expressed intention that they be made into priories or abbeys.[120] And so it was with regard to tenants, lay and clerical, who held property other than churches. Here, too, there were variations on the pattern, for two lords made gifts which were to take effect not after the deaths of their tenants but after the deaths of the tenants' sons, although each tenant was an ecclesiastic.[121]

Because the death after which a post-obit gift was to take effect might occur many years after the gift was made and the decedent would in the interim be in possession of the property, the church might have considerable difficulty in vindicating its right to the property when the occasion arose. Indeed, for the thirteenth century Jean Yver has concluded that a mere act of donation did not obligate the donor to transfer the property and that if a donor remained in possession of what was "given," his or her relatives retained their rights over it.[122] If that conclusion could be applied to the eleventh century, the difficulties posed by post-obit gifts would have been great, for such gifts were by definition not immediately followed by the actual transfer of the gift to the donee. One dispute which probably arose from a post-obit gift may indicate that Yver's conclusion is correct for the eleventh century, too.[123] Yet both the identity in the ceremonial forms used to make post-obit gifts and gifts *inter vivos*, at least when these gifts were to churches, and the absence of special precautions concerning the heirs of donors of post-obit gifts argue the contrary.[124]

Whether the potential difficulties were merely practical or stemmed from a nascent legal rule, it is probably because difficulties were easy to envision that a high percentage of post-obit gifts include, as a sign of the donor's eventual intentions, the immediate transfer of some part of the property. These transfers are sometimes said to be earnest of the eventual transfer of the whole. Roger de Montgomery, for example, gave Saint-Etienne de Caen the bourg of Trun after his death and that of Duke William; "and," he says, "so that this should be certain about the rest, and that no doubt remain in future, I concede at present the house of Aiulf Guirell with all the customs of the house which pertain to me."[125] Even when transfers of this sort—a piece of the property now, the rest later—are not said to be earnest, their close connection with the post-obit gift and the relative insignificance of what was transferred immediately justify regarding them as such.

Sometimes the person whose death must precede transfer of the property became the recipient church's tenant or his service is said to be transferred at once from the donor to the church. Only once is the type of service, a rent, stated.[126] Another rent was used more simply as earnest: Emma countess of Montchamp gave La Trinité de Caen her possessions at Montchamp after her death and "as recognition of the gift the priest of the aforesaid vill gives the Holy Trinity five shillings a year for lamps for the church."[127] Post-obit gifts which, like Emma's, conveyed some small part of the property as present earnest of the future gift outnumber those which transferred the service or lordship of the entire property. The tithes of the property constituting the gift are most common,[128] but earnest might also consist of some of the land itself, a house with its customs, an annual payment of wine produced by the land, money, peasants, the right of hospitality, and the *comparatio* of the vines which are given as of the donor's death.[129] It might also combine various items.[130]

Property given post-obit might, under certain conditions, come to the possession of the recipient before the death of the designated person, for example, if that person decided to become a monk.[131] One transfer was to occur if the designee, a tenant, "should become a monk or go off anywhere or die or withdraw in any manner."[132] Spontaneous surrender was also envisioned;[133]

and, in the two instances in which accelerations of post-obit transfers actually occurred, this rather than becoming a monk was involved.[134]

Gifts might also be given so that they took effect in the future, not post-obit but either at a definite time or after a definite event other than the death of the donor or a designee. Early in his reign, when Duke William gave back to Saint-Wandrille the domain called Ticheville, which his father had seized, Abbot Gradulf allowed him to keep everything there for three years except the churches, the tithe of the vill, and land for one plow, which the abbot "retained at present as if in witness of the aforesaid restoration."[135] Hugh the cleric, "leaving for Apulia," gave Saint-Martin de Sées what he had in two churches "if he should not return from Apulia. . . . But if he should return, he should have all his [property] in his lifetime, if he wishes; after his death, however, the monks" should have it.[136] The latter part of this transaction is a simple post-obit gift. The first part is a gift which takes effect if Hugh does not return although still alive; it is a question, however, whether the gift went into effect when Hugh departed, to be restored if he returned,[137] or only after some unmentioned length of absence. The actual transfer of other gifts depended on chronologically unpredictable events other than death. By compromise with Saint-Pierre de Préaux, Robert count of Mortain retained a disputed estate until "God should enrich him so much that he is able to live honorably without it."[138] When Roger de Montgomery gave various gifts to the abbey he had founded at Troarn, he excluded the island of Robehomme, "which island my son Philip now holds and will hold until he has acquired an honor and then it will go back to the control of St. Martin without contradiction."[139] Roger had given Philip this land on which to support himself; but Philip, as Roger's fourth son, had to "acquire an honor" by his own efforts and merits, not by his father's death.[140]

The considerations which motivated donors to make gifts whose effects were delayed are rarely mentioned; if the charters cite any motive at all, it is the usual one of salvation. The transactions involving Philip de Montgomery and Robert count of Mortain constitute two allusions to what must have been the usual motive. Neither the Montgomery family nor Robert of Mortain was poor, and neither transfer is a post-obit gift; but both indicate that the advantage of a gift whose effect was delayed was that the possessions concerned were thereby made to serve both the important functions of property—to support the one who possessed it and to obtain spiritual benefits for the one who gave it away. Donors who made post-obit gifts wanted, in other words, to have their cake and eat it too. They do not seem, as a group, poorer than the average eleventh-century Norman donor.[141] Instead, the motive of maximizing one's profits from one's property was spread throughout society.

SALES

The most common material countergift was money, and the consequent problem of distinguishing a gift with a monetary countergift from a sale may explain some of the language used by charters to describe gifts and the countergifts they evoked. If that was a problem for eleventh-century Normans, it is also one for modern scholars, for reasons which must be explained at some length.

That it was possible to buy and sell immovables was recognized in eleventh-century Normandy without any doubt. Charters allude casually but clearly to an apparently well-understood distinction between gifts and sales.[142] Gilbert Crispin, in his life of Herluin abbot of Bec, distinguishes between a "sale" and a "free gift."[143] Important lords sometimes included in their gifts to a church a general confirmation of any and all future transactions of their men with the church; these commonly include not only gifts but also sales.[144] Some churches were quite frank about making purchases. Long lists survive of the purchases of the early abbots of Saint-Etienne de Caen, which itemize the sellers, what they sold, and nearly always the price paid.[145] La Trinité de Caen was often careful to state when a transaction which began as a sale ended up as a gift: three pancarts for the abbey include a total of twenty donations by Duchess Matilda of land and other immovables which Matilda herself had bought; there are two similar donations by other individuals.[146] The charters of Saint-Martin de Sées describe a good many acquisitions as partly gifts and partly purchases. Odo Cotinel, for example, "partly gave in alms land for two oxen . . . partly he sold [it] and accepted for the sale thirty-four shillings; for the gift he had prayers and benefit."[147] A similar distinction is made by a charter from Saint-Etienne de Caên.[148]

The difference in the nature of the transfers, therefore, was clear. The problem is the merely practical one of telling one type from the other. No criterion of form distinguishes acts recording sales from acts recording gifts.[149] Moreover, many churches use words of purchase only rarely, if at all, although they grant monetary countergifts freely. Were these sales, or did these churches simply prefer to give money rather than, say, horses? What, for example, is one to think of the case of Fécamp, compared to its priories of Saint-Martin-du-Bosc and Saint-Gabriel? Fécamp fairly often gives monetary countergifts but never refers to the transactions as sales. Saint-Martin often gives monetary countergifts and usually calls the transactions sales.[150] Saint-Gabriel's pancart uses a construction which strongly implies that the priory bought almost all of its endowment: "We gave so-and-so so much money for land (tithes, a mill, and so forth)."[151] These may be simple differences of scribal practice, or they may represent the difference between a church's public records and its documents intended for internal use.[152] It is also possible, however, that the prestige of making a gift to one of the oldest, largest, and most famous abbeys in Normandy was enough to ensure a steady flow of donations to Fécamp whereas its newer, smaller, and less prestigious priories were forced to buy if they wished to expand. In the charters of other churches there seems to be no relation between descriptions of transactions as sales and mentions of monetary countergifts.[153]

Nor is this all, for there were reasons why vendors should wish to appear as donors and purchasers as donees. Because it was apparently the gratuitous, wholly voluntary nature of a gift which earned the donor merit in heaven, it would not be surprising if churches agreed to present transactions into which alienors were forced by necessity[154] or enticed by the prospect of material reward as though they were free of all traces of secular motive. Moreover, there was some official disapproval of the purchase of churches and tithes by monasteries, which would give the monasteries a motive of their own for portraying such transactions in somewhat altered form.[155] In other words, sales or partial sales may often have been described as though they were gifts. This misleading characteristic of eleventh-century charters, not only in Normandy, has come in for considerable scholarly comment.[156]

That sales were disguised as gifts is certain in those few instances when two versions are extant of a transaction which appears as a sale in one version but as a gift in the other.[157] Comparison is possible, for example, for Fécamp's priory of Saint-Martin-du-Bosc. One version of the charter in which Duke William made gifts to the priory and confirmed the gifts of others includes several sales, for which the prices are always quoted; the other replaces *vendere* with *dare* and omits the prices.[158] In one instance, what the first version says was sold the second says was "given in alms,"[159] a phrase sometimes used to denote the purity of a donor's motives as well as the freedom of the church's tenure of what was so given.[160] If only the *dare* version of the charter survived, there would be less reason to suspect that Saint-Martin-du-Bosc purchased some of its possessions than there is in the case of the mother abbey, Fécamp, whose charters at least mention monetary countergifts although they never use words of sale.

In only one instance can a precise motive for the transmutation of a sale into a gift be deduced. Abbot Suppo of Mont-Saint-Michel alienated to Rannulf the moneyer a mill belonging to the abbey; it was recovered by his successor, Abbot Rannulf, from the moneyer's son Waleran. Two charters describe these transactions: the earlier recounts a wrongful alienation by sale followed by a recovery by action in the ducal court; the later version, to which is added an account of a claim to the mill raised by Waleran's nephew John, describes a wrongful alienation by gift followed by a recovery by purchase.[161] Neither even hints that an alternate version of either transaction was possible. Suppo, a controversial abbot, was deposed in 1048, the affair of the mill providing, so to speak, the *casus belli* for his opponents among the monks.[162] Although both charters say that his alienation of the mill was unjust, emphasis on the impropriety of his action is much stronger in the later charter, which calls the alienation a gift. Because public receipt of the price of a sale was strong proof of the legitimacy of the transaction,[163] and, indeed, public receipt of any countergift had considerable evidentiary force,[164] the monks may have felt that their case against Suppo and his alienee would be stronger if the abbey was not known to have received anything of value in return for the alienation. Mont-Saint-Michel is among the churches which most consistently mention countergifts, but in this instance the practice might work to the abbey's disadvantage. Similarly, the apparent discrepancy between the modes of recovery probably results from differing interpretations of a quitclaim, for it was customary for a quitclaim to be sealed by a gift to the quitclaimer just as a gift was sealed by a countergift to the donor.[165] To emphasize the financial loss the abbey incurred in recovering the mill might well strengthen its claim to rightful possession of the mill. John's renewed claim may have made the reinterpretation of both transactions more urgent—or may even have occasioned it.

The motives here cannot have been the usual rationale for disguising sales as gifts, for the mill was alienated by the abbot rather than to the abbey. Presumably, the usual motive was to secure to the vendor the otherworldly advantages of having made a gratuitous donation. This might be a means of reducing the purchase price, spiritual benefits taking the place of part of the material value of what was sold. It might also be an added inducement to the vendor to sell: he or she and the purchasers might both know that the alleged gift was in fact a sale, but one suspects that sometimes both parties thought they could conceal the fact from God.

It is therefore impossible always to know whether a transaction was in fact a gift or a sale. Nor does comparison of the value of the property alienated with the amount of the countergift disclose which transactions were sales, namely, those in which the sums are equal. Not only are values usually impossible to compute; but, in a few early twelfth-century transactions from Troarn for which he felt capable of making a comparison, René Norbert Sauvage noted consistent underpayment by the abbey.[166] Even the redemptory purpose of gifts does not help. To be sure, it is unusual to find a grant of society in connection with a transaction called a sale, and apparently this was a recognized principle.[167] Nonetheless, although there are myriad grants of society in return for gifts, and such a grant may have occurred whenever a gift was made, whether the charter mentions it or not, many more charters do not mention society yet give no other reason to suspect that the "gift" was a sale. It would be rash to argue that all ostensible gifts in return for which the "donors" received monetary countergifts and did not receive society were sales: the charters are too haphazard in what they record. Hence, only when words of sale or purchase occur in the proper context is it certain that a transfer was, in fact, a sale.[168]

Little distinguishes indubitable sales from other permanent alienations except that money was given for some item. If anything, fewer formulas and less ritual are associated with sales than with gifts. Society is not normally granted to the seller, and acts of donation are described much more rarely with regard to sales than to gifts.[169] Some evidence, however, indicates that a special degree of publicity was expected for sales, although this publicity is not usually found in the context of acts of donation. Not coincidentally, most of what meager evidence there is for such practices comes from those abbeys which are least reticent about their purchases.

Saint-Etienne de Caen used several men as almost professional witnesses.[170] Its long list of the transactions of the first three abbots, for example, contains a total of fifty-seven transactions: forty-eight sales to the abbey, four exchanges, three recoveries, and two gifts.[171] Most of the entries name witnesses, usually two or three. Fifty-one men are named, many of them only once but others remarkably often. Of the forty-eight acquisitions of Abbots Lanfranc and William, Wascelin witnessed sixteen, all sales; Geoffrey the cook witnessed seven, six sales and one exchange; Geoffrey de Bras witnessed six sales; two Geoffreys, not otherwise identified, together witnessed the ninth and eighteenth entries, both sales; and one otherwise unidentified Geoffrey witnessed sixteen more, all sales. If, as seems likely, the two unidentified Geoffreys are Geoffrey the cook and Geoffrey de Bras, each would have witnessed at least eight or nine transactions, and one of them may have witnessed as many as twenty-four or twenty-five.[172] Other men also witnessed with highly unusual frequency.[173] The reason may be that they were regarded by Saint-Etienne as especially reliable witnesses to be called upon when needed. If so, their witnessing so many sales might indicate that sales were regarded as needing special precautions. La Trinité de Caen, too, used a small number of men as witnesses to a considerable number of sales.[174]

Saint-Etienne used pledges against claims ten times with regard to sales.[175] Six other documents of this abbey refer to pledges, never in connection with a simple gift. One group guaranteed a donor's separate promises to get the consent of his lord and of all his sons; another stood guarantors of an agreement, and four groups backed up promises to warrant gifts.[176] For such agreements, which could be broken in the future, it was wise to take unusual measures of assurance. That pledges are used ten times in the case of sales suggests that to Saint-Etienne sales, too, were transactions needing unusual precautions. Saint-Martin de Sées appears to have thought similarly, for it also used pledges for sales. Eight of its thirteen references to pledges concern sales, although sales constitute fewer than one-sixth of extant transactions of the abbey.[177] Again, three of the other five charters from this house which mention pledges involve some sort of contractual obligation or as yet unfulfilled promise.[178] Indeed, twelve or more sales from Saint-Martin are called *conventiones*,[179] although the use of the word is puzzling because there would seem to be no obligations outstanding in any of these cases. Nevertheless, both it and the use of pledges suggest that Saint-Martin de Sées thought that sales needed special precautions.

Confirmation comes from both abbeys' use of warranty clauses. At Saint-Martin de Sées four of eight are from charters about sales; and, of the nonsale warranties, at least two, perhaps three, concern disputed gifts.[180] At Saint-Etienne de Caen nine of fifteen warranty clauses relate to sales, and all the nonsale warranties concern transactions to which some element of uncertainty attached.[181] It would seem that these abbeys, nervous about the security of what they had bought, tried to protect such acquisitions by the use of two devices—pledges and warranty—which were otherwise used primarily in connection with more evidently precarious acquisitions. Moreover, three other charters refer to warranty in connection with sales.[182] Given the small number of warranty clauses extant, only about seventy,[183] the sixteen in charters of sale are a high enough percentage to indicate again the apparently especially dangerous nature of sales as transactions. Indeed, the only example of a warrantor who may possibly have been called upon to compensate a church for a lost possession concerns a sale.[184] Also, each of two other churches once mentions pledges in connection with a sale.[185] Only thirty-eight charters mention pledges at all,[186] of which these two plus those about sales from Saint-Etienne de Caen and Saint-Martin de Sées are more than half. Furthermore, a good many of the more interesting references to witnesses concern sales.[187]

All in all, it seems legitimate to conclude that sales were thought to need special protection. The reason, however, is obscure. In practice, the rate of challenge to property sold is not observably higher than for other types of alienations. Moreover, many churches participated in sales without seeming to regard them with apprehension. Even the abbeys at Caen and Sées did not treat all sales with special precautions or, if they did, did not always record them. If some special quality explains the apparently special treatment of some sales, it is invisible: no identifiable element of danger is common to all the sales for which special precautions are taken but absent from those sales for which they are not. On the basis of the evidence available, therefore, no firm conclusion can be reached as to why sales—or some sales—should have seemed dangerous to eleventh-century Normans.

Yet sales are treated gingerly. Moreover, they are often referred to as "agreements," not only in the charters of Saint-Martin de Sées but in many others. One explanation of the use of the term might be that, because immovables tended to be of high value, prices had to be paid in installments although the property was transferred before payment was complete. Thus, a sale would actually constitute, on the purchaser's side, an agreement to pay the purchase price over the course of time. There are two objections to this explanation. First, only one or two references are extant to prices paid in installments.[188] One concerns land at Bayeux which was sold by one individual to another, in which the property had indeed been transferred although the seller had not yet received full payment; but as a sale between individuals this is a somewhat anomalous instance.[189] The second possible example is the notorious incident at the funeral of William the Conqueror when Ascelin son of Arthur laid claim to the land in which William's body was about to be interred. The principal participants at the ceremony, according to Orderic, "for the place of burial alone . . . offered him sixty shillings on the spot, and for the rest of the land that he claimed they promised a sum of equivalent value."[190] Although Orderic presents this as two separate transactions, not two installments, it is conceivable that in the time between the incident and his account of it the detail had become somewhat garbled. Even if the payment was made in two installments, however, the agreement was made in conditions of emergency which render it, too, anomalous. Certainly, charters recording sales to churches are silent on payment in installments.[191] Perhaps the bishoprics and abbeys whose charters have survived were normally rich enough to pay the full price at once. Perhaps the churches, as purchasers, did not feel any need to record their outstanding obligations to others. The latter possibility raises the second objection to the hypothesis that a practice of paying in installments explains why sales were agreements: the charters which suggest that sales were dangerous all involve sales to churches, not by them, but the danger—whatever its source—was clearly to the church, whereas installment payments were dangerous to sellers rather than to buyers. Even if churches sometimes paid for their purchases in installments, therefore, this practice could not explain why those churches perceived sales as dangerous.

Another possible explanation of the danger inherent in sales, though not of why they should be called agreements, might result from the use of money in sales. If money had only recently come into regular use, its very novelty might have made those who used it distrustful. This explanation also seems unlikely, however, for, as many scholars have pointed out, Normandy in the eleventh century, and even in the tenth, was quite familiar with the use of money, which circulated to a remarkable degree.[192]

A sale might be called an agreement because it made the purchaser the tenant of the vendor. The evidence on this point, however, is both scanty and ambiguous. At least one sale by a layman to a layman clearly created such a relationship.[193] Moreover, when Hugh bishop of Lisieux bought a church from a man named Aitard for the use of the nuns of Saint-Désir de Lisieux, "Bishop Hugh bought this benefice so absolutely that neither he nor his successors should do any service or owe anything to Aitard or his successors."[194] If Hugh's freedom had to be emphasized, perhaps sales usually were not this "absolute" but instead created outstanding obligations of the purchaser to the vendor. On the other hand, a charter which specifies that a purchaser was to do service from his land "*although* it was acquired with money"[195] implies that service in these circumstances was unusual, and another contemplated sale was apparently intended to be final in its effects.[196] Moreover, two charters which contrast grants "in benefice" with sales also suggest that sales did not normally establish tenurial relationships.[197] *Conventio* in the context of sales may at least sometimes have been only a meaningless verbal reminiscence of earlier documents which referred to sales as contracts because they had been considered so. [198] Nevertheless, references to service are usually lacking in charters regardless of the context.[199] Thus, their usual absence from charters recording sales cannot be taken as especially significant. Given the prevailing silence about service, the nearly even balance of references to service in connection with sales certainly leaves open the possibility that ales did usually establish a tenurial relationship to which the term *conventio* could accurately be applied. Perhaps this was true specifically of sales to individuals, for all three allusions to service as a consequence of sales concern such transfers.

Even if all sales created tenements, the problem posed by the charters which call sales agreements would not be solved. A tenement created by a sale apparently imposed obligations primarily or entirely upon the purchaser: none of the three charters which discuss service in this context says anything about potential or actual obligations of the vendors. Yet, as already noted, those charters which are concerned to protect parties to sales are concerned to protect the purchasing churches against something vendors might do or not do, not to protect vendors against defaults by purchasers. The reason may be that once a seller had received the entire purchase price the buyer had no effective hold over him or her. If, after a gift, a donor or the relative of a donor seized or claimed or refused to warrant what had been given, the donee could discontinue the spiritual services consequent upon the gift. Once, the threat alone convinced a claimant to abandon his claim; moreover, the heavenly merit earned by a gift might be lost to the donor and any other beneficiaries if the gift were lost by the donee.[200] If, however, a seller or a relative took back or claimed or refused to warrant what had been sold, what could the purchaser do? Against third parties who claimed or disseised, a purchaser could hope to rely on the vendor's warranty and, in the event that the vendor's defense was unavailing, to receive either compensation or the return of the purchase price.[201] If the claimant or disseisor was the vendor or the vendor's heir, however, the purchaser would not be able to exercise a donee's first line of defense, that is, cessation of spiritual services. There is no hint that a suit to recover the purchase price was a possibility. Moreover, a suit to recover the land faced unusual problems, for the very quality which makes money so useful—its ability to store large amounts of value in small, easily moved, easily transferred, even easily concealed things[202]—made it dangerous to a buyer who needed to prove that a purchase had occurred. A seller could deny ever receiving money much more easily than a donor could deny that monks or nuns or canons prayed for him or her or an exchanger deny enjoyment of property which had belonged to a church. Money can be spent or hidden. The only way to demonstrate that it had been transferred was to call in evidence the testimony of witnesses who had seen it transferred. I should therefore like to suggest—hesitantly—that the apparent finality of sales to churches combined with the obvious dangers posed by money together explain the attitude to sales displayed in the charters.

Because sales to individuals are normally mentioned in the documents only when their occurrence affected transactions involving churches, information about them is casual and indirect. They could, and often did, happen; but any differences from sales to churches are hard to see. One, just mentioned, is the attention paid by a few charters to services to be done—or not to be done—by individual purchasers. The only other obvious peculiarity in descriptions of sales to lay persons is the occasional mention that what was purchased—and is now transferred to a church—was bought with the buyer's "own gold and silver," or other similar words.[203] No church ever makes a similar statement about its own purchases. The purpose was probably to stress that the buyer could do completely as he or she liked with what was thus purchased. A rule was developing in Normandy in this period that "conquest," which includes purchases, was more freely alienable than were possessions which had been inherited by the alienor.[204] As a corollary it would be important to a church, when it was given what a donor had bought, to record how the donor had acquired the property so as to forestall possible claims by the donor's heirs.

EXCHANGES

As in the case of sales, some eleventh-century Norman transactions indubitably were exchanges, but others are harder to classify. One fairly common type of exchange occurred between a Norman abbey possessing lands outside Normandy and a non-Norman abbey close to those lands which also happened to possess Norman lands. The motive, explicit or implicit, was convenience.[205] It may have been the deliberate policy of Norman abbeys in the early eleventh century, especially Jumièges, to consolidate their holdings within the borders of Normandy by exchanges or even by sales.[206] A person making a gift to a distant church might well take the possibility of such an exchange into account: when Neil viscount of the Cotentin confirmed to Marmoutier a gift which Duke William had made of land in the island of Guernsey, land William had confiscated from Neil, he added, "If it should happen that the monks . . . should wish to exchange what I have confirmed to them in that island for other land which is closer to them, I confirm [the land] again to those with whom they will have made the exchange."[207] Exchanges might also be made to permit or facilitate the creation of a new abbey, as in the cases of Saint-Evroul and Montivilliers.[208] An abbey might also make an exchange in which the other party was to hold what it received only for life and the abbey was, therefore, in the long run the gainer; these create, in effect, life estates.[209] In addition, charters refer to a good many exchanges between lay persons or between a lay person and a church.[210] Usually these allusions are brief; in exchanges between lay persons, which intrude into the charters only because part of what was exchanged was later transferred to a church, commonly only one side of the exchange is mentioned, the side now donated to the church. Hence, few characteristics of such exchanges emerge. Only twice does a motive appear: once, convenience; the other time, apparently, the desire to be able to give an undivided vill to a church.[211]

Usually, similar items are exchanged, most often land for land, but also houses, quitrents, and castles.[212] There are some contrary cases: tithes for land or for land and money, a market for a house, quitrents for churches.[213] Most charters make no attempt to express any equivalence, however. Indeed, in one instance an exchange was explicitly unequal either in amount or in type: founding a college of canons in his castle at Cherbourg, Duke William "exchanged the land for the cemetery, [giving] for one foot two [feet] of his demesne, so that his chapel should belong to his canons completely quit and in their possession."[214] This exchange seems to have been made with an unnamed third party who possessed either land William wished to make into a cemetery for the chapel or rights over an already existing cemetery. If the latter, it is possible that this exchange was equal in value although unequal in area, for rights over cemeteries were valuable.[215] It is also possible, however, that William gave more both in area and in value than he received so as to induce the third party to make the exchange. All but one of the other charters which mention comparative amounts or values describe equal exchanges.[216]

Warranty clauses which include the warrantor's promise of compensation, a form of exchange, also sometimes specify equivalence, though by no means always.[217] Equal conditions, too, are sometimes specified, as when Robert the Magnificent gave Saint-Taurin to Fécamp in return for Montivilliers;[218] and the equality might concern customs or feudal services due from the lands exchanged.[219]

Only once was there any provision for reexchange. When Abbot Nicholas of Saint-Ouen and Richard Talbot made an exchange of Ancourteville for part of Gouy, "in the presence of Duke Robert [Curthose], it was established between the abbot and Richard that, whenever either of them should wish to withdraw from this agreement, he should pay sixty pounds to the other and thus each will receive back [what he gave] as valuable and unharmed as he gave it." No motive for a desire to cancel the arrangement is mentioned in the charter. The sum of sixty pounds is, however, sufficiently large to ensure that neither party would move lightly to cancel.[220]

The exchanges already discussed use words of exchange,[221] but in other cases each of two parties gives some immovable to the other without such words. Whether these were exchanges or gifts with immovable countergifts is moot. They may appear to be exchanges in all but name. For example, Humphrey de Vieilles and his wife gave to their new abbey of Saint-Léger de Préaux "Graimbouville, with all its appurtenances, for which we gave a certain allod of ours, called Bellemont, . . . to a certain knight named Richard."[222] Presumably, if a transaction was an exchange, there ought to be parity in the value of the two parts of the transaction, whereas, if it was a gift with an immovable countergift, there ought to be disparity; but this rule is impossible to apply. Even in cases of admitted exchanges, apparent disparities exist,[223] and equivalence is rarely stated. Moreover, it is impossible to estimate accurately the value of various immovables in Normandy in the eleventh century. To compound the difficulty, factors such as convenience and sentiment, which probably played their part in determining what transactions occurred, are not given expression in charters. Some transactions appear to straddle the division between gifts and exchanges.[224] Indeed, even in transactions which are called sales the purchase price may consist of or include immovables.[225] Unless something in addition to the form of compensation, something now invisible, was a factor in determining whether an eleventh-century Norman would call a transfer a sale or an exchange, the dividing line between these two types of alienations was apparently no better defined than that between gifts with movable countergifts and sales or that between gifts with immovable countergifts and exchanges.

TENURE IN ALMS

In addition to the various preexisting types of possession which might be transferred—and sometimes modified—by an alienation, one kind of possession could be created only as the result of a permanent transfer to a church, namely, tenure in alms. Jean Yver has ably elucidated the development of tenure in alms in Normandy in the eleventh and twelfth centuries,[226] but he concentrates on the relationship between alms and ducal protection of them and thus leaves room for further study of the subject. In general, moreover, Yver considers the nature of alms to have been rather less clearly defined by the end of the eleventh century than the charters seem to me to indicate that it was.

Transfers to churches were often made "in inheritance," "in allod," "in right," "in perpetuity," "in demesne," and the like. They were also sometimes made "in fee." These terms will be discussed in due course.[227] Most often, however, the quality of a transfer to a church is described as "in alms" or in "perpetual," "free," "absolved," "quit," and/or "pure" alms.[228] These phrases, unlike the others, are, of course, applied only to the possessions of churches. The incidence of the use of such phrases varies enormously from church to church: some abbeys from which large numbers of charters survive never refer to alms, whereas others use the term fairly consistently. Saint-Martin de Sées, the most consistent, uses the formula "absolved and quit as alms in perpetuity" as part of the standard introduction of its charters, with small variations, one of which is the omission of the words "as alms."

By the late eleventh century, alms was a distinct type of tenure. Several charters of Saint-Pierre de Préaux refer to a *ius elemosinae*.[229] Tenure in alms could be sharply distinguished from tenure in fee, as when William de *Claraio* gave Saint-Martin de Sées "Fulcuin's land which the aforesaid monks held from the aforesaid William in fee, not in fee, as at first, but in alms like the rest" of what he gave.[230] The same abbey also clearly differentiated between sales and gifts in alms.[231] This does not mean that no countergifts could be accepted for a gift in alms—they often were[232]—but it does imply that gifts in alms were a distinct sort of transfer. One of Saint-Martin de Sées' scribes committed a tautology which, again, indicates that alms was well understood: when William de *Claraio* quitclaimed to the abbey land his brother had held, he "demised the land to St. Martin . . . as absolved, indeed, and quit as alms ought to be given and demised absolved and quit."[233]

As the adjectives used—free, absolved, quit, pure—indicate, the essence of the tenure was that possessions held in alms were not burdened with services. Saint-Florent de Saumur reports William the Conqueror's assent to the dictum "that alms ought to be given pure."[234] When charters elucidate the meaning of "alms," which is rare, it is by such phrases as "absolved from everything pertaining to him," "free and quit from all customs pertaining to me," or "quit and free from every service."[235] Similar phrases often occur in charters which use neither the word "alms" nor any of the words, to be discussed later,[236] which denoted ownership when applied to churches. The explanatory phrases tend to be somewhat longer and more informative in charters which do not use "alms," perhaps because tenure "in alms" was clearly understood and had only one meaning. The question is whether all these charters—those couched in terms of ownership, those in terms of alms, and those which use neither expression—describe the same type of possession. In other words, when one charter from Saint-Martin de Sées says that a gift was made "absolved and quit in perpetuity" and another says that a gift was made "absolved and quit as alms in perpetuity," do the words "as alms" add anything to the description? Unfortunately, little basis exists for deciding this question. Given the wide variations in the use of the term "alms" from church to church, a grant which was "absolved and quit in perpetuity"—or the like—probably was a grant in alms whether it is said to be so or not, for it does not seem likely that the use or nonuse of the term by different churches reflects a difference in the conditions under which their possessions were given them. Instead, this is probably an especially good indication that the *scriptoria* of different churches, perhaps even individual scribes, had different standards as to what was worth writing down in this period when formulas for recording gifts were, at best, only beginning to develop.

From what services were possessions in alms free? One charter defines "alms" as freedom from "all secular service,"[237] but the other four or five charters which speak of freedom from "secular" or "earthly service" do not use the word "alms."[238] In one for Saint-Martin de Sées, which does not use "alms," the confirmers make a gift "immune and free towards all men from all payments, except those which they [the monks] may charitably and spontaneously make to their [the confirmers'] relatives."[239] A charter for Saint-Sauveur-le-Vicomte is more specific, defining "alms" as freedom "from all services and especially from bernage."[240] Similarly, several for Fontenay, which do not use "alms" in this context, free what was given from "any custom or service or any *gersimonia* or any secular exaction" or a similar phrase.[241] Freedom from all secular service may have been the essence of the matter: one of the charters of Fontenay goes on, exceptionally, to explain why the donor granted these exemptions: "lest the offering which he made to God, who rules all, should have been less acceptable in the eyes of the divine majesty if it should be subordinated to the services of any lay person."[242] One gift included an exemption from episcopal customs as well as from secular obligations, and another included exemptions from all clerical customs as well as all lay ones.[243] Neither of these is said to be "in alms."

A gift seems to have been considered to be "in alms" not only if it was freed from all services, or all secular services, but also if it was merely as free as the donor could make it. "Alms," in other words, meant not only a certain type of tenure but also a certain intention on the donor's part when the gift was made.[244] Thus, although some charters say that the gift is free of all services, others record that the gift is in alms because it is free of all services pertaining to the donor.[245] Moreover, a few donors specify which freedoms were granted by which lords. To cite the most elaborate example, when Robert du Hommet made gifts to the collegial church of Saint-Fromond, he added, "I absolve this church from all secular services and customs which pertained to me. And my lord Richard [II] duke of Normandy, at my request, conceded that the church and its men should be quit of all secular services and customs which pertained to him, Hugh bishop of Coutances also conceding the aforesaid church to be quit and free from all synod dues and circuits and every custom."[246] This is not explicitly said to be a series of gifts in alms. Another man granted a gift, explicitly in alms, "as free and quit as he possessed his honor," doubtless because he could not grant more freedom than he himself had.[247] Yver suggests that "alms" denoted the donor's intention rather than the donee's tenure at an early stage in the history of the term, a stage being superseded in Normandy in the last decades of the eleventh century.[248] The charters cited accord with this in that those which use the word in an intentional sense come from earlier in the century than those which use it in a tenurial sense, where the two meanings can be distinguished. Other indications that the term bore an intentional meaning continue to the end of the century, however. First, in a few of the part-sale part-gift transactions from Saint-Martin de Sées, the gift—and it alone—is said to be "in alms."[249] Because one immovable was transferred by such a transaction, "alms" must here apply to the donor's act of giving rather than to the subsequent tenurial status of the property. Second, although it was possible for an immovable to be sold "in inheritance" or "in allod," descriptions used, I think, to denote ownership on the part of the churches which were the purchasers,[250] no sale is ever said to be "in alms";[251] again, the implication is that "alms" denoted the purity of the donor's intention.

A donor's intention might extend to the assumption of burdens which he or she could not induce a lord to waive. When Warin de la Mare gave Saint-Martin de Sées his hereditary land outside one of the gates of Alençon, he added that the gift was in alms and that "the rent which is owed from it to [my] lords, as long as I shall live and remain capable, will always be paid by me."[252] All of Warin's lords, that is, men at three levels above him in the tenurial hierarchy, consented to this gift, and Warin's immediate lord's lord received ten shillings from Warin as a countergift for his consent; but apparently at least one of the lords was not willing to renounce Warin's rent. Because he could not abolish it unilaterally, Warin had to continue to pay the rent himself to make his gift "alms." Perhaps whenever a donor wished to give in alms but could not get the lord's consent, he or she circumvented the obstacle as Warin did, and Warin's charter is unusual only in stating that this was done. The charter certainly means that a lord's consent to a gift in alms cannot be assumed to constitute his waiver of the services due from the property given. What was to happen after Warin's death is not stated: the abbey's respite from service may have been only temporary.

Although possessions held in alms were free, absolved, quit, and pure, they were not held without any obligations at all. Gilbert de *Brueriecurte* confirmed various gifts to Saint-Pierre de Préaux "in right of alms, so that what other rich men and my peers have had by right in their alms I should also have in mine, seeking nothing more."[253] Apparently Gilbert's peers were accustomed to retain certain rights in possessions they gave away as alms. Perhaps he refers to spiritual services. Unfortunately, however, charters specifying that a gift was in alms or explicitly granting sweeping exemptions from duties do not usually mention details of spiritual services. A few nevertheless show that a close link existed between tenure in alms and an obligation to perform spiritual services. Thus, one says that a gift was made free of all secular service lest the monks "have any excuse to interrupt the church office."[254] Other charters show that the services entailed by tenure in alms were spiritual services only. Robert de Mowbray, for example, gave Saint-Etienne de Caen "what I have in the territory of Villers . . . in alms quit in perpetuity to hold without any service except that the monks of the same convent should always recognize [that they hold] it from me in alms and should always do service to God from it for the health of my soul and [the souls] of all my relatives."[255] There seems, therefore, to have been no contradiction between gifts in alms or with sweeping exemptions from service and requirements that spiritual services be performed. Indeed, services for the souls of donors and others named by them, rather than services owed to ecclesiastics, may be the true contrast implied by the exemptions from specifically "secular" services discussed earlier. Nonetheless, rare though descriptions of spiritual services are, references to the spiritual services due from tenants in alms are conspicuously absent, especially as this is where one might expect to find them. The reason may be that tenure in alms seems to have been one of the better-defined concepts of eleventh-century Norman law; its precise nature did not, therefore, need to be stated when such a tenement was created.

Perhaps the nature of alms in eleventh-century Normandy can best be summed up as follows. As between the donor and the tenant in alms, alms was a tenure characterized by purely spiritual services: it was "free," "absolved," "quit," and "pure" of all "secular services" which had been owed to the alienor or which the alienor might impose on what was being alienated. As among the donor, the donor's lords, and the tenant in alms, the situation was more complex, for a lord might be unwilling to waive service. In such a situation, the donor who assumed as much of the burden of service as he or she could got credit for good intentions: the gift would be "in alms" even though it was not entirely freed from all nonspiritual services. Donors, however, could not completely remove all burdens without the cooperation of others. Episcopal dues, for example, were usually not within a lay donor's control,[256] and some of them—attendance at synods, for example—could not be assumed by a lay person. Similarly, no lesser person could either waive or assume the burden of paying or performing certain ducal rights, such as the rear-ban, the duke's right to summon all in the duchy to its defense. The same may have been true of rights of other lords: hospitality at the place given is one likely example. In such circumstances, what was given "in alms" would not, despite the donor's best efforts, be wholly free from burdens unless the bishop, the duke, or the lord could be persuaded to make a concession. To put the matter in anachronistic terminology, any donor who waived all *intrinsec* service and assumed as much of the *extrinsec* service as was possible would be a donor in alms. This construction is partly theoretical, given the general silence of the charters on what precise services and customs were relinquished by donors and confirmers in alms. If it is valid, it implies what is explicit in the *Summa de legibus* of the mid-thirteenth century, that only the duke could make alms completely free and pure.[257] If, however, "alms" in the eleventh century meant complete freedom from as much service as the donor could remove, the definition changed somewhat in the first half of the twelfth century, for a judgment of Henry II's court at Caen in 1157 admitted that donors could claim something more than mere prayers as service from land held from them in alms provided that they secured ducal charters specifying the additional charges.[258] Was this a small limitation of the previously greater freedom of alms or a large limitation on the previously greater residual interests of donors? On the basis of the eleventh-century documents, I prefer the former conjecture, but the evidence is slight for either side.[259]

CONCLUSION

Given the nature of the documents, it is only to be expected that most known transfers were made to churches, that most were permanent alienations, and that the prevalent type appears to be the gift in return for spiritual services. In the realm of permanent alienations, transactions in which a lay person was the recipient are known only incidentally and only because what was received was later transferred to a church. Sales and exchanges certainly could take place among lay persons and seem, from what little is known of them, to have differed little from transfers to which churches were parties. The charters give no reason to think that true gifts often occurred among lay persons, which is hardly surprising, for gifts to churches were made from pious motives which would not apply to transfers among the laity.

The nature of a permanent alienation seems to have been determined by the recompense it elicited: spiritual rewards for gifts, money for sales, immovables for exchanges. Terminology is not always entirely appropriate, sometimes apparently merely because the art of drafting documents was in its early stages of development in Normandy in the eleventh century. Categories of recompense, too, were not entirely distinct, as in gifts with immovable countergifts or sales which also entailed society or in which the "price" consisted of or included immovables as well as money. In occasional instances a word for one type of alienation is used to denote what otherwise appears to be another.[260] As a result, the different types of permanent alienations shade into one another. This may be merely an example of a phenomenon characteristic of France as a whole in this period, the lack of distinct categories of documents corresponding to distinct types of legal transfers, the formlessness of the instruments accurately indicating the imprecision of legal analysis of the natures of the different acts.[261] Certainly, Norman records of transfers are relatively formless, but I am not convinced that legal analysis was as deficient as the charters might imply. In the case of sales which were presented as gifts, at least, the apparent confusion was probably intentional. Moreover, Norman history was unique in two ways which may render the history of transactions there somewhat different from what it was in the rest of France: the ruling, landholding group was made up of newcomers, whether Scandinavian or continental in origin; and the habit of writing, wiped out for more than half a century, was reintroduced only gradually over the course of another half-century. I am inclined to think that a Norman law concerning the different types of permanent alienations was in the process of formation in the eleventh century and that as the century proceeded the types of transactions became more rather than less distinct in the minds of the scribes of charters and, by inference, in the minds of Normans as a group.

Two complementary processes were probably at work. First, conditions became more settled. Despite temporary lapses into relative chaos during the minority of Duke William and the rule of Duke Robert Curthose, Normans of about 1100 must have had much higher standards concerning stability of possession than did the Normans of the early tenth century who forcibly took possession of the territory which has subsequently borne their name. Indeed, conditions seem to have remained unsettled into the early eleventh century,[262] and the Norman aristocracy of the eleventh century was of very recent origin.[263] In the course of the eleventh century, as immovables came to be held securely by the same persons for long periods of time, transfers would have become increasingly noteworthy as interruptions of continuity. The considerations in return for which transfers were made would, therefore, emerge as a prominent concern; and as, for permanent alienations, these compensations seemed to fall into three types—spiritual, movable, and immovable—so there would seem to be three types of transactions—gifts, sales, and exchanges. Thus, through a kind of settling-out process, the concept of different types of permanent alienations and the definitions of them would gradually emerge. By the end of the century, apparently, this development was almost complete.

The second process is more purely technical: the practice of recording transfers was introduced and the technique of drafting charters subsequently improved. Improvements in drafting may also have contributed to the first process, for they may have reinforced the development of concepts of different types of alienations by giving them names. The improvement of drafting techniques in the course of the century, however, somewhat muddies the waters. Charters of the late eleventh century by and large are easier to understand and give more information more consistently than charters of the late tenth or early eleventh century: but are they easier to understand because concepts were clearer? Do they tell more because there was more to tell? Are they more consistent in what they say because practices were more regular? Or are they simply better at recording concepts and practices which were largely unchanged throughout the period? If, for example, the earliest charter to mention a material countergift dates from 1030,[264] does that mean that material countergifts emerged as a form of compensation only at about that time or that scribes began to record them only then?[265]

My impression is that the apparently greater clarity and precision of the law of the late eleventh century compared with the early eleventh century is real, that, in other words, the legal rules concerning permanent alienations became more fixed in the course of the century. Confusion among gifts, sales, and exchanges is relatively uncommon, and the specialized verbs which existed for buying, selling, and exchanging were rarely used anomalously. All in all, it looks as though when eleventh-century Normans transferred property they had specific purposes in mind and drew distinctions among types of alienations depending on the purposes for which the transfers were made.

About the consequences, as opposed to the motives, of permanent transfers, however, the charters have little to say. Some gifts are said to have been made "in alms," but the meaning of that term is rarely explained; and, as will emerge later, the charters give comparably little explanation of what it meant to transfer a gift "in inheritance," "in allod," "in right," "in perpetuity," "in demesne," or even "in fee." The reason for this silence may be that, as I have conjectured for alms, the meaning of at least some of these terms was so well known that the scribes of the charters did not usually think it necessary to explain them. The absence of reports of arguments presented and cases decided in court may, moreover, be what conceals the eleventh-century definitions of such terms. Certainly, the nearest approach to a definition of what rights a donor transferred by a gift comes from a unique document, Rainald the chaplain's memorandum.[266] Few such documents may ever have been drawn up; but, had more been and had they survived or had charters recording court cases been more explicit about arguments in court and about the grounds upon which decisions were made, the meanings behind the laconic phrases in the charters might be much clearer. On the basis of the extant charters, however, there seems little reason to think that the scribes were unclear about the meanings of the words they used or about the natures of the transactions they were recording. A permanent alienation was, in the first place, intended to be permanent. It was made in return for a specific form of recompense. Although in certain circumstances, such as transfers in alms or transfers which were partly gifts and partly sales, the alienor's intentions played a part in the classification of the transaction, the primary consideration in determining whether a transfer would be recorded as a gift or a sale or an exchange was the form of recompense the alienor received.

4

Conditional and Temporary Alienations

MOST KNOWN ALIENATIONS were made to churches and were intended to be permanent and unconditional, but they are usually recorded so succinctly that a comparable amount of information exists about the exceptions. These include not only grants made with conditions attached, including fiefs, but also rentals, life estates, and mortgages. Because some of these forms of transfers often involved gifts of movables, it seems appropriate to consider that subject here as well.

What was said in the last chapter is equally true here: the law appears to have been only in the process of formation in this period. Indeed, legal rules for the types of alienation now to be considered seem somewhat less advanced by the end of the eleventh century than were the rules about permanent alienations. Not only is it sometimes difficult to tell in a particular instance what form of alienation is involved; but more often than for permanent alienations, even toward the end of the century, scribes seem unable to record the terms of these transfers competently. Perhaps most significant, not all the distinguishable types of alienations had names by the end of the century and only one had a specialized verb: the mortgage has both throughout the century, although even here the terminology is not entirely precise; the fief has a name, though it changed in the course of the century; the *métairie* has a name, as does the farm by the end of the century; but that is all.[1]

CONDITIONAL GIFTS

Many special conditions were attached to gifts in eleventh-century Normandy. Parties apparently could make what arrangements they liked so long as they were in agreement. Therefore, the charters from time to time contain restrictions on how land could be cultivated or on the extent to which a forest might be exploited or any of a number of other provisions. These arrangements, however, are distinguishable from gifts which were made entirely on condition that something be done: the former merely describe some particular aspect of what was given, whereas the latter are true conditional gifts.

All gifts in return for which the recipient church promised to do some religious service for the donor are in form conditional.[2] They were at least occasionally treated as conditional by abbeys, which might cease to do the spiritual service if deprived of the property in return for which the services were done, even when the disseisor was someone other than the original donor.[3] The only indication that in the eleventh century such gifts might be treated as conditional by donors, however, comes from a tendentious twelfth-century source.[4] Equally conditional in form are gifts in return for the creation of a permanent position in a monastery for a monk in place of the donor, the right of the donor to enter the monastery in the future, the education of a son, or someone's entry into the religious life. A few men tried to act on the conditional nature of gifts of the last type. Orderic tells the story of a priest named Adelard who entered the abbey of Saint-Evroul when apparently on the point of death but, upon recovering, left it; "but when he attempted to resume possession of the church of Le Sap which he had given to the monks, Hugh of Grandmesnil, lord of the honour of Le Sap, refused to allow it." When Adelard found that he could not extricate his former church as well as himself from Saint-Evroul, he seems to have decided to regard his gift as conveying a right to reenter the monastery in the future: fifteen years later, when really on the point of death, he again became a monk of the abbey, but Orderic mentions no gift at this moment.[5] There is much less information about the second instance. A charter from Saint-Pierre de Préaux says simply that Robert de Méré seized back, or perhaps never handed over, part of a gift made when his brother became a monk because the brother "fled from the monastery."[6] The third possible example is ambiguous. Duke William's court heard a suit between the Breton abbey of Saint-Magloire de Lehon and a monk named Hugh, son of Warin de Bailleul, who claimed the church of Saint-Cyr de Bailleul, in Normandy, which his father had given to Saint-Magloire. The court's decision went against him because the judges "found that Hugh had been cast out of the monastery by right,"[7] wording which implies that if Hugh had been unjustly expelled his claim would have been valid. Eleventh-century charters sometimes were loosely drafted, however, and the implication may not have been intended. Evidence from Normandy for the treatment of gifts of this type as conditional is therefore inconclusive. Of attempts to act as though they were, only Robert de Méré's was successful, and it may have been based on might rather than right. Moreover, much evidence suggests that in Normandy such donations were not readily recognized as conditional: when charters take contingencies into account, they usually presume that a gift, once made, could not be revoked and that, if the original purpose of the donation could not be fulfilled, injury to the interests of the donor could be prevented by substituting other benefits.[8]

Certain gifts, however, were made to churches on specified conditions, which the churches agreed to fulfill. Most commonly, an abbey was given a church which it agreed to make a priory. Marmoutier might keep in its own hands the decisions as to the "number and quality" of the monks to be sent to a place.[9] It might reserve even the option whether to found a priory at all: an agreement stipulates that if the monks choose not to do so the alienor should return to them one-third of the money he had received for his grant.[10] Other abbeys seem less insistent on complete control than Marmoutier. When Robert de *Peissiaco* gave property to Conches to found a priory, he declared that it should have three monks, though he left the choice of the monks up to the abbey, and he assigned a specific income, five muids of grain, to the monks of the priory.[11] William de Briouze said simply that Saint-Florent de Saumur in its new priory of Saint-Gervais and Saint-Protase should have "only one or two monks, as many as can live from its possessions."[12] In connection with donations of churches on condition that they be erected into priories, some donors also say that, if circumstances warrant, the priory should be elevated into an abbey.[13]

Such conditions were not always simple to fulfill. It was not easy to establish even a priory. Orderic's well-known account of the early history of Saint-Evroul shows not only the problems that abbey faced, first as a priory of Conches and later as an independent house, but also those the abbey of Bec had earlier had in trying to found a priory on the site where Saint-Evroul was later successfully established.[14] In another example, after transcribing the charter by which Ivo de Bellême gave a place called Sainte-Gauberge to Saint-Père de Chartres "so that the monastic order should there serve as soldiers for God," the compiler of Saint-Père's cartulary added a melancholy note: a previous attempt by a monk of Bonneval to found an abbey there, at the instance of Ivo's brother and predecessor, William I de Bellême, had been defeated by "the frequency of wars and the poverty of the place," and Saint-Père's attempt to found a priory had come to an end when the nefarious doings of a monk named Solo "alienated us from the place and the place from us."[15] Poverty and destruction in war, such as plagued Bonneval's efforts at Sainte-Gauberge, were probably more common reasons for the abandonment of cells than were scandals, or at least they are more often cited. Poverty was certainly on the minds of several donors: of Robert de *Peissiaco*, for example, when he specified the income the monks of a priory were to have,[16] or Richard and Turstin de Creully, who explicitly forbade any of the "substance" of the priory of Saint-Gabriel to be removed by Fécamp.[17] In founding Marmoutier's priory of Saint-Léonard de Bellême, Robert de Bellême was careful to prescribe "that during his lifetime nothing should be taken from there to Marmoutier without the same Robert's license. After his death, however, the prior of Saint-Léonard should take annually to Marmoutier ten pounds in coin or in weight, if he is not in poverty and the monks of Marmoutier are; but this is to be demanded by no debt or custom."[18] Founding a priory was difficult enough even when the mother abbey cooperated completely.[19]

One abbey, however, insisted—at least for a while—on its right to share in all gifts to it, even to the detriment of its daughter cells. When, in 1084, Robert

Quadrel gave a church to Saint-Martin de Sées, he provided that its profits should support one monk at the abbey and—depending on how much income there was—one or two at the church. The charter explains that it was Abbot Robert's custom "never to commit a monk of his to serve any church unless he was able to support from that obedience at least one monk in the monastery in addition to the one serving [the church]."[20] I have conjectured that this abbey may have grown very slowly in its early years,[21] and Abbot Robert's rule concerning the creation of cells may have been a reaction to its difficulties. Gifts, or at least gifts of which records survive, began to accrue in large numbers during his last few years as abbot.[22] Perhaps as a result, his successor does not seem to have maintained the same principle: in 1101, Robert son of William de *Polleio* gave the abbey various possessions at *Polleio*, including rights in its church, and the abbey agreed simply to place two monks there.[23] Special circumstances, therefore, may explain the first abbot's caution about the foundation of dependent cells.

What if, despite its best efforts, an abbey was unable to create a priory where a donor had specified that there be one? The compiler of the cartulary of Saint-Père de Chartres does not indicate what happened to Sainte-Gauberge after the monks of the abbey could no longer contemplate establishing themselves there.[24] When the earlier attempt to found a priory there failed, the church had apparently reverted to the donor, perhaps by default. Saint-Evroul eventually became the site of an independent abbey, rather than a priory of Bec; but this was done with the consent—indeed, at the insistence—of the man who had first given it to Bec, and Bec was compensated for the loss of the land by another gift.[25] Conches' attempt to found a priory at Norrey having failed, Norrey seems to have returned to the would-be founders, for it was given to Saint-Evroul as a mere possession, and there is no reference to compensation to Conches.[26] In no other agreement about a priory is the outcome of the attempt known to have been unsatisfactory; and none of the donors in these cases provided in advance for such an outcome.

Instances of the elevation of successful priories into new abbeys, however, give some information. When Duke Robert Curthose confirmed to Bec his parents' gift of a church which became the priory of Notre-Dame-du-Pré, he provided "that, if ever I should wish to make the same church an abbey in itself, I be permitted to do so without any challenge from the monks of Bec, if I give their convent an exchange which will be worth as much to them as the aforesaid church, with all which will then pertain to it, will be worth"; the same right is reserved to his brother William Rufus, king of England.[27] Curthose cannot have feared that the priory would not flourish under Bec's rule, for he would not make the priory an abbey unless the site had proved capable of supporting a sizable number of monks. He may have been afraid that Bec would refuse to relinquish a flourishing site so that it could become a rival abbey. Some earlier donors tried, apparently, to solve that problem by arranging for the new abbey to remain subject to the old one.[28] Such arrangements, however, could lead to disputes between the two abbeys.[29] Perhaps for this reason, Curthose wanted a completely independent abbey and therefore had to find another way.

William de Briouze had had problems in trying to found an abbey in the church of Saint-Gervais and Saint-Protase before he finally agreed with Saint-Florent to found a priory there or, "if the same alms grows enough," an abbey.[30] He had earlier given the church to the abbey of Lonlay, which challenged Saint-Florent's right to the church twice, in William the Conqueror's court at some time between 1080 and 1083 and in Robert Curthose's court in 1093 or 1094. One charter records the decision of both courts; but, because in the second trial the claimants ran away and lost the case by default, the substance of the claim is known only from the account of the first trial. William did not deny that Lonlay had once possessed the church, but

> he showed that . . . he had not given what they were challenging but had commended [it to them] on condition that, when the place had grown a little, there should be an abbey in the same place through their counsel and with the approval of the chapter. He showed also that because of this they relinquished the already mentioned church to him, because he had not given it but commended it, and because they did not wish to create an abbey there—if, at some time, its goods having increased, it would be able to become one—but to have it as a cell, which Lord William had not conceded to them, that is, to hold it as a cell; and because of this they had demised to him all that they were now claiming.[31]

This is the most precise statement extant concerning the nature of a conditional gift: it was "not given . . . but . . . commended on condition," and if the condition was not fulfilled the commended property could not be claimed as a gift and should be "relinquished." It appears that Lonlay feared a rival abbey: William points out that Lonlay did not claim the church while it was held by his mother or by several clerics, although both his mother and the clerics had held after the church had been in Lonlay's hands, but that Lonlay raised its challenge as soon as he gave the church to another abbey.[32] That may explain why, on his next attempt, William gave the church to relatively remote Saint-Florent; it is also probably why he allowed Saint-Florent to maintain a hegemony over the projected new abbey.[33] Before the conquest of England, Duke William's court had heard a similar though considerably more complex case, which originated in Maine, over which William had asserted control in 1063. Although the provenance of the case was not Norman, the court was; and the arguments in this case confirm that, when a conditional gift was made, if the condition was not fulfilled the donor was free to act as though the gift had never occurred.[34]

Conditions about staffing might be attached to gifts of churches. Enguerrand and his wife, Agnes, gave Saint-Etienne de Caen a church and some other possessions "on condition that the monks should place a suitable cleric in that church"; if they did not, Enguerrand would "retain"—that is, withhold or, perhaps, seize back—the gift until the condition was fulfilled.[35] Richard de Rosel, who gave a church to Saint-Etienne on a similar condition, made no provision for enforcement.[36] When, however, William de Montfort confirmed to Saint-Pierre de Préaux a gift of a church and ten acres of land, which had been made considerably earlier so that his brother could become a monk, "he retained in his own hand three acres of those ten which he had given, so that he should find a cleric for the church and should give those three acres to him."[37] William seems concerned not with the suitability of the incumbent of the church but with the adequacy of his support, perhaps because he was to choose the cleric himself, but he used the same method as Enguerrand to ensure the achievement of his ends.

A few other charters containing agreements specify what steps would be taken if the agreement should break down. The abbot of Saint-Martin de Sées and the bishop of Sées entered into a detailed agreement to create a fishpond; they did so in the presence of Robert de Bellême and provided "that if any [complaint of] injustice should arise from this he should do rightful justice between them."[38] Nothing is said of any penalty; and it seems likely that Robert's role would be merely to interpret the agreement, not to adjudge fault and impose a penalty.[39] Two agreements imposing unilateral obligations also avoid the question of penalties. In each a countergift involved an abbey's repeated performance of a duty, and a different obligation could be substituted if, for some legitimate reason, the first one could not be done. The abbot of Saint-Etienne de Caen promised Robert de Beaufour "that he would receive him in hospitality four times per year, each time for one night, provided he came in moderation, that is, not with a multitude, and when he did not lodge with the abbot the abbot would send him a present, if Robert himself should inform the abbot where he is."[40] In return for gifts by Elias de Cagny, Abbot Arnulf of Troarn added "to the fee which he holds from us five hundred eels, and at the time when, in our bogs, we carry off the peat we will give him twelve wagons loaded as they are for sale, three *teras super scaleras*; or, if we should not carry away peat for ourselves or, indeed, if there should not be [enough] to give, we will pay the price which he would have gotten as it is valued this present year, namely, twenty shillings, to him and to his heir."[41] Because these agreements were intended to operate for years in the future, the problem was to arrange matters so that, if nonperformance resulted, not from unwillingness but from inability to perform, the intended recipient could be satisfied, the agreement remain unbroken, and penalties therefore not need to be considered.

A penalty, when specified, is always the loss of the gift to which the condition is attached. Enguerrand provided that he could withhold part of his gift until the donee fulfilled the condition, and William de Montfort apparently actually did so.[42] When Robert de Bellême founded the priory of Saint-Léonard at Bellême, he provided that "the monks of Marmoutier whom he receives to live in his castle . . . should seek no other justice than his concerning all injuries done to them. If they should do so [and] if they do not cease after he has remonstrated with the abbot and the chapter of Marmoutier, they should lose whatever he gave them."[43] Saint-Etienne de Caen granted land to the canon Richard son of William and his heirs, reserving a right to hospitality for the abbot and monks; if ever hospitality should be refused, the land would revert to the abbey.[44] Saint-Martin de Sées, wishing to build a fishpond, obtained control of a mill near the site from William de Sivilly in return for an annual payment of grain. A contingency clause provides for two eventualities. If war or famine makes the mill less productive, the payment dependent on revenue from it is to be reduced proportionally; and Robert Morell, who had given various rights in the mill, "should have three prescribed setiers of grain from the aforesaid mill as long as he keeps his agreements with William de Sivilly." The first part of the agreement is like the arrangements just discussed where nonperformance results from justified inability to perform. If, however, Robert Morell does not keep his agreements—although, it is to be understood, nothing prevented him from keeping them—he loses his payment because he does not deserve it.[45] Similarly, when the duke and the abbey of Jumièges gave Roger de Montgomery permission to construct a market at Montgomery provided that it did not decrease the business of Jumièges' market at Vimoutiers, he agreed both that he would increase Jumièges' revenues by a pound a year for three years and "that, if their aforesaid market should be observed to suffer any detriment on account of mine, which I am now erecting, unless I exert myself to compensate [them] within forty days after their admonition, the agreement being annulled and I losing, the market will revert to the monks."[46]

Additional evidence comes from a very different context: the gifts to or grants by various churches of immovables which are to be held by a layman's wife or daughter until she dies. Some carry the proviso that the wife not remarry or that the daughter live "legally," which presumably means morally. If the wife marries again or the daughter misbehaves, the property goes to the church at once.[47] These lands, in other words, are held on a condition; if the condition is broken by the woman's remarriage or misconduct, she is to lose her tenement.

No charter states both what the penalty would be and that it was put into effect. Nevertheless, instances exist of persons abrogating agreements when a condition was not performed, or trying to do so. William de Briouze received the church of Saint-Gervais and Saint-Protase back from Lonlay because the monks would not make it an abbey, and Sainte-Gauberge reverted to William de Bellême when monks from Bonneval could not make it an abbey. Adelard tried to take back the church of Le Sap when he ceased to be a monk at Saint-Evroul, and Hugh de Bailleul apparently tried to do the same vis-à-vis Saint-Magloire de Lehon. Robert de Méré appears to have been successful in withholding part of what his father had given Saint-Pierre de Préaux to make his brother a monk because the brother did not remain at the abbey.[48] Only two other cases show such provisions being put into effect; both resulted in the eventual buying off of the troublesome provision.[49]

Although conditional gifts are relatively rare, they occur often enough in eleventh-century Normandy to be considered a recognized form of legal transaction. The obligation created might be a standing one, as in Roger de Montgomery's promise to ensure that his market not harm that of Jumièges, or it might be one which could be satisfied once and for all, as in the case of the creation of a priory or an abbey. Intermediate possibilities also existed, as in the countergift Saint-Etienne de Caen gave to Robert de Beaufour or the one Troarn gave to Elias de Cagny, which had to be satisfied annually, or in an agreement whereby Mont-Saint-Michel promised to supply war horses and refuge to Gradelocus and his sons, which had to be satisfied whenever these men "should have to go to war."[50] As violation of an agreement might be either voluntary or involuntary, so two methods of enforcement seem to have been known: either a second obligation would be incurred if the primary obligation was not fulfilled, or a penalty might be imposed. Secondary obligations preserved the agreement and the obligated party's rights when nonperformance of the primary duty was involuntary; only deliberate noncompliance entailed a penalty. Because the obligated party received from the other party not other acts but immovables, when that party did not perform as it should and the agreement was thereby broken the penalty incurred was the loss—temporary, pending resumption or renegotiation, or permanent—of the immovable.[51] The case of Bishop Hugh of Bayeux, who "invaded the lands of Saint-Pierre de Préaux on account of a certain agreement which the builder of that place, named Humphrey, had with him" and was bought off at "great expense," seems to show that enforcement of the penalty of loss of the immovable by forcible seizure was regarded as legitimate at least as late as the middle of the eleventh century.[52]

FIEFS

Unlike most other conditional alienations, the grant of a fief involved obligations on the part both of the alienor and of the recipient: fiefs were contractual in nature.[53] Moreover, most known examples involve both a lay alienor and a lay recipient. Churches could, to be sure, grant fiefs, hold them, even grant them to each other.[54] Furthermore, fiefs are usually mentioned solely for one of two reasons: either the fief was held from a church, or all or part of it was alienated to a church. Nevertheless, most fiefs in Normandy must have been held by lay persons from lay persons. That may be why the charters are remarkably uninformative about the creation of fiefs and the conditions of feudal tenure, a noteworthy omission considering the importance usually attributed to feudal tenure in eleventh-century Normandy. Because of this silence, it is probably better not to accept the usual portrayal of feudal relations in the duchy in this period as highly systematized and hierarchically organized for the duke's benefit.[55]

Even the conclusion that by the end of the eleventh century most of the land in Normandy was held rather than owned is, as will appear, based on an argument from silence, the absence of any reference to ownership.[56] There is a corresponding and much more surprising silence, for hardly anything is said of services due as a result of the transfers of property with which this work is concerned.[57] At best, therefore, it could be only an assumption that transfers normally were infeudations in return for feudal services. Moreover, even if all transfers to churches are excluded from consideration, on the grounds that the products of piety would naturally not be burdened with any but spiritual services, there is evidence that not all the remaining transactions were infeudations of the expected sort, for some tenements were held for rent[58] and life estates granted by churches to lay persons were normally held in return for lump-sum payments, improvements to the property granted, or transfers of additional property on the termination of the estate.[59] To be sure, there were fiefs, though the services for them were by no means always primarily military;[60] and it is possible that among lay persons they were much more common than the exclusively ecclesiastical documents would suggest. All information about secular services is exceptional, however; and, on the basis of existing evidence, there is no more reason to conclude that most tenements were held for feudal services than to assert that most were held for rents or other material considerations.

Fiefs were merely one of a multiplicity of types of tenements which eleventh-century Normans could and did create. It cannot be assumed that they were a more important variety than others or had a special significance in the social, political, or institutional practices of eleventh-century Normans. For this reason, discussion of the ceremony of investiture is deferred to the discussion of public acts of donation,[61].and the questions here asked about fiefs will be those already asked about other conditional alienations: what conditions governed their existence? If the conditions were not fulfilled, what happened?

Because the grant of a fief imposed duties on both lord and tenant, these questions must be considered for each party. The complete absence of charters of enfeoffment greatly hampers investigation. Furthermore, most references to fiefs are succinct. Even when tenements were given to churches, the service due was, apparently, not of marked concern to the clerics who wrote the charters. This is as true of fiefs as of other tenements. An immovable[62] may be said to have been a fief or part of a fief before it was given to a church so as to identify what was given or to report the lord's consent, or it may be said to have been granted out as a fief by the church which possessed it, again to identify it, or canons or monks may complain that their bishop or abbot had granted out possessions of their church without their permission—but in none of these contexts do the documents evince much interest in why or how an enfeoffment was made. Moreover, the contexts are such that what information they provide concerns the obligation of vassals, not lords.

Little, therefore, is known of the duties of lords. During the reign of Duke Robert Curthose, Viscount Rannulf of Bayeux and an unnamed bishop of Bayeux, probably Odo, came to an agreement by which Rannulf was to "serve for those lands which, when Rannulf first held them from the bishop, the king [William the Conqueror] . . . took them away from the bishop and made Rannulf hold them but not from the bishop."[63] According to this document, which restored the feudal relationship between bishop and viscount, lord and tenant each gave the other essentially the same promises: to protect his person from death or wounding, not to plot his capture, to help him in his disputes over land, and to aid him in war against all save the duke.[64] Each, in other words, owed two basic duties: the negative one of not harming and the positive one of support in court and in war. The bishop also promised Viscount Rannulf an annual gift,[65] but the agreement gives no details of Rannulf's service. The only comparable document, an agreement between William Paynel and the abbot of Mont-Saint-Michel, is almost exclusively concerned with what was owed to William from his fief, but it leaves a general impression that the abbot contracted not to make it impossible for William to profit from the fief, even when obligations to the abbot conflicted with obligations to William.[66] The bishop of Bayeux, the abbot of Mont-Saint-Michel, and several other lords were obligated to act as warrantors for the lands they gave to their tenants; indeed, one lord at least, the abbot of Préaux, apparently faced the loss of his lordship if he did not warrant his tenants' possessions.[67]

All the other extant statements of what a lord owed his vassal come from the historians, especially from Dudo of Saint-Quentin. He recounts that Rollo and his brother Gurim promised to aid and protect the members of their Viking band and, especially, to prevent the king of the Danes from depriving them of their lands.[68] By the treaty of Saint-Clair-sur-Epte of 911, he alleges, King Charles the Simple and his magnates "swore to Rollo the patrician by an oath of the Catholic faith [to defend] his life and limbs and the honor of [his] whole kingdom (*regnum*), and especially [concerning] the denominated land [Normandy], that he should hold and possess it and transmit it to his heirs and should have and exploit it in his lineage forever and ever."[69] Dudo also says that, when Arnulf of Flanders seized Montreuil from its count, Herluin, the latter appealed to Hugh duke of France to aid him "because he was his count and knight, prompt in every service."[70] When Hugh repeatedly refused to help, Herluin appealed to Duke William Longsword of Normandy. William, however, sent Herluin again to Hugh, who refused again and informed Herluin that he was allied with Arnulf. Herluin then reproached Hugh, saying, "Since, then, you are not at all interested to succor my necessity, as would be proper, it behooves you not to be angry if anyone else does help me."[71] Hugh having agreed to this, Herluin appealed again to William, who recovered Montreuil from Arnulf. When William gave the castle back to Herluin, the latter protested that he ought not accept it because he could not defend it against Arnulf. Dudo has William reply,

> I shall protect by assisting you. I shall defend by aiding and guarding you. I shall construct this castle again by rebuilding [it] for you . . . ; replenishing it with an abundance of grain and wine, I shall fill it and fortify it all for you by rebuilding [it]. Whomever you may choose of my magnates, they will remain with you, surrounded by a multitude of their vassals. If Arnulf should begin a war against you, I shall quickly come to your aid with the host of my armies. If, however, he should seek a truce

> for negotiating peace, we shall give the advice of our vassals to him; but if in the meanwhile he should wish to come against us in court, using judgment and justice and law, we shall come against him on your account to be judged by the opinion of our [men]. If with obstinate heart he should devastate the estates of your inheritance, with an assembled army we shall burn the whole of his domain for him. [I shall be] your willing benevolent assister, your defender against enemies, docile listener to your complaints, attentive consoler of your calamities, verily indeed the true distributor of fitting benefits to you.[72]

A few years later William's young son Richard I succeeded him as duke of Normandy, and King Louis IV immediately tried to take advantage of the minority to secure control over Normandy. In his account of how Louis came to Rouen to take custody of the young duke, Dudo has Richard's chief protector, Bernard the Dane, address the king as follows:

> Since our lord Duke William was favorable to you in all things, it is fitting that you authorize that Richard . . . possess the land by hereditary right, sanctioning [your authorization] with an oath . . . and that you be harmless to him in the past and from now on, and that you be [his] aider and defender against all earthly men. Thus you should seek to rejoice in our service (*servitium*) and military support (*militatio*), we in your wardship and governance. If anyone should quarrel with you, we shall go against him; and if anyone should revolt against us, by virtue of your power prostrate him to the earth![73]

The king, continues Dudo, deceitfully agreed and swore the oath. These passages certainly cannot be taken as evidence of the obligations of lords in the first half of the tenth century, but they should reflect the ideas of the period when Dudo was writing. If so, then by the third decade of the eleventh century a lord's duties were essentially the same as those the bishop of Bayeux owed Viscount Rannulf toward the end of the century, namely, not to harm the vassal and to aid him in war and—in the case of William Longsword's promises to Herluin of Montreuil—in court. The mutuality of lords' and vassals' duties, again comparable to the agreement between the bishop and the viscount, is prominent in the speech attributed to Bernard the Dane.

The other eleventh-century Norman historians, William of Poitiers and William of Jumièges, do not expatiate on the subject of the duties of lords to their men. Both Norman sources of the twelfth century and English sources of either period are dangerous to use because they, like Dudo, may apply concepts of their own time or place. One passage from Orderic, however, reports an incident similar to Dudo's tale of Herluin of Montreuil. After war broke out between William count of Evreux and Ralph de Tosny, in or before 1091, William apparently attacking first,

> Ralph went to Duke Robert to complain to him of the injuries inflicted by his fellow countrymen and ask him as his . . . lord for help; but he

> wasted his time, for nothing was done. Therefore he looked elsewhere, since he had to seek effective patronage. He sent envoys to describe his misfortunes to the king of England and promised to submit himself and all he owned to William if help were forthcoming. This message was most welcome to the king, and he promised effective support to Ralph in his need. Then he commanded Count Stephen [of Aumale] and Gerard of Gournay and the other military leaders who were in charge of his retainers in Normandy to lend Ralph full support and garrison and provision his fortresses.[74]

Orderic's story resembles Dudo's, among other things, in that the lord's duties included garrisoning and provisioning his men's castles. A good deal of evidence exists that lords garrisoned castles commanded by their subordinates; indeed, it was William the Conqueror's determined policy to do so.[75] This usually seems to have been regarded as an imposition rather than a boon—the reaction of a good many Norman magnates to William's death was to expel the ducal garrisons[76]—but both Herluin and Ralph were under attack, which probably altered their perspectives. Most of the evidence about provisions and repairs suggests that the duty was incumbent on the castellan's subordinates, not his superiors;[77] but here, too, in time of war obligations may have been different, or differently perceived, from peacetime.

Dudo and Orderic also agree that, if a lord, when called upon to give military aid to his man, did not do so, the man was justified in transferring his allegiance—and his fief—to a lord who would. Neither account indicates that the man had to secure a court's judgment before he could exercise his right or even formally to defy his former lord on grounds of refusal of aid. It seems unlikely, however, that lords would voluntarily let their men go, no matter how disinclined they were to protect them. Raw power alone probably lies behind both instances. Robert Curthose was certainly weak enough by the early 1090s to be unwilling or unable either to intervene on behalf of one vassal against another or to prevent an aggrieved vassal from deserting him; and Dudo's account of early Norman history is so pro-Norman that there is no reason to accept at face value his portrait of the legal nicety with which William Longsword and Herluin behaved toward Duke Hugh.[78]

The sources do not say much more about the theoretical obligations of men to their lords than is contained in the passages concerning lords' duties to their men. Only three oaths of vassals are quoted. Dudo says that, when Rollo designated William Longsword his heir, the great men of Brittany and Normandy swore fealty and did homage to him "and vowed that they would be [his] warriors and fight [for him] even against the most remote peoples."[79] According to William of Poitiers, Harold Godwinsson swore an oath to Duke William during his ill-fated visit to Normandy in the early 1060s in which he promised to represent William's interests in England and to construct, garrison, and provision castles there in his behalf.[80] The circumstances, however, make it impossible to take this example as evidence of the contents of Norman feudal oaths. The last oath, sworn by Richard de Sainte-Mère-Eglise to Abbot Ralph of Saint-Pierre de Préaux, also concerns what appear to be truly exceptional promises.[81] The few other passages in the historians on the subject of oaths, all about broken oaths, suggest that a vassal's principal obligation was negative, not to harm his lord.[82]

Legal documents, however, say a great deal more about the vassal's side of the contract than any source says of the lord's side, although the information is fragmentary and almost exclusively from the last three decades of the century. By far the most comprehensive statement of the obligations of tenants is an agreement between William Paynel and the abbot of Mont-Saint-Michel made between 1070 and 1081:

> This charter relates the agreement made at Bayeux in the presence of the queen between the abbot of Mont-Saint-Michel and William Paynel. If William Paynel has war in the land which the king of the English gave him with his wife, the agreement is that Hugh de Bricqueville should do him forty days of watch and ward (*guarda vel custodia*) [with seven horsemen], he himself [being] the seventh of the horsemen, at his own cost. And Hugh's nephew will also do so if he should hold his land in parage (*in parage*), according to what he will hold. Again, if William Paynel should summon Hugh, he will have him in his following (*familia*) with two knights at his own cost or his son if he is free of the abbot's summons. Nor will the lord abbot always have him so that William Paynel does not have it. And so indeed he will have in his following Hugh's nephew and Robert de Chanteloup and William Beceth and the one who will have Scollant's honor. And if he should have a defense or a claim to make, he will have the [suit of the] men whom he holds from St. Michael in such a way that they will be [able to return] to their houses at night. And if the men should default from these services which are apportioned here, they should do right to him at one of the houses which he holds from St. Michael.
>
> He should accept aid from the land which he holds from St. Michael for the capture of his body or for his land, if he forfeits it to the king or the abbot, or for the son of the wife whose inheritance it is, if he should be captured in the service of the king or the abbot from whom the fee is, or to marry one daughter only whom he has from this wife.
>
> The agreement is that in the land which he holds from the abbot William Paynel should appoint one man to whom the abbot will send for the summonses which the same abbot has to make in the land which William Paynel holds from him. If he does the summonses well but he whom he informed should remain [away], the abbot should accept his [the summoner's] forfeit for it. But if the summons remains with the summoner, he will pay a fine of eighteen shillings to the abbot and afterwards the abbot will make his summons by his own messenger.
>
> The agreement is that William Paynel should accept twelve oaks every year, chosen by himself, in the wood of Longueville as far as the water

> which is called *Ars*, nor may he take more unless it should be done by [permission of] the abbot.
>
> The agreement is that the abbot of Mont[-Saint-Michel] should give him every year one provision of wax or twenty shillings, and it is at the choice of the abbot to give whichever he prefers, and this for the reliefs of Chanteloup and for the pasture of La Lande, if the men of Chanteloup are able to deraign it in William Paynel's court. Concerning Lavidande, which William Paynel has been claiming in fee since he came to Mont-Saint-Michel, it is in respite until [it comes] before the king.
>
> The agreement is, concerning the seven peers (*pares*) of the honor which William Paynel holds from the abbot of Mont-Saint-Michel, that he should summon them in his court; [and] if they should be willing of their own accord to go, they will go if they are free of the abbot's service. If they should not be willing to go, William Paynel ought to deraign this in the abbot's court through men who are of the honor which he accepted with his wife [and] who saw them in his service by the custom of his ancestor's.[83]

The obligations of William's men, therefore, involve military service, suit of court, and aids. The agreement also alludes to two feudal incidents: it contains one of the few eleventh-century uses of the term "relief," and the means by which William acquired the land is the clearest eleventh-century example of a lord's right of feudal marriage.[84]

William's vassals' principal military service is forty days of "watch and ward," that is, castle guard, presumably forty days per year. They must also serve in his "following," but whether this means his army or merely his retinue is not clear. Viscount Rannulf and the bishop of Bayeux were obliged to fight on each other's behalf except against the duke, but their agreement says nothing about the duration of the service or about warriors whom either must bring with him. William Paynel's men, however, had fixed quotas: Hugh de Bricqueville must bring six others to do castle guard; he, and perhaps four others, must bring two knights to their lord's following. A somewhat dubious charter from Saint-Amand mentions two knights who serve for forty days per year, one with full arms, the other with "plain" arms.[85] According to Orderic, writing about eighty years after the fact, in 1054 Duke William imposed on Guy count of Ponthieu the duty of providing one hundred knights per year to serve wherever the duke pleased.[86] Gilbert Crispin says in a charter that he held land from his lord the duke "by fighting."[87] St. Anselm's often-used analogy between types of knights and types of Christians is more like a theoretical statement of the obligations of vassals than any other eleventh-century Norman source; in it Anselm assumes that a ruler has some *milites* "who are active in his service in return for the lands which they hold from him."[88] The records of a court case of 1101 show that Robert Samson owed castle guard to the Montgomery family and was not the first tenant of his lands to do so.[89] Orderic says that Abbot Robert of Saint-Evroul transferred two of the abbey's unruly vassals to the lordship of Arnold d'Echauffour, who "piled all kinds of oppressive services upon them, and forced them and their men to perform castle guard at Echauffour and St. Céneri."[90] These meager facts constitute everything known from contemporary sources about the military obligations of vassals in eleventh-century Normandy, not only as to type, amount, duration, and equipment, but even as to the existence of a duty to fight or to guard castles which was consequent upon tenure of land. In addition, the knight Herluin, later the founder and first abbot of Bec, owed messenger service to his lord Gilbert count of Brionne before 1034;[91] and this was the only service owed by two minor tenants, father and son, for a fief they held of Troarn.[92] In the early twelfth century, Humphrey d'Adeville, who held a fief from La Trinité de Caen, served the abbey "by such service as a knight ought to do; this moreover added: that if the lady abbess should have to [travel?] within Normandy or outside Normandy Lord Humphrey [will go?] with her."[93] Here escort service appears to be additional to the ordinary services to be expected of a knight. The few other extant references to messenger or escort service all concern clerics.[94]

Not much more is known about suit of court than about military and quasi-military service.[95] The seven peers of William Paynel's honor apparently owed him suit of court when that service was not preempted by the abbot, unless the reference to their being summoned "in his court" is to a summons for some other purpose. All his men owed suit of court provided that they could return to their homes at night; and all had to answer for default of service but, again, only within a limited geographical area. A charter from La Trinité de Caen describes the suit of court owed by a lay purchaser of land to the lay vendor. So badly drafted that its meaning is obscure, it appears to say that the lord, the vendor, may summon the purchaser, his suitor, to come only to the area in which the land was situated but from wherever the suitor might happen to be when summoned. When the suitor made a post-obit gift of the land to the abbey, it was agreed that after his death the abbess would perform the service.[96] When the same abbess enfeoffed the abbot of Saint-Etienne de Caen with a church, the abbot's only services were an annual payment of twenty shillings and "that he should come to their pleas at the Holy Trinity suitably according to what the fief is."[97] The abbot of Fécamp enfeoffed Gulbert d'Auffay, whose only resulting duty was to "serve the same church in its pleas at Fécamp or at Rouen as often as he should be summoned to do so by the abbot or the monks."[98] When the abbot of Saint-Pierre de Préaux gave the wardship of the sons of a vavassor named Geoffrey to Herluin, who therefore "became the abbot's man," Herluin's only services were "that he should honestly govern and hold Geoffrey's sons and, [when] ordered to St. Peter's pleas, he should come without delay."[99] These scattered references suggest that geographical limits on a tenant's service as a suitor were usual, although it cannot be determined whether all suit of court had to be done as promptly as Herluin's or as often as Gulbert d'Auffay's. Another type of service in court might also be required. The assistance in court which Viscount Rannulf and the bishop of Bayeux owed each other was assistance in the courts of third persons.[100] The memorandum of Rainald the chaplain records Rainald's gift of a garden at Bayeux to one Evremar partly "so that the same Evremar should be present at my pleas, if it is necessary."[101] Because it seems unlikely that Rainald held a court of his own, this probably also refers to aid in the courts of third persons.

Four feudal aids are described in William Paynel's agreement with the abbot of Mont-Saint-Michel. They are not, however, identical with the three later customary in Normandy: ransom of the lord, marriage of one daughter, and knighting of one son.[102] Moreover, no other eleventh-century source refers to any of these aids, with the possible exception of a statement in Viscount Rannulf's agreement with the bishop of Bayeux. The bishop will aid Rannulf in court "by prayers and counsel, not through money, by agreement."[103] Given the generally parallel nature of their mutual obligations, the exception suggests that rendering money as well as advice may have been incumbent upon Rannulf as a tenant or even upon all tenants[104]—and perhaps also upon all lords who did not explicitly repudiate it. Two charters allude to methods used by tenants to raise the money to pay aids: one also mentions actual payment of the aid; the other suggests that a lord might pardon an aid.[105] Neither indicates the purpose of the aid. The evidence is too fragmentary to determine which, if any, aids Norman tenants customarily owed their lords in the eleventh century.

The feudal incidents are also barely attested. As a noun or a verb, "relief" is used in seven extant documents. One from Saint-Wandrille mentions the regrant of a fief "without relief."[106] A donor to Saint-Ouen grants almost every right he has "except the reliefs of vavassors,"[107] and it is likely that the "reliefs of Chanteloup" in William Paynel's agreement with the abbot of Mont-Saint-Michel refer to something similar. Because another charter from Saint-Ouen uses "relieve" to mean "pay an annual rent," it is possible that the reliefs just mentioned were in fact merely payments of rent; but this charter is suspect and therefore not good evidence.[108] In later days, moreover, "relief" could mean a payment on succession when the new tenant was a vavassor or a peasant as well as when he was of higher status;[109] and "relief" certainly did not mean rent when Abbot William of Saint-Etienne de Caen "accepted four yokes of land from Geoffrey *Malsaveir*, three for relief, the fourth for his soul,"[110] or when "William son of Herluin 'the Clerk,' still a little boy, with his mother named Alberada . . . gave God and St. Wandrille a mill in the castle of Brionne with the tithe of *Mesnil Loismer*, for the relief of the land which they held from the saint and for the soul of the aforesaid Herluin."[111] Because they were made up of land rather than of money or valuable items, both these reliefs would later have seemed anomalous.[112] So in another way, too, would the relief William son of Herluin, "still a little boy," and his mother paid, for later a minor such as William would have become the lord's ward during his minority and, upon attaining his majority, would have had to pay no relief.[113] Possibly, indeed, Alberada and the abbey had come to an agreement whereby, in return for the payment here termed "relief," she would have the wardship of her son during his minority.

The final use of "relief" occurs in a charter which records how Roger de

Croismare and the abbey of Saint-Pierre de Préaux worked out their conflicting claims to the possessions Roger's father-in-law Gilbert had held from the Beaumont family. The problem arose because Gilbert, a knight, having no heir, had made a gift of all his possessions to the abbey—apparently post-obit—but then had a daughter who eventually married Roger. After Gilbert's death, Roger naturally wished to succeed to his lands. The claims were reconciled when "Roger de Croismare asked Abbot William that he [William] relieve Gilbert's honor from Roger de Beaumont, from whom the fief came. And if Roger de Beaumont should concede this, he [Roger de Croismare] would afterwards freely recognize Gilbert's honor [as held by him] from Abbot William. Both parties agreed, and the land was relieved from Roger de Beaumont by Abbot William." Furthermore, after the death of Roger de Croismare, the monks should have part of what he held, and the rest "his heir should relieve from the abbot or the monks, as is the usage of the land." Roger de Croismare then became the abbot's man in the presence of Roger de Beaumont.[114] That "relieve" in this charter means "to pay a relief" is only an assumption. It clearly means some sort of payment in the other places where it appears.[115] Moreover, if the verb meant something vaguer, like "take up" the land, that is, accept a grant of it, it would be difficult to understand why Roger de Croismare is not said to "relieve" the land from the abbot as the abbot "relieved" that land from Roger de Beaumont. Assuming that the correct translation is "pay a relief," however, the charter makes sense: as Gilbert's successor in accordance with the post-obit gift, the abbot paid a relief to Gilbert's lord Roger de Beaumont; he then in turn granted it to a new tenant, Roger de Croismare, who "recognized" it as held from the abbot but did not pay a relief because he was not formally inheriting the fief; Roger's heir, in contrast, would have to pay a relief to succeed because he was inheriting the land in form as well as in fact.

Roger did not have to pay a relief, but he accepted from the abbey considerably less than the entire fief his father-in-law had held. This was doubtless the price he paid for the compromise. His heir would hold even less of the land and apparently would have to pay relief as well to secure the diminished fief. This fief, therefore, was to shrink in size in each succeeding generation. The same also happened in both cases when reliefs were paid in land; indeed, those are the only records in which the word is used which state of what the relief consisted. Of the four possible instances of reliefs which do not use the word "relief," only two involve payments of money; the other two involve immovables.[116] Was it a regular practice of eleventh-century Normans to pay reliefs in land rather than in money or other movables? If so, there would have been over the course of time a gradual diminution of fiefs to the detriment of tenants and the advantage of lords. That this practice was normal is not, however, a mandatory conclusion given the nature of the sources: reliefs in land paid to abbeys as lords were much more likely to be noted in charters than reliefs of any other sort.

The earliest of the charters which probably describe reliefs without using the term is worth some discussion. It records that Abbot Henry and the monks of Saint-Ouen bought fifty acres of land from "our knight Gunduin," who, in addition, "freely and without payment gave us ten acres of quite good land which he possessed, on agreement that we should accord to his sons after his death the fief which he had from us, for the same service by which he served."[117] The transaction certainly achieved the same purpose as the payment of a relief, though it is the only known instance in which a relief was paid by the tenant before his death rather than by the heir when he succeeded. Because the charter comes from before 1033, it may mark a stage in the development of feudal tenure in Normandy during which fiefs were not normally hereditary and a father who wanted to pass on a fief to his son or sons had to make a special arrangement to do so. It is the only document from the first half of the century which refers, explicitly or by inference, to a relief.

The most interesting phrase in Roger de Croismare's charter says that the payment of relief by heirs is "the usage of the land" (*mos terrae*). Unfortunately, the custom is by no means clear. Reliefs which were or may have been rents, reliefs in land, reliefs paid by minors, and reliefs paid by fathers all are anomalous when compared to later practice. Indeed, the only description of what appears to be a classic relief does not use the term: Abbot Gilbert of Saint-Etienne de Caen "conceded in fee to Rannulf son of Herfast whatever the same Rannulf's father and mother had in Venoix. Therefore, the same Rannulf became the abbot's liege man and gave him thirty pounds."[118]

The feudal incident of wardship is even less well attested than relief. The rules about who could act as guardian of a minor heir, if there were rules, seem to have included a wider group of persons than was permitted later.[119] While Ralph Taisson II was a minor, the duke held his lands in wardship; but when Ralph Taisson III was a minor, his mother was guardian of his lands.[120] Abbot William of Préaux gave the wardship of the sons of a vavassor to a man named Herluin, thus providing another example of a wardship which belonged to the lord.[121] In contrast, Alberada widow of Herluin "the Clerk" may have bought the wardship of her son from Saint-Wandrille.[122] After the death of Robert de Sully, a vassal of Odo bishop of Bayeux, his wife, brother, and nephews apparently shared the wardship of his son.[123] On his deathbed, William de la Ferté-Macé, a vassal of Duke Robert Curthose, "committed" and "demised" his "honor" to his brother; his children were "very little."[124] In other words, only two of the wardships mentioned in charters were held by lords; the other three or four were held by family members, and in only one of these—*if* the instance from Saint-Wandrille involves wardship—does the lord appear to have had any role in granting the custody. Wardship of the person of the heir, as opposed to wardship of the lands, is mentioned only in the charter from Préaux.

The historians, unlike the charters, often refer to wardship of minor heirs, primarily because two dukes, Richard I and William II, were minors when they acceded. Both had guardians. Richard I is called the ward both of Bernard the Dane and of King Louis IV; and Dudo depicts King Louis as trying to exploit his guardianship both of the person and of the fiefs of his minor vassal, carrying off the ward to his castle of Laon and attempting to rule Normandy as though it were part of the royal demesne, appointing an agent to govern it for him.[125] Bernard the Dane, however, who with the aid of others foiled the king's plots, was the duke's subordinate rather than his lord. Dudo also alleges that Hugh the Great, duke of France, left the wardship of his wife and children to the adult Richard I,[126] but this, again, is not the usual feudal wardship, for Richard was Hugh's vassal, not his lord.[127] King Henry I may have asserted some rights and assumed some duties concerning Normandy during the minority of Duke William,[128] but possession of the duke's person and with it the regency in Normandy was in the hands of a series of ducal vassals.[129] Occasional other wardships among important persons are alleged, but there is little evidence of their juridical nature.[130] Wardships of persons who did not govern states are rarely mentioned by the literary sources, which therefore provide no further help with the problem of feudal wardship.

If feudal wardship is so rarely mentioned, it should come as no surprise that the feudal prerogative of controlling the marriage of the heirs of one's vassals is mentioned even less often.[131] The clearest instance is William Paynel's wife, for his agreement with the abbot of Mont-Saint-Michel is about "the land which the king of the English gave him with his wife." William the Conqueror apparently had the right to choose this woman's husband. Her name is unknown, so exactly why this was so is impossible to decide; but it seems legitimate to infer that she was the heiress not only to lands held from Mont-Saint-Michel but also to lands held from the duke.[132] That William's tenure was only in right of his wife is clear: at the end of the charter reference is made again to "the honor which he accepted with his wife"; the land is said to be his wife's inheritance; moreover, he may take an aid from the land for the ransom of his son or the marriage of his daughter only if the child was born of "this wife."

There may be other examples of feudal marriage in the sources, but they are difficult to discern. The marriage of Alberada daughter of Wimund castellan of Moulins-la-Marche to William son of Walter, which was arranged by Duke William, has sometimes been taken to be one example but probably was not.[133] The duke may have exercised his authority over heiresses in two successive generations of the Bellême family; but in each instance the bride's father was still alive, and political considerations were probably more important than strictly feudal rights.[134] William of Jumièges says that Duke Richard II "gave" his half-brother William "a certain beautiful girl, named Lesceline, daughter of a certain most noble man named Turketil," apparently at the same time he gave him the county of Eu.[135] These seem, however, to have been separate gifts: Lesceline was not heiress to the county,[136] and nothing is said about any other lands she may have brought her husband. Why the duke was able to arrange her marriage is not stated, nor is Turketil known to have been the duke's man. Orderic says that Richard II's great-grandson Richard son of Gilbert de Saint-Valéry "for many years fought for the duke of Normandy, his uncle [Robert the Magnificent], and received from him the hand of the noble

Ada, widow of Herluin the old of Heugleville, with all his patrimony."[137] This case involves a widow rather than a daughter; but, later at least, widows could be subject to feudal rights of marriage.[138] Although it is not known that Herluin was a vassal of the duke, Duke Robert's right to dispose of Ada was probably based on the rights of a feudal lord.

Cases concerning lesser lords are rare. Adeliza wife of William de Bardouville made a complex agreement with Troarn about land she and her husband held from the abbey. One clause sounds very much as though the abbey, as Adeliza's lord, had exercised its right of marriage to give her and her fief first to "her first husband, Robert," and then to William; but it does not say whether Adeliza had inherited the tenement.[139] The other possible examples of lesser lords who exercised this right are more dubious: either it is not clear that the lord had arranged the marriage or it is not certain that the bride had inherited her land.[140] Nevertheless, these ten more or less certain instances are the only possible examples of a lord's right to marry off his men's heiresses or widows which I can find. They indicate little more than that the right was at least occasionally exercised and, in the case of William Paynel's wife, that a husband chosen by the duke apparently had to be accepted by an heiress's other lords.[141]

The obligations vassals owed lords in return for their fiefs might, therefore, include military service, castleguard, messenger service, escort service, suit of court, aids, and three feudal incidents: relief, wardship, and marriage.[142] It is not possible, however, to tell how much of which services any particular vassal—except those of William Paynel—owed. Perhaps most vassals owed most or all of the services just listed. The charter of 1109 from La Trinité de Caen, which talks of "such service as a knight ought to do," implies that a standard definition of knight service—standard in types if not in amount—was in existence by then.[143] It should be noted, however, that sometimes only a few services were required: Gulbert d'Auffay owed only suit of court; the abbot of Saint-Etienne de Caen, rent and suit of court; two minor vassals of Troarn, messenger service alone; a purchaser apparently owed only suit of court and aid to the vendor. One must not, therefore, conclude that eleventh-century vassals owed their lords all the services that were standard in the late twelfth and thirteenth centuries.[144] It is at least equally likely that the conditions under which fiefs were held varied and, perhaps, were still the subject of negotiations between each lord and each vassal at the time of the creation of a fief.

Remarkably few sources say anything directly or indirectly about the duration of enfeoffments. One document may imply that a fief might be only for life;[145] three, that it could be in perpetuity.[146] Adeliza de Bardouville stipulated that the land she held from Troarn would be heritable only by heirs of her body, not by collaterals.[147] An occasional charter shows a son who received his deceased father's fief, and Orderic's narrative is full of hereditary successions to land, often only by inference held in fee. No eleventh-century source asserts as a principle that fiefs were hereditary, however.[148] The seeming relief paid by a father before his death to secure his sons' succession to his fief may imply that early in the eleventh century such tenements were not normally hereditary, but by the second half of the century it seems to have been assumed that sons succeeded to their father's fiefs.[149] St. Anselm's analogy between types of knights and types of Christians suggests as much, and particular fiefs could be described as hereditary.[150] Moreover, the existence of incidents consequent upon the heritability of fiefs—relief, wardship, and marriage—presupposes inheritance as a practice; and the charter which calls relief *mos terrae* presupposes it as a rule.

Whatever the conditions of tenure of a particular fief may have been, what happened if the vassal did not fulfill them? Neither the documents nor the historians mention scutage or anything similar to it; in fact, there is little reference to nonperformance of service for legitimate reasons.[151] If William Paynel's men defaulted, they were to "do right" to him in his court; but the agreement makes no mention of what penalties might be assessed. Abbot Robert of Saint-Evroul, to punish two troublesome vassals of the abbey, transferred them to the lordship of a very exigent lord; the transfer was intended to be permanent, but within a few years the abbot relented and received the men back.[152] One might suppose, by analogy, that a lord's remedy against a tenant who refused to do service would be the same as the penalty applied to conditional alienations when the conditions were not fulfilled, that is, loss of what was granted. The many treasons which occurred in Normandy in the eleventh century complicate the case of fiefs, however: when the duke confiscated a warrior's lands, it is almost always moot whether he did so as lord or as the duke; and confiscations by lesser lords may often have been seizures based purely on might rather than penalties exacted of right. Moreover, confiscation and exile were the usual punishment for serious crimes other than treason.[153]

Nonetheless, in a few eleventh-century instances confiscations seem genuinely to have been based on the legal implications of the contractual nature of fiefs. St. Anselm's analogy between types of knights and types of Christians compares monks to knights "who labour with unbroken fortitude to obey his [a secular prince's] will for the sake of receiving back again an inheritance of which they bewail the loss through their parents' fault.[154] According to Orderic, William the Conqueror confiscated the English fiefs of several Normans who returned to Normandy, without his permission, shortly after the Conquest and seized the land of Baudry son of Nicholas when Baudry went to Spain without permission.[155] A charter mentions a second escheat to the duke because of unauthorized departure for Spain.[156] The final breach between Duke William and his uncle William count of Arques occurred, says William of Poitiers, when the count left the siege of Domfront without permission, "refusing the duty of a vassal."[157] Though he reports that, after his defeat, William of Arques was allowed to keep some of his possessions, William of Poitiers clearly thinks this a product of Duke William's mercy: in justice Count William should have been wholly deprived.[158] Escheat could also occur for reasons other than simple refusal of service. Orderic says that Duke William confiscated the honor of Roger de Mortemer in 1054 because Roger, one of the leaders of the army at the Norman victory at Mortemer, had given shelter after the battle to Ralph of Crépy, count of Amiens-Valois-Vexin—one of the losers but also one of Roger's lords—and had enabled him to escape.[159] Robert Curthose confiscated the land of a vassal, who apparently held of him through the abbot of Fécamp, when the vassal both built an adulterine castle and "withheld the service which the land owed."[160]

Instances involving lords other than the duke are rare. Gilbert count of Brionne seized the possessions of his vassal Herluin, the future abbot of Bec, when the latter refused to deliver to the duke a message he considered nefarious.[161] A vassal of the abbey of Saint-Evroul "was justly condemned" in the monks' court "to lose the whole fief he held of St. Evroul" for having purloined a treasure which he had been supposed to convey to the abbey from southern Italy.[162] William de Breteuil confiscated all the possessions which Ascelin Goel held of him when Ascelin turned over to Duke Robert Curthose the castle of Ivry, which he held from William.[163] This last example, however, verges on being an episode of war rather than an exercise based on legal principles; and such is even truer of other, similar instances which could be cited.

Fiefs were, therefore, contractual tenements. The lord had certain duties, and if he did not perform them he risked losing his lordship. The tenant had duties as well, and if he did not perform them he risked losing his fief. The duties of each party are more difficult to determine. Probably neither the obligations of all lords nor the obligations of all vassals were identical. Duties on both sides may well have developed and become more precise in the course of the century: specific obligations on the part of vassals, at least, hardly appear in the sources before the last third of the century. The standardization of "such service as a knight ought to do" may, therefore, have been a relatively late development. Hence, though virtually all of the types of service which were later owed for fiefs can be shown to have been owed for at least a few fiefs in the eleventh century, it ought not be assumed that an eleventh-century tenement, simply because it is called a fief, owed all of them. There are, moreover, indications that fiefs were normally hereditary by the end of the century although they had not been so at its beginning. A good deal of change probably occurred in the course of the century, and some characteristics of fiefs as they are described by sources from the late twelfth century and later may have developed only in the twelfth century. Feudal tenure was not fixed and static. Nonetheless, the essence of the concept of the fief—a contractual tenement whose continuance depended upon the fulfillment of obligations by both parties to the contract—seems to have remained constant throughout the century.

RENTALS AND GRANTS FOR LIMITED TERMS

Rentals and other grants for limited terms or for life are rarely mentioned in the sources; but the record-keeping habits of eleventh-century Normans, or rather their lack of such habits, may have created a substantial discrepancy between appearance and reality.[164] Léopold Delisle finds evidence that even late in the thirteenth century some grants for short terms were never recorded in writing;[165] and, because there was much greater familiarity with documents in the thirteenth century, what was true occasionally then is more than likely to have been true as a rule in the eleventh century. There was, moreover, especially little reason to retain records because these were grants not to churches but by them. The ecclesiastical institutions, as the alienors, might well be expected to do their best to see that the alienations did not become permanent. Not merely would they have little motive to keep outdated records, they would have every incentive to destroy the records just as soon as the term ended and the property granted out reverted to them. If, furthermore, a grantee acted as though a tenement were his or hers to control and alienated it to some church other than the grantor, the transfer constituted a usurpation and the record would not be likely to mention the alienor's weak title: it would simply say nothing about the earlier transaction. Although there are allusions to rental tenements held by lay persons from lay persons, finally, grants made by lay persons were almost certainly not recorded in writing in this period. For all these reasons, it is likely that tenements for limited terms or for life, whether granted in return for rent or for some other consideration, were a good deal more common than the surviving sources suggest.

Peasant tenements, insofar as anything is known about them, were held for rents, usually combined with labor services.[166] They are not at issue here, however, partly because hardly anything can be known about them in this period and partly because they were the hereditary, quasi-compulsory, "statutory" tenements characteristic of the lower classes, rarely the product of recent transfers.[167] The rental tenements of the inhabitants of bourgs are also excluded here, both because burgesses in this period seem to have been no more than peasants of a particular kind and because their tenure, perhaps more than any other aspect of Norman legal history in this period, has been thoroughly studied.[168]

It was clearly possible in the eleventh century for a person of high status to hold land for rent rather than for feudal service: the abbey of Saint-Martin de Sées held a farm from one layman and an unnamed rental tenement from another; Troarn paid rent to one of its feudal tenants; and a farm was held by Hugh de Rosel, an important man in the eleventh century.[169] Casual allusions to rent paid for tenements held by men of clearly elevated status are also found.[170] In practice, however, distinguishing contractual rental tenements from peasant holdings can be difficult. A tenement whose creation is recorded in a charter falls into the former category, and the same is presumably true of tenements which, although mentioned incidentally, are described in some detail. The real difficulty concerns incidental references so brief as to give only a few details or none. In practice, one major distinction between the two sorts of tenements was the presence or absence of personal service as well as rent—or the character of the services required. Brief allusions to tenements, however, usually do not mention service; and, in any context, references to services usually give no details.[171]

Normandy in the eleventh century seems to have been characterized by an absence of legally defined social classes.[172] Serfdom was rapidly disappearing, if it had not already disappeared,[173] and no legal privileges mark out the upper crust of society as a nobility.[174] Terms indicating social status occur in the documents, the most common ones for peasants being *hospites*, *villani*, and *rustici*;[175] but most persons appear in the documents without any designation of status.[176] As a result, although there was, of course, a great social and economic distance between the duke and the magnates, on one hand, and the laborers on their lands, on the other, between the two extremes social status is often difficult to determine. Moreover, it is doubtful whether, even were a great deal more information available, one could draw through the ranks of Norman society a line separating the peasants from the upper class. Vavassors and serjeants straddle any such line.[177] Groups of peasants are transferred by their lords without their consent, or at least without any reference to it—but so are groups of knights.[178] In later centuries peasants did homage for tenements and could even receive homage, and their tenements could be called fiefs.[179] The same may have been true in the eleventh century, though the absence of sources makes it impossible to know. In the eleventh century, at least some peasants certainly could leave their lands when they wished and make alienations from them; and they could act as witnesses to alienations by others.[180] All in all, no hard and fast rule for distinguishing peasants from aristocrats or peasant tenements from aristocratic tenements seems possible even in theory, much less in confrontation with the documents. The rule of thumb adopted here is to exclude all tenements demonstrably held by persons who were peasants or burgesses or demonstrably held for labor services and to consider all others.

Two types of income-producing tenures already had names. One is the *métairie* or *métayage*. The charters of Saint-Martin de Sées refer repeatedly to tenements called *meteariae*,[181] a word used occasionally by other abbeys. No charter which employs the term describes the conditions under which such a tenement was held, however. The tenure may well have been characteristic of peasants. The land constituting a *métairie* was not considered to have left the lord's demesne,[182] whereas fiefs and other similar tenements apparently were.[183] Moreover, Saint-Taurin d'Evreux gave land "as a *métairie* to Godald according to the custom of the vill,"[184] which implies both that the tenure was well known in at least one area of Normandy and that it was a peasant tenure; the date of the charter is hard to establish, unfortunately. The occasional appearance of a man surnamed *Metearius* in a witness list cannot be taken as evidence that *métayers* were not peasants, for peasants were not excluded from functioning as witnesses in eleventh-century Normandy.[185] In later times in Normandy, as in the eleventh century elsewhere, *métairie* denoted a tenement whose lord supplied land and equipment while the peasant tenant did the work, which usually involved clearing the land; as the name implies, the two parties shared the profits of the land equally. Such an arrangement was often used for the development of vineyards.[186] A charter for Saint-Martin de Sées suggests that this type of tenure existed in Normandy in the eleventh century when it describes the gift of a man named Gilbert: "a vineyard, as he had it proportionally with two brothers who had planted it, namely Durand and William, and their whole land as they and another brother of theirs held it from Gilbert."[187] The document does not call the tenement a *métairie*.

Another charter from the same abbey describes a similar arrangement at greater length, also without giving the tenement a name:

> Richard Paynel, having been made a participant in the benefits of Saint-Martin de Sées, gave . . . the monks . . . thirty pounds, with which the same monks bought—in common for themselves and Richard—a certain [piece of] land . . . on this agreement: that while Richard should live he should, with them, cultivate [it], build [upon it] and receive half both of the land and of all [its] stock, whether in men or in animals or in produce. . . . But if he should die or retire from that land anywhere else, his heir, if suitable to hold the land, should have [it] and either should hold [his] father's aforesaid part from the monks or should receive eight pounds from them.

Richard later demised the land to the monks, retaining nothing except the right for himself or a son to become a monk in the future or, if not, "while he resides in our vicinity . . . to have goods of the aforesaid land to supply his needs. Moreover, of the eighteen mares which he placed there to work the land, he should retain half of the offspring while he should reside in our area."[188] What material contribution the monks made to the creation of the partnership is not stated; it is possible that their only investments were the society they granted to Richard and their expertise in the management of land. Richard, however, was clearly no peasant: he had at his disposal thirty pounds and eighteen mares. Moreover, he did not cultivate the land himself: part of its stock consisted of men. Profit-sharing partnerships of this type may have occurred more than once: this one is described to explain how the monks acquired their land. One certain *métairie*—mortgaged to the abbey for sixteen pounds and redeemed by a gift of most of a cemetery and four parcels of land—must also have been a sizable piece of land.[189] In this instance, as in most, there is no indication as to who the partners were who shared the profits of the *métairie*, unless it is assumed that the alienor who seems able to dispose of it was one of them. Perhaps such profit-sharing arrangements occurred on various levels of society and the word *métairie* cannot be taken to have any social connotation. Such arrangements, in any case, were not, of course, strictly speaking rentals, for the superior partner—if, indeed, it is proper in such a case as Richard Paynel's to speak of one partner as superior to the other—received not a fixed income but a fixed share of variable profits.

True rental tenements were, on the evidence, somewhat more common than *métairies*; they are certainly more often and more fully described. Some of them are called "farms" (*firmae*), and these constitute the second tenure of the income-producing type to have a name. An abbey could hold a farm from a layman. When Saint-Martin de Sées "decided to make . . . a certain fishpond for their abbey between their monastery and the mill which is called *de Valle* . . . they asked . . . William de Sivilly . . . that he give them the revenue of that mill in farm, which is commonly called a *moesena*." William "conceded the transfer of the mill . . . for thirty setiers of grain per year, namely ten of wheat [and] twenty of milled grain which may be either barley or rye."[190] Five years later he sold the abbey "the whole half of that farm, which is commonly called a *moisura*, which the monks owed him—five setiers of wheat and ten of rye— . . . for ten pounds of Le Mans."[191] Here, the "farm" seems to mean specifically the rent; that is, by a lump-sum payment the monks effected a reduction by half of what they would thereafter owe William for the mill. This is the only farm to be called a *moesena* or *moisura*, despite the assertion that the names were in commmon use,[192] but in other ways it is fairly typical.

No term is stated for the abbey's tenure. Because an abbey does not die, the farm was presumably intended to be permanent. Lay tenants do die, however, so the terms of the other farms where no term is stated were probably assumed to be the life of the tenant. In one case a life term is stated.[193] In another, the tenant, Anketil de Cambes, "gave the abbess [of La Trinité de Caen] ten shillings for an agreement that he ought to have it [the farm], and his sons [ought], nor should it be taken away from them because of another who offers more."[194] In effect, this agreement created a farm for the lifetimes of the father and his sons. Only once is a term of years stated.[195]

Saint-Martin's rent in produce, specifically in grain, also seems typical: there are five other examples, one of which also includes cartage for the grain as service due from the tenement.[196] The exceptions are a farm held for an annual payment of more than two hundred shillings[197] and a *firmus fiscus* held for an annual rent of ten shillings.[198] How the rent was to be paid is sometimes, as in Saint-Martin's case, not specified. When it is, it may be once, twice, or three times per year.[199] One farmer had granted out a small portion of his tenement in return for partial payment of his rent.[200]

In addition to the farms already discussed there is one late example of a fee farm:

> Harduin de *Beheriis*, having demised all the claims which he had made about the church of *Merreio*, accepted it from the Lord Abbot Ralph and the other brothers [of Saint-Martin de Sées] . . . in such a way that he should have the priest's portion in his demesne; for the other two parts of the same church, he would pay the brothers . . . every year two muids of wheat and two of barley and two of oats and . . . one pound of incense and one of pepper in recognition. And, accepting this farm in fee, he promised that he would always have a priest [living] legally and without a wife, at the judgment of the congregation of Sées, in the aforesaid church; and, [having been] made the man of the aforesaid abbot, he gave twenty pounds of Le Mans.[201]

For his farm Harduin pays a typical annual rent in grain and also an annual amount of incense and pepper "in recognition"—an unusual payment perhaps intended to prevent Harduin, who had been making claims, from denying the abbey's right.[202] His tenement was not, however, merely a farm but a fee-farm, and Harduin became the abbot's man. Other churches were held as fiefs in Normandy at this time, but no other tenement of priest or lay person is ever called a fee-farm.[203] The later Norman fee-farm was a hereditary tenement for a fixed rent,[204] but this charter says nothing about heirs.

The eight tenements called farms are similar in some ways to eleven rental tenements not given any name by the documents. One was to descend to the recipient's heirs, apparently forever.[205] Six do not state any term; three state a term of one or more lives.[206] The rent is once grain, eight times money, and once a combination.[207] Five charters state when the rent is to be paid; each says that it is to be paid in a lump sum on one day, but each names a different date.[208] In addition, Adeliza de Bardouville rented the land she held from Troarn to the abbey for six years for sixty shillings of the money of Rouen per year "because, on account of the absence of her husband, who had gone to Jerusalem, she was not able to exploit the land to her profit."[209]

Two charters from Saint-Martin de Sées record agreements which probably ought to be added to the unnamed rentals. It may be obvious by now that a striking number of the relatively few detailed records of income-producing tenements come from this abbey. Perhaps this illustrates the varying degrees of interest displayed by the charters of different churches in different types of transactions: Saint-Martin de Sées is not, for example, similarly loquacious about mortgages, indeed the reverse. In any case, the detail with which the abbey records various agreements gives a valuable indication of the flexibility of which eleventh-century arrangements were capable. Of the two to be considered here, the first may cast a little light on rental arrangements between laymen:

> Berlaius and his brother Ralph . . . conceded to St. Martin twenty acres which Roger son of Hermer bought from them which he recognized [as held] from them. By the same Roger's intervention, therefore, both Berlaius and Ralph conceded that whatever Roger thence owed to them he should pay [instead] to the monks and should recognize [the land as held] wholly from them henceforward. Moreover, for this concession the two brothers had between them ten shillings of Le Mans from the aforesaid Roger's money.[210]

The subject of this charter is the transfer, at Roger's request, of Roger's service and payments from the two brothers to the abbey, a usual type of transfer. Before the transfer, however, yet after having "bought" the twenty acres from Berlaius and Ralph, Roger had still "recognized" the land as held from them and owed them payments from it. This may be an example of a sale which created a tenurial dependence of the purchaser on the vendors, but it seems likely that Roger's "purchase" was actually an entry fine for a rental tenement. Certainly, several other rentals or farms also began with entry fines.[211]

The second arrangement seems to have resulted from a son's reluctance to lose his patrimony. When Robert "the Jerusalemite" became a monk at the abbey, he gave it his part of a house at Falaise, and his wife also gave her part.

> And a certain son of theirs named Richard, to whom the remaining third part belonged . . . came to the abbot and monks . . . and made this agreement with them about the same house: that, if the abbot or monks are able to secure from the king of the English that he would give them all the customs of the same house, Robert's aforesaid son Richard would hold the oftenmentioned house from St. Martin and would give twenty shillings each year in recognition—and his heir or heir's heir or anyone to whom, at the urging of necessity, the aforesaid house might be sold [would do] the same. He should not pay it, however, unless it could be done by the same abbot or monks. If, however, they are not able to obtain the customs of the house from the king, as is said above, within the aforesaid year, between the feast of St. Lawrence of the following year and the other [i.e., the next?] feast of the same saint, [then] the abbot or the monks should receive ten pounds from Richard for the complete sale of the whole house.[212]

Richard wanted the whole of his father's house. He was willing to hold it for rent from the abbey, provided that he was not also obligated to another lord. Because the charter does not say that the abbey, having acquired the customs from the king, was to accept twenty shillings per year in lieu of them, it is not clear whether Richard's desire was to have only one lord or to pay only once for the tenement.

Some conditions are known for fourteen unnamed rentals in all. They differ from farms in two significant ways: they tend to entail money rents rather than grain; and they require payment only once a year, whereas the rents for farms might be paid in two or three installments. This difference obviously raises the question of whether farms and unnamed rentals were distinct types of tenements or, instead, "farm" was a name sometimes applied to rentals. The total sample is small, only twenty-two, the disparities are never complete, and some of the tenements are very sketchily recorded. Hence one might argue that any factor selected to divide the sample—no matter what factor is selected as the basis for the division—would be likely to lead to apparent disparities between the resulting groups. If so, then "farm" may be merely a name only sometimes used.

All the charters which refer to farms come from late in the period under consideration, moreover, whereas those which do not use the word are, in general, earlier.[213] Three unnamed rentals are later than 1090; no farm is certainly earlier than about 1080.[214] It may, thus, have been the use of a name—"farm"—which was novel in Normandy in the late eleventh century, rather than the tenure itself. Most significant, a tenement transferred to La Trinité de Caen at some time between 1066 and 1083 is called a farm only by a later account of the gift, written between 1082 and 1113, although otherwise the descriptions of the conditions of tenure are identical in import and only slightly different in wording.[215] The nature of the tenure had not changed in the interval, but it had acquired a name. If "farm" began to be used in Normandy only in the late eleventh century to describe an already existing type of tenure, this was not because the term was unknown anywhere before then. In the form *manufirma* it occurs on the southeastern border of Normandy in the first half of the eleventh century.[216] It must have been known even to the Normans before they began to use it, for the abbey of Jumièges held *manufirmae* in France as early as the late tenth century.[217] *Manufirmae* were rental tenements conceded for one or more lives, indistinguishable from the contractual tenure for rent whose generic name in French is *censive* but for which there were many local equivalents.[218] The word is found in many places in western France from the ninth century on.[219] The Anglo-Saxon *feorm*, Latinized as *firma*, which meant specifically a food-rent paid to the king, would also have been familiar to the Normans after 1066. Indeed, in Anglo-Norman England *firma* was sometimes used to specify a rent paid in produce.[220] It may be that in Normandy by the late eleventh century Normans felt a need for a name by which to designate rental tenements—whether because this type of tenure was becoming more common or because of a general desire to name the different types of tenure—and adopted *firma* from one or both of the possible sources. If so, the Anglo-Saxon and Anglo-Norman connection of the word with rents in kind may have led to its application first to that sort of rent in Normandy as well.

Occasionally the parties entered into an agreement on the subject of the tenant's security in his tenement. Blancardus became a tenant of Saint-Etienne de Caen "for as long as pleases the abbot and monks," and, emphatically, only so long; but, because he was granted the tenement, a church, only after he had surrendered a claim which both his father and he had been maintaining and after he swore never to raise the claim again, the arrangement was hardly an ordinary rental.[221] A more typical tenant, as already noted, paid a fine to protect himself and his sons from ouster by a third party who offered a higher rent.[222] The same danger clearly threatened a man whose lords transferred his tenement to La Trinité du Mont, but the charter is ambiguous as to whether the tenant would be protected.[223] A newcomer certainly might offer higher payment: Saint-Léger de Préaux gave a farm to a man who offered ten shillings per year for land "whence it [the abbey] had no more than six shillings per year."[224] These three charters suggest that, in the absence of special precautions, a tenant's hold on his rent-paying tenement was not secure even within the term of the lease, but a fourth implies the opposite. Abbess Matilda of La Trinité de Caen granted Osmund de *Canvilla* a farm for ten years,

> on agreement that, when the term is up, if it shall have seemed proper to the congregation, they should leave it to him for as long as pleases them. If not, they will give [it] to another. And if, within the same term, they should see that he is burdened beyond measure, it will be in their power if they should wish to have some mercy on him [by means] of some

> remission [of the terms of the agreement]. Finally, they—not he—will also have the power to give the farm to another or leave it to him.[225]

Because this rental, unusually, is for a limited term of years, it seems probable that within that period Osmund would be secure in his tenure, a supposition reinforced by the abbey's concern only with what will happen after the term has expired. The provision that the rent may be reduced if it subsequently appears to the nuns to have been set too high makes it unlikely that a higher bidder could have been found. After the term had expired, Osmund apparently would become a tenant-at-will of the abbey, with no security of tenure. Perhaps one might conclude that tenants for unspecified terms or for one or more lives were in effect tenants-at-will, barring agreements to the contrary, but a tenant for a term of years had security in the tenement for the duration of the term.

How a tenant could be forced to pay his rent is another problem pressing enough to be discussed in a charter. When Richard de Roullours gave La Trinité de Caen "the land which Hugh de Rosel has from him, on agreement that Hugh de Rosel render the church of Caen a muid of wheat annually," presumably the same rent Richard had been receiving, Richard further provided that "if he [Hugh] should not have thus rendered [the rent], the convent of Caen should have the land in its power until the muid of wheat is paid."[226] In France in general at this time, as in Normandy in the thirteenth century, the usual method of punishment for delayed payment was a fine, not the loss of tenement, and the charter concerning the tenth-century *manufirma* which Jumièges held outside Normandy contains such a clause;[227] yet no eleventh-century charter about Norman land contains such a provision for enforcing payment of a rent or, indeed, of any other obligation. Conditions attached to Norman transactions seem, as already noted, to have been enforced either by confiscation, especially for contumacious refusal to perform, or by substitution, especially for involuntary inability to perform, rather than by fines or analogous measures.[228] If Hugh de Rosel's rent is regarded as a condition, temporary confiscation intended to compel him to pay fits Norman practice. Correspondingly, the one remaining reference to nonpayment concerns involuntary incapacity and involves a substitution of sorts: when Robert son of Walo confirmed to Saint-Evroul his father's gift of "two bordars who pay five shillings annually . . . he promised that, if the aforesaid bordars should fall into poverty, he himself would pay the sum which they were accustomed to pay."[229] Despite the frequency with which lords gave peasants to churches, this is the only instance in which an alienor assumed such a responsibility. The charter gives no hint as to why he should have done so.

A few grants were made for a limited number of years for a specific purpose. Saint-Martin de Sées made a complex agreement with a cleric named Oliver in which in effect it gambled the burden of administering Oliver's possessions without any reward for a period of up to two years against the possibility of acquiring a considerable amount of new property for itself if

Oliver should not return within the term.[230] The farm Richard de *Ansgervilla* received from Montebourg consisted of property he had just given the abbey; he was to pay twelve quarters of grain per year, in two installments, but the motive for the grant is said to be that he had "decided to restore the aforesaid possession to better condition."[231] Jumièges conceded the church of Dame-Marie—for no annual remuneration, it seems—to Abbot Albert of Saint-Mesmin de Micy, who had given it to the abbey, so that Albert might build a church there.[232] In the latter two instances the recipient had previously given what he now received, the grant was made on the initiative of the recipient, and the motive was to improve the property further before it returned to the possession of the abbey. The grant to Abbot Albert was to last only until a specific improvement—the building of a church—was completed. Richard's, however, was to last for his lifetime. Indeed, except that he paid rent, the grant he received is very similar to a life estate.

LIFE ESTATES

Life estates form a group of temporary tenements distinct from rentals, even rentals whose term was life. The compensation to the grantor of a life estate was not a rent but an immovable, a unique payment of money, or both, and it usually came to the grantor only when the estate terminated. In addition, rentals were not normally accompanied by the trappings of the more permanent forms of transfer—grants by the recipient of his substance and grants to the recipient of society, of burial, of the right to become a monk, and the like—whereas life estates were.

Some tenements, however, are difficult to classify. Richard de *Ansgervilla*'s arrangement with Montebourg has been treated as a farm because the charter uses that term but has features not only of life estates but also of post-obit gifts. Another rental was granted, says the charter, not for the rent but because the tenants, a man and his wife, "conceded to our church their bodies after their death, for burial, and the whole part of their money."[233] Saint-Martin de Sées was party to a transaction which is even less clearly a simple rental:

> Seric the priest . . . received the land which St. Martin had in the territory of Trun on agreement that, having first given twenty pounds, afterwards he should hold it always and always recognize [that he holds it] from the monks and pay twenty shillings annually in recognition, if indeed there should be sufficient peace, and he is to carry out this agreement no matter who receives that land from him—that is, either a certain brother of his or a certain sister of his or either of the two nephews whom the same Seric had. [The land is] conceded by the monks to these five, for as long as any one of them may live, on the aforesaid arrangement [and is] to return to the demesne of the saint after the death of all of them, no successor of theirs claiming [it]. Know also that all of them—the sister, the brother and the nephews—are received into the benefit of the place

> through Seric himself by the . . . abbot and monks, in such a manner that if, on the death of each of them, [his or her] body is brought to the monastery with all his [or her] money, [it] should be received by the monks for burial; if not, however, wherever the body may lie, St. Martin will nevertheless have the whole portion of the deceased.[234]

In many ways, this seems to be an estate granted for five lives, and each recipient conferred his or her substance in return for a right of burial. Seric, however, was to pay the abbey an annual sum regardless of who of the five held the land. Presumably, should he die before one or more of the others, the actual tenant of the land would make the payments. Because the payment is "in recognition," it may have been intended simply to protect the abbey against any future assertion by Seric's family that they had a right to the land.[235] In two other cases from Saint-Martin de Sées, however, what otherwise seem to be ordinary rents are called payments "in recognition."[236] Moreover, the provision that the sum was to be paid only if conditions were peaceable enough to permit cultivation of the land implies that the payment was intrinsically connected with the agricultural production of the land, that, in other words, it was a rent.[237] Whether the land was cultivated in a particular year might affect Seric's ability to pay a rent; it would not affect his family's ability to claim that the land was rightfully theirs.

The obvious characteristic of a life estate is that it was granted for life. I have found twenty-one transfers which are certainly of this type.[238] There was no name for or set way of expressing such a grant;[239] one usually finds a statement that the grant was to be held by the recipient for life and was to come back to the grantor on the death of the grantee. Several grants to men and their wives were to return to the grantors on the death of the spouses who survived longer.[240] One man specified that if his wife survived him the tenement would return to the grantor when she died or remarried.[241] Other grants to married couples either say nothing about what was to happen when one spouse died or leave the matter unclear.[242] No indubitable life estates were granted to two generations of a family, as rentals sometimes were. Two agreements from Saint-Wandrille provide for later generations, however: one says that, if the couple who receives it has an heir, the heir may hold part of the estate as a benefice after the death of the father; the other provides that if, after the termination of the estate, the abbey should ever again decide to give the land "to anyone, on account of service or remuneration . . . no one will have a better right to follow up the agreement than those who will remain living of their [the recipient couple's] descendants."[243] Yet another life estate was granted on certain conditions; if the recipient could not fulfill them, any one of his relatives was allowed to replace him.[244]

Relatives' rights were an obvious problem, as these instances show, especially given the tendency of Normans, at least in the late eleventh century, to claim as inheritances any property which had once been in the family.[245] The very existence of one life estate is known only from a charter drawn up in the name of an heir who had claimed to inherit the estate but had subsequently repented and returned it.[246] Therefore it was usual when establishing a life estate to declare that no relative of the recipient was to claim the property granted; instead, it should return without difficulty to the grantor at the proper time. These statements are often vehement, and they occur in most extant records of life estates.[247] Strictures on tenants not to alienate are also found, and the danger was real. Fécamp gave a life estate to Wascelin son of Heddo "so that for as long as he should live . . . he should retain [it] in his demesne, giving nothing of the same land to any other man. . . . Thereafter the aforesaid Wascelin, ignoring the agreement [which he] had with the abbot and brothers, not only did not increase the benefice [which he had] accepted, but even reduced it to nothing and distributed it to his men contrary to the established agreement."[248]

Nevertheless, the main threat seems to have been claims by relatives after the death of the tenant.[249] The great concern which two charters from Troarn display to deny the inheritability of a life estate graphically illustrates the danger. The first reports that Richard son of Wascelin de Trun "had the church of Trun with land from the Lord Abbot Durand, but only for his lifetime without any right of his heir to retain it since he did not hold the church by inheritance from his father, from whom the abbot of Troarn had bought that whole honor . . . for forty pounds of the money of Le Mans." In 1100 Richard "came to the chapter of Saint-Martin with his brother William and, recognizing all the aforesaid" facts, mortgaged the church and land to Troarn so that he could go on pilgrimage.

> It pleased the abbot, [now Arnulf] therefore, that William brother of the same Richard should participate in handing over the money to Richard and should have the half part of the income, on agreement that when Richard should return the money [which he] accepted, he should have his things back for his lifetime. But if he should not return the money before [his] death, the abbot of Troarn should return to William as much as he had given [and] the estate should belong absolutely to St. Martin. Therefore, the lord abbot and William gave Richard twenty pounds of the money of Le Mans for his part of the church and land.[250]

Because the estate had belonged to the father and the danger of an assertion of hereditary right was therefore great, possible claims not only by the tenant's descendants but also by his brother are carefully forestalled. Moreover, a second charter reports that "in the same year William brother of Richard begged the Lord Abbot Arnulf and the whole congregation that they retain his part of the same church wholly in their demesne. For he recognized and knew from much experience that it was not useful or honorable for him that he retain in his demesne what his father had sold and conceded to our church." For this renunciation William received a countergift of twenty pounds of Le Mans and the abbot "gave back ten [pounds] which he [William], with the abbot, had given in his brother Richard's mortgage of the aforesaid [possessions] of [their] father."[251] Abbot Arnulf, therefore, appears to have paid out a total of forty pounds to the brothers—only twenty of which he had any expectation of recovering—for an estate his predecessor had bought from their father for the same amount; but he had thereby secured both current temporary possession and eventual permanent possession of the whole for his abbey, with explicit public recognition by both brothers that they had no hereditary claim to the estate. The very vehemence of the charters, and Arnulf's willingness to pay out so much although he thereby acquired nothing new for his abbey, suggest that Richard and William had indeed claimed in the past that they had a hereditary right in the estate.[252]

Given the clear danger that what was granted out as a life estate might be kept permanently by the recipient's relatives or later claimed by them, one might expect such transfers to be hedged round with special precautions. Aside from the charters' denials of the rights of heirs, however, few precautions are to be found. When one life estate reverted to Troarn after the grantee's death, no one was allowed to continue to hold the estate, not even his wife, and all of his kin who might conceivably have made claims participated in the ceremonial public return of the estate to the grantor.[253] There was, however, apparently no ceremony whereby the grant of a life estate was made. At least, none is mentioned by any charter although such a ceremony would have been the appropriate moment for a declaration by the grantee and perhaps his relatives recognizing that the grant was not heritable.[254] The only special precaution which occurs with unusual frequency in connection with life estates is the recognitory payment: in addition to the grant Saint-Martin de Sées made to Seric the priest, Fécamp demanded such a payment from one of its life tenants "as a record,"[255] and Saint-Wandrille retained a third of the tithe of the land it granted out "lest these agreements be given over to the negligent forgetfulness of [our] successors."[256] Recognitory payments are occasionally found in other, similar contexts;[257] it is perhaps surprising that they are not found more often in this connection.

What did the grantor, always a church, gain in return for its temporary loss of the property it granted and for the obvious danger it ran of permanently losing control of the property? Most charters give some indication of the advantages expected.[258] Improvement of the property made into a life estate is the most commonly cited incentive. Abbot John of Fécamp created three life estates for this purpose,[259] and Abbot Rainier and the monks of La Trinité du Mont created one.[260] In all these cases the grantor would have to wait until the estate terminated before it could begin to enjoy its increased wealth, for it was not possible to separate an improvement from the property to which it was made. It was therefore not necessary to specify that the improvements as well as the original estate were to return to the grantor, and this was not always stated.[261]

Compensation might take the form of additional land or appurtenances of land along with or rather than improvements to the estate itself.[262] In such cases also, the compensation did not come to the grantor until the estate returned. Abbot John of Fécamp, however, gave Bishop Hugh of Bayeux a life estate in exchange for the present and permanent transfer to the abbey of property in the bishop's possession.[263] The abbey was, as the charter notes, extremely reluctant to enter into the exchange; perhaps it needed an unusual inducement. Nevertheless, the arrangement may not have been as unusual as it at first appears. At least one other life estate constituted one side of an exchange,[264] and others seem to have served as countergifts.[265] There are also instances when the tithes of land granted as a life estate were given by the grantee to the grantor at the moment of the grant.[266]

Money might serve as compensation in the form of entry fines. When, for example, Saint-Pierre de Préaux had vindicated its right to the churches of Pont-Audemer against a cleric named Hugh son of Turulf, the abbey's patron Roger de Beaumont, "not wishing Hugh to lose completely, for he was his relation, begged Abbot William . . . that he accept ten pounds in coin from Hugh for an agreement that for as long as Hugh should live he should hold the aforewritten churches from Abbot William."[267] It is intriguing that this and the other three extant cases[268] involve clerics and that in three of them the life estate consisted of one or more churches. The evidence is too slight to dictate that it was customary for the newly appointed priest of a church belonging to an abbey to pay an entry fine. No known lay person paid an entry fine for a life estate, however, although some did so for rentals.[269] Compensation could also take the form of a payment of money when the estate terminated.[270] Precise sums are less usual, however, than promises of one's "substance," sometimes accompanied by one's body for burial.[271]

There was one other major reason for the creation of life estates: they were often used as a method of compromising disputes over property—or, rather, tenements for life were so used. The problem in many cases is whether the transaction was considered a life estate or a post-obit gift. The situation is always roughly the same: a dispute between an individual and a church is settled by an agreement that the individual will hold some or all of the disputed property until death, when it will become permanently the possession of the church. The life estate granted to Hugh son of Turulf is typical.[272] Because the property was in the hands of the individual, such agreements can resemble post-obit gifts. Nonetheless, the compromises are usually treated as—and were probably considered—life estates, that is, the property was considered rightfully to belong to the church and to be temporarily in someone else's hands only through the church's generosity. The charters, after all, were written by the churches.

Another motive occasionally suggested for the creation of life estates may hide similar instances. Saint-Wandrille gave a man named Wiger and his wife a life estate in return for their "friendship and aid."[273] Abbot Robert of Jumièges gave Hugh de Montfort one consisting of Adhemar, a servant of the abbey, and the land he held; and "Adhemar himself ought to serve no one else except Hugh alone from that benefice, so that Hugh himself should make it [the land] free and quit of every disturbance and claim and should guard and defend the other possessions of St. Peter which are close to him."[274] These grants are presented as voluntary alienations whereby each abbey secured the protective solicitude of a person of local importance.[275] The suspicion arises, however, especially in the case of Hugh de Montfort,[276] that the person against whom protection was most necessary was the one to whom the life estate was given. These may, in other words, be additional examples of the use of life estates to settle disputes.

One of the most immediately striking characteristics of eleventh-century Norman life estates is that nearly half of them, nine of twenty-one, come from Fécamp. Only three other abbeys—Saint-Wandrille, Saint-Pierre de Préaux, and Troarn—are known to have created as many as two. Moreover, eight of the nine life estates from Fécamp come from the abbacy of John of Ravenna, between 1028 and 1079; and the ninth probably does so as well, for it comes from the reign of Robert the Magnificent, between 1027 and 1035. Of the other twelve, four certainly come from the period after John had become abbot of Fécamp, two may have come from the period of his abbacy but probably were later,[277] and six certainly were later. During John's abbacy, in other words, Fécamp created at least one and one-half times the number of life estates known from the whole of the rest of Normandy during those fifty-one years and probably more than twice as many. Indeed, it is possible that, for Normandy, John invented the life estate. The earliest one not from Fécamp is dated by the editor of the charter to between about 1033 and about 1042 but by Jean Adigard des Gautries to about 1052.[278] The later date is preferable, but even the earlier means that John's earliest closely datable life estate, created in 1034, almost certainly was earlier.

The significant association of life estates with Fécamp can be explained in several ways. Perhaps Fécamp recorded such transactions earlier or kept its records more carefully than other churches. Perhaps Abbot John introduced into Normandy a practice characteristic of his Italian homeland.[279] John was an unusually adept administrator; perhaps he was willing to use somewhat unorthodox methods to improve his abbey's existing possessions and to bring in new ones.[280] Lucien Musset, who has studied John's administration more thoroughly than anyone else, is, however, of the opinion that the explanation lies primarily in the peculiar situation of Fécamp, which rendered it unusually subject to depredations by members of the laity, not excepting the duke himself; he credits John's determination and ingenuity with contriving that Fécamp did not lose its threatened possessions permanently but, instead, managed to maintain lordship over what it was forced to cede and to preserve a right of eventual recovery.[281] This explanation is undoubtedly correct for many of the life estates given by Fécamp and for some of the abbey's grants in other forms; but in the case of some of the less important of Fécamp's tenants, at least, it seems possible that John, as an able administrator, may have made the grants voluntarily in the hope thereby of improving or ultimately increasing his abbey's possessions.[282] Moreover, even if every life estate he granted was, in fact, extorted from him, it is significant for the development of the law that John was able to state the grants under a form which appears to have been—or become—well recognized in Normandy in his day and promised, however mendaciously, a concrete recompense for each transfer.

MORTGAGES

Mortgages are one of the few subjects directly of concern to this work which have received considerable attention from Norman legal historians, in this instance especially from Robert Génestal.[283] Nevertheless, Génestal looks only at transactions in which the mortgagees were churches; and he and the others who have studied mortgages in Normandy, considering the entire period down to the early thirteenth century, after various church councils had prohibited them, understandably concentrate on the more abundant sources from the twelfth and thirteenth centuries. Hence it is not mere repetition to try to determine what form mortgages took in the eleventh century.

A preliminary survey of the documents about mortgages which survive from eleventh-century Normandy leaves two immediate impressions; that some churches never acted as mortgagees and that most mortgages eventually resulted in the permanent alienation by the mortgagors of what was originally mortgaged. These appearances have often been accepted at face value, so that it is asserted that mortgages were relatively rare in eleventh-century Normandy and that churches entered into them primarily in hopes of acquiring the mortgaged property permanently.[284] Both conclusions seem to me erroneous: the patterns of references to mortgages on which they are based are probably to be explained simply by the relative novelty and incompleteness of the habit of making written records in Normandy at this time. Because lay persons did not record transfers, knowledge of mortgages made to lay mortgagees comes only from a few incidental references in the charters of various ecclesiastical bodies. Moreover, it is likely that even ecclesiastics rarely kept beyond the term of the mortgage whatever memoranda they may have made of mortgages which were redeemed. They would be wont to preserve only records of mortgages subsequently converted into permanent acquisitions. These documentary habits are sufficient to explain the apparently very high percentage of mortgages which led to permanent acquisitions.[285] Similarly, scribal and archival habits—the failure to record mortgages or to retain such records, the failure to note that current acquisitions had earlier been mortgaged—probably explains the apparent absence of mortgages to certain churches.

Eleventh-century Normans called the transaction at issue here a *vadimonium*.[286] A *vadimonium* was a temporary transfer for a number of years of property, itself sometimes referred to as a *vadimonium*, to one party by another party, almost always in return for a sum of money; the money must be repaid before what was transferred could be received back.[287] The Norman *vadimonium* is to be classified as a mortgage rather than a vifgage. In the type of loan in return for immovable collateral known as a vifgage, the profits from the collateral were collected by the lender and deducted from the amount of the loan; the loan ceased to exist either upon repayment of the amount outstanding or when the profits from the collateral amounted to the total loaned.[288] Vifgages are not unknown from Normandy in this period, but they are rare.[289] A mortgage differed from a vifgage in that the profits of the collateral, which were collected by the lender, were not deducted from the amount of the loan. They served, instead, as interest on the loan.[290] Because the amount of the loan therefore remained constant, it was more necessary than in the case of a vifgage to specify the duration of the loan: for a vifgage, this could be calculated if the amount of the loan and the annual value of the collateral were known.

Only one Norman charter notes in detail the fate of the profits of the collateral for a loan. In September 1096, "on his way to Jerusalem, William du Vast demised his land to the church of Fécamp . . . for three silver marks, in such a way that when he shall have come back he should give back that money and should receive his land." The charter adds

> that he had all the quitrents of his land for that year in which he demised it; similarly, the church of Fécamp will have all the quitrents of that year in which it gives back the land. But if he shall not have come back, his sisters or his closest relatives should give back three silver marks and they will have the land. Nevertheless, the church of Fécamp will always accept and have the quitrents of that year in which the land is given back either to William or to his relatives; as in the demise of the land they were accepted and had by William, so in the return they will be accepted and had by the abbot and the church.[291]

The obvious inference is that, during those years when William was away, Fécamp would collect the quitrents and keep them; the abbey waxed verbose in its attempt to ensure that it did not lose a year's worth of profits.[292] That, in William's absence, his sisters or other relatives could redeem the land for three marks indicates that the profits were not deducted from the amount of the loan. Although other charters say nothing about the profits of what was gaged, they regularly specify the duration of the loan but are silent on the annual value of the collateral, and many of them state that the amount to be repaid is the same as the amount loaned. All this mandates that an eleventh-century Norman *vadimonium* be understood as a mortgage. Orderic's account of the vision Walchelin, the priest of Saint-André de Bonneval, had on the first of January 1091 confirms the nature of *vadimonia*. Walchelin told Orderic that among the dead who appeared to him was a knight who addressed him thus:

> I am William of Glos, the son of Barnon, who was the renowned steward of William of Breteuil and his father William [fitz Osbern], earl of Hereford, before him. I have been guilty of unjust judgements and annexations in the world, and have committed more sins than I can tell. But most of all usury torments me. For I lent my money to a poor man,

> receiving a mill of his as a pledge (*pignus*), and because he was unable to repay the loan I retained the pledge all my life and disinherited the legitimate heir by leaving it to my heirs. . . . Therefore tell my wife Beatrice and my son Roger that they must help me by quickly restoring to the heir the pledge (*vadimonium*), from which they have received far more than I ever gave.

This is obviously a mortgage: even though by the time of the vision the profits had amounted to well more than the debt, the debt remained outstanding.[293]

Property which was gaged was almost invariably immovable. The few exceptions were neither mortgages nor vifgages, for the collateral produced no income, but simple loans against collateral.[294] Their apparent rarity is especially likely to be because they were never recorded in charters or because the charters in which they were recorded were not preserved or copied.[295]

When the duration of a mortgage is specified, it is almost always a minimum, that is, the mortgagor could not redeem the property before the expiration of the term. When, for example, Richard nephew of William Roher mortgaged land to Saint-Pierre de Préaux for ten years, he provided that if he died before the ten years were up the property was to become a simple gift to the abbey, but "if, indeed, the term is up, [but] I—still alive—do not come back, the aforesaid land will remain in mortgage for the same amount until I come back."[296] There is usually no maximum, that is, at any time after the term specified a mortgagor might redeem the property by repaying the sum lent. Occasionally no term is given; the mortgage is said to terminate whenever the money is repaid. Exceptions to the usual apparently unlimited time for redemption were possible. Adeliza de Bardouville promised Troarn that it could assume any mortgage into which any of her tenants wished to enter, but she insisted that, "if, at the term set for the mortgage, he who had demised the land in mortgage could not or would not redeem [it], the same lady, and no one else, would give St. Martin the money of the mortgage and would retain the land as [its] lady."[297] Here the mortgagor had to be able to redeem the mortgage by the terminal date and must have decided to do so or he would lose his rights to his tenurial superior. Such arrangements, however, seem to have been rare: only one other charter may give evidence of them.[298] The reason seems obvious. Terms are stated as minima rather than maxima and charters display little concern about whether mortgages will ever be redeemed because, during the existence of a mortgage, the mortgagee collected all the profits as though the property were a permanent possession. Adeliza's provision was a boon not to Troarn but to her, for it was to the advantage of mortgagees that mortgages not be redeemed for as long as possible.[299]

Mortgagees expected to receive lump-sum payments in redemption of mortgages rather than to be paid in installments. A mortgagor's desire to pay in more than one installment—the only time there is evidence of it—necessitated special arrangements. Lancelin d'Airan, being able to pay back only half the money he had received from Troarn in return for a mortgage, received back only half his property; somewhat later, still unable to raise the second half of the sum, he came to an arrangement with Troarn which was, in effect, a vifgage: he conceded to the monastery for two years all, or almost all, of what had originally been mortgaged, two years being a term which, it may be presumed, was calculated to be long enough to pay off the outstanding portion of the debt.[300]

Because some mortgages were for considerable lengths of time,[301] because many were made in anticipation of long journeys, including the first crusade,[302] and because life was precarious in the eleventh century, the question might arise of who was to be allowed to redeem a mortgage if the mortgagor died before doing so. Charters which raise the issue usually limit the number of persons who may redeem. Adeliza de Bardouville—and she alone—was allowed to redeem mortgages made by her tenants if they did not do so themselves.[303] It is not clear whether the permission granted to William du Vast's "sisters or his closest relatives" to redeem the mortgage is intended to be exclusive in effect or if, instead, its inclusion stems from that charter's concern with collection of the profits of the mortgaged land.[304] In one instance, however, only the mortgagor or his wife or son is allowed to redeem; another charter excludes all collateral relatives.[305] The presumption must, I think, be that if no limitation is stated the right to redeem mortgaged property normally descended from the mortgagor to his or her heir, no matter how remote that heir might be. If so, the apparent rarity of restrictions argues that mortgagees were not notably eager to restrict the possibility of redemption and thereby increase their chances of acquiring the mortgaged property permanently.

Churches not only accepted mortgages, they also entered into them. Some time before 1018 a man named Albert gave Dame-Marie to Jumièges so that he could become a monk there. Later, having become abbot of Saint-Mesmin de Micy, near Orléans, Albert persuaded the monks of Jumièges to mortgage Dame-Marie to Saint-Mesmin to raise the funds necessary to complete the building of a church he had begun at that vill.[306] Not surprisingly, given the propensity of monasteries to try to retain churches which had been temporarily or conditionally entrusted to them,[307] this transaction resulted in a lawsuit, not settled until 1086. A church might even mortgage some of its property to a lay person and might get into difficulties as a result: William of Volpiano, the great monastic reformer who was abbot of Fécamp, among other places, mortgaged two Norman churches to a man named Atto for one hundred pounds; when he was unable to redeem them, Duke Richard II did.[308]

Mortgages were made entirely between lay persons, but the allusions are usually so brief that it is hard to know anything about them. One was for one hundred pounds, another for four, a third for sixty shillings.[309] In addition to William de Glos, a fairly important man,[310] the mortgagees include two burgesses of Alençon, one of them a draper, who shared equally in one mortgage,[311] several persons in administrative positions,[312] a man and his wife together,[313] at least one woman on her own,[314] three or more men together,[315] and a good many persons of whom only the names are known.[316] One parish priest also served as a mortgagee.[317] It is, however, impossible to tell whether provisions of mortgages to individuals differed significantly from those to ecclesiastical institutions.

The scanty and laconic references to mortgages to lay persons occur only in connection with what later happened to the mortgaged property.[318] Although I do not think that this was the only reason why churches became mortgagees, it certainly happened fairly often that property which began by being mortgaged ended up by becoming the permanent possession of a religious institution; indeed, one charter casually mentions mortgages as one item in a list of ways a person could acquire property.[319] Occasionally a charter outlines how the mortgaged property might pass permanently into the hands of the mortgagee: if it is not redeemed by the mortgagor or his wife or son; if the mortgagor dies within the term of the mortgage; if the mortgagor or, he being deceased, his heir wishes to become a monk at the abbey which is the mortgagee.[320] Mostly, however, mortgagees acquired property mortgaged to them, not by death or default or because the mortgagor became a monk, but by gift; nor was it by any means always the mortgagee who acquired permanent possession.

The purest sort of gift to a mortgagee which a mortgagor could have made would have been one in which the mortgage was first redeemed and the property was then transferred as a gift. Such a transaction is never recorded and may well never have occurred: giving countergifts was so habitual that it was probably natural to both mortgagors and mortgagees to regard the amount of the mortgage as the *quid pro quo* for the gift. Therefore, in the simplest transactions the mortgagor kept the money and, in return, conferred the property on the mortgagee permanently.[321] It seems to have been at least as common, however, for the mortgagor to receive additional compensation from the mortgagee.[322] Cases of both types are sometimes called sales and sometimes not. They give rare indications of the percentage of actual value one could raise by a mortgage, if it can be assumed that the amount of the mortgage plus any additional sum paid to the mortgagor for permanent surrender of the property add up to the value of the property. On this basis, Génestal calculates that, in five eleventh-century mortgages, the mortgagors had received between 57 and 68 percent of the value of what they mortgaged.[323] The assumption is dubious, however, for pious motives on the part of the mortgagors-turned-donors may have discounted the amounts they requested from the donees—as exemplified by those mortgages which were converted into gifts with no additional payment—or desperate mortgagors may have had to accept unusually low prices for their property.[324] Either factor would make Génestal's results too high. Only one charter gives independently both the value of the property and the amount for which it was mortgaged: in it the mortgagor received 50 percent of the value of the property.[325]

A few arrangements other than sales or apparent sales resulted in partial transfers. One mortgagor gave the mortgagee part of the property permanently so as to redeem the rest, an arrangement necessitated by the mortgagor's financial difficulties, which meant that he could not redeem his land but doubtless also that he was unwilling to leave it all in the hands of the monks.[326] Lancelin d'Airan's similar problems were discussed earlier.[327] Another mortgagor redeemed mortgaged land by exchanging other land for it, and a third apparently received back his land and kept the amount of the mortgage in return for giving the mortgagee the tithes of the land.[328]

Each of the transfers just discussed involved a lay mortgagor who turned mortgaged property into the permanent possession of a church which was already the mortgagee. There are no similar instances in which an ecclesiastical mortgagor or a lay mortgagee was involved, although in theory at least a lay person could acquire land permanently by mortgage.[329] In a good many cases, however, a lay mortgagor transferred property which had been mortgaged to a lay person to the permanent possession of a church, or a lay mortgagee similarly transferred property mortgaged by a lay person. It is only because of such transfers that lay persons are known to have served as mortgagees. These cases are necessarily more complicated, for three parties were involved. When a mortgagor wished to endow a church, the usual practice was for the recipient church to redeem the mortgage,[330] but it was also possible for the abbey to give the mortgagor-donor money with which to pay the mortgagee.[331]

Mortgagees gave property they held in mortgage much more rarely than mortgagors gave property they had mortgaged. Sometimes both parties gave their rights so that each benefited by the gift.[332] Occasionally, a mortgagee gave property only for the duration of the mortgage, that is, the mortgage was transferred to a church in such a way that the mortgagor would redeem the property from the church.[333] Sometimes, however, charters ignore the rights of the mortgagors.[334] Conceivably the mortgagor's consent was in each case later secured and the record simply does not survive; but this seems unlikely, for the mortgagor's consent must have been more important than the mortgagee's to the donee's ultimate title.[335] Instead, the mortgagors may have been in such straits and may have had so little prospect of redeeming what they had mortgaged that their consent could be ignored; but this, too, seems unlikely given the evident concern of donees to secure the consent of anyone who ever might raise a claim to what was given.[336] Possibly the mortgagors had used the funds they had raised to go off on journeys from which they had not returned. Finally, these may have been transfers not of the lands mortgaged but of the mortgages themselves, each mortgagor remaining able to redeem the land from the church. Such an interpretation would be strained, however, for the charters all speak of gifts of the land held in mortgage rather than of the mortgage.[337] Whatever the reason, the absence of reference to the rights of the mortgagors remains striking.

The mortgages discussed so far were made by landholders of middling or lesser importance.[338] Normally, it was not necessary for great men to mortgage property to make ends meet or to raise the funds for a journey. Yet one mortgage which took place in eleventh-century Normandy was as large as it could possibly be and involved the most important person of all. This was the mortgage of the duchy of Normandy by Duke Robert Curthose to his brother William Rufus, king of England, a mortgage made in 1096 so that Curthose, not the man to save a reserve fund out of the ducal revenues, could go off on crusade.[339]

This was not merely a mortgage, it was a historical event; but, considered as a mortgage, it seems, so far as its details are known, to follow the rules which governed other mortgages. There is remarkably little information, given the importance of the transaction; and it is possible that no formal record was written.[340] Both Orderic and Robert of Torigny say that Curthose initiated the arrangement.[341] The amount was certainly ten thousand marks of silver.[342] There is less agreement on the term of the mortgage: it is reported as three years, as five years, and as until whenever Robert returned.[343] Both William of Malmesbury and Orderic say that the money Curthose brought back to redeem Normandy was the dowry of his wife, Sybil of Conversano, whom he married in southern Italy on his way back from the crusade; William adds that Sybil's father gave it to him "so that by its means he might redeem Normandy from mortgage."[344]

By the time Curthose arrived back in Normandy, the mortgagee was dead. William II of England was killed in a hunting accident on August 2, 1100, and his—and Robert's—younger brother, Henry I, now ruled England and Normandy. Henry was in England and made no attempt to prevent Robert from resuming control of Normandy.[345] Nor did he make any known demand that the mortgage be redeemed: Robert of Torigny says that the mortgage was not redeemed although Curthose was prepared to redeem it.[346] Henry was doubtless too much occupied in England, of which he had been king for only several weeks, to attempt to keep Curthose out of Normandy.[347] Why he did not demand the money back is harder to understand. Possibly he hoped that, if he made no demands on Curthose or Normandy, Robert would be satisfied to rule Normandy and would accept Henry's fait accompli in England. If so, his expectations were disappointed, but in the accounts of the political maneuverings between Robert's return and the battle of Tinchebray in 1106 Henry is never said to have demanded that the mortgage be redeemed.

The sources allude to two other possible mortgages of large territorial units rather similar to the mortgage of Normandy. When William the Conqueror died, he left his third son, the future Henry I, no land but a large sum of money. The next year Curthose ceded the Cotentin to Henry. Orderic calls this a sale for three thousand pounds of silver. Robert of Torigny says that "some people say" that it was a mortgage. Wace states categorically that the transaction was a mortgage and adds that it was to last for however long it took Robert to pay back the money.[348] Wace and Robert of Torigny, however, are both late witnesses. Whether the cession was, in fact, a mortgage or a sale,[349] Curthose got himself out of it by imprisoning his brother and taking the county back. The other instance again involved William Rufus: both Orderic and William of Malmesbury report that just before his death he was considering accepting the offer of William IX, count of Poitou and duke of Aquitaine, to mortgage his lands to Rufus.[350] No details of the projected mortgage are given.

Did the mortgagee enter into actual possession of the rights and obligations of the mortgagor or merely acquire the right to receive the profits produced by the property mortgaged? William Rufus certainly took possession of Normandy in 1096; he ruled the duchy but never called himself its duke.[351] It would, in any case, be dangerous to take his treatment of Normandy as evidence for what happened in less spectacular instances, for political considerations were at least as much involved here as purely legal ones. Rufus was Curthose's brother, moreover, so that, even if this transaction could be taken as typical, it would not exclude the possibility that a mortgagor's family might remain in possession even if the mortgagor himself was off on a long journey. Génestal concludes that the mortgagee did actually take possession of the property, but his evidence from before the thirteenth century is slight.[352] On this problem the eleventh-century charters say nothing and afford only the merest hints of an answer; but, insofar as they point in any direction at all, they suggest that Génestal's conclusion holds for the period.[353] The general impression given by the documents is certainly that mortgagees took possession, although there is no reference to a ceremony whereby the transfer was publicly symbolized,[354] and only one charter seems incapable of being interpreted in a contrary sense.[355] Those lay mortgagees who transferred possession to churches seem actually to have been transferring the property, not merely the mortgage, and must therefore have been in possession.[356]

In sum, the mortgage was a recognized institution of eleventh-century Norman law, the principal means of borrowing against one's land. With a few possible exceptions, the term of a mortgage was its minimum duration, rather that its maximum, and in such cases there seems to have been no maximum. The profits of the property mortgaged served as interest on the loan, and the full sum advanced had to be repaid for one to redeem the mortgage. Both lay persons and groups of monks mortgaged their property; and both acted as mortgagees, as did one priest. A mortgage sometimes served as the first step in the permanent acquisition of the property by the abbey to which it was mortgaged; whether this was true of mortgages to lay persons is unknown, though one casual remark suggests that it may have been.[357] Moreover, mortgages and mortgaged property were treated as transferable to third parties as long as the rights of the other party to the mortgage were protected and sometimes, apparently, even if they were not.

MOVABLES

Eleventh-century Normans probably recognized movables as a type of property distinct from immovables,[358] and transfers of movables are mentioned both in charters and in the histories. They appear rarely in either, however: the historians mention only the most striking examples; and, of all the types of property which might be transferred, movables were the least likely ever to be recorded in charters.[359] There are, nonetheless, reasons to suspect that large numbers of gifts of movables were made. Thus, for example, several abbeys' eleventh-century charters survive well enough to permit the presumption that records are extant of at least most of their permanent acquisitions of immovables, yet the number of monks known to have entered these abbeys as a result of donations of immovables is quite low.[360] Because at least occasionally a new monk or nun entered a convent with a gift solely of movables, it is a fair conjecture that at these abbeys—and perhaps others—many such entries occurred but went unrecorded.[361] It is all the more likely that other types of transfers of movables were never written down.

Little about the few recorded gifts of movables is remarkable. They are hardly ever said to command spiritual benefits in return, whether society, entry as a religious, or any of the others.[362] Exchanges of movables go wholly unreported, and seldom is there even an incidental reference to a sale. Movables, so far as I know, were never given conditionally or rented.[363] They were rarely granted.[364] A few were pawned.[365] Because gifts of movables are only infrequently mentioned in charters which do not also record gifts of immovables, it is not possible to determine whether the ceremonies surrounding gifts and the various ways in which gifts were made secure were used for movables alone.

The one type of transfer of movables about which considerable information survives is the gift of a person's "part" (*pars*) or "portion" (*portio*) or "substance" (*substantia*) to a convent after his or her death. Such gifts occur most often in conjunction with four types of transactions: grants of life estates, post-obit gifts of immovables, grants of the right to become a monk in the future, and grants of the right to be buried at the convent, when there is no expectation that the latter right will be exercised in the near future.[366] Gifts of one's portion are, however, found from time to time in conjunction with every sort of transaction of which a sizable number of examples is known. The nature of such a gift does not seem to have varied with the type of transfer to which it was attached.

Pars occurs most often to denote a gift of this type, largely because it is the word preferred by Saint-Martin de Sées—most often in such phrases as "all his/her/their proper part"[367]—and about half the extant gifts of this type are recorded in charters from that abbey. Terminology, however, was not yet standardized. Saint-Evroul, whose extant charters include as high a percentage of gifts of this sort as Saint-Martin's, uses *substantia* twice and the phrase *pars substantiae* twice but prefers vaguer phrases expressing the idea "all his possessions."[368] Saint-Martin itself often resorts to phrases of that sort or says *portio* or *substantia*.[369] Other abbeys use *pars* alone or in the phrase *pars substantiae*, *portio* alone or in the phrase *portio substantiae*, *substantia* alone, and various circumlocutions, of which the most revealing are "everything which he should possess and which should fall to him in his lifetime" and "everything which pertains to me."[370] Because a charter from La Trinité du

Mont equates *pars* with *portio*[371] and two charters from Fécamp do the same for *pars* and *substantia*,[372] there can be no doubt that the terms were synonymous or that, although the terminology was still imprecise, the post-obit gift of one's portion was a recognized element of eleventh-century Norman law.

Most references to a post-obit gift of one's portion imply that all the goods belonging to the individual making the gift were to change hands. Such gifts were not made only by persons who had no heir, however, so a donor's portion probably did not consist of absolutely everything of which the donor enjoyed possession during his or her lifetime. Instead, it was literally only a portion. When charters elaborate, they usually appear to do so to limit the scope of the gifts. Two portions seem to be limited to one-third of the donor's goods: "the third part of all my substance," in one instance; "the same Richard's part, that is, the third portion of his grain and wine," in the other.[373] "Part" and "portion" may have been understood generally to mean one-third, but the evidence is indirect and difficult to evaluate.[374] It would be stretching the meager evidence too far to conclude that most donors knew they could dispose freely of only one-third of their goods and, therefore, did not feel it necessary to indicate this limitation, which became the rule in the developed custom of Normandy.[375] The frequent recurrence of "his/her/their" and "proper" as modifiers of "part" and "portion" and the use of phrases such as "all of my part which falls to me,"[376] however, both suggest that some limit may usually have been observed.

Persons who gave their portions to churches seem, in any case, to have had perfect freedom to do so. No prohibitions are extant on giving more than a certain amount, nor are there challenges based on the contention that someone had given more than he or she was entitled to give. Only one donor provided for even the partial redemption of his portion by his heir from the church to which it had been given.[377] Moreover, in only one other known case did an heir recover what his father had given; and this—William Rufus's redemption of the regalia William the Conqueror had given to Saint-Etienne de Caen—is so exceptional that it cannot be taken to constitute evidence of a general tendency of the time.[378] Neither the Conqueror's gift nor the similar one which Queen Matilda made to La Trinité de Caen before her death in 1083,[379] which apparently was not redeemed, is called the decedent's portion.

The most common restriction of one's portion is not a percentage but a limitation to one's portion of certain kinds of possessions, nearly always movables, most often money. Commonly, the donor is said to give simply his or her "part of his [or her] money" (*pars pecuniae suae*) or a variant of that phrase. Occasionally a specific sum is mentioned,[380] but in only two of these cases is the money said to come from the donor's portion.[381] Another donor gave "sixty shillings or the part of all those things which fall to me": either the abbey was given its choice, or sixty shillings was the value of the donor's part.[382] A few additional donors give some idea of the contents of their portions. Thus, for example, Ralph, tutor and chamberlain to Duke William, left to the canons of Saint-Georges de Boscherville everything he might possess at the time of his death "in gold, silver, cattle, ornaments and any other things at all."[383] Again, Richard son of Norman agreed with the monks of Saint-Martin de Sées that if he should at some time in the future become a monk at the abbey he would give them "all his things which he should have at that time"; but if he should die without becoming a monk the abbey should bury him and have his "horses and arms . . . and also his other things if he should have any."[384]

A gift of one's portion after one's death was not restricted to movables. To be sure, most of the gifts which record the constituent elements of a donor's portion list movables alone. A charter from Saint-Martin de Sées makes an apparent distinction between gifts of movables and gifts of immovables, saying that when a donor "approached the last day of his life, already on the point of death, for the remedy of his soul he demised to St. Martin and the brothers . . . all the proper part of his substance falling to him, and he gave a certain plot of land . . . quit and free as alms."[385] In several instances, however, a portion is said to consist partly or entirely of immovable property. One donor defines his portion as consisting of "possessions, both in lands and in monies or any other substances."[386] Another says that his and his wife's portion might consist "either in houses or in fields, gold, silver, books, clothes and all household goods."[387] As post-obit gifts of immovables were commonly made in eleventh-century Normandy, it is not overly surprising to find immovables included in donors' portions. It may be that the words *pars*, *portio*, and *substantia* were normally reserved for movable post-obit gifts and were simply misused by the scribes of a few charters. This is unlikely, however, for these donations differ from post-obit gifts of immovables in their vagueness: no particular immovable is specified. The reason cannot be that these donors had no heirs, for the details were included in the first charter quoted precisely because the donor did have an heir. The solution may be that the charters constitute another instance in which the nascent distinction between conquest and patrimony makes an appearance: the immovables which might form part of a decedent's portion would be those he or she had personally acquired and over which, unlike inherited immovables, he or she therefore had control to the exclusion of all claims by relatives. Although immovable in nature, they could be treated as movable for testamentary purposes.[388]

As well as differing by their vagueness, gifts of a donor's portion differ from post-obit gifts of immovables in that they were never postponed until the death of someone other than the donor. They were like post-obit gifts of immovables in raising a problem when a man and his wife made a joint gift. In all four cases in which an attempt is made to solve the problem, the portion is split so that some goes to the recipient abbey when the first spouse dies and some is retained by the survivor until his or her own death. Moreover, certainly in one case and possibly in all, husband and wife divided the available portion equally. The solution, in other words, resembles the usual solution to the same problem with regard to post-obit gifts of immovables.[389]

CONCLUSION

Eleventh-century Normans made alienations of the various types considered here not only in isolation but in combination. An individual might enter into a series of transactions with a church in which, nonetheless, the different types of alienations stand out distinctly. Sometimes, however, the transactions are so closely dependent one on another that to try to dissect the agreement into a number of distinct types of transfers does violence to the true nature of the whole. For purposes of analysis, it has been necessary to treat each type separately. A few examples of the complexity which was possible will do something to restore the balance. Examples are extant from a good many churches, but the cartulary of Saint-Martin de Sées is especially rich, as I have already had occasion to point out. For this reason and because that cartulary remains unpublished, both illustrations have been taken from it.[390]

In 1089, a cleric named Oliver "did homage to the Lord Abbot Ralph and accepted a certain plot of land from him in order to build a house, which [land] he should have free and quit of any payment while he should wish to hold" it. The agreement incorporates contingencies, including: the transformation of the life estate, if the grantee wishes, into a tenement held by a third party and burdened with customs of some sort, which transformation may be either *inter vivos* or post-obit; the regrant to the original grantor, if the grantee goes on pilgrimage, of the estate plus a church which also belonged to the grantee, not in mortgage but for the grantor to manage gratis for up to two years if the grantee returns within two years; transfer to the grantor of all the grantee's possessions if he does not return from pilgrimage within two years; transfer of the church to the grantor on the grantee's death; the possibility of becoming a monk within ten years after the agreement was made, if the grantee wishes; and a post-obit gift of all the grantee's goods, if the grantee dies as a secular cleric.[391] At some time between 1073 and 1089, a man named Adelard did homage to Abbot Robert and received land in return, apparently as a life estate. The abbey, as grantor, received compensation in the form both of an entry fine of six pounds and of immediate and permanent acquisition of the tithes of the land it gave Adelard and the promise of the tithes of any other land he might acquire. It also received Adelard's homage and his feudal services, which apparently could be assigned to a third party. The estate cannot, however, be called a fief because Adelard serves not "for his fief" but "as if for his fief," that is, presumably, by services like those done for a fief, except—if this is an exception—that there is no limit to his services. Adelard provided for more compensation to the abbey after his death: he left it his whole portion, including land as well as movables. The gift of the "monies or any other substances" in his portion is final, but the land is treated differently: his son is allowed to redeem it—for whatever sum the abbey may choose to demand—provided that he, too, serves for the land "as if for his fief."[392] This charter blurs not only the distinctions between life estates and fiefs but also those among reversions of life estates, post-obit gifts, and deathbed portions. Its imprecision may be conceptually unsatisfactory, but it probably represents the nature of eleventh-century Norman agreements more accurately than does an analysis by categories. Agreements such as Oliver's and Adelard's indicate, moreover, the flexibility which could be attained in practice by combining the various types of transfers of property known in Normandy in the eleventh century.

In sum, conditional and temporary alienations are recorded much less often in the extant charters of eleventh-century Normandy than are permanent alienations, but the difference may well be a product of the archival habits of churches rather than a reflection of reality. Because no obvious purpose was served by preserving documents which recorded arrangements no longer in effect and which had resulted in no permanent acquisition of property, the custodians of medieval archives had little reason to save the original records or have them copied into cartularies. Thus it may be that mortgages, contractual arrangements for rents and for feudal services, life estates, and complicated agreements such as Oliver's and Adelard's were much more common than the documents suggest or than, except in the case of fiefs, most previous scholars have recognized.

Though much less survives than may once have existed, there is enough to permit certain conclusions about these types of alienations. Some were quite well defined by the end of the century. The mortgage is the most fixed in its rules, with relatively few anomalous practices recorded. Although conditional gifts might, by definition, vary greatly in their terms, the rules about how conditions were to be enforced seem, too, to have been widely recognized. Grants for rents and for feudal services partake of the same fluidity in their terms, though at least some types of grants—*métairies*, farms, fiefs themselves—were distinct enough to have names by the end of the century, if not earlier. So far as the subject can be studied at all, these contracts share the same method of enforcement as was used for conditional gifts. The bequest of one's portion, usually but not exclusively of movables, was also a recognized institution of eleventh-century Norman law, though the rules limiting how much could be bequeathed may have been less precise than they later became. As with permanent alienations, therefore, so also with the types of transfers considered in this chapter, by the end of the eleventh century the custom of Normandy seems to have been well on its way to definition, though many practices were not yet as precisely fixed as they would later become.

Another conclusion may be derived from the material in this chapter. The nature of the sources makes the prevalent form of transfer in eleventh-century Normandy appear to be the pious donation. Among the laity, however, onerous transfers must have predominated, both transfers of the sorts discussed in this chapter and sales and exchanges. It has been usual among scholars to assume that in return for their land lay persons did one of two types of services: peasants paid rents and did labor services while their lords performed feudal services. For the elite, in other words, the assumption has been that any reference to tenure or to service means feudal tenure or feudal service. The material studied here, however, argues against any such assumption. Both churches and important lay persons held tenements on other bases: for rent, for lump-sum payments of money, for eventual grants of additional property, for improvements to the property granted. Mentions of service are uncommon, and specifics about types of service are much rarer still. Whether the context is service owed, service canceled, service transferred, or service excepted from transfers, most documents say simply "service" or "all service." Perhaps the most intriguing instance occurs in a charter whereby Duke William confirmed to Mont-Saint-Michel his cleric Neil's gift of Sainte-Colombe, which Neil held from the duke: "And I transfer the customs and all the services which come from the land, according to the usage of Normandy (*secundum morem Normannie*), to the same saint and monks to possess in perpetuity in the same land."[393] This is especially interesting, of course, because, uniquely, it refers to customs and services as "the usage of Normandy." Unfortunately, but typically, the allusion is so vague that the services may be Neil's services to the duke, either secular or ecclesiastical, or peasant services which had been owed to Neil by men on the land. It seems unlikely that they can have been military services, but even this exclusion depends on logic rather than facts. Such vagueness is characteristic. Only the exceptions say anything about particular services; and it is, of course, impossible to know how exceptional the services described were—exceptional only in that they were written down, or exceptional in nature and written down for that reason?

Moreover, even when a new arrangement seems to call for an extensive definition of service, the charters are usually silent. Nowhere, for example, does the agreement whereby Roger de Croismare became the tenant of Saint-Pierre de Préaux say anything about the services Roger's father-in-law Gilbert had owed to Roger de Beaumont, about those the abbot was to owe to Roger de Beaumont, about those Roger de Croismare was to owe to the abbey, about those the knights Robert and Roger had owed to Gilbert and were to owe to Roger de Croismare and his heir, or about those Roger's heir was to owe to the abbey for the reduced tenement he would hold.[394] It seems probable that the two agreements which provide so much of what is known about feudal tenure in eleventh-century Normandy—those between William Paynel and the abbot of Mont-Saint-Michel and between Viscount Rannulf and the bishop of Bayeux—were drawn up in circumstances in which new arrangements made it necessary for lords and tenants to define who owed what to whom.[395] Had more such agreements been reduced to writing, or had more of those which were written survived, much more would be known of conditions of tenure in eleventh-century Normandy. What cannot be assumed, however, is that behind every reference to "service" lie specifically feudal services. To presume so, especially given the evidence for other types of service, is to argue in a circle. It will never be known what proportion of tenements was granted for feudal services as they have usually been understood, that is, an indivisible cluster consisting of military service, suit of court, aids, and incidents. It may seem likely that those tenements granted in return for something else were much more often granted for a rent or for some one particular type of service, whether part of the feudal cluster or something else,[396] than for a lump-sum payment, for the eventual transfer of additional property, or for improvements to the tenement. Yet even this is no more than a hypothesis, unverifiable and perhaps no more tenable than the assumption that every allusion to "service" which does not specify something else means the full range of feudal services. Perhaps because the law was developing rapidly and had not yet been fixed either by long practice or by court decisions, flexibility seems to have been characteristic not only of the terms of individual agreements but also of the exploitation of landed resources in general. Institutions and individuals made the most profitable—or, if they were under pressure, the least harmful—arrangements they could, and they seem often to have construed their best interests in terms other than military service and suit of court.

5

Ownership and Tenure[1]

THE DIFFERENT TYPES of tenure which might be created by transfers of property have been discussed in connection with the types of transfers that created them. One more fundamental question, however, remains to be considered, namely, to what extent were immovable possessions in eleventh-century Normandy owned, to what extent were they instead held in return for services? On this subject, widely differing opinions have been expressed. The many scholars who follow Charles Homer Haskins and Henri Navel in believing that by 1066 Normandy was "one of the most fully developed feudal societies in Europe"[2] assume that all or almost all land in Normandy was held rather than owned by the mid-eleventh century; but few explicitly state that tenure was proportionately much more important than ownership.[3] Of the much smaller group of scholars who, in reaction to the views of Haskins and Navel, deny that Normandy was thoroughly "feudalized" by 1066, only Donald Matthew goes so far as to maintain that as of that date most Norman land was still owned rather than held.[4]

Certainty in this matter may be forever beyond reach. It would be possible to argue from the frequency in the charters of references to lords and especially to their consent to alienations,[5] in contrast to the almost complete absence of references to either an alienor's or an alienee's full ownership of property, that most immovables in eleventh-century Normandy were held rather than owned. Consent of lords, however, is by no means always reported; and one might argue that if no lord is mentioned none existed, or even that ownership was the norm and tenure the exception, which was noted because it was unusual. This question—whether what appears in the charters is the rule or the exception—is the fundamental epistemological problem of working with the documents upon which the study of Norman law in this period must depend. Given that problem, either of the possible arguments just suggested or any other argument *ex silentio* on this subject would be untenable. Evidence other than allusions to the consent of lords is scarce, however, except for one trend which emerges clearly from the charters, namely, that certain terms, which in charters of the first quarter of the century were used to denote ownership, came by the end of the century to be applied primarily to tenements. This trend and its implications are the subject of this chapter.

The categories which eleventh-century Normans used to classify the rights they had over their possessions are not hard to establish: the charters are full of references to possessions and transfers "in alms," "in inheritance," "as an allod," "by right," "in demesne," "as one's own," "in benefice," "in fee," and variations on such phrases. Except for "alms," all these terms could be used for possessions of or transfers to either lay persons or churches.[6] It is possible—and I shall contend—that the meanings of the terms were not identical when they were used for the possessions of the laity and when they were used for ecclesiastical possessions. For the most part, in the course of the century, the set of terms did not change, although from about the middle of the century on "fief" tends to replace "benefice," and in the last decades a few temporary tenures begin to acquire names.[7] The meanings of the terms, however, were not necessarily stable; and I shall argue that they were not, that words which early in the century appear to mean full ownership had by the end of the century come to be applied to tenements.

First, the different categories of possession must be established. Five charters, and only five, draw clear distinctions among the major categories, contrasting ownership with tenure:

> It pleased us . . . to confirm those things which our vassals, with our consent, conceded either from the *precarium* or benefices which were of our right or from the inheritances which they possessed by paternal right.
>
> It pleased us to write down those things which our vassals gave either from their benefices which are of our right or from [their] paternal inheritances.
>
> By our authority we confirm those things which our vassals . . . conceded either from their benefices which were of our right or from [their] paternal inheritances.
>
> I approached my lord the illustrious Duke Richard . . . begging that he complete the vow of my desire . . . [and] he satisfied me by agreeing and offering . . . not only my allods but also the vill called Meslay which I held from his benefice. These are, therefore, the things of my ownership which . . . the aforesaid Duke Richard conceded and gave, namely, the vill called Epinay [and so on, not including Meslay]. . . . Because of all this, from his benefice, the aforesaid Duke Richard conceded . . . in perpetual inheritance the vill which is called Meslay.
>
> I had a certain allod from [my] maternal inheritance, not from anyone's benefice.[8]

The first three charters are not completely independent witnesses: although they come from different abbeys, they contrast "benefices" with "inheritances" in such similar phrases that, on that basis alone, it might seem that one scribe wrote them all, a suspicion supported by other verbal similarities among them.[9] The last two contrast "benefices" with "allods," which one equates with ownership and the other associates with inheritance. All five come from about the last decade of the reign of Duke Richard II, between 1015 and 1026; it is possible that all were written at the same time. There are no earlier examples—but few earlier charters are extant from Normandy. The only two later examples are ambiguous:

> We also concede, in perpetuity, the things which [our] aforementioned vassals from their hereditary things and from our cession deputed to the use of the monks.
>
> These things . . . the women consecrated to God in this . . . convent . . . themselves and their relatives with them . . . gave . . . from their patrimonies and benefices.[10]

In both these statements it is possible that "and" couples correlatives or complete synonyms rather than antonyms, as the explicit or implicit "or" of the earlier five could not.

These distinctions imply that full ownership existed in eleventh-century Normandy, but the more one looks in other charters at the words which in these five seem to mean "ownership" the less they appear to do so. These words are *proprietas* (or more often the adjective *proprius*), *hereditas* (and more rarely *patrimonium*), *alodium*, and one type of use of *ius*.[11] Each is sometimes used as though it meant immovables held from no lord, but each is also used when the immovables at issue were held from a superior for some sort of service.

A fifth term, *dominium*, occasionally appears in a phrase which might be taken to imply that this word, too, meant "ownership," as when a man gave Saint-Martin de Sées "whatever he had in the church of *Marcemaisons*, whether in demesne or in fiefs."[12] From about 1050, such distinctions become common in the charters; but wherever they are expanded at all, *dominium* is clearly the opposite not of tenements held from a lord by the person whose demesne is the subject of discussion but rather of tenements held by tenants from that person. Donors give, for example, "the tithe which they had in Martainville both of their demesne and from their men."[13] *Dominium*, in other words, had to do with the exploitation rather than the possession of land: it meant demesne, not domain. Even when possessions were transferred "in demesne," to a church or to a lay person, this meant only that the donor had exploited them directly and was therefore able to give them to the donee to exploit directly.[14]

Of the four terms which mean "ownership" in the charters of Richard II's reign, the one which might most confidently be expected to retain that meaning is *proprietas*. Yet in fact both the noun and the adjective *proprius* quickly came to be synonymous with *dominium*. The noun is rare, occurring only nine times, five of them in contexts which cast light on its meaning.[15] Once, as quoted above, it appears as a synonym for "allod" in a context in which "ownership" seems the only possible translation;[16] but in another charter Duke Richard says, "I turn things of my *proprietas* into ecclesiastical right . . . and, abstracting them from my use, I transfer [them] in writing . . . to the use of the poor of Christ,"[17] a context in which the word need mean no more than direct exploitation. Earlier, *proprietas* appears as a synonym for the rare term *dicio*.[18] Slightly later, it seems to be synonymous with the phrase "in our own power."[19] The fifth time, it is used as *dominium* often is, the charter saying that a donor gave "two sheaves of the tithe of his *proprietas* and of all his men of Mesnil-Baclay."[20] Moreover, the adjective, when it is not used merely emphatically, is also used to point a contrast with possessions held from a person by his or her subordinates. Two men, for example, gave Saint-Taurin d'Evreux "the pannage of both their own pigs and those of their men."[21] Similarly, a good many charters emphasize the munificence of donors by stating that their gifts came "from their own things": *de suis propriis rebus* or *facultatibus* or (once) *de suis proprietatibus*, or simply *de suo proprio*.[22] *Proprietas*, in sum, like *dominium*, meant not "ownership" but direct exploitation.

To judge by the distinctions quoted earlier, the principal terms for ownership used by early eleventh-century Normans were *hereditas* and *alodium*. One charter notes that these were synonyms, saying that a donor gave "his whole *hereditas*, which we commonly call an *alodum*."[23] Others imply this identification or refer to allods as coming from their possessors' inheritances. The two words, therefore, were probably virtually interchangeable.[24] It is, nevertheless, useful to consider them separately in trying to discover what they meant.

Although a person's inheritance could be contrasted with his or her fiefs, as in the distinctions cited earlier, references to tenements which are also inheritances are more common. The longest and most explicit is the following account of a court case.

> Let everyone know that Warin de la Mare gave Saint-Martin de Sées and hereditarily conceded to the monks . . . a certain land which he had hereditarily outside the gate of Alençon. . . . For Warin's uncle . . . had the aforesaid land hereditarily from his ancestors; and Warin, this same uncle of his having died, acquired it for himself hereditarily through a rightful judgment in the court of Earl Roger [de Montgomery], many of the barons of the aforesaid earl seeing and also judging, namely Saffrid d'Escures, Gerard de *Canaio*, Aimery son of Hamelin [and] Wascelin son of Walter (?), who was the chief lord of the same land after the earl, and from whom Walter son of Seibert held it, from which Walter Warin recognized it [as held] and to whom he contributed two shillings per year in rent, for all income and service of the same land. Therefore, this land, which Warin acquired so rightfully [and], as we said, hereditarily from his ancestors through the rightful judgment and deraignment of the aforesaid court and [which] he held in his demesne as [his] own inheritance,

he gave to the abbey.[25] It is possible that the last words ought to be translated "as a proper inheritance"; in any case, the stress on inheritance in the charter is striking.

References to inheritances which were tenements as well need not mean that all tenements were hereditary. Instead, they destroy the apparently neat antonymy between tenements and inheritances observed in the five ducal charters of about 1025. Part of the explanation may be chronological: most categorical distinctions between "benefice" and "inheritance" date from the early part of the century, whereas most examples of tenements which were also inheritances come from its second half.[26] The change in the language of the charters could easily be explained if tenements became increasingly heritable in Normandy in the course of the eleventh century, a development which is often alleged, for fiefs at least, and which is quite probable.[27]

Even if most tenements had become hereditary by the end of the century, however, the problem would not be entirely solved. First, to say that most tenements had become hereditary is not to say that most inheritances were, or had become, tenements: in addition to those pieces of land which were granted out, heritably or not, there might still have been large amounts of land which were in lay hands and passed from generation to generation yet were held of no one. In the early part of the century such owned lands seem to have been called *hereditates*, though the sources are too poor to indicate whether the term could be applied to possessions which had not in fact been inherited from an ancestor but instead had first been acquired by the person in possession, but acquired in full ownership. If ownership existed in the second half of the century, however, it seems to have had no name, for by then *proprietates*, *hereditates*, and, as will soon appear, *alodia* could all be held. Second, gifts to churches were often described as being made "in inheritance" or a similar phrase, as was one sale from a layman to a layman.[28] Such phrases imply that the participants in the transactions understood certain rights or a certain status to be thus described. Indeed, a few charters speak of the *hereditates* of churches, although a church could hardly have an inheritance in any usual sense of the word.[29]

"Hereditary right" did not necessarily mean rightful possession, for scattered references occur to unjust but hereditary possession.[30] These suggest that a hereditary right might be asserted to any possession an ancestor had held, regardless of how it had been held or whether the ancestor had alienated it. The same attitude appears in two charters which carefully explain why a particular person had no hereditary right over something belonging to a church. When William the Conqueror's aunt Adeliza gave La Trinité de Caen the castle of Le Homme, the charter states that she bought the castle from her brother Duke Robert, then continues, "Afterwards her son Guy, unjustly seizing it from her, gave it to Viscount Neil. If, however, the aforesaid Neil should say that he had had it by hereditary right, it should be known that his father held it in no other way than because he was viscount of the same region and

Countess Adeliza ordered him to serve her therein as [her] agent."[31] Adeliza feared that Neil would assert a hereditary right to the castle although, as he must have known, his father had possessed it only temporarily and as her delegate and although his own possession had been based on a disseisin. Similarly, the charter which records the first stages in the complicated transactions between Richard and William, sons of Wascelin de Trun, and the abbey of Troarn over the church of Trun carefully points out that Richard "did not hold the church by inheritance from his father, from whom the abbot of Troarn had bought that whole honor," but rather as a life estate from the abbot.[32] These two charters—and many of the claims the churches of Normandy had to combat—demonstrate that by the late eleventh century Normans sometimes claimed hereditary rights over their fathers' holdings whether or not such rights were justifiable.

Three cases give the positive side of the picture by showing why a person was able to make a hereditary gift. One is the account of how Warin de la Mare vindicated in court his claim to inherit from his uncle.[33] The second also comes from Saint-Martin de Sées: a series of charters says first that Fulk d'Aunou "conceded whatever he had and ought to have had in the *métairie* of L'Osier which was of his fee," which *métairie* William Judas had given the abbey, and then that "in the same year Bigot de Sainte-Scolasse, who was the rightful heir of the same land since it had been in the marriage portion of his mother and his father had placed it in mortgage to William Judas," sold it to the abbey.[34] The abbey thus acquired, not in logical order, the rights of the mortgagee, of the lord, and of the heir to the land. The monks obviously recognized the force of Bigot's position as "rightful heir" although, because of the mortgage by his father, he had apparently never enjoyed possession of the land. In the third instance a charter declares that "the land which is called Ticheville is certainly a legitimate inheritance of Saint-Wandrille. For the glorious and victorious Duke Richard [II] gave it to St. Wandrille . . . at the request of the matron Emma . . . whose it was hereditarily from her relatives."[35] This forceful assertion was necessary because, as the charter goes on to say, Duke Robert the Magnificent had seized Ticheville from the abbey, which succeeded in recovering it only from his son, Duke William. All three transactions imply that a church's ability to possess something "in inheritance" depended on the alienor's having possessed it in the same way, as do charters which more briefly mention that what was alienated belonged to the alienor's inheritance and those which cite the consent of someone "from whose inheritance" the gift came, when that someone was not the alienor.

Few charters state the rights a person had over his or her inheritance. One right, widely implied but never explicitly stated, is to prevent anyone else from alienating parts of one's inheritance; it emerges from various signs that the consent of those with hereditary rights was avidly sought.[36] The clearest explicit statement of a right over one's inheritance comes from a charter of Mont-Saint-Michel, dated 1066, which begins, "Let everyone present and future know that I, William son of Wimund, holding and possessing the whole tithe of all my vavassors in Luot by hereditary right of my father, did as I pleased concerning it without contradiction from anyone."[37] This passage defines hereditary right as absolute ownership, the definition implicit in the distinctions with which this inquiry began. No other charter, however, gives a similar definition; indeed, it is possible that William was so emphatic because by his day it was unusual to be able to "do as one pleased" with one's possessions "without contradiction from anyone." A later charter from Mont-Saint-Michel equates "inheritance" with "of my right,"[38] but this helps little. Three charters describe lands which La Trinité du Mont acquired first as mortgages and later "in inheritance,"[39] thus implying that possession "in inheritance," at least on the part of a church, meant permanent possession. These are the only additional definitions of the phrase.

For something to be possessed or transferred "in inheritance" probably did imply that it was—or was to be—held permanently and relatively free of interference from others. In the early eleventh century it probably meant, as well, possession without any superior. The charter of William son of Wimund shows that at least one lay person continued to possess rights amounting to ownership into the second half of the century, and this meaning of "inheritance" may have persisted when applied to ecclesiastical possessions. By the second half of the century, however, "inheritance" and "tenure" were no longer antonyms: property could be both. No other term emerges to denote ownership by the laity, which suggests that it became rare or disappeared. "Inheritance" itself, however, when applied to lay tenure in the second half of the eleventh century, can have had only one meaning: property which one's ancestors had also possessed on a permanent basis and which no ancestor had alienated permanently from the familial line of descent, regardless of whether such possessions were held from a superior. Viscount Neil and his father did not establish a hereditary right to the castle of Le Homme because the father held only temporarily, as an agent, and the son's possession was wholly illegal. Richard de Trun had no hereditary right to the church of Trun, although his father may have had one, because his father had permanently alienated it to Troarn; that the abbey had given Richard a life estate in the church was dangerous, as the abbey's subsequent attempts to destroy the life estate[40] show, but irrelevant in law. Bigot de Sainte-Scolasse, on the other hand, still was the "rightful heir" of the *métairie* at L'Osier given to Saint-Martin de Sées because his father had merely mortgaged it, not alienated it permanently. For lay persons in Normandy in the second half of the eleventh century, the true antonym of "inheritance" was not "tenure" but "conquest."

The concept of "conquest"—a term meaning possessions one had first acquired oneself—was at least beginning to become current in Normandy. Eight charters cite grants both of what the alienor now possesses and of what he, and sometimes his heirs as well, may come to possess in the future, in terms such as the following: "He conceded . . . all the tithes of the same things, [both] those which he then had throughout his demesnes and those which he or his heirs shall have conquered and had from now on."[41] One such phrase covers not only the alienor but also the recipient, speaks of conquest coming from gifts and sales, and shows that such conquest could be part of a fief.[42] In later French and English law, conquest was more freely alienable than were inheritances. By the end of the eleventh century, Norman law may not yet fully have incorporated this principle, but it seems well on its way to doing so.[43] In short, the word "inheritance" had clearly, in the course of the century, expanded to cover not only familial possessions which were independent of any superior and therefore fully owned—its earlier meaning—but also familial possessions which were tenements held of lords. In addition, a new distinction had at least begun to develop between familial possessions, regardless of how the family possessed them, and possessions which an individual was the first in the family to enjoy, regardless also of the mode of possession. About 1025 one spoke of "inheritances" as opposed to "benefices"; but by 1100 one could speak of one's tenements as "inheritances" and, if one sought to point a contrast, one spoke not of "inheritances" which were not tenements—or of any other term with the same meaning—but of one's personal acquisitions however they were made.

For the laity, then, as Norman law developed in the eleventh century, "inheritance" ceased necessarily to mean ownership and came instead to mean possessions over which the successive generations of a family had rights—property whose destiny, barring permanent alienations, was to descend in the family according to the recognized order of "rightful heirs." Nonetheless, when an alienation was made to a church "in inheritance" or "to possess by hereditary right," these phrases probably retained their old meaning. To speak of a church as having a *hereditas* in the late eleventh-century lay sense is meaningless, for a church never dies, yet charters occasionally do so. If these terms meant anything when applied to alienations to or property of churches, if they were not mere empty reminiscences of a previous state of affairs, they must have been intended to emphasize either the permanence of the possession—as the frequency of the phrase *in perpetuam hereditatem* may imply—or the degree of control which was transferred. The only charters which cast light on the question are the ones from La Trinité du Mont, which report conversions of mortgages into grants "in inheritance," thus suggesting that the phrase connoted permanence.[44]

The charters quoted at the beginning of this chapter contrast "allod" with "benefice" just as they do "inheritance."[45] As with inheritance, so it was possible to possess or to give, concede, buy, sell, or demise something "as an allod" (*in alodio* or *in alodium*); indeed, one charter speaks of a "gift in allod and perpetual inheritance."[46] And just as there was a *ius hereditarium*, so there was a *ius alodii*, although the term is used only once.[47] The word "allod," however, did not continue to mean in Normandy what it meant in most of the rest of France, that is, a possession which was owned absolutely. In Normandy allods were or came to be held of lords, just as inheritances did. The phrase "to hold an allod" (*tenere in alodio* or *in alodium*) from someone occurs fairly often in charters, beginning early in the century.[48] Two charters suggest that in the first third of the century lords could not dispose of their tenants' allods;[49] but not much later men were given with their allods, which must have been held of the donors.[50] In the last third of the century, allods were given with the consent of the lords of the donors.[51] There are also references from the 1040s on to service done for allods.[52] None specifies the services done, except one in which the service is a money rent.[53] Nevertheless, it is evident that for at least the last three-quarters of the eleventh century allods could be tenements.[54]

It would seem, however, that some distinction persisted between an allod and a fief because, in a charter of between 1080 and 1082, William the Conqueror concedes "all the land which Gerald . . . holds from me as well in allod as in fee."[55] The difference may have concerned inheritability, fiefs being at most de facto heritable whereas allods were so de jure. If this was the case, it cannot be proved.[56] Instead, the observable difference concerns service: there are indications that service for allods was lighter than service for other tenements.[57] One is the most famous appearance of "allod" in Norman history. In describing the transfer of Normandy to Rollo by Charles the Simple, Dudo of Saint-Quentin twice says that Normandy was conferred on Rollo "as an endowment and allod."[58] Even to Dudo, anxious as he was to emphasize the independence of the Norman dukes from the kings of France, the word did not imply independence of any feudal superior, for in the same passage he describes Rollo doing homage to Charles.[59] In connection with the negotiations leading up to the grant of Normandy, Dudo refers vaguely to service Rollo was to do to the king in return,[60] and he makes occasional later allusions to services owed by the Normans to the kings of France;[61] but he also repeatedly states that the Norman dukes owe no service for the duchy.[62] The question of the actual relations of the early dukes to the kings of France is vexed and revolves largely around the problem of Dudo's veracity; but whether accurate or not, his account seems intended to deny the existence of any obligation to the king, and this may be why he chose "allod" to apply to the grant of Normandy.

The other evidence that service from allods was unusual comes from the other end of the social scale. The few available details about those peasants known as "alloders" (*alodarii*) suggest that their status was higher than that of other peasants. Thus, a charter for Jumièges includes a gift of "six free men who are called alloders."[63] Fifteen men, including two priests, who witness a charter for Saint-Ouen are described as "men of this honor and alloders."[64] In recounting Duke William Longsword's refoundation of Jumièges, the historian William of Jumièges says that the duke had "bought back the vill for gold from the alloders."[65] As men whose land had to be redeemed from them, alloders were certainly unusual peasants, for in eleventh-century charters peasants are usually transferred along with their land with no reference even to their consent, much less to redemption of the land from them. Alloders may also have done lighter services than other peasants. The only extant description of their services comes from La Trinité de Caen's early twelfth-century survey of its income: at Ouistrehan "we have six men . . . who are commonly called alloders. Each of them holds his garden and they do service at the neighboring manors and they pay sixteen pennies and four quarters of oats annually." These services seem light by comparison with the services of the villeins at Ouistrehan, described immediately before those of the alloders: each villein "pays four and a half shillings annually and three quarters of wheat and five quarters of malt and two hens at Christmas and twenty eggs at Easter, and they plow one acre per year, half before Christmas and half after Christmas, and they harrow and sow with our seed. [They pay] one penny per year for each of their pigs and, when they capture a thousand herrings, each net pays a hundred."[66] It does not, however, follow from the use of "alloder" as the name of a group of peasants that "allod" implies tenure of low status. On the contrary, as late as the end of the century the duke's own land could be called his allod.[67]

For lay tenure, therefore, "allod" and "inheritance" began as synonyms and continued so even as their meaning changed in the course of the century. A possible partial exception to the synonymy is that a tenement which was an "allod" may have been less burdened with services than one which was an "inheritance." The evidence for this difference is slight, however, and affords no opportunity for comparison of service from one with service from the other.

As with "inheritance," so with "allod," when the term is applied to a church's possessions a corollary of inheritability must be meant, for lands belonging to churches were never actually inherited. In connection with inheritance, two corollaries were suggested: permanence and high degree of control. "Allod" and "inheritance" may have been—and have continued throughout to be—completely synonymous in suggesting either or both of these characteristics. Conceivably, however, the slightly divergent meanings of the terms when applied to lay tenure—if there was indeed a difference—carried over into this area, so that "in inheritance" implied permanence whereas "as an allod" implied a relatively great lack of interference. It may be indicative that transfers to churches "in inheritance" are often said to have been "in perpetual inheritance," but the phrase "as a perpetual allod" is rarely found.

The scant evidence which exists implies that a transfer "in inheritance" to a church meant a permanent transfer. Concomitantly, the one extant description of the meaning of a gift to a church "as an allod" suggests that the phrase was used to indicate freedom from obligations. In a charter of 1034 or 1035, Duke Robert the Magnificent says that his father, Richard II, "gave the monks of the Holy Trinity which is called Fécamp the monastery which is called [Monti]villiers as their own allod for the sustenance and use of the monks, so that they should do with it whatever they wished to do, as with [their] own allod." But, says Robert, he himself decided that Montivilliers would be a good site for a nunnery, and he finally persuaded Abbot John of Fécamp to agree to an exchange.

> Therefore I took it back and I gave [to Fécamp] the monastery of Saint-Taurin at Evreux, so that, by the same agreement and [in the same] way in which they held Montivilliers, that is, as an allod, they should similarly hold the lands of Saint-Taurin which it held of old and which I gave . . . , as its own allod, so that whoever will be abbot of Fécamp in our time and in the future should hold and possess the same place for the use of the monks serving God in the same place and at Fécamp, like the other land which pertains to Fécamp; and the cell should belong to the aforesaid monastery of the Holy Trinity forever.[68]

This suggests that a church which had something "as an allod" possessed it not only in perpetuity but to use directly for its own needs rather than for other purposes and that the monks could "do with it whatever they wished to do." Thus, a transfer to a church "as an allod" was a transfer in full ownership.

Duke Robert's charter, however, was written just when the shift in the meaning of lay allodial possession begins to become apparent and therefore cannot be used to demonstrate that the meaning of "allod" when applied to ecclesiastical possessions did not also shift. Seventy years later, after the death of Abbot Ralph of Saint-Taurin, that abbey's monks refused to receive a new abbot from Fécamp and denied that they were subject to Fécamp in any way. When the case came into the court of Henry I in 1106, Fécamp produced Duke Robert's charter as proof of its rights. The charter of 1106 recording Fécamp's victory summarizes Robert's charter simply as one "in which it was written how the church of Fécamp had the aforementioned abbey [of Saint-Taurin] from Duke Robert . . . in exchange for Montivilliers, which [was] accepted from Duke Richard II in perpetual endowment [and which] Abbot John and the monks . . . freely conceded to the same duke for the exchange of the abbey of Saint-Taurin and so that the same abbey of Saint-Taurin should remain a cell of the monastery of Fécamp in perpetuity." The emphasis here is entirely on the permanence, rather than on the quality, of Fécamp's possession. The court's decision, as recorded in the same charter, was more in accord with Duke Robert's charter: the abbot of Fécamp "should accept the abbey of Saint-Taurin as his own cell and should treat it as he wished, choosing and placing the abbot there from his [monks] and removing or sending monks where and just as he pleased."[69] This echoes the language of the earlier charter but nowhere uses "allod" to describe Fécamp's possession of Saint-Taurin. It is therefore dubious evidence, at best, that ecclesiastical allodial possession had not changed in meaning in the intervening seventy-odd years. Indeed, Henry I's court seems to have interpreted the total freedom "as an allod" granted in the earlier charter as though it meant only that the abbot of Fécamp had complete control over the monks of Saint-Taurin, not absolute ownership of its property. Yet, because monastic subordination was exactly the point at issue in the suit, it was likely to be emphasized in the statement of the settlement of the case. Hence, comparison of the two documents need not indicate that in the interval between them the meaning of ecclesiastical allodial possession had changed. It is therefore unfortunate that no other charter gives a description of ecclesiastical allodial possession. The only relevant charter later than Duke Robert's says that Henry de Grainville gave La Trinité du Mont "as an allod an acre and a half of land which he had held from them as a benefice."[70] Here "as an allod" seems synonymous merely with "in demesne."

The last term used to mean ownership is *ius*. This word, of course, had a wide range of meanings. It is used for the law applying to possessions of a particular type: *ius hereditarium*, *ius alodii*, *ius beneficiale*, and *ius elemosinae* all occur.[71] *Ius* could also mean law in general or status in general. Moreover, *iure perpetuo*—or *perenni* or *eterno* or *sempiterno*—was a popular way of saying that a transfer was made "in perpetuity." Here only two types of phrases are relevant: something is said either to be "of my right" or to be transferred "to the right" of a church.

In the distinctions quoted at the beginning of this chapter, the duke used "of our right" to describe fiefs held of him by his men, and similar phrases are used in other charters in reference to tenements held from the duke and others.[72] Once, the duke contrasts land "of my right and demesne" with land a tenant holds "by [his] own and beneficial right."[73] The implication that "of my right" could equally well mean the tenant's right rather than the lord's is borne out by charters in which land is said to be both a fief and of the tenant's right.[74] Both types of phrases are rare but occur both early and late in the century. "Of my right" is occasionally also used to mean that a person has a solid legal right, as opposed to some other claimant,[75] but this does not define his or her rights. Because no other charter defines "right" in reference to lay persons, little can be said except that it is obvious that, for the laity, "right" did not necessarily mean ownership because what was "of right" could also be held.

There are, however, several definitions of what it meant to give something "to the right" of a church, and these suggest that the phrase meant full ownership. Roger de Montgomery made a post-obit gift to Saint-Etienne de Caen of the bourg of Trun: the bourg was to "enter into the right and possession (*in jus et possessionem*) of the aforesaid convent, so that it should be free to the abbot and monks serving God there canonically to dispose of, give [or] hold it and to do whatever they think [will be] useful concerning it, according to God and the rule."[76] Roger specified that the abbey must act "canonically" and "according to God and the rule," but within these bounds he gave it full control over the future destiny of the bourg. A later pancart for the same abbey includes two donations with clauses similar to Roger's. Neither explicitly permits alienation; but one defines "right and possession" by saying that "it should be free to the abbot and monks . . . to do whatever they wish with it, according to God," and the other grants freedom "to do whatever seems [best] to them concerning it, as they please, without any contradiction" although it does not call this "right and possession."[77] For Saint-Etienne de Caen, therefore, *ius* appears to have meant ownership, extending in at least one case even to the abbey's right to alienate what it was given. Approximately the same definition of *ius* occurs in the foundation charter of Marmoutier's priory of Croth, near Evreux.[78] A very similar grant of ownership in a charter for Marmoutier's priory of Saint-Vigor de Perrières, also in Normandy, is less closely connected to *ius*.[79] No other charter indicates clearly that the church which drafted it acquired ownership when it was given something "by right," but none forbids this meaning. It is therefore possible that when a charter speaks of the *ius* of a church, any church, it means that the church had full ownership.

The relationship between the terms which seem to denote ownership when applied to ecclesiastical possessions and tenure "in alms" is moot. There are ways in which they are similar and ways in which they differ.[80] The synonymy or close correlation of inheritance, allod, and right can be proved through the appearance in the charters of definitions of one in terms of another or of catch phrases using two of them together. In contrast, no gift was ever made "in inheritance and alms" or the like, which implies a difference between alms and the other terms. Moreover, although both are often characterized as "perpetual," there are differences of emphasis between possessions which are conveyed under terms of ownership and those which are conveyed as alms or with sweeping exemptions from service. Absolute control to the point of freedom to alienate is never asserted about alms or its equivalent although it is asserted at least once to be conveyed under terms of ownership. On the other hand, emphatic assertions of freedom from secular services and of obligations to perform spiritual services are not found in connection with ownership. The reason for these differences may be that, because everyone knew what "alms" meant, no one felt the need to define the term fully. "Alms," after all, differs from the other terms in being applicable only to the property of churches; and it is precisely those charters which do not use the word which say the most about such things as freedom from service. Possibly, too, to give something to a church "in alms" was to emphasize a different aspect of the same type of transfer: as there are some slight grounds for suspecting that, when applied to the possessions of churches, "in inheritance" stressed permanence whereas "as an allod" emphasized complete control, so "in alms" might similarly denote freedom from service.

From this inquiry certain conclusions seem permissible. By the end of the eleventh century, if not at its beginning, the terms which have been studied had somewhat different meanings when applied to the possessions of lay persons and when applied to those of churches: by then, the evidence that churches had some of their possessions in ownership is much stronger than the evidence that lay persons did. There may have been some change in the meaning of the terms in the course of the century, but it was either slower or less complete for ecclesiastical possessions than for lay possessions.

For the laity, the results are more dramatic. Of five terms which might seem to mean ownership, that is, possession independent of a superior, *dominium* never had that meaning but, instead, always meant direct exploitation, regardless of the mode of possession. Except in one instance, *proprietas* is synonymous with *dominium. Ius* certainly could mean ownership in reference to ecclesiastical possession, but there is no instance in which the same is incontrovertibly true for lay possession. The two remaining terms, *hereditas* and *alodium*, which indubitably could and did mean lay ownership in the first quarter of the century, subsequently lost this meaning and came, by the middle of the century, to be used for possessions which were held of lords for service. The latest assertion of full ownership by a lay person dates from 1066.[81] It is impossible to prove that in the last third of the century lay ownership did not exist in Normandy. An argument from silence is dubious under the best of conditions, and eleventh-century Norman charters provide anything but the best conditions for studying the law which applied to the laity. Equally, however, it is impossible to prove that in the last third of the century lay ownership did exist. If it did, no term was consistently used for it: all the terms considered here were at least sometimes applied to tenements, and in no instance later than 1066 was any of them applied to a lay possession which was demonstrably owned. Moreover, no new term was coined to fill the apparent gap thus left. It therefore seems legitimate to conclude that ownership, which had been an important mode of lay possession of land early in the eleventh century, was by late in that century at best unimportant and that all or almost all the land in Normandy which had been owned in the earlier period later came to be held.

One obvious question is how this change came about. One author has credited the creation of feudal bonds between the duke and his vassals in Normandy in the eleventh century entirely to one process: when the duke defeated a rebellious subject, he confiscated that man's lands and then granted all or part of them back to the former owner, but granted them back as a fief, in return for homage.[82] Such an explanation seems insufficient. The pattern was, to be sure, repeated many times in the course of William the Conqueror's reign as duke; but it is never clear that, previous to his rebellion, the man concerned had not already held his lands, and sometimes there is reason to suspect that he did already hold them from the duke.[83] Moreover, the process did not occur on a scale sufficient to explain a general shift in type of possession; and it has no application either to the creation of feudal relationships between lesser lords than the duke and their men or to the creation of other types of tenure than fiefs. Haskins and Navel, the great authorities on Norman feudal tenure, devote most of their attention to the date by which "fully developed feudalism" had come to exist in Normandy rather than to the process whereby this alleged development occurred, but both attribute the phenomenon to ducal action insofar as they explain it at all;[84] and ducal action has been given explicit credit by other scholars. As it is charters issued in the name of Duke Richard II in the last decade of his rule, perhaps all in 1025, which establish the existence of a distinction between inheritance and tenure, however, ducal action before that date seems precluded.

Nor does later ducal enactment seem a likely explanation. For one thing, it is difficult to imagine that such a profound change, so suddenly achieved and extending well below the level of ducal tenants-in-chief, should completely have escaped mention in the sources. To a certain extent, modern historians who date the complete "feudalization" of Normandy no later than the first third of the eleventh century are able to ascribe this result to ducal action because they need not explain the silence of the sources: there were few contemporary charters, and the only contemporary historian was Dudo of Saint-Quentin, whose account ends in 996. Beginning about 1030, however, the number of extant charters grows by leaps and bounds.[85] Furthermore, for the reigns of Robert the Magnificent and William the Conqueror three partial contemporaries—William of Jumièges, William of Poitiers, and Orderic Vitalis—have left lengthy historical accounts. A second objection to explaining the change by means of an act of legislation by Duke Robert or Duke William is that such an act would be wholly out of keeping with the causes of legal development in Normandy in the eleventh century: outside the area of the public peace, legal development seems to have occurred without legislation.[86]

The change in mode of possession which lies behind the altered meaning of terms which had once meant ownership probably occurred gradually and therefore escaped the notice of contemporaries.[87] The great magnates of eleventh-century Normandy certainly owed many of their extensive possessions to ducal grants.[88] Although no records survive, probably because none was ever drawn up, it seems likely that such grants created tenure rather than ownership. Perhaps by analogy, lands acquired earlier or in other ways—by usurpation from the church, for example—came to be considered to be held of the duke, the despoiled church, or someone else. Perhaps the generalization of tenure to lower levels of the eventual tenurial hierarchy was the result of similar grants by the magnates to their own followers and of encroachments by powerful men against their less powerful neighbors, encroachments made easier by the breakdown of order during the minority of William the Conqueror, between 1035 and 1047, and by repeated outbreaks of rebellion against the dukes throughout the rest of the century. Moreover, if the definitions of obligations characteristic of later Anglo-Norman feudal tenure were not characteristic of it from the beginning, as I think they were not,[89] if specific amounts of service were not yet assigned on specific pieces of land, confusion between those lands which a person had been granted as tenements, presumably for service but for at best only vaguely defined services, and those lands which he already owned could easily have occurred. Indeed, if the second quarter of the eleventh century, comprising the reign of Robert the Magnificent and the minority of William the Conqueror, constituted as much of a weakening of ducal power in the face of an aristocracy out to seize land and power for itself as David Bates has recently suggested,[90] then that period certainly provided the conditions which would most readily facilitate the rapid spread of tenurial relations; and it may have been then that the forms of tenure which were later characteristic of Normandy and of Anglo-Norman England became predominant in the duchy. J. C. Holt has, moreover, pointed out that every resort to the duke for his confirmation of a transfer strengthened the duke's lordship over the alienor's possessions.[91] The same is equally true for less important lords; and such confirmations, which, I shall argue, were necessary in practice but not legally required, might well seem most desirable in turbulent periods such as the second quarter of the century appears to have been.[92]

If, however the change occurred, by the late eleventh century at least most immovables in lay hands were held rather than owned, a second obvious question arises. What happened to the services due from such immovables when they were transferred to churches? This is perhaps the most perplexing problem raised by transfers of property, for, as already noted, the charters extremely rarely say anything about service, and that includes how the service due from the property alienated was to be performed after possession was transferred. A passage already quoted from the memorandum of Rainald the chaplain implies that a gratuitous alienation carried with it whatever claims were outstanding against the possessions transferred;[93] and this would presumably include claims to service as well as claims of possession. Two charters about possible future sales say that any buyer will be subject to the same conditions as the vendor had been.[94] In a unique transaction, Roger de Rosel, with the duke's consent, sold Saint-Etienne de Caen "his whole allod which he held in Rosel, on condition that he hold it from the saint by such service as before he had rendered from it to the duke, his son Robert consenting."[95] Here the duke permitted a tenant-in-chief to subordinate himself, by sale, to another lord. It is not clear whether the duke expected to continue to receive service from the tenement through the abbot as mesne lord or, instead, truly abandoned Roger's service to the abbey.[96] All three charters about sales nevertheless suggest that tenements could be sold in such a way that the purchaser entered under the terms by which the seller had held, as long as the lord consented to the substitution.

One would think that the same would have been true of gifts, but the situation is, in fact, baffling. Service could be the subject of transactions. The services due from particular immovables or individuals were sometimes given by those to whom they were owed, occasionally even when the immovables or the individuals themselves are not said to have been given.[97] In two instances laymen redeemed their services from their lords; in another, several men may have mortgaged their services; and in yet another, the service of two knights was temporarily transferred as a pledge of performance.[98] One form of earnest for a post-obit gift was the immediate transfer of the service due from the land given.[99] Moreover, in confirming gifts by their tenants, lords often conceded all or part of the services due from what had been given. Such a grant might take the form of acquitting the tenement of service or of transferring the service to the alienee. Were these two ways of saying the same thing? Possibly, instead, one phrasing abolished the service or left the subject of future service to be negotiated between the alienee and its new tenants, while the other preserved the tenants' services in their accustomed form, merely changing the lord to whom they were due.

Charters sometimes say, however, that a lord, in confirming, explicitly excepted his service from the gift;[100] and, confirming future alienations by their men, lords sometimes restricted the amount which could be transferred so as to ensure that the service owed them could still be done.[101] Analogously, when Abbot Gilbert of Saint-Etienne de Caen

> made a concord with William Bellengel concerning the claim which his brothers and he himself had long had to St. Stephen's land of Cléville . . . , the abbot conceded to him [part of the vill] . . . so that he should hold it from the saint, in such a way that what the saint had had in his demesne William should have in his own demesne, and the rest, which other men had held from the saint (nor were they in the saint's demesne), they should hold from the same William for suitable service, so that the saint's service should in no way be disturbed on account of William's service.[102]

In other words, the new service owed to the new mesne lord must not detract from the service already due to the abbey.[103] From such evidence it seems clear that in eleventh-century Normandy only a lord could waive the service due him from a tenement which had been transferred; when he did not, someone must have been obligated to continue to perform the service. This being the apparent rule, alienors and alienees might well be expected to show much concern about which of them was to perform service to the alienor's lord after the transfer. Such is most emphatically not the case: records of alienations rarely say anything at all about service, whether or not they report the consent of lords along with the actual alienations; even separately recorded acts of consent by lords rarely mention service.

The silence of the charters about what happened to service is all but deafening.[104] One charter says that the alienee will assume the burden, the service of suit of court, but only after the death of the alienor.[105] A second says that the alienor will continue to perform the service, a rent, for as long as he lives; nothing is said about what will happen thereafter.[106] Was service done by the alienor but taken over by the alienee on the alienor's death the normal pattern? Two other charters suggest that it was: two alienors to Lire "besought Abbot Hildebert to request the lord of Breteuil to concede to the convent of Lire the service which was incumbent upon them" from what they had given, and the lord did in fact concede it; similarly, when Alvered de Moyon gave land to La Trinité de Caen, Queen Matilda, founder of the abbey, redeemed the service from the lord of the fief.[107] Because in these two instances the service was waived by the lord, the question of what might have happened later does not arise; but both suggest that it was usual for alienors to continue to do the service themselves if their lords would not waive it. On the other hand, one act implies that the burden of certain services was shifted to the donee.[108] It may be anomalous, or poorly drafted, however. Confirmations of future gifts by lords who restrict the amounts which may be transferred imply that the donor normally assumed the burden of doing the service for the portion of the tenement which had been given. Otherwise, why would lords be apprehensive lest alienors give away so much as to be unable to perform their services? Moreover, what evidence there is about the meaning of gifts "in alms" and about the reasons for the consent of lords also implies that alienors usually continued to be burdened with the services from alienated tenements.[109] That the burden always remained with the alienor unless special arrangements were made is never stated anywhere, however.

There is, therefore, very little information about what services were done for tenements held by lay persons and still less about what happened to these services when such tenements were transferred to churches. For these reasons, knowledge of the precise details of what services were owed in eleventh-century Normandy is likely to remain forever unsatisfactory; and knowledge of which types of services were most commonly demanded appears beyond reach, although it seems evident that the range of services was wider than has commonly been thought. Nor is there any way to estimate, for any moment in the eleventh century, the ratio of land owned to land held, though statements maintaining that ownership remained important as late as the last third of the century seem to be excluded by the results of this investigation. On the contrary, the shift in meaning of words which had meant "ownership" at the beginning of the century indicates that a profound change in the modes of possession of land occurred. The details and manner of the process are unlikely ever to be known, but the results are clear: in Normandy, a society in which substantial amounts of land were owned was, in the course of less than a century, transformed into one in which the only demonstrable type of lay possession was tenure.

6

Modes of Assurance: Public Acts

THE PRINCIPAL DIFFICULTY confronting eleventh-century Normans who wished to transfer immovables to churches was not the transfer itself but the danger that the transfer would not last.[1] That the same was true of transfers to lay persons, however likely, cannot be proven: almost all information, here as elsewhere, concerns transactions involving ecclesiastical institutions. The insecurity which menaced the hold churches had on their lands was due partly to outright disseisins perpetrated by men bent on aggrandizing their own possessions, partly to the multiplicity of rights which might exist to any piece of property given both the hierarchical structure of tenurial relationships and the tendency of even temporary concessions to come to be regarded as permanent, but perhaps most of all to the prevalent mental attitude which made it difficult for individuals to accept sudden, complete changes in the juridical status of property.[2] Norman documents refer less often to violent seizures of property than to claims, *calumniae*, raised by individuals connected in some way to the alienor or to the property. Probably in the minds of many claimants, though certainly not in the minds of the scribes who wrote the documents, their claims seemed justified.[3]

Even alienors sometimes raised claims to what they had alienated.[4] Nonetheless, at least at the moment when a transfer was effected, the alienor as well as the recipient had an interest in ensuring that no subsequent claim disturb the transfer. If a church lost possession of what it had been given, the spiritual benefits to the donor consequent on the gift might well be endangered.[5] Even an exchange might raise questions; hence, one donor explicitly granted the recipient abbey the right to exchange his gift for more conveniently situated property if it so wished.[6] Because the danger that alienations might prove impermanent was of such great concern, information about the methods used in hopes of forestalling challenges and preventing misappropriations is relatively abundant. Of course, the vast majority of charters give only the barest details of simple gifts to churches; but even here confirmation clauses, witness lists, signature lists, and the like are informative about assurance in a way in which the phrases "I give" and "he gave" are not illuminating about the gifts themselves. The assurance clauses sometimes form the bulk of a charter and are nearly always, except in the case of certain pancarts, a major component of any charter.

An alienor might simply order that no one dare to disturb the alienation. A few tried this,[7] but a mere command was unlikely to be effective. Instead, Normans of the eleventh century used a large number of devices to assure the permanence of their alienations. Had an especially nervous donor agreed to make a gift to an unusually apprehensive church, they might have assured the stability of the gift by the following means. The gift having been agreed upon, the donor would associate all his living relatives, his lords, and their relatives with him as donors and as recipients of the spiritual benefits consequent on the gift, which benefits would be conferred in a public ceremony. The donor and each relative, lord, and lord's relative would also publicly receive a material countergift, and all together would participate in a public ceremony of donation. The boundaries of the land given would be perambulated by the donor, representatives of the recipient, and witnesses. Anyone who appeared to be a special threat would be asked to take an oath not to disturb the gift. Pledges for the permanence of the gift would be named. The donor or someone else in a position to do so would promise to warrant the gift. The charter recording the gift would then be drawn up, publicly signed, and sealed by the donor or a lord; it would record the names of all the persons participating in the gift in any way and of all the witnesses to the public acts connected with the gift. Anyone who might violate the gift would be menaced with excommunication, declared subject to a fine, and, perhaps, threatened with other penalties. Moreover, any potential claimant who was not present for the ceremonies surrounding the donation would be asked to consent to the gift by signing the charter or by going through a public ceremony indicating consent. Various public authorities—especially the duke and the bishop of the area—would also be asked to consent. Finally, after the donor's death his or her heir would be asked to go through the ceremony again, as would the lord's heir after the lord's death—a process which might be carried over to the third generation and further.

No single charter includes all these measures, some of which are rare. Many charters, however, include several of the common modes of assurance; and there seem to be few, if any, rules as to which methods are likely to appear together. Some modes of assurance were not normally used in connection with temporary or conditional transfers, and others occur with unusual frequency in these contexts.[8] A few types of permanent transfers elicited one type of assurance unusually often: the prime examples are quasi-professional witnessing and warranty in connection with sales and earnest in connection with post-obit gifts, the latter a type of assurance used exclusively for one type of alienation, for obvious reasons.[9] In the main, however, there seems to have been little regularity about the modes of assurance used. Individual churches sometimes appear to have preferred certain forms over others, a situation which probably corresponds to actual practice in some cases but in others only to different scribal habits.

The absence of rules covers not only which modes of assurance were used in any transaction but also which modes were used to express the consent of different parties to the transaction. Relatives and lords might express consent by co-donation, by participation in the act of donation, by a separate act of confirmation, by acting as witnesses or pledges or warrantors, or by signing the charter of gift—or by some or even all of these means. Because of the noncoincidence between the type of assurance used and its purpose, the two must be discussed separately. Thus, this chapter will discuss the formal public acts by which alienations were made, irrespective of the persons participating in them, and the next will consider the roles of confirmer, witness, signer, and pledge, irrespective of the relationship to the alienors of the persons serving in these roles. Chapter 8 will consider the consent of relatives, of lords, of tenants, and of other persons who sometimes give consent, regardless of the means by which consent was expressed. Chapter 9 will discuss warranty and Chapter 10 the various penalties which might be prescribed for future violators. Finally, Chapter 11 will consider the role of charters in assuring the permanence of gifts and the significance of this role for the value of the charters as sources.

COUNTERGIFTS

Countergifts of all the types—spiritual and material—so often granted alienors could also be granted to persons who consented and often were.[10] That a person was the recipient of spiritual benefits cannot, however, be taken to mean that he or she had given consent. The almost obligatory clause which states that a gift was made "for the soul" of the donor often names as beneficiaries, in addition to the donor's ancestors, his or her living relatives, descendants, lords, and friends. At least once, some persons were included in a list explicitly in hopes that their inclusion would serve as an inducement to consent, rather than because they had already given their consent.[11] It seems likely that the same hope would often have motivated the inclusion of persons who had not yet, in fact, consented; hence, a list of beneficiaries cannot be taken as a list of persons who had consented and had received grants of society in return. Because the grant of society was an actual ceremony,[12] however, the mention of persons other than alienors explicitly as recipients of society implies that they had already consented. This was probably one of the reasons why charters include such entries, and, when a charter includes both a list of recipients of society and a list of those "for whose souls" the donation was made, the two by no means always entirely agree, even about living persons. Moreover, large numbers of charters make the connection between consent and society explicit, usually very laconically, saying that one was given for the other. Indeed, one charter states that anyone at all who confirms the gift will share in the benefit which had been conferred on the donor.[13] To assume that lists of recipients of society are equivalent to lists of confirmers but that lists of mere beneficiaries are not would, nonetheless, be too simple. Many donors apparently were content that their charters include only a list of those "for whose souls" the gifts were made, without any mention of a formal grant of society: charters with such lists far outnumber those which mention grants of society. Donors sometimes receive society for persons already deceased, who cannot have consented. One charter records the consent of the adult son of a donor whose gift was made some time earlier, when the son was apparently a minor, and says that the son's consent was in return for the society he had already received.[14] It cannot, therefore, be assumed that anyone not explicitly said to have consented had, in fact, done so.

In some instances someone other than the recipient church gave the countergift. Queen Matilda, sometimes with the cooperation of her husband, William the Conqueror, gave countergifts to donors or confirmers to La Trinité de Caen in at least eleven—perhaps fifteen—different transactions; almost every time, the countergift is explicitly described as a motive for the gift or the consent. This was undoubtedly one way Matilda attempted to secure a large endowment for her foundation. No other person engaged in the practice nor did any other church benefit from it with anything like the same frequency, but other examples occur in which the contributor of a countergift to a confirmer was an alienor or another confirmer.[15] Only one countergift appears to have come from someone wholly unconnected with the transaction involved: William Dastin sold some of his wife's patrimony to Saint-Pierre de Préaux "in the presence of Arnulf de Hesdin, whom Abbot Geoffrey was lodging [while he was] on his way to [Mont-]Saint-Michel; and Arnulf, taking off a foxskin [which he was wearing], gave it to William Dastin in memory of this agreement."[16] Perhaps this was Arnulf's way of repaying the abbey for its hospitality, a valuable favor.

There was obviously an actual ceremony by means of which a donor or confirmer was given his or her countergift, but it was often so closely connected with the ceremony of donation that the two cannot be separated; and I have therefore reserved discussion of the actual form of the ceremony for the moment.[17] That the receipt of a countergift was a public ceremony, however, raises a question which should be discussed here: why countergifts were given and given publicly. The reason for some types of countergifts is obvious enough. In a period when one's fate in the next world seemed all-important to many persons at all times and probably to most, if not all, at some times, inclusion among those who benefited from the prayers of monks or nuns must have seemed to many an adequate motive for a gift or a confirmation. That both donors and confirmers sometimes went back on their actions and tried to reclaim what had been given shows that they could change their minds about the relative value of this-worldly profits as opposed to otherworldly concerns; but almost all known challenges were eventually settled in favor of the churches, with, usually, somewhat more compensation to the challengers than they or their antecedents had originally received.[18] Some challengers probably raised claims with the sole aim of increasing the compensation, rather than with the intent of completely nullifying the gifts and thereby forfeiting the spiritual benefits the gifts had created. Otherworldly concerns also underlie at least partially those gifts and confirmations which were made so that the donor or confirmer or some relative or friend might become a monk or a nun or receive absolution or burial. When the result of a gift was entry into a monastery or nunnery or the education of a child, another obvious connection is that a convent was not expected to house, clothe, and feed an additional member without an increase in its endowment. It is also likely that at least some confirmers—who were, in effect, waiving only future or residual rights—felt adequately compensated for their loss when they received a valuable object in return: the material objects used as countergifts were usually of relatively high value and even the sums of money given appear somewhat to reflect both the value of what was given and the amount of difficulty a potential confirmer's refusal to consent could cause.[19] In all these situations, therefore, the only explanation for the countergift necessary is that it was both an inducement and a compensation to a donor or a confirmer. Charters often briefly state or imply this cause-and-effect relationship between donation or consent and countergift.

This does not, however, exhaust the types of countergifts or the explanations of them in the charters, nor does it explain why the grant of a countergift was so often a public ceremony, frequently intimately connected with the act of donation or confirmation itself. Moreover, to consider all material countergifts as either disguised sale prices or extorted concessions, as most scholars have done, does not seem sufficient.[20] The publicity apparently attached to the receipt of countergifts suggests that another motive was at work. Churches found it hard to hold on to their possessions in part because donors and confirmers changed their minds. The theory behind the practice of giving a countergift for each gift may have been that, if donors or confirmers had publicly received countergifts, they or their heirs would subsequently find it hard to challenge the gift: they had, after all, received something in return, and witnesses had seen them receive it.

Charters which expatiate at all on the reasons for the giving of countergifts point to this motive. Seven or eight say that a material countergift was given "in witness" or "in memory" or "as a sign" or "in recognition" of the gift;[21] others say that a countergift was given so that a gift might remain firm or so that no one would challenge the gift.[22] This reasoning is clearly indicated by a list of disseisins emanating from Mont-Saint-Michel which says, about a loss at the hands of William the Conqueror, "He . . . disseised us of the vill which is called Ceaux which Neil the elder gave to St. Michael when he was made a monk, and half of the water. For the concession of which thing, he [Neil] gave the aforesaid William one hundred and fifty pounds which Ralph the [duke's] chamberlain accepted."[23] The argument implied is that because William had received a countergift his seizure was all the more unjustifiable.[24] It may be significant that in all the charters which make explicit statements about the purposes of countergifts the countergifts consist at least partly and usually entirely of material objects. In other words, it is possible that in material countergifts, publicly given, eleventh-century Normans recognized an evidentiary purpose which was absent from spiritual countergifts. Charters which emphasize the public ceremony in which countergifts were given do not bear this out, however, for they deal with spiritual countergifts about as often as with material ones.[25]

I know of only one case in which a countergift was refused. Some time between 1055 and 1066, Duke William confirmed to Jumièges a gift made by Osbern de Manneville of a mill in the river Risle, which gift Osbern made "so freely that neither he himself nor his sons Roger and Robert wished to receive any reward for this thing." The refusal was probably worthy of mention because it was rare and perhaps also to protect Jumièges's possession of the mill if Osbern, Robert, or Roger later changed his mind about the gift. Each of the three had been offered a countergift and had refused it—publicly, at Rouen, in the presence of the archbishop.[26]

Several fairly common practices of the charters also point to the preventive role of the countergift. Thus, a good many charters record which person—usually a member of the church receiving the gift—physically handed over the money or material objects used as countergifts.[27] Many more list the countergifts given individually to different donors or confirmers or say that some third party, acting as an agent, received the countergift.[28] Such notes were doubtless intended at least partly to help the witnesses remember that countergifts had been given; but the receipt of a countergift would also signify the recipient's approval of the transaction, and the testimony of those who had handed over countergifts might be especially telling should the need for proof arise. Moreover, charters occasionally state the use to which a material countergift was put, apparently exclusively when the use was such as to consume the countergift or alienate it from its initial recipient.[29] Here, presumably, one of the reasons was to prevent a potential challenger from arguing that he had not received a countergift.

The evidentiary role of a countergift is suggested by Rainald the chaplain's memorandum about the lands at Bayeux which he had given to Jumièges:

> And, I have heard, Samson the cleric is making claims to the aforesaid things; but he did not claim [them] at the time when I sold him one of the houses within the city with the land pertaining to that house, for sixty pounds, of which I had fifty pounds and he still owes me ten pounds in recompense (*in weredono*), and I still have the men who received those same coins. And this was done by the witness of the queen, and at that time Samson the cleric was indeed with King William and Queen Matilda, who would have done right to him concerning his claims if he had claimed anything justly; and if he had known that he had any right to that land or those houses, he would in no wise have given me those coins at that time.[30]

The situation is not perfectly analogous to occasions when countergifts were given, for it was the person who gave money rather than the one who received it who later raised a claim. Nevertheless, *mutatis mutandis*, Rainald's principal argument could have been used by any defendant against a claimant who had received something of value during the transfer now challenged. That argument itself could not be clearer: Samson's claim is obviously unjust because he did not raise it at a time when anyone with a just claim would have done so; the simple fact that, in public, he handed over money to pay for part of what he now claims proves that he did not then think that he had a claim and, therefore, that his current claim is unjust; and if he should deny that he had handed over the money, the men who received it from him will testify against him. Not every defendant would have been in a position, as Rainald was, to assert that if the claimant had raised his claim at the moment of the public transfer he could have received instant justice because the proper persons to act as judges were present as witnesses to the transaction. This, however, was not the essence of Rainald's defense; it merely reinforced his argument, which would stand up without it.

No particularly precarious element is apparent in those gifts whose countergifts are described in evidentiary terms. Instead, the implication is that every material countergift served, or at least may have served, the same purpose. Charters which mention any countergift are in the minority, and the extent to which every gift is said to have its countergift varies widely from church to church; but the reason seems to be largely the form in which information about gifts survives. The closer a document is to the original record of the original gift, the higher the likelihood that it will mention these practices.[31] Therefore, although the giving of a countergift for every gift may not have been the consistent practice of every church in Normandy in the eleventh century, it was a wise precaution, which many churches certainly, and most churches probably, often took.

ACTS OF DONATION

The act of donation was the public ceremony by which an alienor formally transferred property or a confirmer formally expressed consent. It was apparently used almost exclusively for gifts and confirmations, as opposed to other types of alienations.[32] The reason for staging such a ceremony is obvious. Challenges to alienations were common, and the primary type of proof presented in answer to such challenges was the testimony of witnesses to the transfer. Indeed, witnesses by their very existence were supposed to prevent challenges.[33] If witnesses were to be able to play their preventive and demonstrative roles, however, there had to be something for them to witness.[34] Hence the careful description by a relatively high proportion of the extant charters of the public acts of transfer. It is a valid assumption that every permanent alienation was supposed to be witnessed and that almost every one was, in fact, witnessed. This implies that for every, or nearly every, recorded alienation there had been an act of donation. By no means every charter, however, not even every one drawn up soon after the alienation it records, mentions an act of donation. Only about 15 percent of the extant charters do. The disparity is doubtless to be explained by the habits of eleventh-century Norman scribes and by the form in which records of alienations survive, rather than on the basis that, except when they are mentioned, acts of donation did not occur: many more charters mention witnesses than mention acts of donation, and there must have been something for the witnesses to witness.

The connection between the act of donation and its witnesses' role in ensuring the recipient's continuous and untroubled possession is implied by the fact that a reference to an act is normally followed by a list of witnesses, usually explicitly said to have witnessed the ceremony. Other indications of the purpose of the act of donation, on the contrary, are remarkably rare. Four charters, only two of which mention challengers specifically, state that the ceremony would render the gift secure.[35] A fifth says that the act was done "as recognition of the donation."[36] In the sixth a confirmer says that by performing the act of donation he was expressing his consent.[37] The seventh, having recounted a memorable action by William the Conqueror during the course of the act of donation, remarks, "Therefore, by this manifest sign and by the testimony of many noble men who stood beside the king, this donation was made,"[38] thus neatly linking the act to the role of the witnesses to it. In the eighth the donor took an oath "on a text of the holy Gospels which Arnold de *Stochis* held in his arms, so that the same Arnold would not be able to deny any of this." This statement is most significant: Arnold was not the donor's lord, and why there was reason to fear that he would raise a claim is unknown; but by holding the holy book while the donor swore—and by contributing his knife to be used in the ceremony—he demonstrated conclusively his abandonment of whatever claim he may have had.[39] Even for eleventh-century Normandy, such terseness—only eight explicit statements of the purpose of the act of donation—is unusual. The likely explanation is that the purpose of the act was so well known or so obvious that it did not need stating.

The most often mentioned form of the act was placement of a symbolic object, most often a book or a knife, on the altar of the recipient church. The ceremony seems to have been standard for all churches, and one charter calls placement on the altar the "custom" (*mos*).[40] Nonetheless, some institutions recorded the ceremony much more often than others, and a few seemingly never did so. The details of the ceremony may have varied from church to church. Scribes certainly sometimes recorded a particular feature of an act of donation precisely because it was unusual and would, therefore, assist the witnesses to the act to remember the particular donation at issue.[41] Few descriptions of the ceremony of placement on the altar are at all detailed, however. The act was usually performed by the donor or the confirmer: many charters say that he or she did so "with his/her own hands" or words to that effect. If an act involved more than one donor or confirmer, all the persons involved often participated. One charter indicates how this might be done: when a man named Aimery and his wife and "both their sons" made a gift to Saint-Martin de Sées, "therefore man and wife and sons, all equally in confirmation of the aforesaid gift, together holding one book, placed [the gift] on the altar of St. Martin."[42] On the other hand, Roger de Beaumont, first, and then Roger de Croismare separately placed on the altar of Saint-Pierre de Préaux the agreement about how Roger de Croismare was to hold his wife's inheritance; and on other occasions, apparently, only some of the alienors and/or confirmers performed the act of donation.[43] The ceremony was usually performed at an altar in the recipient church, but at least some abbeys permitted a gift to be made on the altar of a priory which was the direct beneficiary of the gift. This was especially true of Marmoutier, probably because it was the most distant abbey to which Normans habitually made gifts.[44] Occasionally a gift was made on the altar of a church which was part of the gift or even at some wholly unrelated altar.[45] The ceremony might be further solemnized by being performed during the dedication of the recipient church, if it was a new foundation, or on a feast day.[46] Three sources describe acts of donation as having occurred just before, during, or just after mass;[47] but whether the ceremony was normally incorporated into a liturgical rite is impossible to tell.

The second common form of act of donation consisted of the placement of a symbolic object "in the hands of" the head or a member of the recipient church. Although technical terms relating to seisin are rare in eleventh-century Normandy, such an act could be so described: in this context, "seisin" occurs eight times and "investiture" between four and seven times.[48] The act could be performed by the alienor's agent or lord or the lord's agent as well as by the alienor. It was not usually performed by confirmers of earlier transfers, in striking contrast to placement on the altar.[49] The ceremony could occur just about anywhere: the archbishop of Rouen received seisin of one donation in a wood.[50] Four charters indicate that the alienor might kiss the recipient of the symbolic object as well as hand it over.[51]

The only lengthy description of a ceremony of this sort comes from a charter of Saint-Martin de Sées. John Burnet, having been seriously wounded in a siege, asked Abbot Robert to come to his home and comfort him in his affliction. The abbot responded in person, bringing with him another monk and two servitors of the abbey.

> Then the abbot himself through his staff . . . gave him, that is, John, and his brother Herbert, the whole benefit and society of Saint-Martin de Sées. Both of them, moreover, namely, John and Herbert, holding that staff in their own hands simultaneously, gave to Saint-Martin and to the abbot, who accepted the aforesaid staff with his own hand, the tithe of *Fontanis*, in such a way that John, who held it [the tithe] at that time, gave [it] and his brother Herbert, holding the aforesaid staff with him, conceded [it]. Moreover, John himself added during the gift—and Herbert in [his] concession—that if he [John] should recover from that infirmity and [if] God should give him longer life, he would in future give more things, both in lands and in tithes, to the saint and the monks. All of which things, as John described [them] at length in that donation, his

> brother Herbert, holding the staff with him, conceded without any contradiction, many reasonable men hearing this.[52]

As another charter from the same abbey exhibited a group of donors placing a gift on the altar by all together holding the book which symbolized the gift,[53] the practice may have been usual at Saint-Martin de Sées, whether or not it was so elsewhere. That question aside, the picture drawn by this charter both confirms and supplements the one derived from others. The donor, in this case along with the confirmer, placed an object symbolizing the gift in the hands of a representative of the recipient church, in this instance its abbot, and spoke some words during the ceremony. He seems to have spoken at some length, probably describing the terms and contents of the gift. Then his brother, apparently while both alienors were still holding the object, confirmed the gift, perhaps simply by not speaking any words in contradiction, perhaps by repeating the terms as they had been stated. Whether the abbot also held the staff during the speech or speeches or, instead, received it only afterward cannot be determined.

By and large, allusions to this sort of ceremony are brief, so brief that in many instances it is not certain that the ceremony occurred; and the ceremony appears to have been considerably less common than placement on the altar, perhaps because it was restricted to alienations and their immediate confirmations, whereas placement on the altar could be used also for the many subsequent confirmations to which a transfer might give rise. Nonetheless, that it was well recognized as a way of transferring possession is indicated by a famous, if rather elephantine, example of William the Conqueror's humor: when, in England, he gave an English manor to La Trinité du Mont, "Abbot Rainier was present with two monks, Nicholas and William. This gift was made by means of a knife which the aforesaid king jokingly gave to the abbot as if he were going to stab him in the palm, saying, 'This is the way land should be given.' "[54]

There is barely a trace of investiture as a device to confer fiefs on vassals in eleventh-century sources. Even the ceremony of homage and fealty is mentioned rarely and never described at length: at most, a tenant is said to have become the lord's man "with his hands."[55] Moreover, homage could be done to signify the subordination of tenants who did not hold for military services.[56] William of Poitiers's passage on Harold Godwinsson's homage to Duke William is the only extended description of homage and fealty and the only mention at all of investiture in this context: "Harold in that place swore fealty to the duke employing the sacred ritual recognized among Christian men. . . . The duke on his part, who before the oath was taken had received [Harold] as his man through [his] hands, confirmed to him at his request all his lands and dignities."[57] Investiture apparently followed homage and fealty, but no more can be deduced. A formal act of investiture was also used when Adam de Saint-Brice transferred to the duke the duty of protecting the vill of Roncheville, which Adam had given to Saint-Julien de Tours.[58] According to a document of the early twelfth century, when Lesceline dowager countess of Eu founded Saint-Pierre-sur-Dives about 1046, she used the same ceremony to the same purpose.[59] These two acts and various references to tenants who gave back possessions to their lords so that the lords could transfer them to churches[60] may suggest that, despite the silence of the documents, eleventh-century Norman tenants usually received their tenements by means of investiture.

To return to acts of donation to churches, it was by no means always donors or confirmers who acted personally, although this was the norm. In certain instances, a donor or confirmer acted "through" another person. One reason was to demonstrate the agent's consent. Thus, for example, to cite one of the rare instances of a ducal act of donation, "in the year when Duke Robert went to Jerusalem, he gave Saint-Pierre de Préaux from his own demesne a vill which is commonly called Toutainville. . . . But, since William son of the same Duke Robert, still a little boy, was to reign after him, the father sent him to Préaux so that, by his order indeed, the boy should place the donation of Toutainville on the altar with his own hand."[61] In other instances, the donor or confirmer was prevented from acting by illness, involvement in war, death which intervened before the act of donation could be performed by the donor, even by being "outside the Church";[62] but usually no reason is given. The person through whom the donation was made might be a relative or a lay or clerical agent who was sent to place the donation on the altar, as in all the examples already cited. It might, however, also be a member of the community of the recipient church. In such cases, it is possible that the alienor invested the cleric, who later placed on the altar the object which had been used to perform the ceremony. When, for example, Robert Bertram gave woods to Marmoutier, "I made this gift . . . in my house . . . to two brothers of the aforesaid monastery, namely, Rainald and Robert, who in their abbot's stead gave me and my wife the benefit of their place. And I invested the brothers of Marmoutier with this gift by means of a deerskin which I sent to them in their chapter through one of the aforesaid brothers, named Rainald."[63] There are three similar donations to Marmoutier and three to Norman churches.[64] It is probably not a coincidence that four of the seven extant gifts of this type—and also two in which a representative of the recipient church is said to have "taken up" a gift[65]—come from Marmoutier. That abbey, far away from its Norman donors, had to cope with the relative infrequency with which Normans would visit it. One means was probably to make unusually frequent use of the practice of going to them. Indeed, because a strikingly high percentage of the possible examples of investiture comes from gifts to institutions outside Normandy, though such gifts form only a small percentage of all the extant Norman gifts, this form of the act of donation may have been used especially when the prospects for achieving a ceremony of placement on the altar were slim.[66]

In eight instances both investiture and placement on the altar were used to make the same donation. Few patterns are evident. Placement on the altar followed investiture in five cases, but the order was reversed in the other three.[67] On six occasions the same person performed both ceremonies; on a seventh they were done by different persons. On the eighth a confirmer placed his men's gifts on the altar, then invested the bishop, who gave them to the church in an unknown fashion.[68] The same symbolic object was used in both ceremonies in two cases—in one of which the object was used by different persons—but in a third different objects were used.[69] The form of the ceremonies when combined therefore seems to have been fluid. Six of the eight transfers were wholly or partially quitclaims, an extraordinarily high percentage, which suggests that, not surprisingly, it was thought advisable to induce proven troublemakers to go through especially elaborate assurance procedures. Moreover, the donor of one apparently simple gift had done something to incur judgment of a fine to be paid to the abbey to which he made his gift, at just about the time when the gift was made;[70] and the other apparently simple gift was in fact extremely precarious because, at the time when he made it, the donor had been disinherited and exiled from Normandy and, therefore, could not really make the gift.[71] Hence it seems reasonable to conclude that, in all eight instances, the multiplication of ceremonies—or, perhaps, the scribes' care in recording all the ceremonies which were performed—was a result of the recipients' suspicions that their possession of these properties might well be challenged.

A considerable interval might pass between a gift and the act which symbolized it or between the donor's action and the confirmer's. A charter from Saint-Pierre de Préaux recording the gifts, made individually or together, of two brothers, Gilbert and Turstin Efflanc, notes that after Gilbert's death—how long after is not clear—"because these things were done at different times, finally the same Turstin, restoring [them] to memory, had them all written down together in this charter and . . . placed [them] on the altar." The first of the brothers' gifts occurred in 1044 at the latest, but this charter cannot have been drawn up earlier than 1078.[72] Thus, unless some act or acts of donation have gone unreported, at least thirty-four years elapsed between the first gift and the ceremony which solemnized it. It is also clear that a transaction might take place in several stages, including several acts of donation. When Neil de Brévands, for example, gave the church of Brévands and other things to Fécamp's priory of Saint-Gabriel, he first made the gift on the altar of Saint-Gabriel and then traveled, apparently directly, to Fécamp, where he placed the gift on the altar again and received the abbey's society; but the charter itself was completed at a third place in Duke William's presence and with his and other signatures.[73]

Most charters which say anything about the time of the act of donation relative to the gift itself are vague, saying "afterwards" or the like. A donor might simply appear at a church and make gifts: for example, three Norman knights who spent the night at Marmoutier while on pilgrimage to Saint-Gilles, "because they were amicably welcomed by us and honorably lodged," made individual small gifts to the abbey the next day before they left, receiving the abbey's society in return.[74] This pattern, however, does not seem to have been usual. Instead, there were preliminary negotiations, as a result of which the gift was considered to have been made, before the act of donation occurred. The most detailed picture of such negotiation concerns a confirmation. Benscelinus d'Ecos had made deathbed gifts to Marmoutier and its priory of Saint-Ouen at Gisors. These included "Gilbert de Vesly with all his fief and the land which he [Benscelinus] held from Pain lord of Gisors, if, however, his lord Pain should concede him [Gilbert] to us, which gift was made through the hand of Lord Tetbald our brother, then prior of the cell of Gisors, whom he caused to come to him," that is, probably by means of an act of donation in the form of investiture;

> Afterwards, indeed, when Pain de Gisors was staying at Chaumont with Duke Robert [Curthose], who was making war on his brother, Lord Tetbald [our] monk came to him and asked him to concede to us the gift which the aforesaid Benscelinus had given us. He [Pain] answered him that he would come secretly to Gisors the next day and would take counsel there. When he had done this the next day, having accepted his counsel, he conceded everything which the aforesaid Benscelinus had given us, . . . of which concession he placed the gift on the altar of St. Ouen through the priest Garulf and his own seneschal Gilbert.[75]

Whether Pain said that he himself would steal away to Gisors or told Tetbald to do so is unclear, but it seems likely that Pain was meant. Perhaps he had to steal away and also did not have time to perform the act of donation himself because he was expected to be present in the duke's army.[76] It is also uncertain whether the counsel was a conference between Pain and Tetbald or Pain's consultation with others as to whether he should consent,[77] but Pain seems to have wanted time to think things over. This is not surprising on the part of a confirmer who may well have had no warning in advance that his man had made a gift. Many confirmers must have found themselves in similar situations.

A good many charters say that a gift was suggested to a donor by a member of a recipient church. Four single out or include among the witnesses to a transaction the person who arranged it.[78] At least some donors must have made the decision to give on their own initiative, but even so there was likely to be a preliminary stage before the act of donation. A charter from Saint-Martin de Sées suggests what may have occurred in the two stages. Robert Oisuns partially gave and partially sold the church of Courtomer to the abbey.

> He conceded this gift or sale to the Lord Abbot Ralph . . . before Robert de Bellême, in the presence of [three men] . . . and, since William Oisuns and Arnulf [brothers of the donor] had consented, the aforesaid Robert Oisuns promised that his brother Hugh the cleric would firmly and legally and willingly consent. . . . On another day soon afterwards, after all these aforesaid things had been conceded before Robert de Bellême . . .

> the aforesaid Robert Oisuns conceded all the aforesaid things in the chapter of Saint-Martin, in the same way and with the same words, in the presence of legal witnesses, firmly and legally with his own mouth; and he and his brother William placed the gift of the aforesaid church on the altar of St. Martin by means of a certain book. These men were present as witnesses. . . .[79]

This suggests that when the donor and the recipient had agreed on a gift, its terms were made known to third parties; then, when the donor came to the church to perform the act of donation, as part of the ceremony the terms of the gift were repeated for the witnesses to hear. Many charters indicate that participants in acts of donation spoke words as well as performing actions, but this is one of the few which imply that what was said amounted to a description of the property given.[80] The charter also hints that third parties who heard the initial statement of the terms of the agreement to give were not "legal witnesses" in the same sense as those who saw and heard an act of donation.[81] If this was so, it would obviously be to the advantage of recipient churches to have the act of donation performed by every donor as promptly as Robert Oisuns performed his, although in this they were not always successful.

From his study of acts of donation in thirteenth- and fourteenth-century Normandy, Jean Yver concludes that the various ceremonies were primarily means of publicity and that a legally valid transfer of possession could be effected only by the alienee's actual entry upon the land; at best, the ceremonial acts imposed upon the alienor a moral obligation not to revoke the promise to transfer but to allow the alienee to enter.[82] For England, Glanvill shows that the same was true by the late twelfth century.[83] Samuel Thorne, however, thinks that the rule that, to acquire a right, the donee must be put in possession goes back no earlier: in the early twelfth century, "the donee entered upon actual possession soon after receiving symbolic investiture. His ownership did not depend upon . . . entry."[84] It is difficult to be certain of the legal situation in Normandy in the eleventh century; but the balance of the evidence points toward the conclusion that actual possession, or at least an actual right to possess, was transferred by the ceremonial acts which I have been discussing, without any subsequent formal entry on the land. Certainly the ceremonies of investiture which are described seem all to be symbolic liveries: they did not occur on the land being transferred,[85] they did not even use as a symbol something from the land itself,[86] nor was perambulation a regular part of the ceremonies of transfer.[87] Indeed, no eleventh-century source refers to an actual entry on the land as part of the process of transfer, unless the rare mentions of perambulation are such references. Only one transaction may even possibly indicate that until an actual entry occurred the alienee could claim no right to what had been "given."[88] Moreover, although the legal theory prevalent in Normandy and England from the late twelfth or thirteenth century on mandated that livery be the last in a series of acts of donation, in more than half the known eleventh-century instances in which two acts were performed, investiture preceded placement on the altar.[89] Only one or two documents cite "investiture" as proof of possession,[90] but "investiture" is sometimes used elsewhere to mean a rent, payment, or other device whereby an ultimate right to possess was acknowledged while actual possession was in the hands of someone else.[91] "Seisin," in its rare appearances in contexts other than the act of donation, seems normally to refer to actual possession, usually as of a particular moment.[92] In virtually all places where they are used, both words are clearly connected in some way or another with the idea of a right to possess; but the concept of seisin seems to have been vague as yet or, at least, no clear concept can be deduced from the extant references to the term. All in all, it seems likely that the two forms of act of donation were alternatives with the same legal effect, although placement on the altar probably had—or was supposed to have—a greater moral effect, perhaps precisely because it occurred at an altar. Even the instances in which, for the same transfer, investiture followed placement on the altar are no serious contradiction to this suggestion, in view of the obvious desire of clerical alienees to pile on as many of the modes of assurance as they could induce alienors to perform. Indeed, it may be that for the eleventh century, given the prevalent insecurity of transfers, no obligations should be considered more than morally binding and that the concept of a legal obligation fully enforceable in court was a later development consequent upon more settled conditions, a more pervasive and effective system of courts, and a more highly developed jurisprudence.

My conjecture is that the two forms of the act of donation were virtually equivalent except insofar as placement on the altar usually required the alienor to undertake a journey but also might seem more solemn and therefore create a greater sense of compunction in the alienor. If so, it is tempting to extrapolate a further conclusion, that the preliminary stage in making any gift—except perhaps one made on the spur of the moment while the donor was at the recipient church—would culminate in an act of investiture, after which the recipient church did its best to get the alienor and as many confirmers as there were potential claimants to place the gift on the altar. This conjecture turns investiture from a rather uncommon form of the act of donation into the most common in reference to initial alienations. It advances far beyond the available evidence, in which this form of the act of donation is comparatively rarely attested. Nevertheless, when one contemplates the many charters which say that only after a person made a gift did he or she perform some act of donation and asks oneself how the preliminary gift was made—was it simply a verbal declaration of intent in the presence of at least one third party, if that?—the conjecture is tempting.

With the dubious exception of one possibly deliberate play on words,[93] no object used in any form of the act of donation bears a relationship to what was given. The choice of the symbol seems to have been random; if any principle of selection was at work it was that certain churches preferred to use certain types of objects. In by far the largest number of ceremonies in which the object placed on the altar is identified it was a book, sometimes specified as a text of the Gospels. Books are the only object used at all often which were used exclusively for placement on the altar. Rods and knives were commonly used in ceremonies of both types—the use of knives is the most widely distributed among recipient churches. Other objects occasionally placed on an altar or handed to a representative of the recipient church include candlesticks, sums of money, articles of clothing, ecclesiastical vestments, a ring, a cross of wax, a cuirass, even perhaps the horns of a deer the donor had captured.[94] The charters themselves in which the gifts—and the acts of donation—are recorded were also used.[95] In a few cases two objects were used together.

Usually nothing is known of the source of the object. Two knives belonged to men who acted as witnesses; a third, to the donor's brother; one cloak belonged to the confirmer who used it; and the ring, the cuirass, and a deerskin are each said to have been the donor's own, as of course were the horns of the deer.[96] On the other hand, a fourth knife belonged to one of the monks of the recipient abbey, and the books used so often most probably already belonged to the recipient churches.[97] No rule emerges from these scattered examples: whether donors and confirmers used something of their own, something of the recipient's, or something contributed by a third party seems to have been a matter of chance or negotiation in each case. For a person who was not performing the act of donation to contribute an object would, however, constitute an expression of consent to the transaction.

What happened to an object once it had been used in an act of donation is almost equally unclear: no charter indicates that the object went to an individual, but few say that the recipient kept the object. One abbey still had the knife with which a gift had been made; it had belonged to a layman until the act of donation.[98] The other six charters which say something of the later history of the object connect its fate with witnessing. The first is a bit of a puzzle: at the end of the charter recording the settlement of the lawsuit between Jumièges and Saint-Mesmin de Micy over Dame-Marie, the following note occurs:

> So that it should be known to our posterity what and how much of Courgains we had after our investiture (*post nostram vestituram*), we took care to write [this]. Wascelin de Coulonces, after the seisin (*post saisuram*) of the aforesaid vill, brought us the four *nummi* and one *as* which he had taken off the altar. Afterwards, indeed, in order to record what had been done we distributed those same *nummi* to our men in drinks. The names of the men who thus drank are these: Robert son of Dudo, Godeschal, Ansfrid d'Heurteauville, Robert Maisnil, Rannulf son of Tetbert.[99]

Jumièges seems to have used the blank end of a charter to record a matter having nothing to do with the subject of the charter, a practice it followed at other times.[100] Who gave Courgains to Jumièges or who put the coins on the altar, presumably—but only presumably—as part of an act of donation, is never stated.[101] Wascelin de Coulonces is not mentioned elsewhere in the charter or anywhere else in eleventh-century Norman documents; he seems merely to have been sent by Jumièges to receive Courgains from whoever gave it and wherever it was given. The abbey was concerned primarily with what was done with the money: five men were treated to drinks "in order to record what had been done." Somehow, by drinking, these men became competent to act as witnesses to the transaction of which the money was a symbol, although they had apparently not witnessed the act of donation.

The other five charters which specify what became of the object used to make a gift or a confirmation treat the object itself as a witness. Two charters say that knives give testimony, "both for contemporaries and for posterity," as one adds.[102] A charter from Jumièges recording the gift of a mill by Richard count of Evreux has attached to it a straw and contains, apparently as an afterthought, this final paragraph: "A few days after this [the gift of the mill], however, the monks, coming to me again, asked that I concede them one *hospes* pertaining to the mill. To whom I myself, most willingly agreeing, gave what they asked by the gift of this *lignum* hanging from this charter."[103] Another charter from the same abbey, later by more than half a century, records a gift by Ralph son of Ansered of half of Etables and has attached to it a long, thin strip of parchment with writing on it which says, in full, "Robert duke of the Normans sent the gift of Etables to St. Mary of Jumièges through this *lignum*. The witnesses of this thing were Enguerrand son of Ilbert, Ralph de Mortemer, Walter du Chêne, Robert son of Anketil, Walter Broc. These things, in short, were done at Lisieux through Guntard, abbot of that place."[104] An analogous charter, again recording a secondary and subsequent transaction, exists from Fécamp; it also refers to itself as "this *lignum*" by means of which the donation was made, although this piece of parchment is little like a "rod" even in shape.[105]

The problem raised by these statements is how a mute object could witness. Conceivably, each of the knives was so distinctive in its design or as a result of the wear to which it had been subjected that anyone who knew the donor would immediately recognize the knife as his; if so, then, had one of these gifts been challenged, the recipient could have used the knife as "testimony" by producing it in court for witnesses to recognize as the donor's, arguing that the church's possession of the knife proved that the donor had made a gift.[106] It is also possible that the knives were inscribed in some way at the time of the act of donation: one eleventh-century knife survives, used in an act of donation to the cathedral church of Paris, the sheath of which serves as the charter.[107] Analogously, each of two books from Fécamp bears a brief notice of a gift: it seems likely that each had been used to make a donation and that the fact had been recorded on the object, that is, the book, to identify it.[108] Yet the few other surviving objects which had been used in acts of donation, none from Normandy, were, if they were labeled at all, merely attached to parchment labels which note how each object was used.[109] Moreover, a straw such as that attached to the earlier of the two charters from Jumièges was scarcely capable of any degree of distinctiveness. If the *lignum* of the later charter from

Jumièges refers to the piece of parchment itself, it is remarkable that it does not contain the duke's signature when it could so easily have done so.[110] More likely, a wooden rod or a straw or something to which the word *lignum* would seem to apply better than to a strip of parchment was originally attached to this charter and to the charter from Fécamp, as is the case not only with the first charter from Jumièges but also with considerable numbers of charters from elsewhere in France.[111] It remains hard, however, to imagine how so common and nondescript an object could constitute rationally compelling evidence. The answer to the question of how knives and *ligna* could be witnesses is, therefore, probably not entirely rational. Perhaps a donor or confirmer who was reneging on his or her previous action was expected to feel moral compunction if confronted with the very object with which the act of donation or confirmation had been performed. Perhaps only some magical significance will explain the phenomenon.[112]

A third form of the act of donation involved charters. Numerous charters allude to the process by which they were signed. All of these ought probably to be considered references to some form of act of donation involving charters, but only a few—about as many as refer to investiture—say anything about the ceremony itself. As with the other forms of the act of donation, the extant examples come from many churches, but a few—here La Trinité du Mont and Saint-Pierre de Préaux—either used this form or recorded its use disproportionately often.

Almost all of the charters of La Trinité du Mont end with signature lists, and quite a few of them also say that the charter was signed, in phrases similar to those which abound in the charters of many churches. Of these, five add that the charter was signed "on the altar" of the abbey or "in the presence of the altar."[113] Three late eleventh- or early twelfth-century charters from Saint-Pierre de Préaux portray in slightly more detail what was probably the same ceremony. For example, Helgo d'*Alneio* with the consent of his three sons made a gift in alms to the abbey, "who placing this gift on the altar, his aforesaid sons placed this donation on the altar with him and confirmed [it] with signs of the holy cross drawn with their own hands."[114] Many of the originals extant from the eleventh century bear autograph crosses, although in some cases the crosses appear to have been written by the scribe of the charter instead.[115] When the crosses are autographs, the scribe later wrote the name of each signer close to the cross the signer had made. The ceremony described by the charters from La Trinité du Mont and Saint-Pierre de Préaux may have occurred in each of these instances, perhaps even in the case of most charters which were signed.[116]

Apparently, however, a charter was not always signed at the altar. When Robert de Beaufour confirmed a gift made by Ralph son of Ernost, "he confirmed with the sign of his own hand the charter which the same Ralph had written and, moreover, gave us one acre of his own land . . . and placed the donation on the altar."[117] Here the confirmation was made by signing and only the gift was made by placement on the altar. This could happen even when only one transaction was involved: Geoffrey son of Osbern de *Turvilla* "conceded and confirmed his father's gift with the sign of the cross and placed [the confirmation] on the altar by means of a candlestick."[118] A charter from Saint-Martin de Sées says only that the gift was first agreed to in the abbey's chapter, then "recorded in the chamber";[119] both stages were very much public acts, but if a formal act of donation followed the writing of the charter, it is not mentioned. A charter from Fontenay says that after the charter was written and before it was signed it was read aloud.[120] Finally, a charter from Conches gives possibly the most interesting detail of all: the donor, "himself witnessing, held the horn while the scribe wrote out the above."[121] The horn was probably an inkhorn; that the donor held it would signify that he had cooperated in the writing of the charter recording his gift and had, therefore, indeed willingly made that gift.[122]

A certain logical fallacy is inherent in most of these charters, for they describe what was done with them after they were written. It is possible that, by a well-understood convention, they portray a ceremony the participants had already agreed would immediately follow the redaction of the charter or that a blank parchment was placed on the altar and signed and the body of the charter was subsequently written above the signatures.[123] A few originals, however, betray signs that the description of the act of donation, whatever its form, was added to an already completed charter.[124] This practice may have been more common than the surviving documents indicate: not only do relatively few originals survive, but those which do are disproportionately often charters emanating from the dukes, and ducal acts of donation are relatively rarely described.[125]

Was there a ceremony which made public the extent of land transferred? Berlaius d'*Alneio* gave Saint-Martin de Sées "the whole garden which he had in the Alençon road . . . asserting that there were eighty acres of land there; and if they [the eighty acres] should not be found fully in the garden, they should be made complete by addition from his closest level land; if, however, more than eighty should be [found] in the garden, all should remain to St. Martin."[126] If there was a recognized way of ascertaining the area of land given, however, few documents refer to it. Viscount Wascelin gave La Trinité du Mont the church of Monville and "three gardens in front of the same Monville, as was shown from the public road to the brook."[127] The two extant versions of William the Conqueror's gift to La Trinité de Caen of part of his bourg at Caen show clearly that in the interim between them a perambulation had been made.[128] Norman de Bavent, Richard son of Osmund, and Wimund son of Hugh sold to Saint-Martin de Sées "the land of *Rosellus* as it was seen beforehand and shown and divided by legal men . . . and beyond the boundaries of the same land of *Rosellus* we add a hundred acres and as much more as Norman's share is larger than the other partners' shares."[129] The division and view of the land may have occurred when it was divided among the three "partners" rather than when it was sold to the abbey, but a view had certainly taken place.

Only one charter describes perambulation itself rather than its results. When Robert de *Mesneria* sold Saint-Martin de Sées woods and land in the parish of *Coloncheis*, he "demonstrated the measurements and boundaries by showing [them] to Prior Geoffrey and Ernuceus the monk, these [eight] men [being] with them. . . ." Thereafter the transfer was made in the usual way, by placement on the altar and the receipt of a countergift by Robert, his wife and his brothers.[130] Roger de Montgomery is reported to have made a spectacular gesture to fix a particular boundary in the minds of witnesses; he may have done so in the course of a perambulation, but there is no way of knowing whether he did.[131]

Both the charter from La Trinité du Mont and the later version of William the Conqueror's charter for La Trinité de Caen list the boundaries which had been viewed. Some charters, relatively few and most of them early, contain more or less detailed descriptions of the boundaries of land which was given, though none except these two suggests that there had been a public viewing of the boundaries. I have been forced in the course of this work to argue fairly often that even a few references to a practice may mean that the practice was widespread. For those cases, however, the matter under discussion was one with which charters of donation to religious institutions need not normally have been concerned. Perambulation of the boundaries of land about to be transferred is not in that category. The men who had made a perambulation might be very important witnesses against persons who challenged the transaction or encroached on the land. Therefore, if perambulation of the boundaries of the land transferred had been standard practice, there should be more than a few allusions to it. To see every description of the boundaries of land as the product of a public perambulation would be rash; and, even if all those instances were counted, the number of references to perambulation would remain comparatively low. It would seem, therefore, that, though perambulation was not wholly unknown, neither was it a common feature of transfers of land. This conclusion is confirmed by the fact that acts of donation did not take place on the property transferred. Had perambulation been necessary in law or advisable in practice, one would expect that the formal act of donation would have occurred in close conjunction with it, at least some of the time, if for no other reason than to spare the donor a journey to the recipient church and to spare the recipient the anxiety of waiting for the donor to arrive to perform the ceremony.

There were, therefore, three forms of the act of donation: placement on the altar, investiture, and signing of the charter. Of these three, placement on the altar is mentioned most often by far. In most charters which mention only one form of the act and describe it in sufficient detail to make clear what form was used, that form is placement on the altar; and charters which mention either investiture or signing of the charter often refer to placement on the altar as well. It is possible that there was a normal sequence of steps for making gifts and rendering them secure which included all three forms: in the first stage, alluded to by many charters but described by hardly any, the donor would invest the donee with the gift; then, ideally immediately but perhaps considerably later, the donor would place the gift on the altar of the recipient church and sign a charter which had been drawn up to record the gift. Possibly, however, the preliminary step consisted simply of an agreement between donor and donee, sometimes—or perhaps usually, as donees must presumably have preferred—an agreement announced in public. Moreover, although many charters bear some evidence that they were signed, fewer than one-sixth of them mention placement on the altar and very few indeed include anything which can be interpreted as a reference to investiture. Therefore, a theory that all three were usual is extremely conjectural. A large gap may often have existed between the desires of donees for many public acts to assure their possession of what they were given and the actual performance of such acts by donors. These considerations all apply equally to confirmations, with the exception that the preliminary stage, if there was a public element to it, was probably always a mere announcement rather than an investiture.

One principle emerges clearly from study of the different types of acts of donation: it was to a recipient's advantage to induce as many persons as possible of those who might have some claim to what was being given to participate. Whether participation took the form of placing the gift on the altar, or of contributing one's knife to the ceremony, or simply of witnessing the ceremony along with others—as relatives and lords of donors and confirmers are regularly reported to have done—seems to have been immaterial. What counted was participation in public to demonstrate consent. In short, public performance before as many witnesses as possible of as many acts or statements as a donor or confirmer could be induced to make was considered by eleventh-century Norman clerics one of the best ways to render alienations secure.

In addition to acts of donation as such, one other public act was advantageous to churches wishing to retain control of what they had been given, namely, transfer of a countergift. The importance of countergifts probably rested on the possibility of making a legal argument, in case of a challenge, that the challenger had accepted compensation for what had been given or confirmed and therefore had no right to make a later claim.[132] A resolute challenger, however, could deny receiving a countergift unless it had been received in the presence of witnesses. Hence a good many charters record that countergifts were given in public or simply list the witnesses to them. Few, however, say anything more. Occasionally the place where the act occurred is mentioned: the chapter, the abbot's chamber, the court of the abbey, the provost's grange, the house of one of the witnesses.[133] More often a charter notes who handed over the countergift or who received it.[134] Only one says significantly more: when Ralph son of Ansered, with his lord Ralph de Mortemer's consent, made gifts to Jumièges for a countergift of society and fifteen pounds of Rouen, "Warin the toll collector of the same Ralph received the same fifteen pounds of Rouen by order of the same Ralph in the vill which is called Saint-Victor and Fulk the merchant counted out [the money]." The charter goes on immediately to report that seisin was transferred to the abbey by Ralph's lord's agent.[135] Usually, however, it was the donor or confirmer himself or herself who participated in both act of donation and associated transfer of the countergift.

John Burnet invested Saint-Martin de Sées by means of the same staff with which the abbot had given him his countergift of society.[136] Because he was gravely wounded, these transactions took place in his home. Several features of the event, however, are shared by three or four transactions which occurred at the abbey: the grant of society preceded the act of donation, which except in John's case was placement on the altar; the latter occurred immediately after the former; and the same object, in these cases a book, was used for both parts of the ceremony. At the abbey, the stages of the ceremony up through receipt of the countergift occurred in the chapter, after which everyone moved to the altar for the act of donation.[137] Other charters from the abbey allude more briefly to what is obviously the same set of ceremonies performed in the same order; many of these say that the second one, placement on the altar, was done with a book. Because many of the fifty-four extant eleventh-century charters from the abbey which mention acts of donation say that the gift was made in the chapter and also mention either receipt of the countergift in the chapter or placement on the altar, it appears that this abbey had a clearly established procedure for performing these two ceremonies.

The charters of Saint-Evroul are more loosely worded, but they suggest that the first monks of Saint-Martin de Sées had brought their procedure with them from Saint-Evroul.[138] Was the procedure peculiar to these related abbeys or was it commonplace? It is hard to tell. With Saint-Martin de Sées, the other abbey whose charters most consistently give information on both countergifts and acts of donation is Saint-Pierre de Préaux; but its charters do not give a similar picture of two ceremonies always performed in sequence according to certain forms. Even more than Saint-Martin de Sées, which records a few apparent investitures, this abbey was exceptionally consistent in its use of placement on the altar: aside from the few late instances of signing the charter on the altar,[139] twenty-four of its twenty-five references to the act of donation describe placement on the altar.[140] For countergifts, however, the abbey's scribes were much more interested in what was given to whom than in how it was given. Full as charters from Saint-Pierre de Préaux are of details of who got what, only two of them describe the ceremonies by which countergifts were given. One seems to have been recorded precisely because it was unusual and unceremonious.[141] The other occurred when a donor's son became a monk at the abbey. The ceremony was in three parts, all of which took place at the altar: first the mother and her relatives and friends, standing on one side, offered the new monk to the abbot and monks and their men, standing opposite; then she made the gift in an unstated manner; finally, she placed the gift on the altar.[142] A third countergift was given, at Préaux, "before the parish";[143] whether this meant before the parish church or before its congregation, it indicates that the countergift was made publicly, but nothing is said about the ceremony itself. From other churches, too, for comparison with procedure at Saint-Martin de Sées and Saint-Evroul there is little upon which to draw. The few charters which say that the countergift was given in the chapter are the only confirmatory evidence from Normandy.[144]

What the charters say about the countergifts so far considered, those given in return for donations and confirmations, seems to have little to do with whether they consisted of spiritual benefits, objects, or money. Indeed, an individual donor or confirmer or a group of such persons often was given a miscellany which might include all three. It is possible, however, that a special ceremony was connected with sale prices and perhaps with monetary countergifts as well. Ordinary acts of donation are rarely reported in connection with sales.[145] If this is not an illusion caused by the scribes' reticence, then the fact that witnessing was clearly one of the major modes of assurance of sales[146] raises the question of what the witnesses witnessed. Two charters suggest an answer. The memorandum of Rainald the chaplain cites, as possible witnesses, "the men who received the . . . coins" with which Samson the cleric had bought property from him.[147] Ralph son of Ansered's toll collector "received" a countergift to Ralph from Jumièges "and Fulk the merchant counted out" the money.[148] Ralph's transfer is not called a sale, and the charter gives little reason to think it a concealed sale except for the size of the countergift. Nevertheless, on the basis of these two charters, one can envision a ceremony consisting of the public counting out of money into the hands of the alienor or one or more agents, a ceremony used to publicize the payment of sale prices and perhaps also the conferring of monetary countergifts. If the ceremony occurred on more than these two occasions, it went unreported, though a few charters may hint at it.[149] The silence may stem from the nature of the sources. Mentions of countergifts usually consist merely of lists of who got what, and a large number of the extant references to sales occur in documents which are little more than lists of transactions, each only briefly entered.[150] Rainald's memorandum is *sui generis*, and he cited his agents because he needed them as witnesses against Samson. Jumièges may have noted who counted out its countergift to Ralph because it was unusual for someone other than a member of the church to do so. Certainly, one cannot argue on the basis of two examples that a practice was widespread, but in this instance it is tempting, for doing so resolves an otherwise apparent conflict between conclusions derived from study of the surviving records of sales.

SPEECHES AND OATHS

One of the purposes of ceremonies of donation, in whatever form, was to enable persons present who might have a claim against what was given to raise it—or, rather, to secure the consent at least by silence of all such persons, before witnesses, and thereby forestall future claims. This is the ground of Rainald the chaplain's argument against the claim of Samson the cleric to the property at Bayeux which Rainald had given to Jumièges.[151] At least two acts of donation included formal demands that any claims be presented: one was addressed generally and received no reply; the other was addressed to an individual and was answered in the negative.[152] Every ceremony may have included such a demand; certainly every ceremony implied one. The charters, understandably, are almost unanimously silent about affirmative responses, but two exceptions indicate that claims were at least occasionally raised in this context. When Duke William made a gift to Marmoutier, one of the witnesses was "Hugh the forester, whom he wished to beat with the shoulder of a pig because he was contradicting that gift."[153] Hugh must have renounced his claim, for he is cited as a witness; there is no mention of any countergift to him. Orderic, however, says that the second claim—the one which Ascelin son of Arthur raised at the burial of William the Conqueror to the land in which William's body was about to be buried—was settled on the spot by a payment of money.[154]

In addition to an explicit challenge to potential claimants to present their claims now or never and to their responses, if any, the ceremonies surrounding donations may normally have included other statements. Several charters say that in connection with an act of donation some person spoke certain words. When, for example, William son of Hardred sold property to Saint-Etienne de Caen, the charter says that the witnesses "all heard the aforesaid William recognizing and acknowledging this."[155] It is likely that every act of donation included a speech describing what was given.[156] Only twenty-odd, however, actually quote—directly or by means of indirect discourse—what was said; and in them the speeches thought worthy by different scribes of being quoted turn out to be a miscellaneous collection. A few were doubtless quoted for their memorability. Duke William's joke about how knives ought to be used to transfer property is in this category, as is another remark of his, which displays a more refined sense of humor.[157] When William de *Claraio* became a monk at Saint-Martin de Sées, his gifts included the land of a man who was apparently a vavassor, for "in affirming [his gifts] he said that it was only right that he who demised a hundred vavassors to his sons should retain at least one directly and quit for himself and for the monks with whom he was to live and die."[158] Various other striking statements were doubtless also quoted for their memorability.[159]

More often speeches describe the alienations being made, but they show little consistency about what exact aspects of a transaction an alienor should describe. One version of Richard de Reviers's deathbed gift to Saint-Père de Chartres quotes the words of gift which he spoke on his deathbed.[160] A charter from Saint-Pierre de Préaux makes a mortgagor declaim a full description of the terms of the mortgage and the conditions under which it might become a permanent alienation as he places the gift on the altar and also makes him announce that he has received a countergift of society.[161] Another quotes at length the words a man spoke when he did homage for land he had been claiming from the abbey, in which he promised not to demand compensation should he lose the land once more.[162] Yet a third charter from this abbey quotes a much briefer but seemingly complete statement of a gift.[163] Laconic allusions to speeches during acts of donation may also suggest that it was usual for an alienor to give a complete description of the terms of the alienation, and one charter says that it was read aloud before being signed;[164] but the other direct quotations are more limited in scope: two confirm the purity of alms, one limits the donor's rights over alms, another mandates the use to which alms will be put and provides for their freedom from service, the last is an alienor's order to one of the witnesses to defend the transfer against him should he change his mind.[165] That so many concern alms may not be accidental. Because donors lost more by making a gift in alms than in any other transaction,[166] they or others close to them may have been more than usually tempted to take back such gifts; therefore, it may have been more than usually important to be able to recall to the witnesses both the exact words a donor had spoken and the donor's acknowledgment that the gift was in alms. The number of quotations is, however, too small to be used as the basis for contending that gifts in alms required a public declaration—much less that all alienations did.

In roughly half the extant charters, the alienor speaks in the first person. For obvious reasons, none of these includes a direct quotation; but in a sense each is, as a whole, a direct quotation. Each alienor may have said at the moment of the alienation essentially what is recorded in the charter. It would be farfetched to maintain that in all cases the alienor had done so; certainly this was not so only in these cases, for all the obvious examples of direct quotation come from charters in which the speaking voice is the recipient's. The frequency of charters in the first person varies widely from church to church; and some of the churches for which it seems most probable that alienors actually made speeches during acts of donation—most notably Saint-Martin de Sées and Saint-Pierre de Préaux—rarely use them. Use of the first person may, nonetheless, have been something more than a scribal technique, for in a few charters recording transfers in which two or more persons participated the speaking voice changes from participant to participant. When, for example, Alvered the Giant made gifts to Cerisy, which included land held from Alvered by a priest named Walter, first Alvered related his gift, then Walter and his son together gave their land to the abbey effective as of Walter's death, then Alvered's lord the duke gave his consent, and each of these statements is in the first person.[167] Such charters constitute evidence that alienors often, if not universally, recited aloud the terms of their alienations as they made them.

If alienors did so, the purpose was certainly to make known to the witnesses the contents and/or the terms of the alienations. Witnesses who had seen an act of donation but had no knowledge of what the transaction was about would be of relatively little use in case of a challenge. There must, therefore, have been ways in which recipient churches made sure that witnesses knew the terms of each alienation and the extent of the property alienated; and descriptions by the alienors seem one likely method, especially because perambulation of the boundaries of the property given was not usual in Normandy. Witnesses are often said to have "heard" as well as "seen," or simply to have "heard," what was done. In the case of confirmers, another purpose would be served by their speeches, namely, to demonstrate their consent. A few speeches which relate directly to consent are quoted. When, for example, Lancelin d'Airan entered into a complex series of transactions with Troarn, "the same Lancelin, indeed, brought with him to the concession of this agreement his lady Agnes, from whom he held the same inheritance. And he requested strongly that she voluntarily concede this agreement. Then she, in a loud voice, [said], 'I, in everyone's hearing, willingly concede [this] to God and St. Martin and I will have [it] confirmed by my sons.' "[168] A donor to La Trinité du Mont publicly asked his lord and the lord's wife and sons to concede, but the charter does not quote a reply. William d'*Alneto* confirmed an alienation to Saint-Martin de Sées but did not come to the abbey himself; the charter carefully notes that the man whom he sent publicly stated that William had conceded. A group of six claimants to property of Saint-Ouen publicly declared that their claims were unjust at the moment when they renounced them.[169]

These statements were made so as to commit alienors, confirmers, or quitclaimers before witnesses to stand by their actions. They seem to have involved no ceremonial element. A somewhat more formal statement, accompanied at least by the twelfth century by a manual gesture done in public, was the giving of one's faith.[170] Few eleventh-century charters refer to it, and those which do are too laconic to indicate more about the practice than that it was already known. In three of these, faith was given in connection with a promise to warrant, but two others are vague about what the faith given guaranteed.[171] The exception to this taciturnity is the only extant charter whose primary concern is a transaction between lay persons, which recites at length the promise about which faith was given. As a result of a suit in the court of Robert de Bellême, Picot de Say and Dreux de Coimes came to an agreement to divide between them the dower Picot's wife, Adeloia, had from her first husband, who was Dreux's brother. Then, "in the sight of forty or more knights, in the same court, Dreux gave his faith to Picot that he would bear faith in this to him," and what he promised is set out at length.[172] Although exactly what the witnesses saw is not reported, the wording of the charter strongly implies that Dreux spoke aloud the terms of his promises in the course of the ceremony. It is odd that the giving of faith was not reciprocal, for the suit was settled by a compromise establishing obligations for both parties. The imbalance may result from the bias of the source: the charter is found in the cartulary of Saint-Martin de Sées and may have been drawn up by a scribe from that abbey, to which Picot—but not Dreux—was a donor. Perhaps the monks wanted the record because they hoped someday to acquire some of the land; perhaps Picot asked them to make—or at least to take custody of—a record of the settlement because he distrusted Dreux's sincerity.[173] In either case, those interested in recording the agreement would have been concerned with Dreux's duties rather than Picot's. The pledges whom the bishop of Bayeux and Viscount

Rannulf exchanged were, on both sides, bound by their faith to act in certain ways;[174] and, though one of the parties to this agreement was a cleric, it is easy to imagine that this sort of compact also occurred entirely between lay persons. Guarantors of treaties could be similarly bound.[175] All in all, it seems likely, if incapable of proof, that the giving of faith was a common way of guaranteeing the security of agreements in eleventh-century Normandy.[176]

A third sort of speech was also used to assure transfers—the oath. The oaths recorded in the charters seem to have shared with less formal verbal statements the characteristic of being made in public. As such they committed those who took them because witnesses could testify to their having been taken. Oaths, however, had another virtue: they obligated those who took them before God and would bring on divine punishment if broken.[177] Therefore, an oath taken in public was presumably better assurance to a recipient church than a mere speech. Nonetheless, the use of oaths seems to have been remarkably sparing, or remarkably sparingly recorded.[178]

When Blancardus quitclaimed to Saint-Etienne de Caen a church which not only he but also his father had been claiming, "he swore on the four holy Evangels, not at anyone's request nor coerced by any force, but of his own free will . . . , that never again would he or anyone acting for him raise a claim to the same church."[179] Roger the priest of *Monte Tabal* swore that there were no claims outstanding against a church he gave to Saint-Martin de Sées.[180] Lancelin d'Airan, before he asked his lady to confirm his gift to Troarn, went through an especially elaborate act of donation, in which, "so that this agreement should be firm and stable he himself swore in everyone's presence on a text of the holy Gospel which Arnold de *Stochis* held in his arms—so that the same Arnold would not be able to deny any of this—that he would preserve and keep this agreement firmly and without any bad intentions. Then he placed the same text on the altar of St. Martin [along] with Arnold de *Stochis*' knife, with which the donation was made, which [knife] we have in our possession."[181] Other charters say much more briefly that donors or confirmers took oaths—alone, or with their sons, their heirs, or their men.[182] Past or potential claimants might also be asked to swear to respect an alienation.[183] One charter says that the purpose of the oath was "so that this thing should remain firm"; in another the donors swore "to preserve this agreement forever."[184]

From the few direct quotations in the charters, the following conclusions seem permissible. First, they do not amount to proof that a public speech or an oath was a standard part of the ceremonies surrounding transfers. This is a possibility, perhaps inherently likely, but no more. It may be significant that only one charter quotes more than one type of participant in a transfer, if there were two or more: Lancelin d'Airan's charter both reports the oath he took and quotes his lady as to her consent. Because a scribe who bothered to quote one participant might be expected to quote others, the absence of multiple quotations may imply that no public declaration was mandatory, at least not for each and every participant.

Second, even if statements or oaths were usual, no set form seems to have been required.[185] There is no reason to suppose that all statements except those quoted for their memorability were oaths. One alienor is reported to have recited the lengthy and complex details of his arrangement while performing the act of donation; at the other end of the scale, a potential claimant, asked whether he had any claim to make, said simply, "No."[186] Not only the form and the length but also the content of statements and oaths, as recorded, varied widely. What a person might say obviously depended partly on the nature of the transaction and on his or her role in it; but even when charters can be compared which quote persons playing essentially the same role the statements are not necessarily similar. In other words, statements and oaths, even if obligatory, seem to have been free as to form.

Third, with the exception of those statements apparently quoted for their memorability, most of the quotations—especially the oaths—occurred in situations which posed at least somewhat more chance of challenge than usual. This may mean that public speeches were demanded only or primarily in cases when the likelihood of challenges was unusually high; but it is also possible that scribes bothered to write down declarations only in such cases although, in fact, they occurred much more regularly.

RECOGNITORY PAYMENTS

When a possession of one person or institution was temporarily in the hands of another, especially when property belonging to a church was temporarily alienated, some agreements prescribe the payment on a regular, normally annual basis of sums of money or other valuable goods "in recognition," that is, as a sign that the tenant recognized that the tenement ultimately belonged to the recipient of the payment.[187] A payment of this type not only constituted proof of ultimate possession but also provided periodic opportunities to check on the continued recognition—by the person or institution which should be making the payment—of the right of the recipient of the payment to ultimate possession.

A few charters explain the purposes of such payment in detail. When Saint-Wandrille granted a life estate to a layman and his wife, "lest these agreements be given over to the negligent forgetfulness of [our] successors, we retain the third part of the tithe of that land as [our] sustenance."[188] Payments of small sums annually "in recognition" for churches granted to priests by abbeys are mentioned by two eleventh-century Norman charters, and there may be an example as early as 965.[189] There is also one instance in which a priest made a similar payment for land he held from an abbey.[190] Such a payment might also be used to indicate lordship of an immovable which was permanently alienated.[191] Repeated payments might also be used as earnest of post-obit gifts.[192] Moreover, as with earnest, land too might be used for recognitory purposes: Fécamp gave a life estate to Wascelin son of Heddo, "the land which is called Saintigny being retained in our hand *pro investitura*."[193]

This last phrase evokes the problem posed by the term "investiture," whose meanings seem to vary a good deal. It could be used for the stock with which a piece of land was furnished or its appurtenances,[194] but more often its meaning is connected with the idea of possession or an ultimate right to possess. "To invest" could mean to deliver seisin.[195] "Investiture" is used once as the term for the earnest given for a post-obit gift,[196] a usage very similar, *mutatis mutandis*, to the way Fécamp used it in the life estate given to Wascelin son of Heddo. The somewhat suspect charter recording how William the Conqueror settled a dispute between Saint-Wandrille and William count of Evreux over rights in various forests says that the monks, to prove that they had held certain customs since the time of Duke Richard II and Abbot Gradulf, "thence still point out many investitures and tenures."[197] This obscure phrase might refer to something akin to a rent; but, like another charter from Saint-Wandrille, which cites "investiture and the testimony of many faithful men" as proof of possession,[198] it probably refers to the ceremony of investiture before witnesses. Finally, when Gilbert son of Archdeacon Robert of Evreux gave Jumièges a church and its appurtenances, which "came to me from the demesne of the aforesaid church [i.e., the cathedral of Evreux?] according to paternal investiture,[199] he probably meant no more than that he had inherited the property.

Two charters from Saint-Martin de Sées imply that all rents could be regarded as recognitory payments.[200] It was, of course, true, not only of rentals but of fiefs and their services as well, that the rents or services constituted evidence of merely tenurial possession. The main reason for rents or services, however, was to provide lords with things of value. What distinguishes most instances of payments "in recognition" is that their principal purpose was to signify with whom permanent possession ought to lie. In all the cases except the two from Saint-Martin de Sées, their value, when known, was minimal; it was not supposed to reflect accurately the value of the grants they represented, as rents and services presumably were. Such recognitory payments were, in other words, not considerations in return for which grants of immovables were made but, rather, a technique to ensure that such grants would not become permanent alienations.

7

Modes of Assurance: Confirmers, Witnesses, Signers, and Pledges

ALIENORS AND RECIPIENTS were by no means the only participants in alienations. Other parties very often played a role: they confirmed alienations; they witnessed alienations; they signed charters recording alienations. Confirmers, witnesses, and signers abound in the charters, and their purpose was to render alienations more secure than alienors and recipients could make them by their unaided efforts. Much less often another type of participant, the pledge, appears for the same purpose.

Witnesses and pledges were intended primarily to defeat future claims: recipients must have hoped that their existence would deter potential claimants from raising claims in the first place. In contrast, by confirming—and apparently also by signing a charter—a person renounced the right or desire to make any claim. Functionally speaking, in other words, witnesses and pledges were persons who themselves had no basis for making claims; if a claim was raised, in the resulting lawsuit witnesses and pledges ought to be found on the opposite side from the claimant. On the contrary, confirmers—and at least some signers—were themselves potential challengers; if a claim was raised, it was by someone who ought to have served as a confirmer, in the absence of a confirmation, or because a confirmer disregarded his or her confirmation. Nevertheless, illogical as it may be, no consistent pattern associates particular categories of third parties with particular types of participation. Lords, relatives, and others in a position to confirm often confirm explicitly or by participating in some way in the alienation; but in many charters they appear only as witnesses or as pledges, apparently a sufficient demonstration of their consent. The same person, however, may occur in several capacities. The degree of confusion of roles is indicated perhaps most graphically by charters which record alienors themselves as witnesses.[1] Because the relationship of a third party to the principals in a transaction bears no consistent relationship to the role of the third party in the transaction, discussion of the consent of lords, relatives, and others must be separated from discussion of the forms by which consent was expressed.

Moreover, the relative frequency with which confirmers, witnesses, signers, and pledges occur varies considerably from the charters of one church to those of another. The disparities seem to depend on the habits of different *scriptoria* and on the form in which the charters of a church survive, rather than on objective differences either among the transactions or among the reasons why the names of third parties are recorded. Faced with confirmers, it seems, one church might ask them to participate in the original act of donation or act as witnesses to it, another might prefer them to perform a separate act to symbolize their consent, a third might simply record them as confirmers, a fourth might be satisfied to have them sign the charter recording the original alienation, and a fifth might ask them to become pledges for the security of the alienation. Such differences depend partly on accidents of time and place: a confirmer could not, for example, either participate in or witness the original act of donation unless he or she not only had already agreed to consent but also was present. The form in which the charters of a church survive also affects the matter.[2] Copies in cartularies are less likely than originals to contain signatures or complete witness lists. Entries in pancarts are less likely than charters recording single alienations to mention confirmers, aside from the person whose confirmation is the subject of the pancart; they are still less likely to mention witnesses, and they are least likely of all to list the signers of the individual charters from which the pancart was compiled. The simplest way to describe some of the resulting variations among churches is to tabulate them, as is done in Table 2.[3]

CONFIRMERS

One could confirm an alienation in many ways, most of which involved participation in some way in the acts surrounding the alienation. Confirmation could also, however, constitute a separate act indistinguishable in form from the acts surrounding alienations themselves.[4] Previous chapters have cited examples of confirmations which suffice to illustrate most ways in which consent was expressed. It might occur at the same moment as the alienation: two charters from Saint-Martin de Sées show alienors and confirmers jointly grasping the objects with which the acts of donation were being performed and jointly conveying them.[5] By variations on this practice, a confirmer might perform the act of donation instead of the donor[6] or hold the holy book on which the donor swore an oath[7] or contribute the object with which the act of donation was performed[8] or receive a countergift at the same time as the donor.[9] Confirmation might occur later in the same ceremony,[10] but often it was clearly a separate act subsequent to the alienation itself.[11] In some cases each confirmer came to the church to make his or her confirmation;[12] in others, the church sent one or more representatives to different confirmers to secure their consent.[13] Confirmers seem in all these instances to have given their consent in the same way as alienors made their alienations, that is, by a public act perhaps including a speech or an oath and, at least often, by the public receipt of a countergift. If the ceremony was separate from the donation, the public act, when described, is always placement on the altar, never investiture.[14] Recipients seem to have been eager to have confirmers, like alienors, demonstrate their approval by as many modes of assurance as possible. A confirmation might be repeated by the person who made it, once or even several times, and alienors themselves sometimes confirmed their alienations by similar ceremonies. It was also possible to confirm by signing a charter which recorded an earlier alienation.[15]

Although Normans indubitably knew the difference between an alienation and a confirmation, in two situations the distinction is not entirely clear. Many charters say that several persons made one alienation. Some of these were probably genuinely joint gifts of property held in common.[16] By far the most usual group of joint donors, however, was a man and some of his relatives, especially his wife and one or more children. In a fair number of such charters all or most of the verbs are in the singular; and the charter may, therefore, represent not a joint alienation but an alienation by one individual with the consent of others. Second, in a considerable number of charters a lord is said to give land held by his tenant and sometimes to give the tenant himself. In some the tenant consents, in others not. A few say that the lord acted at the request of the tenant, who chose to have the gift performed in this manner to demonstrate the lord's consent, and it is possible that the same circumstances lie behind many if not all lords' gifts of their tenants' lands. Because this second problem concerns only one type of confirmer, I have reserved discussion of it to the section on consent of lords.[17] Joint alienors, on the other hand, consist sometimes of relatives but at other times of lords and men or even of apparently unconnected persons and, therefore, must be discussed here.

The verbs used to express the actions of joint donors or of lords giving their tenants' lands do not help to solve either problem. In the eleventh century, Norman scribes were only beginning to develop formulas to express the common features of the transactions they recorded, and one of the areas in which there were few rules was the proper verbs for different forms of transfer. Some specific terms—such as verbs of sale and of exchange—were in use; but with verbs for more general actions chaos reigns. To cite only one particularly striking example, in a charter from Cerisy *dare* must mean "confirm" and *annuere* "give," although much more often the meanings of those two verbs are reversed.[18]

In Table 3, I have computed the figures on the use by different churches of verbs of gift and verbs of confirmation.[19] The chaos is not absolute. *Dare* and its various elaborations and *concedere* predominate among verbs of gift: together they account for 88 percent of the entries in the table; *dare* alone accounts for two-thirds. Similarly, *concedere*, *firmare* and its elaborations, and *annuere* account for more than three-quarters of the verbs of confirmation. Nonetheless, the predominance is not sufficient to distinguish donations from confirmations. *Concedere*, the most popular verb of confirmation, is the second most popular verb of gift,[20] occurring not only in conjunction with *dare* and other verbs but also alone. The two partial exceptions to the variation in the meanings of particular verbs are *dare* and *confirmare* themselves, especially the latter. *Dare* is relatively rarely used to express the idea of confirming. *Confirmare* is used only by one charter, a very early one, with a meaning as close to "give" as to "confirm."[21] Elsewhere, the use of this verb can be taken as a sign that a transaction was indubitably a confirmation; but *confirmare* is not used in the problem charters.

Most churches from which sizable numbers of charters survive demonstrate a preference for one verb of gift and one of confirmation. Hence, within each *scriptorium* formulas were beginning to develop. Of these preferences, however, some—Saint-Martin de Sées' for *dimittere* as a verb of gift, or Conches' and La Trinité du Mont's for *annuere* as a verb of confirmation, or Lire's for *concedere* in both meanings, to cite four striking examples[22]—indicate that there was as yet no general agreement among *scriptoria* as to which verbs to use. Moreover, as a general rule, the more charters are extant from a church, the more verbs it uses, as Table 4 illustrates.[23] The implication is that, if all the eleventh-century charters of Normandy were extant, rules would appear to apply even less. One further point deserves notice. The churches which show the least preference for any one verb in either category are the five oldest Norman abbeys, the Carolingian convents refounded in the tenth century. All five also rank among the highest in the number of verbs used, higher than they do according to the total numbers of their alienations extant. These abbeys had the longest scribal tradition of any churches in Normandy with the possible exception of the cathedral church of Rouen,[24] yet formulas to express the ideas of giving and confirming are notably absent. This lack reinforces the conclusion that, with the exception of *confirmare* and possibly of *dare*, the use of different verbs cannot be used as an index of the types of transactions involved.

Joint donors appear at least occasionally in the charters of most churches from which a substantial number of charters survives; in those of quite a few churches they are numerous.[25] In rare instances, the number of co-alienors is fairly high. A few charters say that the alienors were all the men of a vill or, in one instance, "many men," usually without naming any.[26] Others name a considerable number of relatives, such as a transfer to Saint-Martin de Sées by "William son of Antelm with my brother Turstin and our mother Lesceline and our sister Emma, with our sons, namely, William and Robert."[27] Occasionally, the reason for the appearance of co-alienors is stated or can be deduced. Wholly unrelated persons might, it seems, maximize the value of what were individually small transfers—often of parts of the same vill or church—by making them together.[28] More often, two or more brothers made a gift together; very rarely, two sisters did. As there is reason to believe that both joint tenancy and parage existed in eleventh-century Normandy, it is possible that these were alienations by joint tenants or by tenants in parage, even when a charter gives no direct evidence.[29] It is easy to understand why a wife appears as a co-alienor with her husband when the transfer involved her inheritance or dower or dowry.[30] Charters which even hint at the reason for the appearance of co-alienors are in the minority, however. Usually a charter says simply that two or more persons made a gift. It is common for such a charter to have all the verbs—or all of them except the first—in the singular,[31] and the same apparent lack of sense often governs the use of various pronouns and adjectives, such as *ego* and *nos*, *is* and *ei*, *ille* and *illi*, and *meus* and *noster*.

The point is not that the scribes did not always construct documents as coherently as they might have done. That should long since have become obvious. Instead, if a considerable number of charters use a singular verb for multiple alienors or say that several alienors transferred "my" something, or the like, the only explanation which would defend the scribes against the accusation of rank incapacity to handle the simplest Latin is that co-alienation was one way of indicating consent. If this explains some peculiar charters emanating from co-alienors, it may also explain many of those in which, although the verbs and pronouns are plural, there is no obvious reason for more than one person to have made the alienation. Remarkably few charters of this type explicitly indicate consent by any of the persons coupled as alienors with the presumptive actual alienor although such charters mention the consent of other persons about as often as usual. This in itself creates a strong presumption that apparently joint alienors actually represent one alienor and one or more confirmers, but at the same time it means that the presumption usually cannot be confirmed.

WITNESSES

The efficacy of the ceremonial acts described in the previous chapter depended largely on the existence of witnesses to them, and for at least most of the eleventh century[32] the model charter included the names of witnesses. Usually the witnesses are listed toward the end of the charter; but sometimes they, or some of them, are found instead in the body of the charter as those "in whose presence" the transfer was made.[33] When an alienation involved several acts, it was not uncommon to record the witnesses to each act separately, not only when the different acts were separated in time, but even when they occurred consecutively but were done in different places, such as first in an abbey's chapter and then at the altar, or by different persons, such as first by the alienor and then by a lord or a relative.[34]

Witness lists often include participants in the alienations or persons who, as potential challengers, are of types often recorded in other charters as participating in similar alienations. Alienors themselves, as already noted, are sometimes, though rarely, found. Persons in a position to confirm or to challenge alienations occur much more regularly: relatives, lords, and lords' relatives. The abbot or prior and/or some or all of the monks of a recipient monastery are often cited, as are the bishop and/or some or all members of a recipient cathedral. Except for the duchesses, women witnessed very rarely, even women related to male participants; but three charters from La Trinité de Caen include nuns among the witnesses.[35] Other participants or persons in a position to confirm are also listed as witnesses: tenants, both lay and ecclesiastical, of what was transferred; the actual alienors in cases when a transfer was made by the alienor's lord; negotiators of alienations; persons who performed acts of donation along with the alienor or when it was not the alienor who did so; agents who received alienations or handed over countergifts for the recipient church or received countergifts on behalf of alienors; pledges; even some of the viewers of the boundaries in the only instance of perambulation as a ceremony of donation which names the viewers.[36] In records of court cases, the judges are often cited as witnesses, as occasionally are both the defeated claimants and the persons who successfully defended the victorious party's rights.

No charter explains why participants and potential claimants are cited as witnesses. Participants on the recipient's behalf could logically be said to have witnessed what the alienors or confirmers had done and could legitimately be expected to support the recipient church in any defense it might have to make against claims raised by participants or their relatives or lords. Citing participants on the alienors' side, however, seems only slightly less illogical than citing the alienors themselves. Any explanation is no more than a conjecture. Nonetheless, the explanation is probably the apparent rule, which governs all the assurance techniques requiring specific acts from individuals, that any person in a position to challenge an alienation should be induced to affirm his or her consent as often as possible in as many ways as possible. After all, if one witnessed an alienation without protest, one could be presumed to have consented to it.[37] Several charters imply that the rule that silence means consent was in fact the reason for the inclusion of relatives, lords, and tenants among witnesses when they cite as witnesses persons who were none of these but were obviously potential challengers: the men whom two donors made heirs to what they did not give; the new tenant of part of what was given; a former tenant who had been dispossessed so that the gift could be made. Each of these men was a danger, yet they are said not to consent but merely to witness.[38] For some potential claimants, therefore, witnessing served as the form in which consent was expressed. It is harder to explain how those who participated in acts of donation could be cited as witnesses to their own actions. Logically, this is a contradiction, for there is no trace of an act which witnesses themselves performed in addition to being passive spectators to the acts of others.[39] Each inclusion of a participant in a witness list seems to represent the triumph over logic of the desire to emphasize the finality with which the person had consented.

Most witnesses, however, were neither participants in nor potential challengers to alienations. They were genuine third parties who were present for a different reason. Relatively few charters so much as allude to the function of witnesses. Of those which do, three say merely that the purpose was to render the alienation more secure.[40] Most of the others point specifically to the use of witnesses as proof if a challenge was raised and brought into court.

Some charters refer prospectively to this situation. William Paynel's agreement with the abbot of Mont-Saint-Michel provides that, if the seven peers of his honor should refuse to answer his summonses, "William Paynel ought to deraign this in the abbot's court through men who are of the honor . . . who saw them in his service by the custom of his ancestors."[41] Rainald the chaplain cites a witness as follows: "All these things which I have just written Vitalis the cleric, who was with me in all [of the transactions], well knows to be so; and if through fear or love of anyone he should deny the truth of this may almighty God excommunicate him, and I in as much as I can. And he well knows . . . ," and the document goes on to describe the transfer.[42] Witnesses to a gift to Marmoutier would be "able to testify by legal proof to what was . . . done."[43] Philip de Briouze confirmed all his father's gifts to Saint-Florent de Saumur "in the presence of William son of Baderon and Ralph de Gournay, saying, moreover, to William son of Baderon that if ever Philip himself should wish to withdraw from that concession the same William should prove him to have conceded thus."[44] Such instructions may have been given to all witnesses; but this is the only recorded instance, and, as Philip seems to have issued his instructions to only one of the two witnesses, his was probably a special case, reported precisely because it was unusual. Philip may have been appointing William to act as the abbey's champion if the hypothetical case should ever get to the stage of a trial by battle.

These and other, similar references[45] demonstrate that the primary function of witnesses was to testify in defense of the recipient if an alienation was challenged. Some accounts of court suits show witnesses performing this function. When the monks of Saint-Pierre de Préaux complained to Roger de Beaumont that their late abbot, Ansfrid, had given the churches of Pont-Audemer to Hugh the cleric son of Turulf without their permission, Hugh replied that he had received the churches from Roger's father, Humphrey de Vieilles, and from Roger himself before he received them from Ansfrid.

> A plea was therefore appointed for the monks [who were] contradicting [him], so that the men who were witnesses of this thing on each side should come together, and this was done. Therefore, on the monks' behalf Wascelin was there as a witness, and on Hugh's behalf his brother Geoffrey. What more? The witnesses having been assigned and pledges given, a day was named so that battle could be waged by the aforenamed witnesses; but when it came to the battle, by the grace of God Hugh's witness and brother, Geoffrey, who was supposed to contend against Wascelin about that matter, confessed that he was feeble in [his] limbs and especially in the arms and that he did not have the strength for this work.[46]

One witness from each side, therefore, was to attempt to prove his principal's case by engaging in a judicial duel. Other descriptions of what witnesses did are ambiguous but suggest that they spoke rather than fought. Marmoutier called as witnesses "very old men . . . who had seen and heard this, ready to prove, at the king's judgment, what we had said."[47] The abbot of Troarn, in a dispute with Robert Samson, "showed through legitimate witnesses and quite old servants of Earl Roger [de Montgomery] and his son Lord Robert [de Bellême] that he had always had" certain rights; "the abbot also showed in the same plea through his charters and through the aforesaid old witnesses" that Robert had no claims at all in other things belonging to the abbey.[48] Unfortunately, the few other references to the actual use of witnesses as proof say nothing about what they did in court.[49]

Marmoutier's witnesses were "very old" and Troarn's "quite old." This points up the obvious drawback of the testimony of witnesses as a mode of proof, that it was available only so long as the last of the witnesses was alive. Normans of the eleventh century were conscious of this problem. When Duke Richard II sent four men to seise the archbishop of Rouen with a domain which was being restored to the church of Rouen, "they there whipped many little boys and [then] refreshed [them] well in record and memory of this deed."[50] The charter recording how Duke Robert the Magnificent sent his young son and designated heir, William, to make a gift on Robert's behalf to the new abbey of Saint-Pierre de Préaux lists four adults as witnesses, the last being

> Humphrey [de Vieilles], founder of the same place, with his sons Roger, Robert [and] William, who [William], moreover, received a blow from [his] father for the sake of memory. Richard de Lillebonne, who carried the greaves, that is, the hose of Duke Robert, received another blow; and, when he asked why Humphrey had given him such a great blow, he [Humphrey] answered, "Because you are younger than I and perhaps you will live a long time and you will be a witness of this business when[ever] there is need." Moreover, Hugh son of Count Waleran received a third blow.[51]

Humphrey's statement clearly indicates both the function of witnesses to transfers and the consequent desirability of having young men among them. Roger de Croismare's agreement with Saint-Pierre de Préaux was witnessed, among others, by "William, infant, son of Fulk Moirus, who on account of the memory of this thing received a blow at the altar in the sight of many."[52] "Infant" sometimes occurs as a nickname for an adult;[53] but in light of the previous charters, it is likely that this "infant" was indeed a child. His father is mentioned nowhere else in the charter. William may, therefore, have been included in the ceremony precisely to secure an especially long memory of an agreement which was complex in itself and which, because it included provisions relating to a second generation, Roger de Croismare's heirs, was unusually likely to give rise to disputes in the distant future. It is interesting that the blow William received is itself described as having been witnessed. Nevertheless, his role seems to be that of a witness.

A fourth charter displays concern for long memory when it records that, after Marmoutier bought tithes from a woman and her son, "Hubert de *Valnoisia* conceded this, and his sons, and they thence had two shillings on agreement that as long as he himself should live he should be a witness of this and his sons after him."[54] This and the three charters mentioning the buffeting of young men are, however, the only charters which evince interest in prolonging the utility of witnesses by choosing young men. Occasional charters mention as witnesses boys who are not said to be sons of anyone concerned.[55] Presumably, their presence was welcomed because of their youth. Many of the sons who acted as witnesses along with their fathers may also have been minors whose presence was important for the same reason. With the four exceptions noted, however, no charter emphasizes the presence of young men. There was, of course, another often used method of serving the same purpose: every confirmation of an earlier alienation provided a new group of witnesses.

All three charters in which the young witnesses were whipped or struck say that the action was taken "for the sake of memory," that is, to make an indelible impression upon them so that they would never forget the acts to which they might later have to testify. Such drastic measures may have been thought necessary because the boys were too young to have any real understanding of what they observed or of their role in the act.[56] In the only other example of such an action toward a witness, Duke William attempted to beat Hugh the forester "with the shoulder of a pig because he was contradicting [a] gift."[57] Here, however, the near beating seems to have been an expression of the duke's anger, not a device to reinforce the memory of a witness.

Nonetheless, the attempted beating of this witness is relevant to the subject of memorability, for it was probably recorded precisely because it was unusual. Such an event could be used to reawaken the memory of the witnesses if they were later—perhaps considerably later—called upon to testify about the alienation. Hugh the forester and both his fellow witnesses to this act, Roger de Montgomery and William fitz Osbern, were among the witnesses to other acts done by Duke William at about the same time in favor of the same priory.[58] Hugh certainly would have been more likely than otherwise to remember this particular transaction if the danger of being beaten which he had then faced was recalled to him. Roger de Montgomery and William fitz Osbern, Duke William's trusted advisers and close companions, are among the most widely cited witnesses in eleventh-century Normandy.[59] They, too, would probably find it easier to recall this particular transfer if a tussle between Hugh and the duke or something of that ilk were recalled to their memories. Men who participated often in the acts of others must have found it difficult to keep all the details straight, or even the basic facts. Indeed, in at least one instance Duke William proved unable to recall whether he had consented to a transfer.[60] Anything distinctive about a transfer would help solve the problem, and much of what is known about certain aspects of transactions can probably be attributed to this principle of selection of what was written down. It doubtless explains at least a few of the direct quotations recorded in the charters,[61] and probably also some of the more complete descriptions of acts of donation, especially those which seem to have included an unusual element.[62] Indeed, the cause of the problem of whether certain aspects of alienations are typical or atypical is precisely that the distinctiveness of events was one criterion for their inclusion in charters.

Donors probably sometimes staged memorable events to fix their donations in the minds of the witnesses.[63] Perhaps the most remarkable incident, reported by a thirteenth-century document from Troarn, is that, when Roger de Montgomery gave the abbey the marsh which surrounded it, "in the presence of many noble men, he threw his son Robert de Bellême, dressed in a miniver cloak, into the water, in witness and memory that the domain of the abbot and monks extended up to there," that is, to the spot where Robert was thrown in.[64] This action, if it occurred, doubtless fixed the event forever in Robert's mind, and he was only a boy at the time. It must also have been all but unforgettably impressed on the "many noble men" who observed it. Somewhat less dramatic but still unusual actions are reported fairly often. Concern for memorability probably explains certain other features of the charters as well, for example, dating by some military or political event of note, by an event important to the internal history of the recipient church, or even by the comet which appeared in 1066.[65] Some places, too, were probably cited for this reason, as when Duke William is said to have confirmed a gift "while he was sitting on his carpet between the forester's house and the church of Bernouville."[66] When a charter remarks, for example, that a gift was made "in the house of Robert the toll collector, he being a witness, who at that time was lying there on a certain bench,"[67] or another notes that when the duchess performed an act of donation her hair was "disheveled,"[68] it is hard not to conclude that such a detail was cited because it would enable a witness to pinpoint his memory of the alienation; there seems to be no other relevance.

In addition to the few indications that young witnesses were especially desirable because of the potential length of their memories, a few charters say that the witnesses to an act were "suitable" or "legal" or "legitimate" or "authentic."[69] Because all four of the abbeys which used such a phrase more than once used two different terms in similar contexts, it can be assumed that the terms refer to the same quality.[70] What that quality was, however, is not evident. The only reference to the suitability of witnesses who actually testified in court is unhelpful.[71] A charter already cited implies that witnesses to an act of donation were "legal" whereas witnesses to the preliminary statement of the transfer were not,[72] but it is hardly sufficient evidence to warrant a conclusion that the situation in which they witnessed made certain men "legal" witnesses. Moreover, the most revealing of the references to such witnesses indicates that "legality" was a personal quality rather than a function of the situation in which the witnesses found themselves: a charter from Saint-Martin de Sées says, "Indeed, of the many witnesses we place here [the names of] only two men, the best and [those who] seemed to us suitable, namely, Osulf and Ansger; the others, indeed, we dismiss as obscure or not useful."[73] It seems unlikely that this wording can be explained as an abbreviation by the scribe out of exhaustion or laziness, yet Osulf and Ansger, though apparently more distinguished than their fellow witnesses, were not important men.[74]

Moreover, the other witness lists whose members are said to be suitable are, with one exception, not composed either of strikingly distinguished persons or of strikingly undistinguished persons whose suitability needed to be emphasized; instead, they seem to be fairly typical lists.[75]

The scornful tone of dismissal of the witnesses whose names were not worth recording might suggest that there was a class basis for legal suitability to witness, but in fact class does not seem to have been determinative. Burgesses appear regularly as witnesses, as do agents and servants of both alienors and recipients. Cooks, bakers, carpenters, masons, tailors, porters, and other menial servants of abbeys witnessed with great frequency.[76] This leaves only peasants as a possibly excluded class. Here an argument from relative silence could be made, for few charters identify witnesses as peasants. There are, however, three "rustics," two "villeins," and possibly one *hospes*.[77] The appellations "rustic" and "villein" might, in all instances, be nicknames; but occasional charters identify witnesses by rustic occupations, including one early one which says that the witnesses were nine men listed by name "and all the herdsmen who were in the village," apparently the vill of Auzouville-sur-Ry in which the land alienated was located.[78] A man called "winnower" was often a witness for Saint-Martin de Sées, and Anketil the vinegrower and his son witnessed all nine of the entries for Abbot Gilbert in the list of purchases of Saint-Etienne de Caen.[79] If these were occupations rather than nicknames, these men were anomalous in the frequency with which they witnessed; but, in all, thirty or more other named witnesses appear to be rustics.[80] This is a truly insignificant fraction of the total number of witnesses named; but these witnesses are not set off in any way from the others in the lists in which they occur, nor are the charters in which they appear markedly early or late in date. It does not seem, therefore, that the use of peasants as witnesses was rejected or first accepted during the course of the century.

For other reasons, too, a prejudice against peasants as witnesses seems unlikely. First, at least most peasants in Normandy at this time were free, and there seem to be no legal distinctions connected with social status.[81] Moreover, at this time burgesses were no more than peasants who lived in a particular type of settlement, yet they witnessed quite often.[82] Second, the social difference between the monks' cook or baker or other menial servant and the monks' peasant was probably not very great—yet menial servants witnessed very often. The only difference between burgesses and menials on one hand and peasants on the other may have been the purely practical one that a church's own servants and the residents of its bourg were much more likely to be present to act as witnesses than were the peasants who lived scattered about the countryside. Third, many charters from throughout the century list as witnesses, by their first names only, men who were not members of the recipient church. It is true that family names or even personal second names were only coming into use in this period. More usually than not, however, and increasingly as the century progressed, persons of honorable status were identified by a toponymic or a patronymic or a nickname or a title such as "knight." Hence, at least toward the end of the century, some of the men who are cited as witnesses by first name only may have been peasants.[83] Because witness lists often seem to be drawn up in approximately descending order of importance, the usual placement of men with only one name at the ends of lists reinforces the possibility. To return to the point at issue, it therefore seems unlikely that the legal suitability of a witness depended on his class or occupational status.

Contemporaries themselves may have had no clear idea of what a "suitable" witness was or was not.[84] In post-Conquest England, however, the "legal" man was a man—any man of whatever sort or condition—"who had been law-abiding, . . . one who had a good reputation, . . . one who was not tainted with infamy."[85] In Normandy in the thirteenth century the distinctive factor may have been the last of these: any man who had incurred *infamia* by committing perjury was forever debarred from testifying in court and would therefore be useless as a witness to an act.[86] The same may have been true in the eleventh century; yet the text which originally posed the problem does not seem consonant with this explanation, for Osulf and Ansger were "the best," the least "obscure and not useful" of the assembled witnesses, not the only nonperjurors among them.[87] A charter recording a gift to Marmoutier's priory of Héauville might be interpreted to mean that "legal" witnesses were laymen, that is, men who could offer battle as proof, as clerics could not. The donor made his gift, both by investiture and by placement on the altar, in the abbey's chapter with two of its servants as witnesses for the abbey; then, in the presence of the same two men, he "confirmed that gift which he had made, outside in the parlor in the presence of lay witnesses. Those who were present are able to testify by legal proof to what was thus done, namely, Martin de la Chapelle" and four other laymen.[88] One charter, however, is a slight basis on which to build a conclusion; and, again, the description of Osulf and Ansger does not fit well with this hypothesis. The question of what made a man a "suitable" witness in eleventh-century Normandy seems, therefore, unanswerable, except negatively: neither the act witnesses observed nor their class was the determining factor.

Nearly one-quarter of the extant witness lists are subdivided into groups of party witnesses by such phrases as *ex parte eius*, *ex parte nostra*, *ex parte sancti*, and the like. The number and percentage of witness lists so divided varies greatly from church to church.[89] Usually, the division is into two groups, the alienor's witnesses and the recipient's. In a good many instances only one group, usually the recipient's, is explicitly identified as party witnesses,[90] yet even in many of these enough of the witnesses who are not said to be *ex parte* of the alienor are connected with the alienor to suggest that they do in fact constitute the alienor's party witnesses. Whether a charter identifies witnesses by their allegiance to one or the other of the parties to a transfer seems at least sometimes dependent upon scribal whim. The fashion spread, however. The number of abbeys whose charters include divided witness lists increased from one, possibly two, in the 1040s to twenty-seven by 1106; and the number of charters in which witness lists are divided increased steadily in the second half of the century.[91] This is true not only for all the charters as a group but for individual abbeys. In the first three decades of the existence of Saint-Martin de Sées, about one in ten of its witness lists was divided; in its fourth decade, about one in four.[92] At Saint-Wandrille the figures are even more striking: of thirteen certainly pre-1066 lists, none is divided; of sixteen certainly post-1066 lists, thirteen—over 80 percent—are. The increase in recording of party witnesses is, therefore, incontrovertible. Whether it reflects merely the generalization of a scribal practice or, more significant, a growing consciousness of the legitimacy and utility of party witnesses is moot.

It seems likely, however, that eleventh-century Normans recognized the bias of party witnesses and used them accordingly. A charter of Saint-Florent de Saumur concerning a court case says that the opponents "came . . . , each with men of his own party, to dispute about the matter."[93] When William the Conqueror conceded to Saint-Etienne de Caen various parcels of land which two abbots had bought from William son of Hardred, the charter lists seven party witnesses of the abbey, "all of whom heard the aforesaid William [son of Hardred] recognizing and acknowledging this," before it lists William's party witnesses.[94] The construction of this passage, if deliberate, implies that only the abbey's witnesses could be expected to testify to William's words in court and thereby defeat William's denial that he had made the sales. Moreover, the same persons sometimes served as both pledges and witnesses; and the role of pledges is sometimes portrayed as similar to that just suggested for Saint-Etienne's party witnesses, namely, to testify for one side in any court case emerging from the transaction.[95] That witnesses could serve the interests of one party to a suit, therefore, seems to have been recognized in eleventh-century Normandy and may be the legal concept underlying all the appearances in the charters of witnesses described as *ex parte*.[96]

Occasionally all the witnesses to a transfer are said to adhere to one of the parties, nearly always the recipient, or, of the groups of witnesses listed, none is said to belong to an alienor.[97] Such charters imply that it was not necessary for alienor as well as recipient to have party witnesses. The reason may have been practical: in the experience of churches, it was alienors and persons closely connected to them who raised unjust claims, not the churches themselves. The same pragmatism may lie behind the witness lists in which only the recipient's witnesses are singled out as party witnesses. Moreover, the charters show no attempt to list equal numbers of witnesses on behalf of different parties: the numbers in the groups seem, relative to each other, random. Party witnesses were clearly not a necessity—as, of course, the much more numerous charters in which witness lists are not divided also indicate. Occasional charters, however, include groups of witnesses who are said to belong to third parties. In court suits, it was common to list the judges as witnesses in addition to the witnesses on behalf of each of the disputing parties; sometimes they are said to be *ex parte* of the lord of the court.[98] In other charters, the alienor's son or brother or the archbishop or the duchess as patron of a nunnery has his or her own witnesses.[99] One charter lists witnesses for the alienor's brother and his lord only, and another separately lists the witnesses of the donor, his brother, his lord, and the recipient.[100] It is easy to understand why judges should be listed as witnesses, but the reason for the scattering of other witnesses for third parties is obscure. Nevertheless, such entries imply that party witnesses had a specific role to play.

Fairly often a list of witnesses is introduced by a phrase which says that they are "of both parties" or the like. The phrase suggests that those whose names follow were to testify on behalf of either party if a lawsuit developed. Occasionally the implication is very strong, as when a charter lists one witness as "from both parties" and then gives separate lists of the donor's and the recipient's witnesses.[101] More charters, however, state or imply that some of the witnesses whose names follow the phrase were one party's witnesses and some were the other's. Thus, for example, a charter for Mont-Saint-Michel says that a confirmation occurred "in the presence of the Lord Abbot Rannulf of the same place and a cohort of monks and also of many laymen of both parties," but the witness list divides the laymen into two parties.[102] The phrase "from both parties" is, therefore, wholly ambiguous when it occurs without additional information.[103]

Even though the presence of some witnesses at the ceremony was a practical necessity, most witnesses do not seem to have been present because their participation as particular individuals was needed to render the transfer secure. Some witnesses evidently were present merely by chance, such as the men "who were in captivity in my house" who witnessed on an alienor's behalf.[104] Nonetheless, in the lists of witnesses *ex parte* of certain churches the same laymen recur remarkably often. Robert du Cotentin witnessed thirty-seven alienations to Saint-Martin de Sées; of those dated to a particular year, the earliest is from 1088 and the latest from 1111.[105] He witnessed between 22 and 32 percent of the extant transfers to the abbey during his period as a witness.[106] In all seventeen witness lists divided by party in which he appears, he was a witness for the abbey. During roughly the same period, and sometimes within even narrower limits, Richard the cook witnessed at least thirty-one charters of this abbey;[107] Herbert the cook, Martin the baker and Witman the cook each witnessed twenty-two,[108] Ralph the marshal nineteen, Roger d'Evreux eighteen, Roscetus at least seventeen,[109] Papilio the cook between sixteen and twenty,[110] Gerard the baker and Gunfrid the winnower each sixteen, Ansger de *Rufaldeio* fifteen,[111] Hilgerius fourteen, Rainald the baker thirteen, Tedulf the mason and Danfront each twelve. Evanus the baker witnessed thirteen; however, because Evanus is a rare name, he may, under other sobriquets, have witnessed as many as another dozen alienations.[112] In divided witness lists, these men always occur—often together—*ex parte* of the abbey. That such men were virtually professional witnesses is very likely. The possibility of such witnesses has already arisen in connection with sales to the two abbeys at Caen.[113] Signs of their use are also found in connection with other abbeys without a particular link with sales or, indeed, with unusually precarious transactions of any kind. Richard the seneschal, Bernard the cook, and Osbern Bruncosted at La Trinité du Mont,[114] Odo the cook, Humphrey the porter and Hervé the mason at Saint-Evroul, Achard the tailor at Troarn, and so on all witnessed, *ex parte* of their abbeys when the witness lists are divided, a high proportion of their abbeys' charters.

One would think that men who witnessed so often were called upon to do so because they had especially good memories or because they were especially trustworthy and therefore were thought likely to be reliable party witnesses if suits arose, or even because they were doughty fighters who would make good champions. There is not even the faintest hint of such reasoning, however. One characteristic many of these men share indicates another possible reason for their frequent appearance: those of them who are identified by occupation are almost always agents or servants of the recipient church, and such frequent witnesses are identified by occupation much more often than is the norm. The extent to which cooks witnessed is startling: of about 1,100 extant witness lists,[115] 153 name at least one cook; often more than one appears. Moreover, one or more bakers are named as witnesses sixty-two times. It hardly seems likely that any skill characteristic of the occupations of cook and baker rendered the men pursuing them especially suitable as witnesses. The explanation may be simply that bakers and cooks were laymen who were always present at an abbey. One charter implies that such men were often used as agents: Richard de Méré promised Marmoutier "that wherever in the whole of Normandy we should have need of his aid or service he would be of aid to us like one of our servitors from our kitchen."[116] Great laymen's cooks could be men of some property,[117] but nothing is known of the standing of these monastic cooks and bakers who so often served as witnesses. Seneschals, marshals, masons, porters, tailors, and the like may not always have been present; but, because they supplied goods or services to abbeys, they would have to visit more often than the average layman of the period. Therefore, if any abbey wished to augment the number of witnesses to an alienation, or the number of its party witnesses, with men who were not themselves members of the recipient church, the persons available would normally be cooks and bakers in the first place and then whoever happened to be visiting the abbey, including its agents and suppliers.[118]

This explanation implies that a long list of witnesses was in some way advantageous. Logically it should have been, both because more witnesses would mean more testifiers to the truth, more defense witnesses, or more potential champions in any eventual court case and because the more witnesses there were originally the longer at least one of them might survive to testify. Some extant charters have very long witness lists: one from Bernay has 116 witnesses, and lists enumerating 30 or more are not uncommon.[119] On balance, however, the evidence does not point to any special concern for long witness lists. No phrase indicates such a concern. The average length of witness lists varies markedly from church to church.[120] Even original charters sometimes cut short a witness list with a phrase like "and many others."[121]

When witness lists are divided, no attempt was made to make the groups equal in size or to make the church's group always larger—or to follow any other discernible rule about relative size. Moreover, there seems to be no regular correlation between the importance of a transaction and the number of witnesses to it, although in particular cases such a relationship is likely. This evidence, though largely negative, indicates that eleventh-century Normans felt no great urgency about large numbers of witnesses.

SIGNERS

Many charters end with signatures. Extant originals usually end in a sea of crosses, each labeled with the name of the person who made it. These signatures are sometimes autograph—the crosses of lay persons, both crosses and names of clerics—but sometimes not.[122] Charters which survive only in cartularies or in late copies less often include signatures, probably because the copyists did not trouble to reproduce them. Moreover, many copies, instead of redrawing the signatures, simply list the names of those who signed. The difference between actual signatures and lists of signers may, therefore, be disregarded as immaterial; I shall refer to a group of signatures in either form as a signature list. It is also likely that if the originals of all the charters were extant the percentage of charters with signatures would be considerably higher.[123]

In contrast to most modes of assurance, the purpose of signatures is often explained in some detail: more than a quarter of the extant lists are introduced by statements that persons who sign charters render alienations secure. Though they vary in wording from church to church and even from charter to charter of the same church, these clauses are remarkably similar in what they say and very often in how they say it. The same words recur again and again in slightly different combinations. Herbert son of Geoffrey, for example, made a series of gifts to Troarn with William the Conqueror's consent, "all of which I wished to be written down together in this charter and, according to the custom (*secundum consuetudinem*), to be made firm by the authority of the aforesaid king and to be strengthened by the subscription of my lords and other faithful men, so that by this our donation of the aforesaid things should be stable and settled, and safe from and undisturbed by the assault of faithless men." The signatures of the king, the queen, and others follow.[124] All the ideas about assurance which are commonplace in explanatory clauses introducing signatures are here; the special interest of this particular exemplar is that it alone asserts that signing charters for these purposes was custom.

Clauses which explain why charters were signed seem to have been inherited or adopted from Carolingian diplomatic practice.[125] This may explain two facets of the frequency of their use: they introduce signature lists in which the duke appears much more often than lists in which he does not, and they are most common in the charters of four of the five oldest abbeys of Normandy.[126] The second pattern may be attributed to the generally more formal scribal style of these abbeys, which seem to have clung to Carolingian phrases.[127] The first, however, is more likely to be related to the reason why the duke signed so many charters, which will be discussed later.[128]

Signatures are generally recognized as the essential element in the validation of charters, that is, they authenticated the account related in the charter; but scholarly discussions of this matter rarely consider why this was thought to be so or whether signatures had a value in and of themselves.[129] The act of making one's cross seems to have been the essence of the matter, and it served not only to validate the charter but also to confirm the transactions recorded in it. Most explanatory clauses, like the one quoted above, make some reference to the act of writing as the source of the assurance; and many phrases which introduce signatures without alluding to their purpose do the same. Moreover, in some—though relatively few—charters all or some of the crosses are identified not merely by the signer's name but by a sentence saying that he or she confirms: William the Conqueror's signature to Herbert son of Geoffrey's charter, for example, where, as is usual, the sentence is in the first person and, as is nearly as common, it alludes to the *signum* as an expression of consent.[130] Other charters allude in other ways to signatures as expressions of consent. Two of these are especially revealing. In 1047 Hugh bishop of Bayeux disseised Saint-Pierre de Préaux of certain lands and was persuaded to return them only by a large countergift, "which money [having been] received, he affirmed the charter by episcopal authority, as the present subscription demonstrates."[131] His signature follows immediately. The second charter illustrates how firmly a signature was thought to "demonstrate" consent. Mainus d'*Albinnei* and his wife made a gift to Mont-Saint-Michel. Their charter bears nine crosses, including those of both donors and their son Robert. The last cross is identified thus: "The sign which Mainus + made in the person of his son Ralph who was absent but nevertheless conceded this gift."[132] Whether Ralph had at some time stated his consent or it was merely his father's pious wish that he would, he was obviously not present when the charter was drawn up and signed; yet the father thought that by signing for his son he could commit him not to challenge the gift.

It seems, therefore, that signatures in and of themselves committed signers to abide by the terms of charters. At Saint-Pierre de Préaux and La Trinité du Mont, and probably elsewhere, one form of the act of donation was the public signing of a charter.[133] That might imply that the principal function of signing was that it was another public act by which alienors and potential challengers might, in the presence of witnesses, express their consent to transfers. A few charters from other churches indicate that this may have been a subsidiary purpose,[134] but it does not seem to have been the principal one. Certainly no witness saw Ralph son of Mainus sign the charter recording his parents' gifts because he did not, yet "his" signature was thought to commit him. Moreover, it is Bishop Hugh's signature, not his act of signing, which demonstrates his consent; and what that charter says simply renders explicit the implication of statements about signatures in many other charters. A signature, in other words, appears in and of itself to have bound the signer to accept the transfer, regardless of whether anyone had seen the signer sign. It is possible that when charters were used as proof in lawsuits, as they were,[135] it was this intrinsic value of the signatures to them which gave them force as proof. No narrative of a suit says so, however.

The types of persons who signed reinforce the impression, unfortunately dependent on so very few charters, that signatures had an intrinsic value independent of the ceremony of signing, especially when those who signed are compared with those who witnessed. Thus, given the function of witnesses, it is not surprising that few alienors are listed as witnesses; indeed, it is anomalous that any are. Concomitantly, whatever the function of signatures, the signature lists of charters could be expected to include the alienors; and those which do not are rare. The relatives and lords of alienors and the lords' relatives often acted as witnesses. They signed charters at least as often. This, again, is to be expected whether signing was primarily a ceremony to be witnessed or an assurance in itself. Members of the recipient church, however, although they often witnessed, hardly ever signed. Ten of thirty-three signature lists from Saint-Ouen include the abbot among the signatories; two probably also include monks of the abbey.[136] From all of the other Norman churches, however, only seven or eight extant signature lists, at most, include the bishop of the recipient cathedral or the abbot of the recipient monastery.[137] Moreover, with the exception of Saint-Ouen and of La Trinité du Mont, a special case which will have to be considered separately, only two charters are signed by any lesser members of a recipient church.[138] These figures are the more remarkable because bishops and abbots so often signed charters benefiting churches other than their own. More than one-third of the signature lists from Norman churches include at least one bishop; a tenth include at least one abbot. Often a list includes several or even nearly all of the bishops and abbots of Normandy, especially the bishops.[139] Apparently, eleventh-century Normans saw little point in having members of a recipient church sign its charters. The reason cannot have been that their party bias made their signatures valueless, for as witnesses they had exactly the same bias yet played a large role. The explanation may, therefore, be that signatures were dispositive, that is, that they indicated or implied the conveyance of property or rights.

The same point may explain why so few signature lists are divided into *ex parte* groups. Five at most—excluding, again, those of La Trinité du Mont—are so divided, as compared to nearly one-quarter of the witness lists; and all five possible examples are dubious.[140] *Ex parte* witnesses might include not only an alienor's relatives and lords or the members of a recipient church but also third parties on behalf of either of the parties; if signatures were dispositive, however, a church's lay vassals, servants, or friends would do it little good by signing because they were not conveying property to the church.

Indeed, third parties who witnessed contrast markedly with third parties who signed. Briefly, signers were of very much higher status. This is difficult to prove directly, as it is hard to assign status in eleventh-century Normandy in any way on which calculations could be based.[141] There is, however, abundant negative evidence. Excluding the charters of La Trinité du Mont, only two of the remaining signature lists include a cook, as compared to 142 witness lists (excluding, to make the comparison more just, those of La Trinité du Mont) which include at least one cook. These two charters are not even from Norman abbeys, but from Coulombs, where a baker also signs, and from Marmoutier's priory of Croth, in Normandy, where a tailor also signs.[142] That is all: two cooks, one baker, one tailor. There is not one identifiable rustic and no other identifiable menial. Admittedly, more witness lists than signature lists are extant; but the comparison with witness lists is, nonetheless, striking, at least as far as menials are concerned. Moreover, only one signer is identifiable as a burgess, a potter; and because he signed a charter which has to do partly with the street of potters of Rouen, he may not be genuinely a third party.[143] Again, the contrast with witness lists is great. Very few provosts and chamberlains and other such officials signed, although they abound in witness lists. There are not even very many men identified simply as priests or clerics although, again, they are numerous as witnesses. Somewhat more positive evidence is provided by women. Except for the duchesses, women witnessed very rarely. The same rule applies to signatures, with one notable exception, namely, female alienors and confirmers and the female relatives of male alienors and confirmers, who signed quite often.[144] The likely explanation of this pattern is that, because women had virtually no legal capacity, they could play no role in proving that a transfer had taken place or in enforcing compliance with the terms of a transfer and, therefore, were useless as witnesses. If such were the function of signatures, therefore, they should be equally rare as signers. Women who were or were related to alienors and confirmers were renouncing rights, however. That they often signed suggests that their signatures would be useful in committing them to their renunciations; and that, in turn, implies that signatures conveyed rights.

To find a group of quasi-professional signers analogous to the quasi-professional witnesses prevalent in the charters of some churches, one must look to the other end of the social scale, to the duke and his relatives first, then to the bishops and abbots, whose frequent appearance as signers has already been noted, and then to the great magnates of Normandy. Whereas men of little importance witnessed much more often than they signed, the important men signed much more often than they witnessed. Duke William witnessed 49 charters; he signed 160 in which he was not a donor.[145] In fact, nearly three-fifths of the extant signature lists include the duke in some capacity. Introductory clauses of lists often refer explicitly to getting the duke—and usually also the magnates—to sign. In a charter written in the duke's name, also, the clause usually refers not only to his signature but to those of his magnates. Like the duke, the greatest magnates signed large numbers of charters about transfers in which they were not directly concerned.[146]

Although the duke, the bishops, the abbots, and the magnates were all great lords, it seems unlikely that their signatures appear so often because—or only because—they were the direct or superior lords of the actual alienors and, therefore, could and did dispose of certain ultimate rights by signing. This is especially true of the many charters which appear to have been signed wholesale by everyone in attendance at one of the duke's solemn courts. Instead, signatures of this type reflect a feeling, explicit or implicit in the language of most of the clauses which introduce signatures, that every additional signature on a charter made the alienation firmer, more secure, less subject to attack.[147] Eleventh-century Normans seem to have felt that third parties who signed thus became associated in the alienation, even though they may have had no specific rights of which to dispose and that, if one could secure the adhesion of all important persons to a charter, no challenge to the transfers recorded could possibly succeed. Why this was so is obscure. It might have been because all the potential judges of a lawsuit about the property would be committed in advance to support the recipient's side[148] or because all the great lords who might support their tenants' challenges would be committed in advance not to do so; but no charter gives cause to suspect either of these or any other reason.

To sign a charter was apparently an act of some finality, not to be undertaken lightly. When Lonlay challenged a gift which William de Briouze had made to Saint-Florent de Saumur, William the Conqueror "at first did not wish to concede that gift to the monks of Saint-Florent and to authorize their charter, until it could be decided in his court whether the abbot and monks of Lonlay had a just complaint." After his court, sitting at Caen, had decided in Saint-Florent's favor, "when the king heard this he asked for the charter and said he would authorize it with his sign." Oddly, the account continues, "Because the monk Albaldus of Saint-Florent, who was there, did not have that [charter] with him, he hurried back to Briouze, took the charter and found the king, already returning from Caen, at Boscherville. When he offered the charter to him, the king signed it and the queen and their sons."[149] One would have expected Albaldus to have the charter with him in expectation that the king would agree to sign as soon as the case was decided.

Certainly, many charters were presented to various important persons long after they had been drawn up, so that these persons might sign.[150] Moreover, many pancarts seem to have been drawn up so that important persons might, by signing, express their consent to all the transfers made to a church over the course of time. In both situations, the signer is usually the duke, although others may sign with him. To sign a charter after it had initially been drawn up was undoubtedly one way of expressing consent to the alienation the charter recorded, whether it was the consent of a lord or a relative with a potential claim to surrender or the consent of an important personage whose signature added weight to the charter.

In much of my discussion of signers I have excepted the charters of La Trinité du Mont. They are indeed exceptional. In the first place, all the known eleventh-century charters of the abbey survive in a late eleventh-century cartulary whose scribe was careful to copy what are apparently all the signatures to every charter which had any: only eight of the ninety-seven charters in the cartulary are not followed by at least one signature.[151] This goes against the usual practice of cartulary scribes. Second, eleven of the eighty-nine signature lists are divided *ex parte*. This is more than twice the maximum for all other extant Norman charters; indeed, they may be the only divided signature lists.[152] Third, La Trinité du Mont's signature lists often include menials, many more than signed all other extant charters.[153] The explanation for these unusual features is, I think, that La Trinité du Mont—or the scribe of the cartulary—made no distinction between witnesses and signers. Eight signature lists call the persons who sign "witnesses" (*testes*). Even more charters take one of two forms: either the signature list is divided *ex parte* or there are signers plus witnesses, all the witnesses being *ex parte* of the abbey. The latter type of charter again suggests the inutility of signatures *ex parte* of the recipient. What makes both forms significant, however, is that, although many individuals are found sometimes in the abbey's group of signers and sometimes in the witness groups, with a single exception they are never found among an alienor's signers or among the signers of a charter which also has witnesses.[154] In other words, the *scriptorium* of the abbey seems to have called these men—several of them agents and menials who witnessed or signed often—by either term indiscriminately although they correspond to the men who at other abbeys functioned as quasi-professional *ex parte* witnesses.

The identification of signers as *testes* is not peculiar to La Trinité du Mont, but only there does it seem certain that the verbal identification represented a real one. At other churches the identification is much less consistent and may have been purely verbal. In addition to charters which simply call signers "witnesses," a few say explicitly that the witnesses signed, for example, one from Mont-Saint-Michel, which introduces the signature list thus: "The witnesses of this donation are those who marked the sign of the cross below."[155] The relative percentages of charters which are witnessed and charters which are signed vary widely among different churches,[156] and some churches appear to have regarded witnesses and signers as alternative means of guaranteeing the security of transfers. From Saint-Evroul, for example, fifty-one extant charters contain witness lists and eight contain signature lists, but only two contain both. This might imply that "witnesses" and signers were synonymous or, at least, functionally similar. Students of diplomatic in France in this period usually maintain that the witnesses to an act signed the charter which was drawn up to record the transfer symbolized by the act and that witness lists are simply degenerate signature lists.[157] In Normandy, however, signers and witnesses seem usually to have been different persons playing different roles. They were drawn primarily from different social groups. One charter says explicitly that only some of the witnesses signed.[158] More generally, the number of charters which end with two lists, one of witnesses and one of signers, is considerably higher than the number of charters which call signers "witnesses"; and, both in these charters and in those in which the witnesses are named in the body of the charter, the overlap between witnesses and signers is, with occasional exceptions, markedly low.[159] On balance, therefore, and except in the case of La Trinité du Mont, it seems likely that in eleventh-century Normandy witnesses and signers were not identical in function and were only sometimes, and then incidentally, identical in person.

PLEDGES

Relatively few charters mention pledges: I have counted only thirty-eight, which contain in all forty-one sets of pledges.[160] In addition, a rule about pledges was included in the *Consuetudines et Iusticie* of 1091.[161] In view of the usual terseness of the sources, these few references provide more information than might be expected. The use of pledges seems to have been widespread. Thirteen of the charters about them come from Saint-Martin de Sées, sixteen from Saint-Etienne de Caen; but the nine others come from seven other Norman churches plus Marmoutier and Saint-Florent de Saumur. Pledges seem to have become an increasingly common device as the century progressed: the earliest charter to mention them dates from just about midcentury, but most date from late in the century.[162] The number of pledges is never particularly large: the range is from one to seven or nine, and the average is 2.9 or 3.2.[163] The persons whom I call "pledges" were usually denominated *fidejussores* or *plegii*; no discernible difference is reflected in the use of different terms.[164]

Pledges were certainly an assurance device, as their contexts show. Ten of the transactions in which Saint-Etienne de Caen used pledges were sales, and all six others involved outstanding obligations. Eight of those in which Saint-Martin de Sées used pledges were sales, and three of the other five involved some as yet unfulfilled duty.[165] The same is true of transactions of other churches in which pledges were used: they are sales or mortgages or complex tenurial arrangements, or they include promises to warrant if the need should arise or to get the consent of an absent relative. One is the only known exchange with a provision for how either party may withdraw from the exchange; another is a quitclaim by a man who had challenged Jumièges's right to land which his father, too, had unjustly held and then quitclaimed.[166] With two exceptions from Saint-Martin de Sées, none is a simple alienation which posed no evident future dangers. Although by no means all potentially precarious transactions were accompanied by pledges—or at least the charters do not say that they were—it is fair to say that pledges are nearly always found in conjunction with such transfers.

Only one charter says anything about how a person became a pledge. When Rannulf de *Marcemaison* partly sold and partly gave his rights in the church of that vill to Saint-Martin de Sées, one of his party witnesses was "Turstin the man of William d'*Alneto*, who was sent on behalf of his lord, in whose fee the same church was, saying and affirming that his aforesaid lord, namely William, conceded this whole agreement. . . . At another time, however, the aforesaid William d'*Alneto* was a pledge of the aforesaid agreements and of this agreement in the presence of Abbot Ralph, the witnesses being" four men.[167]

As these four apparently saw William become a pledge, there must, at least this once, have been some ceremony by which a person became a pledge. Perhaps it was the ceremony of giving faith, which is mentioned occasionally in connection with pledges, although in two of the three instances it was the principals rather than the pledges who gave their faith.[168]

Pledges identified by more than their names were sometimes members of their principal's family: son, brother, brother-in-law, cousin, in one case the alienor's mother and brother and sisters.[169] In the one bilateral exchange of pledges, each party's pledges were his men; but in all other instances of a tenurial relationship the pledges were their principals' lords.[170] One man's cousin was a "conceder" as well as a pledge; a second pledge also consented; and a third, a lord, consented as well as acting as a "defender and pledge."[171] In two instances, relatives who were pledges also signed the charters.[172] It can, in short, be taken as given that anyone who was in a position to challenge a transfer but who acted as a pledge was considered to have consented to the alienation.

There was more to being a pledge than this, however. Not only were the transactions to which pledges are named characterized by future obligations or unusually likely to be challenged, but charters often say that the pledges were to see to the performance of outstanding duties or to prevent claims to the lands whose transfer they note. The most detailed description of how pledges were supposed to do this occurs at the end of the agreement between Viscount Rannulf and the bishop of Bayeux:

> Therefore Rannulf gave his men—William de Semilly, Herbert son of Gonduin, Hugh de Rosel, Rannulf son of Alan, Neil son of Serlo—as defenders of this agreement and hostages (*hujus conventionis assertores et obsides*) pacifying the bishop by their faith, on Rannulf's order, that they should maintain Rannulf in the aforesaid fealty toward the bishop as much as they are able by their prayers and counsel. If, however, they are not able, they will stand forth as witnesses of the truth for the bishop against Rannulf. Similarly, the bishop gave these men of his—Samson son of William Oger, Helto, Adelold the chamberlain, Robert de Sully—to Rannulf as hostages (*obsides*) promising Rannulf by faith, on the bishop's order, that they will keep the bishop in the aforesaid friendship with Rannulf as much as they are able. If, however, they are not able, they will give testimony about the truth for Rannulf against the bishop.[173]

Each group of pledges is to try as hard as possible to persuade its principal not to raise problems and, if unsuccessful, to serve as witnesses against the principal on behalf of the other party. In his study of pledges in the twelfth century, Jean Yver distinguishes between the "hostage-pledge" and the "influential pledge." The latter was a person of importance who was to exert his influence over his principal—who might well be his vassal—to get the principal to adhere to the compact. Hostage-pledges were less important persons, often their principal's men, who were obliged to surrender to imprisonment by the other party if their principal did not live up to his agreement. The principal "would be morally constrained to free them" by performing his obligations.[174] The first example which Yver cites to demonstrate the nature of the hostage-pledge is this charter.[175] In fact, however, these pledges, though called "hostages" and the "men" of their principals, perform the functions Yver attributes to the influential pledges; and there is no reference in the eleventh century to the imprisonment of pledges, although the treaty of Dover of 1101, between King Henry I of England and Count Robert II of Flanders, describes it.[176] A charter which describes pledges as though they were warrantors, saying that the pledges were to "acquit" the alienations, also implies that eleventh-century pledges were bound to exert pressure on their principals and, if necessary, to testify against them, rather than to surrender to imprisonment, for warrantors sometimes served in this fashion.[177]

The agreement between Viscount Rannulf and the bishop is very much like a treaty between equals: although Rannulf was the bishop's man and did him homage as well as fealty, the promises which lord and man made to each other were virtually identical.[178] Three treaties provide the only analogies as far as pledges are concerned. By the treaty of Dover, Henry I and Robert II each named pledges, twelve on the count's part, eleven on the king's. If the agreement was broken, each set of pledges was given a third of a year in which to try to reconcile their principal to the other party. If their efforts failed, each pledge was to pay the other party one hundred marks or surrender for imprisonment.[179] Strictly speaking, however, this treaty involves no Norman. The other two are, therefore, somewhat more obviously relevant, although no account of either calls the guarantors "pledges."[180] The Anglo-Saxon Chronicle reports that "twelve men of the highest rank on both sides confirmed with an oath" the treaty made in England in 1101 between Henry I and Robert Curthose,[181] but nothing is said there or elsewhere about the enforcement of this treaty. More is known of the similar pact made in Normandy ten years earlier between Curthose and King William Rufus. According to William of Malmesbury, it "was sworn and was confirmed by the oath of the men of both." The Chronicle is more specific: "Twelve of the best men on the king's side and twelve on the duke's swore to this agreement, though it lasted only a little while after." Because the agreement did not last, continues the Chronicle for 1094, the king went to Normandy and he and his brother "came together with the same men who had made that settlement, and also had sworn the oaths, and they blamed all the breach upon the king, but he would not assent to it, nor further keep the agreement."[182] Here, therefore, the pledges acted as impartial judges as to which party had broken the agreement, rather than as party witnesses against their principals.

Only in these treaties and the agreement between Viscount Rannulf and the bishop of Bayeux did both parties present pledges. In all other cases, it was the lay party to a transaction with a church, alone, who did so.[183] Rannulf's agreement with the bishop is also the only charter which explicitly makes the role of pledges encompass the duty to remonstrate with their principal and the duty to testify against their principal if remonstrance failed. The odd locutions of two other charters may, however, be allusions to the same function. One lists four "witnesses and pledges of the performance of the whole agreement" and seven "witnesses from the men of Saint-Martin" de Sées.[184] Although this might allude to a division into witnesses for the two parties, another distinction may be meant, one between the abbey's men, who are simple witnesses, and the alienor's friends or men, who not only may be called upon to witness for the abbey but also are expected to use their best efforts to prevent the need for testimony from arising. The second is a complex agreement whereby, among other things, Lancelin d'Airan made a post-obit gift of tithes to Troarn and his lord William d'Angerville transferred to the abbey the service Lancelin owed him from the church of Airan; the lord and his son, says Lancelin, "are pledges and witnesses and maintainers of this agreement . . . and Wascelin my cousin is a conceder and pledge and a witness on my behalf, and [there were] many others."[185] In this arrangement among three parties, Wascelin may have been Lancelin's pledge vis-à-vis the abbey but his witness vis-à-vis his lord: if Lancelin should refuse to abide by the agreement, Wascelin would try to persuade him to change his mind and, if necessary, act as a witness against him; but if William should refuse, Wascelin would be a simple witness for Lancelin and the abbey. The "many others" whose names and status are not recorded may have been the abbey's witnesses against both William and Lancelin. In short, I am suggesting that a pledge was a special sort of witness, one who had a duty to attempt to prevent a dispute from ever coming into court by reasoning with or applying pressure on his principal. As a last resort if these attempts failed, the pledge would be obligated to act in court against his principal like any other witness for the other party to the agreement.[186] If this was indeed the difference between a pledge and an ordinary witness, it will explain most of the other thirty-seven charters in which there are lists both of pledges and of witnesses, in only two of which are the groups identical.[187] It should be noted, however, that the fact that most sets of lists are not identical might otherwise be taken to imply that pledges and witnesses had separate functions. Moreover, eight charters are difficult to reconcile with my suggestion, for in them some or all of the pledges are also listed as witnesses *ex parte* of the alienors,[188] whereas logically they ought to be among the recipient's party witnesses.

Two charters mention pledges who had a different obligation, namely, to pay money if their principals defaulted on the agreements. Vitalis, a cleric, mortgaged his part of the church of *Marcemaison* to Saint-Martin de Sées for fifteen years for twenty shillings of Le Mans and named four or five men as "pledges in such a way that, if the aforesaid Vitalis shall not have held to this agreement, each pledge will pay the monks twenty shillings of Le Mans."[189] Wascelin, a monk of Saint-Florent de Saumur who was that abbey's overseer of the gifts it had received from William de Briouze,

> gave back to Roger Carpitus the church of Sevrai at Ecouché . . . on agreement that Roger should do him right about everything which he [Roger] had forfeited against him [Wascelin]. And he [Roger] gave in pledge the church and whatever he had held from him [Wascelin], and the pledges were Archdeacon Guy and his nephew Osmelinus: if he [Roger] cannot complete the rectification, they should pay whatever he may have had from the church in the meantime.[190]

What were these payments? They might be, in effect, fines for failure in the pledges' primary duty to control their principals' actions and compensations to the injured parties for the trouble caused by the nonperformance of the agreements, that is, payments which left the principals still obligated. They might, instead, be substitute payments, clearing the principals of their obligations under the agreements but perhaps obligating them to reimburse their pledges.[191]

Both charters are ambiguous. The pledges to Saint-Florent are responsible for compensating the abbey if its trust in Roger turns out to have been misplaced because he rather than the monks will have been collecting the revenues from the church during the period allotted for him to rectify whatever he had done wrong. It may be that the pledges would have to pay only if Roger refused to return the proceeds himself; but it is also possible that the fine assessed on the pledges would be set at whatever figure Roger's illicit profits might attain. In the charter from Saint-Martin de Sées, if the amount to be assessed against the pledges were not the same as the amount of the mortgage, the pledges' payments would clearly be a fine; but the actual identity of the figures does not permit the opposite inference, that their payments would terminate the mortgage, for it might be symbolic or even merely accidental. Neither charter specifies whether the pledges were bound individually or collectively, that is, whether the entire group was to club together to pay the amount or, instead, any one pledge could be asked to pay the full sum. The charter from Sées certainly sounds as though the abbey could collect the full sum not merely from any one pledge but from each of them. If that was indeed the case, if this is not simply an instance of poor drafting of a charter, the pledges' payments would obviously have to be considered fines.[192]

In any case, that the pledges could expect to have to pay if their principals misbehaved would be a strong incentive for them to exert themselves to keep their principals to their agreements. Because one of the pledges in the charter from Saint-Florent is also among the witnesses to that charter, it is possible that pledges who had to pay were expected to testify against their principals, if necessary, as one of their methods of coercing them. It would seem unrealistic, however, to expect pledges to act as witnesses in court when they would thereby prove not only their principals' defaults but also their own liability for monetary losses. The inference that all pledges might have to pay seems even more dubious. The reason most of the charters are silent on this subject might be the bad habits of most scribes, or, perhaps, the principle was so well known that the mere word "pledge" sufficed to cover it. Neither explanation seems likely, however. Only the charter from Saint-Martin de Sées specifies an amount, yet one would expect more than one statement of how much pledges might have to pay if the prospect of payment actually existed in thirty-odd instances. This is especially so because most of the charters which list pledges concern agreements in which the source and, even more, the exact amount of the financial loss to the party protected by pledges would be much harder to pinpoint than in those involving Vitalis and Roger Carpitus. If the pledges were indemnifying the churches for their losses, how much could they be called upon to pay? If they were being fined for their inability to control their principals, how much were the fines? Only if one assumes not only that the payments were fines but also that the fine which a pledge could be called upon to pay was a fixed amount, known to everyone, would one be able to hypothesize that all pledges might be called upon to pay money if their principals misbehaved. Such a hypothesis seems, in light of the evidence, too tenuous to be sustained. Therefore, it seems best to conclude merely that, though all pledges were expected to try to prevent their principals from breaking agreements or raising claims, if they failed they were obligated either to pay money to the injured party or to testify in court for that party.

About actual enforcement of pledges' duties the charters are silent. The only allusion in any eleventh-century Norman source to what might happen is a clause of the *Consuetudines et Iusticie*, which appears to concern pledges for debts rather than pledges to agreements about land. It provides that "no one in Normandy may disturb a merchant except for his own debt and except if he was a pledge."[193] This is quite cryptic but makes best sense if read "except for the merchant's own debt or if the merchant was a pledge."[194] On that reading, merchants must often have acted as pledges, perhaps not as often as they incurred debts but sufficiently frequently for the two roles to be coupled as legitimate reasons for actions against merchants. Whose pledges were they? Because merchants must have had comparatively large amounts of cash at their disposal, if payment was a usual duty of pledges whose principals misbehaved it might be that merchants were often asked to serve as pledges for transactions involving land. One wonders, however, what incentive they would have had to accede to such requests. Moreover, no pledge in a charter is ever identified as a merchant or even as a town dweller. Hence it seems likely that these merchants were pledges for commercial transactions rather than for transfers of immovable property. So little is known about mercantile law in eleventh-century Normandy or about debt in any context except mortgages that it seems impossible to deduce anything further about pledges from this injunction than that some sort of action—perhaps distraint, authorized or extrajudicial, perhaps a suit—could be used against some of them.[195]

Either of these methods might work to force a pledge who was obligated to pay money to fulfill the obligation. Logically, it would seem that distraint would be more effective against a pledge who was unwilling to testify against his principal than would a suit, though conceivably the witnesses who saw William d'*Alneto* become a pledge could have been brought to testify against him in an attempt to force him to testify against Rannulf de *Marcemaison*. Because the parties whose interests were protected in the charters which list pledges were, with the exception of Viscount Rannulf, churches or churchmen, they could presumably have used the threat of excommunication; and if pledges usually gave their faith it may be that they would ipso facto be excommunicate if they proved contumacious.[196] All this is conjectural, however.

It seems certain that a pledge's chief duty was to try to keep his principal from behaving badly and likely that pledges who failed were either to testify against their principals or to pay money to the churches whose interests they had been unable to protect, but there is no way of knowing how effective pledges were as a mode of assurance. Their relative rarity in charters suggests that they were not thought especially useful. Their association, when they do appear, with troublesome transactions indicates that they were considered effective. When the pledges to the treaty of 1091 were called upon three years later to hold William Rufus to the treaty, they were not able to do so; but high politics hardly makes a good test of ordinary law. References in the sources to disputes which came into court are usually brief and uninformative. Moreover, if pledges were effective, potential disputes would not come into court at all; and pledges who failed to prevent disputes and who, therefore, served as witnesses might well be called simply "witnesses" in the records of the suits. Finally, payments of money by pledges were not likely to be recorded in the kinds of documents produced in the eleventh century. For all these reasons, it is scarcely surprising that nothing is known of pledges who actually performed their obligations; but, for the same reason, the question of their effectiveness as assurance cannot be answered with confidence.

8

Consent

THE FORMS DISCUSSED in the two previous chapters were used to confirm particular alienations. Consent could also be given to large numbers of transfers at once: a man might, for example, be called upon to confirm all his ancestors' alienations to a church or a lord to confirm all his tenants'. Such confirmations constitute the entire subject of a good many charters: the duke, especially, often issued global confirmations. Usually charters recording confirmations of this type describe every transfer or list the possessions of the church as of the moment of the confirmation; they often give all the information available about the alienations of lesser individuals. The only type of confirmer who was apparently never called upon to give a general confirmation is—for logical reasons—the tenant of something given: by virtue of the reason why his or her consent was necessary, a tenant's consent could apply only in the particular. General confirmations of the previous gifts of one's ancestors or one's men apparently used the same ceremonies as alienations, just as confirmations of particular transactions did. Functionally, however, consent was different from alienation, of course, and it is now time to turn from form to purpose. This chapter is concerned with consent itself, regardless of the forms by which it was expressed.

Consent is a subject of constant interest to the charters, which often note the consent of the duke, bishops, lords, tenants, and relatives of all these, as well as relatives of the alienor. The principal question to be asked about the consent of all these persons is why it was secured. Was it legally necessary, that is, could a transfer not take place if consent was not obtained? If, for one or more of the categories of persons whose consent was often sought, it was not legally necessary, then why was it nonetheless worth securing? One fruitful source of information on this subject is occasions of refusal of consent. Refusals are rarely reported, both because the documents are charters—records of actual transactions rather than expressions of general legal principles or discussions of things which had not happened—and because it was hardly to the advantage of those who drew up the charters to record them. Nevertheless, consent could be withheld. Many accounts of lawsuits or mentions of disseisins in the charters imply as much, and an occasional charter explicitly mentions a denial of consent and sometimes even gives its legal grounds or consequences.

The most complete statement of the consequences of a refusal to consent comes from a charter for Saint-Etienne de Caen in which Hugh Paynel gave the abbey "by hereditary right in demesne . . . , absolved, free and quit," two thirds of the tithes of Fontenay-Paynel, except for the tithes from the lands of five men. "These," he says,

> I am not able to give in demesne because the aforesaid men held them from my father and now hold them from me in fee. Nevertheless, I concede them and give them to the same convent in such a way that whenever the abbot or the monks should give or do to these men anything in return for which they may recognize and hold them from St. Stephen and the abbot or concede them in demesne in any way at all, St. Stephen should have them free and quit, like the aforesaid [things which I gave], and so that the abbot or the monks or even my aforesaid men should never thence require [anything] of me or my brothers or heirs from the time when those men should wish to hold them from the saint or, as was said, to sell or give [them] entirely to him. And also [this grant is made] in such a way that those men should never have any prohibition or contradiction, open or secret, about this thing from me or my brothers or heirs.[1]

Without their consent, Hugh could not give those tithes which his men held in fee; apparently he could not even transfer lordship over the tithes. Although three of the five men concerned are among Hugh's party witnesses to the charter and one of these three signed the charter along with Hugh, the five apparently were unwilling to give their consent at that time. All Hugh could do, therefore, was to make a gift of all his rights over the tithes as of any future moment when his men might decide to make over the tithes to the abbey either absolutely—by giving or selling them—or by becoming the abbey's rather than Hugh's tenants for the tithes.

There are other indications that a tenant's consent was necessary. The point in Hugh Paynel's charter is made implicitly in another act from Saint-Etienne de Caen; it is made in reverse fashion by a charter which says that William de Sacquenville gave Jumièges a tithe "absolved of any claim, for he then held it in demesne."[2] Baudry d'Epréville gave Jumièges parts of the tithes of two vills, "except the land of two vavassors, Gilbert son of Walter and Gilbert son of Wascelin, who did not wish to concede it."[3] These charters indicate that a tenant who refused consent could block an alienation completely.[4] At least two other cases imply the same: in each a donor acquired by exchange with his tenant what he then gave away, apparently because he wished to give certain particular lands and the holder was not willing either to give them or even to be transferred to the recipient church as a tenant.[5]

In contrast, lords apparently could not block alienations simply by refusing consent.[6] One case seems contrary: when Benscelinus d'Ecos made a deathbed gift to Marmoutier's priory at Gisors of one of his men with the man's whole fief "if, however, his [Benscelinus'] lord Pain should concede him to us," the abbey hastened to get Pain's consent, which was given only after considerable deliberation.[7] Presumably, if Pain had refused, the transfer could not have been accomplished; but this may have been a special condition. A charter from Jumièges says that a lord gave his consent to a gift only after initially refusing but does not indicate whether his refusal had delayed the transfer.[8] Many charters, however, say that a lord gave consent only after—sometimes long after—the tenant had alienated property, and none of these furnishes any sign that lack of the lord's consent had inhibited transfer of the property.[9] Only one says that the lord had initially refused his consent: William the Conqueror, when first asked, refused to consent to a gift to Saint-Florent de Saumur because the abbey of Lonlay claimed already to have received the same gift.[10] The very circumstances make it clear that the gift had been made before William's consent was even requested. The same seems to have been true in many other instances of the consent of lords and possible in all of them. Furthermore, in a charter by which Richard de Méré, son of Humphrey de Bohun, confirmed all his father's gifts to Marmoutier, the monks noted that they "promised him that from the same day [forward] we would neither accept nor buy anything further in that land of his or of his father's, unless we first request his permission, nor would we even receive the inhabitants of the same land on our [land] except in the same way."[11] Stated as it is, this appears to be a special concession granted to Richard in return for his consent. If so, it implies that Marmoutier did not normally recognize a lord's right to prevent his tenants' gifts and sales or even to prevent his peasants from migrating elsewhere.

It seems equally clear that relatives could not block alienations by refusing consent.[12] Two charters say that an alienor's son had refused to consent to a transfer; but each transfer occurred before or despite the refusal, and each son eventually consented.[13] Orderic describes the beginning of one of the notable crises of Duke Robert Curthose's reign, in 1089 or 1090:

> Robert count of Meulan . . . approached the duke at Rouen, and haughtily demanded the tower of Ivry from him. The duke replied, "I gave a fair exchange to your father: the noble castle of Brionne for the tower of Ivry." The count said, "I do not concede the exchange; instead I wish to have what your father gave to my father. Otherwise, by St. Nicaise, I will cause you to regret it. At this the duke flew into a rage and ordered him to be seized and thrown into prison, giving Brionne to Robert son of Baldwin to guard.[14]

Robert of Meulan's father, Roger de Beaumont, who was still alive, had been holding Brionne instead of Ivry for several years although his son had not consented to the exchange. Again, as in the case of lords, there are many instances when a son's or other relative's consent occurred only after an alienation was made, none of which indicates that the delay in any way impeded the transfer. In one instance even the lack of consent of the person to whom the property alienated belonged by right did not prevent the transfer: Berengar Pontuinus sold tithes to Saint-Martin de Sées with the consent of his son and daughter and of his lord and the lord's wife and sons; "then, after a space of many years, Geoffrey son of the aforesaid Berengar's wife, to whom the aforesaid tithes pertained in inheritance, conceded [them] perpetually to St. Martin as his stepfather Berengar and his mother had sold them and all the aforesaid [persons] had conceded them."[15]

The evidence of individual cases, therefore, suggests that, though a tenant could prevent an alienation by refusing to consent, a lord or a relative could not.[16] Against that, however, must be placed the testimony of all the charters as a group: they report the consent of relatives and lords much more often than that of tenants; and many charters mention gifts of tenants' property without saying that the tenants had consented, whereas few mention a lord or a relative in any context without discussing his or her consent. When, for example, Benscelinus d'Ecos made gifts to Marmoutier, the abbey, concerned though it was to get the consent of his lord, showed no interest in the consent of the tenant whom Benscelinus gave with his fief to the abbey.[17] Despite the distinction drawn above, the clear impression left by the charters is that recipient churches were much more worried about the consent of relatives and tenurial superiors than about the consent of tenurial subordinates. This impression may, however, derive from an assumption by eleventh-century Normans that unless a tenant's refusal is mentioned the tenant can be presumed to have consented. Logically, moreover, if the consent of tenants was necessary, when a tenant refused consent there would be no reason to write a charter, for no transfer could take place. The instances cited above which mention tenants' refusals confirm this contention, for each tenant held only part of what the lord wished to give and the refusal is mentioned to explain why more was not given.[18] Had those tenants held all that the lords wished to give, there would have been no gifts.

Whether one was a relative, a lord, or a tenant, there seems to have been a feeling that in order to consent one had to be present or, at least, that consent given personally—preferably either at the moment of the alienation or, if later, at the recipient church—was worth more than consent given by proxy or at a distance. When, for example, Milo son of Osbern de Vesly challenged his father's deathbed gifts to Marmoutier, he did so "because he was in England when his father died, nor was he present for his father's gift"; the charter goes on to say that he had since come to the abbey and "conceded and authorized . . . what formerly he did not wish to concede."[19] A charter of Saint-Evroul cites the consent of the donor's brother "and all their relatives who were able to be present."[20] One from Saint-Martin de Sées notes that, when William de *Polleio* and his wife and son Robert came to the abbey, made a gift, and received in turn the right to be buried at the abbey or, for William, Robert, and another son, named William, to become monks there, "in fact the same agreement was [made] about William his son although he was overseas when the gift was made."[21] This sounds as though to extend such an agreement to an absent relative was unusual; and, in fact, Saint-Martin de Sées much more commonly held out the promise of such an extension to persons whose consent it desired as an inducement to consent, as did other churches.

Although presence was highly desirable, at times a potential confirmer's absence was unavoidable. Hence, various methods of consent by proxy might be used. Mainus d'*Albinnei* signed a charter on behalf of one of his sons.[22] William d'*Alneto* sent one of his men to give his consent to a gift and only later came to the abbey himself to become a pledge for the gift.[23] When a man named Hubert gave Saint-Martin de Sées tithes so that he could become a monk, his two sons consented; "and also, moreover, the same Hubert's daughter to whom he had given half of the aforesaid tithe as a dowry—but only until he should become a monk—gave and conceded [the gift], by the wish and order of her husband. The husband himself, an invalid, was not able to come, but in the presence of many he plainly stated that the tithe was given to him only until the aforesaid Hubert should become a monk."[24] The absence of the son-in-law was an obvious problem because he had an especially important admission to make; therefore, his public declaration from his sickbed is carefully noted.

The usual result of the absence of someone whose consent was considered desirable was a promise by the alienor or a confirmer to secure that person's consent. Thus, when Geoffrey de Vieux with his brother's consent gave land to Saint-Etienne de Caen, "the abbot gave them a hundred shillings on condition that, because Ralph son of Ralph Taisson had their land in [his] power, they would have him concede this agreement."[25] This is somewhat atypical, for the promise usually appears as a simple offer: when Geoffrey, again with his brother's consent, later sold more land to the abbey, "he agreed that he would have Ralph Taisson, from whom he held that land, concede these sales."[26] It was almost always a donor or seller who made such a promise; but it could be a confirmer, as when a gift to Saint-Martin de Sées was confirmed by two brothers who were the donor's lords and their sister, "to whom her father . . . had given them [the lands given] as dowry. She, indeed, conceded them to St. Martin so much that she even promised that, to whichever of her sons or daughters she might demise her dowry on her death, she would have [that child] concede the aforesaid land . . . absolved and quit . . . as she herself and her brother had done."[27] Twenty-eight promises to get someone else's consent are extant in charters from six Norman abbeys and two abbeys outside Normandy.[28] The practice can, therefore, be said to have been fairly widespread, although seven of the cases come from Saint-Martin de Sées and thirteen from Saint-Etienne de Caen. The importance attached to such promises is shown by two uncommon assurance techniques—pledges and warranty—which occur remarkably often in this context.[29] Such promises always concern relatives or lords. They may, therefore, indirectly suggest that the consent of tenants had to be secured in advance of a transfer. Much more obviously, they indicate that the consent of relatives and lords, even if not legally binding, was important. The question which remains to be considered is why that was so.

CONSENT OF RELATIVES

The persons most likely to challenge an alienation were an alienor's relatives. That this was why their consent was important can, unfortunately, be verified only by inference. No report of a relative's claim states the grounds of the challenge, except for one, already quoted, which cites merely a son's absence at the time of his father's gift.[30] Nor does any charter make a theoretical statement on the subject. Nevertheless, the assiduity with which recipient churches sought the consent of relatives demonstrates beyond doubt that their consent was highly desirable. Once in a while, the connection with potential claims is all but stated. The charters of Saint-Florent de Saumur, for example, show that, because Philip de Briouze had originally been reluctant to give consent to his father's gifts, he was asked to confirm them on three or four separate occasions between 1093 and his departure on the first crusade;[31] and there are a good many similar cases of repeated confirmations by one relative. Direct evidence also exists that potential claims were on the minds of both alienors and recipients. Many charters, in describing an alienation, say that it was made "without any claim of my heirs" or a similar phrase.[32] Moreover, when statements of the purpose of some mode of assurance single out particular categories of persons against whose potential claims the assurance is directed, these persons are nearly always "my relatives" or "my successors" or "my heirs." The same is true of many of the clauses anathematizing anyone who challenges an alienation.[33] Preventive actions against heirs might be extensive. When Lesceline dowager countess of Eu founded Saint-Pierre-sur-Dives,

> fearing lest, if she left the monastery which she had constructed in the hand of her sons, it might suffer a diminution of those things which she had ever given it (such is the cupidity of mortals!), profiting by wise counsel, she bought it back from them with money; and, lest they or their heirs should ever be able to claim anything in the possessions of this convent as theirs by hereditary right, she confirmed this same agreement in the presence of William duke of the Normans, afterwards king of the English, they also being present; and at the same time she subjugated that place to the domination of the same duke and his successors through a pastoral staff which she placed in his hand[34]

—all this although, from everything else known about the foundation of the abbey, little as that is, the sons cooperated fully and ungrudgingly with their mother.

A few charters attempt to prevent claims by saying that all an alienor's relatives gave their consent.[35] Only one names the relatives, and the list turns out to be short: the alienor's wife and son and his wife's father and two brothers.[36] In this instance, it is likely that all the relatives were actually present for the alienation: witnesses are said to have seen them give their consent. In the others, it is possible that they were not, that the alienor simply hoped to commit his relatives by stating that they had consented. Given the apparent importance of personal presence to the validity of consent, however, such a device was not likely to be effective, which may explain why the consent of all relatives is rarely alleged. The reason may be, however, that only the consent of near relatives was considered important.

Instead of saying "all relatives," most charters cite the names of the individuals who consented, even when there were considerable numbers of them. Philip de Briouze was joined in one or another of his confirmations of his father's gifts to Saint-Florent de Saumur not only by his father but by his wife, his son, and a cousin. Sons, wives, and brothers consented far more often than others, sons most of all. Relatives who confirmed only occasionally include, in descending order of frequency, mothers, daughters, uncles, husbands, brothers-in-law, fathers, sisters, nephews, cousins, sons-in-law, grandsons, daughters-in-law, fathers-in-law, sisters-in-law, aunts, stepsons, and stepfathers. In addition, a good many *nepotes* occur who may be either nephews or grandsons, as do quite a few "relatives" whose relationship is not specified and several "heirs," some of whom may be sons, plus in two cases an heir's brother. A niece and her husband and a wife's second husband each appear once as a confirmer.[37]

With certain explicable exceptions, the rule seems to be that closest relatives confirmed most often. Grandsons and nephews would be much higher in the list if it were possible in every case to tell which is meant by *nepos*: *nepotes* who cannot for certain be identified as one or the other are the most numerous confirmers except for sons, wives, and brothers. Fathers sometimes endowed their sons during their lifetimes, but they probably did so rarely enough or with small enough properties to explain why they confirmed their sons' alienations infrequently.[38] Husbands consented relatively rarely because relatively few alienations were made by women. Instead, gifts by wives were probably usually made in their husbands' names, the wives appearing either as co-donors or as mere confirmers.[39]

A wife had special rights over possessions which were her inheritance, her dowry, or her dower. In the case of inheritance or dowry, possessions brought into the marriage by the wife, her consent was probably desirable to the same extent and for the same reason as the consent of any heir to a transfer of patrimony; but only the occasional reference to a wife who gave her consent because the property was her inheritance or her dowry indicates so. Most references to dower, property of the husband which was intended to support the wife if she was widowed, take the same form. Two unusually detailed charters show that a man could alienate his wife's dower in the teeth of her refusal, but she could recover the land after his death if she had not consented to the transfer.[40] In later Norman law, dower might take one of two forms: "devised" dower consisted of particular pieces of property designated for the widow's support; "customary" dower was the wife's right to a fraction of the husband's possessions, normally one-third, but specific properties would be assigned only when the wife became a widow.[41] Only devised dowers are known from eleventh-century Normandy, for knowledge of dower comes almost entirely from charters recording wives' consent to their husbands' alienations from their dowers.[42] Many instances of wives' consent for which the charters give no explanation may, however, have been recorded precisely because no dowers had been devised in these marriages and, therefore, each wife, having become a widow, might challenge any transfer to which she had not already consented on the grounds that the property that had been alienated—or part of it—should be part of her dower. Daughters and sisters may appear as confirmers fairly often because they had comparable claims to dowries against their fathers or brothers. In fact, however, only one charter, just cited, concerns a claim by a widow or any other woman in her own right. Most recorded claimants were male relatives of alienors; and few even of these were, so far as is known, relatives by marriage claiming through their wives.[43]

It would seem that the more likely a person was to succeed the alienor, the more likely he or she was to challenge a transfer and, therefore, the more desirable it was to get his or her consent. When Havisa, mother of Audulf de *Braci*, gave tithes to Le Tréport, "her son Audulf conceded this, and, after the death of [his] father, Audulf's son Nuervo."[44] While Audulf was alive it apparently gave sufficient security for the abbey to have his consent as his mother's heir, but once he was dead his son became the immediate heir and his consent was therefore desirable. When Duke William was about to set off on the conquest of England, Marmoutier sent a monk to him to ask "that he would have those things which he himself had given us, or which he had conceded [to us] to have in the land of his power, confirmed by the authorization of his son Robert, because he should indeed already be old enough to give voluntary authorization."[45] The abbey evidently thought it wise to get Robert Curthose's consent before his father embarked on a very risky adventure. Even potential claimants who were not blood relatives were important in this context: each of two men gave his consent to a transaction because the alienor had made him heir to "the other half" of what was given to a church.[46]

One charter provides different evidence that the right to inherit, to succeed to the property, was what made a relative's consent desirable. As already noted, it appears likely that Norman law by the second half of the eleventh century was developing the later distinction between "conquest," property first brought into a family by the current possessor, who could therefore alienate it at will, and "patrimony," inherited property over which the current possessor had only limited rights of alienation.[47] Among the evidence for the existence of this distinction are charters describing purchases by lay persons made with the buyers' "own gold and silver,"[48] one of which says that the donor, Robert, gave possessions "in which his brother Geoffrey had no part, because *(quia)* the same Robert had bought that land with his own income."[49] The charter reports no one's consent; and though it refers to Robert's relatives, living and dead, as beneficiaries of the merits of the gift, it names no relatives except Robert's deceased wife Muriel and his brother.[50] Geoffrey seems to have been mentioned either to explain why his consent was not reported or to forestall any claim he might make to the land alienated by his brother. That he had no rights because Robert had first acquired the land implies that, if Robert had, instead, inherited the property, Geoffrey would automatically have had rights and would have been requested to consent to the alienation.

The apparent relationship between consent and status as heir is borne out by evidence that an eldest son's consent was more important than his siblings'. Five charters, about four different families, say that one named son "and the other sons" consented, witnessed, or received countergifts; in only two is the named son certainly the eldest, but the inference is permissible in all.[51] When a charter enumerates what countergift each alienor and confirmer received, moreover, it is fairly common for one son to receive more than his brothers and sisters or for only one son to receive a countergift although he had siblings.[52] Occasionally in other contexts, too, one son is singled out as the eldest, as though that had a special importance.[53] The evidence is scarcely overwhelming; and because the degree to which primogeniture was the normal rule of succession in Normandy at this time is by no means certain,[54] its significance is debatable. Nevertheless, it tends to confirm that likelihood to inherit was what made the consent of relatives necessary. So do indications that bastards were less important as confirmers than legitimate children, presumably because they had less right to inherit.[55]

Whether or not an heir had consented to his predecessor's gifts before succeeding to an estate, he would probably be asked to do so afterward. The portions of Orderic Vitalis's history devoted to the abbey of Saint-Evroul are full of accounts of how members of successive generations of families came to the abbey, confirmed what their predecessors had given, and, sometimes, made additional gifts themselves. Other abbeys were equally concerned to record such matters. An alienor or confirmer could not commit subsequent generations to the extent that no later confirmations would be necessary. Neil de *Giroldivilla* gave Saint-Sauveur-le-Vicomte a church, "his son Brian conceding in perpetuity if he should die without sons by [his] wife."[56] This cannot mean that the existence of a legitimate grandson of the donor would cause the gift to revert to the donor's family; hence it must mean that Brian could not give the consent of his putative heir. He could concede "in perpetuity" only in the absence of heirs; otherwise the confirmation would have to be repeated by his son. Usually only two generations of confirmers are known, the alienor's and the heir's, but the reasons are practical: the habit of recording gifts in charters developed among the Normans only during the first half of the eleventh century, and many of the abbeys of Normandy were founded after 1030. Only a few generations, therefore, had passed before the end of the century. Nonetheless, the practice of securing the consent of heirs and potential heirs to alienations was well established.

As the next section will show, lords sometimes gave their consent in advance to the alienations their tenants might make, and the charters in which they do so give a considerable amount of information about the respective rights of lords and tenants. No relative ever gave consent in advance, however: no matter how general relatives' confirmations may be, they always refer only to transfers already accomplished. Except inductively, therefore, the consent of relatives is known only in the particular, not on the level of general principles. From the particulars it is obvious that churches to which alienations were made greatly desired the consent of relatives and likely that this desire was a response to the practical problem of preventing and defeating claims rather than to legal necessity. The group of consenting relatives was scarcely larger than the nuclear family: sons, wives, and brothers predominate. Moreover, the importance of consent of any relative was directly related to the likelihood that that person would succeed the alienor whose actions he or she was asked to confirm.

CONSENT OF LORDS

Like the consent of relatives, the consent of alienors' lords was assiduously sought by recipient churches and, at least on the basis of the extant sources, was usually given.[57] As with the consent of relatives, too, no extant assertions of principle explain why the consent of the lord was important. Somewhat more basis for speculation exists than in the case of relatives, however. The introductory clauses of signature lists and phrases in other contexts often say that the lord's consent made a gift more secure, though exactly how it did so is never stated. Because lords challenged alienations much less often than did relatives, the danger of future claims does not seem an adequate reason. Concern for the services exacted from the alienated tenements seems the obvious explanation; but, as already noted, service is mentioned in this context with surprising rarity.[58] Apparently only a lord could absolve property from whatever services the alienor had owed the lord from it, and many lords added to their confirmations gifts of the services due them from the property. Other confirmations, however, say that the lord confirmed "saving the service due to him" or a similar phrase, and most say nothing of service. Apparently, therefore, lords could expect to continue to receive services unless they waived them; yet explicit waivers are less common than silence about service, and explicit refusals to waive service sometimes accompany consent. Hence, that lords were entitled to services does not seem sufficient to explain the fact or the frequency of their consent.

Sometimes a man explicitly identified as the lord's lord consented as well as the direct lord. Three levels of the tenurial hierarchy above him, from his direct lord up to Roger de Montgomery, approved Warin de la Mare's gift to Saint-Martin de Sées.[59] Nothing, however, indicates, explicitly or implicitly, that an alienation had to be confirmed by every level of the tenurial hierarchy superior to the alienor; and, except when the lord's lord is the duke, the consent of more than one level of lords is rarely reported.[60] Sometimes two men are said to confirm as lords although neither is called the other's superior. It is possible, occasionally highly probable, that some of these pairs are the alienor's lord and the lord's lord; but it often turns out that the two lords are related, most often as brothers or as father and son. Thus, the one charter which says that all of a donor's lords confirmed his gift later identifies the lords as two brothers and their sister.[61] Furthermore, at least once in a while confirmation by two lords seems to have been necessary because the alienor held directly from both. When, for example, both Duke William and his uncle William count of Arques confirmed Gerard Flaitel's gifts to Saint-Wandrille, they did so "each for those things of which the donation pertained to him."[62] If the last phrase were not present, it would be natural to assume that the duke confirmed as the count's lord. Caution must therefore be used in interpreting every instance in which two or more lords are said to consent but none is explicitly said to be the superior.

The most valuable information about the consent of lords comes from a type of consent characteristic only of lords, namely, consent to future alienations. Forty-nine clauses are extant, from twenty different churches, in which a lord or a lady confirms transfers which his or her men may, in the future, make to the church. Hugh Paynel's grant to Saint-Etienne de Caen, quoted earlier in connection with refusals of consent by tenants, is an unusually long example.[63] Although it was provoked by Hugh's tenants' refusal to consent to a gift he wanted to make at present, there is no reason to suppose that the same circumstances explain any of the other such clauses. The grants can also be very brief: in his charter of gift to Saint-Florent de Saumur, William de Briouze says simply, "And if any of my men should either give or sell anything, I agree."[64] Such statements usually occur toward the end of charters in which the lords also make gifts of their own and confirm gifts their men have already made; only one charter is solely a confirmation of future alienations.[65] Most of these clauses confirm the gifts the lord's tenants may make in future or speak of the recipient church's general right to acquire property. Twelve add sales, and two add mortgages. One speaks only of sales and mortgages, not of gifts.[66] It is difficult to decide how far to rely on the precision of this language. Charters which mention only gifts may be intended to exclude sales and mortgages, or "give" may be intended to cover all sorts of transfers. Nine charters specify gifts in alms; but one of these also permits sales and another mortgages. In three of the charters which speak of gifts in alms, the lord surrenders some or all of his rights over whatever may be given; the same is true of six charters which do not specify alms.

In another, similar type of clause, which occurs in ten charters from seven different churches, a man grants that if he or his relatives or, sometimes, any of his tenants finds it necessary to sell possessions the prospective alienor must offer them first to the church; three also mention mortgages, three gifts, and one exchanges.[67] Three times the church is awarded only a right of first refusal over the property, but six times it is made the sole potential beneficiary of the transfers. The tenth charter draws a distinction: in his memorandum about his gifts to Jumièges, Rainald the chaplain says that he gave gardens at Bayeux to three individuals, "and none of them may sell those gardens except to the abbot and monks or give them to anyone without their license."[68] These clauses of consent to future alienations are not identical in purpose with the more numerous ones. Those seem to be intended to encourage the confirmer's tenants to make transfers, whereas these seem designed simply to make the best of a potential bad situation by ensuring that, if a person should be forced by circumstance to alienate, the church would benefit from the transfer in preference to anyone else. Several mention the compulsion of necessity,[69] and seven of the ten concern only sales or sales and mortgages. Four are only about alienations the person issuing the charter or his relatives—not his tenants—may later have to make.[70] Nevertheless, the other six, two of which mention gifts as well as sales, are very like the more numerous clauses of consent to future alienations. I shall therefore consider these six together with the clauses of the more common sort in the rest of what follows.

The lords who issued confirmations in advance were usually fairly important men. The duke, however, is conspicuously absent. William the Conqueror seems never to have granted one. From all his predecessors there are only two; each concerns only one potential donor, and one is a sole option to buy or exchange rather than a confirmation of the broader type.[71] Robert Curthose issued three, all in charters drawn up by the *scriptorium* of Bayeux cathedral; they are nearly identical in wording, and two concern the same transaction.[72] The dukes, apparently, were leery of granting unrestricted rights of alienation. Many of the clauses from lesser lords restrict the consent in some way. Four concern only tithes.[73] Like one of the two early ducal examples, Hugh Paynel and four other lords name one or a few specific persons to whom alone the concession applies.[74] Others restrict the territory within which the future gifts may be made.[75]

Restrictions of these types are relatively infrequent, however. The one which is common is a limitation of the amount of property which might be alienated or the conditions under which it might be transferred. Nearly a third—sixteen in all—of the clauses contain such a limitation. Of the others, only one actually says that the confirmer's men may alienate as much as they like;[76] but, because lords were not reticent about stating limits and the limits vary widely, it is likely that when no limit is stated none was intended.

The range is wide even in the way in which the limitation is expressed. Each of three eleventh-century grants to Troarn which survive only in a long confirmation of the abbey's possessions by King Henry II of England says that the lord confirms any transfer which is made "reasonably." The word is not explained, however, and it probably reflects twelfth-century legal terminology.[77] A few charters state the limit in areas of land: one permits alienations of one carrucate, another up to two acres; a third allows the grantor's "greater men" to give up to ten acres, the "lesser" are permitted only one.[78] Again, when Robert fitz Hamo gave the church of *Scai* and its tithes to Mont-Saint-Michel, along with some land, he added "that, if any of my men who cultivate the same vill, driven by any necessity, should wish to mortgage some of his land or possessions to the abbot of the same place, it is permitted that he do so; if, however, he should wish to sell altogether, I agree similarly [that he may sell] up to two acres, except for the dwelling plots and the garden lands."[79] This is unusual in referring clearly to peasants who could engage in the sorts of transactions with which this work is concerned.[80] For the matter at hand, what is significant is that there is a limit on what may be sold but none on what may be mortgaged, doubtless because mortgages were only temporary transfers, whereas sales were permanent. Such a distinction occurs nowhere else. Its effect here is that Robert makes the concession without risking losing his peasants entirely: when they sell, not only may they sell only a limited amount, but they may not sell any of their dwelling plots or gardens, that is, of the lands forming their homesteads as opposed, presumably, to lands in the fields.

When Robert count of Eu founded Le Tréport in 1059, he confirmed the gifts "of all those things which his men have given or will have given to the same church in his whole county, except for the heads of their honors."[81] This is the feudal equivalent of Robert fitz Hamo's prohibition on the sale of his peasants' dwelling plots. Other charters limit alienations of fiefs to a certain fraction. In one the transfer may constitute up to half the fief.[82] In another Robert Oisuns concedes "concerning my lesser men up to the third part of their fiefs, if they should give or sell to the monks; of the greater, however, up to the fourth part."[83] Because by the same charter Robert confirms to the monks "whatever . . . they have already acquired by gift or purchase or in any other way . . . and [what] they are able to acquire at any time in the aforesaid ways,"[84] it may be significant that the limits he states apply only to gifts and sales. "Any other way" in which the recipient might acquire possession would be either an exchange, in which the alienor would be compensated for what he gave up, or one of the modes of temporary transfer. Therefore, like Robert fitz Hamo's, the effect of Robert Oisuns's restriction is to limit his losses through his men's permanent alienations.

These ten are all the clauses which limit transfers to a certain amount of property. Another six state limiting conditions. One contains a phrase—"saving our service and rights"—similar to phrases found from time to time in connection with consent to alienations which had already been made.[85] It probably served the same purpose, to give notice that the services due the lord from the property transferred had not been waived. An analogous phrase—"saving the reverence and obedience due to the holy mother church of Bayeux"—appears in the clause confirming future gifts in a charter by which Bishop Odo made gifts to Saint-Bénigne de Dijon.[86] The four remaining limitations refer to service in a way which probably explains what "reasonableness" was and why the limits in areas or fractions were included, a way which perhaps even casts light on the problem of why a lord's consent was desirable. Each permits alienations unless, in the words of one, what is transferred "should be so much that afterwards he [the potential alienor] is not able to serve us."[87] In other words, these limitations were imposed to protect lords against tenants who might give away so much of their tenements that they rendered themselves or their heirs incapable of performing the services due the lords. This is likely to have constituted a standard of reasonableness for transfers.

The idea that there ought to be a limit on how much one's tenants could transfer seems to have developed in Normandy only in the second half of the eleventh century and to have become common only in the last quarter of the century. The only limitation which certainly comes from before the 1070s is the one which allows alienors to give away all but "the heads of their honors," which is from 1059. Moreover, the fraction which it was reasonable to transfer had apparently not yet been decided even by the end of the century: the two charters which prescribe certain fractions come from the same abbey, Saint-Martin de Sées, and from very late in the century, yet one says that up to one-half of a fief may be alienated and the other is much more restrictive, permitting up to a third of small fiefs and only up to a quarter of large ones.[88] Robert fitz Hamo's limit of two acres for his peasants was probably a much smaller fraction of the average peasant tenement even than one-quarter, though the size of the average peasant holding cannot be calculated.[89] The other limits stated as specific figures are even less capable of being expressed as fractions.[90] Nevertheless, the idea that there ought to be a limit for the lord's protection seems to have been growing—or finding increasing expression—during the course of the century. It seems somewhat odd, however, that one charter which sets different limits for large and small fiefs allows those who hold less to give a larger proportion of what they have; perhaps the lord's material interests had to be balanced against the spiritual needs of his tenants.[91] Moreover, the clauses which give consent to future gifts only within certain limits, especially the four which state the limit in terms of preventing loss of service, are probably the only extant evidence that lords might be concerned about excessively large alienations. No lord, for example, is ever said to have challenged a transfer on the grounds that it was too large or to have insisted that a tenant reduce the size of a grant before the lord would give his consent. Nor does there seem to have been much concern about deathbed or post-obit gifts, transfers in which donors might be especially likely to make overly large transfers.[92]

Although the charters are almost universally silent on who was to do service when the lord did not waive it, this question may have been partially responsible for the eagerness with which the consent of lords was sought. One recipient certainly was to take over performance of the service.[93] In such a situation, the lord's consent would presumably have been necessary, for he and his new tenant would have had to come to a mutual understanding about the terms of the service, especially when, as must often have been the case, not only various payments but also personal services were involved. *Mutatis mutandis*, this is the situation which resulted in the agreement between William Paynel and the abbot of Mont-Saint-Michel, which is so informative about feudal tenure.[94] One tenant certainly continued to do the service so as to exempt the church from the burden.[95] Here, the lord would presumably at least have wished to make sure that his tenant could support the burden of all the services on the basis of a smaller tenement. Either arrangement, therefore, would make it desirable to secure the lord's consent. If, in the absence of the lord's waiver, it was the normal practice for the tenant to continue to perform the services, as I have conjectured,[96] it is even possible that it was not the recipient church but the alienating tenant who was most concerned to get the lord's consent, for by doing so he or she might find the burden of service reduced in proportion to the amount of the tenement transferred.[97]

A few lords protected themselves against losses resulting from grants by their tenants by devices which foreshadow the *retrait féodal* of later Norman law. Troarn accorded Adeliza de Bardouville the right to redeem the mortgages of any of her men who could not redeem them themselves.[98] She therefore was able to substitute herself for the abbey as the beneficiary of such alienations when they threatened to become permanent. When Odo and his wife, Ermengard, gave half their land to La Trinité du Mont after their deaths and established the other half as a tenement to be held by their descendants from the abbey, they provided that if any of the descendants, "compelled by some necessity, should wish to sell the portion of it [the land] which fell to him by hereditary right, he should accept the price for it from the abbot of the monastery or, by his license, from any man."[99] Here the abbey as lord is to be able to substitute itself for any other purchaser if it wishes to do so. On the principle that no one could grant more rights than he or she had, it is possible that every instance of a lord's grant of either a sole option or a right of first refusal implies that the lord had the right himself; but there is no evidence that any such right was exercised in the eleventh century.

Lords expressed their consent to transfers in all the same ways as did relatives. For confirmations contemporary with the initial alienations, there was in addition one form of consent which they alone apparently could use, the ceremony of investiture. Both lords and relatives might, for example, place a donation on an altar along with or instead of an alienor; but, when the act of donation took the form of investiture, if the alienor did not perform the act, it was the lord or the lord's agent, not a relative, who did so.[100] In a good many instances, too, in which both donor and lord were present for the ceremony, the donor "gave back" what he or she wished given to a church to the lord, who then gave it to the church.[101] Such actions may have resulted from the then current theories about seisin and how it could validly be transferred. Nonetheless, only these instances imply that surrender into the lord's hands of what was to be transferred was required, and they are counterbalanced by transfers clearly made in the lord's absence and without his prior consent.[102] Moreover, when a charter alludes to the purpose of giving back land for a lord to transfer, it cites, not any rule about valid transfer of seisin, but instead the security of the grant. Indeed, one such action is explained as an attempt to prevent claims by the real donor's relatives, and the same motive is implied about another.[103] In sum, to transfer property by resigning it into one's lord's hands seems to have been a means to assure the security of the alienation rather than a ceremony expressing the necessity of the lord's consent.

How the double ceremony would render the transfer more secure is never explained. Like any other public action, of course, it made the lord's consent evident and known to witnesses. When the action is explicitly said to protect against claims of the alienor's relatives, however, one can only speculate. Presumably, if a relative should challenge the transfer, the lord, having participated in the donation, could testify to the gift or warrant it to the church or refuse to hear the claim in his court or in some other way prevent it from succeeding. There is one other indication that the consent of a lord as expressed in any form might be a defense against relatives' claims rather than against the lord himself. William de Briouze's gifts to Saint-Florent de Saumur were made for the souls of a good many persons, among them William the Conqueror and Queen Matilda, who are included "in order that they themselves should consent to this alms and, if anyone should wish to commit an injustice therein, they should hold him to right."[104] This suggests that the purpose of obtaining a lord's consent was to secure his support against all third parties, not only relatives, who disseised the alienee or made claims to what had been transferred. Although in all three instances just cited the lord was also the duke, it is possible that any lord who had given his consent would have been expected to assist in defeating claimants if he could, especially if he had benefited materially or spiritually as a result of his consent; but other charters do not display this expectation.

When a tenant gave property back to a lord for the lord to give, the lord is sometimes depicted as the donor. One entry in a pancart for Bec's priory of Saint-Martin-au-Bosc says that, when Hugh de *Morinval* and his wife and sons gave land, "the aforesaid Hugh gave this land back to Wascelin Fretel from whom he held it"; but a subsequent entry in the same pancart refers simply to "the land of Hugh de *Morinval* which Wascelin Fretel gave in alms."[105] Several charters say that a lord gave a tenant's land at that tenant's request; a great many say that a lord gave a tenant's land—and sometimes the tenant—with no indication that the tenant had given consent. Hugh de *Morinval*'s gift is unusual only in that it appears in both forms. It thereby indicates that they were at least sometimes equivalent and demonstrates the problem of distinguishing alienations in which the lord was the prime mover from ones in which the tenant was.[106] In most cases, one simply cannot tell which sort of transfer is at hand. It certainly cannot be assumed that every grant which takes the form "I give X's land" or "he gave X's land" represents a gift by a tenant which the lord confirmed, much less that in every such gift the tenant gave the property to the lord, who gave it to the recipient church. The contrary assumption—that most if not all transfers recorded in this form were made by lords with, at most, their tenants' consent—is equally untenable as a general rule. "X's land" might simply be a place-name. Even when it is not, the form "I give X's land" or "he gave X's land" might be used in varying situations.

Troarn's pancart of about 1068 in which Roger de Montgomery both made gifts of his own and confirmed gifts of his tenants is a good example. Scattered among Roger's own gifts occur the following lands of others:

> (1) Rainald Malleart's land, also (2) the land of Geoffrey, nicknamed "the fool," for which Geoffrey himself was made a monk in the monas-

> tery of St. Martin, and (3) Roger's land in Ranville . . . and (4) the church of Saint-Pair, with all the land which the same Roger's mother holds there for her lifetime . . . , and (5) the church of Saint-Samson, with . . . the land of William the cleric and Ingulf . . . , and also (6) the church of Saint-Sylvain . . . with Morinus the carpenter's land, and (7) [the land] which Roger Tanetin recently gave . . . in Airan . . . , (8) the land of Saint-Hippolyte and Giboury, with the honor of Urse the knight, and (9) whatever Geoffrey the cleric held in Réville from the same Roger [de Montgomery] . . . , (10) the land of Gilbert Berbium which he held in Saint-Sylvain, and also (11) Héritot and Hernetot, as Hugh the seneschal had [them] and gave [them] to St. Martin.

After this last grant, the charter says, "This far from the gift of Viscount Roger"; it then turns to the gift of William the Conqueror and his magnates.[107] These eleven alienations are a sample of the ways in which "X's land" typically appears in the charters. The seventh alienation and the last were certainly gifts by Roger's subordinates with his consent, although they are listed among Roger's own gifts. The second probably was also, for the tenant benefited from the gift by becoming a monk, a type of countergift much rarer for confirmers than for donors. Five others—the first, third, fifth, sixth, and eighth—take the form "X's land." They may be place-names, grants by the persons to whom the lands are said to have belonged, or transfers by the lord of lands held by the persons named: without outside information, which is usually lacking, these cannot be distinguished.[108] The ninth and tenth alienations may represent gifts, either by the men named or by their lord, of actual tenements, or they may represent an intermediate stage in the process whereby a tenant's name became a place-name.[109] The fourth alienation certainly concerns land which was held by a tenant—not merely at the moment when it was given to the abbey but still at the time when the charter was drawn up—but whether the impetus for the gift came from the tenant or her lord is not stated.[110]

Because a great many charters contain entries of these types, it is obviously impossible neatly to separate tenants' grants with their lords' consent from lords' alienations with—or without—their tenants' consent. Nonetheless, three charters from Jumièges make a distinction of sorts: in each, the duke confirms his men's alienations "as if given by us."[111] Hence, Jumièges, at least, seems to have recognized that a lord did not really give his tenants' gifts: he transferred them "as if" he had given them himself. The point may be that the duke could give in a way in which no one else could, more absolutely, freer from all services, in "purer" alms, as some explicit and implicit references to alms suggest,[112] and that it was therefore to Jumièges's advantage to possess all its property "as if" the duke himself had given it. That in itself, however, implies that the abbey could have legal possession of property to whose transfer the duke had not consented. By extension, the same would be true of lesser lords. Here as elsewhere, therefore, the scanty evidence seems to indicate that in eleventh-century Normandy a lord's consent to an alienation by his tenant was not legally necessary. It was, however, advisable in practice. One reason for this may have been that, if they had not consented, lords might raise claims to transfers, but there is no evidence of an actual claim of this sort. Instead, the consent of lords was important primarily because the service for the land transferred was a matter of concern and because lords who had consented might protect alienations from claims by others by upholding transfers with the force of their authority and of their courts.

CONSENT OF TENANTS

That tenants were the only category of confirmer whose refusal to consent could, apparently, prevent transfers from occurring has already been noted, as has the comparative rarity of references to tenants' consent; and I have suggested that these phenomena may be related.[113] Records which say that a lord gave some person's land but do not mention consent are far more numerous than those to which a tenant's consent is noted.[114] That a tenant's consent is not mentioned need not mean that the tenant had not given consent, as the transfer to Saint-Martin-au-Bosc by Hugh de *Morinval* and his lord Wascelin Fretel shows.[115] The vagaries of the charters may depend to a considerable extent on scribal preference, on when—relative to an alienation—the charter was written, or on which of the several charters in which the grant may once have been recorded has survived. Roger de Montgomery's charter for Troarn, analyzed above, illustrates other ways in which such apparent anomalies may be explained. It is also likely that many short charters recording individual alienations as the tenant's rather than the lord's have been lost. Some churches may even have drawn up no charters for relatively minor gifts, but have waited instead until an important lord made gifts of his own and confirmed his men's alienations to note down what those grants were.[116] Because confirmation ceremonies seem to have been identical in form to the ceremonies for initial alienations, it would have been easy for all the lord's acts to be recorded as his gifts.

From certain points of view, the apparent equivalence of transfers by tenants with their lords' consent or by lords with their tenants' consent may be highly misleading. Especially with reference to the service owed by tenants, if a tenant gave away some of his property on his own initiative the situation ought to have been very different from that if a lord gave away part of the tenant's land, even with the tenant's consent, or if he transferred a tenant entirely to a church. Just as the limitations of different sorts which lords imposed on their tenants' future grants seem to have been an attempt to protect their interests in circumstances in which the initiative for the transfer was the tenant's, so the apparent rule that a tenant's consent was needed before a transfer could occur may have been the means by which the interests of tenants were protected in the situation in which the initiative was the lord's. The taciturnity of the charters about what happened to service, however, means that it is impossible to cite more evidence for this contention than the charters of Hugh Paynel and Baudry d'Epréville, which contain the only extant examples of refusals of tenants to consent; and neither charter is explicit on the point.

Because the consent of tenants is so relatively infrequently mentioned, it is difficult to say more about tenants as confirmers than this. When their consent is mentioned, it occurs in virtually all the forms used by other types of confirmers. The practice of getting the consent of tenants seems to have been coeval with the making of gifts to churches: a charter of Duke Richard II for Jumièges says that Duke William Longsword, who died in 942, "restored" to the abbey "the vill which is called Jouy, by the consent and will of Hardred who possessed it at that time."[117] Just as an occasional charter cites the consent not only of the alienor's lord but of the lord's lord, so at least one charter cites the consent not only of an alienor's tenant but of the tenant's tenant.[118] If a tenant's consent was indeed necessary before the lord could give the tenement, cases like these should be expected, for the tenant in possession, rather than any intermediate, would have been the person whose consent was crucial. It is also scarcely surprising that tenants' sons participated with their fathers as confirmers: as likely heirs they were, of course, potential claimants. No other relatives of tenants are known to have consented, but probably only because tenants' consent is recorded so rarely. A rule that, except for sons, tenants' relatives need not consent seems unlikely.

Occasionally a disinherited tenant or a former tenant who would seem to have been adequately compensated for the tenement is said to consent. When one person bought property from another to give it to a church, for example, the consent of the seller and sometimes of his or her relatives is recorded fairly often. One tenant is said to have received an exchange precisely to get his consent to his lord's gift of his former tenement.[119] Like the sellers and their relatives who consent, this exchanger's consent was probably advisable because he might otherwise later challenge the transfer to the church on the grounds that the preceding transfer had never taken place. Analogously, recipient churches probably sought the consent of tenants who had been disinherited because they were unlikely to be resigned to their expropriation and might seize back their former possessions. Moreover, disinheritances often, perhaps usually, were not permanent, and a tenant who was restored to some of his tenement might otherwise insist on having it all. Robert de Vitot did exactly that when he was restored to his fief, part of which the interim tenant had given to Saint-Evroul.[120]

CONSENT OF OTHERS

In praising William the Conqueror's piety, William of Poitiers says, "He gladly conceded his authority to anyone wishing to make a gift [to a church], never harming the saints by any injustice at all by disseising [them] of anything dedicated to them."[121] The latter half of this statement is untrue: like his predecessors as duke, William committed at least occasional disseisins against churches as well as against lay persons.[122] The first part of the statement seems essentially accurate, however: William's only known refusal to approve a grant to a church was temporary, having been occasioned by a dispute between two abbeys over the gift; as soon as the dispute was settled, William gave his consent.[123] It would be unrealistic to expect to be told that the duke refused to confirm a transfer—hardly information a recipient church would wish to publish to the world. Nonetheless, it can, I think, safely be argued from the very large number of William's confirmations that he deserved his biographer's praise for his willingness to agree to others' alienations.

In this, again, he resembled his predecessors. Almost all the surviving acts of the late tenth and early eleventh centuries are ducal donations or confirmations. The percentage of acts in the duke's name falls fairly steadily in the last two-thirds of the eleventh century. Robert Curthose participated in remarkably few of the charters of his reign, probably largely because of his exceptional weakness as duke.[124] The more general trend is to be explained on two other grounds: the number of nonducal abbeys in Normandy began to grow only about 1030; and, as the habit of writing and preserving records of transactions took hold in Normandy, acts of persons less important than the duke were more often recorded and survived. Nevertheless, ducal confirmations remained important: even Curthose's acts are more often confirmations of others' acts than grants of his own.

The duke might, of course, be asked to confirm because he was an alienor's lord. He might also, however, be asked because as duke he was the chief public authority in Normandy, the protector of the church, the highest judge, in short the man most likely to be able to defend a church against loss of its property and the man at least ostensibly most willing to do so. Because, at least occasionally, not only an alienor's immediate lord but that lord's lord, and so on, might confirm a transfer, and because it is likely that many—perhaps most—tenants in eleventh-century Normandy could trace upward a chain of dependence leading ultimately to the duke, it is often impossible in practice to discern whether the duke was asked in a particular case to confirm a transfer to a church as a lord or as the duke.

Why the duke's confirmation added to the security of a transfer is rarely explained. Nothing suggests that it was legally necessary. As a lord, the duke was presumably in the same position as other lords, whose consent seems to have been a matter merely of practical advantage. As duke, his position was unique and his consent might, in theory, be necessary because of some rule of public law: but in all the many references to the duke's consent there is no hint of such a rule.[125] The clearest statement about the force of ducal consent certainly cites his position as duke rather than as lord, but it is concerned with the practical matter of protection of transfers and gives no reason to think that ducal confirmation was required. It comes from a charter for Marmoutier, which, having described a gift, says that "the Lord Abbot Albert . . . , because he did not know how else this donation could remain stable, presuming on their great mutual friendship and esteem, approached William prince and duke of the Normans and—so that what you may discover with difficulty elsewhere may be openly said—king of all his land, and induced him to agree to and authorize the aforesaid donation."[126] Because the charter can be dated to 1055, this passage may perhaps be taken as testimony to the reputation William had gained as a result of his victories of the preceding eight years, especially the defeat his forces had administered to the king of France at Mortemer in the previous year. As the slightly desperate tone of the phrase "because he did not know how else this donation could remain stable" might lead one to suspect, the gift was likely to be challenged, perhaps already under challenge: a charter of 1063 records the quitclaim of the donor's maternal uncle, made in Duke William's court before being repeated at the abbey.[127] Abbot Albert relied on William as a duke so strong as to be kinglike to protect the abbey's possessions.[128] In two other instances, the duke's confirmation was intimately related to his ability to defend an alienation against claims.[129] One of these refers explicitly to legal procedure as the way he will render protection if it becomes necessary, but three charters are no guarantee that the duke's consent was always desirable primarily because he presided over the highest court in Normandy.

When the duke confirmed, he did so in much the same ways as any other confirmer. There are some differences of emphasis in the records: few acts of donation by dukes are reported; the duke is relatively rarely described as receiving a countergift, either as a donor or as a confirmer, although the material countergifts to the duke which are recorded are, on average, unusually large; he confirms by signing more often, proportionally, than do other confirmers. Only two charters say that gifts by the duke were confirmed by someone other than an immediate relative. One is the earliest extant Norman charter, in which Duke Richard I cites his lord Hugh Capet, duke of France, as confirming a gift to Saint-Denis.[130] The other, from nearly a century later, is probably merely a garbled account of an act of donation performed by someone else in the duke's name.[131]

Certain things only the duke, as duke, could do. He was, of course, the only person who could grant ducal revenues or ducal rights. The former were granted rather more often than the latter, but neither was granted at all freely.[132] At the end of the eleventh century, the duke also was the only person who could authorize the building of a castle, and any castle built without his permission was illegal.[133] Grants of permission to build castles are not recorded in charters, however; and the historians, whose works are full of tales of castles built with and without permission, say merely that the latter were built in periods of ducal weakness and destroyed as soon as the duke was restored to strength. They do not discuss the law, only the politics, of adulterine castles.[134] The duke alone could exempt persons or areas from the rearban, the duty of all to defend Normandy against attack.[135] He may also have been the only person who could give permission to construct a bourg: Duke

William granted Bec the right to build a bourg around the abbey and gave La Trinité de Caen the right to increase the size of its bourg at Caen.[136] The latter case is not especially significant, as both the town and the abbey were ducal foundations. Bec was not, however; and there is no extant example of a lesser lord granting license to found a bourg, though many built them.[137] The duke apparently did not claim a sole right to possess or to grant rights over the forests of Normandy,[138] and he lost or abandoned his monopoly of the right to grant markets and fairs in the early eleventh century.[139]

Like the dukes, the bishops of Normandy are cited as confirmers even when they were not lords and for the same reasons: because they were public authorities and because they were the only men who could make certain grants. Their consent was usually expressed through their signatures: bishops who were not donors appear in more than a third of the extant signature lists. Occasionally the body of a charter mentions a bishop as a confirmer or witness, but bishops are rarely said to have participated in acts of donation or to have received countergifts or the like except, of course, as donors themselves, which they often were. As ecclesiastical authorities, bishops could play an important role in rendering alienations secure by issuing anathemas.[140] Part of the desire for bishops to confirm probably stemmed from their ability to excommunicate: presumably, even if a charter does not say that the bishops who signed it or otherwise confirmed the alienation had anathematized potential violators in advance, those bishops would be willing to excommunicate actual violators. Another role which bishops played as public authorities was to act as judges when a dispute arose, again a good incentive for securing their consent when transfers were made. This reasoning applies also, of course, to the abbots and important laymen who often signed charters recording grants with which they had no other connection.

Bishops, however, also drew their importance from another fact: they could grant episcopal customs or freedom from episcopal customs and make other ecclesiastical rearrangements. It is, however, not at all clear whether their consent was necessary to every transfer of episcopal rights which were in private hands, as many were. Duke Robert the Magnificent's charter establishing the abbey of Montivilliers implies that bishops alone had the right to grant out episcopal customs: "First, we establish the same church of St. Mary with the others described below as absolved, immune and wholly free from every episcopal custom, which indeed is not done by the violence of our power but is established and confirmed by the gift, will and concession of Lord Robert archbishop of Rouen."[141] To grant episcopal customs without episcopal permission would, it seems, be an act of violence rather than a legal gift. The language may, however, be a result of the specific circumstances of Robert's reign;[142] and even if the charter alludes to a general rule, it was often broken: about half the grants of episcopal customs not made by bishops themselves were made without recorded episcopal permission. A few donors already held the customs in fee from the bishops who confirmed. For the other cases which recorded consent this is not stated, although it is hard to see how the donors could have given rights they did not possess. It is possible that in every instance the customs were both held from a bishop and transferred with his approval, that is, that faults in the charters explain all the contrary examples; but this can hardly be assumed. Even if it was not necessary to secure the bishop's permission when making such a grant, however, it was certainly wise to do so. Episcopal control over monastic institutions and over the episcopal rights and revenues they held was a vexed subject in eleventh-century Normandy. Indeed, many of the forged charters which come from this period were drawn up to serve the monastic party to some quarrel with a bishop. If one wished one's gift not to lead to such a dispute, a sensible precaution would be to secure the bishop's consent at the time of the grant.[143]

Signature lists regularly include not only the duke and the bishops but also abbots and the great lay lords of the day. All these men, even if they had no connection with the transfers recorded in a charter, were welcome as signers at least partly because they thereby put the force of their authority behind the alienations and perhaps also because they were the persons likely to judge any lawsuit which might arise. Visiting dignitaries also signed charters, but remarkably infrequently. During his twenty-eight years of exile before he became king of England, many of which he spent in Normandy, Edward the Confessor signed or witnessed four extant Norman charters, two along with his brother Alfred.[144] Eliminating the Norman charters of non-Norman churches and the non-Norman charters of Norman churches, only three of the purely Norman charters remaining were signed by the king of France.[145] In addition, each of the following important foreigners attested one or two Norman charters: Odilo abbot of Cluny, Waleran I count of Meulan, Alberic count of the Gâtinais, William count of the French Vexin, Hugh IV count of Maine, Enguerrand count of Ponthieu, Baldwin count of Flanders, a Count Odo, and Junguené archbishop of Dol.[146]

The latest year from which any of these signatures can come is 1048. Once Duke William began to restore order in Normandy as he emerged from his minority, the number of foreign signatures falls; indeed, given the rise in the number of charters extant from the second half of the century, the decrease is marked. King Philip I of France confirmed the possessions of Bec in 1077, but the act may concern only the abbey's possessions outside Normandy; and Hoel bishop of Le Mans signed, after the fact, a charter for Saint-Evroul, which was probably drawn up in 1074.[147] After the conquest of England an occasional English bishop signed a Norman charter but probably only because he had traveled with the court of the duke-king to Normandy and happened to be present when a charter was presented for William's signature. William bishop of Durham signed a few of Robert Curthose's charters while he was in exile in Normandy between 1089 and 1091. At least thirteen papal legations were sent to Normandy between 1055 and 1106, and some legations to England passed through Normandy on their way to the island kingdom.[148] Yet of all the eminent dignitaries on these missions only a few appear in Norman documents. Richard archbishop of Bourges and Warmund archbishop of Vienne were among the judges of a suit between the bishop of Evreux and La Trinité du Mont, which was heard in the duke's court in 1080, and both signed the charter.[149] Although no source calls these men papal legates, it seems possible that they were present in Normandy to represent the pope at the council of Lillebonne of the same year.[150] A charter from Saint-Florent de Saumur, concerning its dispute with Lonlay over the gifts of William de Briouze, shows that in 1093 or 1094 a cardinal named Roger, a papal legate, acted as a witness to a decision by Duke Robert Curthose's court. Lonlay defaulted, but it is possible that Roger would have acted as a judge had the case actually come to trial.[151] Abbot Gerento of Saint-Bénigne de Dijon traveled to England and Normandy on papal business in late 1095 and stayed in Normandy through much of 1096 to arrange peace between Curthose and William Rufus and to preach the crusade.[152] In addition to arranging transactions between his abbey and two different Norman churches, he signed a grant by Duke Robert to the cathedral of Rouen.[153] In all instances, the inclusion of the foreign churchmen as participants in or corroborators of the acts in which they appear seems to have been accidental: because they happened to be present, they were used as judges or witnesses or signers, but their presence was the occasion neither for the acts they attested nor for a general movement to secure their approbation of acts already performed in the past.

Lay foreigners appear even less often than ecclesiastics after the middle of the century. Guy count of Ponthieu, who was probably the duke's vassal,[154] appears in the judgments of 1080 and 1093 or 1094, in each case in the same capacity as the foreign prelates. Neither suit has anything to do with Ponthieu; Guy was probably present simply because he was the duke's vassal and, like the legates, was pressed into service when the cases arose because he happened to be there. Eustace count of Boulogne witnessed an act for Bec along with Curthose.[155] Perhaps the most surprising absence is that, even during the turmoil of Curthose's reign, whatever other measures Norman churches may have taken to assure their possession of their property, they did not try to obtain the protection of the duke's brothers to any marked extent, though both were often in Normandy. William Rufus or Henry signed or otherwise attested an occasional charter but not large numbers of them, even during the years when Curthose was off on crusade.[156] Rufus issued two general confirmations, for Saint-Evroul and Troarn;[157] but there certainly was no rush to secure such confirmations from either brother, whether as a bulwark against anarchy or as a claimant to the duchy.

That there was no recourse, even at the height of the turmoil of Curthose's reign, to the king of France is scarcely astonishing, given the state of political relations between France and the Anglo-Norman realm at the time.[158] There was, however, also little recourse to the pope either then or at any time earlier in the century. Relatively frequent papal legations and correspondence with the papal curia notwithstanding, only two or three papal privileges for Norman churches are extant from the eleventh century; and these are primarily concerned with exemptions from episcopal jurisdiction rather than with monastic property. Saint-Etienne de Caen secured a privilege from Alexander II in 1068; Fécamp secured one from Paschal II in 1103.[159] The authenticity of Benedict VIII's privilege of 1016 for Fécamp, however, is very much disputed.[160] A few other Norman churches secured papal mandates in particular disputes;[161] but in other instances papal bulls relevant to Norman churches were obtained, it seems, only by the non-Norman parties to the transactions involved.[162] Some papal bulls were forged by or for Norman churches, but they, too, concerned privileges of exemption rather than property.[163] In short, although the churches of Normandy seem to have thought that confirmation of charters by the duke, the prelates, and the magnates of Normandy was one of the most useful ways of preserving their possessions intact, they also seem to have had sufficient confidence in these authorities so that they did not, even in times of considerable dislocation, feel the need of supra-ducal or extra-Norman authority as an assurance of the stability of their possessions. Norman independence of all putatively higher political—or even ecclesiastical—powers was as pronounced in this area as in others.[164]

CONCLUSION

Of all the persons whose consent was sought to alienations, therefore, only tenants could actually prevent transfers by refusing to confirm. Neither the consent of lords nor that of relatives can be proved to have been legally necessary, and probably neither was. Relatives' consent was useful because it decreased the likelihood of later challenges. The more likely it was that a relative would eventually succeed to the property had the alienation not taken place, the more important it was to secure that person's consent. There was no evident desire for the consent of large numbers of comparatively distant relatives. The consent of lords was useful for two principal reasons: arrangements had to be made about the services owed from the property transferred, and lords might help prevent the success of claims. As in the case of relatives, so in the case of lords, recipient churches do not seem to have striven unduly to get the more remote ones—here, all the lords in the tenurial hierarchy—to consent. The immediate lord usually sufficed. Hence there is little reason to think that, when the duke was not the alienor's immediate lord, desire for his consent stemmed from his tenurial position. Instead, he was probably asked to confirm because he was the highest public authority in the duchy and, as such, had a special duty to see justice done and a special duty to protect the church. Only the duke, moreover, could grant certain rights, and the same was true of the bishops. Like the duke, too, the bishops—and also abbots and lay magnates—probably appear so often in accounts of transfers in which they had no visible direct interest because, as the holders of courts or as judges in the duke's court, they would be involved in the settlement of such disputes as might arise. They would be likely to refuse to permit the success of claims against grants they themselves had confirmed. A great man might also be willing to use his power and prestige to discourage a claim before it became a suit; he might even be willing to try a suit in his court although his was not the otherwise appropriate venue for the case. One or two references to ducal consent may imply that consent conveyed jurisdictional responsibility,[165] but too little is known of the court system of eleventh-century Normandy to permit this speculation to be carried very far. What does seem certain is that those persons whose consent it was important to secure—repeatedly, if possible, as the preceding chapters have shown—were a comparatively small group: tenants; near relatives but not distant ones; immediate lords but not their superiors; great men, but only those of Normandy, not of the whole kingdom or of the whole church.

9

Modes of Assurance: Warranty

THE VERB "WARRANT" and the noun "warrantor" appear only four times in eleventh-century Norman charters,[1] yet about seventy charters testify that the concept of warranty was known. The verbs used are many and fairly general; most technical and most common is "acquit," that is, acquit of claims. In a typical warranty clause, the alienor promised to defend the alienated property against claims which might be brought against it—or that someone else would do so. A charter from Jumièges in which a man named Odard became a monk in return for his gifts says, for example, "It should also be known that, if anyone at all should try to go against or oppose this gift, Richard brother of the aforesaid Odard will deraign [it] against all men."[2] Although the promise was usually made by the alienor, it might also be made by a confirmer, either a lord or a relative. When someone other than the alienor and/or his heirs is named as a potential warrantor, it is, again, either a lord or a relative. One charter which includes neighbors and friends is the only anomaly.[3]

A few clauses say that the persons named will defend the church's right as much as they can.[4] This might refer not to limited ability but rather to the defender's total commitment to the church's interest; however, one son who confirmed his father's gifts to Marmoutier "promised also that he would acquit them against all claimants as much as he will have been able to acquit by right"—thereby indicating that there were circumstances in which a promiser might be unable to defend an alienee's interests successfully.[5] For this reason, the fully developed concept of warranty contained two duties, not one: first, to defend, that is, to demonstrate that the person or institution which had vouched the warrantor had rightful possession of whatever had been challenged; second, if the defense was unsuccessful and the person or institution which had vouched him to warranty therefore lost possession, to compensate the original defendant for the lost possessions. Most extant warranty clauses go no further than the promise to defend, but fifteen add that if the warrantor's defense is unavailing he will compensate the church for its loss. Bigot de Sainte-Scolasse, for example, having sold his rights in some land to Saint-Martin de Sées, "promised that, if ever he is not capable of acquitting it from any claimant, he will give instead as much land in the territory of Sainte-Scolasse, [and] whatever it is worth the monks should accept it willingly and free."[6]

Apparently, because the compensation Bigot would give would be equal in area to the lost possession, it might not be equal in value. Other charters specify equivalence of type and/or value: one vill for another; one vineyard for another of equal value; land in one vill for land in another, "acre for acre and house for house."[7] Lambert de *Fontanis* partly sold and partly gave Saint-Martin de Sées land, some of which was around the *maceriae* of Saint-Hélier; "and he promised that if he is not able to acquit this land he will give the aforesaid lords [the monks] instead as much of his other land as is equal in value to that which he was not able to acquit, except the *maceriae* of Saint-Hélier, because he did not have others."[8] Lambert seems to have thought that he could not compensate the abbey with property of equal value but of another type. In two other transactions involving the same abbey, however, the alienors offered the monks their choice of an exchange of equal value or, instead, the return of the monetary countergifts the alienors had received; and a charter from La Trinité du Mont states that, if a gift of a garden is challenged, three acres of arable land adjacent to the garden will be substituted.[9] Moreover, William d'Argentelles and his wife and sons gave land to Saint-Wandrille in return for thirteen pounds of Le Mans, promising restoration of the money if the land were lost; and Hugh Paynel promised to return to Saint-Etienne de Caen the money he had received for a tithe, should an outstanding claim to the tithe succeed.[10] Equivalence of type as well as amount was, therefore, not mandatory.

Most warranty clauses were directed explicitly or implicitly against anyone who might challenge an alienation, but a few single out for exclusive or special mention one individual, most often a relative of the alienor.[11] One of these gives some details of how warranty operated. Robert Oisuns partly sold and partly gave a church to Saint-Martin de Sées and

> promised that his brother Hugh the cleric would concede firmly and legally and willingly, as [their brothers] William Oisuns and Arnulf had conceded. But if Hugh for any reason—or anyone else—should bring a claim against the monks about the aforesaid church, the aforesaid Robert [being] a witness and conceding all, he [Robert] firmly promised that, on the same day on which the claim is made, he will give the aforesaid brothers [the monks] the hamlet which is commonly called *Ruiel Morellorum*, with everything pertaining to the same hamlet, which hamlet the monks should have until the same Robert Oisuns should acquit the aforesaid church to them absolved and free.[12]

Obviously, the compensation, though perhaps equal in value, was not of the same type. More important, however, in at least this instance the warrantor was required to compensate the church for the mere fact of a claim, not only for actual loss. Presumably, if Robert's warranty was not sufficient to secure a decision in favor of the abbey and the monks lost the church, they would keep the hamlet permanently, but if vindicated in court they would restore it to Robert. It is likely that this arrangement was unusual, which may be why it is described at length. Most other warranty clauses state or imply that compensation was to occur after the case had been lost in court rather than at the moment when the claim was raised.[13]

Was warranty a special concession or a duty incumbent upon every alienor and perhaps even every confirmer? Jean Yver maintains that, without special arrangements, no duty to warrant existed in Normandy; and the same has been asserted about other regions of France.[14] I find this contention difficult to accept. Yver ties the existence of warranty to the grant of a countergift; but, because countergifts seem to have been usual in connection with transfers, the duty to warrant, too, would be common even when not explicitly stated. Moreover, the contention depends upon the assumption that anything not mentioned in the charter recording a grant did not exist for that transfer, an assumption which seems to me impossible to make—and probably wrong—at least for Normandy in the eleventh century. To be sure, the alienations in connection with which thirteen of the fifteen full warranty clauses occur are characterized by an element of insecurity,[15] and it is likely in the abstract that warranty should be used especially in connection with such transactions if it was not implicit in every transfer. If, however, the more general clauses about defense are included, the correlation diminishes: only eighteen of these fifty-three transactions have an observable element of insecurity.[16] It may be that specific provisions for compensation for losses were written into charters only when the losses seemed especially likely to occur, but there is no reason to conclude that promises to defend were always written into the charters. Like so much else, their appearance may be no more than a matter of scribal whim.

Particular clauses suggest that warranty was an obligation of all alienors or of their relatives or lords. When Odard became a monk at Jumièges, his brother Richard became a warrantor of his gifts "because the same Odard conceded all the rest of his inheritance to him."[17] The same suggestion—that one of the duties of heirs was to warrant their predecessors' alienations—may be implied by a remark of Orderic's.[18] The lord's duty is implied in the speech expressing the ideal view of a lord's duties which Dudo of Saint-Quentin has Duke William Longsword deliver to Herluin count of Montreuil. Inter alia, William promises that if Arnulf count of Flanders "should wish to come against us in court, using judgment and justice and law, we shall come against him on your account to be judged by the opinion of our" men. Later in the same speech, he calls himself "your defender against enemies," using terms found in the charters in passages about warranty.[19] Given the context, this seems to mean that a lord ought to warrant his vassal's fiefs if the vassal's right to them was challenged.

There are no theoretical expressions of an alienor's or an heir's duty and none of a lord's duty except for Dudo's, but several charters suggest that all lords had a duty to warrant their tenants' holdings. The young Duke William promised to restore to Saint-Wandrille what his father, Robert the Magnificent, had seized from it and granted to a layman, "in such a way that within three years he should give his vassal a safe exchange and should give us back all our land and, if not before, then immediately at the end of three years" he should give back all the land, "even if he should still have given nothing to his knight Haimo in exchange."[20] This suggests that every lord had a duty to compensate blameless tenants if their holdings had to be surrendered, as do a promise of the abbot of Mont-Saint-Michel to William Paynel and a grant by one of William's tenants to Saint-Etienne de Caen.[21] A situation similar to Haimo's, that is, one in which a lord gave his vassal in fee something which the vassal might well be forced to surrender because of the decision of a court, may lie behind a cryptic provision of the agreement between Viscount Rannulf and the bishop of Bayeux.[22] Indeed, in one instance when it was likely that the tenant would not be able to retain his tenement permanently, he explicitly waived his rights:

> Richard abbot of Préaux, compelled by many, gave back to Richard son of Ralph de Sainte-Mère-Eglise the land of Graimbouville which he claimed by gift of Abbot William. And the same Richard did homage to the abbot in the chapter, saying this: "I, Richard, become your man in such a way, returning you money in pledge, that if it vexes the king or the count that you gave me back that land which I claim, I shall return the same land to your demesne; or if anyone should be able to vindicate [a right to] the aforesaid land against me, I shall quitclaim the same money to you and shall observe [my] homage to you, not seeking that anything be given me by you in exchange."[23]

That Richard should have been asked to make so specific a renunciation and that it should be quoted at length strongly imply that, in the ordinary course of events, had he lost the land in either way outlined by his statement, he would have been entitled to compensation. All in all, these charters make it likely that tenants could expect their lords' warranty as a matter of course. That, remarkably, most of them concern lay tenants does not make it less probable that churches could rely on the warranty of their benefactors. To the contrary, given the pious motives of donors to churches, any protection which a lay tenant could expect ought to have been at least equally available to a church.

Nor is this all, for several accounts of lawsuits show men acting to defend their own or their ancestors' transfers. Because "he wished to protect his alms against false claimants," William de Briouze participated actively in a suit between Saint-Florent de Saumur and Lonlay over property he had given the former.[24] Guy de Laval became even more deeply embroiled in a dispute between Marmoutier and La Couture over a bourg at Laval which he had given the former, a case which was finally settled in Duke William's court though it was not Norman.[25] Roger de Montgomery and his son Robert de Bellême took active parts in a protracted suit between the church of Saint-Léonard de Bellême and the bishop of Sées about the bishop's rights over the church, which had been founded, protected, and eventually given to Marmoutier by the Bellême family.[26] A charter from La Trinité du Mont says that among the possessions with which its founder Wascelin endowed it was the island of Oissel, which the abbey held peacefully for fifty years before it was claimed by Gilbert bishop of Evreux, Wascelin's grandson. When the case came to the ducal court in 1080, fourteen important persons were present, including Bishop Gilbert's brother "William d'Arques, heir of the deceased [donor], that is, his grandfather Wascelin, who gave the aforesaid island." The charter continues: "The aforesaid William, at the judgment of the plea, in order to satisfy the bishop and completely to abolish the disagreement, came forward as a witness to his grandfather's donation and was prepared to confirm under oath that on the day and hour when the same Wascelin gave that land to the Holy Trinity he possessed it freely and fully in his own power."[27] The duke himself could be vouched to warranty: according to a charter from Saint-Florent de Saumur, "the monks of Mont-Saint-Michel claimed the gift of Ceaux which John of Dol made to Saint-Florent and William king of the English conceded. Therefore, the monks of Saint-Florent sent two of their members, David and Guihenoc, to the king so that he should either acquit the gift which he had conceded or have it [i.e., the case?] for himself."[28] There is even one seeming instance of the performance of a warrantor's second duty, that of providing compensation for possessions which were lost, for an entry in the foundation charter of Saint-Georges de Boscherville says, "Azo gave [the canons] the tithe of the land which he has from the chamberlain in Sahurs in exchange for the tithe of Bourg-Achard, which the same canons bought from him for thirty shillings but which they never had at all."[29] This is scarcely an incontrovertible reference to a duty to warrant, but it does imply a duty to compensate if one's attempt to transfer proved ineffective; and the court cases, while they, too, never explicitly call the defenders warrantors, also imply that alienors and their heirs expected, when it was necessary, to be asked to act as warrantors promised to act. It seems, therefore, all the more likely that a duty to warrant, both by defending and by compensating, was implicit in all grants.

Only one charter, however, so much as hints at what might happen to someone who did not perform his duty; and it is a puzzle. When Theobald son of Norman made gifts to Saint-Pierre de Préaux, as part of his countergift he received "the customs of the viscounty which . . . he [the abbot] had bought from the duke. To this gift he [Theobald] added the tithes of his knights which they had retained in fee, on agreement that as long as the abbot should warrant the customs to them, he should have them [i.e., the tithes?] completely. But if ever he is unable [to warrant the customs], they may do as they wish with them."[30] As long, it seems, as the abbot could warrant the customs to the knights he would be entitled to the tithes; but if he could not warrant the customs the knights would recover the tithes.[31] It is not clear whether these customs were the vicecomital customs, and the record of Duke William's sale of the customs to the abbot provides no help.[32] If the vicecomital customs were meant, then, as the abbot had just given those customs to Theobald, it is possible that Theobald had granted them to his men, in return for their surrender of the tithes, and that there was an agreement that the abbot rather than Theobald would warrant them to the knights. The knights' title certainly would have depended ultimately on the abbot's purchase from the duke. The arrangement seems to follow the ordinary Norman rule about conditional transfers: if the condition, in this instance that the customs be warranted, was not performed, the agreement was terminated, the defaulting party losing what had been conveyed by the agreement.[33] The tithes they recovered would be compensation to the knights.

In all the reports of court cases which show men defending the rights of churches to their property, the churches won their cases. This is hardly surprising, for they were not likely to record their defeats in charters. What did their defenders do to help them? Guy de Laval was willing to prove Marmoutier's right to Laval by his own oath asserting that his account of how the abbey had received its possessions was correct. He was reluctant to go through an ordeal to demonstrate his veracity, however, and the dispute was sidetracked for some time by the question of which method of proof to use. Eventually, Duke William decided that an oath would be sufficient, and the case was settled in Marmoutier's favor after Guy swore his oath.[34] William d'Arques, too, was prepared to swear to his grandfather's gift.[35] In the first trial of the case between Saint-Florent and Lonlay, William de Briouze presented a legal argument as to why the latter abbey had no right to the disputed church. His explanation is rather like Guy de Laval's, but he is not said to have proved his argument by an oath or in any other way.[36] Similarly, in various court appearances concerned with the suit between Saint-Léonard de Bellême and the bishop of Sées, Roger de Montgomery and Robert de Bellême acted as pleaders on behalf of the church.[37]

Although churches did not make records of suits they lost, there is evidence that warranty was an effective technique for protecting possession, for the accounts just cited record three of the five defaults known to have occurred in eleventh-century Normandy.[38] The bishop of Evreux declined to receive the oath William d'Arques was prepared to swear, and the suit was therefore immediately decided in the abbey's favor. Although the first hearing of the suit between Saint-Florent and Lonlay resulted, after William de Briouze had presented his argument, in a decision in favor of Saint-Florent, in the second trial, in which William was prepared to act again, the abbot and monks of Lonlay fled on the eve of the day the case was to be heard. Having raised their claim against Saint-Florent, the monks of Mont-Saint-Michel did not even wait for the hearing: as soon as they learned why two monks of Saint-Florent had been sent to Duke William, they abandoned their claim, although it seems to have had a solid basis.[39] About sixty references occur in the charters and the historians to cases which actually came into court; but only about twenty-five give any details of what happened in court. Most of them and most other references to how claims were settled talk of quitclaims rather than either of compromises or of court decisions. Although many quitclaims seem to have been compromises, for quitclaimers usually received countergifts, and some of these were sizable, it is possible that some were the product of defaults and, therefore, that there were many more defaults than five. Still, it seems significant that, of the five settlements reported as defaults, three are so closely connected with warranty.[40]

In connection usually with grants in alms, another device was occasionally used which somewhat resembles warranty: the duke asserted or a donor conveyed to him a duty to act as guardian of the alienations; in one instance a donor other than the duke asserted such a duty for himself. Yver has discussed ducal protection of the churches of Normandy and the absence of lay advocacy from Normandy in two articles which include most of the extant eleventh-century cases;[41] but, because his principal interest is ducal power, it is worthwhile to look at these cases from the viewpoint of the protection of alienations.

Conveyances of guardianship to the duke were done by means of the ceremony of investiture: four of the five extant cases describe or allude to it.[42] The duty could also be assumed by the duke on his own initiative. Richard II redeemed from mortgages two churches which had been given to—but later pledged by—William of Volpiano, abbot of both Saint-Bénigne de Dijon and Fécamp. The duke then "received the aforesaid churches . . . in his alms and gave [them] back to St. Benignus . . . in such a way that he should be advocate, guardian and custodian of the same benefice and his successors [should be so] forever against all adversaries or claimants."[43] When the abbess of Montivilliers challenged Saint-Riquier's possession of a church given to it by Richard II, Duke William, after deciding the case in Saint-Riquier's favor, returned the church to the monastery "in such a way . . . that henceforward it should hold [the church] free under my advocacy, as it had accepted [it] from my grandfather and father."[44] In a charter of 1068 for Troarn, William asserted a much broader obligation on his own part: "I . . . concede and confirm all the abovewritten alms in churches, in tithes, in land and in customs, as they were made and conceded by me and by my men . . . in such a way that the abbot and monks . . . should hold them firmly in perpetuity and should live quietly under my protection and [that] of my heirs against all adversaries, as the alms of faithful and good Christians ought to be."[45] A very similar formula was used in a pancart prepared so that William Rufus could confirm an even longer list of donations to the same abbey.[46]

Yver discusses the charter of 1068 at some length and concludes that it asserts for the duke a duty to protect all possessions held in alms by any church but that this obligation was not an effective ducal prerogative until the mid-twelfth century.[47] It is possible, however, that William was asserting no more than a duty of all alienors and confirmers to protect tenure in alms. This more general obligation is found in two charters which record William's half-brother Robert count of Mortain's foundation of a priory of Marmoutier at Mortain: "The things given by me should remain in my subjection and guardianship alone and . . . I should be the advocate and, as is commonly said, the guarantor, of my alms, as a layman ought to be of the alms retained in his hand."[48] As this assertion almost certainly is later than William's charter for Troarn, that charter's wording ought probably to be taken in the broadest sense, to mean that the duty to protect alms tenure was incumbent upon every alienor and confirmer. It should also be noted that, although Yver asserts that the duke had a duty to protect all ducal monastic foundations,[49] the obligation is, in fact, stated only in charters from abbeys which were not ducal foundations.

All the charters which use the term "advocate" are from abbeys outside Normandy, and there is no reason to believe that advocacy of the type known elsewhere in France existed in Normandy.[50] Nonetheless, it was possible for the duke to transfer his duty of protection to another person. When Odo Stigand founded a college of canons in the church of Saint-Martin d'Ecajeul, "he presented the canons . . . to his lord William duke of the Normans and commended them and the church . . . to him to guard and defend." The duke, in turn, "entrusted [them] to Roger de Montgomery to guard faithfully in his stead."[51] The power over the church which was transferred to Roger has been differently interpreted.[52] There is no further information about it; but, when Duke William committed to another the custody of the college of canons which he had founded in the castle of Cherbourg, he seems to have provided the custodian with a fixed income.[53] Although the custodian was of much less prominence than Roger de Montgomery,[54] this may suggest that the rights of anyone to whom the duke delegated his guardianship were limited. It should be noted, however, that Duke Richard II had received Saint-Bénigne's churches "into *his* alms" and that Robert of Mortain asserted that a layman should protect "the alms retained in *his* hand." These possessives may suggest that a guardian kept a close and somewhat proprietorial as well as protective eye on possessions held of him in alms. The vague rights which the "rich men" who were Gilbert de *Brueriecurte*'s peers retained in the grants of alms they had made may be relevant here, although it is equally possible that Gilbert was referring to spiritual services.[55]

Two other aspects of the ducal delegations of custody are noteworthy. First, by each a layman was made *custos* of a college of canons, whereas all the custodians who are mentioned elsewhere were ecclesiastics appointed over abbeys.[56] The number of instances is, however, too small to derive a valid general rule from this contrast. Second, both appointments of lay custodians can be dated to 1066 or shortly before. Because Roger de Montgomery probably remained in Normandy as one of the regents when Duke William crossed the Channel to conquer England,[57] it is possible that William delegated his guardianship not only in these cases but also in others which were not recorded and did so because he was about to depart on a protracted, hazardous campaign. Delegation may not, in other words, have been a usual feature of ducal guardianship.

All the references to ducal protection involve grants in alms, whereas warranty also occurred in connection with onerous transfers and applied to lay as well as to ecclesiastical grantees. The ducal obligation may, therefore, have been a special type of protection accorded only to the most privileged type of tenure which existed in eleventh-century Normandy. On the other hand, the duty of ordinary warrantors to compensate alienees whose possession they could not successfully defend entailed an economic sacrifice somewhat like that suffered by Duke Richard when he redeemed Saint-Bénigne's churches; and Duke William's provision of legal protection to Saint-Riquier finds parallels in the defense at law which several men, apparently acting as warrantors, are known to have offered. Hence, ducal protection may have been similar in its essentials to the warranty any alienor might provide to any recipient. Both obligations, the duke's and the ordinary alienor's, provided types of protection which recipients must have been eager to have: legal defense and compensation for losses. How far the duke's duty stretched is difficult to ascertain. The duty of the ordinary alienor, however, was very wide in that the obligation to warrant seems to have been implicit in all grants. To judge by the success which attended appeals to individual laymen to defend transfers in court, warranty was a conspicuously effective method for assuring the permanence of alienations. If it failed, the alienees would at least be indemnified for the loss of what they had originally received.

10

Modes of Assurance: Penalties

If warranty appears to have been an effective means of protecting alienations, the modes of assurance to be described in this chapter do not. About 220 charters prescribe penalties for endangering the security of transfers. By far the most common was anathematization, which occurs about two hundred times.[1] Ten anathema clauses also invoke blessings on those who help the church preserve its possessions, as do three charters without anathemas. Twenty-one of the charters with anathemas also order that each guilty person pay a fine, as do five charters which do not contain anathemas.[2] A few others, with or without anathemas, prescribe other secular punishments. These devices do not appear to have been used in connection with grants to lay persons.[3] It is likely that they were used exclusively in connection with transfers to churches.

Some of the clauses in which penalties are laid down use language as formal and formulaic as any to be found in the charters. Nevertheless, the wording is anything but standardized. The style ranges from long and extremely solemn imprecations to brief notices. Much variation, of content as well as style, depends on the practices of individual abbeys.[4] The five oldest abbeys used both anathemas and fines notably more often than did abbeys established in the eleventh century: they account for more than 60 percent both of the anathema clauses and of the fines extant from Norman abbeys.[5] Indeed, the use of anathemas and of fines seems to have been inherited from the pre-Norman past and declined steadily for most of the century.[6] The usage of individual churches also differs. Mont-Saint-Michel, for example, used anathema clauses with a frequency consistent with its status as one of the oldest Norman abbeys but never prescribed a fine. Another striking example is Troarn, which, as was normal for an abbey founded in the second half of the eleventh century, used anathema clauses rarely, only six times, although many charters from Troarn survive. This one church, however, used blessing clauses as often as anathemas, contributing more than half of the blessing clauses extant from Norman abbeys; all the other Norman churches combined used one blessing clause for every thirty-three anathema clauses.[7]

Few charters say explicitly that the purpose of establishing and announcing penalties in advance was to render alienations secure, undoubtedly because the purpose was patently obvious.[8] Each clause names those against whom it is directed, usually all who threaten the grant. The number of different locutions used is nearly equal to the number of extant clauses, although the charters of an individual church tend to resemble one another.[9] Some references to those who might incur excommunication take the form "anyone who claims," but most say "anyone who dares to claim" or "tries to claim" or even "wishes to claim." The implication usually is that the simple desire to make trouble was enough to bring on the punishments; they did not depend upon conviction of having made a false claim. The words used—violate, infringe, subtract, contradict, invade, and so on—imply that any claim is ipso facto unjustified.[10] Two charters from Marmoutier say that only claimants found to have claimed unjustly would be fined;[11] but the issue is theoretical, for there is no evidence that such a fine was ever actually paid.[12]

Some clauses specify particular categories of persons against whom they are directed. Most often these are the alienors' heirs, relatives, or successors, usually followed by "or anyone else." The reason is obvious: heirs and relatives were the persons most likely to raise claims. Only one alienor included himself among potential claimants,[13] although in practice alienors often reneged on their alienations. A few charters announce that the punishment applies only to claims after the alienor's death—presumably because, at least at the moment when the charter was written, the alienor intended to protect the alienation himself until he died.[14] A few charters name persons other than relatives as subject to excommunication.[15] Several condemn members of the recipient church who alienate what the charters confer.[16] The memorandum of Rainald the chaplain declares that all the facts are well known to a cleric named Vitalis, "and if through fear or love of anyone he should deny the truth of this may almighty God excommunicate him, and I in as much as I can"[17]—the only explicit statement of a penalty for false witness from the whole of the century.

Rainald pronounced this anathema himself "as much as I can." In clauses which identify the person pronouncing the anathema, it was most often the alienor, even when he was a layman.[18] Occasionally, a layman is made to say that—like Rainald, the only cleric to do so—he excommunicates as far as he is able.[19] Explicit recognition that laymen had less power than members of the clergy is rare, however.[20] The principal indication of such a sentiment is the number of anathema clauses attributed to bishops: twenty-one, where the bishop or bishops named have no other apparent connection with the alienation.[21] By comparison, abbots seldom anathematized.[22] Rainald, who was, of course, a donor and whose circumstances were unusual, was the only other cleric to issue an anathema, except for one monk who did so as a recipient.[23]

Anathemas were at least sometimes pronounced during acts of donation,[24] and a few charters indicate that all those present responded, "Amen."[25] Just before he died in 1093, Bishop Geoffrey of Coutances issued a charter in which he "blessed the defenders and consolers of the church of Coutances

[and] smote its invaders and devastators with an anathema of eternal malediction." Moreover, he "often had it recited in his presence, and [so did] the bishops and abbots who came to visit him [while he was] still living in the body, and who were present afterwards at his funeral, namely, Odo bishop of Bayeux, Michael bishop of Avranches, William bishop of Durham, and Gilbert abbot of Caen, Roger [abbot] of Lessay and also Roger [abbot] of Montebourg, all the clergy and people responding, 'Amen.' "[26] Obviously, if the purpose of anathema clauses was to scare off potential claimants before they made trouble, publicity was necessary. Geoffrey's actions on behalf of his own church may, therefore, not have been unusual; but if other prelates acted similarly for their own churches they seem not to have recorded their actions in charters.[27]

Whether the danger of incurring excommunication and its consequences in the next world had a deterrent effect on claimants is difficult to determine, for would-be challengers have not left records of their thoughts.[28] The preamble to a grant by Duke William cites, as his reason for the grant, the risk which disseisors of church property ran, but information is not sufficient to tell whether William was ridding himself of a personal danger.[29] Some charters concern restorations made to annul excommunications which had actually been pronounced against the restorers or their ancestors,[30] but how often the penalty was put into effect is unknown. The sources are unlikely to discuss excommunications which did not sooner or later produce the desired effect, and concern for the sensibilities of quitclaimers may well have led to silence even when excommunication had played a role in securing the restoration of disseisins or the renunciation of claims.

Several considerations imply that excommunication was not a particularly useful weapon. Only one anathema clause was used in connection with a sale, although sales appear to have been considered an unusually insecure type of transfer.[31] More important, in several cases a man died excommunicate and it was his son who made the restoration.[32] Furthermore, anathema clauses become less and less frequent from the middle of the eleventh century on. Part of the decline is to be explained by the establishment during the eleventh century of many new abbeys, for none of these used an anathema clause more than a half-dozen times in its extant charters. For the five oldest abbeys, which used anathema clauses consistently, the decline, though not quite as striking, is nevertheless evident.[33] That anathemas were less often written down as the century progressed is unlikely: in a period when writing was coming increasingly into use, more rather than less evidence of something which occurred at an unvarying rate would be expected. If, therefore, the apparent decline represents an actual one, two explanations are plausible: either excommunication in the event of a disseisin had been found relatively ineffective as a means of preventing and terminating disseisins,[34] or churchmen came to have confidence in secular assurance techniques and in the willingness and ability of the duke and his magnates to protect church property. Probably both factors contributed.

About a quarter of the extant anathema clauses include, about any potential challenger, a phrase "unless he comes to his senses" or "unless he makes amends" or "unless he gives satisfaction"—or any two or even all three. Curses which make a distinction between excommunication in this world and damnation in the next, condemning the claimant to both, always say, in effect, "Let him be excommunicated and, unless he makes amends, let him go to Hell." Exactly what was meant by satisfaction is obscure. A few charters refer to "worthy" satisfaction and one to "worthy satisfaction in public," but they do not specify in what the satisfaction consisted.[35] There are no contemporary allusions to corporal punishment as a penitential act of satisfaction, unless the satisfaction which had to occur in public is one.[36] The only charters which say anything on this point refer to entirely secular ways of making amends; one mandates restitution, the other a fine.[37]

Despite the latter charter, it does not seem that the fines prescribed by more than 10 percent of the anathema clauses were intended as the way for claimants to give satisfaction for having raised claims, for only this charter both talks of satisfaction and prescribes a fine, a strikingly low proportion if there was an intrinsic connection between the two ideas. The silence might be explicable, however, on the grounds that the connection was so obvious that it need not be stated. More important, in my view, is the size of most of the prescribed fines. A few charters propose fines in amounts which, though doubtless intended to be painful, were within the scope of possibility; but the amounts in most charters are unrealistic.[38] One proposes a fine of 1,000 gold pounds plus 60,000 silver pounds.[39] The average number of gold pounds prescribed by twenty-four charters is over 178. An ounce of gold was a recognized monetary unit, though a rare one.[40] Nevertheless, fines in gold—especially the eighteen which amounted to 20 or more gold pounds—cannot have been realistic figures.[41] Their purpose must have been simply to terrify potential challengers. Moreover, the size of a fine seems normally to have little relation to the amount of property involved in the alienation which the fine was intended to protect.

Fines so large as to be meaningless cannot have proved a very effective assurance technique. It is hardly surprising that there is no evidence of the payment of any fine or even of any demand for payment in this context. Moreover, the use of fines decreases steadily throughout the century. The sizes of fines probably also reflect their inutility: in the first half of the century, sixteen fines range in amount from 3 gold pounds to 200 and the average amount is 71; after 1050, there are three fines of 1,000 gold pounds, but the other five range from 3 to only 100, and they average only 29.[42] The amounts therefore polarize after midcentury. It is possible that the clauses about fines were copied blindly from pre-Norman diplomas and were meaningless to the scribes who copied them,[43] but the variation in the amounts of fines suggests otherwise.[44] Both trends are, instead, probably signs of the inefficacy of fines in assuring the stability of church possessions: they were made larger so as to raise the level of terror or smaller either in an attempt to make them realistic or because the size simply did not matter, while at the same time they were used less often because they did not work. Moreover, although most abbeys founded in Normandy in the eleventh century adopted the use of anathema clauses, albeit to a lesser extent than the older abbeys, none ever used a fine—with the exception of Bernay, once, in a charter probably written by a scribe from Fécamp.[45]

The persons to whom fines were supposed to be paid also indicate that fines were not intended as satisfaction to churches for claims which were raised, for fines were rarely supposed to be paid to the churches. Instead, they usually were to go to some public authority: two to the king of France, eight to the duke, two divided equally between the king and the duke, one divided unequally between the archbishop of Rouen and the duke, one to the alienor's lord, one to the judge, apparently whoever he might be, and one to the court, which presumably is the equivalent.[46] One fine was to be paid half to the king and half to the aggrieved church, one partly to the duke and partly to the church, one entirely to the church, and one to the target of the suit.[47] Only one fine was payable entirely in the ordinary coinage, 1248 *d.*, the amount which the abbey had paid out for the land. About this the charter says, ambiguously, "Let him pay . . . or concede satisfaction to the brothers of the same place"; probably the fine was to go to the church, but one cannot be certain.[48] As was discussed earlier, whichever of two parties withdrew from an exchange was to pay the other a fine of sixty pounds in the ordinary coinage;[49] but it is questionable whether this payment was intended as a penalty of the sort under discussion here, and I have not otherwise included it. Rannulf the priest of Pieux committed some act against Marmoutier's priory of Héauville for which he was condemned to pay a fine of forty pounds in the ordinary coinage; being unable to pay, he made over to the monks 140 acres of land instead.[50] A vinegrower named Drogulus, condemned to pay a fine of seven pounds in coin to La Trinité du Mont and also unable to pay, took even more drastic action.[51] These are the only two instances of fines which were actually assessed; in each, the fine was to go to the injured party. It is not stated what either Rannulf or Drogulus had done, however; therefore, I have not otherwise included these fines in my discussion of the penalties for disseisins.

A few charters mandate other penalties, alone or in addition to an anathema and/or a fine, but none suggests that the penalty it names was a usual one which was normally left unstated. In one version of the foundation charter of Saint-Evroul, the duke provides that if anyone challenges any portion, large or small, of the abbey's possessions, "all his patrimony ought to be attributed to our demesne possessions," that is, to the ducal demesne.[52] The only other time forfeiture appears in Normandy in this context, it was more moderate: Fécamp, granting a life estate to a layman, stipulated that if he ever tried to demand anything else from the abbey, he was to lose the life estate.[53] The foundation charter of Saint-Evroul also prescribes, in the passage just cited, that any challenger "know that he is answerable to our majesty."[54] Two other charters are similar: one says that a challenger who resists payment of a fine "will be answerable to public justice"; the other orders that any claimant both pay a fine of ten gold pounds "to the court" and be "marked with the infamy of sacrilege."[55] Public trial followed by disinheritance and outlawry, the usual punishments for serious crimes, or by infamy may, therefore, have been contemplated as punishments for claims, but there is no evidence of the application of these penalties to an actual claimant.

The last type of penalty, prescribed only once, is that the claimant "should be a serf forever with all his posterity."[56] As the same charter also prescribes not only an anathema but the largest known fine, it is likely that this penalty was introduced to terrorize potential challengers rather than in expectation of its actually being enforced. Nonetheless, there is one instance of the use of the penalty. For an unknown reason, the vinegrower Drogulus, who belonged to La Trinité du Mont,

> was vehemently accused before us [the monks] and brought to trial, and there he was found liable, so that he should be burdened with a debt of seven pounds. Not having the wherewithal to pay it, he, with his wife and children, was accepted into servile status by Abbot Rainier. And when he sought mercy, the abbot had mercy. He not only dismissed the debt but also gave him five shillings, for this reason: that he or his heir, completely renouncing his customary sack [of grapes?] at the vintage and what they call a "closerie," should demise [these] to the Holy Trinity as an allod.[57]

It is perhaps more likely that Drogulus was accused of a crime—or simply of being in debt—than that he had perpetrated a claim or disseisin.[58] Nonetheless, he provides an example of a man who actually became a serf and incurred forfeiture because he had committed some offense.[59]

There were thus five penalties which might be prescribed in advance in an attempt to ensure that a church's property would remain to it. Of these by far the most common was excommunication, which, if not removed, was expected to result in confinement in Hell in the afterlife. Excommunications were sometimes actually pronounced against disseisors and claimants. Fines, the next most common penalty, are mostly so large that their purpose can only have been to terrorize potential challengers. Forfeiture, trial followed by outlawry or infamy, and reduction to serfdom, the three other penalties, are encountered only very occasionally.[60] There are few known instances of the exaction of any penalty except excommunication, and penalties in general do not appear to have been effective deterrents to claims.

11

Charters

CHARTERS PROVIDE the bulk of the information available about the private law of eleventh-century Normandy, but the purpose of the charters was not such as to make it likely that all legal matters would receive equally extensive treatment in them. Hence it is necessary to determine as exactly as possible the purpose for which charters were drawn up, not only because this is intrinsically important but also because only so can the information which they give be evaluated.

In both earlier and later times charters were deeds: the authentic document, produced in court, constituted adequate proof of title. Of all the extant eleventh-century Norman charters, however, only one seems to have been intended to serve this way. A charter by which Robert abbot of Jumièges gave a life estate to Hugh de Montfort ends thus: "And to confirm this a testimonial writing was made on both parts, having one and the same form: one would be preserved in St. Peter's place [Jumièges], the other the aforesaid Hugh would retain with him, in such a way that if he should lose it he should also similarly lose the land of which we are speaking."[1] Because, elsewhere, the charter suggests that Hugh may have been causing the abbey sufficient trouble so that he was bought off with a life estate,[2] it seems likely that the unusual function ascribed to the charter was an attempt to prevent further dispute if Hugh lost it or claimed to have done so.

The last line of the charter consists of the words *Cirographum testimonii istius scripturae*, and its description of the nature of a chirograph is the only one extant from eleventh-century Normandy. To make a chirograph, a scribe wrote two or more copies of a charter on one sheet of parchment, which was then cut into the separate copies. The cut was sometimes wavy or jagged, and it often bisected the word "chirograph" or another legend written large between the copies before they were cut apart. Each party to the transaction retained one copy, the evident purpose being to defeat forgeries by using the exact dovetailing of the copies as a test of authenticity. It was probably a fairly effective technique.[3] The extent to which the fully developed technique was in use in Normandy in the eleventh century is unclear. Aside from the charter about Hugh's life estate, fourteen Norman charters refer to themselves or to other charters as chirographs.[4] The word is sometimes no more than a synonym for *carta* or *scriptum* or *privilegium*: this was its original meaning.[5] Bishop Geoffrey of Coutances' charter anathematizing the enemies of his church, in which nothing is transferred and there is no second party, is called a chirograph.[6] Nevertheless, at least some of the charters called chirographs seem to have been multiple copies of the type described. One extant original certainly is.[7] Six of the fourteen charters, including Bishop Geoffrey's, use some variant of the phrase *sub chirographo*, a locution which never occurs with *carta* or *scriptum* or *privilegium* and which implies that a chirograph was not a thing but a form.[8] Nothing inherent in the nature of a chirograph makes it a deed, however; and no charter except Hugh de Montfort's implies that chirographs were, in contrast to other types of charters, used dispositively. That the charter about Hugh and Jumièges is both a chirograph and apparently a deed must be regarded as a coincidence.

In eleventh-century Normandy mere possession of a charter did not prove one's right to the property described in the charter, nor did mere transfer of a charter adequately transfer the property it described.[9] In a period when the habit of writing charters was only developing and had hardly begun to spread to transactions between lay persons, the attitude that charters were deeds would be most unlikely. Moreover, despite the apparent recognition of the importance of recording transfers to churches in writing, eleventh-century Norman charters were not always drawn up as soon as an alienation had been made. Short delays were common. Evidence of long delays is less abundant, and they were probably rarer. The most indicative is one, already cited, concerning gifts made by Turstin Efflanc and his brother over the course of at least thirty-four years. Evidently no earlier written record of the gifts had been made.[10] Under such circumstances, the charter can hardly have been a deed.

Instead, the primary function of charters was to record the facts to which witnesses might be asked to testify and, often, the names of the witnesses themselves. Charters might be used in acts of donation but so might other objects; and the purpose of an act of donation was to be witnessed. A charter was sometimes read out so that some person could express his or her agreement to its contents, but again this was a public ceremony with witnesses. Charters were produced in court as proof, but apparently mainly as an aid to the memory of the witnesses whose testimony constituted the proof. Turstin Efflanc, by finally having his charter written, was "restoring" the gifts "to memory."[11] Only in the unavoidable absence of witnesses were charters themselves used as proof.

The evidence for this last assertion comes mostly from one of two places: the preambles of many charters, on one hand, and, on the other, references to the types of proof used in court. Some charters begin with preambles whose theme is that "if anyone, stirred by love of the celestial life, should wish to give anything of his property to any place of the saints to possess in perpetuity, so that it should remain unshaken he should solemnly make a written record about it, [which record should be] supported by the stipulations of suitable persons about it."[12] Preambles of this sort are nearly as numerous as those whose theme is salvation, and similar sentiments are often found in the bodies of charters. The theme is a natural one in a period when recording transactions was a novelty.[13] Such passages commonly refer to charters as a defense against alterations resulting from the oblivion which time brings or as a substitute for the memory of men. This was no mere literary topos: a letter of St. Anselm as abbot of Bec asks Archbishop Lanfranc, who had been prior of Bec, whether he can remember anything about several transfers to the abbey, which itself evidently had only the haziest recollection of how its possession of some of its lands and its claims to possess other lands had come to be. The matter was urgent, for at least one of these claims was about to come to trial before the Conqueror, who himself could not remember whether he had consented to the transfer.[14] No wonder that preambles stress the utility of written records. Less often they call charters a defense not only against forgetfulness but also against deliberate attempts to subvert the intent of the alienors. The wording varies widely, and most are unlike the example quoted in that they do not refer explicitly to human witnesses as well; but the constant theme of these statements is, as another charter puts it, that "those things which are expressed in writing are firmly held."[15]

Charters, as a reservoir of memory of alienations, could be cited as proof in the context of disputes in addition to or instead of witnesses. When Roger de Croismare claimed the land which his father-in-law Gilbert had given Saint-Pierre de Préaux, the first step in the settlement of the dispute was the reading of Gilbert's charter in the presence of both parties. Roger, the scribe suggests, was convinced by this that he had little hope of complete victory and therefore agreed to a compromise.[16] In eight other cases, one involving two separate trials, charters were alleged as proof; in another the absence of a charter was remarked upon.

Six of these nine accounts, two of them from historical sources, mention charters alone, without witnesses. According to the late eleventh-century *Inventio et miracula Sancti Wulfranni*, at some time between 944 and 953 Gerard de Brogne, abbot of Ghent, tried to recover his abbey's Norman lands from Duke Richard I. He promised to return the body of St. Wandrille, which had been translated to Ghent for safety during the Viking attacks,

> if the lands were given back to him which he should be able to prove his by means of privileges recorded in charters. But he [the duke], on the advice of his magnates, ordered that the charters be produced and read and expounded in the presence of all. When this was done, murmurs and denials began to arise from all of them, who said that they could in no way do without their own honors which warlike strength had won for them by the arms and blood of their predecessors or which they themselves had acquired by long service and much toil.[17]

Gerard was therefore unsuccessful in his claim. No one seems to have challenged the authenticity, veracity, or authority of his charters, however, although it must be remembered both that the source was written more than a century after the incident of which it tells and that at the time of the incident, so far as is known, no Norman had yet had any experience with charters.[18]

In the eleventh century, when they were in the habit of drawing up charters, the Normans seem to have been more receptive to claims of this sort. In his chronicle of Saint-Riquier, Hariulf says that, when in 1048 the abbess of Montivilliers claimed a church which had been given to Saint-Riquier by Duke Richard II, Abbot Gervinus "went to Normandy, taking with him the chirograph which Duke Richard had prepared about the gift of the same church, wishing to deraign it for us by veracious assertion and the testimony of the charter."[19] The charter by which Duke William confirmed the church to Saint-Riquier does not explicitly mention the earlier charter, saying only that Gervinus "explained in the presence of the magnates of my court that the cause of this affair [the church] belonged to him by right by the donation of my ancestors."[20] A charter from Odo bishop of Bayeux says that after he had claimed episcopal rights over the church of Rots, which belonged to Saint-Ouen, he was "shattered by the documents and privileges of Saint-Ouen, which were read aloud," and therefore renounced his claim.[21] In a slightly different procedure, a charter from Saint-Pierre de Préaux says that

> after Abbot Ansfrid had died and Abbot William had replaced him, Roger de Beaumont came at the request of the monks to their chapter, wishing to know how the monastery's affairs were going. Then in his presence the charter about the construction of the place, which his father and he had confirmed, was read and, at his order, expounded. The monks then complained that they had lost many of those things which were written in the charter, and especially the churches of Pont-Audemer, which Abbot Ansfrid had given to Hugh the cleric, son of Turulf, without their consent or license. Roger, therefore, when he heard their claims, ordered that everything which had been dispersed without the license or consent of their convent should return to the monks' demesne just as it was written in the charter.[22]

The matter was not settled this expeditiously: Hugh raised a counterclaim and the case went to trial, eventually to be settled by a compromise by which Hugh was to hold the churches from the abbey as a life estate.[23] Nonetheless, Roger was willing to accept the abbey's charter as adequate proof of the extent of its possessions.

When this matter came to trial, however, the proof brought was not charters but witnesses.[24] The cases involving Ghent, Saint-Riquier, and Saint-Ouen apparently never got to the stage of an actual trial. When Saint-Florent de Saumur's possession of a church was challenged by Lonlay, the monk in charge of the defense did not even bring the charter recording the alienation to court; proof was by oral testimony on the part of the alienor.[25] Rouen cathedral had an old charter which was relevant to Archbishop William's suit to recover land from two laymen to whom it had been granted by his predecessor Robert. The case was settled by compromise, but the record cites the charter as evidence.[26] When, in 1106, Saint-Taurin sued before Henry I for freedom from its subjection to Fécamp, it is not certain whether witnesses as well as a charter served as proof. The case was decided in Fécamp's favor only after "those things which were to be said and heard had been said and heard from each party and also the donation [was] heard and the charter read in which it was written how the church of Fécamp had had the aforementioned abbey from Duke Robert, the father of King William who conquered England, in exchange for Montivilliers."[27] The "things which were . . . said and heard from each party" may have been a conflict among party witnesses; but some legal argument may have been meant instead. Such arguments are occasionally quoted by other charters, most notably the one from Saint-Florent de Saumur which quotes William de Briouze's defense of the abbey against claims by Lonlay.[28] That no witnesses were called in the case between Fécamp and Saint-Taurin would hardly be surprising, for the exchange with Duke Robert had occurred more than seventy years earlier.[29] The charter probably served as proof.

In most other court cases for which the proof presented is known, witnesses alone constituted that proof.[30] Three charters, however, cite witnesses and charters together. The abbot of Troarn used both against Robert Samson, although the witnesses seem more important.[31] One account of a dispute between Marmoutier and La Couture over Guy de Laval's gifts says that the matter was finally settled in Marmoutier's favor when Duke William of Normandy "held a plea concerning this very thing and . . . saw that the monks of St. Peter [La Couture] had neither a letter nor any witness who would say that Guy had ever made them a gift of that land . . . nor had they presented a letter or a witness concerning this matter in any plea against Guy."[32] Either a witness or a charter would have been helpful to the monks of La Couture; it is not evident whether one would have been more useful than the other, but the absence of both was obviously disastrous.

The third case involving both a charter and witnesses is much more complicated. In the newer of the two castles at Bellême was a church dedicated to St. Leonard which was served by a college of canons. At some time between 1070 and 1079, the canons became involved in a dispute with Robert bishop of Sées because they alleged that they were exempt from his jurisdiction. As a result, the bishop excommunicated both the canons and their church; and Roger de Montgomery, then lord of Bellême in right of his wife, Mabel, granddaughter of the founder of the collegial church, complained to the archbishop of Rouen of the bishop's conduct. The case was heard in the court of William the Conqueror and decided in the canons' favor. It is recorded, with significant differences, in two notices.[33] There was also at Bellême a church known as Saint-Martin-du-Vieux-Bellême, which Hugh de Rocé had given to Marmoutier between 1050 and 1064.[34] In 1092 Robert de Bellême, eldest son of Roger de Montgomery and Mabel de Bellême, gave the collegial church of Saint-Léonard, too, to Marmoutier, which then consolidated its two churches at Bellême into a priory thereafter known as Saint-Léonard de Bellême.[35] Marmoutier immediately reopened the case against the bishop, and a notice of this second suit is extant.[36]

In connection with this long dispute a charter was forged, in at least two stages, to support the canons and/or the monks in their claims: it presents itself as the document whereby William I de Bellême, during the reign of Duke Richard II of Normandy, founded the church of Saint-Léonard and conferred on it a complete exemption from episcopal jurisdiction. The earlier of the extant redactions was drawn up between 1089 and 1092;[37] the later one, made between 1092 and about 1096, is accompanied by an equally spurious confirmation by King Philip I of France.[38] In addition to these indubitable forgeries, the second account of the first suit is suspect: it probably is not contemporary with the suit but, instead, was drawn up after the earlier redaction of the forged charter.[39] For the matter at hand, that some of these documents are spurious or dubious is not material, for the documents all date from the late eleventh century. Indeed, the very fact of the forgery is significant for the question of the role of charters at the time: documents would not be forged if they were useless.

The apparently contemporary account of the suit heard between 1070 and 1079 says that in William the Conqueror's court Roger de Montgomery and the canons "narrated how William de Bellême had built the aforesaid church for the forgiveness of his sins and how, at the direction of Pope Leo of blessed memory, he had made it free and absolved, and that from its day of dedication no archbishop or bishop had any custom at all in it, nor was able to excommunicate it in any way. And very old men were also there who had seen and heard this, ready to prove, at the king's judgment, what we had said."[40] The only proof offered was by witnesses. They would, indeed, have had to be "very old men" to testify after 1070 to events alleged to have occurred before 1026. The second account of the suit, however, says that "the canons indeed showed their privilege [their charter] and brought with them old men who saw and heard the same church at [its] dedication thus made free and ordained, so that no Christian should have any custom in it, by Robert king of France and R[ichard] duke of the Normans and Richard bishop of Sées and with them many bishops and abbots and counts and barons."[41] As the details given in this passage and in the rest of the charter correspond almost exactly to the earlier redaction of the forged charter of William de Bellême, this version was probably written to incorporate the alleged use of a charter in the suit.[42] It was probably contemporary with the forgery itself and, therefore, unless there was an earlier redaction of the forgery which is no longer extant, would date from between 1089 and 1092.[43]

The charter recording Robert de Bellême's gift of the church to Marmoutier in 1092 appears genuine.[44] Another seemingly genuine charter says that, "in the year when Robert de Bellême gave it to us," Gerard bishop of Sées again tried to subject the church to his jurisdiction. "Therefore we came to court at Sées and there Lord Robert de Bellême, who gave it to us, showed—through the privileges and precepts of the same church and through the authority of those who made it so absolved and quit—that the bishop should have nothing in it."[45] Because Bishop Gerard died in January 1091 and was succeeded by Bishop Serlo later in that year, the monks, who acquired the church only in 1092, seem to have been carrying on a dispute originally revived while Saint-Léonard was still a collegial church. The account of the suit is curiously incomplete. It does not say whose court heard the case[46] or explicitly refer to a decision. Perhaps the monks were not as successful as they had hoped, for, if they had not already done so, it was within the next few years that they reworked their forgery and forged a royal confirmation of it.[47]

These charters are most illuminating about the roles of witnesses and charters as proof in court. The case heard in the 1070s was apparently decided entirely on the basis of the testimony of witnesses. Although the canons won their case, however, they—or the monks of Marmoutier later—must have felt that a charter would make their position stronger, for they created one for this purpose. Moreover, they rewrote the narrative of the case which they had won so as to incorporate a reference to this charter and to alter the details of the decision to correspond to the details of the charter as forged. The second suit depended entirely on charters, undoubtedly out of necessity: witnesses ten years old when the alleged privilege was originally granted would have been seventy-six years old, at a minimum, in 1092; it is likely that no witnesses were available.

In most of the other instances when charters alone were used as proof, the dates of the charters are known or can be estimated with some accuracy. The results are interesting: the interval between the writing of the charter and the case in which it was used as proof ranges from more than thirty to more than seventy years.[48] All the witnesses in each case may well have been dead by the time the dispute arose and charters remained, by default, the only proof available. It is much more difficult to estimate the interval in the other case, aside from that between Marmoutier and the bishop of Sées, in which both charters and witnesses were used. It seems to have been quite long; but the record of the case places most of the emphasis on the witnesses.[49] In the case involving Marmoutier and La Couture, the interval was probably shorter, but here both witnesses and charters were mentioned because they were lacking.[50] Nothing here contradicts the suggestion that charters acquired most if not all of their evidentiary value only in the absence of witnesses.

There are indications elsewhere that charters were normally used as proof only for lack of witnesses. First, Gradulf abbot of Saint-Wandrille implies that while witnesses still lived the role of a charter was primarily to record their names when, narrating a successful claim which he made in Duke William's court, he says, "I produced many witnesses who were written down in the . . . charter of donation, which is in our possession."[51] Second, the emphasis which eleventh-century Normans placed on long memory as a protection is relevant.[52] It appears, among other things, to explain the inclusion in charters of direct quotations, picturesque details of the ceremonies surrounding transfers, and other seeming irrelevancies. Having little or nothing to do with what was transferred, these would be of no use if charters were deeds and of little use if they were intended primarily as proof; but it is easy to understand their presence if the chief purpose of charters, exclusive of preserving the names of witnesses, was to provide a record from which their memories could be refreshed. The preamble of one charter refers explicitly to this function, saying that among the purposes which charters serve is that they "recall forgotten things to memory."[53] Indeed, in this connection the "lest it be forgotten" theme in many charters is relevant.

The full text of the preamble just quoted raises the third and final point. It reads: "The fugitive memory of deeds done ought to be bound with chains of letters, which both in the present either recall forgotten things to memory or notify [men] of things unknown, and in the future renew ancient [deeds] and manifest bygone [things]."[54] Two other charters make very much the same point:

> I had the purchase . . . which I made . . . noted down in this letter and held by the writing of this charter, so that at the present it should be a testimonial judgment of firmness against the thefts and violences of perfidious men and that in the future it should be a manifest monument of truth against the false pretenses of adversaries and the insolent snares of plots.
>
> Lest, however, what had been done should be able to be removed from memory by a brief life or the lapse of time, I wished this charter to be made according to the usage of the ancients (*secundum antiquorum morem*) so that at present it should be a manifest testimony and in future a judgment of immunity against the plots of depraved men.[55]

Charters, in other words, perform two different functions: in the present, they are testimony, aids to men's memories; in the future, they are monuments or judgments, actual embodiments of the truth. Contemporary charters were at most merely one form of evidence, to be weighed against others and possibly to be impeached, and perhaps only memoranda on the basis of which witnesses' testimony could be prepared, whereas old charters were authoritative and would determine the decision in the case. To the question at what moment a charter passed from the former status to the latter, it makes sense to answer: when human witnesses ceased to be available.

Because no extant trials involved conflicts of evidence between witnesses for one party and charters produced by the other or between different charters produced by the two parties, however, it cannot be known whether, in the first situation, witnesses automatically defeated charters or how, in the second, conflicts between documents would have been handled. By the end of the period, moreover, transactions among lay persons seem still to have occurred entirely without written record.[56] Accounts of suits occasionally show a layman or an individual cleric presenting witnesses as proof, but never a charter.[57] Witnesses for lay persons against churches must, therefore, have had to rely on their unaided memory as the basis of their testimony, except presumably in the case of chirographs; and witnesses for lay persons against other lay persons must have had to rely in every instance upon memory alone.

If the charters which churches drew up existed primarily as memoranda for witnesses and only secondarily as proof in themselves, they would, as indeed they often do, include not only the details of the transfers to which the witnesses might be called to testify but also the details of the things seen or heard by the witnesses, especially any striking details which might help them recall one particular alienation out of the several or many which they might during their lifetimes have witnessed.[58] That is why information about modes of assurance is relatively abundant and there is a dearth of information about the things alienated and the conditions under which they were owned or held before and after the transfer. Because the purpose of each charter was, by and large, to record an act rather than the details of the transfer which that act accomplished, the things transferred need merely be identified, not completely described. Such an identification might on occasion refer to the way an alienor had acquired what is now alienated—"the land which I bought from so-and-so" or "held in fee" or "had in mortgage" and the like. These allusions provide almost everything known about transactions among lay persons. As such they are valuable; but their purpose is identification only, not description of the alienor's title. Little, therefore, is known of transactions among the laity except when, and to the extent to which, they had the same characteristics as transactions between lay persons and churches. Even for the transactions involving churches which are the subjects of the charters, however, only enough was noted down to enable the recipient and its witnesses to recall all.

Despite the weight of the evidence that charters were primarily memoranda, a few elements commonly found in them do not fall into this pattern. One is the anathema clause: charters often not merely note that someone pronounced an anathema but record the sentence in all its lurid detail. Indeed, extensive texts outnumber simple mentions, yet for a memorandum only a notation that an anathema had been pronounced would be necessary. The other anomalous element is signatures. Although charters were usually signed in a public ceremony, the value of signatures went beyond this; and the attitude to them seems to have been the more, the better.[59] Apparently, charters were beginning to be regarded as having a force of their own in protecting alienations: the very fact of recording the exact words of an anathema or an additional signature was, regardless of anything having to do with witnesses, thought to render the transfer more secure.

The same attitude seems to have governed the creation of many pancarts, for pancarts are much less likely than individual charters to contain descriptions of countergifts, acts of donation, and other elements of public ceremonies. This is true not only for the individual acts confirmed, where the omissions can be explained as made for reasons of space, because the acts recording the individual alienations could be consulted on these matters or because of the laziness of the scribe, but also in connection with the confirmation itself. The omission of such modes of assurance in the latter case implies that what was important was the pancart itself or the confirmer's signature to it—in other words, that the charter was an assurance in itself rather than merely a memorandum.[60]

A charter from Saint-Martin de Sées has already been quoted as saying that genuine charters might well "be thought by younger men wholly false or fictitious."[61] It seems, therefore, that charters were not automatically accepted as genuine. Unfortunately, no evidence exists of how charters were subjected to criticism before being regarded as proof, unless the statements that charters produced in court were not only read but "expounded" are allusions to some form of criticism or, at least, some form of defense by the party presenting the charter of its genuineness.[62] Whatever the current methods of authenticating charters may have been, the scribe from Sées seems to have felt that they were haphazard at best, since he cited a danger which could occur only if genuine charters were sometimes condemned as "wholly false or fictitious."[63]

By the late eleventh century there was evidently considerable—indeed, sometimes undue—suspicion of charters in the minds of at least some Normans. There was, perhaps, reason for this. In discussing signatures, I raised the possibility that they had an intrinsic dispositive value, that to sign a charter was to renounce all one's rights over the property conveyed by the transfer recorded in that charter,[64] and the lack of attention paid by pancarts to acts of confirmation may be additional evidence. If my suggestion is correct, the situation was potentially dangerous to the interests of alienors or alleged alienors because signatures were easy to forge. One piece of evidence that signatures had an intrinsic value was the behavior of a man named Mainus, who made the sign of an absent son on a charter to compel the son's consent.[65] If Mainus could forge his son's signature, what could prevent enterprising churches from forging whole charters and the signatures to them and thereby carrying the day in court, perhaps unjustly? The canons of Saint-Léonard de Bellême or the monks of Marmoutier did exactly that in the course of their dispute with the bishop of Sées.[66] Technically there was little difficulty: the "signature" of a lay person usually consisted merely of a cross, and nothing about such a mark was distinctive enough to prevent forgery or enable it to be detected.[67] The intrinsic value of signatures may, therefore, have been one of the factors which made forgery a common clerical practice in this period.

Forgeries were, in any case, a clear and present danger by the end of the period: a good many which were produced then are still extant.[68] One of the devices apparently developed in an attempt to prevent them was the chirograph.[69] Another seems to have been the seal.[70] The use of seals had become fairly widespread in Normandy by the end of the eleventh century, but when it began is much disputed. Some scholars reject the existence of a ducal seal in Normandy before 1066 and therefore condemn as a forgery every pre-1066 charter which mentions the ducal seal.[71] No exemplar of a ducal seal survives from before 1066, but at least seven are mentioned in or described for charters of which the originals are no longer extant.[72] Few nonducal seals are alleged before the conquest of England, and all of these are more or less dubious.[73]

The first nonducal seal which there is no substantial reason to question is mentioned in a charter which must come from 1067, however; and thereafter the use of seals both by the duke and by others proliferates.[74] A few extant originals demonstrate that a charter might be sealed without its text saying anything to indicate that it was;[75] because most charters do not survive in originals, it is difficult to say how rapidly the use of seals spread. By 1106, however, there is evidence of the use of seals in Normandy not only by the duke and by William Rufus and Henry I as kings of England but by the counts of Eu, Mortain, and Meulan, by the viscounts of the Cotentin, by the archbishop of Rouen and the bishop of Bayeux, and by a good many men of somewhat less exalted status.[76] Several alienors used their lords' seals to authenticate their alienations, apparently because they themselves did not have seals.[77] This interpretation is permissible wherever the person who seals does so as a confirmer rather than an alienor, for, with one exception, no extant charter was sealed by more than one person.[78] Conversely, to permit one's seal to be used to authenticate a charter thus became another mode of expressing consent.

Many charters state the purpose of the use of seals but usually only by the same stock phrase, "so that it may remain firm," used in other contexts. Scattered bits of evidence suggest a connection with signatures which went beyond the use of the same introductory phrase for both practices. First, and most striking, the verb *sigillare* and the noun *sigillum* could be used as though they were *signare* and *signum*, especially, though not exclusively, in charters from La Trinité du Mont.[79] Again, of the verbs which say what a person was doing by using a seal, the most common is "confirm" in one or another of its forms, but the second most frequent is "sign."[80] Moreover, of charters which mention seals many are said by the same phrase to have been both signed and sealed, as though those two ideas went together closely.[81] All this suggests that the function of a seal in the eleventh century was to authenticate not so much the charter to which it was attached as, more particularly, the signatures on that charter, which were otherwise easily forged but at the same of compelling effect. Seals are sometimes referred to as testimony.[82] Furthermore, Robert Curthose, in a charter by which he returned to Fécamp land of which he had inadvertently disseised the abbey, says that he performed an act of donation and sealed the charter "lest anyone else should come forward who is able to say that this land was not in the saint's demesne and that I did not return and give it back to the same church."[83] This implies that a seal had considerable evidentiary force; but no reference to a charter used as proof alludes to a seal as part of the reason for the worth of the charter.

In sum, therefore, the principal role of charters in eleventh-century Normandy was as memoranda of the transactions recorded, whose chief function was to preserve the names of the witnesses to the transactions and to record enough of the details of the transactions and of the acts by which the transfers were made to enable the witnesses to refresh their memories if they were called upon to testify to what they had seen and heard. Only in default of witnesses would the charters themselves serve as proof. At the same time, a few elements—anathema clauses, signatures, and seals—go beyond this mnemonic role to imply a dispositive function on the part of the documents in which they are found. The problem of forgery was clearly one of the reasons for the development of authenticating devices such as the seal and the chirograph; but descriptions of the uses made of charters as proof are too few and too chary of details to indicate the means by which, in the course of disputes, the authenticity of documents may have been tested.

12

The Custom of Normandy in the Eleventh Century

PARTICULAR TYPES OF alienations and modes of assurance have already been considered. Broader questions also arise about Norman law in the eleventh century. Did Norman practices in this period constitute a coherent body of law, a distinct custom which was fundamentally and consciously similar for all of Normandy, one which was "internally consistent, distinct from other *coutumes* and clearly territorialized"?[1] In other words, had Norman law "crystallized" by the end of the century? If, as I shall argue, it had done so, further questions emerge. When did the crystallization occur? What, if any, principles characterized the law which existed in Normandy in the eleventh century? How did the rules of this law develop?

The frontier of Normandy was more linear than the frontiers of most states of the eleventh century and also more stable, at least by the mid-eleventh century, perhaps earlier.[2] In later times this frontier coincided neatly with the boundaries of certain peculiarities of practice in several very different areas of human activity, among them the use of the acre as an agrarian measure, the absence of serfdom, the structure of the seigneuries, and the absence of a firm distinction between nobles and nonnobles in everything from the names of their tenures to the rules of succession which governed them.[3] The legal frontier—the area within which Norman customary law was the dominant legal system, with few local variations, and within which the Exchequer, later Parlement, of Rouen had jurisdiction—also coincided almost perfectly with the political boundaries of ducal Normandy.[4] Half a century ago, Robert Génestal demonstrated that the agreement of these frontiers can help to determine the period of formation of the custom of Normandy.[5] In the Middle Ages and later an area of twenty-five parishes known as the Conquêts Hue de Gournay was just within the political boundary of Normandy, but its law incorporated large amounts of Picard custom.[6] This area must, therefore, have been absorbed politically into Normandy after the formation of Norman custom within the then-existing borders of Normandy. There were, unfortunately, two men named Hugh de Gournay who might have made this acquisition, one a contemporary of William the Conqueror; the other, grandson of the first, lived in the first half of the twelfth century. Génestal found it impossible to choose between them and therefore established merely a *terminus ante quem* of about 1150 for the formation of the custom of Normandy. More recently, however, Jean-François Lemarignier has given reasons for preferring the earlier Hugh and for dating his acquisition to 1078 or 1079, and Anne Vallez has suggested that the acquisition may have been made even earlier and merely have been recognized by the king of France at that time.[7] As for the *terminus a quo*, the remote date must obviously be the moment when the early dukes acquired at least most of the territory within the Norman borders, which most recent scholars place in or about 933,[8] for before the union of this area under the dukes its component parts had not formed one political unit. Moreover, Lemarignier and others have pointed out that the Passais normand, the area around Domfront and Alençon over which the dukes of Normandy established their firm control no earlier than just before 1050, was governed by Norman custom and therefore must have been incorporated into the duchy before the formation of its custom.[9]

The crystallization of Norman custom may therefore be dated, on the basis of external information, within early and very narrow limits: the thirty years of William the Conqueror's greatest strength, between his victory at Val-ès-Dunes in 1047 and the beginning of his quarrels with his son Robert Curthose and Robert's supporters among the younger generation of Norman magnates about 1077.[10] Does knowledge of the law governing transfers of property in Normandy in the eleventh century, as it has been developed in this work, help to support this dating? Probably it does.

Here and there in the course of this study references have been encountered to the *mos Normanniae* or *mos patriae* or *mos terrae* or simply *mos*. Individually and even more collectively, these suggest that there was already by the second half of the eleventh century a custom which governed all of Normandy and was recognized by contemporary Normans as doing so. A charter of 1054 or 1055 refers to "the customs and all the services which come from the land, according to the *mos* of Normandy."[11] Between 1078 and 1096 relief was described as "the *mos* of the land."[12] Between 1079 and 1083 the ceremonial act of placing a donation on the altar of the recipient church was called *mos*.[13] Four charters from the second half of the century refer to the writing of charters as the *mos* or even the "*mos* of the ancients," although it was not.[14] In 1068, signatures were "according to custom (*consuetudo*)."[15] In addition, a charter of 1106 refers to "the forfeits . . . which are exacted according to human laws from homicides and also thieves convicted by a capital sentence according to ancestral *mos*"—or "according to the *mos* of the country."[16] Finally, the earliest appearance of *mos* in this sense in a Norman document comes from a charter of between 1031 and 1035 in which Duke Robert the Magnificent gave Fécamp "at Argences the league according to the *mos* of our country, for the market of that vill."[17] Although it is not certain that every one of these statements refers to a custom known throughout Normandy, it is the two earliest—the first and last as just quoted—which most clearly do so. It seems possible, therefore, to conclude that with regard to tenure, transfers, and criminal and public law there was already by the second half of the eleventh century a recognized custom of Normandy.

Not only are there references to a *mos* of Normandy, there are also references to *iures*. *Ius*, of course, could mean the rights of a particular individual, as in the common phrases *iure hereditario* and *iure meo/suo*;[18] but it could also mean a set of rules governing one aspect of life, that is, a particular area of law within the *mos*. Thus, there was a *ius alodii*, a *ius beneficiale*, and a *ius elemosinae*.[19] There was also a customary set of punishments for traitors, in existence by midcentury, which William of Poitiers calls a *lex puniendi* and a charter of 1074 calls a *ius iusticiae*.[20] Here, too, therefore, at least the tenurial and public aspects of the law were already separated out as distinct recognizable sets of rules by the second half of the eleventh century.

The question can be approached from another angle, that of the clarity of rules about particular aspects of the law, the content of the *iures*, so to speak; and the results of this study suggest again that the custom of Normandy was relatively well defined. If not in the minds of alienors and their relatives then at least in the minds of the scribes who wrote the charters, permanent alienations and conditional or temporary alienations were different species of transfer. Permanent alienations, moreover, were divisible into three distinct types—gifts, sales, and exchanges—according to the type of recompense. Certain types of transfers seem to have been particularly distinct: gifts in alms and mortgages are prime examples. Specific rules can occasionally be perceived to underlie a wide variety of phenomena. Thus, for example, the distinction between patrimony and conquest may underlie such otherwise apparently unconnected practices as purchases with the buyer's "own money," the presence of immovables in deathbed portions, divisions of English lands from Norman lands in inheritance by the first generation after the Conquest, and the change in the meaning of "inheritance" in the course of the eleventh century.[21] Similarly, the rule that silence means consent not only is the basis of both arguments in court whose details are known, Rainald the chaplain's against the cleric Samson and William de Briouze's against Lonlay, but also underlies many aspects of the modes of assurance which have been studied, among them the importance of ceremonial acts publicly performed, the importance of the personal presence of confirmers at such ceremonies, and questions put to those present at the ceremonies—either generally to the entire audience or specifically to a potential claimant—as to whether there were any objections to the transfer. Indeed, participation in public acts was the prevalent means of expressing consent. How one participated mattered less than the fact that one participated, and the reason for this may well be precisely that one's unprotesting cooperation was thought conclusive proof that any claim which one might later raise was invalid.

The rules were undoubtedly not entirely fixed: rules never are. The forms by which consent could be expressed were very varied, for example. A second area of seeming fluidity was the types of service in return for which grants other than gifts and, probably, exchanges were made. The appearance of variation may well be partly a result of the charters' taciturnity about service: by the early twelfth century the nuns of La Trinité de Caen seem to have had fairly well defined ideas about what services knights and vavassors ought to do. Yet, at the same time, there are enough allusions to some services to suggest that standardization had not gone very far even by the end of the century. Thus, relief, though it could be called *mos terrae*, was anything but fixed in the form it would later take, and the same seems to have been true of feudal wardship and aids. Indeed, it seems likely both that many aspects of feudal obligations were not nearly so precisely defined as they would be a century later and that specifically feudal services were not as prevalent as they have been thought.

If the rules were not and never became entirely fixed, they also never became entirely uniform throughout Normandy. That the custom of an honor might be more important to its tenants than the custom of the duchy is suggested, indirectly, by a compromise in which it was provided that any future dispute be settled by the lord's court sitting either at Alençon, which was by then in Normandy, or at Lurçon, which was outside it.[22] It is also likely that, in some respects at least, individual families had their own inheritance customs.[23] Moreover, there were—or there later developed—local customs within Normandy which differed on one or more points from the custom of the duchy.[24] Nevertheless, the evidence of charters which refer to aspects of the law as *mos* or *ius* or *consuetudo*, the testimony of William of Poitiers, writing in the 1070s, and the existence of well-defined branches of the law and of widely followed rules of law all suggest that by the end of the reign of William the Conqueror and probably a decade or more earlier "the custom of Normandy" was both a conscious concept and a distinct, territorialized body of rules.

To explain why the custom of Normandy should have crystallized so early is difficult. Jean Yver cites the unusual power of the dukes; but, although he dates the crystallization of Norman custom to the second half of the eleventh century, the specific aspects of ducal power which he singles out for discussion are the jurisdictional dominance of the ducal court and the development of writs of inquest, both of which, especially the latter, are twelfth-century phenomena.[25] More cogently, John Le Patourel suggests that the conquest of England led the Normans to contrast Norman law with English law;[26] although he himself does not believe that Norman custom crystallized especially early, his speculation implies that the Conquest may partially explain the early development of the concept of a custom of Normandy. It certainly seems likely, in the abstract, that sudden confrontation with a substantially different set of rules and practices would lead members of a society to perceive more clearly than earlier that their own rules and practices constituted a distinct body of law. Moreover, a contrast between the two sets of rules must have become obvious in such instances as the punishment of the men who rebelled in England in 1075, which differed depending on whether they were Norman or English.[27] Nonetheless, the Conquest is not likely to have been the only factor at work, partly because some of the clearest references to a custom of

Normandy predate it. It is, of course, possible that the general adventurousness of the Normans, which led many of them to travel widely, to participate in wars in Spain, and especially to begin the conquest of Italy roughly a generation before the conquest of England, had developed among them a perception of how they differed from others, legally as in other ways, on which their most famous conquest merely set a seal. It is even possible that the Normans' consciousness that their Scandinavian origins made them different from their neighbors influenced their thinking about their law, but the degree to which Normans of the eleventh century were aware of standing apart from the French is much disputed.[28] The relative fixity of the borders of the duchy may also have contributed. Of any more particularly legal factors, however, it seems impossible to speak.

If there was a distinct Norman custom by the end of the eleventh century, what were its principles? Only a few very broad tendencies are discernible.[29] In the area of assurance, it seems clear that the performance, even the repetition, of a wide variety of acts by the alienor and those closest to him or her by blood or by tenure was more important than the consent of extensive groups of remote connections. The circle of relatives consistently asked to consent is small: spouses, children, brothers, and *nepotes*. Even the consent of a grandson might be foregone as long as his father was alive.[30] Consent by lords' lords and by tenants' tenants is rarely reported, although close relatives and immediate lords often performed many acts to signify their consent and sometimes performed them over and over again.

In the area of transfers themselves, the principle which emerges most clearly is a preference for substitution of alternative beneficiaries or benefits rather than cancellation of an agreement if for some reason the original terms could not be fulfilled. In conditional alienations, loss of the property granted was the penalty for nonperformance of the condition, but attempts were made to provide alternative conditions to prevent loss if nonperformance resulted from inability to comply rather than from contumacy. It should also be noted that escheats, the variety of the penalty of loss which is most widely recorded, were rarely permanent: men whose fiefs were confiscated were usually restored to their lands, or their heirs were, some fairly soon, others after delays of decades.[31] Warranty as a mode of assurance is itself an embodiment of the principle that agreements are to be preserved by the substitution of alternate benefits if the original benefits cannot be maintained. In transactions of other types, most of which were quasi-conditional in nature, substitution was equally common in preference to cancellation. Relatives replace each other as recipients of the right to become a monk, the right to be buried in a convent, the right to be educated by an abbey; or one of these rights is substituted for another. Few attempts to treat a transfer made on such a condition as truly conditional and, therefore, subject to cancellation if the condition was not fulfilled are reported; and even fewer such attempts were successful. Instead, it seems, the alienor was entitled to a compensatory benefit—either the same benefit for a second person or a different one for the original beneficiary.[32]

The means by which some of the types of transactions current in eleventh-century Normandy became customary law and by which the rules about them were defined while others remained little used are obscure. No instance is known in which the private law of Normandy in the eleventh century was altered by ducal legislation, which seems to have concerned the public peace and criminal law exclusively.[33] Ernest-Joseph Tardif thinks that judicial decisions played a much larger role in determining the development of legal rules in Normandy than did custom in the narrow sense of the word.[34] Samuel Thorne and S. F. C. Milsom have certainly demonstrated how, in late twelfth-century England, customs and courts might interact to produce increased fixity and definition in the law, even to change it.[35] Relatively few court cases are reported from eleventh-century Normandy, however, and most of them ended in a compromise, a quitclaim, or a default. Indeed, compromises were probably preferred to decisions.[36] Moreover, the grounds, principles, or innovations of the rare judicial decisions are never stated. Certain rules covering different types of transfers may be deduced from the arguments which were made in court, when these are reported; but I do not think that there is a single known instance in which a recorded decision established a new legal rule or can be shown to have encouraged or discouraged a new legal practice, nor can enough be deduced about procedure to indicate clearly the ways in which procedural developments may have been at the base of development of other aspects of law. The difference may be merely apparent, the result only of an absence of sources, but the demonstrable preference for compromise makes it likely that litigation played a less important role in the evolution of law than it would a century later.

Moreover, it seems to me that a great deal of the law about transfers of property in this period was the product of the development of custom in the narrow sense, that is, of the invention, out of individual ingenuity, of convenient ways of achieving certain purposes and of the spread of these devices because of their advantages to the parties involved. With modes of assurance, one can sometimes observe the rise or decline of a particular method: anathemas and fines decline; party witnesses, warranty, and seals rise. By comparison, the dearth of information about details of the actual transfers makes it difficult to discern secular trends. The only one which emerges clearly is the change from a society in which significant amounts of land were owned to one in which most, perhaps all, land was held, a change which certainly occurred after the end of the first quarter of the century and probably was substantially complete by the beginning of its last quarter. Growing fixity of rules may be another secular trend. Nevertheless, the charters give the impression that in legal matters the Normans of the eleventh century were quite flexible. Within the established rules, they could make a wide variety of legal arrangements to meet the needs of particular situations. Perhaps it is the lack of formulas for drafting documents and the consequent informality of language of the charters which, alone, create this impression, but I think not. Not only did the Normans know and practice gifts both *inter vivos* and post-obit, sales, exchanges, conditional gifts, enfeoffments, rentals, life estates, and mortgages; but they could also combine these forms or alter their terms to produce transactions which were partly gifts and partly sales, mortgages which might become gifts or sales, a mortgage which became a vifgage, and so on—and others so complex as to defy categorization. Indeed, the final impression left by the charters is that any transaction mutually acceptable to the parties involved was legal. Much of the evolution of the forms of transfers characteristic of Norman law must have occurred as some combinations of provisions proved more useful to one or both parties than others and therefore grew increasingly common over time, whereas the less useful or more troublesome arrangements remained rare or disappeared.

Appendixes

APPENDIX A: TABLES

Table 1: Number of Extant Charters[a]

A: By decade

Decade	Certainly from this decade	Midpoint of span[b]	Total	Rate of increase[c]	Cumulative total
960–69	2	0	2		
970–79	0	0	0		2
980–89	0	1	1		3
990–99	2	0	2	2.00	5
1000–09	4	3	7	3.50	12
1010–19	10	5	15	2.14	27
1020–29	20	14	34	2.27	61
1030–39	22	19	41	1.21	102
1040–49	19	20	39	0.95	141
1050–59	25	42	67	1.72	208
1060–69	55	30	85	1.27	293
1070–79	37	43	80	0.94	373
1080–89	101	51	152	1.90	525
1090–99	128	44	172	1.13	697
1100–06	44	11	55	(0.46[d])	752

B: By ducal reign

Duke	Number	Rate of increase[c]	Length of reign in years	Average number[e]	Cumulative total
Richard I (942–96)	5		54	0.09	
Richard II (996–1026)	53	10.6	30	1.77	58
Richard III (1026–27)	2	0.04	2	1.00	60
Robert I (1027–35)	29	14.5	8	3.63	89
William II (1035–87)	455[f]	15.7	52	8.75	
1035–66	(203)	(7.00)	(31)	(6.55)	292
1066–87	(200)	(0.99)	(21)	(9.52)	544[g]
Robert II (1087–1106)	264	0.58 (1.3)[h]	19	14.89	808

[a] About four hundred charters fall into neither of the categories below and therefore do not appear here.

[b] Charters datable only to a span of years are here included as though they were dated at the midpoint of the span but only if the span covers no more than twenty years.

[c] Expressed as the ratio of the total for the period under consideration to the total for the immediately preceding period.

[d] Because this is not a full decade, I have prorated the number of charters for a full decade (i.e., seventy-nine) and calculated this figure accordingly.

[e] Number of charters per year of reign.

[f] The fifty-two charters not included in the division of William's reign which follows are datable to spans of years which straddle the dividing line of 1066.

[g] The fifty-two charters of note f are added here.

[h] The first figure is by comparison with the whole of William the Conqueror's reign; the second is by comparison with his reign after 1066.

Table 2: Confirmers, Witnesses, and Signers

The table is calculated on the basis of individual alienations. A separately issued confirmation is treated as an alienation and, therefore, not entered in the columns relevant to confirmation unless it, itself, was confirmed. Because forms rather than matters of substance are at issue, this seems the best way of proceeding: in form these acts are indistinguishable from acts of donation per se. Moreover, no alienation without recorded confirmers or witnesses or signatures was eliminated from the basis of computation of percentages unless the very form in which the alienation was recorded means that no mention of confirmers or witnesses or signers could be expected. If, for example, two alienations or an alienation and a confirmation are recorded in a charter as having occurred at the same time before the same witnesses, they are treated as one transaction for the purpose of calculating the percentage of acts for which witnesses are recorded. Again, if even one entry in a pancart records the names of confirmers of the alienation, then every entry in that pancart is treated as a separate alienation for the purpose of calculating the percentage of alienations for which confirmers are recorded; and the same is true of witnesses. Since most pancarts do not record signatures to the individual entries, a whole pancart is usually treated as one item for purposes of calculation as far as signatures are concerned. Had calculations been done on the basis of whole charters, had separate confirmations been treated as confirmations, or had the rule about eliminations been construed less stringently, the percentages would in most cases be considerably higher. Only those churches from which significant numbers of alienations survive are tabulated.

Table 2: Legend

Column

1 Number of relevant transactions

I. Joint alienors

2 Number of alienations naming more than one donor (total number of relevant alienations)

3 Percentage

II. Confirmers

4 Number of alienations naming confirmers (total number of relevant alienations)

5 Percentage

6 Highest number of confirmers named in one act

7 Lowest number of confirmers named in one act

8 Average number of confirmers named in one act, i.e., total of all confirmers ÷ number of alienations naming confirmers

III. Witnesses

9 Number of alienations naming witnesses (total number of relevant alienations)

10 Percentage

11 Highest number of witnesses to one act

12 Lowest number of witnesses to one act

13 Average number of witnesses to one act, i.e., total of all witnesses ÷ number of alienations naming witnesses

14 Number of witness lists divided *ex parte* or said to be *utriusque parte*

15 Percentage of witness lists divided, i.e., total in column 14 ÷ number of alienations naming witnesses

IV. Signers

16 Number of alienations naming signers (total number of relevant alienations)

17 Percentage

18 Highest number of signers of one charter

19 Lowest number of signers of one charter

20 Average number of signers per charter, i.e., total of all signers ÷ number of alienations naming signers

V. Overlap between signers and donors-confirmers

21 Number of charters in which there is any overlap

22 Highest incidence of overlap in one charter, i.e., total number of donors-confirmers who sign/total number of donors-confirmers

23 Lowest incidence of overlap in one charter [includes all charters which have signers]

24 Average incidence of overlap, i.e., total of donors-confirmers who sign as a percentage of all signers in all charters which have signatures

VI. Overlap between signers and witnesses

25 Number of charters which have both signers and witnesses

26 Highest incidence of overlap in one charter, i.e., total number of witnesses who sign/total number of witnesses

27 Lowest incidence of overlap in one charter [includes all charters which have signers]

28 Average incidence of overlap, i.e., total of witnesses who sign as a percentage of all witnesses in all charters in which there are both signers and witnesses

Table 2A

Church	1	2	3	4	5	6	7	8	9	10	11	12	13	14	15
Avranches	9	1 (9)	11	3 (9)	33	6	1	2.7	2 (7)	29	4	4+	2.5+	0	0
Bayeux	13	2 (13)	15	8 (13)	62	2+	1	1.3+	7 (13)	54	50+	3	18.6+	1	4.3
Coutances	9	1 (7)	14	0	0				7 (9)	11	6+	–	6+	0	0
Rouen	33	8 (33)	24	5 (33)	15	5	1	2.6	10 (23)	44	39+	4	11.8+	3	30
Bec	286	44 to 47 (286)	15 to 16	49 or 50 (285)	17	7+	1?	1.3	30 or 31 (285)	11	8+	1	3.1	1	3.3
Beaumont-le-Roger	4	0	0	2 (4)	50	6	1	3.5	2 (4)	50	21+	+	10.5+	0	0
Other priories	42	14 (42)	33	6 (42)	14	5+	1	2+	22 (42)	52	25	8	11.8	2	9.1
Bernay	6	1 (6)	17	3 (6)	50	3	1	2	2 (6)	33	116	34	75	1	100
Cerisy	35	3 (35)	9	23 (35)	66	5+	1	1.7	9 (35)	26	1+	–	1+	0	0
Cherbourg	5	2 (5)	40	2 (5)	40	1	–	1	1 (3)	33	10	–	10	0	0
Conches	34	6 (34)	18	25 (34)	74	9	1	ca. 2	11 (34)	32	12+	1	4.6+	1	9.1

Table 2A (continued)

Church	1	2	3	4	5	6	7	8	9	10	11	12	13	14	15
Fécamp	85	5 (83)	6	34 (85)	40	8+	1	ca. 1.5	38 (84)	45	37+	1	10+	12 or 13	ca. 33
St-Martin-du-Bosc	24	0	0	11 (24)	46	7+	1	ca. 1.5	14 (24)	59	4	1	2.9	0	0
St-Gabriel	69	4 or 5 (63)	ca. 7	13 (69)	19	7	1	2	4 (5)	80	17+	3	ca. 11+	2	50
Fontenay	27	4 or 5 (27)	ca. 17	16 (27)	59	10	1	2.7	8 (27)	30	8	1	3.3	2	25
Jumièges	123	21 (119)	18	44 or 45 (93)	ca. 48	7	1	ca. 1.8	19 (77)	26	37	1	10.5	8 or 9	ca. 45
Lessay	22	10 (21)	48	7 or 8 (22)	ca. 34	2	1	ca. 1.5	16 (21)	76	13	2	5.8+	2	12.5
Lire	29	9 (26)	35	6 (27)	24	1	1	1	22 (26)	85	26	4	ca. 8	10	45
Montebourg	12	2 (12)	17	6 (12)	50	3	2	2.5?	6 (11)	55	25+	3	10.8	2	33
Montivilliers	35	1 (33)	3	19 or 20 (35)	ca. 56	4	1	2	24 (35)	69	11+	1	3.8+	0	0
Mont-St-Michel	62	8 (57)	14	21 (62)	34	6+	1	ca. 2.2	14 (58)	24	12	2	6.9	4	28
St-Amand	24	2 (19)	11	10 (21)	48	4	1	1.4	18 (23)	78	9+	3	5.1+	3	17

Table 2A (continued)

Church	1	2	3	4	5	6	7	8	9	10	11	12	13	14	15
St-Désir de Lisieux	9	0	0	6 (9)	67	5	1	2.3+	1 (9)	11	2+	–	2+	0	0
St-Etienne de Caen	275	31 (250)	12	72 (266)	27	29	1	2.5	162 (222)	73	28	1	6.3	48	30
St-Evroul	108	24 (103)	23	41 or 42 (107)	ca. 39	13	1	ca. 2.8	51 (92)	54	26	1	7.4	17	33
St-Georges de Boscherville	51	13 (50)	26	44 (50)	88	4	1	1.2	14 (42)	33	10	1	4	0	0
St-Léger de Préaux	51	6 (50)	12	14 (51)	28	4	1	1.8+	13 (51)	26	14	1	7	7	54
St-Martin d'Ecajeul	7	1 (7)	14	2 to 4 (7)	29 to 57	1	1?	1	0	0					
St-Martin de Sées	241	51 (232)	22	116 (236)	49	7	1	2.3	162 (227)	71	77	1	8.3	38	23
St-Ouen	83	11 (79)	14	47 or 48 (81)	ca. 59	4 or 5	1	ca. 1.6	16 (50)	32	23?	3	ca. 10.5	6	38

Table 2A (continued)

Church	1	2	3	4	5	6	7	8	9	10	11	12	13	14	15
St-Pierre de Préaux	140	27 (136)	20	54 to 59 (140)	ca. 40	5+	1	1.8	56 (139)	40	17+	1	6.7+	36	64
St-Sauveur-le Vicomte	71	9 (71)	13	23 (71)	32	5	1	1.6	25 (71)	35	14	1	7.6+	5	20
St-Taurin d'Evreux	48	10 (48)	21	21 to 23 (45)	ca. 49	4?	1	ca. 1.5	8 (22)	36	38+	5	13.7+	6	75
St-Wandrille	84	13 (80)	16	42 (81)	52	6	1	ca. 1.8	30 (62)	48	29+	1	9.8	15	50
Le Tréport	80	13 (72)	18	51 or 52 (80)	ca. 64	9	1	3.4+	74 (80)	93	12+	1	3.7+	0	0
La Trinité de Caen	206	43 (182)	24	86 to 89 (194)	ca. 45	5+	1	1.8	30 (186)	16	28	2	7.3	9	30
La Trinité du Mont	132	33 (129)	26	63 (125)	50	5+	1	ca. 1.8	57 (122)	47	19	1	5.5	14	25
Troarn	156	38 (152)	25	42 (154)	27	7+	1	ca. 1.9+	32 (136)	27	18+	1+	8.6+	14	44

Table 2B

Church	16	17	18	19	20	21	22	23	24	25	26	27	28
Avranches	1 (7)	14	10	–	10								
Bayeux	8 (13)	62	25	1	14	7	2/2	1/2	86	2	4/4	–	100
Coutances	0	0											
Rouen	5 (25)	20	10	1	4.2	4	2/2	1/7	46	1	1/18 +	–	<5.6
Bec	9 (285)	3	16 +	1	5 +	8	1/1	1/ca. 10	51	2	2/8	0/3	18.2
Beaumont-le-Roger	0	0											
Other priories	1 (42)	2	12	–	12	1	1/1	–	100	0			
Bernay	1 (6)	17	12	–	12	1	3/3	–	100	0			
Cerisy	20 (32)	63	8	3	4.9	20	5/5	3/4	ca. 97	7	1/1	0/1 +	<80
Cherbourg	0	0											
Conches	1 (34)	3	3	–	3	1	1/1	–	100	1	–	0/4	0

Table 2B (continued)

Church	16	17	18	19	20	21	22	23	24	25	26	27	28
Fécamp	28 (72)	39	37	1	7.4	27	4/4	0/1	84	12	6/?	0/20	<1
St-Martin-du-Bosc	1 (1)	100	4	–	4	0				0			
St-Gabriel	2 (3)	67	14	9	11.5	2	7/11	0/2	54	2	8/18+	7/24+	<36
Fontenay	2 (21)	10	26	19	22.5	2?	4/15	1/?	<27	2	0/1	0/2	0
Jumièges	38 (59)	64	24	1	8.5	36	11/11+	0/3	69	7 or 8	1/5	0/15+	<1
Lessay	4 (18)	22	25+	1	15+	4	1/3	0/3	<19	3	1/19?	0/4	0 or 4
Lire	2 (24)	9	7	4	5.5	2	2/2	–	100	1	1/8	–	12.5
Montebourg	5 (11)	46	27	1	10.4?	4	1/1	1/4	<40	0			
Montivilliers	4 (35)	11	5	1	2.8	3	1/1	0/2	50	2	1/9	0/2	2
Mont-St-Michel	34 to 36 (52)	ca. 68	33 or 34	1	ca. 9.5	30 to 32	3/3	0/5+	ca. 66	4	9/9	0/11	<27
St-Amand	14 (20)	70	18	1	ca. 3.6	14	2/2	0/2	64	12	4/4	0/11	7.2

Table 2B (continued)

Church	16	17	18	19	20	21	22	23	24	25	26	27	28
St-Désir de Lisieux	1 or 2 (5)	20 or 40	12	1?	6.5 or 12	1	2/12+	–	<17	0			
St-Etienne de Caen	15 (200)	8	38	4	15.1	15	3/3	2/11	<55	7	1/1	0/9	<19
St-Evroul	8 (75)	11	19+	1	9.3	7	3/3	2/4	36	2	–	0/17	0
St-Georges de Boscherville	1 (1)	100	7	–	7	1	2/many	–	?	1	–	0/many	0
St-Léger de Préaux	5 (11)	46	20	1	4.8	4	1/1	1/3	50	4	0/7	0/14	0
St-Martin d'Ecajeul	2 or 3 (3)	67 or 100	10	1?	6.3 or 9	2	4/4	1/2	83	0			
St-Martin de Sées	37 (208)	18	10	1	3.5	36	3/3	0/6	48	26	7/15	0/13	7
St-Ouen	33 (46)	72	28	1	ca. 7.4	29	4/4	0/4	<64	8	7/7+	0/15	<11

Table 2B (continued)

Church	16	17	18	19	20	21	22	23	24	25	26	27	28
St-Pierre de Préaux	13 (134)	10	11	1	3.2	12	3/3	2/5	<66	3	1/1	0/6	12.5
St-Sauveur-le Vicomte	1 (70)	1	7	–	7	1	2/2	–	100	0			
St-Taurin d'Evreux	3 (21)	14	5	2	3	3	3/3	0/5	31	3	1/12	0/13	<2.8
St-Wandrille	32 or 33 (55)	ca. 59	24	1	ca. 7.3	30 to 32	4/4	0/1	<72	9	5/5	0/7	<32
Le Tréport	0	0											
La Trinité de Caen	7 (101)	7	37	7	20.1	7	2/2	10/81	22	3	11/11	3/17	40
La Trinité du Mont	89 (97)	92	25	1	7.2	75 to 77	7/7	0/4+	<85	*			
Troarn	18 (74)	24	30	2	8.2	17	3/3	3/15	<56	4	1/1	0/12	<12.5

*Special case: see Chapter 7, at nn. 151–54.

Table 3: Verbs of Gift and Confirmation

Entries are made on the basis of the number of records of individual alienations which use a particular verb; totals do not reflect the actual number of times each verb appears in the extant charters. To illustrate: a charter which says that a donor gave (*dedit*) this and gave (*dedit*) that, and so on, is entered as one use of *dare*; but a charter which says that a donor gave (*dedit*) this and conceded (*concessit*) that and transferred (*transtulit*) the other thing is entered as one use of each verb, as is one which says that he gave and conceded and transferred (*dedit et concessit et transtulit*) one thing. On the contrary, a charter which says that one man gave (*dedit*) something and another gave (*dedit*) something else is entered as two uses of *dare*. Verbal nouns of confirmation, as when a gift is said to be made *ex voluntate uxoris meae* or *ex auctoritate domini mei* or the like, are entered under the verbs from which they derive unless no such verb is ever used.

Table 3A: Verbs of Gift

Church	Verbs[a]														
	dare (+)	concedere	ferre (+)	tribuere	dimittere	largiri	praebere	relinquere (+)	alienare	annuere	constituere	signare (+)	fundere (+)	deputare	[b]	number of verbs used
Avranches	6	4		1						1		1			1	6
Bayeux	8	3	1		1						1				1	6
Coutances	3	2	2	3												4
Lisieux	2															1
Rouen	23	8			1				1							4
Sées	2															1
Bec[c]	176	15	2	1	3											5
Bernay	2	4														2
Cerisy	24	5	2							2					3	7
Cherbourg	2	4			1											3
Conches	29	8														2
La Croix-St-Leufroi	3	1														2
Fécamp[c]	112	35	20	11	2	3					1				4	11
Fontenay	13	9	1	1	1	1	1								2	9
Jumièges	71	34	12	11	2	2	5								1	8
Lessay	14	1	1													3
Lire	6	22														2
Lonlay	1	1	1													3
Montebourg	10	9	1													3
Montivilliers	21	7	1	1		1	1								1	7
Mont-St-Michel	41	22	4	7	4	5							1			7

Table 3A (continued)

Church	Verbs[a] dare (+)	concedere	ferre (+)	tribuere	dimittere	largiri	praebere	relinquere (+)	alienare	annuere	constituere	signare (+)	fundere (+)	deputare	b	number of verbs used
St-Amand	12	8	1	6		1										5
St-Désir de Lisieux	5	2	1													3
St-Etienne de Caen	104	38	3	3	2			4	2						1	8
St-Evroul	71	29	3	3	4	1		1						2		8
St-Georges de Bosch.	32	2							1			2			2	6
St-Léger de Préaux	37	13		2												3
St-Martin d'Ecajeul	4	3	1?													3
St-Martin de Sées	169	86	2	3	32	3										6
St-Ouen	63	12	3	4	1										2	7
St-Pierre de Préaux	117	16	7		3											4
St-Pierre-sur-Dives	1														1	2
St-Sauveur d'Evreux	3	2														2
St-Sauveur-le-Vicomte	54	10														2
St-Taurin d'Evreux	40	6	1	3		1		2								6
St-Wandrille	60	18	2	3	1	11			1				1		4	12
St-Ymer-en-Auge		1	1													2
Le Tréport	69	14	1		1										1	5
La Trinité de Caen	109	20		7	1	1	1		1							7
La Trinité du Mont	102	16	8	2	3	6		1						1		8
Troarn	84	44	1	2	3	4					1					7
Number of churches which use verb	40	38	26	19	18	13	4	4	5	2	3	2	2	2	13	
Total number of uses	1706	534	83	74	66	40	8	8	6	3	3	3	2	3		

Table 3B: Verbs of Confirmation

Church	Verbs																	
	concedere	firmare (+)	annuere	consentire (+)	corroborare	corroborandum tradere	auctorizare	laudare	favere	consulere	jubere	precari (+)	velle	dare (+)	d	e	number of verbs used	total number of verbs used
Avranches	2	1							1								3	8
Bayeux	4	6		3	2	2		1						1			7	10
Coutances		1															1	5
Lisieux		2		1										1			3	3
Rouen	2	5	2		3		2		1					1			7	9
Sées		1				1											2	3
Bec[c]	35	14	1	22	2		1	4		1	1		1	1		1	12	16
Bernay	4	1	1						1							1	5	6
Cerisy	20	5	3		1				1					1			6	10
Cherbourg	2																1	3
Conches	1	4	22	1												1	5	6
La Croix-St-Leufroi		1															1	3
Fécamp[c]	19	13	7	12	7	2	8	9	1	1	2		1	1	6	1	20	27
Fontenay	3	5	1	2	3		1			2		1	1		2	1	12	20
Jumièges	11	31	11	12		14		3	4				2		3	3	14	20
Lessay	5	4	3												2		5	7
Lire	5	1		1													3	4
Lonlay				1													1	4
Montebourg	5	4								1							3	5
Montivilliers	5	3	11	1	2		2	1	5	1		1			2		12	18
Mont-St-Michel	10	18	4	7	8	5		1		2					1		9	15

Table 3B (continued)

Church	concedere	firmare (+)	annuere	consentire (+)	corroborare	corroborandum tradere	auctorizare	laudare	favere	consulere	jubere	precari (+)	velle	dare (+)	d	e	number of verbs used	total number of verbs used
	Verbs																	
St-Amand	4	2	5		1									1			5	8
St-Désir de Lisieux	1	2	6		1										1		5	7
St-Etienne de Caen	59	23	4	1	6	1						1					7	13
St-Evroul	39	16	12	4		1					2			2	1	1	9	15
St-Georges de Bosch.		1	3						1								3	9
St-Léger de Préaux	7	3	2	1				1	1			1					7	9
St-Martin d'Ecajeul		2			1							1					3	6
St-Martin de Sées	104	21	12		2		1	1	7	2					1		9	14
St-Ouen	6	16	6	3	3	1	5		1				1				9	15
St-Pierre de Préaux	42	13	13	3							5	1					6	9
St-Pierre-sur-Dives	1	1															2	4
St-Sauveur d'Evreux	2	1	1	2				1					1		1		7	8
St-Sauveur-le-Vicomte	20	12															2	3
St-Taurin d'Evreux	13	3	7	1				1		1			1		1		8	13
St-Wandrille	6	33	11	6	8	2	16				1		4		4	1	14	24
St-Ymer-en-Auge		1					1										2	4
Le Tréport	43		3					1		2		4			3		8	12
La Trinité de Caen	60	3	24	5								3			1		6	12
La Trinité du Mont	4	9	56	3	7		3	4	3	3	3				2		12	19
Troarn	23	29	1	2	5		1			3		1			2		10	16
Number of churches which use verb	33	38	27	22	17	9	10	15	9	10	6	9	8	8	17	8		
Total number of uses	567	311	232	94	62	29	41	29	27	19	14	14	12	9				
					91 (corroborare + corroborandum tradere)													

Table 3B (continued)

(+) means that this column includes variations on the verb (e.g., *donare* for *dare*).

[a]Excluding specialized verbs (*emere, vendere, commutuare, excambiare, restituere, adquietare, querpire,* etc.)

[b]Verbs used by only one church (the numbers in this column represent the number of verbs used, not the number of uses): *corroborare* (Avranches); *laudare* (Bayeux); *atcrescere, apponere,* and *dotare* (Cerisy); *confirmare, destinare, impartiri,* and *vestire* (Fécamp); *augere* and *munire* (Fontenay); *presentare* (Jumièges); *sencire* (Montivilliers); *prestare* (Saint-Etienne de Caen, twice); *allegare* and *delegare* (Saint-Georges de Boscherville); *obmittere* and *remittere* (Saint-Ouen); *ditare* (Saint-Pierre-sur-Dives); *advehere, auctorizare* (twice), *exhibere,* and *perdonare* (Saint-Wandrille); *indulgere* (Le Tréport, three times).

[c]Including priories.

[d]Verbs used by two to four churches (the numbers in this column represent the number of verbs used, not the number of uses). Total: thirteen verbs.

[e]Verbs used by only one church (the numbers in this column represent the number of verbs used, not the number of uses).

Table 4: Average Number of Verbs Used

A. Computed including the five oldest abbeys in the categories based on the number of surviving transactions

Churches[a]	Average number of verbs used[b]
5 oldest abbeys	20.2
All those from which over 100 transactions survive (10 churches)[c]	16.1
All those from which 48–84 transactions survive (8 churches)[d]	12.5
All those from which 22–35 transactions survive (8 churches)	10.3
All those from which 1–13 transactions survive (15 churches)	5.3

B. Computed excluding the five oldest abbeys from the categories based on the number of surviving transactions

Churches[a]	Average number of verbs used[b]
5 oldest abbeys	20.2
All others from which over 100 transactions survive (8 churches)	14.3
Others from which 48–80 transactions survive, excluding Saint-Sauveur-le-Vicomte[e] (4 churches)	10.8
All those from which 22–35 transactions survive (8 churches)	10.3
All those from which 1–13 transactions survive (15 churches)	5.3

[a]The number of transactions is taken in each instance from Table 2, column 1. The figures for those churches excluded from Table 2 because so few of their transactions survive are La Croix-Saint-Leufroi (3), Lisieux cathedral (2), Lonlay (1), Saint-Pierre-sur-Dives (3), Saint-Sauveur d'Evreux (3), Saint-Ymer-en-Auge (1), Sées cathedral (2).

[b]Sum of the total number of verbs (from Table 3B, last column) ÷ number of churches.

[c]Includes Fécamp and Jumièges.

[d]Includes Mont-Saint-Michel, Saint-Ouen, and Saint-Wandrille.

[e]The disparity between the number of transactions (71) and the number of verbs used (3) for Saint-Sauveur-le-Vicomte is probably to be explained by the fact that its charters survive mostly only in partial copies. Including Saint-Sauveur-le-Vicomte, the average number of verbs used is, for this category, 9.2.

Table 5: Anathemas and Fines

Period	Anathemas[a] Number of charters[c]	Anathemas[a] Percentage	Anathemas[a] Cumulative percentage	Fines[b] Number of charters[c]	Fines[b] Percentage	Fines[b] Cumulative percentage	Fines[b] Amounts in gold pounds	Fines[b] Cumulative average amount[d]
960–99	1 of 2	50		1 of 4	25		5	
1000–09	2 of 3	66.7	60	2 of 6	33.3	30	100, 100	68.3
1010–19	6 of 11	54.5	56.3	2 of 14	14.3	20.8	40, 200	89
1020–29	15 of 21	71.4	64.9	7 of 29	24.1	22.6	10, 20, 100, 100, 100, 200	88.6
1030–39	12 of 21	57.1	62.1	3 of 23	13	19.7	5, 50, 50	77.1
1040–49	12 of 20	60	61.5	2 of 23	8.7	17.2	3, 50	70.8
1050–59	12 of 23	52.1	59.4	2 of 32	6.3	14.5	1000	125.5
1060–69	8 of 20	40	56.2	3 of 44	6.8	12.6	3, 10, 1000	157.3
1070–79	3 of 12	25	53.4	2 of 31	6.5	11.6	10, 21	144.4
1080–87	2 of 15	13.3 } 23.2 (1060–1106)	49.3	1 of 23	4.3 } 4.7 (1060–1106)	10.9	100	142.5
1087–96	1 of 15	6.7 } 13.6 (1087–1106)	45.4	1 of 37	2.7 } 1.9 (1087–1106)	9.7	1000	178.2
1097–1106	2 of 7	28.6	44.7	0 of 15	0	9.2		
	76 of 170			26 of 281			Total: 4227 (24 fines)	

[a]Charters of Fécamp, Jumièges, Mont-Saint-Michel, Saint-Ouen, and Saint-Wandrille only.

[b]Charters of all ten churches from Normandy or with possessions in Normandy which ever used a fine clause: Bayeux Cathedral, Bernay, Fécamp, Jumièges, Marmoutier, Saint-Bénigne de Dijon, Saint-Ouen, Saint-Père de Chartres, Saint-Quentin, and Saint-Wandrille. For the non-Norman churches only their Norman charters are counted.

[c]This tabulation includes all charters dated to particular years and all charters datable to spans of twenty years or less, each of the latter tabulated as though it dated from the midpoint of the span of years.

[d]This column includes only amounts in gold pounds, even when a fine is stated partly in gold and partly in silver. The fine discussed above, Chapter 10 at n. 48, and the fine of one talent of gold in Document 255 (p. 352) are not included.

APPENDIX B: DOCUMENTS CITED

What follows is a list, not of all extant eleventh-century Norman charters or even of the most important ones, but merely of those cited in the notes. Only short titles of published works are given: full citations will be found in the Bibliography. Abbreviations are the same as those used in the notes: their expansions will be found in the list of abbreviations to the notes. When several unnumbered charters occur on the same page or folio, incipits or donors' names have been given to differentiate one document from another. Notes which indicate the sources of corrections are given only when quotations differ from the sources listed here.

Unless otherwise indicated, the dates of published charters are those assigned by their editors or are based directly on the known dates or *floruits* of persons named in them. Dates of unpublished charters are given by the charters themselves or are estimated on the basis of persons and events mentioned in them. Except as noted, the dates are those of the documents rather than of the events they record. The following *sigla* are used:

ca. for circa ("about")
v. for *vers* ("shortly before or in")
x for "between"; e.g., 1000 x 1100 means "between 1000 and 1100"

1. Adigard des Gautries, "Possessions de Saint-Wandrille," no. 1, p. 35 (late eleventh century)
2. Ibid., no. 2, p. 36 (late eleventh century)
3. Ibid., no. 3, p. 37 (late eleventh century)
4. Ibid., no. 4, p. 37 (late eleventh century)
5. Allix and Génestal, "Opérations," p. 625, n. 1 (Troarn, shortly after 1100)
6. Barret, *Cartulaire de Marmoutier*, no. 2, pp. 5–8 (1023 x 1027)
7. Ibid., no. 3, pp. 9–10 (1070 x 1079)[1]
8. Ibid., no. 4, pp. 10–12[2]
9. Ibid., no. 5, pp. 13–16 (1050 x 1064)
10. Ibid., no. 6, pp. 16–17 (1067)
11. Ibid., no. 7, pp. 18–19 (before 1064)
12. Ibid., no. 8, p. 20 (before 1064)
13. Ibid., no. 11, pp. 21–22 (*v.* 1067)
14. Ibid., no. 13, pp. 24–26 (1092)[3]
15. Ibid., no. 14, pp. 26–27 (1092)
16. Ibid., no. 15, pp. 27–28 (1092)[4]
17. Ibid., no. 17, pp. 29–30 (1092 x 1100)
18. Ibid., no. 150, pp. 154–55 (1092 x 1137)
19. Ibid., no. 151, pp. 155–56 (1092 x 1137)
20. Bourrienne, *Antiquus cartularius* (Bayeux cathedral), vol. 1, no. 3, pp. 4–6 (1074)
21. Ibid., no. 6, pp. 11–13 (1089)
22. Ibid., no. 21, pp. 27–29 (1035 x 1037)
23. Ibid., no. 22, pp. 30–31 (1092)
24. Ibid., no. 23, pp. 31–32 (1093)
25. Ibid., no. 76, pp. 95–97 (1087 x 1096)[5]
26. Bourrienne, "Odon," vol. 10, pp. 283–84 (Saint-Bénigne de Dijon and Bayeux cathedral, 1096)[6]

26a. Bouvris, "Bref," p. 150 (Montebourg, 1092)

27. Bréard, *Saint-Ymer*, no. 1, pp. 1–2 (1066 x 1067)
28. *Cartulaire du prieuré de Longpont*,[7] no. 330, p. 260 (1061 x 1066)
29. Ibid., no. 331, p. 261 (1061 x 1066)

30. Ibid., no. 332, p. 261 (1061 x 1066)
31. Chaplais, *Diplomatic Documents*, vol. 1, no. 1, pp. 1–4: Treaty "of Dover" between King Henry I of England and Count Robert II of Flanders (1101)
32. Chevreux and Vernier, *Archives*, plate VI (Fécamp, before 1079)
33. Ibid., plate VII (Fécamp, 1085)
34. Couppey, "Encore Héauville" (priory of Marmoutier), p. 354 (1082)
35. Ibid., pp. 437–38 (late eleventh or early twelfth century)[8]
36. Couppey, "Notes historiques" (Héauville, priory of Marmoutier), p. 438 (1093)
37. Ibid., p. 440 (1093)
38. De Farcy, *Fontenay*, pp. 27–33 (1070 x 1079)[9]
39. Ibid., pp. 38–44 (1066 x 1083)[10]
40. Delisle, *Etudes*, p. 282, n. 47 (Troarn, thirteenth century)[11]
41. Delisle, *Histoire*, Preuves, no. 13, pp. 13–16 (Bayeux cathedral, ca. 1036)
42. Ibid., no. 20, pp. 23–24 (Marmoutier, ca. 1048)
43. Ibid., no. 21, pp. 24–25 (Marmoutier, ca. 1048)
44. Ibid., no. 31, pp. 34–35 (Marmoutier, ca. 1060)
45. Ibid., no. 33, pp. 36–37 (Marmoutier, ca. 1073)
46. Ibid., no. 36, p. 40 (Mont-Saint-Michel, ca. 1076)[12]
47. Ibid., no. 40, pp. 44–45 (Marmoutier, 1081)
48. Ibid., no. 42, pp. 46–47 (Marmoutier, ca. 1081)[13]
49. Ibid., no. 46, pp. 55–58 (Saint-Sauveur-le-Vicomte, 1104)
50. Delisle, *Littérature*, no. 13, pp. 28–29 (Fécamp, 1096)
51. Delisle and Berger, *Recueil*, vol. 1, no. 154, pp. 267–86 (Saint-Etienne de Caen, 1156)
52. Denis, *Saint-Julien de Tours*, no. 19, pp. 29–30 (eleventh century)
53. Ibid., no. 20, p. 31 (eleventh century)
54. Ibid., no. 45, pp. 62–64 (1093)
55. Ibid., no. 46, pp. 64–65 (after 1093)
56. A. Deville, *La Trinité du Mont*,[14] no. 12, pp. 428–29 (1051 x 1077)
57. Ibid., no. 13, p. 429 (*v.* 1065)
58. Ibid., no. 14, pp. 429–30 (*v.* 1065)
59. Ibid., no. 15, p. 430 (probably after 1066)
60. Ibid., no. 16, pp. 430–31 (after 1066)
61. Ibid., no. 17, p. 431 (*v.* 1060)
62. Ibid., no. 20, p. 432 (1051 x 1077)
63. Ibid., no. 25, p. 434 (1059)
64. Ibid., no. 31, pp. 437–38 (*v.* 1074)[15]
65. Ibid., no. 34, pp. 439–40 (1062)
66. Ibid., no. 36, pp. 440–41 (*v.* 1060)
67. Ibid., no. 45, pp. 444–45 (1051 x 1077)
68. Ibid., no. 47, p. 446 (1068 x 1071)[16]
69. Ibid., no. 50, pp. 447–48 (1037 x 1053)
70. Ibid., no. 52, p. 449
71. Ibid., no. 53, p. 450
72. Ibid., no. 57, pp. 451–52 (1066)
73. Ibid., no. 58, p. 452 (1063)
74. Ibid., no. 59, p. 452 (1059)
75. Ibid., no. 60, p. 453 (1051 x 1077)
76. Ibid., no. 62, p. 453 (*v.* 1065)
77. Ibid., no. 63, pp. 453–54 (ca. 1066)
78. Ibid., no. 66, p. 455 (1055 x 1066)
79. Ibid., no. 67, p. 455 (1069)

80. Ibid., no. 68, p. 456 (1077 or later)
81. Ibid., no. 75, p. 459 (1068)
82. Ibid., no. 76, p. 459 (1030 x 1051)
83. Ibid., no. 79, p. 460 (mid-eleventh century)
84. Ibid., no. 81, p. 461 (1051 x 1077)
85. Ibid., no. 82, pp. 462–63 (1080)
86. Ibid., no. 83, pp. 463–64 (1091)
87. Ibid., no. 84, p. 464 (1051 x 1077, probably 1054 or later)
88. Ibid., no. 85, p. 465
89. Ibid., no. 87, p. 465
90. Ibid., no. 88, pp. 465–66
91. Ibid., no. 89, p. 466 (1080)[17]
92. Ibid., no. 90, pp. 466–67 (1084)
93. Ibid., no. 91, p. 467 (1077 or later)
94. Ibid., no. 97, p. 469
95. E. Deville, *Cartulaire de Beaumont-le-Roger*, no. 1, pp. 3–6 (ca. 1088 or 1089)[18]
96. Du Monstier, *Neustria Pia*, pp. 424–25 (Lonlay, ca. 1020)
97. Ibid., p. 479 (Bec, 1066 x 1087, about events 1035 x 1066)
98. Ibid., p. 492 (Bec, 1077)
99. Ibid., pp. 520–25 (Saint-Léger de Préaux, ca. 1040 and later)[19]
100. Ibid., pp. 613–14 (Notre-Dame-du-Pré, 1091 x 1092)[20]
101. Fauroux, *Recueil*, no. 1, p. 68 (forgery: Saint-Cyprien de Poitiers, allegedly 963 x 964)
102. Ibid., no. 2, pp. 69–70 (Saint-Père de Chartres, 965)
103. Ibid., no. 3, pp. 71–72 (Saint-Denis, 968)
104. Ibid., no. 4, pp. 73–74 (Fécamp, 990)
105. Ibid., no. 5, pp. 75–76 (Saint-Taurin d'Evreux, 962 x 996)[21]
106. Ibid., no. 6, p. 77 (Coutances cathedral, *v.* 989 x 996)[22]
107. Ibid., no. 9, pp. 79–81 (Fécamp, 1006)
108. Ibid., no. 10, pp. 81–82 (Rouen cathedral)[23]
109. Ibid., no. 11, pp. 83–85 (dower of Duchess Judith, 996 x 1008)
110. Ibid., no. 13, pp. 87–89 (Saint-Ouen, 1011)
111. Ibid., no. 14, pp. 90–91 (Bourgueil and Jumièges, 1012)
112. Ibid., no. 14 bis, pp. 91–92 (Bourgueil and Jumièges, 1012)
113. Ibid., no. 15, pp. 95–96 (Notre-Dame de Chartres, 1014)
114. Ibid., no. 16, pp. 97–98 (Mont-Saint-Michel, *v.* 1015)
115. Ibid., no. 17, pp. 99–100 (Mont-Saint-Michel, 1015)
116. Ibid., no. 18, pp. 101–2 (Saint-Quentin, 1015)
117. Ibid., no. 19, p. 103 (Saint-Ouen, 1006 x 1017)
118. Ibid., no. 20, pp. 104–5 (Saint-Riquier, 1010 x 1017)
119. Ibid., no. 21, pp. 105–6 (Saint-Ouen, 1015 x 1017)
120. Ibid., no. 24, p. 110 (Saint-Ouen, 1017 x 1023)
121. Ibid., no. 25, p. 111 (Fécamp, 1023)
122. Ibid., no. 26, pp. 112–13 (Jumièges and Saint-Vaast, 1024)
123. Ibid., no. 27, pp. 115–16 (forgery: Saint-Wandrille, second half of the eleventh century, attributed to 1024)
124. Ibid., no. 33, pp. 123–25 (Sées cathedral, *v.* 1025)
125. Ibid., no. 34, pp. 127–31 (Fécamp, 1025)
126. Ibid., no. 35, pp. 132–35 (Bernay, 1025)
127. Ibid., no. 36, pp. 137–41 (Jumièges, 1025)
128. Ibid., no. 38, p. 143 (Fécamp, 996 x 1026)
129. Ibid., no. 39, p. 144 (Saint-Ouen, 1006 x 1026)

130. Ibid., no. 40, p. 145 (Saint-Ouen, 1006 x 1026?)[24]
131. Ibid., no. 41, p. 146 (Saint-Ouen, ca. 1012 x 1026)
132. Ibid., no. 42, pp. 147–48 (Saint-Ouen, ca. 1015 x 1026)
133. Ibid., no. 43, pp. 149–50 (Saint-Ouen, 1015 x 1026)
134. Ibid., no. 44, p. 151 (Saint-Ouen, 1017 x 1024)
135. Ibid., no. 45, pp. 152–53 (Saint-Ouen, 1017 x 1026, probably 1017 x 1024)
136. Ibid., no. 46, p. 153 (Saint-Wandrille, 1017 x 1026)
137. Ibid., no. 46 bis, pp. 154–55 (Saint-Wandrille, 1017 x 1026)
138. Ibid., no. 47, p. 156 (Mont-Saint-Michel, 1017 x 1026)
139. Ibid., no. 48, pp. 157–58 (Lisieux cathedral, ca. 1022 x 1026)
140. Ibid., no. 49, pp. 160–62 (Mont-Saint-Michel, 1022 x 1026)
141. Ibid., no. 50, p. 163 (Saint-Père de Chartres, 1017 x 1026, probably 1023 x 1026)
142. Ibid., no. 51, pp. 164–65 (Jumièges, 1023 x 1026)
143. Ibid., no. 52, pp. 167–68 (Saint-Wandrille, 1024 x 1026, probably 1025 x 1026)
144. Ibid., no. 53, pp. 171–73 (Saint-Ouen, *v.* 1025 x 1026)
145. Ibid., no. 55, pp. 175–76 (Saint-Wandrille, 1025 x 1026)
146. Ibid., no. 56, pp. 177–79 (forgery: Saint-Léonard de Bellême, 1089 x 1092, attributed to Richard II)
147. Ibid., no. 57, p. 180 (forgery: Notre-Dame de Montaure, early twelfth century, attributed to Richard II)
148. Ibid., no. 58, pp. 181–82 (dower of Duchess Adela, 1026 x 1027)
149. Ibid., no. 59, pp. 183–84 (Jumièges, 1027)
150. Ibid., no. 61, pp. 186–87 (La Trinité du Mont, 1030)
151. Ibid., no. 63, pp. 190–92 (Jumièges, 1030)
152. Ibid., no. 64, pp. 194–95 (Cerisy, 1032)
153. Ibid., no. 65, pp. 196–97 (Mont-Saint-Michel, 1027 x 1033)
154. Ibid., no. 66, pp. 198–201 (Rouen cathedral, 1028 x 1033)
155. Ibid., no. 67, pp. 202–3 (Rouen cathedral, 1028 x 1033)
155a. Ibid., no. 68, p. 204 (Rouen cathedral, addition made 1028 x 1033 to a document of 872 x 875)
156. Ibid., no. 69, pp. 205–6 (Saint-Wandrille, 1033)
157. Ibid., no. 70, pp. 206–7 (Fécamp, 1028 x 1034, probably *v.* 1031 x 1034)
158. Ibid., no. 71, pp. 208–9 (Fécamp, 1034)
159. Ibid., no. 72, p. 210 (Fécamp, 1027 x 1035)
160. Ibid., no. 73, pp. 212–14 (Mont-Saint-Michel, 1027 x 1033)
161. Ibid., no. 74, pp. 215–16 (Jumièges, 1027 x 1035)
162. Ibid., no. 76, pp. 217–18 (Mont-Saint-Michel, 1027 x 1035, probably 1033 x 1034)
163. Ibid., no. 80, p. 220 (Saint-Wandrille, 1029 x 1035)
164. Ibid., no. 83, p. 222 (La Trinité du Mont, 1030 x 1035)
165. Ibid., no. 84, pp. 222–23 (La Trinité du Mont, 1030 x 1035)
166. Ibid., no. 85, pp. 225–26 (Fécamp, 1031 x 1035)
167. Ibid., no. 86, pp. 227–28 (Saint-Bénigne de Dijon and Fécamp, 1032 x 1035)
168. Ibid., no. 87, p. 229 (Fécamp, 1034 x 1035)
169. Ibid., no. 88, p. 230 (Fécamp, 1034 x 1035, reworked after 1066)
170. Ibid., no. 89, p. 231 (Saint-Pierre de Préaux, 1035)
171. Ibid., no. 90, pp. 233–35 (Montivilliers, 1035)
172. Ibid., no. 90 bis, pp. 236–37 (Montivilliers, falsified version of the preceding charter, before 1076)
173. Ibid., no. 91, pp. 241–42 (reworking or forgery: Saint-Taurin de la Ferté-Imbault, allegedly 1043, which may be an error for 1032)

174. Ibid., no. 92, pp. 243–44 (Jumièges, 1038)
175. Ibid., no. 93, pp. 244–45 (Fécamp, 1034 x ca. 1040)
176. Ibid., no. 94, pp. 246–47 (Fécamp, 1035 x ca. 1040)
177. Ibid., no. 95, pp. 247–48 (Saint-Wandrille, 1037 x ca. 1040)
178. Ibid., no. 96, pp. 248–49 (La Trinité du Mont, ca. 1040)
179. Ibid., no. 98 B, pp. 251–53 (Bec, 1041)
180. Ibid., no. 98 C, pp. 251–53 (Bec, 1041)
181. Ibid., no. 98 D, pp. 253–54 (Bec, 1077)[25]
182. Ibid., no. 100, pp. 256–57 (Jumièges, ca. 1035 x 1043)
183. Ibid., no. 101, p. 258 (La Trinité du Mont, 1043)
184. Ibid., no. 103, pp. 260–62 (Sigy, priory of Saint-Ouen, 1037 x ca. 1045)
185. Ibid., no. 104, pp. 262–63 (La Trinité du Mont, 1035 x 1047)
186. Ibid., no. 105, pp. 263–64 (Saint-Ouen, 1035 x 1048)
187. Ibid., no. 107, pp. 266–67 (Saint-Ouen, 1046 x 1048)
188. Ibid., no. 108, pp. 268–69 (Saint-Wandrille, 1046 x 1047)
189. Ibid., no. 109, p. 269 (Saint-Wandrille, 1047 x 1048)
190. Ibid., no. 111, p. 272 (Mont-Saint-Michel, 1035 x 1041)[26]
191. Ibid., no. 112, pp. 273–74 (Saint-Ouen, 1037 x 1048)
192. Ibid., no. 113, p. 275 (Jumièges, 1043 x 1048)
193. Ibid., no. 115, p. 278 (Saint-Riquier, 1048)
194. Ibid., no. 116, p. 279 (Saint-Amand, ca. 1042 x 1049)
195. Ibid., no. 117, pp. 280–81 (Saint-Père de Chartres, 1040 x ca. 1050)
196. Ibid., no. 118, p. 282 (La Trinité du Mont, ca. 1040 x 1051)
197. Ibid., no. 119, pp. 283–84 (La Trinité du Mont, ca. 1040 x 1050)
198. Ibid., no. 120, pp. 285–86 (Lire, *v.* 1050)
199. Ibid., no. 121, p. 286 (Saint-Pierre de Préaux, ca. 1050)
200. Ibid., no. 122, pp. 289–92 (Saint-Evroul, 1050)[27]
201. Ibid., no. 124, pp. 294–95 (Saint-Wandrille, 1051)
202. Ibid., no. 128, pp. 300–301 (Saint-Wandrille, ca. 1040 x 1053, probably 1047 x 1053)
203. Ibid., no. 130, p. 303 (La Trinité du Mont, 1053)
204. Ibid., no. 131, pp. 304–5 (Saint-Julien de Tours, 1053)[28]
205. Ibid., no. 132, pp. 306–7 (Mont-Saint-Michel, 1054 x 1055)
206. Ibid., no. 133, pp. 307–8 (Mont-Saint-Michel, 1053 x 1054)[29]
207. Ibid., no. 135, pp. 310–11 (La Trinité du Mont, 1037 x 1055)
208. Ibid., no. 137, pp. 313–14 (Marmoutier, 1055)
209. Ibid., no. 138, p. 315 (La Trinité du Mont, ca. 1050 x 1056)
210. Ibid., no. 139, p. 316 (Fécamp, 1057; somewhat suspect)
211. Ibid., no. 142, pp. 322–23 (Saint-Julien de Tours, 1059)[30]
212. Ibid., no. 144, p. 325 (Troarn, 1059)[31]
213. Ibid., no. 145, p. 326 (Fécamp, 1046 x 1060)
214. Ibid., no. 147 B, pp. 328–29 (Saint-Père de Chartres, 1060)
215. Ibid., no. 147 a, pp. 329–30 (Saint-Père de Chartres, 1060)
216. Ibid., no. 148 D, pp. 331–32 (Mont-Saint-Michel, 1061)
217. Ibid., no. 148 A^3, pp. 332–33 (Mont-Saint-Michel, after 1066)[32]
218. Ibid., no. 150, p. 335 (Marmoutier, 1062)
219. Ibid., no. 151, p. 336 (Marmoutier, 1062)
220. Ibid., no. 152, p. 336 (Saint-Wandrille, 1047 or 1048 x 1063)
221. Ibid., no. 153, p. 337 (Saint-Wandrille, 1047 x 1063)
222. Ibid., no. 154, p. 338 (Saint-Wandrille, 1047 x 1063)
223. Ibid., no. 156 B, p. 340 (Saint-Julien de Tours, 1063)
224. Ibid., no. 156 C, pp. 340–42 (Saint-Julien de Tours, 1063)
225. Ibid., no. 157, pp. 342–43 (Marmoutier, 1063)
226. Ibid., no. 158, pp. 343–44 (Saint-Ouen, 1063)

227. Ibid., no. 159 A, pp. 346–47 (Marmoutier, 1063 x 1066)
228. Ibid., no. 159 A', pp. 347–48 (Marmoutier, 1063 x 1066)
229. Ibid., no. 160, p. 349 (Marmoutier, ca. 1050 x 1064)[33]
230. Ibid., no. 161, p. 350 (Marmoutier, ca. 1050 x 1064)[34]
231. Ibid., no. 162, pp. 351–52 (Marmoutier, ca. 1050 x 1064)[35]
232. Ibid., no. 163, p. 353 (Marmoutier, ca. 1050 x 1064, probably 1062)[36]
233. Ibid., no. 163 bis, p. 354 (Marmoutier, ca. 1050 x 1064, probably 1062)[37]
234. Ibid., no. 167, pp. 358–59 (Cerisy, 1035 x 1066)
235. Ibid., no. 169, p. 360 (Cerisy, 1035 x 1066)
236. Ibid., no. 173, p. 361 (Montivilliers, 1035 x 1066)
237. Ibid., no. 177, p. 363 (Saint-Wandrille, 1035 x 1066)
238. Ibid., no. 178, p. 364 (Bec, 1041 x 1066)
239. Ibid., no. 179, p. 365 (Bec, 1050 x 1066)
240. Ibid., no. 180, p. 365 (Bec, 1041 x 1066)
241. Ibid., no. 181, p. 365 (Bec, 1041 x 1066)
242. Ibid., no. 188, p. 371 (Jumièges, 1046 x 1066)
243. Ibid., no. 189, p. 372 (Bec, 1047 x 1066)
244. Ibid., no. 191, p. 374 (Saint-Ouen, *v.* 1050 x 1066)
245. Ibid., no. 193, pp. 375–76 (Saint-Ouen, 1035 x 1040)[38]
246. Ibid., no. 194, pp. 376–77 (Saint-Pierre de Lisieux, ca. 1050 x 1066)
247. Ibid., no. 195, p. 378 (Cerisy, ca. 1050 x 1066)
248. Ibid., no. 196, p. 379 (Cerisy, ca. 1050 x 1066)
249. Ibid., no. 197, pp. 381–85 (Saint-Georges de Boscherville, ca. 1050 x 1066)
250. Ibid., no. 199, p. 387 (Saint-Florent de Saumur, 1051 x 1066)
251. Ibid., no. 202, pp. 389–90 (La Trinité du Mont, 1051 x 1066)
252. Ibid., no. 205, pp. 393–94 (Saint-Ouen, 1051 x 1066)
253. Ibid., no. 208, pp. 396–98 (Saint-Sauveur d'Evreux, 1055 x 1066)
254. Ibid., no. 209, pp. 398–99 (Saint-Magloire de Lehon, 1055 x 1066)
255. Ibid., no. 210, pp. 399–400 (Saint-Ouen, 1055 x 1066)
256. Ibid., no. 211, p. 400 (Saint-Ouen, 1055 x 1066)
257. Ibid., no. 212, p. 401 (Saint-Ouen, 1055 x 1066)
258. Ibid., no. 213, p. 402 (Jumièges, 1055 x 1066)
259. Ibid., no. 214, pp. 404–8 (Coutances cathedral, 1056 x 1066)
260. Ibid., no. 217, p. 409 (Le Tréport, 1059 x 1066)
261. Ibid., no. 218 A, pp. 411–15 (Saint-Martin-du-Bosc, priory of Fécamp, 1059 x 1066)
262. Ibid., no. 218 B, pp. 411–15 (Saint-Martin-du-Bosc, priory of Fécamp, 1059 x 1066)
263. Ibid., no. 219, pp. 416–17 (Bayeux cathedral, ca. 1060 x 1066)
264. Ibid., no. 220, pp. 418–20 (Jumièges, 1060 x 1066)
265. Ibid., no. 221, p. 420 (La Trinité du Mont, 1060 x 1066)
266. Ibid., no. 222, pp. 422–24 (Saint-Martin d'Ecajeul, ca. 1063 x 1066)
267. Ibid., no. 224, pp. 428–32 (Cherbourg, 1063 x 1066)
268. Ibid., no. 225, pp. 433–34 (Saint-Père de Chartres, 1063 x 1066)
269. Ibid., no. 227, pp. 436–37 (Beaumont-lès-Tours, 1049 x 1066, probably 1066)[39]
270. Ibid., no. 228, pp. 437–38 (Marmoutier, 1066)
271. Ibid., no. 229, pp. 439–40 (Avranches cathedral, 1066)
272. Ibid., no. 230, pp. 441–42 (Coulombs, 1066)
273. Ibid., no. 232, pp. 447–48 (Mont-Saint-Michel, 1066)
274. Ibid., no. 234, pp. 451–53 (Saint-Wandrille, 1082 x 1087)
275. *Gallia Christiana*, vol. 11, Instrumenta, cols. 8–9 (Fécamp, 1006)
276. Ibid., cols. 16–17 (Saint-Victor-en-Caux and Saint-Ouen, 1074; somewhat suspect)

277. Ibid., cols. 19–20 (Saint-Lucien de Beauvais, 1096)
278. Ibid., cols. 76–77 (Saint-Bénigne de Dijon, 1096)
279. Ibid., cols. 123–24 (Lire)[40]
280. Ibid., cols. 127–28 (Fécamp and Saint-Taurin, 1106)[41]
281. Ibid., cols. 128–33 (Conches, pancart of Henry I comprising acts from the foundation, 1031 x *v.* 1040, through the early twelfth century)[42]
282. Ibid., cols. 151–52 (Saint-Martin de Sées, ca. 1060)
283. Ibid., cols. 152–53 (Saint-Martin de Sées, 1073 x 1089)[43]
284. Ibid., cols. 153–56 (Saint-Pierre-sur-Dives, early twelfth century)[44]
285. Ibid., cols. 199–203 (Saint-Pierre de Préaux, pancart of acts from the foundation, ca. 1034, to 1078 x 1087)[45]
286. Ibid., cols. 217–24 (Coutances cathedral, narrative from the late eleventh century concerning events between 836 and 1093)[46]
287. Ibid., cols. 224–29 (Lessay, pancart of acts from the foundation to 1084)
288. Ibid., cols. 229–31 (forgery: Montebourg, allegedly 1096 x 1100)[47]
289. Ibid., cols. 232–33 (Montebourg, early twelfth century)
290. Ibid., cols. 326–30 (Montivilliers, 1035 and later)
291. Génestal, *Rôle*, no. 1, p. 215 (Saint-Etienne de Caen, 1096)
292. Ibid., no. 4, pp. 217–18 (Mont-Saint-Michel, ca. 1033)
293. Ibid., no. 5, pp. 218–19 (Mont-Saint-Michel, 971 x 996)
294. Ibid., no. 6, pp. 219–20 (Mont-Saint-Michel, 1086)
295. Ibid., no. 12, p. 223 (Saint-Pierre de Préaux, 1085 or 1104)[48]
296. Ibid., no. 22, pp. 230–31 (Saint-Wandrille, 1063 x 1089)
297. Guérard, *Saint-Père de Chartres*, pp. 108–9 (1023 x 1027)
298. Ibid., pp. 115–16 (ca. 1025)[49]
299. Ibid., p. 118 (1023 x 1033)
300. Ibid., pp. 147–48 (1077)
301. Ibid., pp. 155–56 (before 1061, with comments by the compiler of the cartulary)
302. Ibid., pp. 162–63 (1033 x 1069)
303. Ibid., pp. 167–68 (1033 x 1069)
304. Ibid., pp. 197–98 (1033 x 1069)
305. Ibid., p. 206 (1033 x 1079)
306. Ibid., pp. 230–31 (1079 x 1101)
307. Ibid., p. 539 (1023 x 1033)
308. Ibid., p. 569 (possibly eleventh century)
309. Ibid., p. 601 (possibly eleventh century)
310. Ibid., pp. 602–3 (1082 x 1112)
311. Gurney, *Gournay*, Appendix III, no. 2, pp. 43–44 (Saint-Ouen, 1037 x 1048)
312. Haskins, *Norman Institutions*, p. 20 (Saint-Amand, 1066 x 1087)
313. Ibid., pp. 21–22 (William Paynel and Mont-Saint-Michel, 1070 x 1081)
314. Ibid., pp. 63–64 (La Trinité de Caen, 1088 x 1100)
315. Ibid., Appendix D, pp. 281–84: "Consuetudines et Iusticie" (1091)[50]
316. Ibid., Appendix E, no. 2, p. 286 (Saint-Etienne de Caen, 1096)[51]
317. Ibid., no. 4 a, pp. 288–89 (Fécamp, 1088)
318. Ibid., no. 4 b, p. 289 (Fécamp, 1088 x 1091)
319. Ibid., no. 4 c, p. 289 (Fécamp, 1089 x 1091)
320. Ibid., no. 6, pp. 290–91 (Jumièges, 1088)
321. Ibid., no. 7 a, p. 292 (Jumièges, 1091 x 1095)
322. Ibid., no. 7 b, p. 292 (Jumièges, 1091 x 1095)
323. Jaffé, *Regesta*, vol. 1, no. 4015, p. 509 (Fécamp, 1016)
324. Ibid., no. 4056, p. 514 (Saint-Vaast and Jumièges, 1022 x 1024)
325. Ibid., no. 4644, p. 582 (Saint-Etienne de Caen, 1068)
326. Ibid., no. 5502, p. 673 (Bec, 1090 x 1094)

327. Ibid., no. 5530, p. 676 (Mont-Saint-Michel, 1094)
328. Ibid., no. 5695, p. 692 (Saint-Bénigne de Dijon, 1098)
329. Ibid., no. 5733a, p. 696 (Bayeux cathedral, 1088 x 1099)
330. Ibid., no. 5900, p. 711 (Saint-Etienne de Caen and Saint-Bénigne de Dijon, 1102)
331. Ibid., no. 5907, p. 711 (Bec, 1102)
332. Ibid., no. 5913, p. 712 (Bec, 1102)
333. Ibid., no. 5957, p. 715 (Fécamp, 1103)
334. Laffleur de Kermaingant, *Le Tréport*, no. 1, pp. 1–7 (1036; highly suspect)
335. Ibid., no. 3, pp. 8–20 (1059 and later)
336. Ibid., no. 4, pp. 21–22 (1101)
337. Ibid., no. 5, p. 23 (early twelfth century)
338. Ibid., no. 6, pp. 25–27 (1107)
339. La Roque, *Harcourt*, vol. 3, p. 34 (Rouen cathedral, 1088 x 1096)[52]
340. Ibid., pp. 167–68 (Fécamp, mid-eleventh century)
341. M.-J. Le Cacheux, *Saint-Amand*, no. 1, pp. 244–46 (ca. 1040)
342. Ibid., no. 2, p. 246 (ca. 1040 x 1049)
343. Ibid., no. 11, pp. 250–51 (1067)[53]
344. P. Le Cacheux, "Charte de Jumièges," pp. 213–16 (1080 x 1108)[54]
345. Le Maho, "Seigneuries," p. 70, n. 45 (Saint-Etienne de Caen, 1079 x 1101)
346. Le Prévost, *Eure*, vol. 1, pp. 156–57 (Saint-Taurin d'Evreux, 1067 x 1118)
347. Ibid., p. 157 (Saint-Taurin d'Evreux, 1067 x 1118)
348. Ibid., p. 160 (Conches, 1080 with a later note)
349. Ibid., p. 248 (Lire, late eleventh or early twelfth century)[55]
350. Ibid., p. 356 (Lire, 1087 x 1103)
351. Ibid., p. 473 (Saint-Pierre de Préaux, 1096 x 1101)[56]
352. Ibid., p. 505 (Beaumont-le-Roger, ca. 1090 x 1118)
353. Ibid., p. 518 (Saint-Pierre de Préaux, ca. 1040 x 1072)[57]
354. Ibid., pp. 536–37 (Saint-Pierre de Préaux, 1078 x 1096)[58]
355. Ibid., pp. 571–72 (Marmoutier, 1060)[59]
356. Ibid., vol. 2, p. 43 (Saint-Pierre de Préaux, 1035 x 1087)
357. Ibid., p. 44 (Saint-Pierre de Préaux, 1101 x 1131, perhaps before 1118)
358. Ibid., p. 136 (Conches, 1046 x 1049)
359. Ibid., pp. 171–72 (Jumièges, before 1109?)
360. Ibid., p. 390, "Roberto comite" (Saint-Pierre de Préaux, 1087 x 1106)
361. Ibid., p. 422 (Lire, late eleventh century)
362. Ibid., pp. 495–96 (Saint-Pierre de Préaux, 1078 x 1096)[60]
363. Ibid., p. 515 (Bec, 1071 x 1103 and later)
364. Ibid., p. 539 (Lire, 1071 x 1103)
365. Ibid., vol. 3, p. 46 (Jumièges, 1099)
366. Ibid., p. 97, "Regnante Roberto" (Saint-Pierre de Préaux, 1087 x 1094)
367. Ibid., p. 97, "Anno incarnationis" (Saint-Pierre de Préaux, 1106)[61]
368. Ibid., pp. 129–30 (Saint-Pierre de Préaux, late eleventh or early twelfth century)[62]
369. Ibid., p. 136 (Saint-Taurin d'Evreux, 1071 x 1112)
370. Ibid., p. 209, "Eodem iterum" (Saint-Pierre de Préaux, 1078 x 1096)[63]
371. Ibid., p. 209, "Multis coactis" (Saint-Pierre de Préaux, 1101 x 1106)[64]
372. Ibid., p. 298, "Mortuo Sturmit" (Saint-Pierre de Préaux, after 1078)
373. Ibid., pp. 357–58 (Marmoutier, 1076)[65]
374. Ibid., p. 358 (Marmoutier, ca. 1100)
375. Ibid., p. 381 (Lire, eleventh century)[66]
376. Ibid., pp. 381–82 (Lire, eleventh century)[67]
377. Lot, *Etudes sur Saint-Wandrille*, no. 7, pp. 37–38 (1024)
378. Ibid., no. 15, p. 57 (1032 x 1048)

379. Ibid., no. 16, p. 58 (1032 x 1048)
380. Ibid., no. 26, pp. 71–72 (1047 x 1055, probably ca. 1048)
381. Ibid., no. 34, p. 80 (1063 x 1089)
382. Ibid., no. 37, pp. 83–85 (1074)[68]
383. Ibid., no. 38, pp. 86–87 (1074)
384. Ibid., no. 39, pp. 88–90 (1082)
385. Ibid., no. 42, p. 97 (*v.* 1086 x 1087)
386. Ibid., no. 43, pp. 99–100 (1066 x 1071, with a confirmation added 1087 x 1102)
387. Ibid., no. 44, pp. 100–101 (1091 x 1126, probably 1091 x ca. 1097)
388. Ibid., no. 45, p. 101 (1091 x 1120)
389. Ibid., no. 46, p. 102 (1092)
390. Ibid., no. 47, p. 103 (1096)
391. Mabillon, *Annales*, vol. 5, p. 627 (Marmoutier and La Croix-Saint-Leufroi, 1070)
392. Ibid., pp. 627–28 (Rouen cathedral and Marmoutier, 1067 x 1079)
393. Ibid., p. 650 (Saint-Ouen, 1049 x 1092)[69]
394. Marchegay, "Saint-Florent près Saumur," no. 2, pp. 667–68 (1055 x 1066)
395. Ibid., no. 11, p. 675 (1083)
396. Ibid., no. 14, pp. 678–81 (1080 and earlier)[70]
397. Ibid., no. 15, pp. 681–82 (1081)
398. Ibid., no. 16, pp. 682–85 (ca. 1080 and 1093 x 1094)
399. Ibid., no. 17, p. 686 (1093)
400. Ibid., no. 19, pp. 687–88 (1080 x 1096)
401. Ibid., no. 20, pp. 688–89 (1126 or after)[71]
402. Ibid., no. 22, pp. 691–92 (1097 x 1100)[72]
403. Musset, *Actes pour les abbayes caennaises*, p. 33, n. 30 (Saint-Etienne, 1079 x 1101)
404. Ibid., no. 1, pp. 51–52 (Saint-Etienne, 1063 x 1066)[73]
405. Ibid., no. 2, pp. 54–57 (La Trinité, 1066)
406. Ibid., no. 3, p. 58 (Saint-Etienne, 1077)
407. Ibid., no. 4 A, pp. 60–62 (Saint-Etienne, 1066 x 1077)[74]
408. Ibid., no. 4 A bis, pp. 63–65 (Saint-Etienne, 1081 x 1087)
409. Ibid., no. 6, pp. 69–70 (Saint-Etienne, 1080 x 1082)
410. Ibid., no. 7, pp. 73–77 (Saint-Etienne, 1080 x 1082)
411. Ibid., no. 8, pp. 82–90 (La Trinité, 1080 x ca. 1082)[75]
412. Ibid., no. 11, pp. 93–95 (La Trinité, 1066 x 1083)
413. Ibid., no. 14, pp. 106–11 (Saint-Etienne, *v.* 1080 x 1083, listing transactions of the first three abbots)[76]
414. Ibid., no. 16, pp. 112–13 (La Trinité, 1066 x 1083, probably 1083)
415. Ibid., no. 17 A', pp. 115–18 (La Trinité, 1083)[77]
416. Ibid., no. 17 A, pp. 115–18 (La Trinité, 1083)[78]
417. Ibid., no. 18, pp. 120–22 (Saint-Etienne, 1079 x 1087)
418. Ibid., no. 20, pp. 127–28 (Saint-Etienne, shortly before 1070)[79]
419. Ibid., no. 21, pp. 128–29 (La Trinité, 1075, old style)
420. Ibid., no. 22, pp. 130–31 (La Trinité, *v.* 1080 x 1085?)
421. Ibid., no. 23, p. 132 (Saint-Etienne, 1079 x 1087)
422. Ibid., no. 24, pp. 133–34 (Saint-Etienne, 1096 x 1098)
423. Ibid., no. 25, p. 135 (La Trinité, 1079 x 1101)
424. Ibid., no. 27, pp. 138–40 (La Trinité, pancart of 1109 x 1113 containing acts from as early as before 1083 through the date of compilation)
425. Musset, "Actes inédits, I" (Saint-Gabriel, priory of Fécamp), no. 1, pp. 132–37 (1058 x 1066)

426. Ibid., no. 2, pp. 137–39 (1069)
427. Ibid., no. 3, pp. 139–41 (1080)
428. Musset, "Actes inédits, III" (Bourgueil), no. 6, p. 53 (shortly after 1015)
429. Musset, "Actes inédits, IV" (Bourgueil), no. 1, p. 10 (1012)
430. Ibid., no. 2, p. 11 (1012 x 1015)
431. Musset, "Actes inédits, V," no. 1, pp. 33–37 (Fontenay, 1049 x 1079)
432. Ibid., no. 2, pp. 37–40 (Fontenay, before 1079, perhaps about 1070)
433. Ibid., Annexe, pp. 40–41 (Saint-Wandrille, after 1066)
434. Musset, "Actes inédits, VI," pp. 125–26 (Saint-Ouen, 1089; suspect)
435. Musset, "Actes inédits, Saint-Martin de Sées," pp. 25–28 (1083 x 1089)
436. Musset, "Cimitière," no. 9, p. 26 (Saint-Martin de Sées, 1089)
437. Musset, "Origines du prieuré de Saint-Fromond" (priory of Cerisy), no. 1, pp. 483–84 (996 x ca. 1025)
438. Musset, "Peuplement," no. 1, p. 206 (church of Marigny, second half of the eleventh century)[80]
439. Musset, "Recherches sur les communautés," Appendix II, no. 1, pp. 32–35 (Auchy, late eleventh century)
440. Orderic Vitalis, *Historiae ecclesiasticae libri tredecim*, ed. Le Prévost, vol. 5, Appendix IV, pp. 180–81 (Saint-Evroul, ca. 1080)
441. Ibid., Appendix VI (Saint-Evroul),[81] no. 1, pp. 182–84 (1093)
442. Ibid., no. 2, p. 184 (1093)
443. Ibid., no. 3, p. 184 (1091 or later)
444. Ibid., no. 4, pp. 184–85 (after 1090)
445. Ibid., no. 5, p. 185
446. Ibid., no. 6, p. 185
447. Ibid., no. 7, p. 185
448. Ibid., no. 8, pp. 185–86
449. Ibid., no. 9, p. 186
450. Ibid., no. 10, pp. 186–87 (before 1093 and later)
451. Ibid., no. 12, pp. 187–88
452. Ibid., no. 27, pp. 188–89
453. Ibid., no. 30, p. 189
454. Ibid., no. 32, p. 190 (1091 or later)
455. Ibid., no. 36, p. 191
456. Ibid., no. 37, p. 191 (1098)
457. Ibid., no. 38, p. 191
458. Ibid., no. 39, pp. 191–92
459. Ibid., no. 40, p. 192
460. Ibid., no. 41, p. 192
461. Ibid., no. 42, paragraph 2, pp. 192–93 (1096)
462. Ibid., no. 42, paragraph 3, p. 193
463. Ibid., no. 42, paragraph 4, p. 193
464. Ibid., no. 43, p. 193 (1091 or later)
465. Ibid., no. 44, pp. 193–94
466. Ibid., no. 45, p. 194
467. Ibid., no. 46, p. 194
468. Ibid., no. 47, p. 194 (1091 or later)
469. Ibid., Appendix VII, pp. 195–96 (Saint-Evroul, 1099)
470. Orderic Vitalis, *Ecclesiastical History*, ed. Chibnall, vol. 3 (Saint-Evroul), pp. 128–30 (ca. 1080)
471. Ibid., pp. 138–42 (1085 x 1087)
472. Ibid., pp. 152–54 (ca. 1080)[82]
473. Ibid., pp. 154–58 (1073)

474. Ibid., p. 158 (probably 1074)
475. Ibid., p. 164, n. 1 (late eleventh century)
476. Ibid., pp. 172–76 (Maule priory, outside Normandy; 1076, probably with later additions)
477. Ibid., pp. 182–84 (Maule priory, 1107)
478. Ibid., pp. 246–50 (1079)
479. Ibid., pp. 250–52 (1087 x 1106)
480. Pigeon, *Diocèse d'Avranches*, vol. 2, Cartulary, no. 3, p. 661 (Avranches cathedral, 1091)
481. Ibid., no. 6, pp. 666–68 (Avranches cathedral, 1027 x 1066)
482. Ibid., Charters, no. III, pt. 3, pp. 674–76 (Sacé, priory of Marmoutier, 1090)
483. Pommeraye, *Saint-Amand*, p. 81 (1067)[83]
484. Porée, *Histoire du Bec*, vol. 1, Appendix, no. II, pp. 645–49 (1077)[84]
484a. Prou, *Recueil*, no. 90, pp. 233–34 (Bec, 1077)
485. Ibid., no. 176, pp. 428–31 (Marmoutier, ca. 1092: contemporary forgery)
486. Prou and Vidier, *Saint-Benoît-sur-Loire*, no. 78, pp. 203–6 (1067)
487. Sauvage, *Troarn*, pp. 220–21 (1100)
488. Ibid., p. 221 (1100)
489. Ibid., Appendix II, pp. 302–3 (1067 x 1068)
490. Ibid., pp. 303–4 (1069 x 1079)
491. Ibid., pp. 304–5 (1098)
492. Ibid., pp. 305–6 (1118)
493. Ibid., Preuves, no. 2, pp. 348–51 (1068)
494. Ibid., no. 3, pp. 352–53 (1077 x 1083)
495. Ibid., no. 5, pp. 360–63 (early twelfth-century pancart)[85]
496. Ibid., no. 12, pp. 376–83 (pancart of Henry II, 1155 x 1157, including gifts from the eleventh century)
497. Ibid., p. 456 (1079 x 1083)[86]
498. Société Jersiaise, *Cartulaire*, no. 148, p. 227 (Mont-Saint-Michel, 1028 x 1035 or 1087 x 1106)
499. Ibid., no. 149, pp. 227–28 (Mont-Saint-Michel, ca. 1052)[87]
500. Ibid., no. 150, pp. 228–29 (Mont-Saint-Michel, ca. 1048 x ca. 1068)
501. Ibid., no. 152, pp. 230–31 (Mont-Saint-Michel, 1066 x 1087)
502. Ibid., no. 167, pp. 244–47 (Saint-Sauveur-le-Vicomte, before 1092)
503. Stapleton, "Pretended Marriage," p. 26 (La Trinité de Caen, 1087 x 1096)
504. Vernier, *Jumièges*, vol. 1, no. 5, pp. 14–15 (984)
505. Ibid., no. 8, pp. 20–22 (1020 x 1030)
506. Ibid., no. 17, p. 57 (ca. 1030)
507. Ibid., no. 18, pp. 58–59 (1037 x 1043)
508. Ibid., no. 24, pp. 71–72 (1054 x 1078)
509. Ibid., no. 28, pp. 79–81 (1069 x 1070)
510. Ibid., no. 30, pp. 83–86 (1077 x 1078)
511. Ibid., no. 32, pt. I, pp. 92–104 (ca. 1080)
512. Ibid., no. 32, pt. III, p. 105 (1079)
513. Ibid., no. 32, pt. V, p. 106 (ca. 1080)
514. Ibid., no. 32, pt. VI, pp. 106–7 (ca. 1080)
515. Ibid., no. 32, pt. VIII, p. 107 (ca. 1080)
516. Ibid., no. 32, pt. XI, p. 109 (1066 x 1087)
517. Ibid., no. 32, pt. XII, p. 109 (1078 x 1087)
518. Ibid., no. 34, pp. 111–13 (1086)
519. Ibid., no. 35, pp. 113–14 (1086)
520. Ibid., no. 36, pp. 114–16 (1087 x 1088)
521. Ibid., no. 39, pp. 122–23 (1097 x 1098)
522. Ibid., no. 42, pp. 126–27 (before 1072)

523. Ibid., no. 46, pp. 132–33 (eleventh century)
524. Wiffen, *Russell*, vol. 1, pp. 521–22 (Saint-Etienne de Caen, last quarter of the eleventh century)
525. Ibid., pp. 522–23 (Saint-Etienne de Caen, 1079 x 1096)
526. Arch. Calvados, série F, fonds de Beausse, année 1926, carton 1, liasse Manche, sub-liasse "Copies de chartes des Archives de la Manche," copy of Manche H 4603, the original (Lessay, 1084)
527. Ibid. (Lessay, 1056 x 1106, probably after 1094)
528. Arch. Calvados, série F, fonds de Beausse, année 1926, carton 1, liasse Mont-Saint-Michel, copy of Manche H 15173 (Mont-Saint-Michel, *v.* 1061 x 1085)
529. Arch. Calvados, H 7745 (Troarn), no. 116, f° 50r (1101)[88]
530. Ibid., no. 160, f° 61r (1088 x 1112 and later)
531. Ibid., no. 209, f° 77r (1082 x 1109)
532. Ibid., no. 237, f° 86v (1092)
533. Ibid., no. 428, f° 148r (1103)
534. Arch. Calvados, H 7858 (Troarn, 1088 x 1114, probably before 1100)[89]
535. Arch. Eure, H 54, cote 1 (Bec, late eleventh century)
536. Arch. Eure, H 262 (Conches), f° 149v–150r (1066 x 1102)[90]
537. Arch. Eure, H 438, no. 1 (Lire, pancart containing acts from ca. 1050 to the late eleventh century)[91]
538. Arch. Eure, H 711 (Saint-Pierre de Préaux),[92] no. 112, f° 50v–51r (ca. 1100?)
539. Ibid., no. 293, f° 101v–102r (*v.* 1040 x 1072)
540. Ibid., no. 306, f° 105r (ca. 1100?)
541. Ibid., no. 307, f° 105r (1096 x 1101)
542. Ibid., no. 320, f° 108r–108v (*v.* 1040 x 1072)
543. Ibid., no. 321, f° 108v (ca. 1100)
544. Ibid., no. 329, f° 111r (ca. 1100)
545. Ibid., no. 330, f° 111r (ca. 1100)
546. Ibid., no. 334, f° 112r (*v.* 1040 x 1072)
547. Ibid., no. 336, f° 112v (1035 x ca. 1090)
548. Ibid., no. 341, f° 113v (1091)
549. Ibid., no. 351, f° 116v (ca. 1100?)
550. Ibid., no. 356, f° 117v–118r (1078 x ca. 1090)
551. Ibid., no. 377, f° 122r (ca. 1100?)
552. Ibid., no. 383, f° 123v (1078 x 1096)[93]
553. Ibid., no. 408, f° 131r (ca. 1100?)
554. Ibid., no. 425, f° 135r (before 1106)
555. Ibid., no. 439, f° 137r–137v (ca. 1053)[94]
556. Ibid., no. 440, f° 137v (1035 x 1071)
557. Ibid., no. 444, f° 138r–138v (*v.* 1040 x 1066, possibly 1054)[95]
558. Ibid., no. 445, f° 138v–139r (1096 x 1101)[96]
559. Ibid., no. 446, f° 139r–139v (after 1101)
560. Ibid., no. 455, f° 141v–142r (1096 x 1101)
561. Ibid., no. 456, f° 142v (1096 x 1101)
562. Ibid., no. 458, f° 143r (1096 x 1101)
563. Ibid., no. 459, f° 143r–143v (1096 x 1101)
564. Ibid., no. 460, f° 143v (late eleventh or early twelfth century)
565. Ibid., no. 463, f° 143v–144r (1035 x 1087)
566. Ibid., no. 464, f° 144r–144v (early twelfth century)
567. Ibid., no. 466, f° 145r (*v.* 1040 x 1072)
568. Ibid., no. 467, f° 145r–145v (*v.* 1040 x 1072)
569. Arch. Eure, H 793 (Saint-Taurin d'Evreux), f° 57r–61r (pancart of 1195 containing acts from the late tenth century on)
570. Ibid., f° 72r, no. 60 (second half of the eleventh century)

571. Ibid., f° 72v, no. 62 (1037 x 1065)
572. Arch. Orne, H 2007, cote B (Marmoutier, 1071 x 1076)[97]
573. Arch. Orne, H 2008 (Marmoutier, 1093)
574. Arch. Orne, H 2009, no. 4 (Perrières, priory of Marmoutier, 1105)[98]
575. Arch. Orne, H 2023 (Marmoutier, 1076)
576. Arch. Orne, H 2369 (Marmoutier, after ca. 1067)
577. *Livre blanc* of Saint-Martin de Sées,[99] f° 1v (before 1070)
578. Ibid., f° 1v, 7r–7v, 3r (1066 x 1070 concerning events before 1066)
579. Ibid., f° 4r (before 1070)[100]
580. Ibid., f° 5r–5v (before 1087)
581. Ibid., f° 5v–6r (1073 x 1089)
582. Ibid., f° 6r, "Deinde post" (late eleventh century)[101]
583. Ibid., f° 6r, "Novem acras" (eleventh century)
584. Ibid., f° 8r–8v (1095?)
585. Ibid., f° 8v–9r (1094)
586. Ibid., f° 9r–9v (1097)
587. Ibid., f° 9v–11r (1096)
588. Ibid., f° 11r–11v (1099)
589. Ibid., f° 11v–12r (1101)
590. Ibid., f° 12v and 16r (1101)
591. Ibid., f° 16r (1108)
592. Ibid., f° 16r–16v (1089)
593. Ibid., f° 16v–17r (1089)
594. Ibid., f° 17r–17v (1099)
595. Ibid., f° 18r (1101)
596. Ibid., f° 25r–25v (1077 x 1089)
597. Ibid., f° 25v–26r (1077 x 1089)
598. Ibid., f° 26r (1095)
599. Ibid., f° 26r–26v (1095)
600. Ibid., f° 26v–27r (1073 x 1089)
601. Ibid., f° 27v, "Notum sit" (1109)
602. Ibid., f° 27v–28r (1091)
603. Ibid., f° 28r (ca. 1100)
604. Ibid., f° 28r–29r (before 1080)
605. Ibid., f° 29r (1089)
606. Ibid., f° 29v–30r (1094)
607. Ibid., f° 30r (1100)
608. Ibid., f° 30r–30v (1099)
609. Ibid., f° 30v, "Eodem die" (1099)
610. Ibid., f° 30v–31r (1077 x 1095)
611. Ibid., f° 31r–31v (1086)
612. Ibid., f° 31v (1090)
613. Ibid., f° 31v–32r (1073 x 1103)
614. Ibid., f° 32v and 45r (1091)
615. Ibid., f° 33r–33v (ca. 1100)
616. Ibid., f° 34r (before 1105, probably before 1095)
617. Ibid., f° 34r–35r (1086)
618. Ibid., f° 35v–36r (late eleventh or early twelfth century)[102]
619. Ibid., f° 36r–36v (1078)
620. Ibid., f° 36v–37r (1073 x 1089)
621. Ibid., f° 38r–38v (1095)[103]
622. Ibid., f° 41v and 43r (before 1091)
623. Ibid., f° 42r (1095)
624. Ibid., f° 42v (1098)

625. Ibid., f° 42v and 34r (1073 x 1087)
626. Ibid., f° 43r (1091)[104]
627. Ibid., f° 43v–44r (1088)
628. Ibid., f° 44r (1081)
629. Ibid., f° 44r–44v (1088)
630. Ibid., f° 44v (1096)
631. Ibid., f° 45r–45v (1073 x 1089)
632. Ibid., f° 45v, "Notum sit" (1093)
633. Ibid., f° 46r–46v (1088)
634. Ibid., f° 46v–47r (1088)
635. Ibid., f° 47r–48r (1088)[105]
636. Ibid., f° 48r (1090)
637. Ibid., f° 48r–48v (1088)
638. Ibid., f° 48v–49r (before 1095)
639. Ibid., f° 49r, "Frogerius filius" (before 1095)
640. Ibid., f° 49r, "Item notandum" (before 1095)
641. Ibid., f° 50r–50v (1089)
642. Ibid., f° 50v–51v (late eleventh century)
643. Ibid., f° 51v (1094)
644. Ibid., f° 52r (1089)
645. Ibid., f° 52v (1089)
646. Ibid., f° 52v–53r (1094)
647. Ibid., f° 53r–53v (1096)
648. Ibid., f° 53v (1095)
649. Ibid., f° 53v–54r (1091)
650. Ibid., f° 54v–55r (1092)
651. Ibid., f° 55v (1096)
652. Ibid., f° 55v–56r (1099)
653. Ibid., f° 56r–56v (late eleventh or early twelfth century)
654. Ibid., f° 56v–57r (1091)
655. Ibid., f° 57r–57v (1101)
656. Ibid., f° 57v (1092)
657. Ibid., f° 57v–58r (1093)
658. Ibid., f° 58r (late eleventh century)
659. Ibid., f° 58r–58v (1092)
660. Ibid., f° 58v, Gervase de Domfront (late eleventh century)
661. Ibid., f° 58v–59v (1106 x 1107)
662. Ibid., f° 60v and 33r (1085)
663. Ibid., f° 44v and 61r (1089)
664. Ibid., f° 61r–61v (1081)
665. Ibid., f° 61v–62r (1083 x 1089)
666. Ibid., f° 62r–62v (1105)
667. Ibid., f° 63v (1088)
668. Ibid., f° 64r–64v (1081)
669. Ibid., f° 64v–65v (1084)
670. Ibid., f° 65v–66v (late eleventh century)
671. Ibid., f° 66v–67r (1073 x 1089)
672. Ibid., f° 67r–67v (before 1095)
673. Ibid., f° 68r–68v (1097)
674. Ibid., f° 76r, "Uxor Sarlonis" (late eleventh century?)
675. Ibid., f° 76r–76v (1088)
676. Ibid., f° 76v–77r (1088)
677. Ibid., f° 77r (1088)
678. Ibid., f° 77r–77v (1096)

679. Ibid., f° 78r (1097)
680. Ibid., f° 78r–78v (1097)
681. Ibid., f° 78v, "Eodem anno" (1097)
682. Ibid., f° 78v, "In alio" (1098)
683. Ibid., f° 78v–79r (1102)
684. Ibid., f° 80r, Warin d'Argentan (1083)
685. Ibid., f° 86r (1089)
686. Ibid., f° 87r–87v (late eleventh or early twelfth century)
687. Ibid., f° 87v (1111)
688. Ibid., f° 87v–88r (1101)
689. Ibid., f° 88r–88v (1113)
690. Ibid., f° 88v and 90r (1108)
691. Ibid., f° 90r (1073 x 1089)
692. Ibid., f° 90r–90v (1083)
693. Ibid., f° 90v (1098)
694. Ibid., f° 90v–91r (1090)
695. Ibid., f° 95r, Gilbert son of Gilbert (before 1095)[106]
696. Ibid., f° 95r–95v (before 1095)
697. Ibid., f° 95v (before 1095)
698. Ibid., f° 96v–97r (1099)
699. Ibid., f° 97r (1089 x 1103)
700. Ibid., f° 97r–97v (1073 x 1103)
701. Ibid., f° 97v–98r (1088)
702. Ibid., f° 98r–98v (1086)
703. Ibid., f° 98v (late eleventh century)
704. Ibid., f° 98v–99r (1083)
705. Ibid., f° 99r, "Anno ab" (1083)
706. Ibid., f° 103r–103v (late eleventh century)
707. Ibid., f° 112r (after 1066)[107]
708. Ibid., f° 112v (1094)
709. Arch. Seine-Maritime, G 4069 (Rouen cathedral, 1096)[108]
710. Arch. Seine-Maritime, G 8739, cote 2 (Rouen cathedral, 1075)
711. Arch. Seine-Maritime, G 8740 (Rouen cathedral, 1105)
712. Arch. Seine-Maritime, 14 H 1, no. 300, p. 56 (Saint-Ouen, 1042 x 1092)[109]
713. Arch. Seine-Maritime, 14 H 18 (Saint-Ouen), no. 273, p. 230 (1067)
714. Ibid., no. 341, p. 278 (1066 x 1067)
715. Ibid., no. 597, p. 487 (1087 x 1092)[110]
716. Arch. Seine-Maritime, 14 H 255 (Saint-Ouen, 1006 x 1033)[111]
717. Arch. Seine-Maritime, 14 H 314 (Saint-Ouen, written between 1112 and after 1119 about events before 1112)
718. Arch. Seine-Maritime, 14 H 327 (Saint-Ouen, 1066 x 1083)[112]
719. Arch. Seine-Maritime, 14 H 344 (Saint-Ouen, 1084)
720. Arch. Seine-Maritime, 14 H 374 (Saint-Ouen, eleventh or early twelfth century)[113]
721. Arch. Seine-Maritime, 55 H, cote A 1 (Saint-Amand, last third of the eleventh century?)[114]
722. Bibl. Avranches, ms. 210 (Mont-Saint-Michel), f° 34 (1087 x 1090)
723. Ibid., f° 35r (eleventh century)
724. Ibid., f° 76v–77r (1056)
725. Ibid., f° 78r–78v (mid-eleventh century)
726. Ibid., f° 82r–82v (1104)
727. Ibid., f° 83v–84r (1066)
728. Ibid., f° 93r–94v (twelfth century)
729. Ibid., f° 94v (late eleventh century?)

730. Ibid., f° 108r–110r (after 1087)
731. Ibid., f° 110v–111r (1061 x 1106)
732. Ibid., f° 111v (possibly eleventh century)
733. Bibl. Rouen, ms. 1193 (Y44) (Rouen cathedral), no. 17, f° 30v–31r (1083)
734. Ibid., no. 48, f° 48v (1079 x 1110)
735. Bibl. Rouen, ms. 1207 (Y 51) (Fécamp), no. 2, f° 3r–3v (1066 x 1083)[115]
736. Ibid., no. 17, f° 21r (1005)
737. Bibl. Rouen, ms. 1235 (Y 201) (Cerisy), f° 86v, Guy de Saint-Quentin (1066 x 1083)
738. Ibid., f° 86v–87r (1066 x 1082)
739. Ibid., f° 87r, Roger de *Montargneio* (1066 x 1087)
740. Ibid., f° 87v–88r (1066 x 1083)
741. BN, fonds Baluze, vol. 77, f° 61r (Marmoutier, 1079 x 1110)[116]
742. BN, ms. fr. 4901, no. 269, f° 198v–199r (Saint-Sauveur-le-Vicomte, late eleventh century?)
743. BN, ms. fr. 4902, f° 30r (p. 55) (Fontenay, late eleventh century)
744. BN, ms. fr. 18953, pp. 21–23 (probable forgery: Saint-Martin de Sées, allegedly 1089)[117]
745. Ibid., p. 211 (Saint-Martin de Sées, ca. 1080 x 1089)
746. BN, ms. fr. n. a. 7384, f° 7r–7v (Saint-Martin au Bosc, priory of Bec, 1106)
747. BN, ms. fr. n. a. 21807, f° 305r–305v (Saint-Martin au Bosc, priory of Bec)[118]
748. BN, ms. fr. n. a. 21812, f° 19r (Lessay, 1106 and 1118)
749. BN, ms. fr. n. a. 21813, f° 750r–751r (Saint-Désir de Lisieux, 1068)
750. BN, ms. fr. n. a. 21815, f° 264r (Saint-Ouen, 1042 x 1092)
751. BN, ms. lat. 1939, f° 171v (Fécamp, 1028 x 1079)[119]
752. BN, ms. lat. 5359, f° 1r (Fécamp, eleventh century)
753. BN, ms. lat. 5441 (Marmoutier), vol. 1, p. 210 (1066 x 1087)
754. Ibid., vol. 2, p. 25 (Bohun priory, 1093)[120]
755. Ibid., pp. 161–62 (Sacé priory, 1094 x 1133 but closer to 1094)[121]
756. Ibid., pp. 403–4 and 404–5 (Mortain priory, 1082 and later)[122]
757. Ibid., pp. 405–6 (Mortain priory, 1088)
758. BN, ms. lat. 5650 (La Trinité de Caen), f° 20r–23v (early twelfth-century list of rents and services)[123]
759. Ibid., f° 24r–24v (1083 x 1084)
760. Ibid., f° 24v, Osbern de Billy (1083 x 1084)
761. Ibid., f° 24v, Ralph Bos (1083 x 1084)
762. Ibid., f° 24v, Richildis (probably 1083 x 1084)
763. Ibid., f° 24v, Geoffrey son of Alberada (probably 1083 x 1084)
764. Ibid., f° 24v, Rannulf and Turstin (probably 1083 x 1084)
765. Ibid., f° 24v–25r (probably 1083 x 1084)
766. Ibid., f° 25r, Amisus son of Ilbert (probably 1083 x 1084)
767. Ibid., f° 25r, Harold (probably 1083 x 1084)
768. Ibid., f° 25r, Gilbert son of Humphrey (probably 1083 x 1084)
769. Ibid., f° 31r–31v (last third of the eleventh century)
770. Ibid., f° 32r–32v (1106)
771. Ibid., f° 32v (before 1082)
772. Ibid., f° 32v–33r (1066 x 1113, probably 1084)[124]
773. BN, ms. lat. 10058, pp. 1–6 (Saint-Laurent d'Envermeu, priory of Bec, 1100 x 1105)[125]
774. BN, ms. lat. 10086 (Troarn), f° 44r (1088 x 1100)
775. Ibid., f° 45v (1100)
776. Ibid., f° 64v (ca. 1100)
777. Ibid., f° 83v–84r (1109)[126]
778. Ibid., f° 102r–102v (1105)

779. Ibid., f° 102v (early twelfth century)
780. Ibid., f° 142v, "Anno incarnationis" (1094)
781. Ibid., f° 142v, "Robertus verneit" (before 1094)
782. Ibid., f° 146v (1099)
783. Ibid., f° 146v–147r (1100 x 1101)
784. Ibid., f° 147r (1102)
785. Ibid., f° 158v–159r (1088 x 1097)
786. Ibid., f° 161r–161v (ca. 1100)
787. Ibid., f° 168v (1101)
788. Ibid., f° 180r–180v (1101)
789. Ibid., f° 182v (1101)
790. BN, ms. lat. 10087 (Montebourg),[127] no. 140/139, p. 64 (after ca. 1093)
791. Ibid., no. 374/373, p. 129 (late eleventh century)
792. Ibid., no. 484/483, p. 153 (after ca. 1093)
793. Ibid., no. 485/484, p. 153 (after Document 792)
794. BN, ms. lat. 11056 (Saint-Evroul), no. 703, f° 34v (late eleventh century)
795. Ibid., no. 704, f° 34v–35r (late eleventh century)
796. BN, ms. lat. 12777, p. 731, Robert de *Peissiaco* (Conches, late eleventh century)
797. BN, ms. lat. 12878 (Marmoutier), f° 230r–231r (1067)[128]
798. Ibid., f° 235v (1092)
799. Ibid., f° 235v–236r (1093)
800. Ibid., f° 236r–236v (Bohun priory, second half of the eleventh century)
801. Ibid., f° 277r (second half of the eleventh century)
802. Ibid., f° 280r–280v (Mortain priory, 1099 x 1104)
803. Ibid., f° 281v–282v (Mortain priory, 1066 x 1083)[129]
804. BN, ms. lat. 12879, f° 8r (Marmoutier, 1105)
805. BN, ms. lat. 12880, f° 224r (Marmoutier, 1087 x 1106, probably 1094)
806. BN, ms. lat. 12884 (Bec), f° 82r–85r (pp. 153–59), no. 97 (1084)
807. Ibid., f° 97r–97v (pp. 183–84), bottom margin (1095)
808. Ibid., f° 102r (p. 193), left margin (1097; somewhat suspect)
809. Ibid., f° 104r (p. 197), top margin (1098)
810. Ibid., f° 177v–178r (pp. 344–45) (second half of the eleventh century)
811. BN, ms. lat. 13905 (Bec), f° 82v (p. 156) (St. Philibert priory, 1097)
812. Ibid., f° 83v (p. 158) (1093 x 1112)
813. Ibid., f° 116v (p. 204), "Quicquid habuit" (1034 x ca. 1040)
814. Ibid., "Postea idem" (1034 x 1078)
815. BN, ms. lat. 17137 (Saint-Sauveur-le-Vicomte), no. 86, f° 85r (late eleventh century)
816. Ibid., no. 97, f° 91r–92r (ca. 1100?)
817. Ibid., no. 122, f° 111v–112r (late eleventh century)
818. Ibid., no. 123, f° 112r (late eleventh century?)
819. BN, fonds Moreau, vol. 21 (Fécamp), f° 20v–21r (1028 x 1079)
820. Ibid., f° 22r–22v (1028 x 1079)
821. Ibid., f° 24r–24v (1057 x 1066)
822. Ibid., f° 25r–25v (1028 x 1079)
823. Ibid., f° 26r–26v (1028 x 1079)
824. Ibid., f° 27r–27v (1028 x 1079)[130]
825. Ibid., f° 28r–28v (1028 x 1079)
826. Ibid., f° 30r–30v (1028 x 1079)
827. Ibid., f° 31r–31v (1028 x 1079)
828. BN, fonds Moreau, vol. 28, f° 192r–192v (Fécamp, 1065)
829. BN, fonds Moreau, vol. 30 (Fécamp), f° 190r–190v (1040 x 1046)
830. Ibid., f° 190v–191r (1080 and 1080 x 1087)[131]

831. BN, fonds Moreau, vol. 40, f° 220r–220v (Fécamp, eleventh or early twelfth century)
832. BN, fonds Moreau, vol. 341 (Fécamp), f° 17r–17v (1047)
833. Ibid., f° 28r (ca. 1060)
834. Bibliothèque de l'Université de Caen, Cartulary of Saint-Etienne de Caen, p. 25, no. LXXX (Deville, p. 19; 1070 x 1079)[132]
835. Ibid., no. LXXXI (Deville, p. 19; 1070 x 1079)
836. Ibid., no. LXXXII (Deville, p. 19; 1070 x 1079)
837. Ibid., no. LXXXIII (Deville, p. 19; 1070 x 1079)
838. Ibid., p. 26, no. LXXXVIII (Deville, p. 19; 1070 x 1079)
839. Ibid., no. XCIII (Deville, p. 20; 1070 x 1079)
840. Ibid., no. XCIIII (Deville, p. 20; 1070 x 1079)
841. Ibid., p. 27, no. XCVI (Deville, p. 20; 1070 x 1079)
842. Ibid., p. 28, no. C (Deville, p. 21; 1079 x 1101)
843. Ibid., no. CI (Deville, pp. 21–22; eleventh century)
844. Ibid., no. CII (Deville, p. 22; 1079 x 1101)
845. Ibid., p. 29, no. CIIII (Deville, p. 22; 1070 x 1090)
846. Ibid., pp. 29–30, no. CVI (Deville, p. 23)
847. Ibid., p. 30, no. CVII (Deville, p. 23)
848. Ibid., no. CVIII (Deville, p. 23; 1079 x 1101)
849. Ibid., pp. 30–31, no. CIX (Deville, p. 24)
850. Ibid., p. 31, no. CX (Deville, p. 24; 1079 x 1101)
851. Ibid., pp. 31–32, no. CXI (Deville, p. 24)
852. Ibid., pp. 32–33, no. CXIIII (Deville, pp. 24–25; 1079 x 1101)
853. Ibid., p. 33, no. CXV (Deville, p. 25)
854. Ibid., pp. 34–35, no. CXVII (Deville, pp. 25–26; 1079 x 1101)
855. Ibid., p. 35, no. CXVIII (Deville, p. 26; 1079 x 1101, probably later than Document 871)
856. Ibid., pp. 37–38, no. CXXI (Deville, p. 27; 1087 x 1096)
857. Ibid., no. CXXIIII (Deville, pp. 27–28; 1079 x 1101)
858. Ibid., p. 40, no. CXXVII (Deville, p. 28; 1079 x 1101)
859. Ibid., pp. 40–41, no. CXXVIII (Deville, p. 28)
860. Ibid., p. 42, no. CXXXI (Deville, pp. 28–29; 1079 x 1101)
861. Ibid., no. CXXXII (Deville, p. 29; 1079 x 1101)
862. Ibid., p. 43, no. CXXXV (not in Deville; 1079 x 1101)
863. Ibid., p. 44, no. CXXXVI (Deville, p. 29; 1079 x 1101)
864. Ibid., p. 45, no. CXXXVIII (Deville, pp. 29–30)
865. Ibid., no. CXL (Deville, p. 30; 1079 x 1101)
866. Ibid., pp. 45–46, no. CXLI (Deville, p. 30; 1079 x 1101)
867. Ibid., p. 46, no. CXLII (not in Deville; 1079 x 1101)
868. Ibid., pp. 46–47, no. [CXLIII][133] (Deville, p. 30; 1101)
869. Ibid., p. 47, no. CXLIIII (Deville, p. 30)
870. Ibid., pp. 50–51, no. CLI (Deville, p. 31; 1079 x 1101)
871. Ibid., pp. 51–53, no. CLIII (Deville, p. 32; 1089 x 1091)[134]
872. Ibid., pp. 57–58, no. CLIX (Deville, p. 36; 1101 x 1106)
873. Ibid., p. 61, no. CLXV (Deville, pp. 37–38)
874. Ibid., no. CLXVI (Deville, p. 38; 1094 x 1110)
875. Ibid., no. CLXVII (Deville, p. 38)
876. Ibid., p. 63, no. CLXIX (Deville, p. 39; 1080)
877. Ibid., no. CLXX (Deville, p. 39; before 1082)
878. Ibid., p. 66, no. CLXXVII (Deville, p. 41)
879. Ibid., pp. 68–69, no. CLXXXI (Deville, pp. 41–42; 1095)
880. Ibid., pp. 76–77, no. CC (Deville, p. 46)
881. Ibid., pp. 77–78, no. CCIII (Deville, p. 47)

882. Ibid., pp. 79–80, no. CCVI (Deville, p. 48)
883. Ibid., pp. 81–82, no. CCX (Deville, p. 49)
884. Collection Mancel, vol. 74 (Saint-Evroul), f° 197r (last third of the eleventh century)
885. Ibid., f° 197r–197v (1091 x 1123)
886. Collection Mancel, vol. 300 (Marmoutier), no. 10, f° 224v (p. 2404) (second half of the eleventh century)
887. Ibid., no. 98, f° 239r (p. 2433) (before 1090)
888. Ibid., no. 141, f° 248r (p. 2449) (1070)

Notes

ABBREVIATIONS IN NOTES

Arch.	Archives départementales.
Bibl.	Bibliothèque municipale.
BN	Bibliothèque nationale.
Dudo	Dudo of Saint-Quentin, *De moribus et actis primorum Normanniae ducum*, ed. Jules Lair (Paris and Caen, 1865).
EHD	*English Historical Documents*, vol. 2: *1042–1189*, ed. David C. Douglas and George W. Greenaway (London, 1953).
HF	*Recueil des historiens des Gaules et de la France.*
ms. fr.	manuscrit français.
ms. fr. n. a.	manuscrit français nouvelle acquisition.
ms. lat.	manuscrit latin.
ms. lat. n. a.	manuscrit latin nouvelle acquisition.
OV	Orderic Vitalis, *Historia ecclesiastica.* Unless otherwise indicated, citations are to the edition by Marjorie Chibnall, *The Ecclesiastical History of Orderic Vitalis*, 6 vols. (Oxford, 1969–80), and translations are by Chibnall, on the facing (odd-numbered) pages.
OV, interp.	Orderic Vitalis, interpolations to William of Jumièges, *Gesta*, ed. Marx, pp. 151–98.
PL	Jacques Paul Migne, *Patrologiae cursus completus . . . , Series latina.* 221 vols., 5 supplements (Paris, 1844–1903, 1958–74).
RT	*Chronique de Robert de Torigni . . .* , ed. Léopold V. Delisle, 2 vols. (Rouen, 1872, 1873).
RT, interp.	Robert de Torigny, interpolations to William of Jumièges, *Gesta*, ed. Marx, pp. 199–334.
Summa	E. J. Tardif, *Coutumiers de Normandie*, vol. 2: *La Summa de legibus Normannie in curia laicali* (Rouen and Paris, 1896).
TAC	E. J. Tardif, *Coutumiers de Normandie*, vol. 1: *Le Très Ancien Coutumier de Normandie*, pt. 1: *Texte latin* (Paris, 1881), pt. II: *Textes français et normand* (Rouen and Paris, 1903).
WJ	William of Jumièges, *Gesta Normannorum ducum*, ed. Jean Marx (Rouen and Paris, 1914).
WM	William of Malmesbury, *De gestis regum Anglorum libri quinque*, ed. William Stubbs, 2 vols. (Rolls Series, 1887, 1889).
WP	William of Poitiers, *Gesta Guillelmi ducis Normannorum et regis Anglorum*, ed. Raymonde Foreville (Paris, 1952).

CHAPTER 1

1. For simplicity, I refer to the rulers of Normandy always as dukes, although they used many titles in the eleventh century; see, most recently, Bates, *Normandy*, pp. 148–50, and the references there in n. 6. I also refer to Duke William II, the Conqueror of England, as Duke William, after as well as before 1066; his great-great-grandfather, Duke William I, is called William Longsword whenever it is necessary to refer to him.

2. Preeminently by Robert Génestal in the last generation and by Jean Yver in the current generation. For an overview of the work of Génestal, see Yver, "Coutume." For bibliography of the study of Norman law, see Astoul, "Histoire," and Génestal, "Histoire." Study of the law of Normandy can best be followed in the *Semaines d'histoire du droit normand* held annually or biennially since 1923; summaries can be found in the relevant volumes of the *Revue historique de droit français et étranger* for the conferences held through 1974 and *Annales de Normandie* since 1975. Norman law also appears often in the papers of the biennial *Journées d'histoire du droit et des institutions des pays de l'Ouest de la France*, which are summarized in the *Revue historique de droit français et étranger* through 1975 and in *Annales de Normandie* since 1977.

Lagouëlle, *Essai*, p. 42, says that his study was to be in three parts, the second and third being "Conception familiale de la terre" and "Notion interne du droit réel foncier." These two parts never appeared. Astoul, "Histoire," p. 68, says that the third part "devait avoir pour objet la notion interne du droit réel foncier, c'est-à-dire l'étude de ce droit considéré en lui-même, indépendamment des relations féodales ou familiales, étude de droit tout particulièrement technique, soulevant entre autres les questions délicates de la saisine, de la propriété temporaire, des formes dans la transmission de droits fonciers: étude que l'auteur n'a pas reprise lui-même jusqu'à ce jour et qui n'a pas été abordée sur le terrain spécial du droit normand." See also Lagoüelle, *Essai*, pp. 15–16. It is, in a way, Lagouëlle's third part which I am attempting to write, for the eleventh century.

3. Tardif, ed., *Coutumiers*, vol. 1: *Le Très Ancien Coutumier de Normandie*, pt. 1: *Texte latin*; pt. 2: *Textes français et normand.*

4. See esp. below, Chapter 12.

5. Of all Norman abbeys from which eleventh-century charters are extant, only Saint-Martin de Sées regularly dated its charters, and even it did not do so always: 123 of the 202 eleventh-century charters in the *Livre blanc* of Saint-Martin are dated. I have counted as "eleventh-century" all charters dated 1106 or before and all undated charters which might come from 1106 or before. This procedure maximizes the number of undated charters and therefore minimizes the percentage of charters which are dated. On the other hand, I have counted as dated those which begin with the words *eodem anno* and the like. The count includes charters concerning the abbey's possessions in England. The total is nevertheless less than the total number of Norman transactions of the abbey which is given elsewhere because a good many charters refer to more than one transfer. The earliest dated charter in the *Livre blanc*, Document 707, is dated 1061 but must in fact have been written after 1066, unless the reference to Duke William "qui postea Dei gratia effectus est rex Anglorum" was added by the copyist. The next dated charter comes from 1078.

6. Barlow, "Effects," p. 140.

7. D. C. Douglas, "Norman Conquest," pp. 71–72, makes this point about pre-Conquest Norman history as a whole; see also Le Patourel, *Norman Empire*, pp. 260–61, on legal matters specifically.

8. Keeton, *The Norman Conquest and the Common Law*, despite its title, does little to advance this effort.

9. Milsom, *Legal Framework*, passim. The word "ancient" is used on p. 103.

10. See below, Chapter 4, at nn. 57–60, for a summary of the evidence.

11. Below, Appendix A, Table I.
12. For examples in this work of cases which may be misleading because of the importance of the persons concerned, see: below, Chapter 3, n. 101; Chapter 4, n. 4; Chapter 4, at nn. 125–30, 132–37, 339–50, 378; Chapter 7, last paragraph.
13. Below, this chapter, at nn. 20–25.
14. The longer (French) version of the Bayeux Inquest is published in *HF*, 23:699–702, and in Navel, "Enquête," pp. 13–23. The shorter (English) version is published in *HF*, 23:698–99, and in *Red Book*, 2:645-47. The Inquest of 1172 is published in *HF*, 23:693–98, and *Red Book*, 2:624–45.
15. Tabuteau, "Definitions," esp. pp. 21–40. See also Bates, *Normandy*, pp. 168–69; Chibnall, "Military Service."
16. See also D. C. Douglas, "Norman Conquest," p. 70; Guillot, *Comte*, 1:ix–x.
17. Génestal, *Tutelle*, p. 15, argues that Louis IV's actions with respect to Duke Richard I in 942 are an example of seigneurial wardship as it was practiced in Normandy in the early thirteenth century. The passage reads in full: "Les textes de cette époque lointaine sont trop rares et trop peu explicites pour permettre d'étudier les règles de l'institution. Les origines du droit normand ne peuvent être étudiées que sur la base du droit mieux connu du XIIIe siècle; si des textes postérieures ne nous faisaient connaître l'institution de la garde seigneuriale, nous ne comprendrions rien aux récits touchant la minorité de Richard Ier." See also ibid., pp. 3–4. Below, Chapter 4, n. 125, argues against Génestal's conclusions on the particular point of law about which he makes the assertion quoted.
18. For comparable reasons I have eschewed the use of sources, even eleventh-century ones, from Anglo-Norman England and from Norman Italy.
19. Below, Chapter 2, at and in n. 3.
20. It is denied by Génestal, "Histoire," p. 79, and "Formation et développement," pp. 50–53.
21. Below, Chapter 4, at and in n. 55.
22. A few words of apparent Anglo-Saxon origin are found in Norman charters. "Geld" is one item in each of two lists of ducal rights: Documents 344 (p. 215) and 409 (p. 70). The word *gersimonia*, which appears in several charters from Fontenay (below, Chapter 3, at n. 241), may be the Anglo-Saxon *gersuma*: see below, Chapter 4, n. 211. For the possibility that the Anglo-Norman *feorm* influenced the introduction of the word *firma* into Normandy, see below, Chapter 4, at n. 220.

On the other hand, even so obviously useful a device as the writ, which William the Conqueror began to use in England virtually immediately, was rarely used in or for Normandy until the reign of Henry I. See esp. Bates, "Earliest Norman Writs." See also Yver, "Bref," p. 317; Le Patourel, *Norman Empire*, pp. 244–45, 268; Chaplais, "Anglo-Saxon Chancery," p. 162 and n. 18; Bates, "Origins," pp. 7–8; Bates, *Normandy*, p. 54; Bouvris, "Bref"; Musset, "Huit essais," pp. 141–43. On the general absence of English influence on Norman diplomatic by 1087, see Chaplais, "Anglo-Saxon Chancery," pp. 161–62.
23. Valin, *Duc*, strongly supports the idea that England (and Anjou) influenced Normandy, but only after 1106; see esp. pp. 11, 107–8. On Henry's English orientation, see Barlow, *William Rufus*, pp. 39–40 and n. 165.
24. Matthew, *Norman Monasteries*, p. 28; Le Patourel, *Norman Barons*, pp. 25–26; Le Patourel, *Norman Empire*, passim, esp. pp. 199–200, 330–34. For a somewhat dissenting opinion, see Davis, *Normans*, p. 122.
25. This point is made most forcefully by Le Patourel, *Norman Empire*, chap. 7; pp. 260–77 concern law and its enforcement specifically.
26. Génestal, "Formation et développement," p. 50, rejects the importance of the influence of neighboring customs on Norman law. Goebel, *Felony*, pp. 130–31, 171–72, 180–81, 190–92, and 191, n. 5, however, thinks such influence may have been considerable in the field of public law. See also Yver, "Caractères originaux de l'Ouest,"

for similarities between Norman law and neighboring legal systems.

Génestal, "Formation et développement," pp. 53–55, also rejects the importance of the influence of Roman and canon law before the thirteenth century, with the exception of two particular points of family law which were modified in the mid- to late twelfth century under this influence. His works on specific elements of the law bear out this dating; see, e.g., *Tutelle*, p. 136 and passim. Besnier, *Coutume*, pp. 47–50, is both more general and more positive but seems to think that major influence began only in the twelfth century. Yver, "Droit romain," concludes (p. 16), for the whole period down through the thirteenth century: "Influence très faible du droit savant sur la coutume de Normandie." Foreville, "Ancien droit," pp. 153–54, emphasizes the Romanity of some legal observations by William of Poitiers; but this is unlikely to have had any influence on practice in Normandy.

See below, this chapter, at nn. 37–39, for the few possible influences I have found, all from customary rather than civil or canon law.

27. Génestal, "Formation et développement," pp. 44–46. None of these groups is any longer seriously mentioned. Of them, the Saxons were given the most prominence. Guinet, *Contribution*, states a case, based largely on linguistic evidence, for heavy settlement by Saxons in the future area of Normandy between the third and the seventh centuries; he explicitly attributes to the Saxons many place-names and a good many other linguistic phenomena which have usually been taken to indicate Viking settlement and influence. His conclusions imply an even less dense settlement of Scandinavians in Normandy in the tenth and eleventh centuries than the current scholarly consensus envisions, because most of the evidence about density of settlement is linguistic. Even Guinet, however (ibid., p. 108), doubts that the Saxons influenced the law of Normandy.

28. For a bibliographical sketch of the legal aspect of the subject in the sixteenth through nineteenth centuries, see Lagouëlle, *Essai*, p. 5, n. 1. Haskins, *Norman Institutions*, p. 5, sees the problem as insoluble; Powicke, *Loss*, pp. 1–2, 36–37, is pessimistic and thinks the question of little importance. Since then, however, a great deal of scholarly work has reopened the subject. For recent summaries of the state of the question, see D. C. Douglas, *William*, pp. 19–30; Musset, *Invasions*, pp. 253–61; Musset, "Naissance"; Musset, "Monachisme"; Davis, *Normans*, pp. 19–27; Bates, *Normandy*, passim, esp. pp. 10–11, 15–24, 36–38, 163, 179–80, 239–41. The case for predominantly Scandinavian influence is presented by M. de Boüard, "Neustrie"; see also Breese, "Persistence"; van Houts, "Scandinavian Influence." The case for predominantly Carolingian influence is presented most forcefully by Yver, especially in "Premières institutions." Le Patourel, *Norman Empire*, pp. 4–8, 12–13, 280–83, attempts to reconcile the two views, with a special reference to the question of "institutional continuity" (p. 282). See also Searle, "Frankish Rivalries." The works cited here list further bibliography. The book by Guinet discussed in the preceding note is also relevant in a negative way.

29. On this subject, see Musset, "Apports scandinaves," and the earlier studies to which he refers there. His contentions concerning the Scandinavian origins of the terms "acre" and *mansloth* (ibid., p. 566) have been challenged by Guinet, *Contribution*, pp. 91–94, 98–99; on the acre, see also Navel, "Recherches sur les anciennes mesures," esp. pp. 166–70. See also Bates, *Normandy*, pp. 21–22; Musset, "Huit essais," pp. 55–59.

30. The "genius" and the adaptability the Normans showed in their expansionary and organizational feats of the eleventh and twelfth centuries are often attributed to their Scandinavian origins, e.g., by Yver, "Premières institutions," p. 366. Le Patourel, *Norman Empire*, pp. 285–92, however, gives an explanation of Norman expansiveness which credits specifically Norman conditions without attributing those conditions to Scandinavian influence; it covers only expansion led or sanctioned by the dukes but could easily be extended to cover the private ventures as well. Bates, *Normandy*, also

argues that Norman military and governmental achievements were not due to some innate characteristic of the Normans, whether it was their Scandinavian heritage or anything else.

In more narrowly legal matters, Yver, "Premières institutions," p. 321, suggests that "un sentiment, poussé à l'extrême, de l'égalité entre héritiers," characteristic of Scandinavia, influenced the Norman law of inheritance; see also Yver, *Egalité*, pp. 108, 279–89. De Boüard, "Apogée," p. 101, credits to a specifically Scandinavian aspect of Norman law William's ability to become duke of Normandy in 1035 although he was illegitimate. Musset, "Actes inédits, II," p. 150, notes "un esclavage domestique et personnel, de caractère sans doute scandinave, vers la fin du Xe ou le début du XIe siècle"; see also Bates, *Normandy*, pp. 13, 23. M. de Boüard, "Duché," p. 4, describes the fact that in the tenth century most transactions occurred without being written down as a "trait original qui dénote une solide survivance des moeurs scandinaves." Villers, "Aperçus," p. 149, suggests that "le caractère ethnique de la noblesse normande" is at least partly responsible for the supposed fact that, "controuvée pour la plupart des régions françaises, la thèse de Guilhiermoz sur l'équivalence des *vassi*, des *milites* et des nobles, se révèle au contraire exacte en Normandie." For a denial of Guilhiermoz's thesis, even for Normandy, see, most recently, Bates, *Normandy*, pp. 106–11.

31. The general tendency of Génestal, "Formation et développement," pp. 46–50, is to reject this source of Norman law, as he rejects all others except the Frankish.

32. In addition to the works cited above, this chapter, n. 28, see esp. Carabie, *Propriété foncière*, pp. 120–23; Lemarignier, *Recherches*, chap. 1; Navel, "Recherches sur les institutions féodales," pp. 87–89, 101–3, 106–7, 112–15, 147, 149–50, 162–63, 164–65, 171, 173, 174, and his earlier articles as cited in these places; Musset, "Ruine," p. 275; Yver, "Développement," pp. 183–204; Matthew, *Norman Conquest*, pp. 60–65; Bates, *Normandy*, passim.

33. On non-Normans who became important landholders in Normandy, see, most recently, Musset, "Aristocratie," pp. 74–78, 81–83, and Bates, *Normandy*, pp. 99–100.

34. Le Patourel, *Norman Empire*, pp. 282–83 and 283, n. 1.

35. Cf. Yver, *Contrats*, pp. 304–5, who, as part of his conclusion, asserts the absence of Scandinavian influence on the Norman law of obligations.

36. There have been few studies of the diplomatic of the documents on which this work is based. The only ones known to me are Duhamel, "Diplomatique"; Bénet, "Etude"; Fauroux, *Recueil*, pp. 41–65; Musset, *Actes*, pp. 25–41; Brown, "Some Observations." All of these concern ducal acts alone. The only study devoted solely to the diplomatic of an individual church is Colmant, "Actes," on Marmoutier; but that abbey, although it possessed much property in Normandy, was not Norman. The editor of the charters of a church sometimes discusses diplomatic briefly, and there are a few articles on particular charters.

For various ways in which the five oldest abbeys distinguished themselves diplomatically from the other Norman abbeys of the eleventh century, see below, Chapter 7, after n. 23, with Appendix A, Table 4; Chapter 7, at and in n. 126; Chapter 10, at n. 5, with Appendix A, Table 5; Chapter 11, n. 4. Monastic life at all five abbeys was disrupted, and all but Mont-Saint-Michel were deserted for a time. Of the seven Norman bishoprics, only Rouen and Evreux were continuously occupied throughout the Viking invasions and the tenth century; there are, however, no relevant eleventh-century documents from Evreux, and the documents from the cathedral church of Rouen do not exhibit to any marked degree the characteristics shared by the charters of the five earliest refounded abbeys. One possible explanation for these shared characteristics is that the five abbeys and only these five—not the bishoprics, not Frankish houses refounded later—managed to preserve their Frankish diplomas and therefore were able to follow Carolingian models. This cannot be proved for two reasons. First, Carolingian documents are known to have survived, among abbeys, only at Jumièges and Saint-

Wandrille, but also at Rouen cathedral; see Carabie, *Propriété foncière*, p. 181; Musset, "Aspect," p. 135 and n. 18; Document 155a. Second, Carolingian diplomas of the bishoprics and of Frankish houses which were not refounded until the eleventh century cannot be proved to have been lost by the eleventh century.

For Carolingian reminiscences elsewhere in this work, see below, Chapter 3, at and in n. 94; Chapter 4, n. 358; Chapter 6, n. 197; Chapter 8, n. 128. See also Brown, "Some Observations," p. 150. On the problem of the degree to which such reminiscences can be taken literally, see below, Chapter 4, n. 358, and the references there.

37. Below, Chapter 4, at nn. 181–204 and 213–20.

38. Below, Chapter 4, at nn. 277–80.

39. Tabuteau, "Definitions," p. 59. In actuality, it seems more likely that the post-1066 developments occurred approximately simultaneously on both sides of the Channel.

40. See also above, this chapter, at and in n. 22, on the slightness of evidence for Anglo-Saxon influence on Normandy between 1066 and 1106.

CHAPTER 2

1. The technical diplomatic distinction between charters and notices (e.g., Giry, *Manuel*, p. 8) is irrelevant to this study; see also Sauvage, *Troarn*, p. 306; Brown, "Some Observations," p. 160. For its application to the documents used here, see the works cited above, Chapter 1, n. 36, and A. de Boüard, *Manuel*, 1:49–50, and 2:119–20. I shall use "charter" to mean documents which are technically notices as well as those which are technically charters.

2. The only exceptions are two charters recording dowers of duchesses; one concerning a suit over dower between two lay persons, which was probably drawn up by an abbey on behalf of one of the parties to the suit (on these three, see below, this chapter, at and in n. 11); and a few written by ducal scribes (below, this chapter, at and in n. 12).

3. Document 102, dated 965, is for—and was doubtless drawn up by—the abbey of Saint-Père de Chartres; it comes from Walter count of Dreux but concerns Norman land and was signed by Duke Richard I. The earliest charter which emanates from a Norman is Document 103, from Duke Richard I for Saint-Denis. The earliest charter not only issued by a Norman but also drawn up for—and presumably by—a Norman institution is Document 104. Document 101, allegedly of 963 or 964, is a forgery. Nineteen other charters may be earlier than one or more of these: Documents 105 and 293 and the possible lost charters referred to in Document 106 and in Fauroux, *Recueil*, pp. 19–23, nos. 1–11, 13–17, and nn. 4–14, 16–20. Most of the last sixteen alienations, however, were probably made orally alone, if at all: see below, this chapter, at n. 6.

4. Below, Appendix A, Table 1.

5. In addition to the charters cited in the next note, see Documents 125 and 143. Two of these charters are dated 1025; the other two can be dated to that immediate period. The language of three—Documents 125, 127, and 144—is very similar. They were probably written by the same scribe (see below, Chapter 5, at and in n. 9). Document 144 has no signature list; the signature lists of the other three overlap considerably.

6. Documents 127 (p. 139) and 144 (p. 171). The former of these charters is for Jumièges; see below, Chapter 5, n. 65, for a suggestion that Duke William Longsword, Richard II's grandfather, may have issued at least one charter for Jumièges.

7. Below, Appendix A.

8. On the new foundations, see D. C. Douglas, *William*, pp. 105–6, 111–15. On the dates of foundation of individual abbeys, see Knowles, *Monastic Order*, pp. 701–2;

Bates, *Normandy*, Map 11, p. 274; and esp. Laporte, "Origines," pp. 49–68. After the early eleventh century, the only ducal foundations were the two abbeys at Caen, Saint-Etienne for monks and La Trinité for nuns, founded by William the Conqueror and Matilda in the decade before the Norman conquest of England.

On the new aristocracy, see D. C. Douglas, *William*, pp. 84–96; Le Patourel, *Norman Empire*, pp. 286–88, 292–96; Rioult de Neuville, "Orbec," p. 716; Yver, "Institutions féodales," p. 276; Musset, "Aristocratie," pp. 75–87; Le Maho, "Seigneuries," pp. 7–48; Holt, "Feudal Society, I," p. 203. That the aristocracy of Normandy was new in the eleventh century is denied by Bates, *Normandy*, esp. pp. 34–36, 134–35; for some arguments against this attempted revision, see my review of the book, pp. 612–14. The latest word is Hollister, "Greater Domesday Tenants."

9. See below, Chapter 11, on the use of charters in rendering transfers secure.

10. Document 494, as quoted below, Chapter 11, at n. 55; Documents 217 (p. 332), 499 (p. 227), 521 (p. 122). In addition, quite a few preambles whose subject is the reasons why charters should be written allege that it was ancestral practice to do so.

11. Respectively, Document 313, for which see below, Chapter 4, at n. 83; Document 25, on which see below, Chapter 4, at and in nn. 63–65, 100, 103; Document 617, for part of which see below, Chapter 6, at and in n. 172; Document 109; and Document 148.

12. Document 110 (p. 89); Document 116 (p. 102 with note i). The first is drawn in the name of Dudo's patron, Ralph count of Ivry, rather than of the duke himself. Dudo was in Normandy from before the death of Richard I in 996 at least through the late reign of Richard II, who died in 1026 or 1027 (Prentout, *Etude*, pp. 13–15). Two other charters of about the same time refer to other men as *cancellarius* (Document 125, p. 131) or *notarius* (Document 107, p. 81).

13. Fauroux, *Recueil*, pp. 41–43. She gives more weight to the evidence for a ducal chancery during the reign of Richard II than do most scholars. The consensus is that there never was a ducal chancery before 1066; see, however, Bates, *Normandy*, pp. 154–55; Brown, "Some Observations," pp. 151–53.

14. In the case of warranty, for example; see below, Chapter 9.

15. There are no extant eleventh-century charters from the monasteries of Cormeilles and Saint-Sever or from the nunnery of Almenèches. Until recently the same was thought true of Grestain, but David Bates has now found its "earliest *pancarte*"; see Bates, *Normandy*, p. 139, n. 41. I am grateful to him for providing me with a transcript of the act.

16. Below, Chapter 4, at and in n. 285.

17. It is also possible that some such agreements were never recorded in writing, although I doubt that this was usually so, once the habit of writing had become established in Normandy, for contracts whereby churches established that certain obligations were owing to themselves. On this subject, see Musset, "Contribution," p. 63; and the references below, Chapter 4, nn. 164 (concerning rentals) and 285 (concerning mortgages), and at n. 295 (concerning gages of movables).

18. Document 274 (p. 451). Also Documents 123 (p. 115, which repeats the identical phrase), 154 (p. 199), 481 (p. 666). On the material in this paragraph, see also Chibnall, "Charter," pp. 9–12, and the references there.

19. On Norman cartularies, see Besnier, *Coutume*, pp. 38–39; Fauroux, *Recueil*, pp. 38–39; Musset, "Actes inédits, I," pp. 117–18.

20. Respectively, A. Deville, *La Trinité du Mont*, in which the latest dated act (Document 86) comes from 1091; OV, ed. Le Prévost, 5:182–95. On the latter, see Chibnall, "Charter," pp. 9–10.

21. Copies by J.-L. Lenoir of many documents from the Fécamp cartulary are in various volumes of the fonds Moreau in the Bibliothèque nationale. For the Marmoutier cartulary, see Colmant, "Actes," p. 52.

22. Fauroux, *Recueil*, p. 38; Musset, *Actes*, pp. 25–35; Lemarignier, *Etude*, Appendix I; Colmant, "Actes," p. 54; Chibnall, "Charter," pp. 11–12; Bouvris, "Date," pp. 129–30.

23. The excerpts quoted below, Chapter 8, at n. 107, from the 1068 pancart of Troarn are typical of these brief entries.

24. Document 662 (f° 33r): "Verumtamen quia diversa diversis temporibus vel data vel empta fuisse ratum habetur, singulis tractatibus singulisque cartis ea scribere disposuimus, ne si in eodem scriberentur, aut ex toto falsa aut ficta pueris haberentur."

25. Arch. Orne, *Livre blanc* of Saint-Martin de Sées, from which Documents 577–708 come.

26. For example, much of the work concerning Viking settlement in Normandy is based on the evidence of place-names.

27. Document 515.

28. For Rainald's memorandum (Document 344), see esp. below, Chapter 3, at nn. 2 and 189; Chapter 4, at n. 101; Chapter 6, at n. 30; Chapter 7, at n. 42; Chapter 8, at n. 68. The astonishing part of Rainald's account says that Stephen, his predecessor as possessor of the property, "habuit puerulum ex quadam muliere vidua nomine Oringa . . . ; quo puerulo mortuo, nesciente Stephano, femina illa ingeniosa, dando pretium x^{cem} solidorum per annum, emit puerulum a quadam muliere . . . , et illa femina vocabatur Ulburga; quem Stephanus credens suum jure heredem hereditavit illum de suis alodiis . . . ; deinde, mortua femina Stephani prius et postea ipso mortuo, supradicta femina [i.e., Ulburga] . . . , non habens pretium sui pueruli quod solita erat habere, reclamavit suum infantem et non potuit habere pro parentibus femine Stephani; cujus femine clamor perveniens ad Willelmum ducem . . . , fecit rex inde tenere placitum, qua probatione mulier illa rehaberet suum puerum, et dijudicavit . . . quod femina illa . . . per judicium ferri calidi rehaberet suum filium, si Deus eam servaret illesam . . . . [Q]uo judicio portato . . . fuit mulier illa . . . Dei judicio illesa . . . ; quod rex . . . audiens . . . accepit in suum dominium possessionem Stephani" (Document 344, pp. 213–14).

29. For another example, contrast the charter discussed below, Chapter 4, at n. 252, with the charters discussed there at nn. 250–51.

30. Besides Rainald's memorandum, the only document which actually rehearses arguments in court is 398, for which see below, Chapter 4, at n. 31. For examples of other records of claims and court cases which cast light on something other than procedure, see below, Chapter 4, at and in nn. 34, 89, 114, 306–7; Chapter 5, at n. 69.

31. See below, Appendix A, Table 2. For other examples, see below, Chapter 3, n. 66; Chapter 6, at nn. 136–43; Chapter 7, n. 126; Chapter 7, at and in nn. 136–38; Chapter 7, at nn. 151–54; Chapter 10, at nn. 4–7, 45.

32. E.g., below, Chapter 3, at n. 34; Chapter 3, n. 146; Chapter 3, after n. 228; Chapter 4, after n. 209; Chapter 4, before n. 277; Chapter 4, at and after nn. 284–85. Three of the four references to necessity as a motive for sales (below, Chapter 3, n. 154) come from Saint-Martin de Sées. Eight of the twelve certain instances of corodies (below, Chapter 3, at nn. 72–83) come from Saint-Etienne de Caen. The word "fief" appears in the charters of Conches much more often than is usual, as does the word "allod" in the charters of La Trinité du Mont. For other examples, see Bates, *Normandy*, pp. 107, 148.

33. See also Pollock and Maitland, *History*, 1:26.

34. Below, Chapter 7, at n. 124.

35. Especially, among Norman churches, Saint-Martin de Sées (e.g., above, Chapter 1, n. 5). The most striking example encountered in connection with Normandy, however, is the abbey of Marmoutier at Tours, on which see Colmant, "Actes"; Le Roy Ladurie, "Rôle," pp. 322–23; Fauroux, *Recueil*, pp. 47–48 and n. 55. For other indications of similar, though less extensive, formulas from other churches, see Fauroux, *Recueil*, pp. 51, 54–55 and nn. 167, 56; Musset, *Actes*, pp. 35–37.

36. Especially, again, Saint-Martin de Sées; see below, Chapter 3, at and in n. 147; Chapter 3, after n. 228; Chapter 4, at and in n. 367. For examples from other churches, see below, Chapter 3, at and in nn. 98–99. Körner, *Battle*, pp. 244–45, discusses several stock phrases in a group of charters from La Trinité du Mont; he suggests that the recurrence of these phrases is attributable to the copyist of the cartulary, but the argument is not convincing.

37. See below, Appendix A, Table 3, with Chapter 7, at nn. 19–24. For other examples, see below, Chapter 3, at nn. 228 and 235 and after n. 236; Chapter 5, n. 24; Chapter 7, at and in n. 164; Chapter 10, at and in n. 9; Carabie, *Propriété foncière*, p. 336; Musset, "Aristocratie," pp. 89, 90, 91 (n. 1); Le Maho, "Seigneuries," p. 67; Bates, *Normandy*, p. 123.

38. See also Giry, *Manuel*, p. 818.

39. Dudo of Saint-Quentin, *De moribus*. The fundamental destructive work was done by Prentout, *Etude*. Attempts have been made since to rehabilitate Dudo's reputation as a historian, especially by Steenstrup, "Normandiets Historie," pp. 292–94. They have failed. The sensitive treatment of Dudo's purposes in writing by Searle, "Fact," does not claim to rehabilitate the work's reputation for accuracy, indeed, quite the reverse. See ibid., p. 121, n. 12, for the date of the work, which Searle suggests was written not between 1015 and 1026, as has usually been thought, but between the 990s and 1015. Huisman, "Notes," suggests an original written between 996 and 1015 and "a second redaction after 1015" (p. 135). Van Houts, "Scandinavian Influence," pp. 109–11, is more sanguine than most about Dudo's reliability.

40. On the problem of the date of WJ, see WP, pp. xxv–xxx; Davis, "William of Jumièges," esp. pp. 604–5. On the date of WP, see WP, pp. xvii–xx; Davis, "William of Poitiers," pp. 71–93. Both the exact dates and the relative priority of the works of the two Williams seem still far from certain. On William of Poitiers's interest in law, see Chibnall, "Charter," p. 5, and the references there.

41. RT; Marx, in his edition of WJ, publishes Robert's interpolations, pp. 199–334. Wace, *Le roman de Rou*.

42. OV. The older edition, *Orderici Vitalis Historiae ecclesiasticae libri tredecim*, is still useful for the notes and the ancillary documents (among them Documents 440–69) published in vol. 5. Marx, in his edition of WJ, publishes Orderic's interpolations, pp. 151–98.

43. OV, 1:29–31. Van Houts, "Quelques remarques," p. 220, demonstrates that Orderic must still have been making interpolations in 1113.

44. For the dates, see OV, 1:31–34, 45–48; 2:xiv–xv; 5:xii. For possible anachronism, OV, 2:xxxiv–xxxvii; 4:xix–xx; Chibnall, "Droits"; Chibnall, "Some Aspects," p. 404. See also below, Chapter 4, n. 148. Yver, "Autour de l'absence," pp. 273–76, rejects a charge of anachronism in an area in which it seems at first obvious. Bourrienne, "Odon," 8:514, accuses Orderic of not telling the truth about Odo of Bayeux for fear of King Henry I. Ray, "Orderic," pp. 128–34, cites the reverse problem: he sees Orderic as interpreting various aspects of the changing relationship in his day between church and state in the light of an old-fashioned theocratic ideal.

Many historians have found Orderic in error on particular points of information, but only two all-out attacks have been made on his veracity. Le Hardy, "Dernier des ducs," is a partisan defense of Robert Curthose against Orderic's account of him; see especially p. 6. Du Motey's two books, *Origines de la Normandie* and *Champion de la Normandie*, are intended to rehabilitate the lords of Bellême from Orderic's very negative account of them. Neither attack has done much damage to Orderic's reputation as a historian. For the most recent discussion of the two points at issue, see Chibnall's "General Introduction," in OV, vol. 1, esp. pp. 91–97; she concludes, "He was certainly partisan, for Giroie and Grandmesnil against Bellême, for Henry I against Robert Curthose; but he did not tell deliberate lies" (p. 92). On Orderic's reliability in general, see Chibnall, *World*, passim.

45. OV, 1:31–34; 2:xv–xvi.

46. Ibid., 1:63–76, 98 and n. 4; 3:xxi–xxiv; Chibnall, "Charter," pp. 12–14, 16; S. Perrot, "Catalogue." Both commentators suggest the need for a certain amount of caution in treating the charters in Orderic's text as exact copies.

47. WM.

48. Document 286 is a work on the history of the see of Coutances from 836 to 1093, usually known as *De statu hujus ecclesiae*, datable to shortly after 1093. For comments on its value and its relationship to the closely associated *Miracula ecclesiae Constantiensis*, see Delisle, "Notice"; Le Patourel, "Geoffrey," pp. 130–32.

A short tract usually called *De obitu Willelmi ducis Normannorum regisque Anglorum* is appended in some manuscripts to William of Jumièges's history. It is published by Marx, in WJ, pp. 145–48. Until recently this was accepted as a nearly contemporary, independent, and valuable account of William's last days and actions. Engels, "De obitu," however, demonstrates that the work is almost entirely taken from the *Vita Hlodowici Imperatoris* and Einhard's life of Charlemagne; ibid., pp. 223–30, publishes the texts in parallel columns. Ibid., pp. 253–55, suggests a date in the early twelfth century. The value of the work as a source for Norman history seems to have been destroyed, though Engels himself is hesitant to reach such a conclusion.

Marx, in WJ, pp. 335–41, publishes the so-called *Additamenta ad historiam Normannorum*, an anonymous work of the twelfth century. It is also found, with minor textual variants, as part of the material added to the end of the anonymous *Brevis relatio de origine Willelmi Conquestoris*, ed. Giles, pp. 15–21. As Giles notes, pp. ix–x, the bulk of the *Brevis relatio* appears to have been written before the death of Henry I, but "the legendary portion with which the tract concludes," which includes the *Additamenta*, "was evidently added to the work by a later copyist" (p. x). Lot, *Fidèles*, p. 232, asserts that the *Additamenta* was written by Robert of Torigny. Chibnall, "Charter," p. 7 and n. 39, suggests a connection with Saint-Ouen.

The *Notitia de libertate Beccensis monasterii circa professionem episcopis ab abbatibus faciendam*, in *HF*, 14:270–77, is a mid-twelfth-century work, certainly later than 1136, written primarily to deny episcopal rights over Bec. It is translated in Vaughn, *Abbey*, pp. 134–43. Saltman, *Theobald*, pp. 4–5, dates it to 1137. Vaughn, *Abbey*, p. 26, dates it "shortly after 1136"; see also ibid., pp. 58–59, 64. I have used it, with reservations, below, Chapter 4, at and in n. 4; Chapter 5, n. 10.

49. Document 315, on which see below, Chapter 12, n. 33.

50. Bessin, *Concilia; Mansi, Sacrorum conciliorum collectio*, vols. 19–20, passim; Delisle, "Canons." On these councils, see Foreville, "Synod." The canons of the council of Rouen of 1072 are found in OV, 2:286–92; those of Lillebonne, 1080, are ibid., 3:26–34; those of Rouen in 1096 are ibid., 5:20–22.

51. Gilbert Crispin, *Vita Sancti Herluini*; Eadmer, *Vita Sancti Anselmi.*

52. Document 758. The date is difficult to determine. Carabie, *Propriété foncière*, p. 151, suggests a date in the second half of the twelfth century. Although his discussion there refers only to the section of the list on Carpiquet, he consistently gives the same date in citing other parts of the list elsewhere in the book. At the other extreme, Legras, *Bourgage*, p. 35, calls the list part of a charter of William the Conqueror, which it clearly was not. Delisle, *Etudes*, cites the list but does not give a date; see, e.g., p. 80, nn. 140, 143. In BN, ms. fr. n. a. 21831, f° 88r, however, he dates it "saec. XII ineunte"; ibid., f° 345r, he dates part of it to 1106. The reason for the specific date is that the second entry in the list, for Colleville, refers to a mortgage made in the year when "the count," presumably Robert Curthose, was captured (Document 758, f° 20v). The same entry refers to a second mortgage made the next year, however, so the list would appear to be later than 1107. The first of these mortgages was to last for eight years, the second for twenty. On the assumption that in such a list a mortgage would be mentioned only while it existed, not once it had been terminated (see below, Chapter 4, at and in n. 285), one might calculate that the list must have been drawn up

within eight years after 1106; but unfortunately the terms of mortgages were *minima* rather than *maxima*. Nevertheless, it seems unlikely that a list drawn up in the late twelfth century (or even in midcentury) would mention mortgages falling due in 1114 and 1127 without saying something about what had happened in each situation. Few names are given in the list. Of these few, two men—Richard Rufus and Helto the steward (both on f° 21v)—are mentioned in a charter from the abbey (Document 770) which must come from 1106; and one—Richard son of Herluin (Document 758, f° 23v)—occurs, among other places, in charters for the abbeys at Caen (Documents 410, 411, 412) datable to between 1066 and 1083. All in all, it seems likely that the list was drawn up shortly after 1107. Chibnall, *Charters*, pp. xxix–xxxi, arrives at a similar conclusion in attempting to date the series of surveys, English as well as French, of which this list forms part: it "dates from some time between 1106 and 1131, and may have been made before 1113" (p. xxxi).

CHAPTER 3

1. Document 719: "donatione legali"; Document 642 (f° 50v): "firmiter dono et donando legaliter . . . concedo." Document 113 (p. 95) uses the phrase "donatione directa" but gives no hint as to what the phrase means.
2. Document 344 (p. 214).
3. Below, this chapter, at nn. 244–51; Chapter 5, at and after nn. 33–35; Chapter 5, at and in nn. 94–95; Chapter 9, at nn. 4–5.
4. Below, this chapter, at and in n. 143.
5. On such preambles in ducal acts, see Fauroux, *Recueil*, pp. 50–51. For preambles emphasizing the utility of written documents, see below, Chapter 11, at nn. 12–15. Both types were characteristic of France as a whole in this period, as was a third, citing secular legal texts, which is rare in Normandy; see A. de Boüard, *Manuel*, 1:271–73.
6. The series of types of countergifts which I shall now discuss has also been set forth by Sauvage, *Troarn*, pp. 125–33; he explicitly accepts the donors' expressed pious motives as their dominant motives. For a more cynical view of these pieties, see Chesnel, *Cotentin*, pp. 231–32.
7. That there was no difference is assumed by Le Cacheux, *Saint-Amand*, p. 140. Sauvage, *Troarn*, p. 126, suggests that the two were distinct.
8. These words appear to be synonyms: they occur not only singly but in almost all possible pairs and combinations. "Fraternity" needs more comment than the others. The phrase *frater factus esse*, or the like, occurs often in contexts which clearly do not mean the man became a monk; that is always expressed by the word *monachus*, although men already monks are sometimes called *fratres*. Women are sometimes included in grants of *fraternitas*, though none is ever, understandably, said to have become the *frater* of a church. There are no uses of the word *sororitas* in this context, even in connection with gifts from women to nunneries, and only four uses of the word *soror*: Documents 298 (p. 453), 513 (p. 305), 685 (f° 61v), and 690. On fraternity, see Chibnall, *World*, pp. 67–70.
9. Documents 143 (p. 104) and 520.
10. Documents 158 (p. 150), 164 (p. 158), 176 (p. 191), 317, 365 (p. 244), 499, 531 (p. 81), 745 (f° 78r).
11. Documents 66, 418 (p. 667), 494 (p. 130), 508 (p. 205), 811.
12. Documents 58, 269 (p. 375), 418 (p. 667), 494 (p. 130), 695, 797 (f° 83v), 811.
13. Documents 84, 456, 701 (f° 98r), 792.
14. Documents 356, 565 (f° 144r), 792.
15. Documents 67, 470 (p. 130), 486 (p. 205).
16. Documents 337, 392 (p. 628), 470 (p. 130), 792.
17. Document 67.

18. Document 394 (p. 667).
19. Document 151 (p. 191).
20. Documents 245 (p. 375), 394 (p. 667), 470 (p. 130), 486 (p. 205), 514 (p. 107), 828, 831 (f° 220r), and possibly 516 and 517.
21. This does not, of course, mean that when society alone is mentioned a donor received only the minimal services. The terseness of the charters is likely here as elsewhere to mean that they do not always mention the details.
22. Document 509 (pp. 80–81).
23. A. de Boüard, *Manuel*, 2:147–48; Sauvage, *Troarn*, pp. 129–31.
24. Documents 229 and 230.
25. Document 293; the exact relationship of donor and claimant is not stated. Analogously, in Document 394, when the abbot of Saint-Florent de Saumur writes to ask Duchess Matilda to restore lands in the Cotentin which his abbey had once possessed, he says that by doing so "non solum eorum qui prius contulerunt sed et ipsorum qui postea abstulerunt animas letificas."
26. One gift might cover the entry into the convent of several men or women at once. In addition, a few persons made gifts to become hermits or hermitesses attached to conventual abbeys: Documents 169, 272 (p. 441), 297 (p. 109). On such solitaries, see Chibnall, *World*, pp. 79–82.
27. Génestal, in "Formes," pp. 225–26, is, so far as I know, the only student of Norman law to remark on the different varieties of donations for entering the religious life. He briefly describes those made to secure immediate entry for the donor or another and those to secure immediate entry for a donor on the point of death, but not those to be discussed here.
28. OV, 3:126; Documents 347, 726 (f° 82v), and perhaps 276 (col. 16).
29. OV, 3:164.
30. Documents 91, 118 (p. 104), 486 (p. 205), 718.
31. This number does not include transactions in which the incumbent of a parish church given to an abbey or the canons of a collegial church given to an abbey were granted the right to become monks if they so wished. On canons, see below, this chapter, at n. 119.
32. Documents 604 (f° 28v) and 706 (f° 103v).
33. Document 225 (p. 342).
34. Below, Chapter 4, n. 389; Document 645.
35. Of the eleven such transactions, five are dated to specific years between 1088 and 1091 and three others must have occurred in or before 1089. One must have occurred between 1073 and 1095; the other two can be dated only to the late eleventh century.
36. Musset, "Premiers temps," p. 23.
37. Of 178 eleventh-century charters from Saint-Martin de Sées concerning Normandy, 112 are dated to a specific year. Of these, excluding one problem charter (on which see above, Chapter 1, n. 5), only one is dated before 1080, specifically to 1078; but 7 undated charters must be attributed to before 1080 by virtue of their references to various persons. In contrast, 102 dated charters (12.75 times as many) come from between 1080 and 1100, the earliest from 1081. Adding the undated charters which can be dated to before the end of some decade and those from some short span of years (counted as though they came from the midpoint of the span), the figures rise to 10 by 1079 and 125 between 1080 and 1100.
38. For other evidence on this point, see below, Chapter 4, at and in nn. 20–23.
39. Above, this chapter, at n. 32.
40. Eleven reservations come from Saint-Martin de Sées, five from Saint-Etienne de Caen, four from Troarn, and three from Saint-Pierre de Préaux. The other two come from Marmoutier; see above, this chapter, at n. 33; Document 888.

41. Préaux was founded in William's father's reign. Its charters are very hard to date within narrow limits. The three with reservation clauses are Documents 552, 557 (f° 138v), 568.

42. Musset, "Origines d'une classe," pp. 59–61, 80, concludes that the opposite was true, that after the conquest of England the lords of Normandy, having large amounts of English land to give away, became less generous with their Norman lands than they had been before. Certainly some of the religious houses of Normandy acquired large amounts of land in England (Matthew, *Norman Monasteries*, pp. 1–70). Not all families, however, may have desired, or been able, to follow the same plan; or some may have insisted on getting more in return for a gift of land in Normandy precisely because they now regarded Norman land as more valuable than English land.

43. Sometime shortly after William's coronation, the bishops of Normandy drew up an ordinance imposing penances on those who had fought in the campaign to conquer England. It is edited by Cowdrey, "Bishop Ermenfrid of Sion," pp. 241–42, and translated in *EHD*, pp. 606–7. Cowdrey, pp. 233–40, argues for a date during the new King William's triumphal visit to Normandy in 1067, although others have accepted 1070, the date of Bishop Ermenfrid's confirmation, as the date of the ordinance.

Even if the ordinance was not strictly obeyed, it suggests that a good deal of psychological tension must have gone along with the material satisfactions of the Conquest. The warriors who gradually won England for William and themselves were, as a group, the same men who had sponsored the astonishing revival of monasticism in Normandy in the years after 1030. They must, therefore, have had strong, if intermittent, pious impulses and would be likely to feel the force of ecclesiastical condemnations of the sins committed in conquering and holding England. Indeed, Orderic notes several instances of men who refused to accept land or position in England on the grounds, at least according to Orderic, that this would be theft (OV, 2:270–80, and 3:254–56). Yet most Normans, given the opportunity, gladly accepted both lands and positions in England; and it is doubtful that many of them willingly submitted to the penances prescribed in the ordinance or, indeed, to any penances at all. The result may well have been that many salved their consciences with gifts to monasteries and with the resolve to enter a monastery later.

44. William's hold on his kingdom and on the county of Maine (which he took in 1063) was never entirely secure, and his hold on Normandy itself was less secure after 1066 than it had been in the decade before the conquest of England. See D. C. Douglas, *William*, pp. 211–44, 346–47, 354–58, for the details of William's many campaigns and numerous enemies; Le Patourel, "Norman Colonization," pp. 409–29, for the effects of this pressure on the way of life of the Normans in England; Bates, *Normandy*, pp. 248–50, for William's relative weakness in Normandy after 1066. There was never a danger of a surplus of fighting men. Nonetheless, by the early 1070s, after the Normans had consolidated their hold on England, their wars reverted to the usual pattern of responses to revolts and outside attacks, rather than the expansion of the decade 1060–70.

45. Document 267 (p. 429) is an exception.

46. Documents 528, 671 (f° 67r: "si autem indignum eum viderent nichil ei plus quam alicui extraneo concederent"). Other examples are Documents 359 and 607; Document 774 is partly analogous.

47. Document 798: "unum ex parvulis suis Hunfridum nomine receperunt tali conventione, quod illum aut apud Bohonium aut in aliqua domorum suarum facient nutrire et docere donec perveniat ad illam aetatem qua monachus possit et velit fieri, et in riga esse. Interim autem si parvulus mortuus fuerit, et pater ejus Richardus velit monachari, recipient eum: et si ipse non vult fieri monachus, et de quodam filiorum suorum velit facere monachum, illum solum recipient hac conventione et non amplius: ita tamen quod si parvulus est, faciet ipse idem, et non monachi illum docere et nutrire,

donec perveniat ad illam aetatem qua possit esse in riga." Richard was a son of Humphrey de Bohun, who had founded the priory of Bohun. A *riga* is a furrow or a line; therefore, the idiosyncratic expression *esse in riga* probably means something like "to follow the straight and narrow," that is, to conform to the full austerity of a monk's life; Round, *Calendar*, p. 438, no. 1213, translates it "to be a monk." Document 799, recording the act of donation by which Richard made his transfer, states the agreement thus: "concessit . . . propter amorem cujusdam parvuli filii sui quem dederat eidem loco ad nutriendum et imbuendum litteris usque dum tante esset etatis ut monachatum pati posset si tamen monachus fieri vellet." It does not include the provisions about what will happen if the son dies.

48. Document 476 (p. 176).

49. The cases are too numerous to cite; but for a woman who is to be buried like a monk, see Document 566 (f° 144v).

50. Documents 283, 584 (f° 8r), 593 (f° 17r), 645, 654 (f° 56v), 701 (f° 98r).

51. See below, Chapter 4, at nn. 366–89, on such bequests.

52. Below, Chapter 4, n. 234; Document 386 (p. 99): Ralph son of Ansered and his wife Gerberga promise at their deaths all the gold and silver the couple have "citra Sequanam," but only Gerberga is to be buried at the abbey; Document 356: if the donor dies outside Normandy, the monks will have one hundred shillings, but if he dies in Normandy the monks will bury him and have all his *substantia*; Document 448 (p. 186): if a confirmer dies on the same side of the Seine as the abbey, the abbey will have all his goods, but if he dies elsewhere "quod sibi placuerit de suis rebus huic loco dabit"; Document 625 (f° 42v): William, brother of Hugh de *Burei*, promises either himself or his goods to the abbey after his death; Document 645: Ruello de Courtomer will be buried at Saint-Martin de Sées "si haberi et deferri convenienter valeret corpus ejus," and the abbey is to have all his rightful portion, whatever is decided about burying his body.

53. Document 719: "illius amplius nichil exigentibus nisi ex mea meorumve voluntate prodiret."

54. OV, 3:16–18.

55. Document 786 (f° 161r) and the next note.

56. Document 39 (p. 39).

57. Document 645, as above, this chapter, n. 52.

58. Same side of the Seine: Document 386, as above, this chapter, n. 52. In Normandy: Document 356, as above, this chapter, n. 52; Document 727.

59. Documents 214 and 215, two versions of these events.

60. Document 711.

61. Préaux: Document 556. Saint-Evroul: OV, 3:124–26, and Document 440; Orderic (p. 124) interpolates that Ralph's purpose in coming to Saint-Evroul was to seek absolution ("veniam petiit"). Caen: Document 872. Saint-Martin de Sées: Document 633 (f° 46r): "multis modis . . . ecclesie nimium nocuerat et inde apud districtum judicem accusari metuebat."

62. Unspecified: Document 543. Absolution, excluding charters in which *absolutio* appears to mean the general absolution of sins which every Christian needed: Document 752, and probably 428. In Document 113 (p. 95), Duke Richard II makes gifts to Chartres cathedral "injuriae causa non modicae quam in vicinia ejus graviter exercueram"; but he speaks of his motive as *satisfactio* rather than *absolutio*. For what this may have meant, see below, Chapter 10, at nn. 35–37.

63. For examples, see below, Chapter 6, at and in nn. 52 and 160 (the charter contains precautions other than the one cited there). See also the elaborate precautions in the following instances in which, although the donor was not on his deathbed, his life was at unusual risk in the immediate future: below, Chapter 6, at n. 61, with Chapter 7, at n. 51; Chapter 8, at n. 45. On the basis of scattered eleventh-century examples like these plus a great deal more evidence from succeeding centuries, Génes-

tal, "Formes," pp. 230–35, presents a coherent picture of the nature of a Norman deathbed gift such as cannot be drawn on the basis of the eleventh-century evidence alone. See also Sheehan, *Will*, p. 109.

64. Many charters which record deathbed gifts say that the donor's heir(s) or lord consented, oversaw the transfer, or, in the case of heirs, inherited what remained after the gift—or all three. As Génestal points out ("Formes," pp. 224–25), neither the deathbed gift nor the more common post-obit gift (for which see below, this chapter, at nn. 97–124) was a true testament. Nevertheless, the unsupported assertions of Matthew, *Norman Conquest*, p. 56 ("it is certain that Norman custom did not allow landlords to dispose of their property by wills") and p. 146 ("Normans did not make wills and did not admit death-bed wishes") are misleading. On the lack of prejudice in eleventh-century Normandy against deathbed gifts, see Génestal, "Interdiction," p. 683. See below, this chapter, n. 101, for a charter which may refer to deathbed gifts as a usual type of transfer. Only one charter, cited below, Chapter 8, n. 92, shows any sign that lords were aware of the dangers of posthumous alienations.

65. Below, Chapter 6, at nn. 10–31 and at nn. 132–50.

66. The charters of Saint-Pierre de Préaux, in Arch. Eure, H 711, are an especially informative source on the objects used as countergifts. Saint-Pierre was probably not especially inventive; rather, it recorded countergifts of all sorts much more often than any other church. Its gifts of objects other than money and horses, as a percentage of all its countergifts, are, at most, only slightly higher than other churches'; but Saint-Pierre notes the giving of countergifts much more consistently than other churches do.

67. Below, this chapter, at nn. 149–68.

68. Document 443, on which see also below, this chapter, at n. 70. See also Document 393: "non tamen mea monitus petitione, sed sua spontanea voluntate."

69. Documents 686 (f° 87r) and 780.

70. Quotation from Document 443. Journeys: Documents 35 (p. 438), 99 (pp. 521, 523), 170, 473 (p. 156), 711. Ransoms: Documents 99 (pp. 521, 523), 592 (f° 16r), 594 (f° 17r), 619 (f° 36r), 748, 871. Mortgages: Documents 558 (f° 139r), 668 (f° 64v), and perhaps 683 (f° 79r).

71. See also Chibnall, *World*, pp. 55–56, who suggests that the principal purpose of some of the transactions involving horses was to transfer the animal, rather than the immovable.

72. See, in general, Sauvage, *Troarn*, pp. 235–39, based mostly on documents of the twelfth and later centuries; Allix and Génestal, "Opérations," pp. 618, 630–36, which does not refer to any examples before the thirteenth century.

73. Document 413 (p. 108). The problem is Document 566, which is dated "evolutis plurimis annis" (f° 144r) after some point between 1096 and 1100.

74. Respectively, Document 413 (p. 108); Document 877, which is summarized in Document 409 (p. 69), without mention of the service as a shoemaker; below, Chapter 4, at and in 188; and below, this chapter, at n. 79.

75. Document 88, in which the corody is granted in return for "terram de Belcaisne," may be an exception.

76. For *victus* and/or *prebenda*, see Documents 409 (p. 69, twice), 696 (f° 95v), 877, 880, and 566, which specifies "unius monachi victum" (f° 144v). For precise amounts of grain, see Documents 88, 587 (f° 9v), 778 (f° 102r), 843, 876. Document 846 gives a detailed list of types of food. Document 413 (p. 108) says simply "alatur"; Document 881 says merely "pasceretur." See below, Chapter 4, at and in n. 188, for another vague expression.

77. Per year: Documents 88, 587 (f° 9v), 778 (f° 102r), 846, 876. Per day: Document 843.

78. Documents 413 (p. 108), 696 (f° 95v), 846 (which gives a detailed list of the clothes to be provided), 881.

79. Document 778; on this transaction, see also below, Chapter 4, at and in n. 300.

80. Document 843.
81. Document 880: "versus finem caligans oculis, sua sibi penitus deficiente substantia."
82. Document 696: "tam mariti prius defuncti quam filii destituta solatio."
83. The others are Documents 409 (p. 69), 566 (f° 144v), and 846.
84. Below, Chapter 4, at n. 209.
85. Below, this chapter, at and in n. 154.
86. Documents 297 (p. 108) and 340 (p. 168). The other three are Documents 201 (p. 294), 712, and 713. On anathema clauses in general, see below, Chapter 10, at nn. 1–34.
87. Documents 216 (p. 332) and 823 (f° 26r).
88. Document 201 (p. 294): "neque in benefitio neque pro pretio tribuatur" (repeated in Document 274, p. 452); Document 823 (f° 26r): "nec . . . potestatem vendendi sive in beneficio alicui dandi habeat." See also Document 712, a French summary of a charter which survives only fragmentarily in the Latin, which says that one condition was that "la dicte terre ne seroit enffaye"; for the Latin, see BN, ms. fr. n. a. 21815, f° 264r.
89. Document 340 (p. 168).
90. Respectively, below, Chapter 5, at n. 76, and this chapter, at n. 207.
91. E.g., below, Chapter 4, at n. 243. If the story told below, Chapter 4, n. 4, can be trusted, heirs of donors were also capable of acting as though this were recognized practice.
92. Documents 84 and 274 (p. 453).
93. Document 226 (p. 344).
94. G. Mollat, "Restitution," pp. 400–401. As one of the pre-Viking abbeys which was refounded in the tenth century, Saint-Ouen made considerable use of Carolingian formulas in its charters.
95. Document 529: Odo de Tilly "terram . . . Rogerii Guiet concessit . . . tali divisione ut si heres Guiet voluerit a domino Ottone recuperare terram, dominus Otto vel heres eius eque valentem terram reddet Sancto Martino." This, however, is at least as much a warranty by the donor as a potential *retrait lignager*.
96. On the absence of the *retrait lignager* in eleventh-century Normandy, see also Génestal, *Rôle*, pp. 26–27, whose evidence is Document 291 (discussed below, Chapter 4, at n. 305), on the grounds that "si les parents avaient un droit propre et reconnu par la coutume à racheter le bien, ils ne pourraient être écartés par une simple convention entre l'engageant et l'engagiste" (p. 27).
97. Post-obit gifts, however, were not always recorded as such, as a series of documents from Fécamp shows. Muriel d'Amblie made a gift to Fécamp which is mentioned in Document 829 (f° 190r) and a reference to which is interpolated into Document 166 (p. 226n); it is also discussed in a letter of Abbot John of Fécamp to William the Conqueror (*PL*, vol. 147, col. 476, no. 9) and in Document 830 (f° 190v), which is presumably later than Abbot John's letter. Only the last of these, apparently the latest of the references, calls the gift post-obit: "terras quas Muriel de Amblida post suum decessum sancte Trinitati in dominio dedit." These transactions are discussed by Musset, "Contribution," p. 63, and "Vie économique," pp. 70–71, 79 (with n. 79); but he does not consider this problem.
98. Document 411 contains five post-obit gifts, of which the dispositive clauses read as follows: "de ecclesia eas teneret in vita sua, et post obitum ejus in sua possessione propria possideret ecclesia" (p. 83); "teneret in vita sua, post obitum vero suum . . . sancta possideret ecclesia" (p. 84); "in vita sua eam teneret, et post mortem suam mater ecclesia in sua proprietate possideret" (p. 85); "teneret in vita sua et post obitum ejus dicta possideret ecclesia" (p. 87); "teneret in vita sua, et post obitum suum predicta possideret ecclesia" (p. 88). Because all five examples come from the same pancart, one scribe, rather than the abbey, may have been responsible for their great similarity.

99. Document 531: "donamus et concedimus . . . ex toto in fine"; Document 534: "do et f[irmiter concedo ex toto in fin]e"; Document 779: "dono et ex toto in fine . . . concedo."

100. Above, this chapter, at nn. 63–64.

101. Génestal, "Formes," pp. 224–36, makes this distinction clearly, but his treatment of post-obit gifts of immovables is regrettably brief (pp. 227–28). So are the discussions of Sheehan, *Will*, pp. 108–9, and Holt, "Feudal Society, I," pp. 197–98.

The only indication in a charter that post-obit grants to lay persons were possible is the clause "[s]in autem eam alicui homini vel in vita aut post vitam dimitteret" in the charter cited below, Chapter 4, at and in n. 391; but "post vitam" may refer to a deathbed bequest. It has been argued that the conflict between Harold of England and Duke William of Normandy in 1066 was, juridically, a conflict between a post-obit gift made by Edward the Confessor to William and a gift *in articulo mortis* by Edward to Harold; see Foreville, "Aux origines," pp. 61–70; Foreville, "Hastings," pp. 39–41; Beckerman, "Succession," pp. 259–60. Unfortunately, only the English side of the alleged conflict is explicit in WP, pp. 172–74; the Normans do not reply in kind. For a possible explanation, see below, this chapter, n. 123. Beckerman, "Succession," pp. 258–59, also argues that William the Conqueror had made a post-obit gift of Normandy to Robert Curthose.

102. Below, Chapter 4, at n. 296.

103. In addition to the charters cited in the discussion, see Documents 73, 88, 117, 197 (p. 283), 410 (p. 75; also in Document 417, p. 121), 531, and possibly 823 (f° 26r).

104. Documents 97 and 484 (p. 647) both refer to one gift; the other instance is Document 851.

105. Documents 58 (p. 429), 580 (f° 5v), and 670 (f° 66r–66v). For similar distinctions with regard to deathbed portions, see below, Chapter 4, at n. 389. With regard to life estates, the matter is less clear, but the survivor seems usually to have kept the entire estate until his or her death (below, Chapter 4, at nn. 240–42).

106. Document 84, and perhaps either or both of the charters cited below, this chapter, n. 108.

107. Document 878, as quoted below, this chapter, n. 109.

108. Documents 386 (p. 99) and 851.

109. Document 878: "si vir sine haerede ante mulierem finierit pars pecuniae viri Sancto dabitur et terra mulieri, quia de ejus haereditate est, remanebit. Post mortem autem mulieris et viri si mulier absque haerede mortua fuerit, terra Sancto remanebit. Si vero haeredem habuerit aut de primo viro sive de secundo haeres terram possidebit." Documents 261/262 (p. 415) are another example.

110. Documents 410 (p. 75) and 441 (p. 183); and both charters cited in the next note.

111. Documents 57 and 616.

112. Documents 117, 119 (twice), 128, 163, 366, and possibly 534.

113. Document 80.

114. Document 413 (p. 109).

115. Mother: Document 531. Uncle: Document 413 (p. 108). Sister: Document 410 (p. 76); Document 411 (p. 84), in which William the Conqueror and his wife Matilda give the bourg of Le Homme after the death of William's sister or half-sister Adeliza countess of Aumale (Adeliza is not called William's sister by the charter, but she was the illegitimate daughter of Robert the Magnificent; whether she had the same mother as William is debated). Brother: Document 441 (p. 183). Step-daughter and her son: Document 84. Nephew: Document 410 (p. 76: In form this is a post-obit gift on the uncle's death or decision to become a monk, with a life estate in the house to his nephew. In practice, full control of the house would not pass to the abbey until the nephew's death; if he was required to pay rent or do service to the abbey in return for his tenement, the charter does not say so.)

116. Document 410 (p. 73); in Robert's case, of course, his lord was also his half-brother. The original of Roger's gift, Document 406, does not differ in wording from the version in Document 410 with regard to the post-obit gift. In Document 404, the same gift eliminates the reference to Roger's wife, although she was very much alive.

117. Below, Chapter 8, at nn. 100–106.

118. Below, Chapter 8, at nn. 1–5.

119. Musset, "Recherches sur les communautés," passim, esp. pp. 18–19.

120. E.g., Document 757 (p. 406).

121. Documents 247 and 441 (p. 183).

122. Yver, *Contrats*, pp. 34–38.

123. Below, Chapter 4, at and in n. 114. It is not inconceivable that William of Poitiers's failure to have the Normans make the obvious reply to Harold of England's statement of his claim to the throne of England—that it was good because, among the English, a deathbed gift canceled a prior post-obit gift of the same property (above, this chapter, n. 101)—was caused by the author's knowledge that the rule was already recognized in Normandy that a post-obit gift conferred no right to possess; but this is sheer speculation.

124. See below, Chapter 6, at and in nn. 32–150, on the act of donation; there is no observable distinction between donations *inter vivos* and donations *post obitum*. Génestal, "Formes," p. 228, treats post-obit gifts as transactions *inter vivos*. Sheehan, *Will*, p. 109, asserts that post-obit gifts "were considered to be irrevocable donations *inter vivos*," but he offers no evidence.

125. Document 404.

126. Document 117. Others: Documents 120, 411 (p. 83), 575, 779, and probably 198 (p. 285). In one case (Document 845) the property which constituted the post-obit gift was held by the donor from the eventual recipient, and the service which might otherwise have constituted an earnest was, therefore, already being done to the donee. Document 732, which is difficult to date, may be another example. Cf. Document 733 (f° 31r), in which the recipients of a life estate created to settle a dispute will serve the church from which the estate is held for as long as they hold the estate.

127. Document 411 (p. 88).

128. Documents 119 (twice), 285 (col. 200), 732 and 769 (f° 31v).

129. Respectively, Document 531; above, this chapter, at n. 125; Documents 58 (p. 429), 877, 358, 410 (p. 76), 163. For the payment called *comparatio vinearum*, see Delisle, *Etudes*, p. 468. For a general survey of types of earnest, see G. Mollat, "Restitution," p. 403, which cites no Norman examples.

130. Below, this chapter, at n. 135; Document 410 (p. 73): the priest, his land, the church, the tithe, and one *hospes*; ibid. (p. 76): hospitality and three cartloads of hay per year.

131. E.g., Documents 366, 410 (pp. 74, 76) and 425 (p. 133).

132. Document 531: "quando monachus factus fuerit aut alicubi perrexerit sive obierit vel quoque modo defecerit."

133. Document 366.

134. Documents 482 (pp. 675–76) and 673.

135. Document 177 (p. 248). The abbey did indeed recover Ticheville, although whether only three years later is unknown; see Adigard des Gautries, "Possessions," p. 23.

136. Document 643: "pergens in Apuliam, . . . si ab Apulia non rediret . . . ; revertens vero omnia sua haberet in sua vita, si vellet, in morte autem monachi."

137. As in the agreement below, Chapter 4, at and in n. 391, which also involves Saint-Martin de Sées.

138. Document 539 (f° 101v): "si deus tantum eum cresceret quatinus absque illa honoratus vivere posset."

139. Document 494.

140. OV, 4:302, asserts categorically that only the two eldest sons inherited, the eldest in Normandy, the second in England. Ibid., 3:148–50, notes that Earl Roger secured endowments for his third and fifth sons during his lifetime but says nothing about Philip. Mason, "Roger," p. 15 and n. 4, says that Philip never had any land in England and cites only this charter as evidence that he had possessions in France. Philip eventually became a cleric and died at Antioch on the first crusade (OV, 4:302).

141. See also Document 99 (p. 522), in which Saint-Léger de Préaux, having received from Humphrey de Bohun property he had mortgaged to Hildulf *Parvus*, redeemed the mortgage for the full amount but allowed Hildulf to keep the land until his death; on his death the land would go to the nuns "pro redemptione sua, suorumque." Because Hildulf was well enough off to become a mortgagee, it is unlikely that poverty induced him to wish to retain the mortgaged property for his lifetime.

There is one possible exception, but it is not certain that the gift was intended to take effect only post-obit. Document 551: "Helgo de alneio cadens in nonposse, et non habens unde posset terram suam deservire, concedentibus filiis suis, Adelardo, Giroldo, Radulfo, donavit sancto petro et monachis eius sex agros terre . . . , ut esset omni tempore vite sue quittus ab omni servitio, quod antea faciebat, et tali tenore hoc fecit, ut eo moriente pro anime eius redemptione, sanctus petrus et servientes sibi perpetuo in elemosinam eandem terram haberet." The last clause may mean that the gift was to take effect only after Helgo's death, or it may merely be intended to emphasize the permanence of the gift and forestall claims by Helgo's sons or other heirs.

142. E.g., Document 290 (col. 330): "concedo . . . ea quae . . . vel alii contulerunt, vel abbatissae emerunt."

143. Gilbert Crispin, *Vita*, p. 94: "seu venditione seu gratuita donatione."

144. Below, Chapter 8, at nn. 63–70.

145. Document 413; Document 418 is a repetition of eighteen of the twenty-three acquisitions attributed to Lanfranc by Document 413, with no substantial differences.

146. Documents 405 (p. 55), 411 (pp. 83–87), 412 (p. 94). Several of the gifts are repeated in two or all three of the pancarts; two of them are repeated in Document 420 as simple gifts. Other donors to other churches occasionally indulged in the same practice, but the frequency with which Matilda used it is unparalleled. If the difference is real, if La Trinité was not merely less reticent than other abbeys, it probably stemmed from Matilda's desire to create a large endowment for her new nunnery as quickly as possible.

147. Document 656: "partim in elemosinam donavit terram ad duos boves . . . , partim vendidit et xxx^{ta} iiii^{or} solidos pro venditione accepit, pro dono vero orationes ac beneficium habuit." See also Documents 583, 606, 641 (f° 50r), 650, 657 (f° 57v), 659 (f° 58r), 662 (f° 33r), 694 (f° 91r). All the charters which use the *partim* . . . *partim* formula, except for one (Document 583) which is hard to date, come from a period of nine years; hence, one scribe may have been responsible for this particular formulation of the distinction between sales and gifts. The distinction is equally clear, if less strikingly expressed, in several other charters from this abbey.

148. Document 864.

149. For transactions explicitly called sales, references to the benefits accruing to one's soul are rare, as are references to grants of society (below, this chapter, at and in n. 167) and to acts of donation (below, this chapter, at and in n. 169). Yver, *Contrats*, p. 40, discussing primarily the thirteenth century, thinks that any transfer characterized both by a statement that it was made for someone's soul and by the description of the countergift as *ex caritate* was certainly a gift. Such references are by no means universally present in records of eleventh-century transfers which otherwise appear to have been gifts, however, and there is reason to think that sales were sometimes disguised as gifts (below, this chapter, at nn. 154–68).

Several studies of other regions of France concentrate on the gradual disappearance of the legal distinction between sales and donations, the blurring of the forms in which different sorts of transfers were recorded, whereby all became donations in form: Chevrier, "Evolution"; Chevrier, "Remarques"; Lemarignier, "Actes," esp. pp. 53–71; de Fontette, *Recherches*, pp. 15–28; Vigneron, "Vente." Most date the change to the early eleventh century, though Lemarignier thinks that it occurred several centuries earlier north of the Loire. All in all it seems likely that eleventh-century Norman scribal practice knew no distinction of form between sales and gifts (but see below, this chapter, at and in n. 198, for a possible instance of the use of a vestige of the older contract of sale). If so, the reason may be connected with the date of the disappearance of the distinction elsewhere, for the recording of transfers in writing in Normandy became common at just about the same time.

150. Documents 261 and 262.

151. Document 425. Musset, "Actes inédits, I," pp. 119–24, is an extended comment on the document which treats it as a record of sales. See also Musset, "Contribution," pp. 64–65, for a discussion of both Saint-Gabriel and Saint-Martin-du-Bosc.

152. In the articles cited in the preceding note and in "Vie économique," Musset emphasizes that the deliberate purpose of Abbot John of Fécamp was the source of the priories' methodical efforts to expand; the chance survival of frankly financial documents which were intended only for internal use gives glimpses of the process. See below, Chapter 4, at nn. 277–82, for more on John as a financial organizer. Musset makes the same point about the much greater frankness of documents intended for internal use in "Actes inédits, Saint-Martin de Sées."

153. This disorientation seems especially characteristic of Jumièges, Marmoutier, Mont-Saint-Michel, Saint-Pierre de Préaux, Saint-Père de Chartres, and La Trinité de Caen.

154. For necessity cited as a motive, see below, Chapter 4, at and in n. 212; Chapter 5, n. 94; Documents 641 (f° 50r) and 642 (f° 51r). Olivier-Martin, *Histoire*, p. 265, suggests that the excuse of poverty exempted an alienor from the full need to get the lord's consent to the alienation; ibid., p. 273, suggests the same about the vendor's family's consent. This does not, however, seem to have been the motive in Normandy or, at least, there is no evidence that it was.

155. G. Mollat, "Restitution," pp. 416–17; OV, 3:124; see also Giry, *Manuel*, p. 857.

156. On Normandy: Génestal, *Rôle*, p. 128; Allix and Génestal, "Opérations," p. 621; Sauvage, *Troarn*, pp. 129–33; Musset, "Actes inédits, I," pp. 122–23; Musset, "Vie économique," p. 69; Musset, "Actes inédits, Saint-Martin de Sées," p. 20; Musset, *Actes*, p. 46. References to the phenomenon in France as a whole are too numerous to cite; the works cited above, this chapter, n. 149, may be consulted as examples.

157. In addition to the instances discussed here, see above, this chapter, n. 146; compare Document 200 (p. 290) with OV, 2:36; compare Document 199 with Document 555.

158. Documents 261 and 262.

159. Documents 261 (p. 412) and 262 (pp. 412–13), the gift of William de Colombiers.

160. Below, this chapter, at nn. 244–52.

161. Documents 216 (p. 332) and 217 (p. 333). John's claim (Document 46) was raised about fifteen years after the return of the mill, that is, about 1076. It seems likely that the reworked version (Document 217) dates from the time of the second claim. The signature list is not consistent with any date later than 1067; but it appears to be a partial copy of the signature list of no. 216 and, therefore, cannot be used as an aid in dating. One signature in no. 217 is not, it is true, in no. 216; but, because the latter survives only in two copies, both of which may be incomplete, the full signature list may have included this name.

On the family, see Musset, "A-t-il existé," pp. 292–94; *Complete Peerage*, vol. 12, pt. 2, pp. 268–69 and Appendix B, p. 11.

162. On this episode and the later conflicts between Suppo's detractors and his supporters, see Herval, "Moine," p. 42; Laporte, "Abbaye," pp. 74–76; Quivy and Thiron, "Robert," pp. 348–49. Alexander, *Norman Illumination*, p. 12, suggests that the true reason for Suppo's ouster may have been political; he is followed by Bates, *Normandy*, p. 82.

163. Below, Chapter 6, at and in n. 30, and perhaps at nn. 145–50.

164. Below, Chapter 6, at nn. 20–31.

165. In general, see A. de Boüard, *Manuel*, 2:147–48; G. Mollat, "Restitution," p. 420. There are a good many Norman examples.

166. Sauvage, *Troarn*, pp. 132–33 and p. 132, n. 3.

167. See above, this chapter, at and in n. 147, for an explicit indication of this; a similar distinction is found in some of the other charters cited in n. 147. Other explicit dissociations of grants of society from sales are found in Documents 413 (p. 108) and 763. I have noted only the following grants of society in connection with sales: Documents 261 (pp. 412–13; not repeated in no. 262, which treats the sale as a gift), 405 (p. 55), 413 (p. 107), 611 (f° 31r), 652 (f° 56r), 850, 858, 862, and perhaps 413 (p. 108), in which society is given specifically in return for a promise to warrant what was sold. The same abbeys are responsible for the dissociations as are responsible for many of the associations; this is, therefore, presumably not a matter of scribal practice.

168. The verbs of sale and purchase are, preeminently, *vendere* and *emere*, depending on whether the charter speaks in the name of the seller or the buyer. In the passage quoted above, Chapter 2, n. 28, *emere* and the noun *pretium* are used of a rental, albeit a very peculiar one. Other verbs for buying and selling are also used. *Comparare* appears infrequently but consistently. *Appretiare* is used only by Fontenay, but the noun *pretium* occurs often. *Mercari* is used only twice, both times by the abbeys at Caen: Documents 413 (p. 108) and 419 (p. 129). See Musset, *Actes*, pp. 35–36, for the possibility that the abbeys at Caen sometimes shared the same scribes.

169. I have noted only the following references to acts of donation in connection with sales: Chapter 6, at n. 130; Documents 99 (p. 523), 203, 413 (p. 109), 424 (p. 139), 544, 545, 558 (f° 139r), 594 (f° 17r), 840. Document 357, as cited below, Chapter 6, n. 42, is probably too late. In Document 869, the act may be related to the bequest of the vendor's *substantia* rather than to the sale. The ceremonies cited here must, of course, be distinguished from the many acts of donation performed by persons who confirm sales by others.

170. See below, Chapter 7, at nn. 105–18, for other examples of quasi-professional witnesses, not in connection with sales.

171. Document 413.

172. A third Geoffrey also witnessed in this document; see the next note. Musset seems to think that Geoffrey the cook was meant by all the single unidentified Geoffreys; see the entries in the index of names under "Godefridus cuisinier" and "Godefridus de Bras," in Musset, *Actes*, p. 162. The Geoffrey meant may, however, be sometimes one and sometimes another. Moreover, if the unidentified Geoffrey was always the same man, he cannot have been the cook, for one purchase from Geoffrey the cook (Document 413, p. 106) was witnessed by "Godefridus." Geoffrey the cook once acted as a witness for La Trinité de Caen (Document 405, p. 55), again to a sale, but otherwise charters from Caen do not help in solving the problem.

173. Anketil the vinegrower and his son witnessed all nine entries for Abbot Gilbert, all sales; Sasfredus witnessed five of these acts. Rannulf witnessed seven of Abbot Lanfanc's purchases; Warin witnessed six of Abbot William's acts, five sales and an exchange; Geoffrey the *pratarius* witnessed five of William's acts, four purchases and an exchange; Durand de Dive witnessed four of William's acts, three sales and a gift. Five of these men also appear in Document 410, a pancart of sixteen gifts to Saint-Etienne: Wascelin witnessed four; Durand de Dive, three; Geoffrey the *pratarius*, two; an unidentified Geoffrey, two; and Warin, one.

174. In the list of ten small purchases by Abbess Matilda which constitutes Documents 759–68, twenty-one men occur as witnesses, many only once; but Wimund witnessed seven acts; Geoffrey, six; Ralph Folenfant, four; and Bernard, four. In other documents of La Trinité, Ralph Folenfant witnessed two sales to Duchess Matilda of land which she then gave to the abbey: Document 405 (p. 55). Bernard witnessed a simple gift (in which there may have been some threat of a claim on the land) and a lease granted by the abbess: Documents 771, in which he is called "homo abbatisse," and 791.

175. Documents 413 (p. 110), 841, 848, 849, 850, 864, 866, 868, 869, 870. For pledges, see below, Chapter 7, at nn. 160–96.

176. Respectively, Documents 854, 403, 410 (p. 76), 873, 876, 883.

177. Documents 599, 606, 610, 650, 656, 659, 681, 704. Of 213 relevant transactions extant from this abbey, 31 are wholly or partly sales. Four of the eight sales involving pledges are the partly-sale partly-gift type referred to above, this chapter, at and in n. 147.

178. Documents 592 (f° 16r), 607, and 612.

179. Documents 590, 595, 606, 610, 624, 629, 638, 650, 652, 656, 657, 694. In the following, *conventio* may refer to a sale or to the entirety of the more complex transaction described in the charter: Documents 589 (f° 11v), 597, 704.

180. Sales: Documents 641, 650, 681, 694.

Of the others, in Document 683, the abbey receives property currently being claimed from the donor by a third party, and the donor's warranty is directed specifically against the possibility that the claimant will vindicate his claim. In Document 634, William de *Claraio* returns land which he had claimed because his brother, who is still alive, had held it. Document 697 is a writ from Roger de Montgomery to his son Robert de Bellême ordering Robert to warrant gifts made to the abbey by one of Roger's vassals. Only Document 612 is a simple gift; its warranty clause is atypically short.

181. Sales: Documents 51 (p. 282), 413 (p. 107), 841, 849, 850, 866, 868, 869, 870. Not sales: Documents 410 (p. 76), 852, 855, 873, 876, 883.

182. Documents 13 (p. 22), 62, 532.

183. On warranty, see below, Chapter 9.

184. Below, Chapter 9, at n. 29.

185. Documents 13 (p. 22) and 528.

186. Below, Chapter 7, at nn. 160–96, esp. at n. 160.

187. E.g., below, Chapter 7, at and in nn. 54 and 94, and Document 203.

188. Yver, *Contrats*, p. 279, n. 1, proposes but rejects—correctly, I think—an interpretation of Document 63 which would make it a third instance of a price paid in installments; ibid., p. 279, unfortunately, misconstrues the charter on the subject of lords' consent, about which it says nothing.

189. Below, Chapter 6, at n. 30.

190. OV, 4:106. For a commentary, see Musset, *Actes*, pp. 45–46. WM, 2:337–38, speaks of one payment, in the amount of one hundred pounds.

191. Yver, *Contrats*, pp. 29–31, thinks that sales in which the payment of the purchase price was partly or wholly postponed were rare in Normandy throughout the period he studies; the earliest instance he cites comes from 1190. De Fontette, *Recherches*, pp. 53–61, agrees for the region around Paris but finds some evidence that in the twelfth and thirteenth centuries more sales were made on credit than the documents indicate.

192. Allix and Génestal, "Opérations," pp. 620–23; M. de Boüard, "Neustrie," p. 8; Musset, "Notes sur l'histoire"; Musset, "Recherches sur Bayeux"; Musset, "A-t-il existé"; Musset, "Actes inédits, Saint-Martin de Sées," pp. 23–25; Musset, "Vie économique," pp. 72–74; Musset, "Naissance," p. 107; Musset, "Conditions"; Musset, "Deux âges," pp. 191–92; D. C. Douglas, *William*, pp. 135–36; Matthew, *Norman Conquest*, pp. 33, 44, 53; Powicke, *Loss*, pp. 48–49; Strayer, review of Fauroux,

p. 608; Mason, "Roger," pp. 11–12; Breese, "Persistence," pp. 54–56; Bates, *Normandy*, pp. 96–97.

193. Below, Chapter 4, at and in n. 96. For another possible example, see below, Chapter 4, at and in n. 210.

194. Document 749 (f° 751r): "Hoc beneficium ita absolute emit Hugo episcopus ut nullum servicium faciat nullum debitum reddat ipse vel successores sui Aitardo vel successoribus suis."

195. Below, Chapter 4, at and in n. 392.

196. Below, Chapter 4, at and in n. 212: if Richard bought his father's house from the abbey, he was apparently to maintain no connection with the seller.

197. Above, this chapter, at and in n. 88.

198. The works cited above, this chapter, n. 149, trace the processes whereby, in other areas of France, the contract of sale as a form of document disappeared, leaving at most vestigial traces, because the legal situation to which it corresponded also disappeared. I am suggesting that in Normandy the use of the word *conventio* for sales may be such a vestige. The word was, however, in use in other contexts in which it clearly meant an agreement creating obligations for the future on the part of at least one of the parties.

199. Below, pp. 92–93, 110–12.

200. Above, this chapter, at nn. 24–25.

201. In the charters discussed below, Chapter 9, at n. 10, the return of the countergifts is the only compensation envisioned: neither transfer is absolutely certainly a sale. In two other instances discussed below, Chapter 9, at n. 9, one a sale, the other a gift with a monetary countergift, return of the money is an alternative to substitution of other land. All other warranty clauses which discuss compensation propose substitution of other property alone; see below, Chapter 9, at nn. 6–9.

202. The *Dialogus de Scaccario*, II.13, ed. Johnson, p. 108, uses this characteristic of money to explain why town dwellers, unlike persons in the countryside, were subject to seizure of their immovables in payment of debts to the king. The *Dialogus* was written in England in the late twelfth century. I cite it in default of explicit eleventh-century Norman evidence of the currency of the idea.

203. Below, Chapter 5, at n. 65; below, Chapter 8, at n. 49; Document 129: "auro et argento meo"; Document 344 (p. 213): "suo auro atque suo argento"; Document 419 (p. 129): "de auro suo."

204. Below, Chapter 5, at nn. 41–43.

205. Explicit in Documents 316, 428, 812. Implicit in Document 122. For further discussions of the motives for such exchanges, see Musset, "Recherches sur la consistance" and the works cited in the next note.

206. D. C. Douglas, *William*, p. 110; Musset, "Destins"; Lemarignier, "Paix," esp. pp. 444–46, 468–69; Bates, *Normandy*, pp. 58, 225.

207. Document 43 (p. 25).

208. Saint-Evroul: OV, 2:14–16, and Document 200 (p. 289). Montivilliers: below, Chapter 5, at n. 68.

209. Documents 158 and 413 (p. 107).

210. Aside from the instances already cited, there are about seventy mentions of exchanges.

211. Respectively, Documents 832 (f° 17r) and 179 (pp. 251–52).

212. Respectively, Documents 413 (p. 110) and 794, and RT, interp., p. 289.

213. Tithes for land: Documents 274 (p. 453) and 364. Tithes for land and money: Document 842. A market for a house: Document 125 (p. 130). Quitrents for churches: Document 478 (p. 248).

214. Document 267 (p. 430).

215. Musset, "Cimitière," p. 11.

216. Equal: below, Chapter 4, at n. 27; Documents 99 (p. 522), 413 (p. 106), 837

(a statement concerning the four exchanges in Documents 834–37), and possibly 538 (f° 50v). Unequal: Document 839.

217. Below, Chapter 9, at nn. 6–10.

218. Below, Chapter 5, at n. 68.

219. Customs: Document 413 (p. 110). Services: Document 633 (f° 46r).

220. Document 715: "Atque hoc presente Roberto comite ita stabilitum est inter abbatem et Ricardum ut quicumque illorum aliquando primus ab hac cunventacione resilire voluerit sexaginta libras alteri persolvet et ita recipiet quisque similiter sicuti dederat valens et illesum." Le Maho, "Seigneuries," p. 51, suggests that the abbey's interest in the exchange came from its fear of the castle Richard had just built at Cleuville, near Ancourteville. Richard later gave Ancourteville to the priory of Longueville (ibid., p. 43, no. 41a). No reexchange can, therefore, have taken place.

221. *Commutare* (or *commutuare*), *cambiare*, *concambiare*, *excambiare*; the nouns are *mutuum*, *cambium*, *concambium* and *excambium*.

222. Document 99 (p. 521).

223. In the case cited above, this chapter, at and in n. 220, for example, the whole of Ancourteville is exchanged for one-quarter of Gouy.

224. Sizable countergifts consisting of or including immovables can be found in Documents 251 (p. 390), 639, 698 (f° 96v), 813.

225. Documents 82, 273, 413 (p. 106), 590.

226. Yver, "Boutade"; the title of this article refers to the remark quoted below, this chapter, at n. 234, and Chapter 6, n. 157. See also Yver, "Autour de l'absence."

227. Below, Chapter 4, nn. 53, 149; Chapter 5, at nn. 6–79.

228. These adjectives occur, often in combination, in the descending order of frequency in which they are listed. That, when the quality of the transfer is specified, it is most usually "in alms" cannot, of course, be used to argue that in the eleventh century Norman churches held most of their possessions in alms. Most records of transfers specify no quality and give no information to imply a quality.

229. Below, this chapter, at and in n. 253; Documents 295, 563 (f° 143r), 566 (f° 144r). Cf. Document 559 (f° 139v): "iure ecclesiastico"; and Document 259 (p. 405): "prebendarum jure."

230. Document 635 (f° 47v): "terram Fulcoini quam predicti monachi a prefato Willelmo in feodo tenebant non in feodo, ut prius, sed in elemosinam sicut cetera."

231. Above, this chapter, at and in n. 147.

232. See above, this chapter, at n. 159, for the extreme case: a transfer is recorded once as a gift in alms and once as a sale.

233. Document 634 (f° 46v): "dimisit Sancto Martino terram . . . ita quidem soluta et quieta sicut elemosina soluta et quieta debet dari et dimitti."

234. Below, Chapter 6, n. 157.

235. Respectively, Document 800 (f° 236r): "elemosynam absolutam ab omnibus sibi pertinentibus"; Document 818: "in perpetuam elemosinam liberam et quietam ab omnibus consuetudinibus mihi pertinentibus"; Document 787: "elemosinam . . . ab omni servitio quietam et absolutam." See also Documents 493 (p. 350) and 707.

236. Below, Chapter 5, esp. pp. 102, 104–7.

237. Document 534: "sic quietam ab omni seculari servici[o eam concedo sicut melius potest] manere quieta elemosina."

238. Below, this chapter, at nn. 241 and 246; Documents 92 (p. 467) and 740 (f° 88r). In Document 739, two lords "concesserunt . . . quicquid terrenum iuris in ea habebant preter recognitione domini"; for the meaning of the last phrase, see below, this chapter, at and in n. 255.

239. Document 578 (f° 3r): "immunem et liberam erga omnes homines ab omnibus redditionibus, preter ea que caritative et sponte sua exhiberent parentibus eorum."

240. Document 817: "liberam et quietam ab omnibus servitiis et maxime de b.nagio [*sic*]." BN, ms. fr. n. a. 21815, f° 132r, a copy of the same charter, reads

"benagio"; but *bernagium*, a payment to the duke which was made in oats (Fauroux, *Recueil*, p. 456, sv° *bernagium*), was probably intended.

In addition to this charter and those cited in the next note, see Document 808: "in perpetuam et puram elemosynam liberam et quietam omnino de omni auxilio et tallagio et consuetudine et omni alio servitio et exactione"; but this is a somewhat suspect charter.

241. Documents 38 (p. 28) and 39 (p. 41, twice).

242. Document 38 (p. 28).

243. Respectively, below, this chapter, at n. 246; Document 14 (p. 24). A good many charters from eleventh-century Norman churches are entirely concerned with exemptions from obligations to other ecclesiastical persons or churches. These are not considered here; on them, see Lemarignier, *Etude*.

244. See, for post-Conquest England, Pollock and Maitland, *History*, 1:241; Lennard, *Rural England*, p. 324.

245. Above, this chapter, at and in n. 235 (citations from Documents 800 and 818); Documents 38 (p. 32), 740, and probably 535.

246. Document 437 (p. 484). Yver, "Autour de l'absence," p. 196, n. 21, finds this clause exceptional because, he contends, churches occupied by canons were more subject to the rights of their founders than were monastic houses (see esp. ibid., p. 205); he attributes "cet octroi exceptionnel de libertés" to "l'origine franque de l'église et la participation du duc à la fondation." Saint-Fromond later became a priory of Cerisy.

247. Document 335 (p. 15).

248. Yver, "Boutade," pp. 784–86. A. Douglas, "Tenure," esp. p. 111, however, implies that the change was a twelfth-century phenomenon in England.

249. E.g., this chapter, above, at and in n. 147.

250. Below, pp. 102, 104–6.

251. The instance cited above, this chapter, at n. 159, might be an exception but seems rather to be the extreme case of concealment of the true nature of the transaction.

252. Document 665 (f° 62r): "Census qui de ea dominis debetur a me quamdiu in propria potestate vixero semper reddetur." For the bulk of this charter, see below, Chapter 5, at and in n. 25.

253. Document 560 (f° 142v): "iure elemosine, ita ut quod alii divites paresque mei in suis elemosinis iure habebant et ego in mea habeam, nichil aliud querens."

254. Document 740 (f° 88r): "ne occasione intermittendi officium ecclesiasticum aliquam haberent."

255. Document 410 (p. 75). The charter quoted above, this chapter, n. 238, in which lords concede everything secular "preter recognitione domini" should perhaps be understood similarly. For other examples, in which "alms" is not used, see Documents 49 (p. 57) and 249 (pp. 383–84). OV, interp., p. 177, says that the founders of Saint-Evroul decided to give the duke custody of their abbey "contra nos et posteros nostros omnesque mortales . . . ut videlicet, si preter spirituale beneficium aliquid servitii seu muneris violenter exegerimus, principali severitate salubriter coherciti tirones Dei molestare vel inviti cessemus." In his *History*, however, he sticks closer to the actual foundation charter (Document 200), which, though it certainly evokes ducal protection, makes no similar statement of its purpose.

256. Some episcopal customs were in lay hands, which may explain those grants of episcopal customs which were made neither by a bishop nor with one's recorded consent. On this subject, see below, Chapter 8, at nn. 141–43.

257. *Summa*, XXX.2, p. 100; see also Lagouëlle, *Essai*, pp. 264–65; Yver, "Boutade," p. 795. See also below, Chapter 8, at nn. 111–12, for charters from Jumièges which may imply this theory.

258. *Acta* of Robert of Torigny, abbot of Mont-Saint-Michel, in RT, 2:252, no. 35.

259. Rabasse, *Régime*, pp. 62–63, also thinks the former conjecture correct but

does so on the basis of a misconstruction of the meaning of "allod" in eleventh-century Normandy (ibid., pp. 59–62). Other commentators do not raise the issue; see Lagouëlle, *Essai*, pp. 261–62; Senn, *Institution*, pp. 98–99; Yver, "Très Ancien Coutumier," p. 372, no. 2.

260. For example, above, Chapter 2, n. 28, where *emere* and *pretium* are used for a rental; Documents 99 (p. 523) and 558 (f° 139r), where *donum* and *donatio*, respectively, are used for sales; below, Chapter 4, n. 239, where *mutuum* is used for a life estate; below, Chapter 4, at and in n. 392, where a quasi-relief is called an exchange and treated as a sale.

261. Above, this chapter, at and in n. 149. See also Giry, *Manuel*, esp. pp. 507, 795; A. de Boüard, *Manuel*, vol. 2, pt. 1, esp. pp. 96, 119–24; Tessier, *Diplomatique*, pp. 208–10.

262. The relative amount of destruction caused by Viking raids and by the Norman settlement itself is debated; it is much involved with the twin questions of continuity in Normandy after 911 with, on one hand, previous Scandinavian custom and, on the other, the Carolingian institutions characteristic of the area before its conquest by the Vikings. For discussions of these questions, see above, Chapter 1, at and in nn. 28–32. The recent emphasis on continuity with the Carolingians implies relatively little destruction. No one, however, can or does deny that life in the part of the Carolingian kingdom which became Normandy was markedly disrupted. Moreover, most recent scholars agree that in 911 Rollo received only part of the territory known as Normandy; the rest was taken in the years between 911 and 933 by military means, and for a century new bands of Vikings came to aid their Norman brethren or to join them as settlers. As late as 1013 a band arrived to help Duke Richard II in a war with Odo of Chartres. Patterns of landholding must, therefore, have been unstable throughout the tenth century at least in certain areas of Normandy. On all this, see, most recently, Le Patourel, *Norman Empire*, pp. 3–21, 282–86, who emphasizes the great fluidity of the situation well into the eleventh century and cites the major scholarly studies preceding his own; and Bates, *Normandy*, passim, esp. pp. 9–10, 36–38, 239–41, who stresses elements of stability.

263. Above, Chapter 2, at and in n. 8. Remarkably little, indeed, is known of the tenurial conditions or the family destinies of the Normans of the tenth century; see Rioult de Neuville, "Orbec," pp. 716–17; M. de Boüard, "Duché," p. 4; Stenton, "Scandinavian Colonies," pp. 11–12; Yver, "Développement," p. 191; Yver, remarks in "Discussione sulla lezione Yver," p. 592; Musset, "Aristocratie," pp. 72–74. Even Bates, *Normandy*, admits that hardly any evidence exists on the tenth-century aristocracy; see esp. p. 35.

264. Document 151 (p. 191). Even this charter is not wholly Norman: the donor is the count of Amiens, the land given is not Norman, and the charter is confirmed by the king of France.

265. Musset, "Conditions," p. 308, appears to favor the former alternative.

266. Above, this chapter, at n. 2.

CHAPTER 4

1. Mortgage: below, this chapter, n. 286; the verb is *invadimoniare*. Fief: below, this chapter, n. 53. *Métairie*: below, this chapter, at nn. 181–89. Farm: below, this chapter, at nn. 190–204, 213–20.

2. See also Sauvage, *Troarn*, pp. 126–27.

3. Above, Chapter 3, at nn. 22–25.

4. *Notitia*, p. 272: at some time between 1088 and 1090, Robert count of Meulan, having been given the castle of Brionne as part of his demesne by Duke Robert Curthose, tried to make the abbey of Bec part of his demesne as well; but "Willelmus Crispinus et Willelmus de Britolio et Rogerius de Benefacta . . . magna indignatione

commoti . . . terribilibus juramentis protestati sunt, quicquid sui parentes ecclesiae Becci dederant, se auferre, si comes . . . coenobium . . . in suo dominio quoquo modo haberet." Although the work is tendentious, it is mainly concerned with the relationship between the abbey and the archbishop of Rouen. It may therefore be relatively reliable in its account of the relationship between the abbey and laymen; but it is hard to reconcile with Orderic's account of Brionne in these years, for which see below, Chapter 8, at n. 14. If the story can be accepted, these great lords thought that their ancestors' gifts were conditional on the abbey's remaining independent of lay control and regarded their reversion to the donors' descendants as the proper penalty if the abbey lost its independence. No charter ever imposes such a condition, however; and even if the story is true political considerations undoubtedly at least partly motivated the magnates' threat. Hence this evidence is dubious at best. On this source, see above, Chapter 2, n. 48. The story is accepted by Bates, *Normandy*, p. 222; and Vaughn, *Abbey*, pp. 32–33, though on page 34 she admits that "the account has overtones of apocryphal exaggeration."

5. OV, 2:46.

6. Document 370.

7. Document 254 (p. 399). The charter does not say that Saint-Cyr had been given to Saint-Magloire in return for Hugh's entry into the abbey, but the inference seems justified.

8. Above, Chapter 3, at and after n. 48; below, this chapter, at nn. 24–52 and 226–29; Chapter 9, at nn. 30–33.

9. Document 797 (f° 230v–231r): "numero et qualitate." See also Document 355 (p. 572).

10. Document 42, in which the countergift is said (p. 24) to have been forty pounds; Document 43, in which the countergift is said (p. 25) to have been thirty-five pounds. Neither version explains why the alienor should pay money if the monks do not perform. Perhaps the reason is that the monks would make their decision based on the wealth of the site: if they found that it was too poor, they would have paid him too much.

11. Document 796.

12. Document 396 (p. 679).

13. Below, this chapter, at and in n. 30; Documents 269 (p. 436) and 427 (p. 140).

14. OV, 2:14–16, 20, 32.

15. Document 301 (pp. 155–56).

16. Above, this chapter, at and in n. 11.

17. Document 427 (p. 140).

18. Document 14 (p. 24).

19. About the creation of new priories and abbeys and the attendant difficulties, see Musset, "Recherches sur les communautés"; Laporte, "Origines," pp. 49–68; Bates, *Normandy*, p. 221. For particular cases, see Musset, "Contribution," pp. 64–66; Quivy and Thiron, "Robert," pp. 349–52; Bourrienne, "Odon," 10:286. On the sizable costs of founding a priory or an abbey, see Musset, "Actes inédits, I," pp. 120–24; Musset, "Vie économique," pp. 70–71.

20. Document 669 (f° 65r): "enim moris domni abbati [*sic*] Rotberti fuit semper quatinus nunquam monachum suum alicui ecclesie serviturum committeret nisi de ipsa obedientia preter ipsum servientem saltem unus in monasterio sustentare prevaleret."

21. Above, Chapter 3, at nn. 35–39.

22. Robert, the first known abbot, was probably in fact the first. Ten charters survive from the abbey's first two decades (above, Chapter 3, at and in n. 37); another fifty-eight must also be dated to Robert's abbacy, which ended in 1089. Forty-one of these are dated to particular years, of which seventeen come from 1078 through 1087; fourteen come from 1088 alone and ten from 1089. For the years of the next abbot, Ralph, 1089–1103, sixty-nine dated charters survive (excluding those of 1089), and

two others must come from those years. Both calculations exclude undated charters which cannot with certainty be assigned to one abbacy.

23. Document 655.

24. The church eventually became Sainte-Gauberge de la Coudre (later Saint-Cyr de la Rosière), a priory of Saint-Denis de Nogent (Flament, *Répertoire*, p. 60 and the references there).

25. OV, 2:16.

26. Ibid., p. 32; Orderic's only other reference to the matter is ibid., p. 20.

27. Document 100 (p. 614). The priory was also known as Notre-Dame-de-Bonnes-Nouvelles.

28. Below, this chapter, at and in n. 33; Document 269 (p. 436); and the next note.

29. For example, the dispute between Fécamp and Saint-Taurin d'Evreux, on which see below, Chapter 5, at nn. 68–69, and Chapter 11, at n. 27. On this see also Laporte, "Origines," p. 67; Bates, *Normandy*, p. 221.

30. Document 396 (p. 679).

31. Document 398 (p. 683).

32. Ibid.

33. Document 396 (p. 679): the abbot of the prospective abbey was to be chosen by the abbot and monks of Saint-Florent.

34. The case involved a bourg near Laval which Guy de Laval had given to Marmoutier; the gift was challenged unsuccessfully by Saint-Pierre de la Couture on the grounds that Guy had previously given the bourg to their priory at Auvers-le-Hamon. There are two records of the case: Documents 227 and 228.

The story must have been as follows. Warin, a monk of Saint-Calais, was put in charge of that monastery's church at Auvers, which may already have been a small priory. Warin subsequently renounced his allegiance to his abbey but kept those of its possessions which were in his hands. He then entered into an agreement with Guy de Laval to create an abbey at Laval, of which Warin would be the first abbot. Its endowment would consist of possessions at Laval, including a bourg, conveyed by Guy, plus all those possessions of Saint-Calais which Warin had abstracted from that abbey's control. Work on the new abbey had barely begun, however, when Warin died. This seems to have ended Guy's hopes of establishing an abbey, but he now had effective possession of the church of Auvers. He did not return it to Saint-Calais; instead, he gave it—but nothing at Laval—to La Couture. La Couture then either established or reestablished a priory at Auvers. Still later Guy gave the bourg at Laval to Marmoutier, with no apparent intention that it become the site of either an abbey or a priory. The gift to Marmoutier was then challenged by La Couture on the grounds that the bourg had once belonged—and therefore of right ought to belong—to its priory at Auvers. Guy denied the claim on two grounds: that the bourg had not belonged to Auvers but rather both had belonged independently to the projected abbey at Laval, and that at that time Auvers had had no connection with La Couture. By decision of Duke William's court, Marmoutier kept Laval: for some of the details, see below, Chapter 7, n. 49; Chapter 11, at n. 32.

Thus by Guy's agreement with Warin the church at Auvers, the bourg at Laval, and the abbey of Laval were to form one unit; but the abbey never came into existence. Guy therefore felt himself free to treat the church at Auvers and the bourg at Laval as though they had no connection with each other—he gave them at different times to different abbeys—and William the Conqueror's court agreed with him.

35. Document 410 (p. 75). Whether Enguerrand and his heirs retained the right to oversee the suitability of incumbents of the church after the first is not stated.

36. Document 524 (p. 521).

37. Document 351.

38. Document 586 (f° 9v): "ut si qua inde oriretur injustitia ipse rectam teneret inter eos justitiam."

39. This is unusual both as a bilateral agreement and because no alienation is

involved. A few other bilateral agreements are recorded, but none says anything about enforcement. For another example, see below, this chapter, at and in n. 188.

40. Document 853: "Convenit etiam ei abbas quod quatuor vicibus per annum illum hospitio reciperet, una quaque vice una nocte, si tamen mensurate id est non cum multitudine veniret, et cum apud abbatem minime hospitaretur, abbas ei caritatem mitteret, si tamen ipse Robertus abbati se adesse mandaret."

41. Document 777 (f° 84r): "ad eius feudum quod nobis tenet, ad hunc de anguillis dimidium miliarum addimus, et tempore quo in mariscis nostris terram ad ardendum trahemus duodecim onerata plaustra sicut onerantur ad vendendum tres teras [*sic*] super scaleras ei dabimus, aut si non traxerimus nobis terram vel eciam si defuerit ut non possit dari, precium eius sicut presenti anno appreciata est, scilicet .xx. solidos, ipsi et heredi eius persolvemus."

The passage is published by Allix and Génestal, "Opérations," p. 623, n. 1, in connection with their discussion of the abbey's sale of peat from its bogs; they print the problem phrase as "tres terras super scaleras" but do not attempt to explain what it means. The passage is also published by Delisle, *Etudes*, p. 285, n. 59. He prints the phrase as "tresteras super scaleras" and comments, "Les mots 'trestella' [*sic*] et 'scalera', désignent sans doute quelques parties de la charrette. On reconnaît dans ces mots les mêmes radicaux que dans nos mots français 'tréteau' et 'échelle.' " Sauvage, *Troarn*, pp. 260–61, also discusses this charter in the context of the sale of peat by Troarn.

42. Above, this chapter, at and in nn. 35 and 37, respectively.

43. Document 14 (p. 25).

44. Document 879 (p. 68).

45. Document 587 (f° 10v): "Hoc etiam in eadem conventione definitum fuit, ut si quando tanta guerra seu famis pestilentia unde hec patria vastaretur, his partibus ingrueret, secundum tempus, ad mensuram praestitam redditio mitteretur, et Rotbertus Morellus tam diu de prefato molendino tres prestitutos sextarios annone haberet, quamdiu Willelmo de Sivilleio suas conventiones servaret; si vero non servaret, eadem redditio ex toto remaneret." See below, this chapter, at and in n. 234, for a similar provision about reduced payments in another charter from this abbey.

46. Document 161.

47. Above, Chapter 3, at n. 114; Documents 274 (p. 453) and 386 (p. 99), two versions of the same transaction; Document 851. For another—but highly dubious—example of permanent confiscation, see below, this chapter, n. 228.

48. Respectively, above, this chapter, at nn. 31, 15, 5, 7, and 6.

49. Below, this chapter, at and in nn. 50, 52.

50. Document 292 (p. 217). Some time later the abbey "broke the agreement about the horses, because it was burdensome," and the donors seized back the church. Later still, they restored the church to the abbey for eight pounds "in testimonium." The provision about refuge was to remain in effect.

51. Yver, *Contrats*, p. 76 and n. 1, expresses a similar opinion about the eleventh century but cites no evidence.

52. Document 285 (col. 202).

53. Feudal tenure is a well-worked topic, although most previous studies either concentrate on the period from the twelfth century on or rely on the use of and assumptions derived from twelfth-century evidence in discussing the eleventh century. Rabasse, *Régime*, must be used with great caution: it depends heavily on evidence which is late and/or English and sometimes gives a remarkably static picture of Norman feudal tenure from the tenth through the fifteenth centuries (see also Haskins, *Norman Institutions*, p. 6, n. 8). The following works are more profitable: Lagouëlle, *Essai*; Carabie, *Propriété foncière*, esp. pp. 230–97; Navel, "Recherches sur les institutions féodales." Haskins, *Norman Institutions*, pp. 3–24, is specifically on the eleventh century. For critiques of the work of Haskins, see Tabuteau, "Definitions"; Bates, *Normandy*, pp. 168–69, 258–59; Chibnall, "Military Service."

The term "fief" (*feodum*, *feudum*, etc.) came into use in Normandy only in the middle of the eleventh century. The earliest use of it which I have found, from between 1031 and about 1040, is in Document 305 (col. 129): "[concedo] ecclesiam et decimam cum feodo Farmanni presbiteri . . . et foefum [*sic*] Osuli de Monasterio." For one implied suggestion as to the word's meaning, see below, Chapter 5, n. 53. The earlier term for a grant made on condition of services of honorable types was *beneficium*, which continued in use throughout the eleventh century. It can have three different specific meanings in Norman documents of that time—a fief, an ecclesiastical benefice, and the spiritual benefits of the prayers of monks and nuns—as well as any benefit in the most general sense. *Feodum* did not become the exclusive term for a fief until the mid-twelfth century, and it soon came to mean any tenement: see below, this chapter, at and in n. 179. On the general history of these terms, see, especially, Carabie, *Propriété foncière*, pp. 245–60, though some of his conclusions need to be modified; see also Chibnall, "Military Service," pp. 66–67; below, this chapter, n. 149.

54. For one church which held from another, see below, this chapter, at n. 97. In Document 810 (f° 178r, p. 345), the bishop of Evreux holds a mill from the archbishop of Rouen, but the type of tenure is not stated.

55. See also Tabuteau, "Definitions," and the references there in n. 2, to which should be added Le Patourel, *Norman Empire*, pp. 253–54, 262, 290; Bates, *Normandy*, passim, esp. pp. 122–28, 133, 168–72; Chibnall, "Military Service"; Chibnall, *Anglo-Norman England*, pp. 2–3, 13–14, 15–16, 28–29, 32–35.

56. Below, Chapter 5.

57. Below, pp. 93, 110–12.

58. Below, this chapter, at nn. 169–229.

59. Below, this chapter, at nn. 233–76.

60. Below, this chapter, at nn. 85–101 and 142–44.

61. Below, Chapter 6, at nn. 48–66.

62. Most known fiefs consisted of immovables, but there are a few exceptions: above, this chapter, at and in n. 41, a fief consisting in part of annual renders of eels and peat; Document 552, a fief of twenty shillings annually; Document 478 (p. 248), a fief of two wagonloads of wine annually, held by a layman from the duke; OV, 6:296, an allegation in 1120 that the right to convey William the Conqueror to England by ship had been held as a fief. See Lyon, *Fief*, p. 33, for the possibility that the money fief granted by the kings of England to the counts of Flanders in the twelfth century was first granted by William the Conqueror in 1066.

63. Document 25 (p. 95). Bourrienne, *Antiquus cartularius*, 1:95, dates this charter merely to before 1147. Because both parties to the agreement reserve their fealty to a Count Robert, who must be Duke Robert Curthose, it must come from between 1087 and 1106. The viscounts of Bayeux were named Rannulf from before 1047 through 1153, and the bishop of Bayeux is never named by the agreement. He is usually assumed to be Odo, who left on crusade in 1096 and died in Sicily in 1097. Navel, "Recherches sur les institutions féodales," p. 17, offers an explanation of the circumstances surrounding the agreement which implies a date in 1087 or very shortly thereafter; it is plausible but based on conjecture. See also Haskins, *Norman Institutions*, p. 22, n. 70. A good many persons named in the agreement are—or may be—mentioned elsewhere in eleventh-century Norman sources, but no such reference mandates a particular terminal date for the document.

64. Document 25 (pp. 95–96): "fecit enim Rannulfus fidelitatis securitatem episcopo, sicut domino suo, fide et sacramento de vita sua videlicet episcopi, et de menbris quae corpori suo adhaerebant, et de captione sui corporis, quod nullo modo eam quaereret dampno episcopi; fecit etiam sibi fidelitatem ligiam idem Rannulfus jurejurando de tota terra quam episcopus ea die tenebat, et de tota illa terra, quam ipse episcopus consilio Rannulfi adquireret, hoc modo quod ipse Rannulfus inde episcopum juvaret ad hoc ut ipse episcopus eam ex integro optineret; juvaret autem, salva fidelitate comitis Roberti, contra omnes impugnare volentes. . . . Fecit igitur episcopus Rannul-

fum sicut suum hominem securum per fidem de vita sua, id est Rannulfi, et de menbris quae corpori suo adhaerebant, et de captione sui corporis, quod nullo modo eam quaereret dampno Rannulfi, et de tota terra quam idem Rannulfus ea die tenebat, et de tota illa quam ipse consilio episcopi adquireret, hoc modo quod ipse episcopus Rannulfum fideliter adjuvaret contra omnes impugnare volentes, salva fidelitate comitis Roberti." In addition, the agreement contains several provisions concerning aid which the bishop and the viscount will render each other in court about particular disputed possessions, for one of which see below, this chapter, at n. 103. On liege fealty, see Tabuteau, "Definitions," pp. 55–57.

65. Document 25 (p. 97): marten skins and an ermine pelt or thirty pounds of the money of Rouen every Easter. The annual amounts of wood and wax or money in William Paynel's agreement, below, this chapter, at n. 83, are only accidentally similar to this provision: they are discussed because the amounts William may take are limited.

66. Below, this chapter, at n. 83, especially the obscure phrase "Nec si[c] eum donnus abbas semper habebit quin Guillelmus Paginellus hoc habeat." The emendation is Haskins's.

67. Below, Chapter 9, at nn. 30–33.

68. Dudo, p. 142.

69. Ibid., p. 169. For Normandy as a *regnum*, see below, Chapter 8, at and in n. 128.

70. Dudo, p. 203. For the background to this episode, see Searle, "Frankish Rivalries," esp. p. 212.

71. Ibid., p. 204.

72. Ibid., pp. 204–5.

73. Ibid., p. 226.

74. OV, 4:214; translation adapted from Chibnall, ibid., p. 215. She translates "erile adiutorium ab eo poposcit" as "ask him as his liege lord for help"; but I do not think that "liege" in the technical sense is necessitated by Orderic's language. See ibid., p. 214, n. 4, for the date of this incident.

75. Yver, "Châteaux forts," pp. 60–62; Bates, *Normandy*, pp. 165–66.

76. OV, 4:112–14.

77. Ibid., p. 296; Documents 306 (p. 230), 314 (p. 63), and possibly 567.

78. Gilbert Crispin, *Vita Herluini*, pp. 87–88, however, says that Herluin, while still a vassal of Gilbert count of Brionne, withdrew from his service because his lord had done him an injury and later voluntarily returned. There is no indication that Gilbert attempted to punish him during or after the hiatus in his service, although he did so when Herluin left without apparent cause (below, this chapter, n. 95).

79. Dudo, p. 182.

80. WP, pp. 102–4. Körner, *Battle*, pp. 105–6, 109–21, 124, 137, doubts that Harold actually took this oath and can find no independent evidence that he did. For the argument here, it makes little difference: either he did, or William of Poitiers knew that in the circumstances he was describing Harold should have done so.

81. Below, Chapter 9, at and in n. 23.

82. WP, p. 114, about Harold; WJ, p. 123, about Guy of Burgundy; ibid., p. 133, about Harold.

83. Document 313. My translation is indebted to those by Stapleton, "Letter," pp. 24–25, and Round, *Calendar*, pp. 255–56, no. 714. The translation "watch and ward" is Haskins's. Less trustworthy translation and paraphrase are given in Chesnel, "De quelques usages féodaux," pp. 544–48, and Chesnel, *Cotentin*, pp. 215–18.

84. It is also the only eleventh-century document to use the term "parage" or to use the word "peer" in a technical sense (for the only other use of *pares* in a document, see above, Chapter 3, at and in n. 253, where it is used in a social sense). Largely on these grounds, Bates, *Normandy*, pp. 258–59, denies that the document can be taken as valid evidence for the eleventh century. It seems to me, however, that, because the document

is unique, its terminological peculiarities need not cast doubt on its authenticity; they merely remind the investigator of how much of eleventh-century Norman law went unrecorded. See also my review of Bates's book, p. 612. On parage in the eleventh century, see Chibnall, *Anglo-Norman England*, p. 165.

85. Document 312. For a denial of the authenticity of the document, see Bates, *Normandy*, p. 258; cf. my review of Bates's book, p. 612 and n. 4. For more detail on most of what follows concerning military service, see Tabuteau, "Definitions," pp. 40–58. On length of service, see now also Chibnall, "Military Service," pp. 74–75.

86. OV, 4:88.

87. Document 242: "benefitium . . . quam a . . . meo domino militans obtineo."

88. Eadmer, *Vita Anselmi*, p. 94v; translation by Southern, ibid., p. 94r.

89. Documents 788 and 789.

90. OV, 2:80–82. See also below, this chapter, at n. 152. The incident must have occurred between 1059 and 1061.

91. Below, this chapter at n. 161.

92. Document 776.

93. Document 424 (p. 139): "per tale servitium quale miles facere debet hoc etiam adjecto quod si donna abbatissa [ ]rtura sit per Normanniam vel extra Normanniam, donnus Hunfridus secum [ ]ia." The brackets represent gaps in the manuscript.

94. Documents 392 (p. 628) and 758 (f° 22r); canons of the council of Lillebonne in OV, 3:28.

95. Bates, *Normandy*, p. 127, points out that "the earliest mentions of lords holding courts to adjudicate between their tenants come from the 1070s." See ibid., n. 141, for these courts, which include those cited below, Chapter 5, at and in n. 25, and Chapter 7, at and in n. 46. Gilbert Crispin's *Vita Herluini*, p. 90, says that Gilbert count of Brionne held a court to try Herluin for refusing to perform messenger service; this would have been about 1034, but Gilbert Crispin wrote the *Vita* only in the early twelfth century. On this instance and another purported pre-1066 example from Orderic (cited below, this chapter, at n. 162), see Chibnall, "Military Service," pp. 75–76.

96. Document 769: "Rogerius de salam et hosmundus frater eius vendiderunt unam terram Radulfo filio anseredi et heredi suo, eo conventu quod si in plaga qua ipse moraret, adiuvaret eum in placitis suis si ab illo requireretur, et ubicumque eum residentem inveniret, illud idem auxilium ab eo haberet si requireret. Adiuncto etiam quod quando de sua terra dominica auxilium daret, aut radulfus quantum rectitudo foret de terra tali scilicet vastata dare daret aut quietum eum dimittere faceret. Nunc autem ipse radulfus de hac terra hereditat sanctam trinitatem et abbatissam facturam illud idem auxilium Rogero post obitum Radulfi quod ipse faciebat illi, concesso eidem radulfo quicquid habebat abbatissa in eadem terra, ipse vero e [*sic*] decimam illius terre. Post obitum autem suum et terram et decimam." The documents in this cartulary are often difficult to understand, but few are as baffling as this one.

97. Document 423. The last words of this passage—"secundum quod fedium est"—are ambiguous: if *fedium* is translated as "the fief," they suggest that the suit of court was in some way proportional to the fief; if it is translated as "a fief," they suggest that suit of court was a normal part of feudal service. Having found no neutral translation, I have used the first one; but the second may be more in line with analogous statements in the documents of this abbey, for which see below, this chapter, at and in n. 143.

98. Document 33. For the surrounding circumstances, see Le Maho, "Seigneuries," p. 97.

99. Document 370: "eo tenore . . . ut filios Gaufridi honeste regeret et teneret, et mandatus ad placita Sancti Petri sine dilatione veniret. Inde quoque ipse Herluinus homo abbatis factus est."

100. Document 25.

101. Document 344 (p. 215). Evremar's other services were hospitality for Rainald

and his horses and up to one hundred shillings of credit at Bayeux (ibid.). The grant to Evremar must have been made between 1066 and 1079; his tenement is never said to be a fief.

102. Lagouëlle, *Essai*, p. 174 and the references there, to which should be added Viollet, "Coutumiers," pp. 50–51, 189. Haskins, *Norman Institutions*, p. 22, and M. de Boüard, "Duché," p. 14, comment briefly on the discrepancy. Even in the twelfth century, some men owed aids other than the customary three; see Navel, "Enquête," pp. 57–59; Gleason, *Ecclesiastical Barony*, pp. 50–51. On aids and incidents, see also Chibnall, "Military Service," p. 75.

103. Document 25 (p. 96).

104. Perhaps this is what was meant by the aid William Paynel could take if his land were confiscated.

105. Respectively, Document 490, and above, this chapter, n. 96, in which *auxilium* appears to mean suit of court as well as "aid" in the usual sense. In the following, *adiutorium* or *auxilium* certainly or probably means a payment by peasants: Documents 535, 788, 789, 808, 815. Document 334 is a highly suspect charter dated 1036 which contains (p. 7) a clause about peasant *auxilia* which is not in Document 335, the genuine version.

106. Bates, *Normandy*, p. 145, n. 142.

107. Document 244. On vavassors, see below, this chapter, at and in n. 177.

108. Document 434 (p. 126): "eam per quatuor denariorum libras uno quoque anno in termino festivitatis sancte Marie . . . relevaverit."

109. Delisle, *Etudes*, pp. 67–68; Lagouëlle, *Essai*, pp. 175–76 and the references there; Carabie, *Propriété foncière*, pp. 67–68.

110. Document 413 (p. 109).

111. Document 389. Lot identifies the donor as William I, son of Herluin III viscount of Mantes, who was nicknamed "the Clerk."

112. For later practice, see Lagouëlle, *Essai*, pp. 175–76 and the references there. Ibid., pp. 176–77, discusses how reliefs paid in money developed. On this see also Navel, "Enquête," pp. 19, 56–57; but his assumption that the Bayeux Inquest reflects eleventh-century conditions is unwarranted (Tabuteau, "Definitions," pp. 21–30).

113. *Summa*, XXXI.12, p. 104. The same rule is implied but not quite stated in *TAC*, LXXXIV, ed. Tardif, I.i, pp. 93–94, and I.ii, p. 79 (in which the chapter number is LXXXV). Barlow, *William Rufus*, p. 254 and n. 187, suggests that in England the rule may have developed only in the late twelfth century.

114. Document 354: "petiit Rogerus de Crucemaris abbatem Willelmum quatinus relevaret honorem Gisleberti de Rogero Bellemontis, de quo beneficium erat. Et si hoc ipse Rogerius Bellemontis concederet, libenter postea honorem Gisleberti, ex abbate Willelmo recognosceret. Fit ex utraque parte consensus, et de Rogerio Bellemontis terra ab abbate Willelmo relevatur, ea tamen ratione ut medietatem Condedi quandiu viveret Rogerus de Crucemaris haberent monachi. Post exitum vero suum quicquid in predicta villa habebat ex toto, exceptis triginta acris terre et domo cum curte et viridario et duobus militibus, Roberto scilicet et Rogero. Quod vero aliis in locis habebat, cum triginta acris terre et domo et duobus suprascriptis militibus, relevaret heres ejus de abbate vel monachis, sicuti mos est terre . . . . Rogerus de Crucemaris . . . donationem hujus rei supra altare misit, et inibi homo abbatis, presente Rogero Bellemontis, effectus est." For the preceding steps, see below, Chapter 11, at n. 16. On the charter, see also Holt, "Feudal Society, II," p. 200, n. 39.

The dates of these transactions are difficult to establish. Le Prévost, *Eure*, 1:536–37, gives no dates. Round, *Calendar*, pp. 109–10, no. 320, dates the charter to between 1066 and 1087. The arrangement involving Roger de Croismare must have been made between 1078 and 1096, when William was abbot of Préaux, and the notice was presumably contemporary with the transaction. Because the notice begins, "Regnante Willelmo," and contains no reference to Duke William's death or to Robert Curthose as his successor, it was presumably written before William's death in 1087; but the reference to William's reign applies most directly to Gilbert's original grant. That grant is said to have been made with the concession of Robert son of Humphrey, almost certainly Humphrey de Vieilles, founder of the Beaumont family and of the abbeys at Préaux. His son Robert was killed in the disorders of the minority of Duke William (OV, 3:88; ibid., 4:302). These disorders were at their height about the year 1040. If "Robert son of Humphrey" is not an error for his brother Roger (as Round, *Calendar*, p. 109, n. 2, appears to think it was), then Gilbert's grant must have occurred between 1035 and the early 1040s.

If Yver's conclusion that an act of donation did not legally obligate the donor to transfer the property concerned in the gift (see above, Chapter 3, at n. 122) can be applied to the eleventh century, Roger's claim had a sound basis and the abbey's acquiescence in the elaborate arrangements which followed becomes easier to understand. It is noteworthy that the charter does not present Roger's claim as obviously unjust.

115. This statement is perhaps too strong in relation to the relief paid by William son of Herluin and his mother (above, this chapter, at n. 111), where *relevatio* refers to the acquittance of the land in general rather than specifically to the transfer of land.

116. Below, at and in the next note, where the relief is in land; below, this chapter, at and in n. 118, where the relief is in money; below, this chapter, at and in n. 392, where a quasi-relief is in money; Document 782, where the relief is in land.

117. Document 716: "a quodam Gunduino milite nostro . . . comparavimus. . . . Ad hoc etiam idem Gunduinus supradictus gratis et sine precii taxatione dedit nobis x acros de meliori terra quam possidebat eo rationis tenore ut beneficium quod ex parte nostra habuit post mortem eius etiam filiis filiis [*sic*] suis sub eodem servitutis respectu quo et ipse servivit consentiremus." Henry was abbot from 1006 to 1033; Adigard des Gautries, "Noms des lieux de la Seine-Inférieure," 6:130, dates the charter to about 1015.

118. Document 852 (p. 24): "Rannulfo filio Herfasti concessit Gislebertus abbas in feudium totum quicquid pater et mater ipsius Rannulfi habuerunt in Venuncio. Ipse vero Rannulfus ob hoc devenit homo ligis ejusdem abbatis, et XXX libras dedit ei."

119. See also Chibnall, "Military Service," p. 74. For later Norman practice, whereby feudal wardship belonged to the lord of the fief, see *TAC*, XI.1, ed. Tardif, I.i, pp. 10–11, and I.ii, pp. 9–10; Powicke, *Loss*, pp. 41–42; Génestal, *Tutelle*, esp. pp. 7–38. Yver, "Très Ancien Coutumier," pp. 354–56, suggests that this rule was established or perhaps first clearly enunciated by twelfth-century ducal legislation; see esp. ibid., n. 63. *TAC*, LXVI.2, says that the rule, insofar as it pertained to the duke's vassals, was stated by an inquest held during the reign of Henry II (ed. Tardif, I.i, pp. 60–61, and I.ii, p. 53, in which the chapter is numbered LXVI bis). On this inquest, see Haskins, *Norman Institutions*, pp. 160–61; n. 22 dates it to before 1174, perhaps considerably before.

120. Respectively, Documents 432 (p. 38) and 38 (pp. 32–33).

121. Above, this chapter, at and in n. 99.

122. Above, this chapter, at n. 111.

123. Document 785. Odo of Bayeux left on crusade in 1096, dying in Sicily in 1097. If Robert died after Odo's departure, the arrangements he made might conceivably have been an interim measure taken in the lord's absence and only because of it.

124. Documents 54 (p. 63) and 55 (p. 64).

125. Dudo, pp. 224–27; WJ, pp. 45–48. Even Prentout, *Etude*, chap. 4, esp. p. 355, accepts the story. Génestal, "Tutelle," p. 708, not only accepts it but argues on the basis of it that seigneurial wardship "est bien dès lors une coutume normande, puisqu'on n'en retrouve pas trace dans le droit parisien et qu'au contraire la garde seigneuriale se développe en Normandie." He elaborates this conclusion in *Tutelle*, pp. 8–15. See also Lauer, *Règne*, pp. 93, 102–3, and 103, n. 1.

Génestal's interpretation of Louis IV's actions is based on the reasoning quoted above, Chapter 1, at and in n. 17. I find it difficult to accept. The Normans had been settled in Normandy for only thirty-two years by the accession of Richard I, and "settled" is inapt because immigration of Vikings from elsewhere and expansion of Normans beyond the boundaries granted in 911 characterized this period; see above, Chapter 3, at and in n. 262. Moreover, if King Louis was unfamiliar with such a custom in his own demesne, it does not seem likely that he would have known of it to use it in Normandy (but cf. Génestal, *Tutelle*, pp. 12–14). More probably, a purely political act of Louis's, based on some high-sounding assertion of a moral duty to protect the young duke, was transmuted by Dudo, writing about three-quarters of a century later, into what may have been by Dudo's day a recognized seigneurial right. Even as evidence of the state of the law only by Dudo's day, so clear a description of a lord's right over his vassals' minor heirs is surprising: the charter evidence begins much later, and the evidence in the historians for the first half of the eleventh century which is independent of Dudo does little to confirm the impression he leaves that this practice of feudal law was already fully developed. Why Dudo wrote his work is not known. It is possible that here as elsewhere he distorted past events to provide evidence for a present claim of the duke, in this instance a claim to the wardship of the minor heirs of his vassals. For accusations that Dudo was writing to justify current claims, see Powicke, *Loss*, p. 79 and the references there; Chesnel, "Traité," p. 324; Chesnel, "Département," p. 46; M. de Boüard, "Duché," pp. 3–4; Lemarignier, "Political and Monastic Structures," p. 110.

126. Dudo, p. 263; WJ, p. 60.

127. Dudo, pp. 250–51; Document 103 (p. 71).

128. Stenton, *William*, pp. 73–74, and D. C. Douglas, *William*, pp. 41–47, present Henry I as having had wardship of William, but the evidence comes mostly from twelfth-century historians writing in England; for the contrary view, that Henry did not assert a right to wardship of Normandy, see Dhondt, "Relations," pp. 469–70; Bates, *Normandy*, pp. 61, 74–75.

129. D. C. Douglas, *William*, pp. 37–52; M. de Boüard, *Guillaume*, pp. 11–13. Lepelley, "Jeunesse," p. 60, says that for most of the period William's maternal relatives had actual custody of the boy duke; see also D. C. Douglas, *William*, p. 40. Henry of Huntingdon, *Historia*, pp. 189–90, says that at the time when King Harold I of England exiled his stepmother Emma, daughter of Duke Richard II of Normandy, William was residing with King Henry. This is late evidence and from England. Moreover, because the remark is incidental to Huntingdon's story at the point at which he makes it—it seems to be intended to explain why Emma took refuge in Flanders rather than in Normandy—it may be based on an assumption on Huntingdon's part rather than on knowledge. As Maitland says, "It is difficult to square this story with the known facts" (Pollock and Maitland, *History*, 1:71, n. 3).

130. See David, *Robert*, pp. 7–11, for William the Conqueror's custody of Margaret sister of Count Herbert II of Maine; but she was in William's custody as the fiancée of his son Robert Curthose even before Herbert's death, and William's claim to Maine was based on Herbert's post-obit gift of it if he died without children, not on his wardship of Margaret. Lemarignier, *Recherches*, p. 117, asserts that when Geoffrey-Berenger count of Rennes went on pilgrimage in 1008 he gave custody of Brittany and of his two sons to Richard II of Normandy and that when he died on the pilgrimage Duke Richard kept the wardship; but Geoffrey-Berenger and Richard married each other's sisters, so this may be familial rather than feudal wardship. Rioult de Neuville, "Orbec," p. 715, n. 3, deduces on the basis of twelfth-century sources that Gilbert count of Brionne had wardship of the children of William count of Eu after the latter's death; but Gilbert was the son of Geoffrey count of Eu and nephew (or half-nephew) of Count William, so either familial wardship or Gilbert's hereditary pretensions rather than a feudal relationship would have been involved here, presuming that the deduction is correct.

131. For the law of Normandy on this subject in the twelfth century, see Petot, "Mariage," pp. 32–35. For the situation about 1100, see Holt, "Feudal Society, IV," p. 7.

132. On who she was not, see Tabuteau, "Definitions," p. 47, n. 102. Farrer and Clay, *Early Yorkshire Charters*, 6:1–2, suggest that she may have been the heiress to Hambye, which the Paynel family later held in chief from the duke.

133. Several of her brothers were alive long after William became lord of Moulins (Ménager, "Inventaire," pp. 332–36).

134. On the descent of the Bellême lands and the marriage of Mabel de Bellême to Roger de Montgomery, see Chibnall, in OV, 2:362–65, and the references there; Chibnall, *World*, p. 52, n. 19; Searle, "Women," p. 160; Bates, *Normandy*, pp. 79–81; Holt, "Feudal Society, IV," p. 4, n. 7; Thompson, "Family." On Roger de Montgomery, see Chibnall, in OV, 2:362–65, and the references there; Chibnall, *World*, p. 52, n. 19; Searle, "Women," p. 160; Bates, *Normandy*, pp. 79–81; Holt, "Feudal Society, IV," p. 4, n. 7; Thompson, "Family." On the marriage of Mabel and Roger's son Robert de Bellême to the heiress to the county of Ponthieu, see OV, 4:158. For Guy count of Ponthieu as a vassal of Duke William, see below, Chapter 8, at and in n. 154.

135. WJ, p. 75.

136. The county of Eu seems to have been created for William at this time; see D. C. Douglas, "Earliest Norman Counts," pp. 135–40.

137. OV, 3:252; translation adapted from Chibnall, ibid., p. 253. Mistaking Richard's parentage in the genealogical table, ibid., p. 367, she makes Duke Robert his "great-uncle." She translates "senis" as "the elder," but there seems to have been no other Herluin de Heugleville. She translates "cum toto patrimonio eius" as "with all her inheritance"; but, because Ada's second husband, Richard, took the name "de Heugleville" and that estate passed to his descendants, the lords of Auffay, it seems likely that it was Herluin's lands, including Heugleville, rather than lands belonging to Ada, which Richard acquired.

138. Ada is the only particular example given by Génestal, *Tutelle*, p. 21 and n. 2, to prove that "[o]n sait . . . , par un assez grand nombre d'exemples, que le seigneur avait le droit de marier non seulement l'orpheline en garde, mais toute fille ou veuve possédant fief"; the passage from the *TAC* (LXVI.2, ed. Tardif, I.i, p. 61) which he cites concerns only daughters. There are later instances of a ducal right which applied to all female vassals; for early thirteenth-century examples, see Rabasse, *Régime*, p. 218, n. 4, and p. 220, n. 3; Petot, "Mariage," p. 34, n. 22, and p. 39 with nn. 40–41. The king's right to marry off the widows of his tenants-in-chief was, of course, well known in England in the twelfth century and later. Nonetheless, Petot, "Mariage," p. 34, concludes that in Normandy "il ne s'agit que d'actes isolés, d'une pratique fugitive qui n'a pas passé en coutume."

139. Document 491 (p. 305): if Adeliza should not be survived by a son or daughter, then on her death the land was to revert to the abbey's demesne, "unde vir ejus et ipsa acceperat [*sic*] pro ipsa."

The lands Adeliza held from Troarn were Héritot and Hernetot (Document 492). They had been given to the abbey by Hugh the seneschal by 1068 (below, Chapter 8, at n. 107, no. 11). Document 497 is a charter from Hugh concerning these lands, which is datable to between 1079 and 1083; it is so badly mutilated that the dispositive section can no longer be completely deciphered, but it presumably records the confirmation of an earlier gift. None of these documents makes any connection between Hugh and Adeliza, and I can find no evidence elsewhere that there was one. Document 497 is signed by a Robert, called brother of Corbet, who might be Adeliza's first husband; but there is no reason except the coincidence of names to think that he was, and Robert was one of the most popular names in Normandy at the time.

140. Documents 47, 720, 865.

141. This last rule was asserted as such by an inquest held during the reign of Henry II (*TAC*, LXVI.2, ed. Tardif, I.i, p. 61, and I.ii, p. 53 [as LXVI bis]). On this inquest, see also above, this chapter, n. 119, and the references there; Petot, "Mariage," pp. 32–33.

142. The obligation of hospitality is mentioned occasionally in eleventh-century Norman documents but never in a demonstrably feudal context; for examples, see above, Chapter 3, n. 130; this chapter, at and in n. 40; this chapter, n. 101.

143. Above, this chapter, at and in n. 93. Two considerations reinforce this implication. First, the knight's escort service is expressed in a way which suggests that it was additional to other services which were standard. Second, Document 758, the early twelfth-century list of peasant rents and services owed to La Trinité de Caen (on which see above, Chapter 2, n. 52), uses similar phrases about services in such a way as, again, to suggest that the services the nuns did not feel it necessary to describe were those which were typical; e.g., f° 20v–21r: "habemus . . . .ix. bordarios . . . et serviunt sicut bordarii"; f° 22r: "habet ecclesia . . . duos dimidios villanos .x. inter bordarios et censarios . . . et serviunt sicut debent, et .ii^{os}. vavasores. Unus commodat palefridum suum. . . . Alius servit sicut vavassor"; f° 22v: ".iiii^{or}. bordarios . . . et serviunt sicut debent"; f° 23r: ".iiii^{or}. bordarios . . . servientes sicut debent." See also above, this chapter, at and in n. 97, for a possible example in a feudal context.

144. See also Tabuteau, "Definitions," pp. 18–19, 58–59.

145. In Document 832 (f° 17r), what is clearly a life estate (below, this chapter, at and in n. 248) is twice called a *beneficium*.

146. Documents 542 and 546 are two copies of a charter which says that Abbot Ansfrid (ca. 1040–72) of Saint-Pierre de Préaux granted a *beneficium* without the monks' consent; the heading of Document 546, alone, says that the grant was "tenendum in perpetuum." This may be the interpretation of the scribe of the cartulary, which was compiled about 1227 (Fauroux, *Recueil*, passim, in entries about this abbey).

Document 286, written in the late eleventh or early twelfth century (above, Chapter 2, n. 48), says (col. 218) that Bishop Robert (ca. 1025–48) of Coutances gave prebends which rightfully belonged to the canons to his relatives "in feodum et hereditatem," the only appearance in Normandy of the phrase "in fee and inheritance" in connection with the eleventh century.

In Document 84, the donors' heirs and their heirs are to hold from the abbey by hereditary right, but the tenement is never called a fief.

147. Above, this chapter, n. 139.

148. Document 20, dated 1074, which gives (or restores) to the cathedral of Bayeux the tenements Grimold du Plessis forfeited for rebellion in 1047, comes closest: "ipse perfidus, pro reatu . . . , ea jure justiciae sibi *et heredibus suis* perdidit" (p. 5, emphasis added).

Because the inheritability of fiefs is one of the subjects about which Orderic has most cogently been accused of distorting eleventh-century evidence to fit his own ideas, his assertions must be discounted as evidence for the eleventh century. See Chibnall, "Droits"; Chibnall, in OV, 2:xxxvi–xxxvii; ibid., 4:xix–xx. Cf. the riposte by Holt, "Feudal Society, II," pp. 215–16.

149. On the state of development of rules of inheritance in eleventh-century Normandy, see Chibnall, *World,* pp. 22–23, 122–25; Chibnall, *Anglo-Norman England,* pp. 165–66, and, by implication, 174–76.

It is often asserted that fiefs were from the beginning hereditary. Carabie, *Propriété foncière*, pp. 245–50, draws a distinction between *feoda*, which were hereditary, and *beneficia*, which were not, and seems to think that the change in terminology whereby *feodum* replaces *beneficium* in the course of the eleventh century demonstrates that by the end of that century fiefs were hereditary; he is widely followed, most recently by Bates, *Normandy*, pp. 122, 126. These processes, however, even if both occurred, could have been contemporaneous without being connected; and without the semantic change as evidence for the legal change, very little remains to indicate whether there was a legal change. Carabie, *Propriété foncière*, p. 247, makes too much of the phrase "beneficium quod Gislebertus tenuit de me quando erat eques" (Document 27, p. 1) as constituting an example of "un benefice qui n'était pas héréditaire, pas même viager, mais simplement concédé pour la durée d'un service de chevalier": Gilbert may merely have renounced his benefice to become a monk; perhaps he became a monk at Saint-Ymer, beneficiary of the transfer, and his lord, like many another, here ratified the gift Gilbert had made to the abbey. The deduction from the same phrase by Musset, "Aristocratie," p. 92, that "apparemment quand le lien de dépendance a été rompu, le *statut* de chevalier a pris fin" (emphasis added), seems also to place much too much weight on a very brief remark.

150. Anselm's analogy: below, this chapter, at and in n. 154. Particular fiefs: below, Chapter 5, n. 26; Documents 264 (p. 418), 616, 755 (p. 161).

151. Above, this chapter, at n. 83: William Paynel will have the service of Hugh de Bricqueville or his son "if he is free of the abbot's summons"; but nothing is said about what will happen if Hugh or his son is not free except, by inference, that William will simply lose the service. WP, p. 260, says that one of the regents of Normandy in 1066 was Roger de Beaumont, who was "ob maturitatem aevi liberior ad negotia quae domi geruntur; filio adolescenti . . . officio militari tradito"; in other words, Roger's son did the military service which his father was too old to do well. In Document 208 (p. 313), Guy de Laval, "cum ipsi grandaevus esset et senio gravis," gave his eldest son, John, a knight, the two vills in Normandy which had been Guy's wife's dowry, "quia longinqua erant"; but, as the charter gives no reason to connect this endowment with the need to do service for the distant vills, this is probably not parallel to the case of Roger de Beaumont and his son.

152. OV, 2:80–82, for which see also above, this chapter, at n. 90.

153. Musset, "Autour des modalités"; Musset, "Apports scandinaves," pp. 571–72; Bates, *Normandy*, pp. 166–67.

154. Eadmer, *Vita Anselmi*, p. 94v; translation by Southern, ibid., p. 94r. Although this does not say that the inheritances had been fiefs before they were lost or would be fiefs after they were recovered, the context (e.g., above, this chapter, at n. 88) makes it likely that Anselm was thinking of tenements.

155. OV, 2:218–20; ibid., 4:100. The former incident occurred about 1067; the latter, possibly early in 1087 (ibid., 4:100, n. 2).

156. Document 262 (p. 412). Bourrienne, "Odon," 8:521–22, suggests that the offense for which William the Conqueror imprisoned Odo of Bayeux in 1082 was Odo's attempt to depart, unauthorized, with an army. Bates, "Character," pp. 16–17, discusses the evidence for Odo's alleged attempt to seize the papacy by force but does not try to explain why, if the allegation is true, the attempt should have been offensive to William. See also Mason, "Norman Earls," p. 156, n. 14.

157. WP, p. 52.

158. Ibid., p. 62. The other historians agree that William of Arques was disinherited and/or exiled: WJ, p. 120; OV, 1:159; ibid., 4:84. William of Arques signs Documents 204 and 211, two ducal acts for Saint-Julien de Tours dated after his rebellion. Both are also signed by the other great rebel of Duke William's reign, his cousin Guy of Burgundy. WP, p. 20, says that Guy, too, was pardoned and allowed to remain in Normandy after his revolt but chose not to do so; the passage says nothing about his possessions except that his castle of Brionne was surrendered to the duke. Guy, but not William of Arques, also signed Documents 64 and 246. Because none of these charters survives in the original, it is not possible to tell whether the rebels' signatures were added after the fact, perhaps, so far as the two for Saint-Julien de Tours are concerned, while they were in exile in the vicinity of Tours, like the probable supporter of one of them whose gift is the subject of Document 211 and whose disinheritance is likely to be another example of the escheat of a fief (below, Chapter 5, n. 83). The signature list of

Document 211 is uncomfortably similar to that of Document 204 and may have been copied from it, though the contents of the charter are rehearsed in Documents 223/224, which do not otherwise seem tainted. On the grounds of the signatures of William of Arques and Guy of Burgundy, Bates, *Normandy*, pp. 91 (n. 88), 256, rejects the authenticity of Documents 204 and 211. Holt, *What's in a Name?* p. 19, n. 80, however, accepts the charters' authenticity and says that they "confirm William of Poitiers' statement" about Guy of Burgundy.

159. OV, 4:88.

160. Document 319. On this affair, see Le Maho, "Seigneuries," pp. 56–57, 92–93.

161. Gilbert Crispin, *Vita*, p. 90.

162. OV, 2:60–64; quotation from p. 65. Document 432 may include an example of escheat for departure; see the interpretation of Musset, "Huit essais," p. 53 and n. 35.

163. OV, 4:198.

164. See above, Chapter 2, at and in n. 17, for the general tendency not to preserve documents recording temporary alienations. With reference specifically to rental tenements, see Delisle, *Etudes*, p. 55; Carabie, *Propriété foncière*, p. 308. For France in general, see Schnapper, "Baux," p. 349; for Anglo-Norman England, see Lennard, *Rural England*, pp. 174–75.

Except for Carabie's book, which is primarily on the thirteenth century, little has been written on these tenements in Normandy. Schnapper, "Baux," does not discuss Normandy; Lennard's book provides illuminating insights into post-Conquest English practice but does not attempt to look across the Channel. Delisle's pages on the subject in *Etudes* are rarely helpful, and his references are almost entirely to transactions dating from the late twelfth century or later. Apparently on that basis, Yver, *Contrats*, concludes that such arrangements were virtually nonexistent before the late twelfth century; see pp. 13 (with n. 3), 16, 21, 79 (with n. 2). M. de Boüard, as quoted below, this chapter, n. 167, thinks that they existed from the beginning of the twelfth century at the latest.

165. Delisle, *Etudes*, p. 55.

166. Ibid., chap. 2; Carabie, *Propriété foncière*, passim. The earliest list of peasants' rents and services of which I know which is intended to be a complete list is Document 758, on which see above, Chapter 2, at and in n. 52. Incomplete lists may be found in Document 730, a record of disseisins of such rents and services perpetrated upon the abbey of Mont-Saint-Michel after the death of William the Conqueror; and Document 731, a record of similar disseisins perpetrated between 1061 and 1106. Document 314 is another list of disseisins, but it does not mention peasants' services as such.

167. Carabie, *Propriété foncière*, passim, distinguishes "contractual" tenures from the "statutory" tenures characteristic of domainal organization. Of the latter, the type I am attempting to exclude from consideration here, he gives the following definition, ibid., p. 179: "Aucun rapport contractuel n'intervient entre le seigneur et chacun de ses tenanciers. Ceux-ci héritent, avec la tenure qu'ils reçoivent de leurs ancêtres, de toutes les charges qui pèsent uniformément sur les tenures de l'espèce dont la leur fait partie"; see also ibid., p. 227. M. de Boüard, "Normandie," p. 160, adopts the same distinction; he adds, p. 161, "La Normandie fut, de tous les Etats de la France féodale, la première à pratiquer, dès le début du XIIe siècle au plus tard, ces formes contractuelles de concession foncière," i.e., those forms which will be discussed here.

Domainal organization in Normandy in the tenth and eleventh centuries was subject to many forces leading to change. No matter how many of the peasant inhabitants of the area in Carolingian days survived into tenth-century Normandy, there must have been considerable resettlement of areas of Normandy which had been devastated in the course of the Viking attacks. Some of the settlers were doubtless Scandinavian in origin and some Frankish. The evidence on these matters is scanty, and scholarly interpretations vary considerably; see above, Chapter 1, at nn. 28–34 and the references in those notes. In the eleventh century settlement continued with the founding of bourgs and the clearing of forests and other wastes; see the references in the next note; Deck, "Formation"; Deck, "Essai"; Le Maho, "Seigneuries," esp. pp. 9–11, 17–18, 106. Nevertheless, most peasants in most areas of eleventh-century Normandy were inhabitants of old areas of settlement; they were probably descended from previous inhabitants and probably held on terms similar to those of their ancestors. On the basic continuity of domainal organization from Carolingian to eleventh-century Normandy, in addition to Carabie, see Navel, "Recherches sur les anciennes mesures"; Musset, "Notes pour servir"; Musset, "Observations historiques"; Musset, "Autour de la seigneurie"; Bates, *Normandy*, pp. 22–23, 32; and many of the articles on vavassors cited below, this chapter, n. 177.

168. The fundamental works are Génestal, *Tenure en bourgage*, and Legras, *Bourgage de Caen*. For more recent studies, see Boussard, "Hypothèses"; Musset, "Transformation"; Musset, "Recherches sur Bayeux"; Musset, "Recherches sur les bourgs"; Musset, "Invasions"; Musset, "Actes inédits, VI"; Musset, "Peuplement"; Piletta, "Bourgs."

It is doubtful that burgage was a distinct type of tenure or status at this time, although the term had appeared by the end of the century (Yver, "Droit privé," p. 137). Ibid., p. 157, suggests that burgage as a category of tenure was the creation of the author of the mid-thirteenth-century *Summa de legibus*. Musset, "Peuplement," pp. 199–200, goes even further.

169. Saint-Martin de Sées: below, this chapter, at and in nn. 190–91; Document 623. Troarn: below, this chapter, at n. 209. Hugh: below, this chapter, at n. 226. For Hugh as a lord, see below, Chapter 8, at and in n. 1. Wightman, "Famille," p. 272, suggests that a substantial part of the Lacy family's holding from the bishop of Bayeux may have been at rent rather than in fee in the late eleventh and twelfth centuries; see also Wightman, *Lacy Family*, pp. 215, 220–21. The charter cited below, this chapter, n. 228, would provide another example of a highly placed person, Gerald son of William the Conqueror's butler Gerald, holding a rental tenement—if it could be used with confidence; but it cannot.

170. E.g., below, Chapter 5, at and in nn. 25 and 53.

171. Below, pp. 92–94, 110–12.

172. Musset, "Autour de la seigneurie," p. 161. Cf. for the thirteenth century, Carabie, *Propriété foncière*, pp. 244–45, 293.

173. Delisle, *Etudes*, pp. 17–25; Duval, "De l'état," pp. 35–36; Legras, *Bourgage*, pp. 34–36; Lagouëlle, *Essai*, pp. 131–32; Powicke, *Loss*, p. 48 and n. 58; Prentout, "Règne," p. 65; Gleason, *Ecclesiastical Barony*, pp. 56–57; Musset, "Autour de la seigneurie," p. 160; Musset, "Peuplement," p. 195; Musset, "Observations sur l'histoire"; Musset, "Quelques observations"; M. de Boüard, "Duché," p. 17; M. de Boüard, "Sur les origines," pp. 185–86; Yver, "Caractères originaux de l'Ouest," pp. 20–21 and 21, n. 1; Yver, "Caractères originaux de Normandie," pp. 320–21; Bates, *Normandy*, pp. 23, 94–95.

For some expressions of doubt or disagreement, see Chesnel, *Cotentin*, pp. 237–50; Corbett, "Development," p. 490; Carabie, *Propriété foncière*, pp. 217–19; Musset, "Notes pour servir," pp. 68–69; Musset, "Actes inédits, II," pp. 150–51; Musset, "Apports scandinaves," p. 565; and possibly below, this chapter, n. 211, on *gersimonia*.

174. Bates, *Normandy*, pp. 106–9, 111.

175. One also finds *agricola*, *alodarius* (on which, see below, Chapter 5, at and in nn. 63–66), *bordarius*, *censarius*, *colonus*, *conditionarius*, *cottarius*, *mansionarius*, *ortolanus* and *vernaculus*. *Servus*, *ancilla*, *mancipia*, and so on, are very rare. On the terminology of the Norman social classes, see Delisle, *Etudes*, chap. 1; Musset, "Notes pour servir," pp. 70–75; Gleason, *Ecclesiastical Barony*, pp. 54–57. See also Musset, "Tenure," on *bordarii*.

The meaning of *hospites* is a special problem. There is general though tentative agreement that they probably were characterized by somewhat more favorable conditions than other peasants but no agreement as to what their conditions were; see Delisle, *Etudes*, pp. 8–14; Chesnel, *Cotentin*, p. 243; Corbett, "Development," p. 490; Musset, "Notes pour servir," pp. 72, 75 and n. 204; Musset, "Peuplement," p. 182; Yver, "Droit privé," pp. 136–37.

The phrases *franci* or *liberi homines* also occur, sometimes in contradistinction to one or more of the terms for peasants, but the meaning of "free men" and which peasants were members of the group are unsettled questions; see Delisle, *Etudes*, pp. 3–8; Guilhiermoz, *Essai*, pp. 360–61, n. 39, and p. 363 and n. 43; Gleason, *Ecclesiastical Barony*, pp. 55–57; Musset, "Notes pour servir," pp. 71, 75 and n. 204; Hollyman, *Développement*, pp. 76–77; and many of the discussions of vavassors, below, this chapter, n. 177.

176. This is equally true for persons known to be in the upper class; see, for example, Musset, "Aristocratie," pp. 88–93, though not all his conclusions can be accepted (e.g., above, this chapter, n. 149, and below, Chapter 5, n. 53). See also Gonthier and Le Bas, "Analyse," p. 26.

177. For attempts to define the status of vavassors in Normandy and the nature of their tenure(s) and services, see especially Navel, "Recherches sur les institutions féodales," pp. 77–115, and his earlier works as cited there. See also Delisle, *Etudes*, pp. 5–7, 32–34, 78, 126–27; Guilhiermoz, *Essai*, pp. 183–88; Sauvage, *Troarn*, p. 196; Corbett, "Development," p. 490; Gleason, *Ecclesiastical Barony*, pp. 54, 76–77, 78; Bloch, *Feudal Society*, p. 177; Carabie, *Propriété foncière*, passim; Musset, "Notes pour servir," pp. 71, 74–75 and n. 204; Musset, "Autour de la seigneurie," pp. 161–62; Hardouin, "Clécy," p. 38; Hardouin, "Manses," pp. 361–63; M. de Boüard, "Duché," pp. 7–8, 14; Chanteux, "Quelques notes"; Matthew, *Norman Conquest*, pp. 63–65; Brown, *Normans*, p. 40.

Like "vavassor," the words *serviens*, *famulus*, and *minister* are found in some contexts which imply honorable status and others which imply peasant status; but they are rarer than "vavassor" and have been much less studied. For a *famulus* who was a knight, see below, Chapter 7, n. 74. For the status of such persons in Normandy, see Chesnel, *Cotentin*, p. 113; Génestal, "Histoire," p. 87; M. de Boüard, "Duché," p. 29; and esp. Navel, "Vavassories," pp. 143–48, suggesting that, at least in the two vills which are the subject of the article, serjeanties were the same as vavassories.

178. The land Roger de Croismare's father-in-law Gilbert gave to Saint-Pierre de Préaux (above, this chapter, at and in n. 114) included two knights whose consent is not reported. For other transfers of knights without their reported consent and references to knights as mere appurtenances of land, see below, Chapter 6, at and in n. 75; Bates, *Normandy*, p. 110 and the references there in n. 64, to which should be added Documents 166 (p. 225), 250, 255 (p. 400), 297 (p. 108), 410 (pp. 75–76), 616, 832 (twice), and perhaps 749 (f° 750).

179. Legras, *Bourgage de Caen*, pp. 4–5 and p. 4, n. 2; Carabie, *Propriété foncière*, pp. 254–58, 284–93; Gleason, *Ecclesiastical Barony*, p. 55; Yver, comments on Navel, p. 301; Navel, "Recherches sur les institutions féodales," pp. 40–58, 168–69; M. de Boüard, "Duché," p. 7. On the incompleteness in Normandy, even in the thirteenth century, of the distinction between nobles and nonnobles, see Yver, "Caractères originaux de Normandie," passim, esp. pp. 317–19.

180. Leaving: below, Chapter 8, at and after n. 11. Alienating: below, Chapter 8, at and in nn. 79–80; a good many of the charters cited below, Chapter 7, n. 26, probably also record alienations by peasants. Witnessing: below, Chapter 7, at nn. 77–83.

181. Documents 436, 626, 629 (f° 44r), 651, 653 (f° 56r), 664 (f° 61r), 666 (f° 62v), 679, 680 (f° 78r), 681, 683 (f° 79r). *Metearius* is used as a last name or an occupational designation in Documents 436, 623, 635 (f° 47v), 670 (f° 66r), and the charters witnessed by *metearii* cited below, Chapter 7, n. 80. *Mediatoria* and *mediator* are alternative latinizations of the terms.

182. Documents 273 (p. 447), 635 (f° 47v), 758 (f° 22v).

183. Below, Chapter 5, at and in nn. 12–14.

184. Document 569 (f° 60v): "ad medietariam Godaldo secundum consuetudinem ville."

185. Below, Chapter 7, at nn. 77–83, where n. 80 lists the places in which witnesses called *metearii* can be found.

186. Delisle, *Etudes*, pp. 50–51, 461–64. See also Bouvris, "Possession," p. 171.

187. Document 695: "vineam suam, sicut ipse eam parcionaliter habebat cum duobus fratribus qui eam plantaverant, Durando videlicet et Willelmo, quorum etiam totam terram sicut ipsi et quidam alius eorum frater a Gisleberto tenebant."

188. Document 672: "Ricardus Paganellus particeps factus beneficii Sancti Martini Sagii, dedit . . . monachis . . . .xxx^ta^. libras unde ipsi monachi quandam terram . . . communiter inter se et Ricardum emerunt. Hoc quidem pacto ut dum Ricardus viveret totam terram cum illis excoleret, edificaret, ac tam terre quam tocius vestiture sive in hominibus sive in animalibus sive in frugibus medietatem reciperet. . . . Si autem vel ipse obiret vel alicubi ab hac terra recederet heres suus si congruum ad tenendam terram haberet, aut predictam partem patris a monachis teneret, aut octo libras ab eisdem reciperet. Quam totam conventionem . . . ipse Richardus . . . dimisit. . . . Nisi quod hoc solum retinuit, quod si ipse . . . unquam monachus fieri vellet predictum monasterium vel ipse intrare vel quendam filium suum si ei placeret monachum intromittere . . . valeret. Si autem neutrum faceret, dum in vicinitate nostra maneret . . . de supradicte terre bonis ad explendas suas necessitates habere valeret. De decem et octo autem equabus quas ipse ibi ad exercendam terram addivit, medietatem fructus dum in confinio nostro maneret sibi retinuerit."

189. Document 436.

190. Document 587 (f° 9v): "Cum domnus abbas Radulfus ceterique fratres . . . inter monasterium suum et molendinum quod dicitur de Valle quoddam vivarium abbatie sue . . . facere disposuissent . . . , Willelmum de Sivilleio . . . rogaverunt ut illius molendini redditus ad firmam que vulgo dicitur moesena sibi daret. . . . Constituto itaque die . . . ipse Willelmus . . . pro xxx sextariis annone per singulos annos, x quidem frumenti, xx vero annone multuragensis que valeat aut ordeum aut sigalum, dimissionem molendini de Valle concessit."

191.Document 589 (f° 11v): "totam medietatem illius firmae, que vocatur vulgo moisura, quam monachi ei debebant . . . pro x^{cem} libris Cenomannensium vendidit, quinque sextarios frumenti et x^{cem} ordei."

192. For this term, see Fourquin, "Au seuil," p. 586; Du Cange, *Glossarium*, 5:441, sv° *moiso*; *Novum Glossarium mediae latinitatis*, vol. *Ma–Nysus*, col. 700, sv° *moisona*.

193. Document 790.

194. Document 758 (f° 21v): "dedit abbatisse .x. solidos eo conventu quod eam debet habere et filii eius nec auferetur ab eis pro altero qui plus offerat."

195. Document 772 (f° 32v): ten years.

196. Below, this chapter, n. 200; this chapter, at and in nn. 201 and 226; Documents 758 (f° 22v) and 790 (includes carting).

197. Document 772 (f° 33r). The rent was to be paid in three installments, two of a hundred shillings each; the third of "alios [solidos]."

198. Document 99 (p. 524). It is not absolutely certain that *firmus fiscus* is synonymous with *firma*; but, in view of the scant details given, it seems likely. On the meaning of *fiscus* in eleventh-century Normandy, see Carabie, *Propriété foncière*, p. 248, n. 62 (on pp. 249–50). See also below, this chapter, n. 203.

199. Document 99 (p. 524): at the first Sunday in Lent; Document 790: half at Michaelmas and half at Christmas; Document 772 (f° 33r): at a term which is left blank in the manuscript, at Pentecost, and at the feast of St. Peter and St. Paul. Musset, "Sur les mutations," p. 292 and n. 5, suggests that the term left blank in the last instance cited should be Christmas; ibid., p. 293, suggests a date for the charter in Robert Curthose's reign.

200. Document 758 (f° 21r–21v): "Anschitillus . . . habet terram . . . in firma pro .xx.ix. minas avene et .iii. sextarios frumenti. . . . Sed femina putei factoris habet inde .iii. virgas et reddit inde .i. minam de his triginta minis." Because the document does not state how much Anketil held, it is impossible to calculate whether the amount his subtenant owed was proportional to the amount of land she held.

201. Document 688: "Harduinus de Beheriis ecclesiam de Merreio, dimissis omnibus calumniis quas de ea faciebat, sic a domno abbate Radulfo ceterisque fratribus . . . accepit ut presbiterium quidem in suo dominio haberet; de ceteris vero duobus ejusdem ecclesie partibus unoquoque anno duos modios frumenti et duos ordei et duos avene et . . . de recognitione unam libram incensi et unam piperis . . . fratribus redderet. Et hanc firmam in feodo accipiens legalem et sine uxore presbiterum ad judicium Sagiensis congregationis in predicta ecclesia se semper habiturum promisit, et factus homo predicti abbatis xx^ti libras cenomanensium dedit."

202. See below, Chapter 6, at nn. 187–200, for other examples of payments "in recognition" and the reasons for them.

203. One rental, in Document 824, is called a *beneficium*: the charter begins (f° 27r), "Convenientia inter abbatem johannem et filios Gilduini presbiteri: reddidit eis abbas collaudatione monachorum beneficium quod pater eorum ipso die per rectum tenebat . . . . " Because the father was a priest, however, *beneficium* probably means an ecclesiastical benefice, not a fief. The *firmus fiscus* which paid ten shillings annually (above, this chapter, at n. 198), might be a fee-farm, if *fiscus* was a synonym for *feodum* in Normandy at this time, but that is not certain (see Carabie, as cited above, this chapter, n. 198).

204. Delisle, *Etudes*, p. 45; Carabie, *Propriété foncière*, pp. 312–13, commenting primarily on the charter at issue here (but assuming that *feodum* meant hereditary tenure by this date); Navel, "A propos," p. 329; de Bieville, "Fieffermes, mode"; de Bieville, "Fieffermes, institution."

205. Document 879.

206. Documents 117, 734, 824 (f° 27r). The last charter and Document 381 present themselves as renewals of tenements held by the recipients' fathers; Document 381 may, therefore, also be relevant. So may the charter discussed below, this chapter, at and in n. 234. For the eleventh charter, see below, this chapter, at and in n. 221.

207. Grain: Document 824 (f° 27v): "unum modium puri frumenti." Money: Document 879 (p. 68): ten shillings; Document 381: ten shillings; Document 94: four shillings; Document 833: ten shillings; Document 636: twelve coins (*nummi*); Document 699: four shillings; Document 734: thirty shillings; Document 874: one hundred shillings; cf. below, this chapter, at and in n. 234, for a "rent" of twenty shillings. Both: Document 403: "II^os modios annone, octo scilicet frumenti sextarios, octo ordei, octo avene et XV solidos." Document 117 does not specify the amount of rent.

208. Document 381: the feast of St. Martin; Document 403: the fair of Le Pré; Document 734: Easter; Document 833: Pentecost; Document 879: the feast of All Saints.

209. Document 491.

210. Document 613 (f° 32r): "Concessit etiam idem Berlaius et Radulfus frater ejus Sancto Martino XX acras terre quas Rogerius filius Hermerii ab ipsis emerat quod ab eis recognoscebat. Ipsius igitur interventu Rogerii, concessit uterque Berlaius videlicet ac Radulfus ut quidquid eis inde Rogerius debebat Sancto Martino et monachis redderet et ab ipsis in antea omnino recognosceret. Pro hac quoque concessione habuerunt inter se duo fratres X solidos cenomanensium de pecunia predicti Rogerii."

211. Above, this chapter, at and in n. 201; Document 772, where the entry fine was twenty-six pounds and the rent over two hundred shillings per year; Document 699, where the entry fine was forty shillings and the rent was four shillings. In Document 99 (p. 524), the tenant gave Saint-Léger de Préaux the tithes he possessed in the vill which was granted to him as a *firmus fiscus*. Above, this chapter, at and in n. 194, may be another example, but the fine there is presented as a payment for a special purpose.

Legras, *Bourgage de Caen*, pp. 137–40, and Carabie, *Propriété foncière*, pp. 265–67, think that similar transactions in the late twelfth and thirteenth centuries were basically sales; e.g., Carabie, pp. 266–67: "le concédant cherche essentiellement à se procurer une somme d'argent contre l'abandon de sa terre; mais comme il veut conserver la satisfaction de pouvoir éventuellement recouvrer cette terre, il prend soin de retenir un cens, si modique soit-il." The rents in the eleventh-century cases which can be calculated are, however, comparatively high percentages of the fines: 10 percent in Document 699; at least 38 percent in Document 772. These sums scarcely seem so modest as to justify concluding that what was true a century later was already true at the time of these charters. I am inclined to think that such a fine represents the payer's desire to occupy the land rather than the recipient's desire to dispose of it. The few instances of references to tenants' security of tenure (below, this chapter, at and in nn. 221–25) imply that persons desirous of becoming tenants outnumbered the tenements to be had and, therefore, that aspiring entrants might have to proffer fines.

The only other possible evidence of entry fines for rental tenements in eleventh-century Normandy is a series of references to *gersimonia* in the charters of Fontenay, for which, see above, Chapter 3, at n. 241. I can find the word nowhere else. It must, I think, be a variant of *gersuma*, which in Anglo-Saxon and Anglo-Norman England could mean an entry fine (Lennard, *Rural England*, pp. 180–81). Du Cange, *Glossarium*, does not list *gersimonia*; under *gersuma*, 4:61, he gives the definition "apud Forenses Anglicos ut plurimum usurpatum legimus pro *fine*, seu pecunia, data in pactionem, et rei emptae vel conductae compensationem," and one of the passages which he cites in proof is Document 39 (p. 41), from Fontenay, where he reads *gersumis* for *gersimoniis*. As used by Fontenay, however, *gersimonia* sounds more like a regular burden upon agricultural land than an entry fine for a particular type of tenure; and the *Revised Medieval Latin Word-List*, which collects English usage, gives, p. 211, sv° *gersuma*, the definition " 'gersum,' premium, fine, esp. merchet." As merchetlike payments were known at least occasionally in Normandy in the thirteenth century (Carabie, *Propriété foncière*, pp. 218–19), that may have been what the charters of Fontenay intended by the use of the term.

212. Document 702: "Quidam vero eorum filius nomine Ricardus cui reliqua tertia contingebat pars . . . venit ad abbatem et monachos . . . , et talem cum eis de eadem domo conventionem fecit, ut si abbas vel monachi a rege anglorum impetrare possent, quod de eadem domo eis consuetudines omnes donaret, predictus filius Rotberti Ricardus sepedictam domum totam a Sancto Martino teneret et per singulos annos .xx^{ti}. solidos de recognitione donaret. Et hoc idem heres suus vel heredis heres vel aliquis cui urguente [*sic*] necessitate prefata domus venderetur. Quod tamen non nisi per prefatum abbatem vel monachos fieri posset, persolveret. Si autem a rege per predictum annum ut predictum est consuetudines domus obtinere non possent, a festivitate Sancti Laurentii sequentis anni usque in aliam festivitatem eiusdem sancti .x. libras a Ricardo abbas vel monachi pro tocius domus omnimoda venditione reciperent."

213. The striking exception is the statement in RT, interp., p. 259, that Esperleng, second husband of Duke William Longsword's wife Sprota, "molendina vallis Pistris ad firmam solitus erat tenere." As William Longsword was murdered in 942 and, according to ibid., p. 258, Sprota married Esperleng in a hurry to protect herself, this might be evidence of a farm in Normandy about 940. Robert of Torigny, however, was writing in the mid-twelfth century and may well have used a contemporary term to convey his meaning to his readers.

214. Late rentals: Documents 491, 874, 879. The designation *firmarius* occurs, in Document 259 (p. 407), more than a decade before 1080.

215. Documents 412 (p. 94) and 424 (p. 138).

216. Document 307, about Armentières, on the non-Norman bank of the Avre; Document 304, about the Corbonnais.

217. Documents 149 (p. 183) and 504.

218. Du Cange, *Glossarium*, 5:239–40, sv° *manufirma*; *Novum glossarium*, vol. *Ma–Nysus*, col. 167, sv° *manufirma*; Giry, *Manuel*, p. 862; E. Perrot, *Précis*, p. 225. The definition given by Guérard, *Saint-Père de Chartres*, 1:ccxxviii–ccxxx, and 2:847, sv° *manus firma*, is too specific to be relevant to the Norman examples.

219. *Novum glossarium*, vol. *Ma–Nysus*, col. 167.

220. Lennard, *Rural England*, p. 180.

221. Document 874: "tenere quanto duntaxat tempore eidem abbati et monachis placeret. . . . quanto idem abbas et monachi tempore vellent, ita scilicet ut quando voluerint possent eamdem ecclesiam cui voluerint alt[er]ius commendare absque ulla contradictione."

222. Above, this chapter, at and in n. 194.

223. Document 94: "Notum sit . . . quoniam Rainaldus, filius Vileberti Pain, et Eva et Auffrida, soror [*sic*] ejus, dederunt Sanctae Trinitati . . . pratum unum, quod unoquoque anno reddit IIII solidos . . . ; et si Willelmus, filius Rainerii, reddiderit bene IIII^or solidos, tenebit quandiu voluerit; et si alius venerit qui amplius reddere voluerit, Willelmus supradictus libere reddet, et nos ad libitum nemini alio plus reddenti dabimus." I should like to translate the last clause as: "if another should come who should wish to render more, the aforesaid William should surrender [the tenement] freely and we will give [it] as we wish to anyone else who renders more." My interpretation, however, depends upon the conjecture that the double negative of his native French influenced the scribe of this charter into using *nemo* without an accompanying *non* to mean "anyone" rather than "no one"; but in the eleventh century the double negative was by no means required. The use of *ad libitum* seems to make it difficult to translate the clause, as would otherwise be plausible, as "the aforesaid William should render [the higher rent] freely, and we will give [the tenement] to no one else who offers more." The charters of La Trinité du Mont are usually comparatively well drafted, but this seems to be an exception.

224. Document 99 (p. 524). Nothing is said about the preceding tenant, if there was one.

225. Document 772: "eo pacto ut transacto termino si congregationi visum fuerit ipsi eam relinquent quamdiu illis placuerit. Sinautem alii dabunt. Infra ipsum quoque terminum si viderint eum supra modum gravari in ipsis erit si aliquam misericordiam remissionis cuiusque illi facere voluerint. Denique in ipsis similiter erit facultas firme alii dande vel ei relinquende, non in ipso."

226. Document 412 (p. 94). The later version of this gift, in Document 424 (p. 138), differs somewhat in wording but not in sense. There may be a second example, for which see below, this chapter, n. 228.

227. Document 504 (p. 15). For Normandy, see Carabie, *Propriété foncière*, p. 270. For France, see Giry, *Manuel*, p. 862; Schnapper, "Baux," pp. 350–51; G. Mollat, "Restitution," p. 404.

228. Above, this chapter, at nn. 5–8, and the references in n. 8. Document 879 apparently specifies confiscation only for refusal of hospitality (above, this chapter, at n. 44), not if the rent is not paid, though poor drafting may be responsible. Document 434 may be an example, concerning a rent, in which even nonfraudulent inability to perform would lead to permanent confiscation: a claimant against Saint-Ouen receives the land which he claims in return for fealty and an annual rent of four pounds; the tenement will be held by the claimant and his son; "cum vero ab hac conventione in aliquo declinaverit, sive pauperitatis adtenuatione, vel etiam qualibet fraude, igitur demum si placet illum ab eadem possessione amo[ve]re, licebit, ut sic imperpetuum ad illam non reverteretur" (p. 126). The emendation to *amovere* is Musset's. For Musset's arguments for the authenticity of this charter, see "Actes inédits, VI," p. 120 and n. 7; I do not find them convincing.

229. Document 445.

230. Below, this chapter, at and in n. 391.

231. Document 790: "Et quia predictam possessionem in melius restaurare decrevi."

232. Document 519. The grant was later turned into a mortgage: below, this chapter, at n. 306.

233. Document 734: "quia idem Turaldus et uxor sua emma corpora sua post mortem sepelienda et omnem partem pecunie sue nostre ecclesie concesserunt."

234. Document 700: "Sericum sacerdotem terram quam sanctus Martinus habebat, in territorio Trumi tali pacto . . . recipisse ut datis in principio XX[ti] libris postea quamdiu ipse eam teneret semper a monachis recognosceret ac de recognitione in uno quoque anno XX[ti] solidos persolveret, si tamen tamta [*sic*] pax in patria esset ut predicta terra im [*sic*] pace excoli valeret, et hanc eandem conventionem est executurus quicumque illam terram per se est habiturus, scilicet quidam frater suus vel quedam soror sua vel aliquis duorum nepotum quos ipse Sericus habebat. His enim quinque, quamdiu aliquis eorum vixerit, predicto pacto a monachis habere concessa, post eorum omnium mortem nullo successore eorum reclamante in dominium sancti reditura. Sciendum enim quod omnes isti, tam soror quam frater vel nepotes per ipsum Sericum in beneficio loci recepti sunt a . . . abbate et monachis hoc modo ut si in fine uniuscujusque eorum corpus cum omni sua pecunia ad monasterium deferretur a monachis sepeliendum reciperetur, sin autem tamen ubicumque corpus jaceret sanctus Martinus totam partem defuncti haberet." Perhaps in the same connection Seric and his brother-in-law Ernuceus rented from the abbey a plot at Trun on which to build a house: Document 699, which has been treated as an ordinary rental tenement.

235. Below, Chapter 6, at nn. 187–200.

236. Above, this chapter, at and in nn. 210 and 212.

237. See also Duval, "De l'état," pp. 35–36. For another example of a payment whose amount depended on whether there was peace or war, see above, this chapter, at and in n. 45.

238. All are cited in the following notes. Document 823 (discussed below, this chapter, n. 242) and Document 418 (discussed below, this chapter, at n. 264) are not included in this count. Another possible instance is Document 410 (discussed above, Chapter 3, n. 115).

239. Document 550 (f° 117v) refers to one as a *mutuum*.

240. Documents 822 and 826 (f° 30v). Document 159 says that the estate granted to a man alone is to come back "post decessum autem ejus et uxoris sue," which presumably means that, if the wife survived her husband, she was to keep the entire estate until she died.

241. Document 274 (p. 453).

242. No specification is made in Document 387. In Document 823, Ansfrid son of Osbern sets up a life estate for his wife because he is about to go to Jerusalem; he provides that she will hold it for life but may not alienate it, and then adds, "nec etiam ego si reversus fuero" (f° 26r). Whether this means that he and his wife would become joint tenants if he returned is not stated. For the date and for more on Ansfrid, see Musset, "Recherches sur les pèlerins," pp. 142–43.

243. Respectively, Documents 274 (p. 453) and 387 (p. 101).

244. Document 402 (p. 692).

245. Below, Chapter 5, at nn. 30–32.

246. Document 710.

247. Of the twenty-one certain life estates, only six do not contain such statements: Document 387, where the relatives' rights are considered in a different manner (above, this chapter, at n. 243); Documents 274 (p. 453) and 386 (p. 99), two versions of one transaction, where the same is true; and Documents 87, 522, 550 (f° 117v), 751. The last of these seems to be a summary of a charter rather than the charter itself (below, Chapter 6, n. 108); it is therefore possible that the full charter would have included a prohibition of inheritance. Eliminating this case from consideration and counting the

two cases from Saint-Wandrille among those which discuss the problem of relatives, only three of twenty charters are silent on this subject. Even a proportion of fifteen out of twenty-one is conspicuously high compared to the rate of mentions of relatives' rights in all transfers considered as a group.

248. Document 832 (f° 17r): "ut quoad viveret . . . in sua dominicatura retineret, nulli alio homini quicquam de ipsa terra tribuens. . . . Porro jam dictus Gozelinus parvipendens convenientiam cum abbate et fratribus habitam, beneficium acceptum non solum non auxit, sed etiam ad nihilum redegit, atque suis hominibus contra statutam pactionem distribuit." The events occurred between 1028 and 1035. Document 159, which records the grant of the life estate, says that it was given "tali modo ut in vita sua habeat . . . , post decessum autem ejus et uxoris sue . . . in proprium jus prefati monasterii redeat absque calumnia cujuscumque ordinis vel persone," but does not mention any prohibition on alienation while Wascelin was alive.

249. Document 499 is a letter of Hugh bishop of Avranches renouncing the right of anyone else to claim on his death the life estate which he holds from Mont-Saint-Michel; it anathematizes anyone "sive successor seu parens aut heres" who might raise a claim. Document 213, his similar letter about a life estate held from Fécamp, anathematizes only "aliquis ejus quomodo successor." In each of these letters *successor* may be intended to refer to any later bishop of Avranches, the appropriate counterpart for this grantee of relatives in the case of a lay grantee.

250. Document 487.

251. Document 488.

252. Document 5, a short notice from the abbey, reports that, apparently soon after these actions, Richard and William surrendered all their rights at Trun to the abbey and that Richard placed the gift on the altar; it says nothing about the life estate or the mortgage and, by itself, would give the misleading impression of a simple initial donation.

253. Document 785 (f° 158v).

254. Below, Chapter 6, esp. at nn. 151–86.

255. Document 820 (f° 22v): "ob recordationem." For Seric, see above, this chapter, at and in n. 234.

256. Below, Chapter 6, at n. 188.

257. Below, Chapter 6, at nn. 187–200.

258. Six charters say nothing on the subject. Of these, two are letters Bishop Hugh of Avranches wrote to Fécamp and Mont-Saint-Michel: above, this chapter, n. 249. Hugh hardly gives a complete account of either life estate and stresses the spiritual benefits to himself of his making sure that the estates return to their grantors, rather than the material benefits to the grantors. Another is the probably summary notice of a life estate granted by Fécamp, above, this chapter, n. 247; it is possible that the original charter did give this information. The fourth is a son's brief reference to his father's life estate, above, this chapter, at n. 246; as the son is concerned with his own sin in trying to keep the estate, it is not surprising that he does not say why it was granted in the first place. In other words, it is easy to see why these four charters are silent. The fifth charter, the one about Richard son of Wascelin de Trun, is much more concerned with arrangements for the future than with arrangements in the past; the mention of the life estate is subordinate to the description of the mortgage, except for the question of inheritability. The sixth charter, Document 823, is laconic; and the estate it records was arranged under special circumstances: above, this chapter, n. 242. Moreover, the land of which the estate consisted had earlier been given to the abbey, Fécamp, by the husband of the recipient. It is, therefore, possible that this life estate was created by Fécamp without expectation of reward as a favor to a benefactor, especially since he was about to go off on a pilgrimage to Jerusalem.

259. Document 159: "tali modo ut in vita sua habeat, edificet, amplificet et carrucis, porcariis, pecudibus repleat"; Document 820 (f° 22v): "eo tenore ut ipsam eccle-

siam quam perficere decrevimus in quantum potuerit ope et adjutorio nobiscum expleat"; Document 821 (f° 24r): "tali scilicet tenore ut in vita sua habeat et in quantum potuerit decimas et terram adcrescere et multiplicare studeat."

260. Document 87: "terram, ad unam domum construendam, in castello Archensi . . . : eo conventione ut, post obitum ejus, eadem terra cum domo libere monachis redeat." See below, this chapter, at and in n. 391, for another example of this form of compensation.

261. Documents 87 (as quoted in the preceding note) and 821 (f° 24r) do so; the other two instances do not. Document 790, on which see above, this chapter, at n. 231, also does so.

262. Documents 159, 386 (p. 99) with 274 (p. 453), 541, 822 (f° 25v). See also the analogous clauses in the complex agreements made by Saint-Martin de Sées, below, this chapter, at and in nn. 391 and 392.

263. Document 158.

264. Document 418 (p. 128). Document 274 (p. 453) may be another example, although the other version of the same transaction (Document 386, p. 99) makes it seem less similar to these.

265. Document 386 (p. 99); Document 785 (f° 158v), for the return of which estate see above, this chapter, at n. 253.

266. Documents 175 and 550 (f° 117v).

267. Document 285 (cols. 202–3). The charter continues with standard phrases about return of the churches when Hugh dies. For the dispute and how it was treated in court, see below, Chapter 7, at and in n. 46; Chapter 11, at and in n. 22.

268. Above, this chapter, at and in n. 234; Documents 820 (f° 22v) and 821 (f° 24r).

269. Above, this chapter, at and in n. 211. See also below, this chapter, at and in n. 392, where the grantee is a layman but the transaction is too complex to be called a simple life estate.

270. Documents 87 and 821 (f° 24v).

271. Documents 274 (p. 453) with 386, 820 (f° 22v), 826 (f° 30v), and probably 550 (f° 117v). Génestal, "Formes," p. 226, states that the purpose of grants of life estates was precisely to induce the grantees to make post-obit gifts of themselves (for burial) and their movable possessions; but this seems too narrow. See below, this chapter, at nn. 366–89, on bequests of *substantia*.

272. Above, this chapter, at and in n. 267. For other examples, see above, this chapter, at and in n. 114; Documents 539 (f° 101v) and 733; and perhaps above, this chapter, at and in n. 201, and below, this chapter, at n. 274. The agreements above, Chapter 3, at and in n. 138, and this chapter, at and in n. 221, are analogous. The charter quoted above, this chapter, n. 228, would be another example if it could be used with confidence. See also below, this chapter, at nn. 279–81, and the references in n. 281.

273. Document 387 (p. 100).

274. Document 522 (p. 127).

275. Lennard, *Rural England*, pp. 166–67, finds a very flexible use of the life estate in Anglo-Norman England, up to and including to secure "the patronage or friendship of a powerful lessee" (p. 167), which is similar to the apparent flexibility of the Norman grants. For similar instances to the south of Normandy, see S. D. White, "*Pactum*," pp. 295–96.

276. Partly because of another unusual clause in the charter, for which see below, Chapter 11, at and in n. 1.

277. Documents 285 (cols. 202–3) and 550 overlap John's abbacy but by only one year.

278. Document 499; Adigard des Gautries, "Noms des lieux des îles," p. 30.

279. Musset, "Vie économique," p. 67, n. 3, attributes Fécamp's "plus grand usage des pièces administratives écrites"—greater than that of any other Norman church of

the time—to John's Italian origins, but not the types of transfers recorded in those acts. See also Musset, "Actes inédits, I," p. 121.

280. Musset, "Actes inédits, I," p. 119; Musset, "Contribution," pp. 64–65; Musset, "Notes sur la gestion"; Musset, "Vie économique," passim. See also Musset, *Actes*, p. 46.

281. Musset, "Contribution," pp. 62–63; Musset, "Vie économique," pp. 75, 77–79. See also Chibnall, "Fécamp," p. 127. Guillot, *Comte*, 1:161 and n. 137, finds similar behavior—leading to the same sort of transfer—on the part of the counts of Anjou in the late tenth and eleventh centuries vis-à-vis the abbey of Saint-Aubin d'Angers.

282. No life estates granted by Fécamp are extant from the abbacy of John's successor, William II, who was abbot until 1108. This may mean little, for the charters of Fécamp do not survive particularly well. It may mean that Fécamp grew disenchanted with the life estate as too dangerous; indeed, this may have happened while John was abbot, for all the life estates he granted which can be narrowly dated come from approximately the first three of his five decades of rule. Or it may reflect some easing of the pressure on Fécamp which Musset describes.

283. Génestal, *Rôle*, pp. 1–86; Allix and Génestal, "Opérations." See also Delisle, *Etudes*, pp. 206–11; Sauvage, *Troarn*, pp. 218–27; Yver, *Contrats*, pp. 170–75.

284. On rarity, see Sauvage, *Troarn*, p. 226; Musset, "A-t-il existé," p. 288; Musset, "Vie économique," p. 74. On purpose, see Génestal, *Rôle*, pp. 73–77; Allix and Génestal, "Opérations," pp. 618–20, 629.

285. See above, Chapter 2, at and in n. 17, for the general tendency not to preserve documents recording temporary alienations. With reference specifically to mortgages, see Génestal, *Rôle*, pp. 16–18, 74; Allix and Génestal, "Opérations," pp. 624–25; Sauvage, *Troarn*, pp. 225–26; Legras, *Bourgage de Caen*, pp. 146–47; Musset, "Notes sur la gestion."

Of charters which mention mortgages or mortgaged property, alone or in simple contexts (that is, excluding charters which sum up whole sets of transactions between a donor and a church including one or more mortgages), thirty-seven refer to mortgages in the past (thirty-nine in all) in connection with more recent gifts or sales; only nine refer to current mortgages (thirteen in all). Moreover, of the forty-six charters, six are originals, of which three concern a total of six current mortgages, whereas the other three concern five past mortgages. In other words, half the originals concern current mortgages but only 17.5 percent of the nonoriginals do; and knowledge of 46 percent of the current mortgages depends on originals, but originals account for only 12.8 percent of the past mortgages. The conclusion must be that the relatively rare survival of originals is a major reason—perhaps the principal one—for the apparent preponderance of mortgages which were converted into gifts and sales. Presumably, when a *scriptorium* decided to draw up a retrospective charter or to compile a pancart or a cartulary from the charters in its charge, it relatively infrequently bothered to include out-of-date agreements which had resulted in no permanent acquisitions.

286. The use of the term *vadimonium* was not entirely standardized. A synonym was *pignus*; see this chapter, quotation at n. 293, and Document 167 (p. 227), which explicitly identifies *pignus* and *vadium* as synonyms which mean a mortgage. For three other uses of *pignus* in this context, see Document 99 (pp. 521–22). For other uses of *vadium* in this context, see Documents 296 (p. 230), 409 (p. 69), 413 (p. 109), 838, and probably below, this chapter, n. 322. Moreover, just as *pignus* normally meant a "pledge," so could *vadimonium* or *vadium*; see Documents 96 (p. 425), 309 (col. 202), 312, 440 (p. 180, echoed in OV, 3:124–26), 756, and perhaps below, Chapter 9, at and in n. 23. Document 267 records Duke William's endowment of canons in the chapel of Notre-Dame at Cherbourg, which was made as the result of a vow William had made when gravely ill; it refers to "comitissa . . . que . . . super altare posuit comitis vagium" while William was ill (p. 432). The word *vagium*, which Fauroux, *Recueil*, p. 469 (the Index rerum, compiled by Lucien Musset), refers to as a "terme corrompu, non iden-

tifié," seems to be *vadium* used in the sense of a pledge; it is so understood by Couppey, "Abbaye," p. 58, and by Stenton, *William*, p. 137 (see below, this chapter, n. 378). These, however, are anomalous instances. In the vast majority of its appearances in the charters, *vadimonium* means a loan of the type under discussion.

287. In Document 461 (p. 192) the mortgagor receives a horse; only the value of the horse need be restored, not the horse itself. In Document 291, a mortgagor receives both money and a horse; only the money need be repaid, "relicta sibi equitatura."

288. On the differences between these transactions, see Génestal, *Rôle*, pp. 1–3. Vifgages could be so arranged as to provide the gagee with interest: the duration could be set overly long or the profits of what was gaged could be deliberately underestimated; see Génestal, *Rôle*, pp. 2–3; Allix and Génestal, "Opérations," pp. 627–28.

289. See below, this chapter, at n. 300, for one example of a mortgage later converted into a vifgage. Génestal, *Rôle*, pp. 3–16, concludes, for the entire period from the eleventh through the thirteenth centuries, that mortgages greatly outnumbered vifgages. See also Delisle, *Etudes*, pp. 208–10. I do not know the source of the assertion in Chibnall, *World*, p. 56, that abbeys "frequently made use of the contract known as a *vivum gagum*."

290. It is almost impossible to calculate the interest rate on mortgages because charters never directly state the annual profits of the mortgaged property. Calculations have been attempted, on the basis of the mortgage cited below, this chapter, at n. 300, by Allix and Génestal, "Opérations," pp. 626–27, who conclude that the rate was 50 percent per year, and by Sauvage, *Troarn*, pp. 223–24 and p. 224, n. 2, who concludes that it was slightly less than 25 percent per year. Génestal, *Rôle*, p. 61, on the basis of his calculations, which are discussed below, this chapter, at n. 323, concludes that the usual rate was 15 percent; but he does so only by assuming that the annual rate of return on land was about the same in the eleventh century as it was when he was writing.

291. Document 50.

292. Probably for the same reason, Documents 461 (p. 192) and 462, both from Saint-Evroul, specify that mortgages must be redeemed on a particular date at the end of the term or on the anniversary of that date and include provisions about the produce of the land. See also Génestal, *Rôle*, pp. 40–42.

293. OV, 4:244. Ibid., p. 248, says that Orderic heard the story from Walchelin himself. Sauvage, *Troarn*, p. 227, says, "L'*usura*, telle que la décrit Orderic Vital dans un passage de l'anecdote fameuse . . . , n'est pas à confondre avec le mort-gage." I do not see why not: as described, the transaction fulfills all the criteria for a mortgage.

294. Movables gaged: Document 249 (p. 385), a cape; Document 592 (f° 16v), a sword; Document 668 (f° 64v), a horse. In one instance service may have been gaged: see below, Chapter 5, at and in n. 98. On such loans, see Génestal, *Rôle*, p. 21 and n. 1.

295. Yver, *Contrats*, pp. 168–69.

296. Document 295. Génestal dates the charter to 1142. It has a very unusual dating clause, which Delisle, in BN, ms. fr. n. a. 21831, f° 479r, deciphers as 1085, 1104 or 1123. Round, *Calendar*, p. 111, no. 327, dates it 1085 or 1104. The few witnesses who can be identified flourished in the last decade of the eleventh century and the first decade of the twelfth, which makes either 1085 or 1104 more likely than 1123. Génestal, *Rôle*, p. 29, n. 1, gives an ingenious explication of the transaction of which these provisions form part; he thinks that it was a transfer of the mortgage from an English abbey to a Norman one.

297. Document 491 (p. 305). Allix and Génestal, "Opérations," pp. 629–30, interpret this clause as a restriction intended to increase Troarn's chances of securing permanent possession of any lands which might be mortgaged by Adeliza's tenants. It seems to me, rather, to be intended to preserve Adeliza's rights against such an eventuality, to insure her against the possibility of the entry of third parties (for how this happened, see below, p. 85) and perhaps to enable her to oust her tenants' heirs if the tenants

should die during the existence of the mortgages.

298. Document 724 is an account of a mortgage to a layman in the course of which the mortgagor remarks (f° 76v) that "cum vero reddendi terminus appropinquasset" he found himself unable to pay, which implies that the mortgage had to be paid off by the arrival of its term. The implication is not absolutely necessary, however.

299. Génestal, *Rôle*, pp. 40–44, 70–73; Allix and Génestal, "Opérations," p. 628; Yver, *Contrats*, p. 174. In the thirteenth century the mortgagee could eventually establish a prescriptive right to the mortgaged property (Génestal, *Rôle*, pp. 44–46); but no evidence exists of any rule on this question in the eleventh century.

300. Document 778 (f° 102r), also discussed by Allix and Génestal, "Opérations," pp. 626–28; Sauvage, *Troarn*, pp. 223–24.

301. Document 758 (f° 20v) mentions a mortgage for twenty years (above, Chapter 2, n. 52); so does Document 296 (p. 231), which Génestal, *Rôle*, p. 40, cites as the longest term he can find. Document 607 mentions a mortgage for fifteen years. The number of mortgages for ten and for twelve years is sizable, especially considering that most references to mortgages give no details, not excepting the duration of the mortgage.

302. Aside from Robert Curthose's mortgage of Normandy to William Rufus (below, this chapter, at nn. 339–44), no mortgage is explicitly said to have been made so that the mortgagor could go on crusade. This can sometimes be inferred, however: the mortgage cited above, this chapter, at n. 291, was made in 1096 by a man "vadens in Jerusalem"; the two cited above, this chapter, n. 292, were made in 1096 by a man who received a horse in return for one of them; the charter cited above, this chapter, at n. 300, refers in 1105 to a man who made a mortgage before he went to Jerusalem years earlier; Document 291 is a mortgage made in 1096 by a man who was about to leave for somewhere. Document 487, discussed above, this chapter, at n. 250, records a mortgage made in 1100 by a man who "volebat . . . peregre proficiscere"; but this may refer to a simple pilgrimage, for the destination is not stated. Although the evidence is indirect, most scholars have assumed that these mortgages were associated with the first crusade; see Allix and Génestal, "Opérations," p. 624, n. 2; Sauvage, *Troarn*, p. 223; Musset, "Recherches sur les pèlerins," p. 150; David, *Robert*, pp. 228–29, nos. 44, 52.

Other mortgages occurred in connection with the campaign to conquer England and with trips to Apulia; see Allix and Génestal, "Opérations," p. 624; Sauvage, *Troarn*, p. 226, n. 3; Musset, "Recherches sur les pèlerins," pp. 149–50; G. H. White, "Companions," p. 421, and the references there.

303. Above, this chapter, at and in n. 297.

304. Above, this chapter, at n. 291.

305. Respectively, Documents 291 and 296.

306. The gift: Document 142. The mortgage: Document 519. Albert was abbot of Saint-Mesmin from about 1018 to 1036.

307. E.g., above, this chapter, at nn. 31–32.

308. Document 167 (p. 227); the events occurred between 1001 and 1026.

309. Respectively, above, at the preceding note; Documents 622 (f° 41v) and 852.

310. Above, this chapter, quotation at n. 293.

311. Document 622 (f° 41v).

312. Document 261 (p. 415) mentions what appears to be a mortgage to three men, one of whom bears the cognomen *dispensator*. In Document 68, Hugh *pincerna* of Ivry holds a mortgage; he may be the Hugh *pincerna* to Duke William who was a frequent signer of ducal charters at about this time. Document 425 (pp. 134, 135–36) includes five references to mortgages too brief to be clear; it is possible to interpret each as meaning that the priory bought mortgaged property from a lay mortgagee, one of them a *senescallus* named Osmund.

313. Document 73.

314. Document 413 (p. 109). Document 425 (p. 134) probably also refers to a woman as a mortgagee; see above, this chapter, n. 312, on the problem this charter presents.

315. Document 261 (p. 415).

316. Documents 99 (p. 522, twice), 183, 409 (p. 69), 592 (f° 16v), 681, 724 (f° 76v), 852, and possibly Documents 425 (p. 134, three times; see above, this chapter, n. 312, on the problem this charter presents) and 758 (f° 20v, twice).

317. Document 71.

318. A good many mentions of mortgages in the same connection do not indicate the mortgagee. Presumably these mortgagees were usually lay persons: they clearly were not the churches to which possession of the property eventually came, and it seems likely that a church which was a mortgagee would be reluctant to allow the property to go to some other church rather than to itself.

319. Document 645: "decimas quas vel de sua terra haberet vel de alia emptione, recta et vadimoniis adquireret." Document 872 (p. 58) may provide a second instance.

320. Respectively, Document 291, as cited above, this chapter, at n. 305; above, this chapter, at n. 296; Document 557 (f° 138v).

321. Documents 89, 90, 292 (p. 217), 490, 513, 548. Document 875 is another example but cannot be definitely dated to the eleventh century. In Documents 376 (p. 382) and 683 (f° 79r) the transactions may also be of this type, or the alienors may instead have been raising money by their gifts to pay off mortgages held by someone other than the recipient abbeys. In Documents 588 (f° 11r) and 779, two other possibly similar instances, it is not certain that the debt canceled by the transaction was a mortgage.

322. Documents 65, 74, 221, 293, 560 (f° 142r), 615.

Document 840 says that Rannulf son of Ascelin sold the monks of Saint-Etienne de Caen land at Caen which Abbot William "prius habuerat, partim vadio, partim emptionis conventione." This, however, might refer not to one transaction in two stages, i.e., a mortgage which became a sale, but to two separate transactions. Several of Rannulf's sales to Abbots Lanfranc (1063–70) and William (1070–79) are recorded (Document 413, pp. 107, 109), but I have found no other record of either a sale or a mortgage of the land in Document 840.

323. Génestal, *Rôle*, pp. 58–60.

324. Ibid., pp. 59, 60–61, notes the second of these objections.

325. Document 487, on which see above, this chapter, at nn. 250–52.

326. Document 81.

327. Above, this chapter, at n. 300.

328. Respectively, above, this chapter, at n. 189; Document 4.

329. Document 645, as quoted above, this chapter, at and in n. 319, where the person whose acquisitions are at issue is a layman.

330. Documents 68, 99 (p. 522), 183, 249 (p. 381), 261 (p. 415), 300 (p. 147), 622 (f° 41v), 843, 852 (p. 33).

331. Document 196. Some charters are ambiguous; e.g., Documents 66, 637, and several of those cited above, this chapter, n. 321.

332. Below, Chapter 5, at and in n. 34; Documents 71 and 724 (f° 76v).

333. Documents 99 (p. 522) and 285 (col. 201, twice).

334. None of the following mentions the consent of the mortgagors or any other participation by them: Documents 73, 409 (p. 69), 413 (p. 109), 773 (p. 3).

335. Moreover, all but the first of the documents cited in the preceding note were drawn up after the fact rather than at the time of the transfer; had the mortgagors' consent been secured, one might expect it to be mentioned. The consent of the *rectus heres* of the land was secured after the fact and recorded in a separate charter in the case cited below, Chapter 5, at and in n. 34.

336. Below, Chapter 6, especially pp. 114 and 133, and Chapter 8.

337. Compare the wording of the charters cited above, this chapter, n. 333, with the wording of those cited in n. 334. As the transactions cited in n. 333 come from the abbeys at Préaux, it is possible that these sister foundations shared a common scribal tradition which may have differed on this point from the general practice and been more precise in doing so. I do not think this likely, however.

338. Not, however, so far as one can tell, by peasants; as Génestal, *Rôle*, p. 32, points out, "les cultivateurs eux-mêmes . . . n'auraient pu se déposséder, fût-ce pendant peu de temps, de la terre qui les nourrit." See also ibid., pp. 61–62, 68–69. Ibid., pp. 55–56, 69, notes that the amounts of money involved in mortgages were relatively large sums for their day. Ibid., p. 69, also notes that the items mortgaged were beyond the means of peasants. From all this, Génestal concludes (p. 70) that "l'engagement n'a servi qu'aux riches." The term "riches" must be taken relatively, however. Génestal himself notes that necessity is the most commonly cited motive for mortgages (ibid., pp. 63–64) and that mortgages sometimes ruined mortgagors (ibid., pp. 65-67); and the names of known mortgagors are not (with the one exception to be discussed in the next few pages) among the famous names of eleventh-century Normandy.

339. Sauvage, *Troarn*, p. 226, n. 4, asserts that the agreement between Curthose and Rufus "paraît avoir été une sorte de vif-gage." There is, however, considerable evidence that Robert, on his return in 1100, was prepared to repay the full amount he had borrowed; see below, this chapter, at nn. 344, 346. The gage was therefore indubitably a mortgage.

340. Barlow, *William Rufus*, p. 363.

341. OV, 5:26; RT, interp., p. 274.

342. David, *Robert*, p. 91 and the authorities cited there in n. 16; Hollister, "Strange Death," p. 644; Barlow, *William Rufus*, p. 363 and n. 104.

343. Barlow, *William Rufus*, p. 363, n. 104, and the references there. See also David, *Robert*, p. 91, n. 16; Haskins, *Norman Institutions*, p. 79.

344. WM, p. 461; OV, 5:280.

345. David, *Robert*, p. 123.

346. RT, interp., p. 282.

347. Exactly when Curthose returned to Normandy is uncertain. Le Hardy, "Dernier des ducs," p. 128, asserts that he had returned before Rufus's death; but his work is untrustworthy. The consensus of more recent scholars is that Curthose returned in late August or September; see David, *Robert*, p. 123; Hollister, "Strange Death," passim; Le Patourel, "Norman Succession," p. 243; Barlow, *William Rufus*, p. 414.

348. OV, 4:118–20; RT, interp., p. 269; Wace, *Roman de Rou*, 2:234, line 9383; ibid., p. 235, lines 9393–96.

349. Modern scholars are divided. David, *Robert*, p. 49 and n. 38, raises the question but does not try to resolve it; the same is true of Yver, "Châteaux forts," p. 77; Le Patourel, *Norman Empire*, p. 342; Barlow, *William Rufus*, pp. 69–70. Chesnel, *Cotentin*, pp. 21–22, asserts that it was a sale; see also Chesnel, "Bel arbre," p. 234. Le Hardy, "Dernier des ducs," p. 53, insists vigorously that it was only a mortgage; ibid., n. 1, attacks Orderic for calling it a sale. Génestal, "Formation du droit," p. 168, asserts that it was an infeudation. Génestal, "Note," pp. 769–70, says, however, "Je considère . . . que le duc Robert fait un démembrement [of the ducal demesne], quand il engage [*sic*] à son frère Henri le comté du Cotentin. Du moins, rien ne permet de croire que des services quelconques, qu'un lien quelconque de vassalité soit réservé." Several objections can be raised to this statement. First, because nothing is known in any eleventh-century case about what happened to the feudal service due from land which was mortgaged, that nothing is known here can hardly be the basis for a conclusion. Second, Henry did homage to Curthose at some point, for Curthose released him in 1101, and the most likely moment for the bond to have been created is when Curthose transferred the Cotentin to Henry (OV, 5:318; David, *Robert*, p. 134; Le Patourel, *Norman Empire*, pp. 343–44 and p. 344, n. 1).

Léonard, *Histoire*, p. 42, asserts that Curthose's cession of the counties of Eu and Aumale to Rufus in 1091 was a gage; but he seems to be alone in this opinion, and there is little warrant for such an assertion in the sources: see David, *Robert*, p. 60, and the authorities cited there.

350. OV, 5:280; WM, p. 379. The story is accepted by Barlow, *William Rufus*, pp. 416–19; Hollister, "Strange Death," p. 645; Corbett, "England," p. 527.

351. Barlow, *William Rufus*, pp. 367–68.

352. Génestal, *Rôle*, pp. 33–39, 49; see also Yver, *Contrats*, pp. 171–72, as quoted below, Chapter 6, n. 8.

353. The one apparent exception is probably merely the result of poor drafting. Document 758 (f° 21v) says, "decimam de graieo habemus in vadimonio ab eudone et ipse tenet eam de nobis." This might mean that Odo held the tithe from the abbey while it was in mortgage, rather than except while it was. The entry is very brief, however, and the early documents of La Trinité de Caen which are copied in this manuscript are often characterized by awkward phrasing; see also Musset, *Actes*, pp. 36–37. All that may be meant is that Odo was the nuns' tenant before he mortgaged to them a tithe which he held from them: mortgagees were often the mortgagors' lords.

354. Below, Chapter 6, n. 8.

355. Below, Chapter 5, at and in n. 34, where the *rectus heres* to land was not in possession of it because it had been mortgaged.

356. So also William de Glos, who "retained" mortgaged property "all my life and disinherited the legitimate heir by leaving it to my heirs": above, this chapter, at n. 293.

357. Above, this chapter, at and in n. 319.

358. Document 249 (p. 381): "ea quecumque a fidelibus christianis ecclesiis Dei conferuntur . . . , sive in agris, sive in aquis, in vineis quoque, silvis et pratis, sive in mancipiis et peccoribus, necnon in rebus mobilibus aut immobilibus." This clause, however, is a distinct reminiscence of a clause characteristic of Carolingian diplomas; see Musset, "Notes pour servir," p. 59; Musset, "Actes inédits, II," p. 150, which points out, in connection with words like *mancipia* which appear in such clauses, that it is impossible to know to what extent they corresponded to eleventh-century reality. See A. de Boüard, *Manuel*, 1:282–83, on mindless copying of Carolingian formulas by scribes of later centuries. See, however, Document 368 (p. 130) for another use of *mobilis*, in which it seems certain that the scribe knew what he meant: the donor gives his portion, consisting of "equos suos atque arma cum omni parte sue pecunie mobili." De Fontette, *Recherches*, pp. 44–45, thinks that the distinction between movables and immovables as legal categories "n'est pas encore établie de façon rigoureuse" even in the thirteenth century.

359. Génestal, "Formes," p. 227. This excludes, of course, the use of movables as countergifts. Probably the most detailed record of gifts of movables is Document 435.

360. This seems especially noteworthy at La Trinité du Mont, Saint-Pierre de Préaux, and Saint-Martin de Sées. The late eleventh-century cartulary of La Trinité du Mont, edited by Achille Deville, which preserves all ninety-seven of the abbey's extant charters from the century, includes 132 gifts, of which only 10 were made for the entry of a new monk. The minimum number of monks necessary for a house to be considered an abbey rather than a priory was twelve, and Norman abbeys seem to have obeyed the rule; see Berlière, "Nombre," 41:248–52; Quivy and Thiron, "Robert," p. 350. Because La Trinité du Mont was founded about 1030, two generations of monks—at least—had lived there before the compilation of the cartulary, in which, obviously, charters concerning the entry of well fewer than half the monks were recorded. Arch. Eure, H 711, the cartulary of Saint-Pierre de Préaux, founded during the 1030s, records 141 relevant donations, but only 22 mention the entry of new monks. The *Livre blanc* of Saint-Martin de Sées, founded shortly before 1060, records only nine entries of monks in 213 relevant donations; another eleven transactions include the right for one or more men to become monks at some time in the future, but it is impossible to verify

that any of these men ever exercised his option. OV, 2:86, says that Saint-Evroul, founded about 1050, already sheltered forty monks when Robert de Grandmesnil was abbot, between 1059 and 1061; ibid., 3:118, says that Abbot Mainier (1066–89) admitted ninety-two monks to the abbey. Despite these sizable numbers, only six of the transfers to the abbey extant from the period between 1050 and 1106 were explicitly made for admissions of monks.

361. Orderic Vitalis, for example, entered the abbey of Saint-Evroul as a result of his father's gift of thirty silver marks (OV, 3:146). In ibid., p. 150, Goisbert, a citizen of Chartres, becomes a monk at Saint-Evroul in return for thirty pounds of the money of Chartres; he was, like Orderic himself, not from Normandy, and the abbey may have found this sizable amount of money a more convenient gift than the house at Chartres which Goisbert sold to raise it. Goisbert, however, also benefited in entering from a gift by his patron, Ralph de Conches (ibid., pp. 124–26). Le Cacheux, *Saint-Amand*, p. 142, assumes that money that abbey was able to spend very soon after its foundation came from the nuns' dowries.

In Document 435, many movables are given to Saint-Martin de Sées so that it can buy property whose early revenues are to be used to acquire various ornaments and whose later revenues, after those purchases, are to be part of the general income of the monks. This is wise management, but was it normal practice or highly unusual? If it was at all typical, it implies that churches would rather receive immovables than movables because only the former continue to produce wealth.

362. Eadmer, *Vita Anselmi*, pp. 47v–48v, says that one of the ways in which Providence saw to the fiscal needs of the abbey of Bec was "quemlibet de divitibus terrae fraternitatem aecclesiae quaerentem cum magna pecunia adventare"; this seems to mean that during Anselm's abbacy, at least, the abbey regularly granted society in return for gifts of money alone. The charters of Bec never so indicate, however. Bec's charters survive mostly in highly abbreviated form and are, therefore, hardly conclusive; but the charters of other abbeys also rarely mention society in connection with gifts of movables alone.

363. See above, Chapter 2, n. 28, for what was in effect the rental of a child, but a child is scarcely a usual type of movable property.

364. Above, this chapter, n. 62.

365. Above, this chapter, at and in n. 294.

366. Génestal, "Formes," pp. 225–26, considers that gifts of movables of this type were always of *se et sua*, that is, not only of one's portion but also of one's body for burial. The eleventh-century examples, however, by no means always mention burial or anything else to imply it, such as becoming a monk or a nun; and they occasionally make distinctions between the two, e.g., above, this chapter, at and in n. 234.

367. The phrase "omnem suam rectam partem" is used in Document 645. Similar phrases, never identical, occur above, this chapter, at and in n. 234; below, this chapter, at and in n. 385; below, this chapter, n. 392; and in Documents 632 (quoted below, this chapter, n. 389), 597 (f° 26r), 602 (f° 28r), 609, 612, 623, 625 (f° 42v), 628, 646 (f° 53r), 654 (f° 56v), 664 (f° 61r), 667, 671 (f° 67r), 686 (f° 87r), 693, 706 (f° 103r).

368. "Pars substantiae" is used by Orderic at two points where he is transcribing eleventh-century charters: OV, 2:30; Document 473 (p. 156). *Substantia* will be found in Documents 456 and 466. Other phrases will be found in Documents 442, 448 (p. 186, for which see above, Chapter 3, n. 52), 452 (p. 189), 453, 457, 458 (p. 192), 459, 464, 465 (p. 193), 467.

369. Below, this chapter, at and in nn. 384 and 391.

370. Respectively, Documents 249 (p. 383) and 88.

371. Document 80.

372. Document 820 (f° 22v) and 827 (f° 31r).

373. Respectively, Document 724 (f° 76v): "tercia parte tocius substantie mee"; Document 80.

374. The priest's portion of a church (*presbiterium*, *presbiteratus*) was normally understood as one-third, as a few charters indicate; for an example, see above, this chapter, at and in n. 201. Moreover, when fractions of tithes, rather than whole tithes, were given to churches, the fraction is nearly always stated as two *garbas*, occasionally as two *manipulos*. There are a few references to *tertia garba* but none to *una garba*. The meaning of the phrase *duas garbas* is discussed by Navel, "Monographie," 38:426–30; he concludes that two *garbas*, literally two "sheaves," meant two-thirds of the tithe and that the third third belonged to the priest, i.e., that his share was again one-third. See also Musset,"Aperçus sur la dîme," p. 544. Both kinds of references imply that one-third was a customary fraction when things were to be divided. On the other hand, both concern matters of church law and may not be symptomatic of the law which applied to the laity. Moreover, in both the part freely disposable by the proprietor of the church is two-thirds rather than one-third. William the Conqueror allegedly pondered on his deathbed "quid ecclesiis, quid pauperibus, postremo quid filiis largire deberet . . . " (*De obitu*, p. 146, on which see above, Chapter 2, n. 48). Even if the source could be accepted without hesitation, I do not think that the statement refers to a formal division into thirds.

375. Génestal, "Formes," pp. 226–27: a married man with children could dispose of one-third; a married man without children could dispose of half. In the same place, Génestal insists that the phrase "all my portion" is different only semantically from an expressed fraction, but it must be remembered that his emphasis is much more on the twelfth and thirteenth centuries than on the eleventh.

376. Above, this chapter, at n. 370; below, this chapter, at and in n. 382; this chapter, at and in n. 385; Document 83. Some variation of the phrase *ei/sibi contingere* occurs in connection with donors' portions in Documents 456, 602 (f° 28r), 609, 628, 667, 683 (f° 79r), 685, 687 (f° 87r).

377. Below, this chapter, at and in n. 392. The agreement above, this chapter, at and in n. 212, is somewhat analogous.

378. Document 422. Similarly, OV, 3:200, reports that when Ansold de Maule died in 1118 he left Saint-Evroul a horse for which his son and successor Peter subsequently gave the monks some land and confirmed his father's gifts; not only is this incident too late, however, but Maule is not in Normandy.

Stenton, *William*, pp. 136–37, cites Duke William's gift to the college of canons of Cherbourg of "reliquiis sanctorum . . . carioribus quas in sua capella gestabat" (Document 267, p. 430), and says that "the said reliquary was subsequently redeemed by grants of land to the church which had received it in pledge." As Stenton notes, however, the charter is the only source of information on this transaction; it is very poorly drafted, and I can find no clear statement in it that William ever redeemed the relics, although he made many later gifts to the church. Indeed, it is only an assumption that the "pledge" (*vagium*) of Document 267, p. 432, was the relics of ibid., p. 430. On the pledge, see also above, this chapter, n. 286.

379. Document 414.

380. In addition to the citations in the next two notes, see Documents 445 (twice), 467, 620 (f° 36v).

381. Documents 87 and 821 (f° 22v). In Document 386 (p. 99), "pecunia uel substantia" appears to mean that *pecunia* and *substantia* are synonyms. The charter quoted above, this chapter, at and in n. 234, appears to assume that *pecunia* and *portio* are synonyms. Cf. a passage above, this chapter, n. 358, in which the word *pecunia* may mean "wealth" rather than "money," for the donor specifies "the movable part of his *pecunia*."

382. Document 368 (p. 130): "et cum obiero .lx. solidos vel partem omnium rerum mihi contingentium"; *vel* is substituted from the manuscript for the editor's *aut*.

383. Document 249 (p. 383). See also Document 386 (p. 99) with Document 274 (p. 453), for gold and silver; Document 198 (p. 285), for jewelry.

384. Document 701 (f° 98r): "omnes res suas que tunc temporis haberet. . . . Si autem sine monachi habitu moreretur, cum equis et armis suis ad predictum locum se deferri faceret, et secum etiam alias res sibi proprias si quis haberet." For other portions including horses and arms, see above, this chapter, n. 358; Document 888.

385. Document 685: "dum ad sue vite extremum diem appropinquaret, pro sue anime remedio, jam in ipso mortis articulo positus, Sancto Martino fratribusque . . . omnem sue substantie rectam partem sibi contingentem dimisit et quamdam masuram terre . . . quiete et solute ut eleemosinam donavit." See also the instances of the apparent synonymy of one's *pecunia* with one's portion noted above, this chapter, n. 381.

386. Below, this chapter, n. 392.

387. Document 820 (f° 22v): "ut si quid substantie habuerint vel quidquid a modo adquisierint, sive in domibus sive in agris, auro, argento, libris, vestibus, omnique suppellectilivia." Document 537 (second paragraph), which says "omnem partem mei census in morte," may be another example, if *census* here means the profits from land. By saying "totam substantiam suam, praeter terram," Document 849 (p. 31) strongly implies that a portion could contain land.

388. For the other evidence for this distinction which is discussed in this book, see below, Chapter 5, at and in n. 43. In addition, evidence is provided, again in a testamentary context, by the numerous instances in which, after the Conquest of England, a man's lands were divided between his two eldest sons, the elder receiving the Norman lands (his father's patrimony), the younger receiving the English lands (his father's conquest).

389. Documents 83, 620, 663 (f° 61r), 878 (quoted above, Chapter 3, n. 109). When, in Document 632, Hamelin de *Condeto* "et in vita et in morte ad suum corpus sepeliendum cum omni sua rerum recta parte, se et suam uxorem nobis conjunxit," he may be providing merely that his wife should fulfill this part of the agreement in the event of his death; otherwise, this is a fifth example. For post-obit gifts of immovables, see above, Chapter 3, at nn. 103–8.

390. Above, p. 70. An edition by Jean-Michel Bouvris is promised.

391. Document 593: "domno Radulfo abbati hominagium fecit, et ab eodem quandam mansuram terre ad domum faciendam accepit; quam dum tenere vellet, solute et quiete sine aliqua redditione haberet. Sin autem eam alicui homini vel in vita vel post vitam dimitteret, successor, secundum consuetudines quas monachi tunc temporis ei constituerent, si vellet, ab eisdem acciperet et haberet. Quod si ipse Olivarius peregre proficisci vellet, ipsam domum et ecclesiam Sancti Petri de Castello Sagii, ceteraque omnia sua supradictis monachis dimitteret: ita tamen ut si infra duorum annorum spatium rediret, omnia sua cum redditionibus in illo intervallo inde habitis recuperaret; si vero ultra prescriptum terminum moraretur, omnia sua Sanctus Martinus solute et quiete in perpetuum haberet. Prefatam autem ecclesiam Sancti Petri, vel iret vel non iret, Sancto Martino remota omni fallaci retardatione post suum ab hoc seculo discessum perpetuo dimittebat. Quod si ipse a supradicto anno usque ad decimum monachalem habitum expetere vellet, securus de hac re ad monasterium Sagiense veniret; et si sine monachi habitu in hac terra moreretur, omnibus suis Sancto Martino derelictis a monachis sepeliretur."

392. Document 631: "Notum sit omnibus quod quando Adelardus terram quam Sanctus Martinus habebat apud Bellum fontem a domno abbate Rotberto recepit, totam decimationem tam illius quam omnium aliarum quas undecunque vel emere vel adquirere posset terrarum supradicto sancto eternaliter remanendam concessit. Et hoc non tantum post mortem suam sed etiam in vita. Deinde ipse Adelardus pro eadem terra sex libras predicto abbati dedit et insuper manibus suis homo illius devenit et se pro eadem terra serviturum cuicunque abbas vel fratres preciperent sicuti pro feodo suo sine ulla determinatione pepigit. Insuper etiam quiddam quod melius estimamus addidit, quod uxorem quoque suam et filios gratanter concedere fecit ac etiam ipse scripto firmari precepit, hoc scilicet quod quando ipse obiret, nullo resistente herede, de omni-

bus possessionibus suis, tam in terris quam in pecuniis seu quibuscunque substantiis, partem suam Sancto Martino dimitteret, nisi heres suus partem patris a monachis commutando pecuniam pro eorum arbitrio redimere satageret. Hec tamen redemptio de sola quidem concessa est terra, et hoc pacto quod semper eam suus heres a monachis teneret et eis sicuti pro feodo suo pro eadem parte patris quamvis nummis adquisita deserviret."

Whether there were any widely recognized limitations on feudal services in eleventh-century Normandy is difficult, perhaps impossible, to determine; see above, this chapter, at nn. 85–93, and Tabuteau, "Definitions," pp. 40–59. If it were certain that fiefs were hereditary at law as well as in fact by this date, as many scholars maintain, the reason why Adelard's tenement was merely analogous to a fief might be that the tenement was not inherited, and the same would apply to his son's tenure of the same land, which would have been transferred to the abbey in the interim. I am not at all certain, however, that fiefs were indubitably hereditary at this time. On this question, see above, this chapter, at and in nn. 145–50. It seems unlikely that the analogy is merely to some other fief, which Adelard already held from the abbey, because the fact that his son will have paid money for the land somehow affects the matter.

393. Document 205 (p. 306).

394. Above, this chapter, at and in n. 114. For another striking example, see below, Chapter 5, at n. 102, where, given the circumstances, it seems remarkable that Abbot Gilbert did not define either the old service due to his abbey or the new service to be due to the mesne lord (whose own putative service to the abbey may not be mentioned because there was none, this being an extorted concession).

395. Above, this chapter, at and in nn. 63 and 83 (with this chapter, at n. 132).

396. E.g., the messenger service required above, this chapter, at n. 92. See also Bates, *Normandy*, p. 123. The instance cited there, at and in n. 118, of an *eques* "qui . . . prata custodit" (from Document 410, pp. 75–76) may be another example, although the tenement is not called a fief and it is not certain that guarding the meadow was this knight's only duty.

CHAPTER 5

1. The bulk of this chapter first appeared in the *American Journal of Legal History* 21 (1977): 97–124.

2. Haskins, *Norman Institutions*, p. 5. In general, see the works cited above, Chapter 4, n. 53.

3. Lagouëlle, *Essai*, p. 118: "dès avant la conquête [i.e., 1066], toutes les terres normandes se trouvent asservies et rentrent dans l'organisation féodale et seigneuriale"; his statements, ibid., pp. 120, 121, are slightly less sweeping. Corbett, "Development," p. 484: by the end of the reign of Duke Richard I in 996, "most of the important landowners . . . held their estates on a feudal tenure, rendering the duke military service and doing him homage. Allodial ownership, however, was not altogether obsolete." Haskins's conclusion, *Norman Institutions*, p. 6, that "the greater part of the land seems to be held by hereditary tenure of some lord" concerns heritability more than tenure.

4. Matthew, *Norman Conquest*, p. 146: "it seems likely that allodial lands were still the most common type of tenure." It would appear from Matthew's definition of an allod, for which see below, this chapter, n. 54, that on p. 146 "tenure" means no more than "possession"; see also below, this chapter, n. 10. Musset, "Aristocratie," p. 93, partially agrees with Matthew, asserting, "L'alleu a constitué, jusque vers le troisième quart du XIe siècle, le mode le plus courant de tenir des terres importantes en Normandie. . . . Cependant, à partir de la seconde moitié du XIe siècle, l'alleu décline constamment, face à la montée du fief." Musset, however, thinks—correctly—that

allods were tenements; for the difference he alleges between them and fiefs, see below, this chapter, n. 53. For others who question the conclusions of Haskins and Navel, see above, Chapter 4, at and in n. 55.

5. Below, Chapter 8, at nn. 6–11, 57–112.

6. See Yver, "Boutade," p. 787, for some remarks on the significance of this phenomenon.

7. Above, Chapter 4, n. 53, on "fief" and "benefice"; above, Chapter 4, at nn. 181–204 and 213–20, on temporary tenures.

8. Document 125 (p. 130): "placuit . . . firmare ea que fideles nostri, nostro consensu, aut precario vel beneficiis que nostri juris erant, vel de hereditatibus quas paterno jure possidebant, concesserunt."

Document 127 (p. 140): "His subscribere placuit ea que fideles nostri vel de suis beneficiis que nostris [*sic*] sunt juris vel de paternis hereditatibus contulerunt." Some copies correctly read *nostri.*

Document 144 (p. 172): "nostra auctoritate firmamus ea quae fideles nostri . . . concesserunt, aut de beneficiis que nostri juris [era]nt, aut de paternis hereditatibus"; *erant*, obliterated in the earliest surviving copy, has been restored from later copies.

Document 133: "domini mei Ricardi illustrissimi comitis presentiam adii . . . deprecans ut desiderii mei votum perageret, . . . michi satisfecit annuendo et tribuendo . . . non tantum alodos meos, sed etiam villam que dicitur Meslet quam de beneficio ejus tenebam. He sunt igitur res mee proprietatis quas . . . predictus comes Ricardus concessit atque dedit, videlicet villa (*sic*) que Spinetum vocatur. . . . Propter hec omnia de beneficio suo predictus comes Ricardus perpetua hereditate villam que Meslet dicitur . . . concessit."

Document 142 (p. 164): "erat michi quidam alodus ex materna hereditate, non ex alicujus beneficio."

9. The similarities among these charters are catalogued in Fauroux, *Recueil*, pp. 42–43. See also above, Chapter 2, at and in n. 5.

10. Document 150 (p. 186): "in perpetuum concedimus, sed et res quas memorati fideles ex rebus hereditariis suis et ex nostra cessione in usum monachorum . . . deputaverant."

Document 420 (p. 130): "Hec autem . . . mulieres in hujus . . . ecclesie cenobio . . . Deo consecrate ex patrimoniis et beneficiis suis ipse parentesque earum secum . . . tradiderunt."

One reported eleventh-century incident may also be relevant. The *Notitia de libertate Beccensis monasterii*, p. 272, says that when Robert count of Meulan, having been given the castle of Brionne by Duke Robert Curthose, attempted to assert his lordship over the abbey of Bec, Abbot Anselm's reply consisted in part of the statement, "Non enim est haereditas vestra hoc castrum; sed donum domini principis, qui, quando voluerit, ut rem propriam repetet." Matthew, *Norman Conquest*, p. 255, accepts this without question and says that it "shows that there were two types of tenure still distinguished in Normandy about 1090." The statement is not good evidence, however, for two reasons. First, although the incident, if it occurred, must have happened between 1087 and 1093, the work itself dates from the mid-twelfth century (above, Chapter 2, n. 48), and it was certainly a tendentious work. Second, even if the *Notitia* reports the incident accurately and without bias, Anselm's assertion concerned a castle, and castles were exceptional. William the Conqueror's policy was to keep them firmly in his own hands and to allow their castellans no permanent rights in them. One of the signs and causes of Robert Curthose's weakness was his inability to do the same. Castles, therefore, cannot be used as examples of any other sort of immovable. On ducal policy toward castles in the eleventh century, see Yver, "Châteaux forts," esp. pp. 60–62; Bates, *Normandy*, pp. 165–66.

11. *Precarium* appears in no charter except Document 125, as quoted above, this chapter, at and in n. 8.

12. Document 606 (f° 29v): "quidquid ipse habebat in ecclesia de Marcemaisons, sive in dominio sive in feodatis."

13. Document 360.

14. E.g., below Chapter 8, at and in nn. 1 and 2. For an especially clear indication of the meaning of *dominium* in a different context, see below, this chapter, at n. 102.

15. For the other four, see above, Chapter 3, n. 8; below, this chapter, n. 22; Documents 69 (p. 448) and 753.

16. Document 133, as quoted above, this chapter, at and in n. 8.

17. Document 125 (p. 131).

18. Document 110 (p. 88).

19. Document 341 (p. 244): "res proprietatis nostre concedimus et de propria potestate in donum ejus transponimus."

20. Document 473 (p. 156).

21. Document 369. Carabie, *Propriété foncière*, p. 236, thinks that the adjective indicates "la terre reçue des ancêtres, le propre de succession." Although I argue (e.g., below, this chapter, at nn. 41–43) that the distinction between "propres" and "acquêts" was already known in Normandy by the late eleventh century, the usage of such charters as the one quoted indicates that *proprius* meant "own," i.e., exploited directly, rather than "inherited."

22. *De suis proprietatibus* occurs only in Document 341 (p. 245).

23. Document 175 (p. 244).

24. Implied identification: Documents 344 (p. 213), 506, 832. Allods from inheritances: Document 142, as quoted above, this chapter, at and in n. 8; Documents 127 (p. 140), 179 (p. 252), 181 (p. 254), 201 (p. 294), 320 (p. 290), 381, 521 (p. 122), 829 (f° 190r).

Musset, "Réflexions sur *alodium*," thinks the difference between *alodium* and *hereditas* partly a matter of the preferences of different *scriptoria*. The unusual frequency of "allod" in the charters of La Trinité du Mont (above, Chapter 2, n. 32) supports this conclusion. On both terms, see also Holt, "Feudal Society, II."

25. Document 665: "Notum sit omnibus quod Guarinus de Mara dedit Sancto Martino Sagii et hereditabiliter concessit monachis . . . quandam terram quam hereditabiliter habebat ante portam Alenci. . . . Predictam igitur terram quidam avunculus Guarini nomine Herbertus Carboneta hereditabiliter ab antecessoribus suis habuit et Guarinus, ipso avunculo suo defuncto, eam per rectum iudicium in curia Rogerii comitis sibi hereditabiliter acquisivit, videntibus et etiam iudicantibus pluribus ex baronibus predicti comitis, Seifrido videlicet de Scuris, Girardo de Canaio, Hamerico filio Hamolini, Gotscelino filio Gualterii, qui capitalis dominus post comitem ipsius terre erat et a quo Gualterius filius Seiberti eam tenebat, a quo Gualterio Guarinus ipsam recognoscebat et per unum quemque annum duos solidos de censu pro omni redditu et servitio ipsius terre ei tribuebat. Hanc itaque terram quam ita recte ut diximus hereditabiliter ab antecessoribus suis per predicte curie rectum iudicium et dirratiocinationem Guarinus acquisiverat et in suo dominio ut propriam hereditatem tenebat." On this act, see Musset, "Huit essais," pp. 135–36.

26. The clearest exception is Document 96 (p. 424), the foundation charter of Lonlay, in which the founder, William de Bellême, describes his gifts to the abbey as coming "de nostris haereditariis beneficiis." At so early a date, the Bellême area cannot yet be considered part of Normandy or subject to Norman law.

27. The change in language being discussed is a typical example of the existing evidence. For others, see above, Chapter 4, at nn. 106–41, 145–50. For the most recent argument for heritability of tenements in eleventh-century Normandy, see Holt, "Feudal Society, II," esp. pp. 200–201, 204–7, 210–13.

28. Document 164.

29. Below, this chapter, at n. 35; Documents 491 (p. 305) and 832 (f° 17r). See also Fauroux, *Recueil*, p. 27, n. 34, from the *Chronicon Beccensis abbatiae*, a° 1063.

30. Documents 99 (p. 523), 336 (p. 21), 755 (p. 161), and, obliquely, 713.

31. Document 419 (p. 129). The sale of the castle must have occurred between 1028 and 1035, the reign as duke of Adeliza's brother Robert. Yver, "Châteaux forts," p. 47, thinks that the castle was still in Neil's hands in 1075, but this inference is not necessary. Adeliza's son, Guy of Burgundy, and Neil viscount of Saint-Sauveur were two of the principal rebels defeated by Duke William at the battle of Val-ès-Dunes in 1047. The viscount of Saint-Sauveur who rebelled in 1047 was Neil the younger, who succeeded his father, Neil the elder, in 1040 or 1042; see Delisle, *Histoire*, pp. 3–4. Neil the younger died only in 1092 (ibid., p. 24) and would have been well able to raise a hereditary claim in 1075 based on events which had occurred in 1047 or earlier.

32. Above, Chapter 4, at n. 250.

33. Above, this chapter, at and in n. 25.

34. Document 679: "Fulco de Alnoo . . . concessit quicquid ipse habebat et habere debebat in metearia de Osario, que de suo feodo erat"; Document 681: "Eodem anno Bigotus de Sancta Scolastica qui rectus heres eiusdem terre erat quippe cum maritagium matris eius fuisset et pater eius in vadimonio Willelmi iude posuisset . . . eandem metеariam . . . vendidit."

35. Document 177 (p. 247). In translating, I have read *vocatur* for the document's *vocat*. Emma's charter, Document 145, does not use words of inheritance.

36. Below, Chapter 8, at nn. 30–56, but cf. Chapter 8, at nn. 12–15.

37. Document 727 (f° 83v): "Notum sit omnibus presentibus et futuris quod ego Guillelmus Guimundi filius jure hereditario patris mei tenens et possidens totam decimam omnium vavassorum meorum de Luoht, absque contradictione cujuslibet quod inde michi placebat faciebam." The gift was confirmed by Michael bishop of Avranches but apparently only as a friend, not as William's lord.

38. Document 294: "concedo de hereditate a parentibus meis michi relicta . . . ecclesiam quandam de villa quadam mei patrimonii, . . . cum decima . . . , excepta quadam parte duorum scilicet vavassorum, qui non sunt mei juris."

39. Documents 65 (p. 440), 81, 89.

40. Above, Chapter 4, at nn. 250–52.

41. Document 38 (p. 30): "Concessit . . . omnes decimas rerum ipsarum, quas tunc temporis habebat per omnia dominia sua, et quas etiam ipse vel heredes sui conquisituri erant et habituri, ex tunc in antea." For the others, in addition to the charter cited in the next note, see ibid. (p. 32); above, Chapter 4, n. 319; Documents 39 (p. 41), 198 (p. 285), 200 (p. 291), 432 (p. 39), 584 (f° 8r). Most of these charters use the verb *adquirere* (source of the French term "acquêt") rather than *conquirere* (source of the English term "conquest"). OV, 3:142, makes the same distinction in describing Roger de Montgomery's gifts to many abbeys; but his terminology is different ("de acceptis honoribus, quos de paterna haereditate non est adeptus"), and he might be importing a twelfth-century legal concept into his account of the eleventh century. *Adquirere*, however, was sometimes used in the eleventh century to describe what William the Conqueror did to England in 1066; e.g., Document 267 (p. 432).

42. Document 642 (f° 50v): "dono . . . quicquid terrarum, ecclesiarum, decimarum, omniumque ceterarum rerum predicti monasterii fratres dono vel emptione vel quoque alio modo in toto meo foeodo [*sic*] quod in presentiarum habeo et quod per totam vitam meam adquirere potero, sibi suisque posteris huc usque adquisiverunt atque supradictus modis omni tempore adquirere poterunt."

43. E.g., above, p. 34; above, Chapter 4, at and in n. 388; below, Chapter 8, at nn. 47–50. Olivier-Martin, *Histoire*, pp. 271–72, dates the acceptance of the rule in French customary law in general to about 1200. It had certainly become accepted in England by the late twelfth century (Glanvill, *Tractatus*, p. 71). It died out in England soon after Glanvill's day, however. Le Patourel, "Norman Succession," denies that such a legal principle existed in eleventh-century Normandy; see also his *Norman Barons*, pp. 25–26, and *Norman Empire*, p. 183, n. 1. I intend to refute his argument at a later

date. The degree to which the rule was accepted in Normandy in the eleventh century is also discussed by Génestal, "Formation du droit," p. 168; Yver, "Caractères originaux de l'Ouest," pp. 58–62; Holt, "Politics," pp. 12–19, 45; Holt, "Feudal Society, I," pp. 198–99, 204–5; Holt, "Feudal Society, II," p. 213.

44. See also Holt, "Politics," p. 40. Holt, "Feudal Society, II," pp. 201, 204, 210, suggests that grants in inheritance to churches buttressed the donors' "inherited right" and "heritable claim" (p. 204) to their estates.

45. For a different interpretation of the meaning of "allod" in these charters, see Bates, *Normandy*, pp. 124–25; cf. my review of Bates's book, p. 615.

46. Document 158 (p. 208).

47. Document 209. Document 99 (p. 521) also suggests that allods constituted a separate type of tenure, but its meaning is none too clear.

48. Documents 136 and 137 (p. 154) are the earliest instances.

49. Documents 41 (p. 15) and 127 (p. 140).

50. Documents 176 (p. 246, four times) and 287 (col. 226). In regard to one of the examples from Document 176, Musset, "Vie économique," p. 76, says, "[I]l arrive à Guillaume le Bâtard de qualifier indifféremment *alodum* ou *beneficium* une terre qu'un chevalier et ses frères tiennent de lui." The charter, however, actually says, "Dedi quoque Godeboldum militem et omnes fratres ejus, cum omni eorum alodo, absque beneficio quod habere videntur." Although this certainly indicates that allods could be given by the lord from whom they were held—here the allod is given and the benefice is not—it suggests that they were in some way not identical with benefices.

51. Documents 181 (p. 254), 511 (p. 102), 806 (f° 82v).

52. Document 179/180 (p. 252) is the earliest instance; see also Document 181 (p. 254). All these refer to a gift to Bec by Gilbert count of Brionne of the services the brothers of Abbot Herluin did to Gilbert "pro alodiis suis" (p. 252).

53. Document 381. Musset, "Aristocratie," p. 93, asserts that the difference between allods and fiefs was that allods were held "à charge de services dont quelques-uns sont de nature publique et qui, en tout cas, ne sont point militaires." He cites no evidence for this distinction, which he also makes, even more explicitly, in "Naissance," p. 124. Given the state of available information on service for any and all tenements in eleventh-century Normandy (above, Chapter 4, at nn. 393–95), I do not see where such evidence could be found.

54. This has been generally recognized by most scholars of this century; see Pollock and Maitland, *History* 1:70; Lagouëlle, *Essai*, pp. 87–89, 118–20, 125–26, 246–47; Corbett, "Development," p. 487; Carabie, *Propriété foncière*, pp. 230–43; Musset, "Réflexions sur *alodium*"; Strayer, review of Fauroux, p. 609; Bates, *Normandy*, pp. 123–24. Matthew, *Norman Conquest*, p. 145, says that the Normans of 1066 "understood that an 'allod' was family property for which the holder did no homage to a lord, but which he could not alienate without the whole family's consent; the present occupier had the slenderest right to prejudice the expectations of his heirs"; see also ibid., pp. 55, 58, 146. There is little evidence to support this unsubstantiated assertion: lords give allods and give consent to transfers of allods with some frequency, and there are no signs that relatives consented more often or in larger numbers or only in return for larger than usual countergifts—or the like—when what is given is called an allod than when it is called something else or given no name.

55. Document 409 (p. 69).

56. It is asserted or assumed by many of those who have noted the tenurial nature of Norman allods, e.g., Lagouëlle, *Essai*, p. 119; Carabie, *Propriété foncière*, pp. 235–36; Bates, *Normandy*, pp. 122–26.

57. See also Carabie, *Propriété foncière*, p. 238 and n. 39; Musset, "Réflexions sur *alodium*."

58. Dudo, p. 168: "quasi fundum et alodum, in sempiternum"; ibid., p. 169: "in alodo et in fundo."

59. Ibid., p. 169. Cf. Searle, "Frankish Rivalries," p. 205.

60. Ibid., pp. 166–67. Lagouëlle, *Essai*, pp. 86–87, and Prentout, *Etude*, pp. 243–47, put more emphasis on this passage in connection with Dudo's intentions than I think it can be made to bear; they conclude that he used "allod" to emphasize the permanence of the grant of Normandy to Rollo. See, similarly, Carabie, *Propriété foncière*, pp. 238–39, followed by Chibnall, "Military Service," p. 68, n. 24.

61. E.g., above, Chapter 4, at n. 73.

62. See esp. Dudo, pp. 247, 250, 265.

63. Document 264 (p. 418).

64. Document 244.

65. WJ, p. 40. Chibnall, "Charter," p. 6 and n. 35, suggests that this passage may have been taken from a charter which is now lost.

66. Document 758 (f° 20v): "Unusquisque eorum reddit per annum .iiii^or^. solidos et dimidium et tres quadrantes frumenti et v. minas brasii et .ij. capones ad natale domini et .xx. ova ad pascha et i acram terre arant per annum dimidiam partem eius ante natale et dimidiam post natale et erciant et seminant de nostro semine. De uno quoque porcorum suorum .i. denarium per annum et quando ad milia capiunt allecra reddit quodque rete .c. Sex homines ibi habemus quos aloers vulgo vocant. Quisque eorum tenet ortum suum faciuntque servitia ad propinqua maneria et reddunt per annum .xvi. denarios et quattuor minas avene." Descriptions of peasant services of any sort are extremely rare for Normandy in this period; see above, Chapter 4, at and in n. 166.

It is conceivable, though impossible to demonstrate or disprove, that the alloders at Ouistrehan were not better off than the villeins but worse off and that their apparently lesser services were the result of their smaller holdings: the mention of their gardens might imply that alloders, like bordars and cottars, had little or no land but gardens. How much land the villeins of Oustrehan had is not stated.

67. Document 424 (p. 139). The only other charter which calls ducal land *alodium* is Document 138.

68. Document 168. Duke Richard II's gift of Montivilliers to Fécamp is mentioned in Document 125 (p. 129), but no details there elucidate the meaning of the quotation given here.

69. Document 280 (col. 127). In translating, I have read "tractaret" for the edition's "traderet," following BN, fonds Moreau, vol. 42, f° 88v–89r.

70. Document 78.

71. *Ius hereditarium* occurs often, usually in the form *iure hereditario*; for an example, see above, this chapter, at and in n. 37. For the others, see below, Chapter 12, n. 19.

72. Documents 127 (p. 138), 251 (p. 389, twice), 489 (p. 302), 505 (p. 21), 511 (p. 103).

73. Document 139 (p. 158): "tradidi . . . quandam mei juris ac dominii terram . . . , et terram cujusdam Anchitelli, quam jure proprio et beneficiali tenebat."

74. Documents 182, 202 (p. 301), 211 (p. 322), 410 (pp. 74, 76), 507, 713, 782.

75. Documents 123 (p. 115), 214 (p. 328), 274 (p. 451), 384 (pp. 88, 89), 542 (f° 108r), 675 (f° 76v), 733 (f° 30v).

76. Document 404 (p. 51).

77. Document 410 (pp. 73, 76).

78. Document 355 (p. 572): "omnia hujus nostre oblationis dona . . . , solida et quieta et ab omni cujuslibet mortalis consuetudine calumniave liberrima, de nostro jure in jus et dominationem Sancti Martini Majoris Monasterii transferimus atque transfundimus, ita ut ab hodierna die . . . liceat illis jure perpetuo possidere et quicquid exinde agendum decreverint, sine ulla vel mea vel cujusque [*sic* for *cujuscumque*] successorum meorum contradictione liberam potestatem habeant faciendi, ordinandi et qualitercumque eis placuerit meliusque visum fuerit disponendi, tam presentibus quam futuris temporibus."

79. Document 572: "aliquid ex meis rebus que hereditario iure mihi contingunt et

annuens concedo et concedens annuo iure perpetuo possidendum. . . . Que omnia . . . libera et quieta ab omni interpellatione calumnie facio ita ut ab hodierna die sine ulla vel mea vel cuiusquam [*sic*] successorum meorum contradictione supradicta congregatio Sancti Martini et omnes abbates qui eidem congregationi pro tempore preerunt liberam potestatem habeant faciendi, ordinandi et qualitercunque eis placuerit meliusque visum fuerit disponendi ea tam presentibus quam futuris temporibus."

80. On alms, see above, Chapter 3, at nn. 226–59.

81. Above, this chapter, at and in n. 37.

82. Matthew, *Norman Conquest*, pp. 67–68.

83. Grimold du Plessis clearly held from the church of Bayeux the land confiscated from him for his part in the revolt of 1047 (Document 20, p. 5). Perhaps the clearest instance at the level of direct tenants of the duke is Document 211 (p. 322), though there are problems with the document. It records that Adam de Saint-Brice, while "exheredatus a comite Normannorum Willelmo," gave land at Roncheville to Saint-Julien de Tours and the duke subsequently—but before Adam was restored to favor—confirmed the gift "ita quiete et libere ut eam tenuerat Adam ab ipso comite." As the charter is dated 1059 and records Adam's restoration as well as these events, it seems likely that Adam was disinherited for playing a role in one of the rebellions which took place between 1047 and 1053. This conjecture may be strengthened by the signatures on the charter of the leaders of the rebellions of 1047 to 1053, but those signatures in turn raise problems about the authenticity of the charter, for which see above, Chapter 4, n. 158. The substance of Document 211 is repeated in Documents 223 and 224, dated 1063. For the second phrase just quoted from Document 211, Document 223 has Duke William say, "trado . . . sicut Adam meus vassallus de me tenuit"; but Document 224 (p. 341) says that Duke William gave the land "sicut ipsa die in manu mea eam tenebam." Document 224 also calls Adam the duke's vassal and says that two knights had served him from the land given to the abbey. Neither version of the charter from 1063 actually calls the land a fief.

84. Haskins, *Norman Institutions*, pp. 10, 11, 14; Navel, "Recherches sur les institutions féodales," pp. 60, 173–74.

85. Below, Appendix A, Table 1.

86. Below, Chapter 12, at and in n. 33.

87. See also Chibnall, *Anglo-Norman England*, p. 165. In a period of much more abundant sources, England in the thirteenth century, an analogous change occurred in similar silence, namely, the drastic reductions in the quotas of military service owed by the king's tenants-in-chief; see Painter, *Studies*, pp. 38–45.

88. D. C. Douglas, *William*, pp. 84–92; Musset, "Aristocratie," pp. 72–87; Le Patourel, *Norman Empire*, pp. 285–88; Bates, *Normandy*, pp. 99–103, 153, 170–71.

89. Above, Chapter 1, at n. 21; Chapter 4, at nn. 55–60 and 85–94; and Tabuteau, "Definitions." See also the references above, Chapter 4, n. 55.

90. Bates, *Normandy*, passim, esp. pp. 99–105, 114–18, 125–28, 133–35, 165–66, 196–98.

91. Holt, "Feudal Society, II," p. 210.

92. On lords' consent, see below, Chapter 8, at nn. 57–112. In "Feudal Society, II," p. 202, Holt is somewhat imprecise about the need for a lord's consent in eleventh-century Normandy: "a grant made without his approval was infirm"; various expressions of his approval "were an important, often the essential, element in the emerging notions of warranty," an intriguing suggestion which is not elaborated. The tenor of Holt's suggestion, however, seems to me to necessitate that a lord's consent was not legally requisite: if it had been, the argument would be circular.

93. Above, Chapter 3, at n. 2.

94. Above, Chapter 4, at and in n. 212; Document 84: if necessity should force a member of a family who held from the abbey to sell land, "ab abbate . . . precium pro ea sumeret, aut, per ejus licentiam, a quovis homine, qui eam ejusmodi lege teneret."

95. Document 51 (p. 283). In translating, I have read *eam* for the document's *eum*. The transaction must have occurred between 1079 and 1101.

96. In the Inquest of 1172 into the feudal services due to the dukes of Normandy, Saint-Etienne de Caen owed the service only of one knight, and that service was assigned to the fief of Taillebois (Haskins, *Norman Institutions*, p. 9 and n. 20). If Roger de Rosel's service was military, which is not indicated, the abbey apparently did not become obligated to the duke for it.

97. The occasional instances may be conflated accounts of the consent of lords to gifts of the immovables or the individuals: Documents 41 (p. 16), 179/180 (p. 252) with 181 (p. 254), 198 (p. 285, twice), 335 (p. 13), 407 (p. 61), 420 (p. 131). This list excludes clearly agricultural or ecclesiastical services.

98. Redemptions: above, Chapter 3, n. 141; and Document 372, where three men buy back their service for five years. Mortgage: Document 261 (p. 415); but cf. Document 262 (p. 415), where the gage appears to concern land. Pledge: Document 312; see, however, above, Chapter 4, n. 85, on this document.

99. Above, Chapter 3, at and in n. 126.

100. Below, this chapter, at nn. 102–3; Documents 274 (p. 453), 531, 791. This list excludes clearly agricultural or ecclesiastical services. Confirmations without saving clauses cannot be taken to mean that the lords had waived the service due them.

101. Below, Chapter 8, at nn. 77–97, esp. at n. 87.

102. Document 345.

103. Cf. Document 407 (p. 61), completed by Document 408 (p. 64): the duke gives the service of the men of a vill "ita ut servientes qui ibi manent michi servian[t et propter] servitium monachorum, servicium meum non remaneat."

104. Stenton, *First Century*, p. 170, notes a similar reticence in twelfth-century England.

105. Above, Chapter 4, at and in n. 96.

106. Above, Chapter 3, at and in n. 252. OV, 3:186, says that a donor to Saint-Evroul agreed that his "heredes qui terram habebunt omne seruitium domino de cuius feodo illa [i.e., the gift] est facient." Ibid., p. 188, implies the same concerning another gift, that of Geoffrey de Marcq. Both these transfers, however, were made by non-Norman donors to Saint-Evroul's priory of Maule, which was not in Normandy, in the early twelfth century. They cannot, therefore, be used as evidence for eleventh-century Normandy.

107. Lire: Document 537 (paragraph 11): "Ricardus Mahiart et Symon de Gutteriis petierunt abbatem hildebertum ut a domino brittolii impetraret quatinus servitium quod illi impendebant de mancellis cenobio lirensi concederet. Dominus itaque brittolii . . . idem servitium quod de mancellis sibi debebatur . . . concessit . . . multis presentibus . . . [including] ipsis dominis ipsius feudi Ricardo et Symone." Richard and Simon may themselves have been confirmers, since they were "domini feudi." If so, then nothing is said of the original donor; but it is possible that Richard and Simon were willing to waive the service due them from their tenant the alienor only if their own lord would waive whatever service they owed him with respect to the same land.

Caen: Document 411 (p. 85). The many instances in which Queen Matilda provided countergifts to confirmers of gifts to the abbey, for which see the charters of La Trinité de Caen in Musset, *Actes*, may represent similar transactions; but only this instance is explicit. Behind Documents 261/262 (p. 412) may lie a similar action by the duke, but neither version is at all clear. Document 851 may possibly constitute another example; but it, too, is obscure.

108. Document 873: Three men concede another's gift and "convenerunt . . . quod ipsam terram de omni servitio contra omnes bene adquietarent, excepto eo solo servitio quod pertinerent [*sic* for *pertinet*] ad dominum terrae."

109. Above, Chapter 3, at nn. 244–52; below, Chapter 8, at nn. 57–112, esp. at nn. 87 and 95. Pollock and Maitland, *History* 1:245, think that later in England, where

charters say nothing, the burden of service fell on the donor, at least when the gift was in alms. Génestal, *Tutelle*, p. 34, n. 7, asserts, for thirteenth-century Normandy, "Le tenant peut donner sa terre en aumône sans le consentiment de son seigneur, à condition de garantir le donataire, c'est-à-dire de se charger sur la terre qui lui reste des services dûs par la terre donnée." The document cited to prove this (namely, Delisle, "Jugements," p. 349, no. 461) does not, however, seem to do so.

CHAPTER 6

1. This is a commonplace of legal studies for all of medieval Europe. Indeed, eleventh-century Normans were probably better off than residents of many other areas because the dukes maintained notably strict standards of public order and justice. Nevertheless, that strictness was relative only, even in the best of times. Order broke down at least twice in the course of the century: during the early part of the reign of William the Conqueror, from 1035 to 1047 or 1053, and during the whole of the reign of Robert Curthose. Even when the duchy as a whole was at peace, some part of it might be troubled, most especially the southern border, plagued by the endemic warfare of the houses of Bellême and Giroie-Grandmesnil, which Orderic's detailed account has made famous. The dukes themselves sometimes lapsed from the high standards they set. In the early part of his reign, Robert the Magnificent was a notorious disseisor of churches. For disseisins committed by William the Conqueror, see below, Chapter 8, at and in n. 122. The fortunes of some of the great Norman families of the eleventh century were founded in large part upon lands seized from churches; for the example of the Montgomery family, see Musset, "Premiers temps," esp. pp. 20–21. For a particularly graphic demonstration of the pressures to which a Norman abbey of the eleventh century, and one of the most ducal of Norman abbeys at that, might be subjected, see Musset, "Contribution," and "Vie économique." Le Maho, "Seigneuries," considers, inter alia, many examples of disseisins and usurpations in one area of Normandy in the eleventh and early twelfth centuries.

2. On this last point, see esp. de Fontette, *Recherches*, p. 87.

3. On *calumniae* and how they were settled, see, most recently, S. D. White, "*Pactum*."

4. The point is forcefully made by Document 44, in which Neil viscount of Saint-Sauveur confirmed to Marmoutier a gift of six churches in Guernsey made by Duke William and also, in very general terms, the gifts of tithes in those churches made by his own men, and then added: "Omnes vero qui suas partes [i.e., of the tithes] sancto Martino, me interveniente, dimiserunt, ad convincendum eos, si quandoque id negare temptaverint, hic nominatim designati sunt," and then listed ten names. In other words, these donors were so likely to claim what they had given that the charter had better include their names so that they would be recognizable as alienors making claims when they made them—and could be defeated because they had been recognized. In addition, of course, a good many charters refer to actual claims or disseisins by alienors.

5. Above, Chapter 3, at and in nn. 25–26.

6. Above, Chapter 3, at n. 207.

7. Documents 141 and 335 (p. 15).

8. Recognitory payments are often found: above, Chapter 4, at and in nn. 255–57; below, this chapter, at nn. 187–200. The rare forms include the ceremonial acts of transfer discussed below, this chapter, at nn. 32–150, expressions of consent by various interested parties (below, Chapters 7–8), warranty (below, Chapter 9), and penalties (below, Chapter 10).

Yver, *Contrats*, disagrees with my conclusions on two of these points. Ibid., p. 136, alleges, "Conférer un gage immobilier a été longtemps impossible au tenancier sans l'autorisation de son seigneur; et il fallait peut-être une nouvelle autorisation pour permettre l'attribution définitive du gage au créancier." For the eleventh century this statement seems much too sweeping. Lords sometimes gave consent in advance to mortgages which their tenants might make (below, Chapter 8, at nn. 66–67); but where consent is reported in connection with actual mortgages it is always to the subsequent permanent transfer, not to the gage itself. This is true even of Document 65, the one document Yver cites (ibid., n. 2) to prove his statement. Génestal, *Rôle*, pp. 22–24, agrees with Yver, but the only eleventh-century evidence he cites, on pp. 24–25, is an instance of consent in advance.

Yver, *Contrats*, pp. 171–72, alleges, again about mortgages in this early period, "Une terre est transférée immédiatement en pleine propriété, *au moyen des formalités d'usage*, mais elle pourra au bout d'un certain délai être reprise par l'aliénateur moyennant remboursement de la somme fournie par l'acquéreur" (emphasis added). Again, this seems too simple. Both of the eleventh- or early twelfth-century charters which he cites were more than simple mortgages: one was a truly anomalous transfer, for which see above, Chapter 4, at and in n. 296; the other, Document 291, includes provision for the conversion of some or all of the mortgaged land into the abbey's permanent possession. A third charter, Document 557, which Yver, *Contrats*, p. 172, n. 1, cites as an example of the mortgage as an "aliénation . . . faite . . . sous condition suspensive," describes two mortgages, with regard to neither of which is there any reference to the "formalités d'usage." Génestal, *Rôle*, pp. 25–26, 28, differs from Yver, saying, "Dans l'engagement . . . le transfert se fait généralement sans aucune solennité" (p. 28); ibid., pp. 28–30, explains why the two charters Yver cites "présentent un caractère spécial" (p. 28) which makes them anomalous.

9. Above, Chapter 3, at nn. 125, 169–84.

10. In rare circumstances, a countergift might be given to a witness or to someone else with no intrinsic connection with a gift or whose connection was of a type not normally remunerated. For witnesses, see Documents 60, 320 (p. 291), 686. Below, Chapter 7, at and in n. 54, a confirmer and his sons are given two shillings specifically in order that they be witnesses of the gift for as long as they live. The references to countergifts to witnesses are, however, sufficiently rare that it seems impossible to deduce from this one instance a conclusion that witnesses were regularly remunerated in order to compel them, morally if not legally, to witness should the occasion arise.

For other anomalous instances, see Documents 249 (p. 381), 341 (pp. 245–46), 353.

11. Below, Chapter 8, at n. 104.

12. Below, this chapter, at nn. 132–44.

13. Document 774.

14. Document 786 (f° 161r). The only exceptional feature of this charter is that it explicitly links the earlier grant of society to the later confirmation, perhaps to explain why the son was given no countergift at the time of his confirmation. The events recounted in the charter are not unusual in themselves.

15. For the eleven certain examples from Queen Matilda, see Documents 405 (p. 55), 411 (pp. 83, 85 five times, 87 twice, 88), 412 (p. 94, eight times), 424 (p. 139). Some of these items are repetitions of others, but the details often differ. Indeed, two of those in Document 412 are reported as sales to Matilda in Document 411; these are not counted among the eleven instances. In four additional cases men made gifts to La Trinité "pro adjutorio quod regina ei [or *eis*] faciebat" or "pro adjutorio regine": Documents 411 (p. 88, three times) and 424 (p. 139). For another way in which Matilda worked to secure the abbey a large endowment, see above, Chapter 3, at and in n. 146.

For other examples, see below, this chapter, n. 21; this chapter, at n. 23; Chapter 8, at n. 34; Documents 69 (p. 448), 170, 511 (p. 102), 596 (f° 25r), 613 (f° 32r), 665 (f° 62r).

16. Document 558 (f° 139r): "hec definitio facta est coram ernulfo de hesdin quem abbas Gaufridus hospitaverat euntem ad sanctum michaelem, qui etiam ernulfus se

exuens Wlpino renone dedit eum Willelmo dastin ob memoriam huius conventionis." Arnulf was Flemish in origin and a tenant-in-chief in England after the Conquest. Geoffrey was abbot of Saint-Pierre de Préaux from 1096 to 1101. Arnulf went on crusade with Duke Robert Curthose and died at Antioch, so this grant must have been made in 1096; see David, *Robert*, p. 222; Musset, "Recherches sur les pèlerins," p. 131.

17. Below, this chapter, at nn. 132–50.

18. Churches were undoubtedly not as successful as the charters make it appear, of course, for successful disseisins were hardly likely to be described in charters. They are mentioned occasionally in passing in connection with other matters and in internal memoranda such as those cited above, Chapter 4, n. 166, and below, this chapter, at n. 23.

19. E.g., below, this chapter, at and in n. 129, where the partner with a larger share receives a larger countergift; below, Chapter 8, at and in nn. 51–53, where alienors' eldest sons alone receive countergifts or receive larger countergifts than their siblings.

20. For the former view, see the references above, Chapter 3, n. 156; Lemarignier, "Domaine," p. 355, also argues against it. For the latter view, see the articles by Musset cited above, this chapter, n. 1, and A. de Boüard, *Manuel*, 2:147–48.

21. Above, this chapter, at and in n. 16; Document 217 (p. 333): "ob memoriale sempiternum"; Document 292 (p. 217): "in testimonium"; Document 393: "pro signo"; Document 543: "e cognitione huius dati"; Document 716: "pro signo et testimonio"; Document 783 (f° 147r): "ut ista concordia perenniter firmaretur et memorialiter teneretur." The eighth possible example is Document 210: "pro testimonio hujus conventionis"; the charter is somewhat suspect.

Document 450 (p. 186) says, of a donor to Saint-Evroul, "Pro quibus dedit ei domnus Rodbertus in Angliam suam retributionem." Lord Robert is Robert of Rhuddlan, the donor of Document 449, who died in either 1088 or 1093 (OV, 4:140 and n. 1). What the "retribution" was is not stated, but I think that the word must refer to a countergift. If so, it too indicates the "tit for tat" relationship of countergift to gift or confirmation.

22. Remain firm: Documents 32, 167 (p. 227), 182 (p. 257), 249 (p. 385), 348, 379, 393, 410 (p. 76), 500 (p. 228), 533, 642 (f° 51r), 666 (f° 62v), 782, 783 (f° 147r, as quoted in the preceding note), 784, 883 (p. 81). No challenge: Documents 182 (p. 257), 191 (p. 274), 507 (p. 59), 784.

23. Document 501 (p. 230). For the later disposition of Ceaux, see below, Chapter 9, at n. 28. If "Neil the old" is Neil viscount of Saint-Sauveur, whose son of the same name was one of the principal rebels at Val-ès-Dunes in 1047, it is likely that William's seizure of Ceaux was in some way connected to the confiscation of the younger Neil's possessions, which followed the defeat of the rebels. That confiscation was only temporary, yet Mont-Saint-Michel seems to have lost Ceaux permanently. Bates, *Normandy*, p. 82, thinks that this and other contemporary confiscations were intended to punish the abbey for involvement in the rebellion.

24. See also the conjecture above, Chapter 3, at and after nn. 162–65, as to why a charter from Mont-Saint-Michel eliminates all references to a sale by the abbot.

25. Many scholars have noted the connection made by eleventh- and twelfth-century charters between countergifts and the security of transfers. That these countergifts were not necessary to the legal validity of transfers (unlike, for example, the Lombard *launegild*, without which a transfer was of no effect) is generally agreed; see, for example, Chevrier, "Remarques," p. 75; Castaing-Sicard, "Donations," p. 62; de Fontette, *Recherches*, p. 27 and n. 42 bis. Few scholars, however, have considered the question of precisely how a countergift rendered an alienation less subject to rescission or successful challenge than it would otherwise have been. Castaing-Sicard, "Donations," p. 63 and n. 264, suggests that part of the explanation may be that alienors rescinding their alienations or confirmers seizing alienations would have been obliged to return the countergifts. This cannot be part of the explanation for countergifts in

Normandy, I think, for there are no Norman examples of provisions for legal cancellations of transfers (except one for possible reexchange: above, Chapter 3, at and in n. 220) and it would have been unrealistic to expect disseisors to return countergifts. Chevrier, "Remarques," p. 77, thinks that a countergift "accroît la solidité du don en créant une sorte d'amitié entre les parties" and "atteste . . . la réalité de la tradition dont dépend l'avenir irrévocable du don." Again, there is no evidence from Normandy that countergifts created *amicitia*, but in his suggestion that they "attested" to the transfer Chevrier comes closer to my explanation than anyone else I have read.

Yver, *Contrats*, pp. 33–34, thinks that the similar payments, usually of small amounts of money but occasionally of small objects, which he finds in connection with many thirteenth-century transactions, including sales and grants for service or rent as well as donations, "servaient principalement à constater la formation du contrat" (p. 34); they are said by the documents to be made "in recognitione" or "de recognitione." He concludes (ibid., pp. 39–41), in discussing donations alone, that wholly unremunerated donations did not bind the donor to hand over actual possession of the property whose transfer had been promised or to warrant the gift against third parties and, therefore, that countergifts served two purposes: "Transformer la donation en un contrat réel, se créer par une rémunération fournie au donateur un droit acquis à la donation, tel sera précisément le moyen employé par nombre de donataires pour obliger le donateur à garantie. Le '*Launegild*' lombard avait eu un rôle analogue. . . . Le but de la rémunération . . . , c'est, d'une façon large, de consolider, d'affermir la donation. . . . Mais, parfois, et notamment au XIIIe siècle, le but de la rémunération est indiqué de façon plus précise: ce que le donataire paie au donateur, c'est l'obligation pour ce dernier de garantir sa donation" (pp. 39–40). He does not discuss publicity given to transfers of countergifts. I do not find any obvious connection in the eleventh-century documents between countergifts and warranty (on which see below, Chapter 9). Nor can it be proved that a countergift was as necessary to every transfer as the analogy with the *launegild* would suggest that it should have been; and the one instance in which a countergift was explicitly refused (below, at the next note) may be evidence against that analogy.

26. Document 258.

27. Charters very often say that the abbot and/or the monks or the abbess and/or the nuns or the bishop and/or the canons gave the countergift. This note lists only those countergifts which some individual other than an abbot or abbess or bishop is said to have given. In the following, material countergifts or sale prices are handed over by individual, named monks or nuns: Documents 32, 66 (p. 441), 204 (p. 305), 233, 295, 388, 396 (p. 681), 425 (p. 133), 463, 465 (p. 193), 543, 768, 781, 810 (f° 178r, twice), 812; OV, 3:132. The following charters include spiritual countergifts conferred by individual monks: below, this chapter, at and in n. 63; Document 32. In the following, the men who hand over material countergifts are or may be laymen: below, this chapter, at n. 135; Documents 349 and 759 (f° 24r). Document 830 (f° 190v) is another instance of a material countergift handed over by two individuals associated with an abbey; Musset, "Vie économique," p. 71, thinks that the two were "deux laïcs qui appartenaient à l'entourage de l'abbaye (sans qu'on puisse y préciser leur place)," who not merely handed over the money but contributed it themselves.

28. The examples of individual recipients are too numerous to list. For third parties, see above, this chapter, at n. 23; below, this chapter, at nn. 30 and 135; Documents 830 (f° 190v) and 855.

29. For countergifts used to ransom captives, redeem mortgages, provide money or horses for journeys, and, in one instance, provide a horse for another purpose, which, like a journey, was likelier than most to lead to the rapid demise of the animal, see above, Chapter 3, at n. 70. In addition, Document 490 notes that most of a monetary countergift was used to contribute an aid to the lord of the recipient of the countergift; Document 454 notes that a monetary countergift was to be used "ad emendum

psalterium filio suo quem ad scolam miserat"; Documents 170 and 886 note that a horse or a mule given as a countergift was transferred to a third party; and Document 425 (p. 133) may mean that a monetary countergift was used to purchase property.

30. Document 344 (pp. 215–16). The translation of *weredono* as "recompense" is suggested by ibid., p. 215, n. 1.

31. This is not a universal rule; see Musset, "Vie économique," p. 70, for one case from Fécamp in which, of three relevant documents about a transaction which was challenged, only one mentions that the duke had received a countergift for his confirmation of the original transaction. Countergifts to the dukes are, in general, rarely reported.

32. For its nonuse in connection with sales, see above, Chapter 3, at and in n. 169. Such a ceremony seems to have been thought inappropriate for any temporary alienation; concerning mortgages, see above, this chapter, n. 8.

33. Below, Chapter 7, at nn. 40–49.

34. See also Thorne, "Livery," pp. 348–52. The *Additamenta ad historiam Normannorum*, p. 341, and the *Brevis Relatio*, p. 21, say that Duke Richard II gave Vimoutiers to Jumièges in secret, by placing an object on the altar of the church in the dead of night and unobserved, and only later revealed to the mystified beneficiaries what the object symbolized. If such a story could be accepted as an account of actual events, it would pose a problem in this context; but I see no reason to consider it more than a twelfth-century legend. On these sources, see above, Chapter 2, n. 48.

35. Documents 287 (col. 228), 351, 385, 720.

36. Document 669 (f° 65v): "pro recognitione donationis"; cf. Document 591: "pro perenni concessu."

37. Document 497.

38. Document 79. See below, this chapter, at n. 54, for what William did.

39. Below, this chapter, at and in n. 181; the charter also calls Arnold a witness. See also below, this chapter, at and in n. 168, where the same charter refers to the consent of the donor's lady Agnes and her sons.

40. Document 497. For the objects used, see below, this chapter, at nn. 93–95.

41. Below, Chapter 11, at nn. 52–53 and 58.

42. Document 619 (f° 36r): "Haimericus de Valle Framberti et uxor ejus Manselina et ambo filii ejus, Guarinus videlicet atque Torbertus, . . . dederunt. . . . Ad predicti igitur doni confirmationem omnes pariter, vir et uxor et filii, unum librum insimul tenentes super altare Sancti Martini posuerunt." That this was not anomalous is indicated by Document 357, which is probably too late to fall within the scope of this book: the vendors "[p]osuerunt . . . terram super altare . . . per quandam regulam, tenentes illam uterque." See also OV, 3:162: in 1112 a donor, his wife, and their three sons, confirming an earlier gift, "donum super altare omnes pariter . . . posuerunt."

43. For the two Rogers, see Document 354; the transaction is discussed above, Chapter 4, at and in n. 114. For instances wherein not all participated, see Documents 99 (p. 522), 281, 287 (cols. 227–28), 347, 446, 468, 606 (f° 29v), 800 (f° 236r), 847.

44. Below, this chapter, at and in n. 75; Documents 574 (Perrières), 755 (Sacé), 800 (f° 236r, Bohun), 802 (Mortain).

Examples are found from other abbeys, both within and outside Normandy. For Bec, see Document 811 (Saint-Philibert) and probably Document 747 (f° 305, Saint-Martin au Bosc). For Fécamp, see Documents 32 (Mantes) and 426 (p. 138, Saint-Gabriel). For Saint-Père de Chartres, see Documents 300 (p. 147, Planches), 302 (p. 162, Planches), 306 (p. 230, Planches). For Longpont, see Document 28 (Touques); Longpont itself was only a priory, but that a group of monks lived at Saint-Arnoult de Touques is proved by Document 30.

45. In Documents 10 (p. 16), 669 (f° 65v), and 773 (p. 5), the gift is said to have been made at the church which was given, but only Document 669 specifically mentions placement on the altar. In Documents 4 and 561, the gift was placed on the altar

of a church which was apparently not concerned in the gift. In Documents 206 (p. 308) and 240, the confirmation is said to have been made at a church which was apparently not concerned in the gift; but neither charter specifically mentions placement on the altar.

46. In addition to the documents cited in the next note, see Documents 99 (p. 521), 131, 206 (p. 308), 219, 262 (p. 412), 295, 335 (p. 17), 339, 368 (p. 129), 395, 443, 669 (f° 65v), 703, 745, 773 (p. 5). In addition, Documents 335 (p. 17) and 804 note that the act of donation was performed on a Sunday. At least some of these notations were probably simply dating devices to make it easier for the witnesses to remember the donation.

47. Respectively, Documents 399 and 711 and OV, 3:130.

48. In Document 856 (p. 38), an exchange, for example, Abbot Gilbert of Saint-Etienne de Caen "[d]e terra . . . et aliis . . . rebus Sancti Stephani saisivit . . . Willelmum [de Tornebu] et uxorem ejus in Leredo. De terra vero de Lu saisivit abbatem Radulfus Loret armiger Willelmi praecepto ejusdem Willelmi et uxoris ejus." For other uses of "seisin," see Documents 26a, 52 (p. 30), 108 (p. 82), 269 (p. 436), 320 (p. 291), 526. In addition, below, this chapter, at n. 99, "seisin" appears to refer to placement on the altar. For "investiture," see below, this chapter, at and in n. 63; Documents 121, 476 (p. 176), 755; probably below, this chapter, at nn. 99 and 198; and possibly below, this chapter, at n. 199.

49. For acts not done by the alienor, see below, this chapter, at n. 135; Documents 26a, 49 (p. 57), 108 (p. 82), 269 (p. 436), 755, and perhaps also Documents 165 (p. 223), 503, and 527. Only in Document 840 does a relative—the alienor's eldest son—perform such an act, and he appears to have done so at the time of the transfer.

50. Document 108 (p. 82).

51. Documents 52 (p. 30), 53, 211 (p. 323), 480. In OV, 3:166, a boy, confirming his father's confirmation, about 1111, "per capitulum ductus fratres osculatus est."

52. Document 604 (f° 28v): "Deinde autem ipse abbas per baculum suum . . . dedit illi scilicet Johanni ac Herberto fratri eius, totum beneficium et societatem loci Sancti Martini Sagii. Ipsi autem utrique Johannes videlicet et Herbertus eundem baculum insimul manibus tenentes dederunt Sancto Martino et abbati manu predictum baculum propria accipienti decimam de Fontanis, ita ut Johannes qui eam tunc temporis tenebat daret, ac Herbertus frater ejus predictum cum eo tenens baculum concederet. Adiecit etiam ipse Johannes in eadem datione et Herbertus in concessione quod si de illa infirmitate resurgeret et Dominus ei vite longioris incrementa tribueret, plura sancto ac monachis et de terris et decimis in futuro contraderet. Que omnia ut ipse Johannes in ea donatione peroravit frater ejus Herbertus predictum cum eo tenens baculum multis rationabilibus audientibus viris sine ulla contradictione concessit."

53. Above, this chapter, at and in n. 42.

54. Document 79. Descriptions of acts of donation performed by the dukes of Normandy are rare; see Fauroux, *Recueil*, p. 56 and n. 192. See also Haskins, *Norman Institutions*, p. 73, who thinks that evidence that Duke Robert Curthose performed such acts is "another indication of the small weight attached to Robert's seal" and suggests that during Curthose's reign "the ducal charter did not differ fundamentally from a private agreement."

55. E.g., above, Chapter 4, n. 392. Document 882 reports, uniquely, that when William son of Herbert d'*Aldreio* "fecit ei homagium de terra de Condeto," the abbot of Saint-Etienne de Caen gave him one hundred shillings.

56. E.g., above, Chapter 4, at and in n. 391. In the case cited below, Chapter 9, at and in n. 23, nothing is said about the conditions of tenure.

57. WP, pp. 102–4; translation from *EHD*, 2:218, except that it translates "satelliti suo accepto per manus" as "had received ceremonial homage from him." Dudo of Saint-Quentin's fanciful description, p. 169, of the homage Rollo did to Charles the Simple does not mention livery.

58. Document 211.

59. Below, Chapter 8, at n. 34. On the date of foundation, see Laporte, "Origines," p. 58.

60. Below, Chapter 8, at and in n. 105; Chapter 9, at n. 51; Documents 49 (p. 57), 201 (p. 294), 236, 243, 269 (p. 436), 271 (p. 439), 277 (col. 20), and possibly 672 (f° 67v).

61. Document 170. Lepelley, "Jeunesse," p. 59, expresses some doubt as to this event, which seems unnecessary to me, but points out that this "aurait été le premier acte officiel de Guillaume." It may have been connected with Robert's designation of William as his heir before he left on his pilgrimage.

62. Illness: Document 267. War: Document 300, and possibly below, this chapter, at and in n. 75. Death: Documents 77, 421, and probably 513. Excommunicate status: Document 305.

63. Document 801: "Hoc autem donum . . . feci in domo mea . . . , duobus fratribus de supradicto monasterio, scilicet Rainaldo et Rotberto, qui vice abbatis sui dederunt mihi et uxori meae benefactum loci sui. Et hoc dono revestivi fratres Majorismonasterii per unum corium cervinum, quod misi eis in capitulum eorum per unum de supradictis fratribus nomine Rainaldum."

64. Marmoutier: below, this chapter, at and in n. 75; Document 755 (twice). Norman churches: Documents 493 (p. 350), 665 (f° 62r), 675 (f° 76v).

65. Documents 10 (p. 17) and 482 (p. 676).

66. Of the thirty-one relevant transfers among those cited above or in the next note, thirteen—or 42 percent—come from outside Normandy: seven from Marmoutier, three from Saint-Julien de Tours, and one each from Beaumont-lès-Tours, Saint-Florent de Saumur, and Saint-Lucien de Beauvais. Of the three from Saint-Julien, however, two were made "in the hands" of the prior of the Norman priory to which the gift was given; and one of those from Marmoutier was made at the abbey itself. Excluding these, ten of twenty-eight transfers fit the case. Moreover, of the cases from Norman churches, four or five were transfers by non-Norman donors. Therefore, at most half of the cases are purely Norman. In general, however, Normandy was relatively insular in both these respects: nothing like 35 percent of all extant gifts by Normans were made to non-Norman institutions or 22 percent of all gifts to Norman institutions by non-Normans.

67. Investiture comes first in Documents 36, 211 (p. 322), 400 (p. 688), 710, 754. Placement on the altar comes first in Documents 49 (pp. 56–57), 711, 755.

68. The actor was the same in all five instances when investiture came first and in Document 711. The one simple case of two actors is Document 755. The more complex case is Document 49 (pp. 56–57).

69. The object was the same, a knife in both cases, in Documents 400 and 755. In Document 711, placement on the altar was done with a knife and, later, investiture was done with a rod.

70. The donor in Document 36. For the judgment against him, see below, Chapter 10, at n. 50.

71. Document 211.

72. Document 362. The brothers' earliest gift was made in the time of Abbot Evrard, who died in 1044 (Le Prévost, *Eure*, 2:495); the charter mentions Abbot William, who was abbot from 1078 to 1096.

73. Document 426 (pp. 137–38).

74. Document 573: "Cumque a nobis amicabiliter fuissent suscepti et honorabiliter hospitati."

75. Document 805: "Gislebertum de Verliaco cum toto suo fevo et terra quam de Pagano Gisorcii domino tenebat si tamen Paganus ejus dominus eum concederet nobis, quod donum factum est per manum domini Tetbaldi fratris nostri quem ad se venire fecerat, eo tempore prioris cellae Gisorciensis. . . . Postea vero cum Paganus de Gisortio

morabuntur [*sic*; correct to *morabatur*] apud Calvum montem cum Rotberto comite qui faciebat guerram fratri suo, ivit ad eum Domnus Tetbaldus monachus et rogavit eum, ut donum quod prefatus Bencelinus nobis dederat, concederet nobis, qui respondit ei quod in crastino venire [*sic*; correct to *veniret*] occulte Gisortium et inde caperet consilium, quod cum in crastino fecisset, accepto consilio suo, omnia quae supradictus Bencelinus nobis dederat, concessit . . . , cujus etiam concessionis donum misit super altare sancti audoeni per Garulfum presbyterum et Gislebertum Siniscalcum suum." This charter was obviously not drafted by the most capable of scribes, which is unusual for Marmoutier. Gilbert was so common a name in Normandy in the eleventh century that there is no reason to think that Gilbert de Vesly and the seneschal Gilbert were the same man.

76. Cf. a case cited above, this chapter, at and in n. 62.

77. Charters fairly often mention that a potential alienor consulted his friends, barons, magnates, counselors, and the like, before making the gift or confirmation.

78. Documents 3, 249 (p. 385), 413 (p. 108), 482 (p. 676).

79. Document 641: "Hoc autem donum sive venditionem predicto anno ante Rotbertum de Belismo, Rainfrido filio Bosonis, Gualterio preposito et Herberto calcante salem presentibus, domno Radulfo abbati concessit; et sicuti Willelmus Oisuns et Arnulfus concesserant, Hugonem clericum suum fratrem predictus Rotbertus Oisuns firmiter et legaliter libentique animo concessurum promisit. . . . Altera autem die proximo subsequente postquam ista omnia supradicta fuerunt ante Rotbertum de Belismo concessa, . . . in capitulo Sancti Martini predictus Rotbertus Oisuns omnia supradicta simili modo eiusdemque [*sic* for *eisdemque*] verbis sub presentia legalium testium suo proprio ore firmiter atque legaliter concessit; et super altare Sancti Martini de ecclesia supradicta ipse et frater eius Willelmus donum per quendam librum posuerunt. Isti vero viri testes affuerunt." The names of twenty-one witnesses follow.

80. See below, this chapter, at nn. 151–86, for a discussion of words actually quoted or paraphrased.

81. On legal witnesses, see below, Chapter 7, at nn. 69–75 and 84–88.

82. Yver, *Contrats*, pp. 34–38.

83. Glanvill, *Tractatus*, pp. 69–70.

84. Thorne, "Livery," pp. 353–62; quotation from p. 361.

85. If, as I shall argue, there was no difference of legal effect between investiture and placement on the altar, then those acts of donation performed at the altars of churches being given (above, this chapter, at and in n. 45) are an exception.

86. Below, this chapter, at n. 94.

87. Below, pp. 131–32. Thorne, "Livery," pp. 348–50 and n. 16, thinks that the recording of boundaries in charters verifiable by witnesses liberated donors from the need to perform livery of seisin on the land itself after perambulation of its boundaries.

88. Above, Chapter 4, at and in n. 114; see also above, Chapter 3, at and in n. 123.

89. Above, this chapter, at and in n. 67.

90. Below, this chapter, at and in n. 198 and possibly n. 199.

91. Below, this chapter, at and in nn. 193–97.

92. Canons of the council of Lillebonne of 1080, in OV, 3:34; canons of the council of Rouen of 1096, in ibid., 5:22; Documents 14 (p. 24), 289 (col. 232), 518 (p. 112), 634 (f° 46v).

93. In Document 543, the donor gives three virgates (*virgas*) by placing a branch (*virga*) on the altar.

94. The horns of the deer are mentioned in Document 279 (col. 124), an account of the foundation of the abbey of Lire in the 1040s, but written much later, certainly after 1066; the story it tells smacks of legend, and the horns of the deer, too, may be legendary. See above, this chapter, at and in n. 63, for a deerskin used in an act of donation.

95. A. de Boüard, *Manuel* 2:116 and n. 2, suggests that, for France in general, in

every case where a charter says simply that the "donum" was placed on the altar the object used was the charter itself. Many such references occur in Norman charters, but I do not think that they necessarily have this meaning: the difference between "posuit donum super altare" and "posuit donum super altare per quendam librum," or the like, seems at least as apt to be a matter of whether the scribe bothered to name the object used as to represent a real difference in what was placed on the altar. Explicit mention of the use of charters is rare in Normandy; see below, pp. 130–31.

96. Respectively, below, this chapter, at and in n. 181; Documents 350, 673 (f° 68v), 755, 785 (f° 158v), 513; above, this chapter, at and in nn. 63 and 94.

97. For the knife, see Document 399. See below, this chapter, at and in n. 108, for the possible identification of two of the books used at Fécamp.

98. Below, this chapter, at and in n. 181.

99. Document 518 (p. 113). This transaction was presumably not earlier than 1086, the date of the settlement of the lawsuit. As only *denarii* circulated in Normandy in this period, the only explanation of the "quattuor nummos et unum assem" which I can suggest is that they were four *denarii* and one fraction of a *denarius*. I am indebted to Alan Stahl, curator of medieval coins, American Numismatic Society, for confirmation that this speculation is not unreasonable. See above, Chapter 4, at n. 306, for the suit over Dame-Marie.

100. Document 112 (p. 92 and note a); Document 264, which has two final paragraphs apparently having nothing to do with the body of the charter or with each other. Document 174 (cited below, this chapter, at and in n. 103) is a charter in which the additional paragraph is relevant to the body of the charter, as is Document 359.

101. Musset, "Destins," maintains that Courgains was continuously in the possession of Jumièges from before the Viking invasions on; neither it nor the nearby Dame-Marie is in Normandy. The wording of the note in the charter of 1086, however, seems to mandate that someone had granted, or possibly regranted, Courgains to the abbey shortly before the note was written.

102. Document 29; Document 745: "in pignore cultellum super altare obtulit, qui ad notificandam supradictam traditionem tam presentibus quam futuris in testimonium ab ipsius monasterii fratribus posset reservari." Document 856 (p. 38) makes a similar statement about seals—"Ad testimonium . . . et confirmationem hujus excambii habemus in hoc monasterio sigillum Willelmi . . . regis anglorum et Roberti ducis Normannorum"—but there is no indication that the seals had been used to transfer the land concerned.

103. Document 174. Fauroux, *Recueil*, p. 243, note b, notes that the handwriting of the charter becomes somewhat smaller with the first word of this paragraph, which suggests that it was added after the charter was written.

104. Document 322.

105. Document 319: "inde donationem hoc lignum in manus abbatis misi." The word *per* is missing in the original although "per hoc lignum" would seem necessary to the sense of the sentence. For the shape of this charter, which is a rectangle more than half as wide as it is long, see Haskins, *Norman Institutions*, p. 288. *Lignum* was by no means the only term used to denote a "rod"; *baculus* is more common, and *ramus* and *virga* are also found. Whether it is significant that the three charters at issue here all use *lignum* seems impossible to decide.

106. Clanchy, *Memory*, pp. 206–7, gives essentially this explanation of a twelfth-century English instance in which the knife survives. Ibid., p. 207, suggests that the apparently greater durability of knives over parchment may have played a role in their conservation.

In later days a knife could be produced in court, at least in England, to prove that a transfer had occurred: e.g., *Curia Regis Rolls*, 1:323, 361, both concerning a suit over dower from 1200. I am grateful to Robert C. Palmer for this information and for the references.

107. De Lasteyrie, "Notice." Ibid., p. 313, says that this is rare but cites a second example from Angers about 1130, which was seen by Mabillon; ibid., n. 1, cites an analogous example of a rod around which an inscribed lead sheet had been fastened, which comes from Tours from 1144. Ibid., p. 315, cites a piece of wood used as a symbol on which a notice of the act was written in ink, coming from Paris cathedral from the late eleventh century. For English examples, see Clanchy, *Memory*, pp. 206–7.

108. BN, ms. lat. 5359, is a liturgical book from Fécamp from the early eleventh century on f° 1r of which a notice (Document 752) was written in a late eleventh-century hand, which reads, in its entirety, "Walterius reddidit decime sue partem super altare sancte trinitatis et nos absolvimus patrem eius Matheum de Fraxino et Adelais matrem eius." BN, ms. lat. 1939, is a mid-eleventh-century manuscript from Fécamp of works of St. Augustine, which similarly contains one notice of a transaction, this time on the verso of the last folio and in a hand roughly contemporary with the manuscript. The notice, Document 751, is considerably longer than Document 752; it begins, "Noticia facta ab abbate . . . cum quodam milite nomine Rannulfo . . . posteris recitanda." On these manuscripts and the notes added to them, see Branch, "Development," pp. 60, 124; ibid., pp. 85, 87, 89, concern other miscellaneous notices added to leaves of manuscripts from Fécamp, but none is a reference to a transfer. I am grateful to Branch and to the Department of Classical Studies at Duke University for permission to cite this dissertation.

None of the sources cited in the next note discusses the possible use of books in this connection. Chaplais, "English Diplomatic Documents," p. 23, n. 1, notes an analogous set of inscribed manuscripts which were exchanged when Edward the Elder's daughter Edith married Otto I.

109. Giry, *Manuel*, pp. 569–70, 656–57, and the references there; de Lasteyrie, "Notice," pp. 312–13; Delisle, "Lettre," pp. 118–19 and 119, n. 1; Halphen, "Institutions," p. 301 and n. 3. Most of the examples cited come from the twelfth century or later. For some English examples, see Clanchy, *Memory*, pp. 23–24, 127, 206.

110. His signature occurs on the charter proper instead (Document 321).

111. A. de Boüard, *Manuel*, 2:104–6, 111 and n. 2, 124 and n. 2.

112. Gurevič, "Représentations," attributes magical significance to many of the practices discussed here. Ibid., pp. 536–37, contends, "L'objet qui appartenait à un homme portait la marque de la personnalité de cet homme précis, comme s'il imprégnait l'objet de ses qualités." Although Gurevič does not connect this remark with acts of donation, it would provide a psychological and nonrational explanation of the attitude to those objects used in acts of donation which had previously belonged to the lay participants. It would not apply very well to *ligna*, however.

113. Documents 57, 59, 64 (p. 438), 70, 265.

114. Document 551: "Qui ponens hoc donum super altare, filii eius prescripti com [*sic*] ipso donationem hanc super altare posuerunt, signisque sancte crucis propriis manibus depinctis confirmaverunt." For the gift, see above, Chapter 3, n. 141. For the two similar charters from Préaux, see Documents 544 and 545. In addition, Document 368 (p. 130), also from Préaux, is one of the few eleventh-century Norman charters which says, without any doubt, that a gift was placed on the altar by means of a charter.

115. Below, Chapter 7, at and in n. 122.

116. The following charters from other churches certainly or probably allude to the ceremony: Documents 49 (p. 58), 268 (p. 434), 521 (p. 123), 642 (f° 51r). See also OV, 3:132.

117. Document 775: "cartam quam idem Radulfus scribi fecerat signo manus sue firmavit, insuper et unam acram terre sue . . . nobis donavit et donationem super altare posuit."

118. Document 547: "concessit et confirmavit donum patris sui signo crucis, et posuit super altare per unum candelabrum."

119. In Document 587 (f° 11r), a long witness list is followed by the remark: "Hi testes quos prescripsimus primam conventionem quae fuit facta in capitulo audierunt. Isti vero subtitulati recordationem ipsius conventionis quando fuit recordata in camera," which is followed by another long witness list.

120. Document 38 (p. 33).

121. Document 536 (f° 150r): "ipso domino Radulpho testante qui tenuit cornu dum scriptor notavit supradicta."

122. A. de Boüard, *Manuel* 2:116–17, mentions as fairly common elsewhere in France a ceremony whereby the alienor handed the parchment and the inkwell to the scribe, thus acting out his order to have the charter written. There is no evidence of such a ceremony in Normandy except insofar as this charter is one.

123. Gurevič, "Représentations," pp. 532–33, attributes magical significance to all the objects used in acts of donation. About charters, ibid., p. 533, says, "Durant le haut Moyen Age beaucoup de peuples germaniques avaient l'habitude de la *levatio cartae*: avant la constitution de la charte, le parchemin qui devait être utilisé, ainsi que les accessoires pour écrire, étaient déposés dans le terrain qui faisait l'objet de la transaction. Le sens de cette procédure était que le parchemin posé sur le sol s'imprégnait de 'la force de la terre.' Conséquemment, l'acte, scellé sur ce morceau de parchemin, devenait inaltérable et actif. Cette habitude de considérer la charte comme un moyen magique s'est perpétuée dans une période beaucoup plus tardive," by which he seems to mean the twelfth and thirteenth centuries. If this had been the case in eleventh-century Normandy, the blank parchment could have served as the object and later have been inscribed (like the knives and other objects discussed above, this chapter, at and in nn. 107–8) with a record of the gift in a perfectly logical fashion. Unfortunately, I know of no evidence to justify regarding this explanation as valid for eleventh-century Normandy, and it runs counter to the otherwise apparently prevalent dissociation of the act of donation from the land given.

124. E.g., above, this chapter, n. 103; Haskins, *Norman Institutions*, p. 290, discussing Document 320 (on which see below, this chapter, at n. 135).

125. Documents were also sometimes rewritten so that they would be all in one hand; see below, Chapter 7, n. 122.

126. Document 613 (f° 32r): "totum corileturn quod ipse habebat in via Alerci . . . , asserens ibi .lxxx. agros terre esse qui si in corileto non plene invenirentur, de sua proxima plana terra adiungendo perficerentur; si autem in corileto plures quam .lxxx. essent, omnes sancto Martino . . . remanerent."

127. Document 165. As the charter continues, "Hec omnia . . . coram testibus trado," perambulation certainly did not constitute the sole act of donation.

128. Documents 415/416 (pp. 115–16). Both charters record William's resolution of a dispute between the nuns of La Trinité and the monks of Saint-Etienne de Caen in 1083. Document 415 is a preliminary memorandum; 416 is the final version.

129. Document 638 (f° 48v): "terram de Rosello sicut est previsa et ostensa et per legales homines divisa . . . et extra metas ipsius terre Roselli adiungimus centum acras et tantum plus quantum est maior pars Normanni ceteris partibus sociorum." Document 640 records that Norman got seven pounds of Le Mans and Richard and Wimund each got six, thus confirming that Norman's gift was somewhat larger. Why these men shared the land and why their shares were unequal are not explained. Document 638 (f° 49r) records other gifts they made together and the consent of five men called "domini ad quos pertinet ipsa terra."

130. Document 652: "predictus Rotbertus metas et terminos ostendendo demonstravit Gaufrido priori et Ernuceo monacho et istis hominibus cum eis"; eight names follow.

131. Below, Chapter 7, at and in n. 64.

132. Above, this chapter, at nn. 20–31.

133. In addition to the charters cited in what follows, see Document 807: the

chapter; Document 850: the chapter; Document 809: the abbot's chamber; Document 868: the court of the abbey; Document 465 (p. 193): the provost's grange; Document 349: a witness' house.

134. Above, this chapter, at and in nn. 27–28.

135. Document 320 (p. 291).

136. Above, this chapter, at and in n. 52.

137. Documents 620, 634, 686 (f° 87r). Document 649 follows the same pattern except that society is not said to have been conferred with the book which was used to place the gift on the altar.

138. Documents 441 (p. 183), 443, 444, 446, 447, 448 (p. 186), 450 (p. 187), 457, 464, 466. In addition, Documents 442 and 445 clearly refer to grants of countergifts in the chapter.

139. Above, this chapter, at and in n. 114.

140. The exception is the first transaction in Document 561: the donor merely "venit . . . et fecit donationem"; by contrast, and typically, in the second transaction the same donor "venit . . . et dedit ibi donationem super altare."

141. Above, this chapter, at and in n. 16.

142. Document 351; the gift was made between 1035 and 1087. Porée, "Abbaye," p. 427, describes the ceremony by which oblates were offered at Bec in later centuries but without reference to any ceremonies by which the gifts accompanying the oblates may have been transferred.

143. Document 543: "ante parochiam."

144. Above, this chapter, at and in n. 133. Documents 12 and 303 (p. 167) portray ceremonies similar to those of Saint-Martin de Sées; but the abbeys involved, Marmoutier and Saint-Père de Chartres, respectively, were not in Normandy.

145. Above, Chapter 3, at and in n. 169.

146. Above, Chapter 3, at nn. 170–74 and at and in n. 187.

147. Above, this chapter, at n. 30.

148. Above, this chapter, at n. 135.

149. Of the twenty instances, aside from the one involving Ralph son of Ansered, which are listed above, this chapter, n. 27, where the names of those who handed over material countergifts are given, four are sales, those in Documents 233, 759, 768, and 812. Document 812 also names the person who received the money. Moreover, Document 66 concerns money paid out to redeem a mortgage, and Document 295 concerns mortgage money.

150. This is especially true of the records of sales at Saint-Etienne and La Trinité de Caen, the two abbeys which consistently used the same men over and over again as witnesses to their purchases. It is, however, conspicuously not true of Saint-Martin de Sées, which, with the two abbeys at Caen, provides the bulk of the evidence for the seemingly risky nature of sales.

151. Above, this chapter, at n. 30. For another legal argument, not in the context of presence at an alienation, that a claim was invalid because the claimants had not made it at the right time, see above, Chapter 4, at n. 32. Because the extant examples of legal arguments are extremely rare, it is significant that two of them include this line of reasoning. See also Thorne, "Livery," p. 351.

152. Respectively, Document 99 (p. 521) and below, this chapter, at n. 186.

153. Document 219. The duke was probably dining or hunting at the time.

154. Above, Chapter 3, at n. 190.

155. Below, Chapter 7, at n. 94. For other examples, see above, this chapter, at and in nn. 52 and 79.

156. Thorne, "Livery," p. 348, points out that this was so in the earlier Germanic practices from which these ceremonies descend. Besnier, *Coutume*, p. 41, asserts that it was so whenever a lord confirmed a donation.

157. Respectively, above, this chapter, at n. 54; and Document 250: "Monachis

enim dicentibus helemosinam mundam debere dari, ipse, ut vir prudentissimus, respondit: 'Licet Normanni simus, bene tamen novimus quia sic opportet fieri, et ita, si Deo placuerit, faciemus.' "

158. Document 635 (f° 47v): "Namque affirmando rectum esse dicebat ut qui suis filiis .c. vavassores dimittebat sibi atque monachis cum quibus victurus et moriturus erat unum saltim ex illis proprie et solute retineret." The charter never explicitly calls the man given a vavassor.

159. Below, Chapter 7, at nn. 44 and 51.

160. Document 214 (p. 328). Document 215 contains most of the same information but not as a quotation. See above, Chapter 3, at n. 59, for more on this gift.

161. Document 295. For the gist of the agreement and its date, see above, Chapter 4, at and in n. 296.

162. Below, Chapter 9, at and in n. 23.

163. Document 368 (p. 130).

164. Above, this chapter, at n. 120.

165. Respectively, above, this chapter, n. 157; Document 559 (f° 139v); above, Chapter 3, at and in n. 253; Document 665 (f° 62r; see above, Chapter 3, at and in n. 252, for the freedom from service); below, Chapter 7, at n. 44.

166. Above, Chapter 3, at nn. 234–52; Yver, "Autour de l'absence," p. 205.

167. Document 247. For other examples, see Documents 187 (p. 266), 234, 235, 248, 347, 534, 570, 774, 795. It is also common for an anathema clause to be added, in the speaking voice of one or more bishops, to a charter in the speaking voice of an alienor. In addition, in the following charters the body is stated by two or more persons in the first person plural, but an additional gift or confirmation—made by one of the participants in the main transaction and, to all appearances, at the same time—is recorded in the first person singular, or vice versa: Documents 154, 550 (f° 117v), 691. This note includes only charters in which the persons concerned certainly or almost certainly all participated in one act.

168. Document 778 (f° 102v): "Idem vero lancelinus ad concessionem huius pactionis secum adduxerat dominam suam agnetem de qua ipsam hereditatem tenebat. Rogavitque obnixe, ut istam conventionem sponte concederet. At illa elevata voce, '[Ego] audientibus omnibus, libenter concedo deo et sancto martino et a filiis meis faciam annuere.' " The word I have restored as *Ego* is too worn to read.

169. Respectively, Document 64 (p. 438); below, Chapter 7, at and in n. 167; Document 717. Document 851 is probably another instance of a renunciation of a claim.

170. Yver, *Contrats*, pp. 44–58, discusses *fides data* through the end of the thirteenth century and concludes that it was distinct from the oath, that it involved actions (whose exact form is not recoverable) as well as words, that it created primarily a religious obligation, and that violation might entail pecuniary, moral, and/or religious sanctions. Most of his evidence for the eleventh century is taken from Dudo of Saint-Quentin.

171. Warranty: Documents 2, 292, 681. The others are below, Chapter 7, n. 189, and Document 253 (p. 397).

172. Document 617 (f° 35r): "Ad ultimum, videntibus .xl. vel eo amplius militibus in predicta curia, dedit Droco fidem suam Picot, quod fidem inde portaret nec damnum suum quereret vel consentiret in aliqua de supradictis particionibus, quamdiu Adeloia viveret uxor eius. Misit etiam Droco in eadem fiducia quod similiter fidem eis portaret de omnibus quecunque Picot cum uxore sua de remanentibus dotis calumpniis per placitum sibi adquirere valeret. Si autem Droco vel aliquis suus homo Picot vel uxori eius de aliquo supradictorum iniuriam postquam ad rationem missus fuerit, ante quadragesimum diem iusticiam faciet ei, secundum iudicium curie Alentii vel Luercii, quod etiam per predictam fidei dationem fiduciavit, et similiter debet facere homini Picot si ipse vel uxor eius in hac terra non fuerit. Hanc concordiam et fidei dationem viderunt

Rotbertus de Belismo et multi alii." On the case, see Musset, "Huit essais," pp. 133–34; on Picot, see ibid., p. 137.

173. Elsewhere in France abbeys were at least occasionally used as depositories for lay charters. Although the charter is poorly drafted by comparison with most of the other eleventh-century charters in the cartulary, it begins with a dating clause similar to those used in charters of transfer to Saint-Martin de Sées. It is also possible that a monk of the abbey was present in the court when the compromise was arranged. Robert de Bellême was the patron of the abbey, which had been founded by his parents. The case was heard at Bellême, which is close enough to Sées so that it would not be unlikely that a monk of Sées might be there. If my conjecture, below, Chapter 11, n. 46, is correct that the court in another case was Robert's, his court certainly might include monks from Sées at least when it met at Sées.

174. Below, Chapter 7, at n. 173; for the agreement itself, see above, Chapter 4, at nn. 63–65 and 100.

175. Below, Chapter 7, at nn. 181–82.

176. Yver, *Contrats*, pp. 82, 84, thinks that this was the case, at least for compromises and the creation of pledges, in the twelfth and early thirteenth centuries.

177. Ibid., pp. 60–61, says that oaths entailed only ecclesiastical penalties plus the closely allied civil disability of infamy; no eleventh-century document specifies what will happen if an oath is broken.

178. See also Duhamel, "Diplomatique," p. 30. Yver, *Contrats*, pp. 58–63, finds oaths increasingly common in later centuries.

179. Document 874: "Juravit etiam super sancta quatuor Evangelia, nullius tamen requisitione ut [*sic* for *aut*] vi coactus sed propria voluntate . . . , quod nunquam amplius, nec ipse, nec alius pro se, aliquam calumpniam de ipsa aecclesia moveret." See above, Chapter 4, at and in n. 221, for the concession he received in return.

180. Document 694 (f° 91r).

181. Document 778 (f° 102v): "Et ut hoc pactum firmum ac stabile esset iuravit ipse coram omnibus super textum sancti ewangelii quod Ernaldus de Stochis tenebat in brachia sua, sicut idem ernaldus nichil [?] potuit disserere, quod ipse hoc pactum firmiter et absque ullo malo ingenio servaverat ac tenerat. Deinde detulit ipsum textum super altare sancti martini cum cultello Ernaldi de stochis de quo largitio facta fuit, quem apud nos habemus." The word I have deciphered as *nichil* is difficult to read.

182. Alone: Documents 184 (p. 261) and 488; in addition, in Document 292 (p. 217) two brothers who were co-alienors give their faith. Sons: Document 2. Heirs: Documents 161 (p. 216) and 348. Yver, *Contrats*, p. 61, says that such coswearing occurred because an oath bound only the one who swore it; heirs would not be bound unless they swore personally. Men: Document 296 (p. 231). Yver, *Contrats*, p. 59, suggests that in the twelfth century such coswearing reflected the influence of the coswearers in compurgation and/or of the pledges used to increase the security of treaties (for which, see below, Chapter 7, at nn. 179–82), whose role was to exert pressure on their principals to see that the agreements were kept. Of these, the latter explanation seems much more plausible.

183. Documents 724 (f° 77r) and 741.

184. Respectively, Documents 161 (p. 216) and 348.

185. Yver, *Contrats*, p. 59, concludes for an oath taken in 1177 that the only formally necessary element was the use of the word *juro*.

186. Respectively, above, this chapter, at n. 161; and Document 525 (p. 522).

187. Yver, *Contrats*, pp. 33–34, finds that in the thirteenth century countergifts were sometimes said to be "in recognitione" or "de recognitione." I have found only one eleventh-century instance of the use of the word this way, though analogous terms are somewhat more common: above, this chapter, at and in n. 21. The payments at issue here differ from countergifts in that they are regularly repeated.

188. Document 387 (p. 101). The word which I translate "successors," *sosseden-*

tium, is, I presume, an error for *succedentium*; if it should, instead, be *possidentium*, the point is only slightly different.

189. Above, Chapter 4, at and in nn. 201 and 255. In Document 102 (p. 70), Walter count of Dreux confirmed a gift by one of his vassals of a church in Normandy to Saint-Père de Chartres and provided: "Ad cavendam autem, quod minime credimus, subsequentium inimicorum calumniam causa recognitionis, singulis annis, missa Sancti Remigii quae evenit kalendas Octobris, trium solidorum pensionem solvere eis statuimus." Much about this transaction is obscure, including who was to make the payment to whom. Because the intention was to protect the abbey, rather than the donor or the lord, against "future enemies," it seems possible that the payment was to be made by the priest to whom the monks would give the church as a benefice.

190. Above, Chapter 4, at and in n. 234.

191. Document 392 (p. 627). A charter of Cerisy in which the donor's lord and the lord's lord "concesserunt . . . quicquid . . . habebant preter recognitione domini" may refer to a similar payment but more probably refers to some patronage right or spiritual service from the abbey: above, Chapter 3, n. 238. For another possible instance, see above, Chapter 3, at and in n. 255.

192. Above, Chapter 3, at n. 127 (where the payment is explicitly "pro recognitione"), and Document 117, cited above, Chapter 3, at n. 126.

193. Document 159. The charter in which William count of Arques eventually gave the land back says of this stage in the transaction: "Retinuit quoque predictus abbas de ipso alodo pro investitura villam quae dicitur Santiniacus" (Document 832, f° 17r).

194. Above, Chapter 4, at and in n. 188; Documents 159, 734, 776.

195. Above, this chapter, at and in n. 48, the first four examples of "investiture."

196. Document 285 (col. 200).

197. Document 382 (p. 83). The charter is suspect because, as Lot, *Etudes*, p. 82, n. 1, points out, its introduction and one sentence of its conclusion are copied from an 854 act of Charles the Bald for the abbey. There is, however, no obvious flaw in the substance of the charter. Moreover, it was not at all unusual for scribes of this period to draft charters by copying the formal portions of earlier documents; see A. de Boüard, *Manuel*, vol. 1, passim, especially p. 124. It is likely that the monks of Saint-Wandrille in fleeing before the Vikings were able to preserve at least some of their documents: the charter of Charles the Bald certainly survived; see Musset, "Aspect," p. 135, n. 18. This charter is accepted as genuine by Round, *Calendar*, p. 58, no. 165; *Regesta*, 1:19, no. 73; Lemarignier, *Recherches*, p. 68, n. 163.

198. Document 274 (p. 451).

199. Document 365.

200. Documents 613 (f° 32r) and 702, discussed above, Chapter 4, at n. 236.

CHAPTER 7

1. Documents 23 (p. 30), 52 (p. 30), 96, 155, 283 (col. 153), 335 (p. 15), 379, 423, 431 (p. 36, twice), 513, 717, 773 (p. 2). There are, in addition, four Norman charters from Marmoutier: Documents 7 (p. 10), 17, 44, 47. See also A. de Boüard, *Manuel*, 2: 93–94, who notes a similar phenomenon in southern France.

2. For a detailed study of the vagaries of a limited number of documents, see Musset, *Actes*, pp. 25–35, esp. p. 31.

3. Below, Appendix A.

4. Sauvage, *Troarn*, p. 17, n. 1; Colmant, "Actes," p. 55.

5. Above, Chapter 6, at and in nn. 42 and 52; see also Chapter 6, at and in n. 114.

6. Above, Chapter 6, at nn. 37 and 61.

7. The only extant charter which depicts such an action is quoted above, Chapter 6, at and in n. 181.

8. Above, Chapter 6, at n. 96.

9. Above, Chapter 6, at n. 130.
10. Above, Chapter 6, at and in nn. 167 and 168.
11. Above, Chapter 6, at and in nn. 75 and 104.
12. Individual examples are too numerous to cite. For the importance of being present, see below, Chapter 8, at nn. 19–21.
13. Above, Chapter 6, at and in n. 75.
14. Above, Chapter 6, at n. 49.
15. Below, this chapter, at n. 149.
16. E.g., above, Chapter 6, at and in n. 129. For other examples, see Holt, "Feudal Society, II," pp. 212–13. On joint possession of tithes in Normandy in the eleventh century, see Musset, "Aperçus sur la dîme," p. 545; his information comes, of course, from documents recording joint alienations of tithes.
17. Below, Chapter 8, at nn. 101–16.
18. Document 738: "Ego Walterus Brech cum fratribus meis hugone et Rogero do ecclesiam de villa que dicitur seon . . . deo et sancto vigori Cerasii quam Robertus convains avunculus noster donno Warino abbati in elemosina primitus annuerat et insuper annuimus rectam decimam de bestiis nostris caseis et fructibus herbarum."
19. Below, Appendix A.
20. Guillot, *Comte*, 1:303, suggests that *concedere*, when used by the count of Anjou, "signifie tout à la fois qu'il confirme ce qui existe, et qu'il concède à ce droit existant un caractère officiel nouveau." In Normandy, however, at least as used for private individuals, the word sometimes governs what appear to be initial alienations.
21. Document 104 (p. 73): "Constituo etiam atque confirmo . . . hanc ecclesiam . . . et duodecim ecclesias ad eam pertinentes, ab omni episcopali consuetudine immunes."
22. Below, Appendix A, Table 3.
23. Below, Appendix A.
24. Above, Chapter 1, at and in n. 36.
25. Below, Appendix A, Table 2 A, cols. 2–3.
26. Documents 112 (p. 92: "multi . . . viri"), 260, 411 (p. 86; repeated in 420, p. 131), 424 (p. 139), 502 (p. 245), 816 (f° 92r). See also Delisle, *Etudes*, p. 142; Musset, "Aperçus sur la colonisation," p. 37.
27. Document 691: "ego Willelmus filius Antelmi cum Turstino fratre meo matreque nostra Ledscelina et sorore nostra Emma, cum filiis nostris scilicet Willelmo ac Rotberto."
28. There are many cases in which this may have happened. For examples which seem fairly certain, see Documents 618 and 651.
29. For a typical example of the evidence which suggests joint tenancy, see above, Chapter 6, at and in n. 129. Some charters are explicit. In Document 207 (p. 310), for example, Roger the bishop's son is "particeps et coheres" of an allod with Ralph de Warenne. William Paynel's charter, above, Chapter 4, at and in n. 83, is the only eleventh-century Norman document which uses the word "parage." For other likely instances of the practice, see Document 484, as quoted below, Chapter 8, n. 5; and Document 542, on which see also Bates, *Normandy*, p. 127 at n. 140. On parage in Normandy the fundamental study is Génestal, *Parage*, but it barely mentions the tenth and eleventh centuries. For works which assert that parage existed in Normandy by about 1100, see Guilhiermoz, *Essai*, p. 214, n. 71; Génestal, "Formation du droit," pp. 173–74, which cites William Paynel's charter and two examples taken from Orderic; Wightman, *Lacy Family*, p. 220.
30. Below, Chapter 8, at nn. 39–43; Génestal, "Origine," pp. 570–71.
31. The only discernible rule emerges from the charters of Bec, which consistently link the names of the co-alienors either with *et* followed by a plural verb or with *cum* followed by a singular verb. The force of this evidence is vitiated because most of the charters from Bec survive only in late and obviously summary versions. The regularity

of the usage may derive from the copyists, not the original scribes. No other church consistently follows the usage: *cum* is often followed by a plural verb. In general, however, a disproportionately high percentage of singular verbs is preceded by *cum* as opposed to *et*, *atque*, *quoque*, *-que*, and so on.

32. Disproportionately many of those charters which contain no evidence of either witnessing or signatures are early ducal charters. This may indicate that in Normandy as elsewhere the late tenth and early eleventh centuries saw a transition—on the part of the acts of the ruling authority—from the old Carolingian diploma, which did not necessitate witnesses or large numbers of signatures, to the new notice form, whose main purpose was to record the names of the witnesses. On this shift, see A. de Boüard, *Manuel*, 1:49–50, 237; Thorne, "Livery," pp. 349–50; Lemarignier, *Gouvernement*, pp. 42–46, 72–74; Guillot, *Comte*, 2:5–8.

33. The difference seems to me to be almost purely stylistic. Witnesses listed within the bodies of charters often were persons of relatively high status, as though these were singled out for special mention from among the throng of onlookers. The duke or duchess, for example, if named as a witness, almost always appears in the body of the charter as someone "in whose presence" the transfer occurred. A functional difference might exist between those "in whose presence" the act was done, mentioned because of their status and authority, and those listed at the end of the charter, who could be called upon to testify in court should the need to prove that the transfer had occurred arise. Guillot, *Comte*, 2:17–19, distinguishes important persons, whose witness was intended to ensure that the act would be effective, from witnesses of lesser importance, whose function was to be ready to fight a judicial duel if the act was challenged. In practice, a distinction seems likely: to cite the extreme example, it cannot have been expected that William the Conqueror, because he had witnessed an act, would serve as the recipient's champion should the act be challenged. Guillot does not remark on any difference in the place and form in which the two sorts of witnesses are mentioned. It would be difficult to prove or disprove a connection in Normandy, for accounts of the participation of witnesses in court proceedings are few (below, this chapter, at nn. 46–49), the names of such witnesses are rarely given, and the charter recording the transfer being defended rarely survives to make comparison possible. Oddly enough, Guillot himself (ibid., p. 20) finds an almost complete lack of coincidence between the witnesses to acts and the witnesses brought to court to defend the same acts against challenge in those cases from Anjou and Touraine where a comparison can be made. See also below, this chapter, at and in n. 39.

34. The occasional allusions to witnesses to transfers between individuals are too brief and scattered to permit discussion of witnesses in this context. The only charters devoted to transactions between lay persons cite no witnesses or cite them only in the most general terms: Documents 109 and 148 cite none; Document 617 says that the agreement occurred in the court of the lord of both parties and names some of those present (partially quoted above, Chapter 6, at and in n. 172).

35. Documents 423, 424 (p. 139), 768. The last charter was witnessed also by Adeliza abbess of Winchester. Only one other charter for any Norman church may have been witnessed by any nun: Emma abbess of Almenèches witnessed—or signed—Document 474. At most three other charters name as witnesses women who appear not to be related to the male participants: Documents 252 (p. 394), 753, and possibly 228 (p. 348; cf. no. 227, p. 347). Only five charters list female relatives of male witnesses among the witnesses: Documents 19 (p. 156), 112 (p. 92), 260, 482 (p. 676), 581 (f° 6r). I have counted twenty-six additional alienations in connection with which a female relative of a male participant in the transfer serves as a witness; all told, there are eighteen wives, three daughters (two as witnesses to one alienation), and four mothers of alienors, plus three wives of lords. These calculations do not include alienations witnessed by duchesses of Normandy, of which there are many.

36. Above, Chapter 6, at and in n. 130; of the eight viewers of the boundaries,

three are named as the *ex parte* witnesses of the seller. For *ex parte* witnesses, see below, this chapter, at nn. 89–103.

37. Above, Chapter 6, at nn. 30 and 151–54. The presumption is all but explicit in Document 661 (f° 59r), where two brothers, listed only as witnesses, are given a countergift "pro hoc concessu."

38. Respectively, below, Chapter 8, at and in n. 46; Documents 682 and 319. Bouvris, "Date," p. 129, n. 78, points out that the heir who witnesses Document 579 is, instead, said by Document 577 to confirm the same transaction.

39. The distinction between those "in whose presence" an act occurred and listed witnesses (above, this chapter, at and in n. 33) might be taken to indicate that the latter group had done something which made them witnesses in a sense in which other onlookers were not; but this is pure speculation.

40. Documents 159, 299, 544. The preambles of some charters make similar allusions, e.g., below, Chapter 11, at n. 12.

41. Above, Chapter 4, at n. 83.

42. Document 344 (p. 215).

43. Below, this chapter, at n. 88.

44. Document 400 (p. 687). Philip was in England at the time.

45. Documents 18 (p. 155), 203, 225 (p. 343).

46. Document 285 (col. 202). The case probably occurred in the year of Ansfrid's death, 1078, or soon afterward. Despite the default, the abbey did not triumph completely: Roger de Beaumont arranged for Hugh to hold the churches as a life estate from the abbey; see above, Chapter 4, at n. 267. See below, Chapter 11, at n. 22, for the basis of the monks' claim.

47. Below, Chapter 11, at n. 40. See below, Chapter 11, at nn. 33–47, for a discussion of the problems connected with this case and the use of charters in it. The second version of the case, below, Chapter 11, at n. 41, does not say what the witnesses were to do.

Document 309, a possibly eleventh-century charter recording a quitclaim, lists sixteen men under the rubric "Hii autem sunt quorum testimonio calumpnia eadem depulsa est, offerentium se ad omnem quecunque adjudicaretur probationem, quod terra de qua agitur juris ecclesie nostre foret, quodque super ea nobis injusta calumpnia fieret."

48. Document 788: "Abbas vero ostendit per legitimos testes et antiquiores servientes Rogerii Comitis et domini Roberti eius filii quod semper habuerat. . . . Monstravit etiam abbas in ipso placito per cartam suam et per prefatos antiquos testes." Document 789, the other version of the case, does not discuss the evidence adduced. For another possible example, see below, Chapter 9, at n. 27; but cf. Chapter 9, n. 40.

49. Above, Chapter 6, at n. 198; below, this chapter, at nn. 93 and 173; Chapter 11, at nn. 32 and 51; Document 19.

Valin, *Duc*, pp. 198–99, thinks that none of these cases involved battle; he does not discuss the cases from Documents 285 and 309. On the use of witnesses as proof in eleventh-century Normandy, see Besnier, *Coutume*, p. 41; Goebel, *Felony*, pp. 410–11, 416 and n. 276. On duels, see Canel, "Combat."

The case between Marmoutier and La Couture about possessions in Maine (above, Chapter 4, n. 34) was delayed for several years by a procedural dispute over whether Guy de Laval, a warrantor rather than a witness, could prove Marmoutier's right to the possessions by oath or would instead have to do so by ordeal. The issue was finally decided by Duke William, between 1063 and 1066, on the grounds given below, Chapter 11, at n. 32. Guy was allowed to prove his statement by an oath alone. Although the case was not Norman, the decision was rendered in the duke's court. It may be evidence of Norman familiarity with oaths as proof. There are several instances of the use of ordeals in Norman courts in the eleventh century, but these were undergone by one of the parties to each case, not by witnesses.

50. Document 108 (p. 82).

51. Document 170. See above, Chapter 6, at n. 61, for the act of donation. Bates, *Normandy*, pp. 118 (with n. 98), 157, identifies Richard de Lillebonne as viscount of Rouen and "the duke's leg-armour bearer" (p. 157) and thinks that he had been functioning as a viscount since 1025 at least. This charter, which seems to depict Richard as a mere boy in 1035, makes at least the early references to a Viscount Richard unlikely to be to this Richard de Lillebonne, and Richard was a very common name in eleventh-century Normandy. Bouvris, "Contribution," pp. 303–4, thinks that the Richard of 1035 may be a Viscount Richard who apparently flourished 1057 x 1066.

52. Document 354 (p. 537): "Willelmus, infans, filius Fulconis Moiri, qui ob memoriam hujus rei colaphum unum coram altari videntibus multis suscepit." See above, Chapter 4, at and in n. 114, for the agreement.

53. E.g., below, Chapter 9, n. 21.

54. Document 576: "Concessit hoc Hubertus de valnoisia, et filii eius, et habuerunt inde duos solidos, tali pacto, ut quamdiu vixerit ipse sit testis huius rei, et filii eius post eum."

55. In many instances, of course, it is not possible to tell whether the appellations are age designations or nicknames. For "infants" or "boys" who were fairly certainly children, in addition to the instances already cited, see Documents 99 (p. 524), 392 (p. 628), 395, 460, 549, 869. Document 17, quoted below, this chapter, n. 121, cites *pueri* as a group as witnesses but does not name them. For squires, see Documents 3, 99 (p. 524), 306 (p. 230), 320 (p. 291), 426 (p. 138), 529, 548, 549, 594, 658, 854 (p. 35). See also below, this chapter, n. 83. "Squires" were probably older than "boys," but they were still young, apprentices in the military arts. On squires, see Brown, *Normans*, p. 47 and the references in n. 152; Guilhiermoz, *Essai*, pp. 432–35; van Luyn, "Milites," pp. 28–29.

56. On these practices in general, see A. de Boüard, *Manuel*, 2:144–48, esp. p. 145.

57. Document 219, as quoted above, Chapter 6, at n. 153.

58. Documents 218 and 233. See also Document 232, a seventeenth-century abbreviation of another charter, now lost, in which the incomplete witness list consists of William fitz Osbern, Roger de Montgomery, and two of the other witnesses to Document 233; Hugh the forester may have been named as a witness in the complete charter. It seems probable that all four of these charters were issued at the same time in 1062; but Couppey, "Notes," 7:433, suggests that Document 233 is earlier than 219.

59. For their dominant presence in ducal acts as witnesses or signers, see Fauroux, *Recueil*, p. 62; D. C. Douglas, *William*, p. 144; Musset, "Gouvernés," p. 462; Bates, *Normandy*, p. 159.

60. Anselm, Epistles, p. 216, no. 89: Anselm abbot of Bec writes to Lanfranc archbishop of Canterbury, once prior of Bec: "Mortuo . . . archiepiscopo Iohanne quaerimus terram de Ramsoneto ex dono Willelmi, filii Osberni. Sed cum rex requirat utrum ipse donum illud concesserit, nullum omnino invenimus qui hoc meminerit. Si ergo aliquid de regis concessione meministis, . . . prout vobis videtur expedire mandate nobis et regi."

61. Above, Chapter 6, at nn. 157–59.

62. E.g., above, Chapter 6, at and in nn. 16, 121, and 181.

63. Matthew, *Norman Conquest*, p. 75, thinks that William the Conqueror's playful stab at the hand of the abbot of La Trinité du Mont (above, Chapter 6, at n. 54) was done for this purpose.

64. Document 40. The gift is reported in Document 493 (p. 348). That charter makes no mention of this incident; but, because it is a pancart which includes no acts of donation, its silence does not imply that the incident did not happen. Sauvage accepts the story as true (*Troarn*, pp. 15, 256, 301).

65. Document 271 (p. 440), which also gives the date A.D. and says that Alexander II was pope, Henry (IV) was emperor, and Philip (I) was king of France in that year. On

dates cited for their memorability, see A. de Boüard, *Manuel*, 1:297, 313. On the dating of Norman ducal acts, see Fauroux, *Recueil*, pp. 63–65.

66. Document 48 (p. 47).

67. Document 592 (f° 16v): "in domo Rotberti telonearii, teste ipso qui ibi iacebat in quodam scanno."

68. Document 267 (p. 432). Presumably, Duchess Matilda was distraught because Duke William was, as the charter notes, gravely ill at the time.

69. *Idonei*: below, this chapter, at and in n. 73; Chapter 11, at and in n. 12 (two charters); Documents 32, 60 (p. 430), 112 (p. 92), 167 (p. 227), 193, 571, 737, 751. *Legales*: above, Chapter 6, at and in n. 79; Documents 176 (p. 247), 346 (p. 156), 594 (f° 17r), 614 (f° 45r), 629 (f° 44v), 642 (f° 51r), 662 (f° 33r), 667, 719. *Legitimi*: above, this chapter, at and in n. 48; Documents 99 (p. 521) and 456. *Auctentici*: Document 152 (p. 194).

70. Fécamp, Saint-Taurin d'Evreux, and Saint-Martin de Sées use both *idonei* and *legales*. Cerisy uses both *idonei* and *auctentici*. A. de Boüard, *Manuel*, 2:141–42, implies that *autentica persona* was functionally synonymous with *legalis vir*. See also below, this chapter, n. 81.

71. Above, this chapter, at and in n. 48.

72. Above, Chapter 6, at and in n. 79.

73. Document 615 (f° 33v): "Ex plurimis vero testibus duos viros optimos nobisque visos idoneos, scilicet Osulfum et Ansgerium, tantum hic posuimus, ceteros vero tamquam ignotos vel non necessarios dimisimus."

74. They are among the witnesses to Document 592, the only other charter they witnessed together.

Osulf witnessed seven other charters for the abbey. In Document 596 (f° 25r), he is called "Osulfus famulus abbatis"; in 610 (f° 31r), he is called both "famulus abbatis" and "homo Sancti Martini"; in 642 (f° 51r), he is called "homo monachorum." In 604, he is called "Osulfus famulus" twice (f° 28v, 29r); on f° 29r one of the men also called a *famulus* when Osulf is on f° 28v is called a *miles*, but Osulf is not. Hence, *famulus* was a word this abbey, at least, might use of a person of knightly status, but it is not certain that Osulf was a knight. For the other places where Osulf appears, see Documents 601, 634 (f° 47r), 644.

Ansger, often called Ansger de *Rufaldeio*, witnessed thirteen other charters for the abbey. In Document 669 (f° 65v), he is said to be a layman and—like all the other witnesses to the charter—is entitled *dominus*; in 605, he is called "homo monachorum." For the other charters, see Documents 584 (f° 8r), 585 (f° 9r), 608 (f° 30v), 627 (f° 44r), 633 (f° 46v), 636, 641 (f° 50v), 659 (f° 58v), 667, 705, 708.

75. The exception is Document 112, whose witnesses were the duke and his mother, wife, eldest son, and three brothers, one of whom was the archbishop of Rouen, as well as William count of Poitou and his wife, another bishop, and a viscount and his wife, mother, and brother. This charter, however, records a very important transaction, an exchange between Jumièges and the Poitevin abbey of Bourgueil.

76. Below, this chapter, at nn. 107–18.

77. Rustics: Documents 540, 545, 564, all three from Saint-Pierre de Préaux. Villeins: Documents 348 and 349. *Hospes*: Document 773 (p. 3): "testimonio . . . Willelmy [*sic*] hospitis monachorum." This is a careless copy of the charter, as can be seen by comparison with the partial, more careful copy in BN, ms. lat. 13905, f° 80r, p. 151; it is possible that the monastic official called a *hospitarius*, rather than the peasant known as a *hospes*, should be understood here.

78. Document 716: "harum rerum testes sunt . . . et omnes pastores qui erant in vico."

79. Respectively, below, p. 155, and Document 413 (p. 110).

80. *Vinitores* (vinegrowers): Documents 302 (p. 163), 544, 545, 563 (f° 143r), 858, 862, 866, 872. Documents 553, 862, and 866 include the brothers of *vinitores*. *Porcarii*

(swineherds): Documents 589 (f° 12r) and 690 (f° 90r). A *bubulcus* (herdsman): Document 547. *Piscatores* (fishermen): Documents 361, 363, 594 (f° 17v). A *viridarius* (verderer): Document 618 (f° 36r). Two *bercarii* (shepherds) may be among the witnesses to Document 652 (f° 56r): the word is hard to decipher. Individuals called *metearii*, at least some of whom may have been peasants (above, Chapter 4, at nn. 181–86), witnessed Documents 76, 99 (p. 524), 268 (p. 434), 302 (p. 163), 554, 587 (f° 11r), 598, 660, 708. One of these witnesses is said by Document 635 (f° 47v) to have cultivated (*colebat*) land. An *asinarius* (ass-driver): Document 594 (f° 17v). The *quadrigarii* (teamsters) who witnessed Documents 621 (f° 38v, 41v), 630, and 652 (f° 56r) may have been town dwellers rather than countrymen.

81. Above, Chapter 4, at nn. 172–80. It is often alleged that at this time in France in general serfs could not testify in court and were therefore useless as witnesses; see, for example, Olivier-Martin, *Histoire*, p. 249. This is denied by Guillot, *Comte*, 2:18–19 and n. 55, who thinks that the lower social classes were, instead, "la catégorie social prédestinée à l'époque pour les duels judiciaires" (p. 18). To his evidence may be added Document 227 (p. 346), an instance from Laval in Maine in which proof was to be by the ordeal of hot iron (see Document 228, p. 348). By this time in Normandy peasants, however lowly, were rarely if ever serfs (above, Chapter 4, at and in n. 173), so the subject casts at best an indirect light on the situation there.

Guilhiermoz, *Essai*, p. 351, n. 8, says that in Normandy by the time of the *TAC* a *legalis homo* was the possessor of a knight's fee or a vavassory but that earlier "on ne parlait que de chevaliers"; cf. the slightly different interpretation of Besnier, "Inquisitiones," p. 198. The instances under discussion here seem sufficient to disprove the contention so far as the eleventh century is concerned.

Le Maho, "Seigneuries," p. 8, suggests briefly that the phrase *testes legitimi* was synonymous with *testes mei* and says that both terms "suggèrent un lien personnel, un engagement féodal précis" between the donor and his witnesses. This seems dubious as a general rule even for a donor's *ex parte* witnesses and a dangerous assumption on the basis of which to identify feudal *mouvances*. In Document 349, for example, a father witnesses *ex parte* of the abbey of Lire while his son witnesses *ex parte* of the donor. Moreover, the context in which *legitimus* and its synonyms appear has nothing to do with *ex parte* witnessing, on which see below, this chapter, at nn. 89–103.

82. For burgesses and burgage, see above, Chapter 4, at and in n. 168.

83. Appert and Bernier, "Essai," pp. 280–81, in comparing and analyzing the witness lists of two versions of a transaction between the abbey and William de la Ferté-Macé, assert that the knights who have surnames in the list in which not all knights do are accorded them "parce que seuls ils étaient chefs de famille, tandis que les autres n'étaient que de simples écuyers ou bacheliers faisant leur apprentissage militaire au service du baron," i.e., William de la Ferté. They do not attempt to demonstrate the truth of this hypothesis, although the existence of the second list makes this one of the few instances where it might be possible. Their explanation, if correct, might imply that laymen who appear in other witness lists only by first name were not peasants but unendowed knights and squires; but there seems to be no reason for generalizing it, even if it is correct in this instance. On toponymics, see also Musset, "Aristocratie," pp. 94–95; Bates, *Normandy*, pp. 113–14.

84. Boulet-Sautel, "Aperçus," p. 305.

85. Odegaard, "Legalis homo," p. 192; the article discusses the term's meaning in England from 1066 to the thirteenth century and concludes that it could mean rustics and even Jews. The author does not, however, specifically discuss *legalis testis*.

86. Yver, *Contrats*, pp. 55, 60.

87. *Infamia* is mentioned only once in the eleventh-century charters, as a penalty to be imposed on challengers to one alienation: Document 263, quoted below, Chapter 10, at n. 55. Two other charters may refer to the same penalty in different terms: below,

Chapter 10, at and in nn. 54–55, if *reus esse* is taken to mean something like "repugnant to" rather than merely "answerable to."

88. Document 36.

89. Below, Appendix A, Table 2 A, cols. 14–15.

90. I have counted thirty-eight charters in which only the recipient's witnesses are identified as such. In contrast, five charters identify only the alienor's witnesses as such: Document 3, 412 (pp. 94–95), 566 (f° 144v), 758 (f° 21v), 765.

91. One church which used the practice in the 1040s is Saint-Pierre de Préaux (Document 285, col. 202, an act from 1047). Another might be Lire, if the editor's date for Documents 375 and 376 could be accepted: see below, Appendix B, n. 66. With the exception of Cerisy and Montivilliers, the ones which did not use the practice by 1106 are cathedral churches, of which only Rouen ever used it, or churches from which few charters are extant, or those whose transactions, numerous as they may be, are recorded in one or a few pancarts.

After the one, perhaps three, charters from the 1040s which divide witness lists, of charters which can be dated by decades, there are six from the 1050s, eight from the 1060s, six from the 1070s, sixteen from the 1080s, thirty-one from the 1090s, and nineteen from between 1100 and 1106. Of charters which can be dated by reigns, thirteen come from the thirty-one years of Duke William's reign before he became king of England; twenty-nine from the twenty-one years of his reign after the Conquest; and ninety-one from the nineteen-year reign of Duke Robert Curthose. The increase is real, that is, the rate of increase is higher than the rate of increase of all charters (as calculated in Appendix A, Tables 1 A and 1 B, below), except for the decade 1070–79.

92. Except for Saint-Martin de Sées, the abbey with the highest number of divided witness lists is Saint-Pierre de Préaux. Unfortunately, however, the charters of this abbey are almost impossible to date within close limits.

93. Document 397 (p. 681).

94. Document 409.

95. Below, this chapter, at nn. 174–77 and 184–88.

96. Valin, *Duc*, p. 199, maintains that the witnesses adduced in court "ne donnaient au sentiment de justice qu'une satisfaction médiocre, car ces témoins étaient les hommes de la partie qui les amenait avec elle, et leurs dépositions pouvaient à juste titre passer pour suspectes." He thinks that this is the reason for the increasing use of inquests in Normandy in the late eleventh and twelfth centuries (ibid., pp. 199–200).

97. Only the recipient's witnesses are listed in Documents 390, 544, 545, 551, 555 (f° 137v), 559 (f° 139v), 610 (f° 31r), 819 (f° 21r), 850, 860, 861, 862, 865, 868. Document 563 (f° 143r) lists only the alienor's witnesses to one of the transactions it records; see the next note for three other examples from charters recording lawsuits, which list no witnesses for alienees.

No group belongs to an alienor in Documents 365 and 525 (p. 522), where each second group of witnesses belongs to the archbishop of Rouen, and in Document 532, where there are pledges plus the abbey's witnesses.

98. Documents 33 and 280, in each of which the judges are witnesses *ex parte regis* and the loser and victor both have their own witnesses; Documents 518 (p. 112) and 788, in each of which only the judges and the losing party's witnesses are listed; Document 398 (p. 685), where one group of witnesses is probably the judges and the losing party and the victor's warrantor both have their own witnesses.

99. Respectively, Documents 566 (f° 144v; the son is also listed among his father's witnesses) and 503; above, this chapter, n. 97, twice; Document 771.

100. Respectively, Documents 534 and 793.

101. Document 584 (f° 8r): "Hujus rei testes fuerunt: Johannes archidiaconus ex utraque parte. Ex parte vero Rotberti. . . . Ex parte vero monachorum."

102. Document 500.

103. I have nevertheless included charters which describe the witnesses they list in such terms among the entries tabulated in Appendix A, Table 2 A, cols. 14–15, because they indicate the existence of the concept of *ex parte* witnesses.

104. Document 349: "Ex parte mea testibus . . . filiis Goelli, qui erant in captione in domo mea apud essarz."

105. Documents 676 and 677 come from 1088; 687 comes from 1111. On Robert and the other frequent witnesses cited in this paragraph, see Adigard des Gautries, "Etudes," p. 18. Bouvris, "Possession," pp. 178–79, n. 64, disagrees with Adigard des Gautries about the site of the Cotentin from which Robert came.

106. One hundred and thirteen witness lists are dated to years between 1088 and 1111. If all thirty-seven lists in which Robert appears fall within this period, he would appear in 32.7 percent of all the witness lists. Only twenty-nine of the witness lists in which he appears—or 25.7 percent of those between 1088 and 1111—bear dates. One of the undated ones, Document 597, may possibly have been drawn up as early as 1077, though it probably comes from 1079 or later. A total of 166 witness lists may (not must) have been drawn up between 1077 and 1111, of which Robert's thirty-seven are 22.3 percent.

107. Richard the cook appears in thirty-one charters, dated from 1089 to 1113. In addition, Richard brother of Witman the cook witnessed Documents 655 and 688. A man called Richard the baker witnessed five charters between 1089 and 1096 and one in 1113. The last charter, Document 689, is also witnessed by Richard the cook. In that year, therefore, there were clearly two Richards; but the gap from 1096 to 1113 makes it possible that the baker of 1113 was not the same man as the one of 1089–96, who may be the same man as the cook of 1089–1113. Compare Evanus, below, this chapter, at and in n. 112. Richard, however, was a very common name in the eleventh century; Evanus was not.

108. Witman the cook occurs in charters dated from 1090 to 1101. In addition, Witman brother of Herbert the cook witnessed Document 644. It is possible that the monks had three brothers—Herbert, Witman, and Richard (see the preceding note)—working in their kitchens. If so, Herbert, who witnessed between 1081 and 1094, was probably the earliest employed.

109. In charters dated from 1090 to 1101. He is sometimes described as a goldsmith. It therefore seems likely that Adigard des Gautries, "Etudes," p. 23 and n. 9, is correct in identifying him with Roscelinus, also called a goldsmith, who appears in three charters of 1090–92. Adigard des Gautries finds this man appearing a total of twenty-three times; but, although the name is very rare, I do not think that it is safe to identify him with the Roscetus de Beaumont of Document 683, the Roscelinus de *Sancta Radegunda* of Document 634, or the Roscellus of Document 608.

110. "Papilio cocus" witnessed sixteen acts. In addition, Documents 647 and 678 are witnessed by a cook named William "Papilio"; Document 684 is witnessed by "Willelmo qui cognominatur Papilio," who is not called a cook; and Document 654 is witnessed by "Willelmo coco."

111. Above, this chapter, n. 74.

112. Aside from the person or persons named Evanus in the charters of Saint-Martin de Sées, I have found only one man of this name in any charter: Evanus the steward of Harscutus in Document 887, who is the same man as Evanus Secar in Document 482 (pp. 675–76).

Of the thirteen charters witnessed by "Evanus pistor," Document 677 comes from 1088, 436 comes from 1089, and the other ten which can be dated to one year come from between 1096 and 1101. "Evanus cocus" witnessed seven alienations; the six which can be dated to one year come from between 1094 and 1096. It seems likely that these two are the same person: either Evanus went from being a baker to being a cook to being a baker or the scribe of the cartulary got confused when transcribing the charters from the 1080s. An Evanus who may be a cook witnessed Document 651.

"Evanus de Sagio" witnessed Document 642 and Document 16, for Marmoutier, which was also witnessed by the abbot of Saint-Martin de Sées and which calls Evanus a layman; "Evanus burgensis Sagii" witnessed Document 584. As no other charter from any abbey ever calls a cook or a baker a burgess, it may be that the last charter, or all three which do not cite Evanus by occupation, refer to a second man. An "Evanus monachus Sancti Martini Sagii" appears in Document 618 (f° 35v), dated "post multum vero temporis" in reference to the preceding act, dated 1094. Cooks and bakers were at least usually laymen. Given the vague date of Document 618, however, it is possible that either the cook-baker or the burgess had become a monk by the time of the purchase. Only the rarity of the name Evanus makes the identification of all these men at all likely, however.

113. Above, Chapter 3, at nn. 170–73.

114. Below, this chapter, n. 154.

115. Counting only those lists which name at least one person and including non-Norman as well as Norman abbeys.

116. Document 754: "quod in tota Normannia ubicumque haberemus opus ejus adiutorio vel servitio esset nobis in adjutorium sicut unus de famulis nostris ex coquina nostra."

117. In Document 207 (p. 310), Ralph de Warenne sold his cook's tenement for ten pounds. In Document 75, Odo the moneyer son of Humphrey the count's cook sold land for twenty-five pounds; but this man's wealth may have come from his own position as moneyer rather than his father's position as a cook. On the mediocre wealth of royal cooks mentioned in Domesday Book, see Barlow, *William Rufus*, p. 144; on royal bakers, see ibid., p. 143, and Round, *King's Serjeants*, pp. 232–33.

118. See also Adigard des Gautries, "Etudes," p. 18; Musset, *Actes*, p. 39; Musset, "Actes inédits, VI," p. 124, although the charter to which his discussion relates is suspect.

119. Below, Appendix A, Table 2 A, col. 11, indicates the highest number of witnesses in a list from each church tabulated. The charter from Bernay is Document 126 (pp. 134–35). From churches not tabulated, one charter, Document 391, includes the names of forty-three witnesses.

120. Below, Appendix A, Table 2 A, col. 13.

121. This might represent an attempt to make the group of witnesses appear larger than it actually was; but it more probably is in each case an abbreviation of the list, as a few charters imply by the phrases they use: above, this chapter, at and in n. 73; Document 8 (p. 11): "et multi alii quorum nomina propter prolixitatem tacuimus"; Document 17 (p. 30): "et alii quamplures . . . milites, pueri et venatores, quos nominare nescimus omnes"; Document 23 (p. 30): "multisque aliis quos longum est enumerare"; Document 95 (p. 6): "multis aliis, quod enarrare longum est"; Document 335 (p. 15): "et alii multi quos longum est nominare."

122. Fauroux, *Recueil*, pp. 44, 57; Musset, *Actes*, pp. 34, 38–39. A. de Boüard, *Manuel*, 1:322, holds that signatures in the form " + (ego) N. subscripsi" are—or were on the original—autographs whereas those in the form "Signum + N." are not. Giry, *Manuel*, pp. 595–97, who notes the same difference of form, thinks that by the eleventh century it did not correspond to a difference of fact; and the distinction does not appear to hold for Normandy in the eleventh century. Bénet, "Etude," pp. 3–4, thinks that the originality of a charter of this period depended on the existence of autograph signatures. Musset, however, has demonstrated, both in *Actes*, p. 34, and in "Expédition," that *scriptoria* of the eleventh century preferred that their documents be in a uniform hand and therefore sometimes recopied "originals" to achieve uniformity, even of the signatures. Guillot, *Comte*, 2:10, cites charters which indicate that in Anjou, at least, the requirement that a subscription be done *manu propria* was satisfied if the "signer" merely touched the parchment on which the "signature" would be recorded. See also Colmant, "Actes," p. 54, and, more generally Giry, *Manuel*, pp. 598–

99; A. de Boüard, *Manuel*, 2:89–94, 109–10; Tessier, *Diplomatique*, p. 221; Brown, "Some Observations," pp. 156–59.

123. For the percentages, see below, Appendix A, Table 2 B, col. 17. That they are low is suggested in several ways. First, in a few charters which survive only in copies the body of the charter refers to signatures but no signatures follow. Because many charters which end with signatures refer in no other way to the fact that they were signed, these few charters imply that many other nonoriginal charters without signatures were signed in the original. Second, there are instances of originals, the copies of which do not include the signatures, e.g., Document 709 and its copy in Bibl. Rouen, ms. 1193 (Y 44), f° 47r, no. 43.

124. Document 489 (p. 303). For the duke's signature see also below, this chapter, at and in n. 130. The version published as Document 489 does not, in its current damaged state, include the donor's signature; but the version copied into BN, ms. lat. 10086, f° 151v–152r, does, giving his name as Herbert de l'Epinay. The latter list is published by Round, *Calendar*, p. 166, no. 466.

125. A. de Boüard, *Manuel* 1:292. In this case, at least, the formulas seem to have had meaning to eleventh-century Normans despite their Frankish origins; they were not the result of blind copying.

126. Of 124 charters in which such clauses are extant, the duke signed 86, or 69.4 percent, sometimes as an alienor but often not. Ten of these charters are from Fécamp (7 of whose signature lists are not explained), 17 are from Jumièges (19 lists not explained), 20 are Norman charters from Mont-Saint-Michel (12 Norman lists not explained), and 13 are from Saint-Wandrille (22 lists not explained). In other words, 60 of 124, or 48.4 percent, of all the explanatory clauses come from these four abbeys; and 60 of 120, exactly half, of their signature lists have such clauses, which is roughly twice as high a percentage as average. Saint-Ouen is, among the abbeys of pre-Norman origin which were refounded in the tenth century, the exception: only 3 of its 33 signature lists are introduced by such clauses.

127. Above, Chapter 1, at and in n. 36.

128. Below, this chapter, at nn. 145–49.

129. Giry, *Manuel*, pp. 612–14; A. de Boüard, *Manuel*, 1:321; Haskins, *Norman Institutions*, p. 73; Chaplais, "Charte," pp. 94–95; Guillot, *Comte*, 2:5–16. Ibid., p. 13, n. 35, notes, "Pour la France médiévale, . . . il n'y a pas d'étude très approfondie."

130. Document 489 continues immediately after the sentence quoted above, this chapter, at n. 124: "Ego Willelmus, Dei gratia Anglorum rex et Normannorum princeps, hanc cartam agnovi et hoc nostre auctoritatis signo firmavi +." Usually, when more than one cross is identified by a whole sentence, each sentence is in the first person with a different subject. See above, this chapter, n. 122, for the possible significance of signatures in this form.

131. Document 285 (col. 202). See above, Chapter 4, at n. 52, for more on this transaction.

132. Document 725 (f° 78v): "Signum quod fecit Mainus + sub persona filii sui Radulfi qui absens erat et tamen hoc donum concessit."

133. Above, Chapter 6, after n. 112 and at nn. 113–16.

134. Document 186 (p. 264): "signum, cunctis fidelibus meis astantibus, impono"; Document 299: "vos . . . testes estis . . . quia ego manu mea illam firmavi."

135. Below, pp. 213–18.

136. Documents 117, 119 (p. 106, probably also monks), 129, 130, 135 (p. 153, probably also monks), 184 (p. 261), 226 (p. 344), 255 (p. 400), 256, 714.

137. Document 124 is signed (p. 124) by Saffrid bishop of Sées; Document 166 is signed (p. 226) by John abbot of Fécamp; Document 213 is signed by Hugh bishop of Avranches, who, in this charter, received a life estate and was, therefore, personally the recipient; Document 318 is either witnessed or signed by Abbot William and John the

cellarer of Fécamp; Document 316 (p. 286) records an exchange between Saint-Etienne de Caen and Saint-Bénigne de Dijon and is signed by both abbots, perhaps as alienors, but they were also recipients; Document 708 is signed by Archbishop William of Rouen. Document 271 is signed (p. 440) by John bishop of Avranches, but he is the donor as well as the head of the recipient institution. Document 176 is a more difficult problem. At the end of this charter for Fécamp is an additional paragraph recording a few more gifts by the donor, Duke William, which ends, "Ad hoc testes sunt Rotbertus de Moretuli et Johannes archiepiscopus Rotomagensis et Rogerius de Belmont et Stigandus + et Johannes abbas Fiscannensis. Signum Willelmi regis +." Since the original is not extant, it is unclear whether only Stigand and King William signed or whether all these *testes*, including the abbot of the recipient monastery, did so.

The absence of signatures of members of the recipient church is noted briefly in Fauroux, *Recueil*, p. 59, with regard only to abbots (two of the three examples cited in ibid., n. 237, come from a non-Norman abbey and have therefore not been considered here), and in Laporte, "Abbaye," p. 74.

138. See the cellarer John of Fécamp in Document 318, as cited in the previous note. Document 153 is signed by two monks from the recipient church. In addition, Document 24 seems to contemplate the possibility that the clergy of the recipient cathedral might sign; but the only actual signer was the alienor. Indeed, in this case *signa* may be a synonym for *nomina*. It is, of course, possible that some of the individual signers whom many charters identify only by first names were members of recipient churches, but there is no way to determine this.

139. The relative dearth of signatures of abbots is briefly noted by Fauroux, *Recueil*, p. 59, D. C. Douglas, *William*, p. 144; Haskins, *Norman Institutions*, p. 275.

140. Because the number of possible divided signature lists is so small, this information is not included in Appendix A, Table 2. The problem in each instance is that the list may be of witnesses rather than of signers. They are Documents 39 (p. 42), 318, 417 (p. 122), 521 (p. 123), and 729, the last of which may not be from the eleventh century.

141. Above, Chapter 4, at nn. 172–80.

142. Respectively, Documents 272 (p. 442) and 355 (p. 572).

143. Document 226; see also Fauroux, *Recueil*, p. 343, n. 1. He witnesses as well as signs the charter.

144. For women as witnesses, see above, this chapter, at and in n. 35. Except for duchesses, women with no apparent connection to alienations signed only six charters. Document 200 is signed (p. 292) by a woman named Emma, who may be the mother of another signer, William son of Osbert, if he is actually William fitz Osbern, as is likely. This would not be the only instance in which William's father's name is rendered Osbert; and Orderic's version of the charter, OV, 2:38, includes William fitz Osbern (not Osbert) among the signers, but not Emma or any other woman. Emma wife of Osbern, however, had become abbess of Saint-Amand by 1049 at the latest (see Document 194), and the Emma of Document 200 is not so described. Document 264 is signed (p. 419) by the wives of two of the men who sign; one is not explicitly called a wife. Document 510 may be signed (p. 84) not only by the alienor's wife but also by an apparently unrelated woman. Document 523 is signed (p. 133) by the mother and sister of an alienor and also by an apparently unrelated woman. Document 282 is signed (col. 152) by the unnamed abbess of Almenèches, and Document 579 is signed by Adelasia abbess of Almenèches; Almenèches was the sister abbey of Saint-Martin de Sées, for which both charters were drawn up.

145. These figures are minimal: cases in which the duke may have been an alienor or was or may have been the direct lord of a donor are not included. The charters of La Trinité du Mont are included.

146. Haskins, *Norman Institutions*, pp. 54, 275–76; Fauroux, *Recueil*, pp. 59–62; D. C. Douglas, *William*, p. 144; Brown, "Some Observations," p. 156.

147. See also A. de Boüard, *Manuel*, as quoted below, Chapter 8, n. 6; Guillot, *Comte*, 2:9–10, 12–13; Brown, "Some Observations," pp. 156–57.

148. See also Guillot, *Comte*, 2:14–16.

149. Document 397.

150. E.g., Document 145. Brown, "Some Observations," p. 158, points out that in the extreme case (Document 155a) Duke Robert the Magnificent signed an act over 150 years old.

151. The entire cartulary is printed by A. Deville, *La Trinité du Mont*; twenty-two of the charters are ducal charters from before 1066, which are included in Fauroux, *Recueil*, from which I cite them when citation is necessary. Document 93 is incomplete, and therefore its inclusion among those without signatures may not be justified.

152. Above, this chapter, at and in n. 140.

153. No man explicitly identified as a monk appears as either a signer or a witness in the charters of La Trinité du Mont.

154. Thus, Richard the seneschal witnessed twenty-six charters and signed six "ex nostra parte"; Bernard the cook witnessed twenty-one and signed seven "ex nostra parte"; Osbern Bruncosted witnessed eight and signed two "ex nostra parte." For other men the figures are: Ansfred the cook, two and four; Richard de Drincourt, three and three; Osmund the marshal, three and one; Ralph brother of Bernard the cook, five and one. Four men witnessed one charter and signed another "ex nostra parte": Turold brother of Richard de Drincourt, Isnel the baker, Bernard son of Hermer, and Robert d'Aulage. Geoffrey *del Bec* signed one "ex nostra parte" and witnessed one or two (in Document 72, p. 452, the name appears as *del Busc*). In addition, a man named Evrard brother of Simon who witnessed two, an Evrard who witnessed one, and Evrard the deacon, who signed one, may all be the same person. The exception referred to is Warner the forester, who signed one charter "ex nostra parte" and witnessed one in which the witness list is not divided and a second in which he seems to have witnessed *ex parte* of the alienor. Several of these men also signed charters whose signature lists are not divided.

155. Document 205 (p. 306). Some of the charters cited above, this chapter, at and in n. 1, in which alienors appear as witnesses may also be examples of the use of *testes* to mean signers.

156. Below, Appendix A, Table 2, cols. 10 and 17.

157. E.g., Giry, *Manuel*, pp. 600, 608–9; A. de Boüard, *Manuel*, 1:328; ibid., 2: 89–94, 109; Colmant, "Actes," pp. 54–55.

158. Document 24, this chapter, n. 138.

159. Below, Appendix A, Table 2 B, cols. 25–28. See also Brown, "Some Observations," p. 156.

160. In addition to those charters cited in the following notes, see above, Chapter 3, nn. 175–78, and Document 603. Yver, *Contrats*, pp. 83–86, 135–66, gives an extended discussion of pledges, primarily in the twelfth and thirteenth centuries.

161. Below, this chapter, at n. 193.

162. The earliest is Document 557. Of the other charters mentioning pledges which can be dated by decades, one comes from between 1060 and 1069, one from between 1070 and 1079, four from between 1080 and 1089, and eight from between 1090 and 1099. Of those charters which can be dated by reigns, only Document 557 comes from William the Conqueror's reign as duke, six come from his reign as king, and fifteen come from Robert Curthose's reign as duke. The increase is real, that is, the rate of increase is higher than the rate of increase of all charters (as calculated below, Appendix A, Tables 1 A and 1 B), except for the decade 1060–69.

163. Alternatives are given because a few charters give two sets of pledges to one transaction: if these are counted together, the highest total is nine and the average is just under 3.2; if they are counted as separate groups of pledges, the highest number is seven and the average is over 2.9.

164. *Fidejussor* is used twenty-six times, *plegius* fourteen times; the words are never used together to refer to the same persons, although Document 528 (described below, this chapter, n. 187) uses *fidejussor* once and *plegius* three times, and Saint-Martin de Sées, in different charters, uses *fidejussor* three times and *plegius* ten times. Document 779 says that the *fidejussores* are also *manutenentes*: below, this chapter, at and in n. 185. One charter (below, this chapter, at and in n. 173) uses *obses*. Yver's contention, in *Contrats*, p. 137, that *plegius* came into use only in the twelfth century is clearly wrong.

165. See above, Chapter 3, at nn. 175–78, where the use of pledges is one of the arguments on which the conclusion that sales were regarded as an insecure type of transfer was based. As there are other reasons for that conclusion (and other reasons for the conclusion that pledges tended to be used in connection with insecure transfers), the argument is not entirely circular.

166. Respectively, above, Chapter 3, at and in n. 220; Document 523.

167. Document 606: "Turstinus homo Willelmi de Alneto, qui ex parte sui domini de cuius feodo ipsa ecclesia erat, missus fuit, dicens et affirmans suum dominum predictum scilicet Willelmum hanc totam conventionem concedere. . . . Alias quoque predictus Willelmus de Alneto prelocutorum conventionum et ipsius conventionis plegius coram abbate Radulfo fuit, teste. . . ."

168. Below, this chapter, at and in nn. 173 and 189; Document 681: "Fide sua data plegios etiam . . . donavit." Yver, *Contrats*, p. 152, thinks that giving faith occurred only some of the time.

169. For sons, see Documents 410 (p. 76) and 849. For brothers, see Documents 592 (f° 16r), 704, 850, 854. For brothers-in-law, see Documents 656 and 659 (f° 58v). For a cousin, see below, this chapter, at and in n. 185. For mother, brother, and sisters, see Document 523 (p. 133).

170. Men: below, this chapter, at n. 173. Lords: above, this chapter, at and in n. 167; below, this chapter, n. 189; Document 661 (f° 59r), and perhaps Document 599 (f° 26v). The pledges to the treaties of 1091 and 1101 (below, this chapter, at nn. 180–82) were, of course, their principals' men. One of the pledges in Document 681 may have been the alienor's tenant, if Fulk de *Peneio* (or *Peveio*) is Fulk du Pin. Yver, *Contrats*, p. 136, thinks that it was the duty of tenants to act as pledges for their lords; his evidence proves that this was so in the thirteenth century but does not concern the eleventh.

171. Respectively, below, this chapter, at and in n. 185; Document 599 (f° 26v); Document 661 (f° 59r): "ipso concedente et defensore et fideiussore."

172. Documents 523 and 592 (f° 16r).

173. Document 25 (p. 97). Rannulf's pledges are *assertores* as well as *obsides*, and the bishop's are not; but the difference in wording seems not to correspond to a difference of function.

174. Yver, *Contrats*, pp. 139–45, quotation translated from p. 140.

175. Ibid., p. 140. Yver accepts Bourrienne's date for the charter, namely, before 1147.

176. Below, this chapter, at and in n. 179. This treaty renewed an arrangement originally negotiated in 1066 between William the Conqueror and Count Baldwin V, ruptured after 1071, and renewed by William Rufus with (probably) Robert II in 1093 (Lyon, *From Fief*, pp. 33–34, 201; Barlow, *William Rufus*, pp. 325–26). Texts of the earlier treaties do not survive, and it is impossible to know whether their terms were substantially the same as those of 1101. If they were, the hostage-pledge was known in eleventh-century Normandy.

177. Document 850.

178. Above, Chapter 4, at and in n. 64.

179. Document 31 (p. 3): the count's pledges have the following duties: "Si comes Rotbertus de predictis conventionibus exierit et ipsi [i.e., the pledges] eum infra iij

quarantenas reconciliare regi non potuerint, quod unusquisque ex predictis obsidibus dabit regi c marcas argenti et hoc facient infra tres quarantenas. Et si non fecerint, in captione regis Henrici se ponent pro predictis marcis argenti. Et rex ab eis non plus exiget quam quod predictum est. Et ponent se in captione in Turri London' vel in aliquo loco ubi rex eos libere possit retinere ad proficuum suum"; ibid. also lists each of the count's pledges as "pro c marcis." About the king's pledges, the document says (p. 4) only: "Et isti tali conditione sunt obsides erga comitem quali conditione comitis obsides erga regem"; one of the eleven, Robert fitz Hamo, was a pledge "pro cc marcis," the other ten "pro c marcis."

180. These two treaties also differ from the agreement between Rannulf and the bishop in that, at least according to the Chronicle, the numbers of pledges on each side were equal, always twelve. The equality is consistent with the nature of a treaty, an agreement between full equals. In Rannulf's agreement with the bishop, Rannulf, presumably because he was the subordinate, gave his lord more pledges than his lord gave him. The same was true in the Anglo-Flemish treaty of 1101, although the values of the pledges add up to the same amount, twelve hundred marks.

181. *Peterborough Chronicle*, p. 29; translation by Whitelock et al., *Anglo-Saxon Chronicle*, p. 177. WM, 2:472, says only, "satagentibus sanioris consilii hominibus." OV, 5:318, says, "Remotis omnibus arbitris soli fratres scita sua sanxerunt," but he seems to have been mistaken; on his discussion of this treaty, see Chibnall, *World*, pp. 197–99. David, *Robert*, p. 136, accepts the oath of twelve magnates, as does Hollister, "Anglo-Norman Civil War," p. 329. Hollister publishes, ibid., p. 334, a new source on the treaty, which says that it was made "mediantibus utrorumque baronibus" and "sacramento et affidatione inter eos facta." Ibid., p. 331, points out the similarity of many of the terms of the treaty of 1101 to those of the treaty of 1091 and proposes that the former was modeled on the latter; perhaps this included the arrangements about pledges. See also Le Patourel, *Norman Empire*, p. 199 and n. 5.

182. WM, 2:363; *Peterborough Chronicle*, pp. 18–19, 21 (translations adapted from Whitelock et al., *Anglo-Saxon Chronicle*, pp. 169, 171). See also David, *Robert*, pp. 60–61, 83–84; Barlow, *William Rufus*, pp. 281–84, 327, 331–32, 416.

183. Document 617, the one extant record of a pact between laymen, says nothing on the subject.

184. Document 610 (f° 31r): "testes atque tocius conventionis exequende fideiussores. . . . Testes . . . de hominibus Sancti Martini."

185. Document 779: "Huius conventionis sunt fide iussores et testes atque manutenentes ipse Willelmus de Ansgervilla et Robertus filius eius, et Goislenus cognatus meus est concessor et fide iusso [*sic*] atque mea parte testis, et plures alii."

186. De Fontette, *Recherches*, p. 102, makes a similar conjecture for the Paris region in the twelfth century.

187. Documents 13 (p. 22) and 715 (p. 487).

Document 528 records a complex series of small transfers—a gift, two sales, and four mortgages—which is probably also relevant here. The charter appears to record an instance in which a group of men coordinated their alienations, for a purpose which is not clear. Four men are said to have witnessed all the transactions. In addition, witnesses, pledges, or both are listed separately for each transfer except one of the sales. Those with at least one pledge are the other sale and three of the mortgages. One man served as a witness or a pledge in all six transactions which have either, always as a pledge when there were pledges. Two of the alienors served as pledges or as witnesses to one or more transfers other than their own, again always as pledges when there were pledges.

188. Documents 99 (p. 524), 410 (p. 76), 557 (f° 138v), 848, 849, 854, 873, 883.

189. Document 607: "suum fidem dedit in plegio et .iiii.^{or} homines: Rannulfum scilicet, dominum eiusdem ville, Hugonem filium Rainaldi de Polleio et Hugonem car-

pentarium de Boisco, Albertum et Rotbertum de Plaisseio. Et sic sunt isti plegii ut si predictus Vitalis hanc conventionem non tenuerit, unusquisque plegius .xx. solidos cenomannensium reddat monachis." Rannulf had given the abbey his part of the church six years earlier (above, this chapter, at and in n. 167).

190. Document 402 (p. 691).

191. Yver, *Contrats*, pp. 138–47, insists that the first alternative was the only one in the eleventh and twelfth centuries and that the second emerged as the rule in the course of the thirteenth century; but he cites no eleventh-century evidence.

192. The silence of both charters about obligations of the principal to his pledges should they have to pay cannot be taken as evidence that the payments were fines because the matter was of no interest to the abbeys which drew up the charters. Moreover, Yver, *Contrats*, pp. 164–65, shows that even in the thirteenth century the sources, both custumals and documents of practice, are silent on this subject, yet he concludes that the pledges' right of recourse "ne paraît pas douteux" (p. 165).

Document 31, the Anglo-Flemish treaty of 1101, if it can be considered relevant, may cast some light on these matters. See above, this chapter, at and in n. 179, for the clauses about pledges. Each pledge was to pay, individually, a preset amount, 100 or, once, 200 marks. The total owed by the king's pledges is 1,200 marks, but Document 31 (p. 4) gives the king's fee to the count as 500 pounds, i.e., 750 marks, a sum which bears no obvious relation to the pledges' obligation. An alternate reading of the sum—given by Rymer's *Foedera* (as cited by Chaplais, *Diplomatic Documents*, p. 4, n. 5) and preferred, without explanation, by Barlow, *William Rufus*, p. 325—is 400 marks, exactly one-third of what the pledges would owe. If the king's pledges would overcompensate the count, the amount owed by the count's pledges would probably not adequately compensate the king. The count owed the king one thousand knights for a campaign, to serve "quamdiu illa necessitas duraverit" (Document 31, p. 2). Taking the later standard minimum, forty days' service, the count's pledges were obligated to pay the king only 4.8 *d.* per knight per day. If the term of service expected was longer, the wage would be correspondingly less: sixty days, for example, would yield a wage of only 3.2 *d.* per knight per day. No rates of wages are known from the Anglo-Norman realm in the eleventh or early twelfth centuries. In the early years of Henry II a knight's wage seems to have been 8 *d.* per day (Round, *Feudal England*, pp. 271–72). In Stephen's reign, it may have been no more than 6 *d.* per day (Holister, *Military Organization*, pp. 160, 208–11, 285–86). In ibid., pp. 211–12, Hollister calculates that in Edward the Confessor's England it was 4 *d.* per day for a sixty-day period of service. See also ibid., pp. 89–94, 286–88, for the prevalence of a two-month term of service in wartime in England in the century after the Conquest. The assumption of both Round and Hollister that the scutage rate was set at exactly the product of the daily wage of a knight and the number of days of service has often been challenged, most recently by Keefe, *Feudal Assessments*, pp. 37–40. If it is valid, however, the wage rates which result from the figures in the Anglo-Flemish treaty of 1101 seem anomalously low. If Count Robert defaulted and King Henry had to hire a thousand mercenary knights for the duration of an emergency, he would probably have to expend a good deal more than 1,200 marks. The incongruity of all these figures, in turn, suggests that the sums paid by pledges were fines, not compensation.

193. Document 315 (p. 283), c. 11.

194. Yver's arguments to this effect, in *Contrats*, p. 157, n. 1, are quite convincing.

195. On the type of judicially authorized distraint which may have been involved, see Hall and Sweeney, "'Licentia de Nam,'" pp. 2–4. (Cf. Musset, "Huit essais," p. 122, n. 48, who thinks that the license was something else entirely, a *licentia de navi*.) Yver, *Contrats*, pp. 156–58, argues against the existence of extrajudicial distress against pledges in Normandy; but on pp. 252–56, 271–73, he is less categorical, especially for the earliest period. Ibid., p. 157, n. 1, and pp. 252, 272–73, discusses this

clause of the *Consuetudines et Iusticie*. Cf. the apparent allusion to extrajudicial distress, above, Chapter 4, at n. 52.

196. Above, Chapter 6, at and in n. 170.

CHAPTER 8

1. Document 871: "jure hereditario in dominio . . . solidas liberas et quietas. . . . Has enim non possum dare in dominio quia praedicti homines tenuerunt eas de patre meo et nunc tenent de me in fedio. Verumtamen tali modo concedo eas et do eidem coenobio ut quandocumque abbas vel monachi dederint vel fecerint ipsis hominibus tale quid pro quo eas a Sancto Stephano et abbate recognoscant et teneant aut omnino qualicumque modo in dominio concedant eas Sanctus Stephanus libere et quiete sicut supradictas habeat et ita ut nunquam abbas vel monachi aut etiam praedicti mei homines me sive fratres aut haeredes meos inde requirant quandocumque ipsi homines velint eas tenere de Sancto aut ut dictum est vendere vel ei dare omnino, et ita etiam ut nunquam pro hac re ipsi homines habeant prohibitionem vel quodlibet contrarium in aperto sive in occulto a me aut a fratribus vel haeredibus meis."

2. Respectively, Document 863: Hugh de Rouvres "[t]erram . . . Gualterii hominis sui . . . promisit se daturum sancto si eam posset excambire. Si vero non posset, concessit ut ipse Gualterius terram illam se vellet sancto vel in elemosinam daret vel venderet"; Document 520 (p. 115). On the meaning of *dominium* as "demesne," see above, Chapter 5, at nn. 12–14. Document 520 is one of the clearer examples of the meaning of the word, because it is written in the name of William's lord, who was present and consented when the gift was made, yet considers the tenement the tenant's demesne. Moreover, given the lord's consent, the only claims which could have been relevant here would be those of William's tenants, had he had any: demesne would be beside the point if the putative claimants were relatives.

3. Document 517. The charter shifts abruptly from a gift of tithes to an exception of land; presumably Baudry meant the tithes of this land.

4. The same rule seems to underlie a provision of the charter recording Geoffrey Infant's sale of the tithes of eighty acres of his demesne to Saint-Etienne de Caen, "tali conventione ut si ipsa terra non est tota in suo dominio perficiet decimam ipsa ex alia terra" (Document 848). In other words, if the land or its tithes—the record seems unclear—are in a tenant's hands, the lord's gift will not be valid. Geoffrey Infant was one of the tenants of Hugh Paynel who would not consent to Hugh's gift of tithes to the abbey.

Only one charter might say that a tenant's consent had not occurred until a time subsequent to the alienation—Document 708—but this is probably in fact a confirmation of a gift by an ancestor of the tenant.

5. Documents 34 and 259 (p. 407). Document 756 (p. 403) is analogous, but as the tenant is a church a different rule is probably involved. In Document 484 (p. 648), a pancart from Bec, Alvered gave "dimidium quod frater ejus ab eo tenebat, si frater ejus concesserit." This might be another example of the need for tenants' consent, but it might also be a special condition like that discussed below this chapter, at n. 7.

6. Corbett, "Development," p. 487, asserts the exact opposite, that lords' consent was necessary and tenants' consent was not. Few other scholars have commented on tenants' rights in this matter, but the consensus has been that lords' consent was necessary. See Génestal, *Rôle*, pp. 22–24; Lagouëlle, *Essai*, pp. 115, 242–43; Yver, *Contrats*, p. 136 (quoted above, Chapter 6, n. 8); Carabie, *Propriété foncière*, pp. 246–47; D. C. Douglas, *William*, pp. 96–97. Goebel, *Felony*, pp. 289–90, denies the necessity; see also below, this chapter, n. 125. A. de Boüard, *Manuel*, 2:141–42, asserts, in a more general context, that the submission of charters to lords for their signatures was not an expression of a need for consent but, instead, "c'est en qualité de *vir bonus* ou *legalis*, de *persona autentica* qu'il est sollicité de souscrire"; ibid., p. 141, n. 4, says

that the lord's consent "était explicitement exprimé par le formule 'cum consensu N. senioris mei.'" I do not think that this distinction can hold for eleventh-century Normandy.

7. Above, Chapter 6, at and in n. 75.

8. Document 512.

9. Bouvris, "Plus anciennes chartes," p. 329, describes a late eleventh-century charter of Gilbert Crispin for Saint-Laumer de Blois conceding them a tithe "que les moines de cette abbaye avaient acquise sans son consentement." Here, it seems, the transfer had certainly taken effect despite lack of the lord's consent.

10. Above, Chapter 7, at n. 149.

11. Document 373.

12. There has been little discussion of this question for Normandy in the eleventh century, but it is sometimes asserted that relatives' consent was legally necessary. See, for example Génestal, "Interdiction"; Génestal, *Tutelle*, p. 41; Matthew, *Norman Conquest*, p. 57. Olivier-Martin, *Histoire*, p. 78, notes, for France as a whole, a conflict at this time between ecclesiastical insistence on freedom of alienation and a popular feeling that the family's rights were to be preserved, a conflict resolved only in the twelfth century. Because the documents used here were written by clerics and record transactions of interest to churches, it is possible that their silence on this subject is deliberate.

On the absence of the *retrait lignager*, see above, Chapter 3, at nn. 95–96.

13. Below, this chapter, at n. 19; Document 476 (p. 174).

14. OV, 4:204; translation adapted from p. 205. Roger de Beaumont eventually managed to secure his son's release from prison, but disputes over Ivry and Brionne remained one of the major problems of Robert Curthose's reign. For the significance of Ivry and Brionne to the magnates who disputed possession of them, see Yver, "Châteaux forts," pp. 67–69. On the date, see Barlow, *William Rufus*, p. 271 and n. 35.

15. Document 581 is the sale. Geoffrey's confirmation is Document 582: "Deinde post multorum spatia annorum Gauffridus filius uxoris predicti Berengarii ad quem supra dicta decima hereditabiliter pertinebat, sicut vitricus suus Berengarius et mater sua vendiderant et omnes supra scripti consenserant, Sancto Martino perpetualiter concessit." The manuscript has blank spaces after "filius" and "mater sua," apparently for the name of Berengar's wife, which is given nowhere. The charter is ambiguous as to whether the tithes belonged by inheritance to Geoffrey or to his mother.

16. The only charter which might suggest that a relative's refusal to consent could block an alienation is Alvered's gift to Bec of what his brother held from him if the brother would consent: above, this chapter, n. 5. As his brother was also his tenant, however, this proviso, if it was not a special condition, was probably not an exception to the rule about relatives but rather an expression of the rule about tenants.

17. Above, Chapter 6, at and in n. 75, and this chapter, at n. 7.

18. Above, this chapter, at and in nn. 1 and 3.

19. Document 374.

20. Document 441 (p. 183). OV, 3:192–96, tells the story of how, in 1118, Ansold de Maule became a monk at Saint-Evroul and died there. Ibid., pp. 192–94, says, "Monachi . . . per biduum tamen propter absentiam primogeniti filii sui et haeredis futuri quod petierat [i.e., to become a monk] distulerunt. . . . Denique biduo transacto ut filium aduenisse audiuit, coniugem suam cum eodem ad se protinus accedere iussit," and he became a monk at the abbey. This example is too late to be of direct concern, but it is significant of what seems already to have been the attitude earlier. Ansold was not Norman; but, as it was the monks, not he, who insisted on the delay, the incident can stand as an example of Norman practice.

21. Document 654: "Idem enim pactum fuit de Willelmo filio eius licet ultra mare esset quando donum fuit factum."

22. Above, Chapter 7, at and in n. 132.

23. Above, Chapter 7, at and in n. 167.
24. Document 605: "Nec non etiam filia eiusdem Huberti, cui ipse medietatem supradicte decime in mariagio dederat, tamdiu donec ipse monachus fieret, dedit atque concessit, voluntate et iussu sui mariti. Ipse enim maritus infirmus venire non poterat, sed coram multis aperte dixerat sibi tantum decimam esse datam, donec predictus Hubertus monachus fieret."
25. Document 844: "abbas dedit eis centum solidos tali conditione quod ex quo Rodulfus filius Radulfi Taisson haberet terram suam in potestate facerent eum hanc conventionem concedere."
26. Document 850: "conveniens quod Radulfum Taisson de quo illam terram tenebat faceret has venditiones concedere."
27. Document 600 (f° 27r): "cui pater eius . . . ea in maritatu dedit. Ipsa vero in tantum ea Sancto Martino concessit ut etiam promitteret quod cuicumque filiorum filiarumve suarum maritatum suum in fine suo dimitteret supra dictam terram . . . solute et quiete . . . , sicut ipsa et fratres eius fecerant, concedere faceret." For a second example, see above, Chapter 6, at and in n. 168. In Document 214 (p. 329), the duke is asked to secure the consent of the brothers of a donor who was on his deathbed and does so. See above, Chapter 3, at n. 59, for more on this gift. Document 215, the other version, does not mention this request to William.
28. In addition to the charters cited here, see Documents 214 (p. 329), 310 (p. 602), 372 (reading *concederet* for *conjugi* or *conjugis*, which, though it is what the manuscript says, makes no sense in the context), 448 (p. 186), 642 (f° 51r), 786, 804, 857, 859, 860, 861.
29. Ten charters, from four different abbeys, couple a total of eleven promises to secure someone's consent with the creation of pledges: Documents 13 (p. 22), 592 (f° 16r), 659 (f° 58v), 704, 779, 850, 854 (twice), 864, 868, 870. As there are only forty-one mentions of pledges in the extant charters, this degree of coincidence is significant. Four of these ten charters and two others, from four different abbeys, couple a promise to secure someone's consent with a promise to warrant the alienation: Documents 13 (p. 22), 562, 641 (f° 50r), 850, 868, 870. Warranty does not occur in anything like a fifth of the extant charters: see below, Chapter 9.
30. Above, this chapter, at n. 19.
31. See Document 399 for the description of Philip's earlier reluctance and for his first confirmation. For the others, see Documents 400 (pp. 687, 688) and 401 (p. 688). William de Briouze's original gifts were made before 1080 (Document 396).
32. Document 205 (p. 306) is quoted. The other similar examples are too numerous to cite.
33. Below, p. 206.
34. Document 284 (cols. 154–55). This account is not contemporary with the foundation of the abbey, about 1046. The editors of the *Gallia Christiana* date it to 1108 (col. 153), but Musset, "Recherches sur les pèlerins," p. 144, n. 99, calls it "un récit mal daté (du XIIe siècle?)," and Yver, "Autour de l'absence," p. 203, says only that it is "postérieure de plus d'un demi-siècle aux événements." Both scholars nevertheless accept it as substantially accurate.
35. In addition to the charter cited in the next note, see Documents 222, 247, 507 (p. 59), 723, 866, 867, 885 (f° 197v), and probably 521 (p. 122).
See also above, this chapter, at n. 20. In Documents 51 (p. 282) and 868 alienors promised to secure the consent of all their heirs.
36. Document 755. The charter says nothing to indicate that the church given had been the wife's property, as the list of confirmers might suggest.
37. For the heirs' brothers, see Documents 185 (p. 262) and 597 (f° 26r; three sons either of the heir or of his brother also consented). For the niece and her husband, see Document 578 (f° 7v), where Mabel de Bellême and Roger de Montgomery consent to a gift bv Ivo de Bellême, bishop of Sées; the connection is close, for Mabel was to

inherit her uncle's share of the lordship of Bellême on his death. For the second husband, see Document 433 (p. 41). Document 688 (f° 88r) includes the participation as witnesses of the alienor's brother-in-law and of men who are either the alienor's or the brother-in-law's *nepos* and son-in-law. For corroborating evidence from a different source that family circles were small, see Barlow, *William Rufus*, pp. 9–10.

38. If there was a rule that fathers could not inherit from their sons unless there were no other possible heirs, it has left no trace in the extant documents.

39. Génestal, "Origine," pp. 570–71.

40. Respectively, Documents 433 and 538.

41. *TAC*, LXXIX, ed. Tardif, I.i, pp. 80–83, and I.ii, pp. 66–69.

42. The exceptions are the two charters recording devises of dowers to duchesses, on which see above, Chapter 2, at and in n. 11.

43. The widow's claim is in Document 538. Roger de Croismare claimed his wife's inheritance (above, Chapter 4, at and in n. 114); Picot de Say and his wife claimed her dower from her first husband's brother (above, Chapter 6, at and in n. 172).

44. Document 335 (p. 16). Cf. Document 722, in which, when Robert count of Mortain and his second wife, Almodis, made gifts of land in England to Mont-Saint-Michel, "caritatem istam concessit Robertus filius comitis Moretonii ille quem de Almodi comitissa habuit et Willelmus ejus alter filius concessit ita si de Almodi supradicta non remaneret heres et ad ipsum Willelmum reveniret terra quod concederet." This seems to mean that William gave his consent so that, in case his half-brother, Robert, should die and Robert's mother, Almodis, to whom what was given had apparently belonged, should die without other heirs and her possessions should therefore revert to her husband and thence to her stepson, the stepson, William, would already have given his consent to the gift. This case therefore differs from Havisa's in that the remoter heir's consent was secured before the death of the closest heir, but both charters show much the same concern to secure the consent of whoever might at some point be the closest heir.

45. Document 270.

46. Document 271 (p. 440): "heredem alterius medietatis"; Document 577 (repeated in Document 579): "ex alia medietate heredem." Bouvris, "Date," p. 128, n. 74, suggests that the place concerned in Document 577 is in Maine rather than Normandy. See also above, Chapter 4, n. 249.

47. Above, Chapter 5, at nn. 41–43.

48. Above, Chapter 3, at and in n. 203.

49. Document 438.

50. Farrer and Clay, *Early Yorkshire Charters*, 7:34–35, publish a French paraphrase of the charter (taken from *Inventaire Sommaire, Manche, H*, 1:7), conjecture that Robert's heir was a daughter named Lucy and suggest a date in the early 1090s.

51. Documents 1, 2, 13 (p. 148), 204 (p. 305), 729. The son who is singled out by name was certainly the eldest only in the third and the last of these instances.

52. E.g., Documents 529 and 207 (p. 310), respectively.

53. Above, Chapter 6, n. 49; this chapter, n. 20; Documents 208 (p. 313), 309, 383 (p. 87), 448 (p. 186), 743.

54. Powicke, *Loss*, p. 43; Génestal, "Formation du droit," pp. 160–63; G. H. White, "First House," pp. 85–88 and 88, n. 2; Le Patourel, "Norman Succession," p. 226; Bates, "Notes," esp. p. 15; Bates, *Normandy*, pp. 118–20; Holt, "Feudal Society," passim, esp. "II," pp. 211–13; Chibnall, *Anglo-Norman England*, pp. 174–76.

55. The strongest indication comes from Document 10 (p. 17), in which the last of fourteen witnesses to a confirmation by Hugh de Rocé is "Girardo bastardo filio ipsius Hugonis de Roceto, qui et donationes supradictas patris sui, quantum ipsius esse poterat auctorizavit." This clearly implies that Gerard's confirmation was not worth much because he was a bastard: no other son is ever said to confirm "quantum ipsius esse poterat" or a similar qualification. See also Document 11 (p. 19), in which Walter du

Pin made a gift "annuentibus filiis suis, hoc est: Gualterio et Haloissa matrimonialibus; Gradulfo et Hugone cognomento Taleboto, atque Roberto bastardis"; this, again, suggests that in matters of consent there was a significant difference between "matrimonial" children, even daughters, and bastards. Both examples, however, come from a non-Norman abbey and from the Bellême area, which was only marginally Norman. Both are confirmed by Ivo bishop of Sées; Walter du Pin's charter is also confirmed by Geoffrey count of Anjou. There is, therefore, little reason to consider these charters to embody elements of Norman law.

From Normandy itself, the evidence is very scant. The considerable concern with legitimacy in connection with post-obit gifts (above, Chapter 3, at nn. 110 and 113–14) certainly suggests that legitimate children had much more right to inherit than did illegitimate children. About their relative capacities to consent, however, there is no direct evidence.

Modern scholars are not agreed on the rights of bastards in eleventh-century Normandy. Chesnel, *Cotentin*, passim, esp. p. 169, asserts that from the eleventh century on bastardy was a shameful and socially disabling condition; but he does not discuss its legal implications. Lepelley, "Jeunesse," p. 59, and M. de Boüard, *Guillaume*, p. 10, assert that there was still no prejudice against bastards in 1035, when Duke Robert the Magnificent named his bastard son William his successor; but D. C. Douglas, *William*, p. 37, disagrees. Regnault, "Condition," says that in the tenth and eleventh centuries "le bâtard noble, de grande famille, avoué par son père" was not debarred from succession. He cites as evidence the succession of Duke William Longsword in the tenth century (but not that of William the Conqueror in the eleventh), the succession of Eustace son of William de Breteuil in 1103 (see OV, 6:40), a case from Saint-Vincent du Mans, and the gift of Hugh de Rocé cited above. None of these seems to me to be good evidence, and the last item seems to argue the contrary view.

56. Document 502 (p. 247).

57. Not only lords but also their relatives are often said to have given their consent to alienations. The participation of a lord's relatives, however, falls into the category of consent of relatives rather than consent of lords. Figures on the numbers of charters in which lords are said to consent are, unfortunately, impossible to give, for many charters cite the consent of persons who do not seem to be relatives or tenants but are not identified as lords. That they were lords cannot be verified unless some other source attests to the relationship, which is rare. The problem is further complicated by the use of the term "lord" for the duke: it does not always mean that the alienor was a tenant-in-chief.

58. Above, Chapter 5, at nn. 93–109.

59. Above, Chapter 3, at and in n. 252; Chapter 5, at and in n. 25.

60. In addition to the charter cited in the previous note, see OV, 2:34–36 (a passage which is not in Document 200 and may be an interpolation by Orderic into the charter), and Documents 300 (p. 147), 302 (p. 162), 534, 739.

61. Document 600 (f° 26v): "omnibus dominis suis"; see also above, this chapter, at and in n. 27.

62. Document 188 (p. 269).

63. Above, this chapter, at and in n. 1. On such grants, see also Holt, "Feudal Society, II," pp. 202–4.

64. Document 396 (p. 679).

65. Document 642.

66. Document 560 (f° 142r).

67. In addition to those cited in the next four notes, see Documents 183 and 200 (p. 292, note x, with OV, 2:30).

68. Document 344 (p. 215).

69. E.g., below, this chapter, at n. 79.

70. Below, this chapter, at n. 99; Documents 81, 296 (p. 231), 778 (f° 102r).

71. Documents 116 (p. 102) and 127 (p. 141).
72. Documents 21 (p. 12), 26 (p. 284), 278 (col. 76). See Haskins, *Norman Institutions*, pp. 66–67 (nos. 2–4), 75–76, on the verbal similarities among these charters.
73. Documents 347, 349, 410 (p. 76; also in Document 417, p. 121), 537 (paragraph 13).
74. Above, this chapter, at and in n. 1; below, this chapter, at n. 79; Documents 349 and 697.
75. Below, this chapter, at n. 79; Document 496 (p. 378).
76. Document 432 (p. 39).
77. Document 496 (pp. 378–79): "rationabiliter." The first grant must have been made before 1095; the others can be dated only to the eleventh century. The second use of "rationabiliter" actually covers grants by four different lords, so there was presumably a total of six similar grants to the abbey originally. The fact of this condensation increases the probability that the word "rationabiliter" is a twelfth-century interpretation of whatever the eleventh-century documents had actually said. On twelfth-century usage, see Lagouëlle, *Essai*, pp. 245–46, and the references there.
78. Respectively, Document 388; Document 623; Document 854: "Concedo . . . ut liceat meis melioribus hominibus usque ad decem acris de suis terris quas de me tenent . . . dare. Minoribus vero unum tantummodo." Neither in Document 854 nor in the analogous provision quoted below, this chapter, at and in n. 83, is the difference between "lesser" and "greater" defined.
79. Document 294 (p. 220). See also Génestal, *Rôle*, p. 25.
80. For other indications, which are less certain, see above, this chapter, at n. 11; and Document 249 (p. 384), a gift of tithes in two vills, "ipsis annuentibus viris qui in villa manent, Hoel et fratribus ejus." If Hoel and his brothers were peasants, the charter gives the only indication that peasants ever consented to their lords' transactions. Legras, *Bourgage de Caen*, pp. 57–58, 96–97, emphasizes the ability of the burgesses of Caen as early as the eleventh century to alienate their tenements with their lords' consent.
81. Document 335 (p. 11).
82. Document 648.
83. Document 642 (f° 51r): "concedo de minoribus quidem hominibus meis usque ad tertiam partem feodi sui si dederint vel vendiderint monachis, de maioribus autem usque ad quartam partem." At the end of the charter Robert's brother Arnulf makes the same concession, but its terms are not repeated.
84. Above, Chapter 5, n. 42.
85. Document 531: "salvo nostro servicio et rectitudinibus." For reservations of service concerning current alienations, see above, Chapter 5, at nn. 100–103.
86. Document 278 (col. 76).
87. Quotation from Document 39 (p. 42). The others are Documents 473 (p. 156), 476 (p. 174), 477 (p. 184); in the last two, the donors were not Normans but came from Maule, near Meulan. Document 744 (p. 22) says that alienors may give "si tamen haeres dantis ex toto exhaereditus non sit"; this is almost certainly a forgery, however.
88. In later times the customary limit was one-third of the property (*TAC*, LXXXIX.1, ed. Tardif, I.i, pp. 99–100); but few discussions of this limit so much as mention the eleventh century. Sauvage, *Troarn*, p. 125 and n. 1, implies that the limit of one-third already existed in the eleventh century. Goebel, *Felony*, p. 290, asserts that "there was no demonstrable rule of law in the eleventh century, as there was later, limiting gifts in alms. On the contrary, such grants were encouraged by the suzerain." Matthew, *Norman Conquest*, pp. 57–58, regards the dukes as indifferent to the problem.
89. Document 758, the early twelfth-century list of peasant rents and services due to La Trinité de Caen (on which see above, Chapter 2, at and in n. 52) does not state the sizes of the tenements of its "typical" tenants; it is impossible, for example, to calculate even indirectly the size of any villein's holding. The list includes incidental

mentions of vavassors' tenements ranging in size from forty acres down to one virgate (i.e., one-quarter of an acre), of four bordars each of whom held half an acre, and of other tenants who held between one virgate and six acres; but these references are likely, given the construction of the list, to be exceptions in no way indicative of the rule for the size of tenements.

Carabie, *Propriété foncière*, pp. 75–77, calculates that at Verson in the thirteenth century a "full" villein tenement consisted of between 13 and 30 acres, with a certain concentration at 24 acres, though by then only two such tenements remained undivided; most individual villeins in 1247 held between 3 and 12 acres. Vavassors at Bretteville and Verson held between 5 and 120 acres (ibid., p. 65 and n. 48); bordars there held no more than "quelques acres" (ibid., p. 79). See also, in general, Navel, "Recherches sur les institutions féodales," pp. 96–100; ibid., passim, gives figures for individual estates, taken mostly from documents of the thirteenth and later centuries, which are of comparable magnitudes to those cited here. On the relationship of the virgate to the acre, see Delisle, *Etudes*, pp. 535–36; Navel, "Recherches sur les anciennes mesures," pp. 37, 117.

90. Above, this chapter, at and in nn. 78–79.

91. Document 642 (quoted above, this chapter, at and in n. 83), but cf. Document 854 (quoted above, this chapter, at and in n. 78).

92. On deathbed gifts, see above, Chapter 3, after n. 62. Only two charters may allude to post-obit gifts in this context. One, otherwise unlimited, may intend to exclude post-obit gifts from the types of alienations which are approved in advance, saying, "et si quis hominum vivorum aliquid in feodo meo . . . conferre voluerit . . . concedo" (Document 796). On the other hand, "any living man" may be merely a hyperbolic way of saying "anyone." Document 287 (col. 226), a considerably earlier charter, may explicitly allow post-obit gifts, saying that the lord and his son "annuerunt . . . ut si quis suorum se viventibus aut post mortem suam aliquid de terra sua . . . dare voluerit, nullo modo impediatur." "While alive or after their deaths" may be intended to include post-obit gifts by their tenants within the scope of the confirmation, or it may merely mean that the confirmers were trying to extend their confirmations beyond their own lifetimes: the question is whether *se* and *suam* refer to the donors or to their men. Together, these charters permit, but are hardly sufficient to justify, the interpretation that as the century progressed lords became aware that their tenants' heirs were more likely to be effectively disinherited by post-obit gifts than by any other type of alienation and therefore began to exclude post-obit gifts in an attempt to preserve the service due to them.

93. Above, Chapter 4, at and in n. 96.

94. Above, Chapter 4, at n. 83.

95. Above, Chapter 3, at and in n. 252.

96. Above, Chapter 5, at nn. 104–9.

97. The case cited above, Chapter 5, at and in n. 107, implies as much.

98. Above, Chapter 4, at n. 297.

99. Document 84.

100. Above, Chapter 6, at n. 49. It is, of course, possible that this apparent rule is merely an accident of the haphazard survival of sources.

101. Above, Chapter 6, at and in nn. 58–60.

102. Above, this chapter, at nn. 7–11.

103. Respectively, Documents 271 (p. 439) and above, this chapter, at n. 34. On the former, see also Holt, "Feudal Society, II," p. 208.

For the same reason, that is, the emphasis upon assurance, it also seems unlikely that the principal purpose of the ceremony was to make the recipient church the direct tenant of the lord rather than of the alienor, although that would appear to be the effect of the use of the ceremony if its tenurial implications were recognized. No charter comments on the tenurial consequences of the ceremony.

104. Document 396 (p. 678). Ibid. (p. 680) records the king's and queen's subsequent consent.

105. Document 747 (f° 305r): "Hanc terram predictus Hugo reddidit Goscelino Fretel de quo eam tenebat"; ibid.: "terra Hugonis de Morinval quam dedit in elemosina Goscelinus Fretellus." The pancart is difficult to date. I have used it, nevertheless, because it alone records one transfer in both these forms.

106. See also Génestal, *Rôle*, p. 95, n. 1; Holt, "Feudal Society, II," p. 208, who points out Documents 214 and 404 as another example.

107. Document 493 (p. 349).

108. See below, this chapter, n. 110, for a reason to think that the land given in Ranville was actually held by a man named Roger. Document 212 contains an account of some of these gifts, which implies that Morinus the carpenter no longer held his land at the time of the gift but says that the clerics William and Ingulf did then hold their land in Saint-Samson. Document 789 indicates that by 1101 "terra Ursi de Giburi" was a place-name.

109. In charters in the present tense, such phrases indicate the latter alternative, at least on the supposition that scribes always used the proper sequence of tenses, which there is some reason to doubt; but this charter is in the past tense: it says Roger "gave," not "gives."

110. The Roger whose mother this tenant was is not Roger de Montgomery but the Roger whose land in Ranville was given to the abbey. Because she was still alive at the time of the charter, it is probable that "Roger's land in Ranville," the third gift in the list, is not a place-name but a tenement.

111. Documents 127 (p. 141), 264 (p. 419), 511 (pp. 99, 103).

112. Above, Chapter 3, at nn. 244–59.

113. Above, this chapter, at nn. 1–5 and 16–18.

114. Génestal, *Rôle*, p. 132, notes a similar absence of records of consent of tenants in thirteenth-century sales of rents, where expressions of the consent of the tenants would seem to be logically necessary. He concludes that the tenant's consent was not necessary.

115. Above, this chapter, at and in n. 105.

116. Colmant, "Actes," p. 54; Matthew, *Norman Conquest*, p. 50.

117. Document 127 (p. 138).

118. Document 614. Document 183 seems to be another instance: Warulf licenses his lord Robert to sell land belonging to Osbern, apparently Warulf's tenant, and Osbern consents. In Document 451 (p. 188), the consent of a tenant's former tenant is included.

119. Document 34.

120. For Robert de Vitot, see OV, 2:120. For examples of other persons disinherited by the duke and subsequently restored, see above, Chapter 4, at and in nn. 154 and 158, and Chapter 5, at and in n. 83. On the impermanence of confiscations see also Delisle, *Histoire*, pp. 19–21; D. C. Douglas, *William*, p. 375; Matthew, *Norman Conquest*, pp. 74–75; Le Patourel, *Norman Barons*; Chibnall, "Feudal Society," pp. 38–39; Musset, "Huit essais," pp. 51–53.

121. WP, p. 122.

122. He disseised the bishopric of Bayeux of Viscount Rannulf and his land (above, Chapter 4, at n. 3). He disseised Mont-Saint-Michel of various things, including what Neil the old had given it (above, Chapter 6, at n. 23). He disseised Fécamp of land which Robert Curthose finally restored (Document 317, p. 288). He may have disseised Ascelin son of Arthur of land at Caen (above, Chapter 3, at n. 190). For other examples, see the articles by Musset cited above, Chapter 6, n. 1; Musset, "Actes inédits, VI," p. 121.

123. Above, Chapter 7, at n. 149.

124. For the surviving acts of Curthose, see Haskins, *Norman Institutions*, pp. 66–

70, which lists a total of 39 in fifteen years (excluding the time when Curthose was on crusade). For others, see Bouvris, "Bref" and "Aux origines." From his father's reign as duke before the conquest of England, thirty-one years, Fauroux, *Recueil*, contains 142 acts; this is nearly twice as many per year, even though for the first twelve years of his reign William was at least as weak as his son later was, the habit of writing was less well established, fewer abbeys were in existence, and fewer documents of any sort survive from these years than from later. On the various ways in which Curthose's charters illustrate his weakness, see Haskins, *Norman Institutions*, pp. 66, 70–78.

125. For brief statements of opinions that a ducal confirmation was important as a practical matter only, see D. C. Douglas, *William*, p. 152; Matthew, *Norman Conquest*, pp. 51–52. Goebel, *Felony*, pp. 289–90, however, maintains that ducal confirmation of grants to monasteries was a legal necessity and that the necessity was based not on "an alleged rule of feudal law requiring the consent of the lord for any vassal alienation" or even on "a milder rule of feudal law requiring the lord's consent to such vassal grants as work a change in the nature of the services" (which rule did not exist, he thinks), but rather "on the narrow ground that the duke's protection, assumed over the acquisitions of ecclesiastical establishments, is generally recognized." In other words, this was a necessity of ecclesiastical rather than feudal (or public) law. The argument is interesting. Its point is to deny the existence of a theory of judicial franchises in eleventh-century Normandy; see ibid., pp. 291–92. I think, however, that Goebel misconstrues some of the evidence. Brown, "Some Observations," p. 150, also considers ducal consent a necessity. For the duke as protector of all the churches in Normandy, see also Haskins, *Norman Institutions*, p. 36; Yver, "Autour de l'absence"; D. C. Douglas, *William*, pp. 153–54; Brown, *Normans*, pp. 32–33; Bates, *Normandy*, pp. 207–8. That he was is denied by Sauvage, *Troarn*, pp. 61–62, and Matthew, *Norman Conquest*, p. 51.

126. Document 208 (p. 314).

127. Document 225. The land was originally the donor's mother's, i.e., the claimant's sister's.

128. For other examples, from before the conquest of England, of Normandy as a *regnum*, see Documents 103 (p. 71), 150 (p. 187), 155 (p.202), 161 (p. 215), 174 (p. 243), 177 (p. 248), 200 (p. 289), 226 (p. 344); Prou, *Recueil*, p. 406, no. 163; Dudo, passim, e.g., p. 142, as quoted above, Chapter 4, at and in n. 69; Durand of Troarn, "Liber," col. 1422. On the subject of Normandy as a *regnum*, see Strayer, review of Fauroux, p. 608; Le Patourel, *Norman Empire*, pp. 181, 231; Hollister, "Normandy," pp. 211–12; Werner, "Quelques observations," pp. 707–9. Dudo is emphatic on the subject. Most of the charters, however, use the term in such a way that it may be no more than a locution proper in a Carolingian diploma copied for the sake of elegance into a Norman one where it does not belong. That Document 103 both calls Normandy a *regnum* and records the consent of the duke's lord (see below, this chapter, at n. 130) merely confirms the general impression; see Lot, *Fidèles*, p. 198, n. 5. In Document 208, in contrast, the scribe calls William a *rex* rather than Normandy a *regnum*, a locution which is, I think, unique for the period before 1066.

129. Above, this chapter at nn. 103 (the first example) and 104.

130. Document 103 (p. 71).

131. Document 239: William the Conqueror gave Bec "omnes ecclesias de Algia quas tunc in suo dominio habebat. . . . Istam donacionem confirmavit Ricardus filius Gilberti comitis, mittens donationem ipsarum super altare monasterii." Like nearly all the extant charters of Bec, this is an abbreviation: probably all that was meant was that Richard performed the act of donation in the duke's stead. It is also possible that the scribe carelessly imputed what was appropriate in most instances when someone other than the alienor performed the act of donation, namely, that doing so signified consent. Richard was William's second cousin, but so remote a relationship is unlikely to explain the wording of the charter.

132. Musset, "Vie économique," p. 69. In contrast, Matthew, *Norman Conquest*, chap. 2, passim, esp. p. 45, emphasizes the freedom with which ducal rights were granted.

133. One of the longest chapters of the *Consuetudines et Iusticie* of 1091 is on this subject: Document 315 (p. 282), c. 4. The interpretation of this clause, and how much earlier than 1091 it was in effect, are not entirely settled questions; see Powicke, *Loss*, pp. 180, 185; Haskins, *Norman Institutions*, pp. 38, 278; Corbett, "Development," p. 496; Aubenas, "Châteaux forts," pp. 566–68; Yver, "Châteaux forts," pp. 60–62; Brown, *Normans*, p. 45 and n. 142; M. de Boüard, "Apogée," p. 99, n. 1.

134. See, however, above, Chapter 4, at n. 160, where the building of an adulterine castle was one of the causes of the confiscation of a fief.

135. This is implied by several exemptions granted by lords other than the duke from all service except the duke's *generalis expeditio*: Documents 408 (p. 64), 478 (pp. 246–48), 479 (p. 250). Document 744 (p. 22), which includes a detailed exclusion not only of ducal wars but also of the immediate lord's wars from an exemption, is almost certainly a forgery. In Document 103 (p. 72), Duke Richard I exempts the domain of Berneval "ab omni hoste aut curte vel districto." The persons whose army service is at issue are clearly burgesses in one of these cases and peasants in the others. On the rear-ban in Normandy, see Haskins, *Norman Institutions*, pp. 22–23; Génestal, "Histoire," p. 97; Navel, "Enquête," pp. 54–56; Gleason, *Ecclesiastical Barony*, pp. 77–79; M. de Boüard, "Duché," p. 22; Yver, "Premières institutions," pp. 336–37. On peasants who fought in Normandy in the eleventh century, see M. de Boüard, *Guillaume*, pp. 11–12, 50.

136. Bec: Documents 181 and 238. La Trinité: Documents 415/416 (pp. 115–16).

137. See Musset, "Peuplement," passim, on the foundation of bourgs, and ibid., p. 187, on this point; he thinks that ducal permission was probably not necessary. M. de Boüard, "Duché," p. 12, says that from the early eleventh century on "le duc et les seigneurs hauts justiciers peuvent seuls donner à un bourg le privilège de banlieue."

138. Besnier, *Coutume*, p. 26; Lemarignier, *Recherches*, pp. 67–68; M. de Boüard, "Duché," p. 5; Matthew, *Norman Conquest*, p. 151.

139. Musset, "Foires," pp. 15, 17, 22.

140. Below, Chapter 10, at n. 21.

141. Document 171 (p. 233).

142. In the first part of his reign Robert the Magnificent had committed much violence against the church, and he had revised his behavior very largely as a result of the influence of Archbishop Robert. The charter may, therefore, merely allude to Duke Robert's own past.

143. See below, Chapter 11, at and in nn. 33–47, for one such dispute and the forgeries which resulted. On this subject, see Lemarignier, *Etude*, passim, esp. chaps. 3 and 4. Ibid., pp. 72 (n. 35), 85, 156–58, thinks that before about 1060 grants of episcopal customs were made by the dukes but after about 1060 by the bishops and that the change was the result of deliberate ducal policy. Ibid., pp. 70–71, maintains that in eleventh-century grants by private individuals of episcopal customs, "lorsqu'elles sont cédées, le consentement du duc de Normandie est généralement exprimé; parfois aussi celui du seigneur; et lorsque ce seigneur est l'évêque, c'est en qualité de seigneur et non pas d'évêque, qu'il paraît intervenir." See also Chibnall, "Ecclesiastical Patronage," p. 106.

144. Documents 156 (with Alfred), 157 (with Alfred), 166, 190 (also published in Document 160, p. 214). Edward also made a gift to Mont-Saint-Michel: Document 162. On these charters, see Haskins, *Norman Institutions*, pp. 261, 273 (no. 16), 275; Matthew, *Norman Monasteries*, p. 25; D. C. Douglas, *William*, p. 162; Barlow, *Edward*, p. 40 and n. 3; M. Mollat, "Seigneurie," p. 75. There is some doubt about the authenticity of Documents 162, 166, and 190, the latter two extant originals, in all of which Edward is styled *rex* before 1042; but see Fauroux, *Recueil*, p. 217. For Edward

in Normandy, see Barlow, *Edward*, pp. 34–48, esp. pp. 39–42; D. C. Douglas, *William*, pp. 160–65.

145. Robert the Pious signed Document 124, which is only marginally Norman because the donor is William de Bellême and at this time Bellême was still at least as much subject to the count of Anjou and the king of France as to the duke of Normandy. In 1033, when he sought refuge in Normandy briefly, Henry I signed two charters for Saint-Wandrille: Document 145, which had been written seven or eight years earlier; and Document 156, which cannot be dated closely except by Henry's signature. Documents were rarely even dated by the reigns of the kings of France. See also Le Patourel, *Norman Empire*, p. 239 and n. 2.

146. Odilo: Documents 145 and 156. Waleran and Alberic: Document 185; the identification of Alberic is only probable. Waleran also appears in Document 187. William: Document 192. Hugh: Document 187. Enguerrand: Documents 163 and 166. Baldwin: Document 166 and 171. Odo: Document 22 (p. 28), where he appears as a judge; D. C. Douglas, *William*, p. 39, n. 2, suggests either Odo II of Blois or Eudo of Penthièvre. Archbishop Junguené: Document 166. In addition, Document 824 mentions an Abbot Remigius who appears to be the head of a non-Norman house; for who he may be, see Bouvris, "Contribution," p. 171. This discussion excludes the signatures or other confirmations of persons, such as Mauger count of Corbeil and son of Duke Richard I of Normandy or Robert count of Meulan and son of Roger de Beaumont, who were lords of non-Norman lordships but were themselves members of Norman families.

147. Bec: Document 484a. Saint-Evroul: Document 474 (the date comes from OV, 3:158, n. 1).

148. Normandy: Schieffer, *Päpstlichen Legaten*, pp. 53–54, 65–66, 79–80, 93–94, 107–8, 129, 141–42, 142–43, 143, 175; Musset, "Notules," pp. 596–97, Annexe II.1, paragraphs 4 and 8, for the dates of which see ibid., pp. 592, 593. England: Tillmann, *Päpstlichen Legaten*, pp. 10–23. The only known legation to Normandy before 1055 occurred in 991 (Schieffer, *Päpstlichen Legaten*, p. 37). There may well have been other visits: the evidence for some of those Schieffer documents is scanty, and the two in the source published by Musset apparently are mentioned only there.

149. Document 85 (p. 463). They and Count Guy of Ponthieu are the only members of the court named in the charter who are said to have signed it, aside from the duke and his relatives.

150. Neither Schieffer nor Tillmann notices a legation by these two men in 1080 or at any other time, and Foreville, "Synod," pp. 25–27, by implication denies that papal legates attended the council of Lillebonne. The extant texts of the council are OV, 3:24–34 (also in Mansi, *Sacrorum conciliorum*, XX, cols. 559–64); Mansi, ibid., cols. 555-59; Teulet, *Layettes*, pp. 25–28, no. 22. Each of these says only that Duke William, Archbishop William, and "bishops, abbots and counts and other Norman magnates" were present; there is no extant list of the names of all those who attended.

The council of Lillebonne took place at Pentecost (OV, 3:24; Mansi, *Sacrorum conciliorum*, XX, col. 555; Teulet, *Layettes*, p. 25). Document 85 dates the trial in which the two archbishops participated "in paschali solennitate," that is, seven weeks earlier; the place where the court met is not named.

151. Document 398 (p. 685). On Roger's legation at this time, see Schieffer, *Päpstlichen Legaten*, pp. 142–43; Tillmann, *Päpstlichen Legaten*, p. 19. For the case, see above, Chapter 4, at nn. 30–33.

152. Haskins, *Norman Institutions*, p. 75; David, *Robert Curthose*, p. 91; Schieffer, *Päpstlichen Legaten*, p. 143; Tillman, *Päpstlichen Legaten*, pp. 21–22; Barlow, *William Rufus*, pp. 362–65.

153. Document 709. Gerento's companion, the historian Hugh of Flavigny, participated only in acts concerning the abbey of Dijon; see Haskins, *Norman Institutions*, pp. 75–76.

154. Le Patourel, *Norman Empire*, pp. 19–20, 77; Tabuteau, "Definitions," p. 51 and n. 113.

155. Document 100.

156. For Rufus's acts issued while he was in Normandy or for Norman churches, see Haskins, *Norman Institutions*, pp. 80–81; of the fifteen, eleven are for French religious establishments, of which most are confirmations, many of them including or concerning Norman land. For Henry, see ibid., p. 69, nos. 19, 20, 24, in all of which he consents to particular grants in Normandy; two of these certainly come from 1088 and the third may do so. For other acts for Norman abbeys in which Henry participated before 1106, see *Regesta*, vol. 1, no. 320, and vol. 2, nos. 524, 533, 601, 623, 764, all of which concern English land only; ibid., vol. 2, no. 679, confirms Norman as well as English land to Marmoutier before 1106.

157. Saint-Evroul: OV, 4:254; Troarn: Document 495 (p. 363), on which see below, Chapter 9, at and in n. 46.

158. Tabuteau, "Definitions," p. 26, n. 39, and the references there, to which should be added Bates, *Normandy*, chap. 2, esp. pp. 59–62.

159. Respectively, Documents 325 and 333.

160. Document 323; the editor judges it spurious. Lemarignier, *Etude*, p. 37 and n. 38, argues for its authenticity, and his conclusion is accepted hesitantly by Yver, "Autour de l'absence," p. 236 and n. 26. Goebel, *Felony*, p. 310, also thinks the privilege genuine. Werner, "Quelques observations," p. 709, n. 49, thinks it a forgery. Lemarignier and Werner, as cited, refer to earlier scholarship on the subject.

161. Document 326: Urban II protects Bec's rights at Pont-Isère against interference from the archbishop of Rouen or the canons of Pont-Isère. Document 327: Urban II orders the bishop of Avranches to judge a dispute between Mont-Saint-Michel and the knight Harscutus. Document 329: Urban II orders that no harm should come to the church of Bayeux because of the imprisonment of Bishop Odo. Documents 331 and 332: Paschal II confirms grants of churches to Bec by the archbishop of Rouen and the bishops of Chartres and Paris.

162. Document 324: Benedict VIII confirms an exchange between Saint-Vaast and Jumièges. Document 328: Urban II confirms Bishop Odo of Bayeux's grant of Saint-Vigor de Bayeux to Saint-Bénigne de Dijon. Document 330: Paschal II confirms an exchange between Saint-Bénigne de Dijon and Saint-Etienne de Caen and all the other possessions of Saint-Bénigne.

163. See Lemarignier, *Etude*, passim, esp. pp. 29 (n. 10), 180–202, 264–66. Ibid., pp. 214–15, however, notes that the real age of forgery of papal bulls by or for Norman monasteries began only about 1130 with a series of spurious papal privileges for Saint-Ouen; the eleventh-century forgeries are more likely to be of ducal documents. Levison, *England*, pp. 207–18, in discussing the same material from Saint-Ouen, implies that its date was earlier because the self-confessed forger died "obviously in old age" at some time between 1119 and 1131 (p. 210). Yver, "Autour de l'absence," p. 236, notes that the flow of genuine papal privileges also dates primarily from after 1130; and Chibnall, in OV, 1:76, notes, about Orderic, "Papal bulls . . . rarely or never came his way." In "Charter," pp. 8–9, she discusses "a crude forgery of a supposed bull of John XIII" perpetrated by the monks of Mont-Saint-Michel between 1058 and 1060; ibid., p. 10, argues that the "clumsy" nature of the forgery itself shows that "papal bulls were rare until towards the close of the century." Because forgers would have little incentive to forge a document whose genuine variety was not widely known and considered valuable, it is scarcely surprising that there should be few spurious papal documents from the eleventh century.

164. On Normandy's effective political independence, see most recently Hollister, "Normandy," pp. 202–14; Le Patourel, *Norman Empire*, pp. 217–19, 238–43. Bates, *Normandy*, pp. 59–62, argues that Normandy became effectively independent only in the reign of William the Conqueror. For the expression of independence in the dating of

charters, see Musset, "Huit essais," pp. 5–17. For its expression in ducal religious policy, see Lemarignier, *Etude*, pp. 153–54; Foreville, "Synod," pp. 34–37; Chibnall, in OV, 1:96–97; Bates, *Normandy*, pp. 57–58. See above, Chapter 3, at n. 206, for the analogous withdrawal of Norman monastic property within the borders of the duchy. Musset, "Huit essais," p. 146, finds an analogy in the administration of the lands of the family of Bellême-Montgomery.

165. Above, this chapter, at n. 104; below, Chapter 9, at and in n. 28.

CHAPTER 9

1. Below, this chapter, at and in nn. 30 and 48 (twice); Document 746 (f° 7r): "Praeterea vero concedo et hac praesenti carta garantizo Deo et Sancto Martino de Bosco omnes subscriptas donationes quas eidem Ecclesiae pro suarum salute animarum homines mei fecisse noscuntur." There is a fifth use of the word, as a verb, in Document 288 (col. 230); but it is a forgery.

2. Document 521.

3. Document 195 (p. 281). See Document 205 (p. 306) for a more general appeal to friends to combat claimants; here the alienor was a cleric and, at law, had no relatives.

4. Documents 476 (p. 174), 537 (paragraph 10), 634 (f° 47r).

5. Document 373 (p. 357). In Document 855, a quitclaimer promises no more than that, should another, specified man challenge the transfer, he would not support that claimant.

6. Document 681: "et si quo calumniante eam adquietare aliquando non valeret, tantum terre in territorio Sancte Scolastice se redditurum promisit, quam que valentem monachi gratis et libenter acciperent." See above, Chapter 5, at and in n. 34, for more on this transaction. It is noteworthy that Bigot was not the current possessor but was the "rectus heres" to what was transferred.

7. Respectively, Documents 257, 62, and 841: "acram pro acra et domum pro domo." See also above, Chapter 3, n. 95.

8. Document 650 (f° 55r): "Et promisit si hanc terram non posset adquietare tantum de sua alia terra se redditurum predictis dominis quod eque valeret illi quam adqueitare non posset preter macerias Sancti Helerii quia alias non habebat." *Maceria* properly means a wall, but it is also an alternate form for *macera*, *macella*, *macellum*, meaning a butcher's shop, an abattoir, a meat market.

9. Respectively, Documents 683 (f° 79r), 694 (f° 91r), 64 (p. 438).

10. Respectively, Documents 2 and 855.

11. Brothers: Documents 13 (p. 22), 292 (p. 217), and the next note. A tenant's heir: above, Chapter 3, n. 95.

In Document 683 (f° 79r), Robert de Neuville, the donor, promises to warrant "tam a filio Fulconis quam ab omni ei calumpniam faciente." The Fulk whose son was apparently a claimant was either Fulk d'Aunou, who gave his rights in the same place five years earlier (Document 679), or Fulk du Pin, who did the same in the same year (Document 680) and acted as a pledge to Bigot de Sainte-Scolasse's concession of rights in the same place (for which see above, this chapter, at and in n. 6), also in the same year. Robert de Neuville and Fulk d'Aunou may have been related: OV, 2:82, says that one of Fulk's brothers was Richard de Neuville.

12. Document 641 (f° 50r): "et sicuti Willelmus Oisuns et Arnulfus concesserant, Hugonem clericum suum fratrem predictus Rotbertus Oisuns firmiter et legaliter libentique animo concessurum promisit. Quod si ipse Hugo aliqua de causa vel aliquis alius calumniam contra monachos de supradicta ecclesia inferret, predicto Rotberto teste et omnia concedente, ipso die in quo calumnia fieret, vicum qui dicitur vulgo Ruiel Morellorum se predictis fratribus traditurum cum omnibus ad eundem vicum pertinentibus firmiter spopondit. Quem vicum monachi tamdiu haberent donec ipse Rotbertus Oisuns predictam ecclesiam eis solute et libere adquitaret."

13. This is most clearly stated in Document 158 (p. 209), in which it is evident that the land alienated was not free of claims at the time of the transaction, and Document 694 (f° 91r).

14. For Yver on Normandy, see above, Chapter 6, n. 25. For other regions, see S. D. White, "*Pactum*," p. 296, n. 72; Castaing-Sicard, "Donations," pp. 56–57.

15. Four are sales: above, this chapter, at and in n. 6, and Documents 13, 62, 841. Three are partly sales and partly gifts: above, this chapter, at and in nn. 8 and 12, and Document 694. One seems to be a sale recorded as a gift: Document 2. One is a post-obit gift: Document 257. Two are exchanges, one of them already being claimed: Documents 158 and 308. One is a gift of land to which there was a claimant: above, this chapter, n. 11. One is a quitclaim of property to which there was another claim: Document 855. Only two are simple gifts: above, Chapter 3, n. 95, and Document 64. Because there are other reasons for conjecturing that sales were dangerous, because post-obit gifts were obviously uncertain until the donor or the designee died, and because one of the gifts and one of the exchanges were under immediate threat, it is not quite circular to argue both that the correlation with warranty proves that sales were dangerous and that the correlation with sales proves that warranty was used in dangerous transactions.

16. Twenty-seven gifts, seven confirmations, and one confirmation plus additional gifts, in contrast to two feudal agreements, one agreement about a mill, ten sales, four quitclaims, and one case actually decided in court.

17. Document 521 (p. 123). See above, this chapter, at n. 2, for the immediately preceding phrase.

18. OV, 2:126: when Arnold d'Echauffour made his son Rainald a monk at Saint-Evroul, "terram unius carrucae apud Sanctum Germanum . . . concessit, quam pro infortuniis quae ipsum haeredesque eius perpessos esse retulimus aecclesia iam dudum perdidit."

19. Dudo, pp. 204–5 (translated above, Chapter 4, at n. 72), esp. the words "contra adversarios tibi defensor." Searle, "Fact," p. 126, n. 33, cites passages like this one and the one cited above, Chapter 4, at n. 68, to suggest that by the late tenth or early eleventh century the dukes saw their ability to warrant their men's possessions as one of the principal "advantages" of their "lordship."

20. Document 177 (p. 248). See also Musset, "Actes inédits, II," pp. 146, 148.

21. For William Paynel, see above, Chapter 4, at n. 83, the promise about the pasture of La Lande. In Document 868 (p. 46) Peter son of Geoffrey Infant of Fontenay sold tithes and two acres of land to Saint-Etienne de Caen, "convenitque quod hanc venditionem concedere faceret omnes heredes suos, et si aliqua inde calumnia moveretur, bene totum hoc adquietaret Sancto Stephano usque dum Willelmus Paganellus ipsam venditionem concederet." The tenurial relationship between the Paynel and Infant families is established by Document 871 (for part of which see above, Chapter 8, at and in n. 1), for Geoffrey Infant was one of the men whose tithes Hugh Paynel was there unable to transfer. Hence, Document 868 implies that a lord ought to assume the duty of defense when he confirmed his tenants' alienations. It is tempting to try to explain the difference between Peter's apparently permanent warranty of the tithes and his apparently only temporary warranty of the land as somehow connected to the consent in advance which Hugh Paynel gave to a gift of tithes by Geoffrey Infant.

On the other hand, in two instances when men lost their fiefs through no fault of their own, nothing is said about compensation to them: Document 319; OV, 2:120. Because both references are incidental, however, silence does not necessarily mean that there was no compensation in one or both of the cases.

22. Document 25 (p. 96): "Terram autem, quam Adam habuit de Sancto Bricio, ita recognovit Rannulfus ab episcopo, ut si aliquis eam super Rannulfum reclamaret, ne episcopus eum cogeret, ut inde nisi vellet alicui responderet." This may mean that if anyone claims this part of his fief from Rannulf his lord the bishop will warrant the land, that is, will defend the case in court; and Rannulf need only be affected if the

bishop loses the case and, therefore, has to order Rannulf to surrender the land.

23. Document 371: "Multis coactis, Ricardus, abbas Pratellensis, reddidit Ricardo, filio Radulfi de Sancta Maria Ecclesia, terram Grinboldiville, quam dono abbatis Willelmi reclamabat. Ipse quidem Ricardus fecit homagium abbati in capitulo, ita dicens: Ego Ricardus tali tenore devenio vestrum hominem, denarios vademonii vobis reddendo, ut si piget regem aut comitem eo quod mihi reddideritis eam terram quam clamo, reddam eamdem terram in vestro dominio; aut si quis disseruerit super me predictam terram, clamabo ipsos denarios quietos vobis et homagium servabo vobis, non querens aliquid in concambium mihi donari a vobis." William had been abbot from 1078 to 1096. Richard was abbot from 1101 to 1131. As it seems likely that the "rex aut comes" to whom the transfer might be irksome are King Henry I and Duke Robert Curthose, the charter is probably to be dated to between 1101 and 1106.

I have quoted the whole of the charter except for the witness list. There is, therefore, no information as to why the grant to Richard should annoy either the king or the duke. Nor is it clear what the *denarii vademonii* are. *Vadimonium* normally meant a mortgage but could mean a pledge: above, Chapter 4, n. 286. I have translated it here as "pledge" and understood it to mean that Richard transferred an unstated sum of money to the abbey as a guarantee, that should the king or the duke object to the grant, he would restore the land to the abbey's demesne or forfeit the money permanently and that in addition he promised not to demand the money back if he lost the land because of a successful claim by anyone else. Possibly, however, the land at issue had been mortgaged to the abbey and Richard, to receive the land, agreed to pay off the mortgage.

24. Document 398 (p. 684). For the case, see above, Chapter 4, at nn. 30–33.

25. Above, Chapter 4, at and in n. 34; below, Chapter 11, at n. 32.

26. Below, Chapter 11, at nn. 40 and 45.

27. Document 85 (p. 463). The charter does not point out the relationship between the claimant and the warrantor; for the genealogy of the family, see M.-J. Le Cacheux, *Saint-Amand*, p. 41.

28. Document 395. The last phrase—"ut aut donum quod concesserat adquietaret, aut illud sibi haberet"—is a problem. Round, *Calendar*, p. 400, no. 1117, translates the second alternative "or to take it into his hands," meaning the gift rather than the case. It seems unlikely, however, that the monks should ask the duke, even as an alternative, to take one of their possessions from them. Perhaps they meant that he should try the case personally.

29. Document 249 (p. 384).

30. Document 555 (f° 137v): "consuetudines vicecomitatus quas a comite . . . emerat. Huic dono addidit decimas militum suorum quas in beneficio retinebant, tali tenore ut quam diu abbas eis consuetudines guarantiret, haberet eas ex integro. Quod si aliquando minime posset, facerent inde quod vellent."

31. *Inde* must refer to the tithes. It cannot, logically, refer to the customs because, if the abbot proved unable to warrant them, the knights would lose them.

32. Document 199. There has been a considerable amount of comment on the duke's sale of these vicecomital customs; see the works cited by Fauroux, *Recueil*, p. 286. Unfortunately, no one has gone on to discuss, on the basis of the subsequent charter, what the abbot then did with the customs. Yver, "Premières institutions," p. 346 and n. 120, is a partial exception; but he does not go beyond the initial transaction between Theobald and the abbey, which he calls an exchange.

33. Above, Chapter 4, at n. 8, and the references in that note.

34. Documents 227 and 228.

35. Above, this chapter, at n. 27.

36. See above, Chapter 4, at nn. 31–32, for his lines of argument. The silence of the charter does not necessarily mean, of course, that no verification of William's argument was made.

37. Below, Chapter 11, at nn. 40 and 45.
38. The only others are above, Chapter 7, at n. 46; Document 851.
39. Above, Chapter 6, at and in n. 23.
40. Language typical of warranty clauses is used with regard both to William de Briouze's participation in the second suit brought by Lonlay (quoted above, this chapter, at n. 24) and to what the monks of Saint-Florent wanted William the Conqueror to do against Mont-Saint-Michel (above, this chapter, at n. 28). It is not used in the account of the dispute between Gilbert of Evreux and La Trinité du Mont, nor does the charter recording the gift (Document 150) contain a warranty clause. It should be noted, however, that fifty years separated the gift of Oissel to the abbey from Bishop Gilbert's claim. It is unlikely, therefore, that William d'Arques was an ordinary witness who had seen the orignal transfer. He is not mentioned in Document 150; but that may not be strong evidence, for the charter contains no witness list and few signatures.
41. Yver, "Autour de l'absence," and "Boutade." On the absence of advocacy in Normandy, see also Senn, *Institution*, pp. 95ff. Yver denies that anything like advocacy existed in Normandy and minimizes the power of founders of monastic houses over their foundations, attributing this absence to the duke's position as protector of the churches of Normandy; he thinks that founders and their families had considerably more control over collegial churches. Although all scholars agree that advocacy in Normandy was of minimal importance when compared with other areas, not all deny its importance as completely as Yver; see Valin, *Duc*, pp. 85–88; Sauvage, *Troarn*, pp. 61–62; Haskins, *Norman Institutions*, p. 36 and n. 143; Génestal, "Histoire," pp. 83, 102; M. de Boüard, "Duché," p. 22.
42. Above, Chapter 6, at n. 58; Chapter 8, at n. 34; below, this chapter, at n. 51; Document 269. The exception is Document 405 (pp. 55–56).

Document 267 (p. 431) may contain another example of ducal guardianship of alms, saying that William de Vauville gave "quadrugatam in Aurenoio, quam Willelmus emerat de elemosina Turgoti Turlacville ad opus canonici concessu consulis [i.e., the duke], et concessit Willelmus de Walvilla ut consul esset inde protector et dator hoc pacto ut consul daret ei quietanciam et costumas sicut aliis." This is so concise as to be baffling. The *elemosina* here may merely be part of the glebe of the church of Tourlaville; for *elemosina* to mean "glebe," see Chesnel, *Cotentin*, p. 161; Yver, "Boutade," p. 785, n. 7.
43. Document 167.
44. Document 193. Document 118, the charter in which William's grandfather Richard II originally gave the church to Saint-Riquier, does not include a clause establishing the duke as advocate.
45. Document 493 (pp. 350–51).
46. Document 495 (p. 363). What Sauvage reads as "sicut / / concesse elemosine fidelium" can be corrected to "sicut [debent] esse elemosine fidelium" from BN, ms. lat. 10086, f° 7r. William Rufus's confirmation is followed by one from Henry I, "rex anglorum et dux normannorum," which is wholly different in wording from those of Henry's father and brother. This document is an unsigned and seemingly unfinished pancart. Hence it is not certain that either William Rufus or Henry ever issued the confirmations attributed to them.
47. Yver, "Boutade," pp. 786–92; Yver, "Autour de l'absence," pp. 206–7. He appears to be unaware of the repetition of this clause in the pancart of William Rufus.
48. Document 803: "ut in mea solius subjectione ac tuitione permaneant res a me datae, et ego sim advocatus et ut vulgo dicitur garantus eleemosinae meae, sicut homo laicus esse debet eleemosinae in sua manu retentae." The second charter is Document 756 (p. 403): "ita ut sit in subjectione comitis et ipse comes advocatus et guarantus sit illius elemosine sicut laicus homo debet esse illius elemosine quam in manu sua retinet."
49. Yver, "Autour de l'absence," p. 201. See also above, Chapter 8, n. 125.
50. See Yver, "Autour de l'absence," p. 213 and n. 66, on the charters from Saint-

Riquier and Saint-Bénigne. He does not discuss Robert of Mortain's charters for Marmoutier. In "Châteaux forts," pp. 75–76, Yver perceives an abortive tendency in the direction of real advocacy in Normandy during the reign of Robert Curthose; but see "Autour de l'absence," pp. 217–19.

51. Document 266 (p. 424). Musset, "Recherches sur les communautés," p. 21, thinks that Roger was not created *custos* until after Odo Stigand's death, but the charter sounds as though William transferred custody to Roger as soon as he received it from Odo. Yver, "Autour de l'absence," pp. 198, n. 27, appears also to think the transfer to Roger immediate.

52. Yver, "Autour de l'absence," pp. 198–99 and n. 27, discusses this charter at some length because exemption of collegial churches from their founders' control was unusual. He thinks that the exemption occurred some time after the foundation (see also ibid., p. 196, n. 21), perhaps when the church was becoming a center of pilgrimage, and that Roger received "une véritable délégation de la *custodia* ducale" (p. 199), not permission to exploit the church as collegial churches were normally exploited by their founders. Musset, "Recherches sur les communautés," p. 21, thinks that Roger may have had the same powers over the church as a founder normally had over a college of canons.

53. Document 267 (p. 432): "Posuit . . . custodem ecclesie Anschitillum cui dedit tantum quod fuit computatum quinquaginta et duos solidos."

54. Yver, "Autour de l'absence," p. 201.

55. Above, Chapter 3, at and in n. 253.

56. Yver, "Autour de l'absence," pp. 198–99.

57. D. C. Douglas, *William*, pp. 185–86.

CHAPTER 10

1. Some charters make a clear distinction between excommunication in the present world and condemnation to Hell in the afterlife, whereas others allude only to one or the other or simply express a hope that persons who trouble the church may never go to Heaven. I do not think that these differences were functionally significant. Fauroux, *Recueil*, p. 54, however, thinks that there was a real difference between a malediction and an excommunication or an anathema; see also Little, "Morphologie," pp. 50–51; Zimmermann, "Protocoles," pp. 56–62.

2. These figures are for all charters relevant to this inquiry. The figures for the charters of Norman churches alone are as follows: 174 anathema clauses; 9 blessings in connection with anathemas and 2 elsewhere; 13 fines in connection with anathemas and 5 elsewhere.

3. Below, this chapter, at and in n. 53, is an exception in form, but it was nevertheless a church which stood to lose by any infringement of the agreement.

4. On variations among the charters of different abbeys, see Fauroux, *Recueil*, pp. 54–55. For another indication of the wide variations, see below, this chapter, n. 9. For a detailed study of the composition of one anathema clause, see D. C. Douglas, "First Ducal Charter," pp. 51–53. Only one charter, cited below, this chapter, n. 27, actually quotes the words by which the anathema would be imposed if necessary. Little, "Formules," publishes and discusses a pre-Viking anathema formula from Saint-Wandrille which could be used against an actual disseisor; some of its language is similar to the language in the anathema clauses under discussion here.

5. There are twenty anathemas and five fines from Fécamp; twenty anathemas and four fines from Jumièges; twenty-three anathemas but no fines from Mont-Saint-Michel; twenty-seven anathemas and four fines from Saint-Ouen; and twenty-two anathemas and three fines from Saint-Wandrille.

6. See below, pp. 207, 208–9, and Appendix A, Table 5.

7. Five of the anathema clauses from Troarn also include blessings; one does not and one blessing appears without an anathema. Subtracting the charters of Troarn

leaves 168 anathema clauses and five blessing clauses from all the other Norman churches.

8. See also A. de Boüard, *Manuel*, 1:280, 283; G. Mollat, "Restitution," p. 419.

9. Eighty verbs are used at least once to express the idea of challenging an alienation. The most common, *violare*, appears thirty times. Forty-four verbs are used only once each. Often a clause uses more than one verb.

10. Only two charters modify the verb or verbs used by "unjustly": Documents 99 (p. 521) and 343 (p. 251). Both use *injuste*.

11. Documents 231 (p. 352) and 572. The earlier charter prescribes an anathema for a mere claim.

12. See below, this chapter, at nn. 50 and 57, for two fines which were commuted into other penalties. There is no reason to think that either of these was a fine of the sort prescribed in connection with anathemas.

13. Document 135 (p. 152).

14. Documents 134, 470 (p. 130), and probably 32.

15. Document 146, a forgery of the late eleventh century, which purports to come from the reign of Duke Richard II, in which the church of Saint-Léonard de Bellême is granted an especially sweeping exemption from both episcopal and lay customs, says (p. 178) that "si quis in posterum archiepiscopus sive episcopus ipsam ecclesiam quocumque modo inquietare presumeret, . . . anathematis vinculo . . . teneretur." The reason for this peculiarity is obvious: the charter was forged in the course of a dispute between the church and the bishop of Sées, for which see below, Chapter 11, at nn. 33–47. As several of the secondary sources cited in connection with my discussion of the case point out, the forged charter was apparently not based on a genuine charter. There is, therefore, no reason to think that such a clause might, earlier in the century, have been written into a genuine charter. Cf., however, above, Chapter 4, n. 249, where a bishop apparently prohibits his successors as bishops from raising claims; this is not in the context of an anathema.

16. Above, Chapter 3, at and in nn. 86–87.

17. Above, Chapter 7, at n. 42.

18. The duke as an alienor or confirmer pronounced thirty-three anathemas. The mother of a duke, who did so once, is the only woman to do so on her own. Other laymen as alienors or confirmers did so forty times. Bishops as alienors or confirmers did so twelve times. Abbots as alienors did so twice. Rainald is the only cleric who was not a prelate to do so as an alienor. Many charters do not say who prounounced the curse. See also Brown, "Some Observations," p. 159.

19. Documents 202 (p. 301), 237, 335 (p. 11).

20. In Document 276 (col. 17), a suspect charter for Saint-Victor-en-Caux, Archbishop John of Rouen, from whom the charter emanates, issues the anathema along with four of the other Norman bishops, but it is Duke William who prescribes the fine. This might imply that anathemas most properly came from a religious authority and fines from a secular authority; but no such rule was consistently followed, and the charter, being suspect, is not a good authority. Cf. the opinion of Goebel cited below, Chapter 11, n. 40.

21. A. de Boüard, *Manuel*, 2:142, suggests that the primary reasons for seeking the signatures of bishops to charters were "leur prééminence morale et . . . leur pouvoir spirituel armé de l'anathème." See above, Chapter 7, at n. 139, on the great frequency with which bishops signed charters in Normandy.

22. An abbot, head of the recipient monastery, acts alone in Document 338 (p. 27). Abbots certainly or probably act together with others in Documents 171 (p. 235), 200 (pp. 291–92), 281 (col. 129), 336, 338 (p. 25), 378, 750. See above, Chapter 7, at and in n. 139, on the comparative absence of abbots as signers of charters.

23. Document 306 (p. 230), where the monk is the abbey's *procurator* of its possessions at Planches in Normandy.

24. Documents 49 (p. 57), 70, 99 (pp. 521, 523), 206 (p. 308), 265, 336 (p. 22),

338 (p. 27). See also the following charters in which anathemas are closely connected with the act of signing: Documents 133 (p. 150), 187 (p. 267), 191 (p. 274), 388, 471 (p. 140).

25. In addition to the work cited at the next note, see Documents 49 (p. 57), 439 (p. 35), 826 (f° 30v). An additional thirty or so of the extant charters which refer to anathemas end the anathema clauses with an "Amen" or a "Fiat" or two or three of either or both words. The most elaborate is Document 259 (p. 408): "Amen, amen, amen, fiat, fiat, fiat, sitque anathema. Maranatha." On the word "maranatha," see Little, "Morphologie," pp. 50–51. Each set of these words may indicate by its inclusion that the imprecation had been publicly pronounced and affirmed; see also ibid., p. 48.

26. Document 286 (cols. 223–24). On Geoffrey's charter, see Le Patourel, "Geoffrey," p. 158.

27. The only other extant charter whose sole subject was an anathema was issued by Archbishop Mauger to assure the permanence of an alienation which he and his brother, William count of Arques, had made to Saint-Ouen: Document 311. The charter of gift, Document 191, itself includes (p. 274) a very brief anathema clause.

28. See, however, Boussard, "Thomas," for a description of the reaction of a claimant to his excommunication, recorded in a charter of Mont-Saint-Michel from 1106 x 1131.

29. Document 246 (p. 377).

30. Above, Chapter 3, at nn. 59–62.

31. Document 380 (p. 71).

32. Document 177 (p. 248), suggests that Duke Robert the Magnificent himself died while under an excommunication for having disseised Fécamp.

33. As Appendix A, Table 5, below, makes clear, the number, percentage, and cumulative percentage of anathemas in the charters of these five abbeys all peak in the decade of the 1020s. Moreover, the cumulative percentage for the century from 960 through 1059 is 59.4 percent, whereas the cumulative percentage for the years 1060–1106 is only 23.2 percent. For the Norman charters of all churches, the comparable figures are 41.4 and 10.1 percent.

34. See Goebel, *Felony*, pp. 308–9, on its ineffectiveness against habitual disturbers of the peace.

35. Documents 104 (p. 74), 175 (p. 245), 472 (p. 154), 825 (f° 28v). The last charter specifies publicity.

36. In Document 728, a charter slightly too late for this study, Richard son of Robert Malmarche was corporally and publicly disciplined as part of his reception of absolution for himself and his deceased father for disseisins which they had perpetrated against Mont-Saint-Michel.

37. Restitution: Document 714. Fine: Document 174 (p. 243).

38. See below, this chapter, at n. 48, for a fine of 1248 *d.* in ordinary coin. For other figures, see below, Appendix A, Table 5. The fines of £10 or less in gold may not have been wholly beyond possibility of payment.

39. Document 242.

40. Very occasionally, a monetary countergift is stated partially or entirely in ounces of gold; see the next note for one example. A few other charters mention gold bezants or gold marks; see Musset, "Actes inédits, I," p. 122; Musset, "Actes inédits, Saint-Martin de Sées," p. 23. Musset, "Réflexions sur les moyens," p. 330, emphasizes the degree to which gold circulated in Normandy, but it is high only in comparison with neighboring regions of northern France.

41. See also Matthew, *Norman Conquest*, p. 52. There is only one indication of how much gold was worth in eleventh-century Normandy: Document 425 indicates (p. 136) that an ounce of gold was worth thirty shillings. Musset, "Actes inédits, I," p. 122, calculates that this means that a pound-weight of gold was the equivalent of eighteen pounds in coin. Twenty pounds of gold was therefore 360 pounds in coin; 178

pounds of gold was 3,204 pounds in coin; 1,000 pounds of gold was 18,000 pounds in coin. Such amounts are ridiculous. Unfortunately, Document 425 does not specify whether the money was of Rouen, of Le Mans, or of one of the other coinages which circulated in Normandy more rarely than those two. The money of Le Mans was worth twice as much as that of Rouen (Document 560, f° 142r; Dieudonné, "Numismatique," p. 343).

42. The sample is so small that the addition or subtraction of even one item can make a substantial difference to the statistics. Nevertheless, as Appendix A, Table 5, below, shows, the trend of the figures on the frequency of fines is almost steadily downward in number and percentage, and entirely so in cumulative percentage, from a peak in the 1020s, the same decade in which these figures peak for anathema clauses. Moreover, the cumulative percentage for the century from 960 to 1059 is 14.5 percent, whereas that for the years 1060–1106 is only 4.7 percent. The trend is even more striking if the dividing date is moved back two decades, for up through 1039 the cumulative percentage is 19.7 percent, whereas thereafter it is only 5.4 percent.

43. A. de Boüard, *Manuel*, 1:282–83, says that this was true for France in general after the ninth century.

44. The variation is characteristic not merely of the fines as a group but even of most of the individual churches from which more than one fine survives. The most regular is Fécamp, four of whose five fines were of £100; but one of these (Document 275, col. 9) also included one hundred talents of silver, and the fifth was of £50. At Jumièges, the amounts run from £10 to the largest of all the fines (above, this chapter, at n. 39). At Saint-Ouen, they run from £20 to £200; at Saint-Wandrille, from the one realistic fine (below, this chapter, at n. 48) to £50; at Saint-Père de Chartres, from £3 to £1,000.

45. Document 126 (p. 134). For why this charter was probably written by a scribe from Fécamp, see Fauroux, *Recueil*, pp. 42–43; Chanteux, "Abbé Thierry," p. 69. Matthew, *Norman Conquest*, p. 52, thinks that such a clause was a matter of ducal favor, saying, "Such protection was not accorded to the monasteries of other lords." It seems to me more properly a question of scribal practice.

46. King: Document 149 (p. 184), a case concerning Jumièges's possession of land outside Normandy, which was heard in the king's court; Document 736, a gift by King Robert the Pious. Duke: Documents 26 (p. 284), 125 (p. 131), 126 (p. 134), 127 (p. 141), 144 (p. 173), 156 (p. 205), 157 (p. 207), 268 (p. 434). King and duke: Documents 110 (p. 89) and 116 (p. 102). Archbishop and duke: Document 276 (col. 17). Lord: Document 102 (p. 70). Judge: Document 215 (p. 330). Court: Document 263 (p. 417). Of all those which designate a single recipient, only Documents 215, 263, and 268 are at all specific; the rest say "to our demesne fisc," or something of that sort, so that only the speaking voice of the charter determines the recipient.

Document 110 is the only charter from a Norman abbey about Norman land in which a fine is to be paid even partly to the king of France. It was written by Dudo of Saint-Quentin, who not only wrote but also was the alienor of Document 116. Dudo was, of course, not Norman himself; and his influence may explain the appearance of the king in the fine clause of Document 110, although Dudo as a historian was at pains to deemphasize the subordination of the dukes of Normandy to the kings of France.

47. Respectively, Documents 275 (col. 9), 242, 174 (p. 243), 135 (p. 152).

48. Document 377 (p. 38).

49. Above, Chapter 3, at and in n. 220.

50. Document 37.

51. Below, this chapter, at n. 57.

52. Document 200 (p. 289). This clause is not in Orderic's transcription of the charter. The anathema clause in this charter, which is in both ibid., pp. 291–92, and Orderic, is separate. Chibnall, *World*, p. 48, suggests that complete disinheritance was proposed because Saint-Evroul lay "in a frontier region rent by conflicting territorial

claims." It was, presumably, more likely than other abbeys to be troubled.

53. Document 822 (f° 25v). The presence of this stipulation and its tone imply that the life estate itself may have been created to settle a claim. Cf. Documents 453 and 454, where forfeiture plays a role in an agreement between the abbey of Bourgueil and a knight of Dreux about the monks' peasants at Coudres in Normandy.

54. Document 200 (p. 289): "noscat se nostre reum esse majestatis." This phrase, too, is not in Orderic's transcription of the charter.

55. Document 377 (p. 38): "publici reus erit iudicii"; Document 263 (p. 417). Yver, *Contrats*, pp. 55, 60, finds that in the twelfth and thirteenth centuries *infamia*, whose chief secular consequence was inability to testify in court, was one of the normal penalties for breaking one's faith or one's oath; but Document 263 mentions neither of those modes of assurance.

56. Document 242.

57. Document 56. A *closeria* is a croft or other small enclosed plot.

58. Yver, *Contrats*, p. 272, n. 2, in discussing what Drogulus might have done, considers only the first two of these possibilities. Ibid., pp. 271–72, is a commentary on this case, in the course of which Yver maintains that, in return for his surrender of his rights, Drogulus received not only the cancellation of his debt and five shillings but also his freedom. I see no warrant in the charter for concluding that Drogulus was enfranchised, however.

59. For commentary on this case, in addition to Yver, as cited in the preceding note, see Delisle, *Etudes*, pp. 17–18; Musset, "Actes inédits, II," p. 150. Delisle, *Etudes*, p. 18 and n. 89, finds a somewhat analogous case in which, "à la fin du XIe siècle, un homme d'Isigni, miraculeusement guéri dans la cathédrale de Coutances, se constitue serf de cette église." Musset, "Recherches sur les communautés," p. 26, suggests that Document 290, the foundation charter of the collegial church of Saint-Martin d'Ecajeul (later called Sainte-Barbe-en-Auge), may provide another example of "l'asservissement volontaire par dévotion." For the practice and its evolution through the thirteenth century, see Gonthier and Le Bas, "Analyse," pp. 7, 11, 12, 31–33. For discussions of the development of reduction to serfdom as a punishment, see Goebel, *Felony*, pp. 86–87, 94 and n. 100; Petot, "Hommage," pp. 80–81.

60. Duhamel, "Diplomatique," p. 30, notes concerning William's charters, "Les peines dont elles menacent son peu variées." The action which one would most expect to find required of disseisors, restitution of what had been wrongfully seized, is rarely mentioned in advance, although it must have been the normal prerequisite for absolution from an anathema or for the avoidance of that or any other penalty. It was not, of course, itself a penalty, which may be why it is rarely discussed before it occurred.

CHAPTER 11

1. Document 522 (p. 127).

2. Above, Chapter 4, at n. 274.

3. For the form of chirographs, see Giry, *Manuel*, pp. 510–11; A. de Boüard, *Manuel*, 1:365–66. For their superior value to other charters and their disadvantages, see ibid., pp. 368–69; ibid., 2:144; Colmant, "Actes," p. 52; Chrimes, *Introduction*, pp. 13–14.

4. In addition to the charters cited in the notes below, see Documents 104 (p. 73), 191 (p. 273), 217 (p. 333), 386 (p. 99), 523 (p.132). It is noteworthy that the only Norman churches to use the term are the same five abbeys of pre-Norman origin and tenth-century refoundation which share so many other diplomatic characteristics. Historians, however, also sometimes use the word; see below, this chapter, at n. 19, for one example.

5. Giry, *Manuel*, pp. 10, 511. Documents 220 and 274 (p. 451) are clear instances.

6. Document 286 (col. 223).

7. Document 33. The surviving fragment of the Anglo-Flemish treaty of 1101 is also in this form (Chaplais, *Diplomatic Documents*, p. 4).

8. Documents 111 (p. 91), 118 (p. 104), 123 (p. 115), 274 (p. 451), 286 (col. 223), 821 (f° 24v). Document 134 calls itself a *carte cirographum*.

9. See also Colmant, "Actes," p. 53; Sauvage, *Troarn*, p. 301; Yver, *Contrats*, p. 77 and n. 6; A. de Boüard, *Manuel*, passim; Thorne, "Livery," pp. 350, 353.

Diplomatists sometimes distinguish between acts in the present tense, which had a dispositive force, and acts in the past tense, which were merely evidentiary; see, e.g., Lemarignier, "Actes," pp. 40, 47 and n. 41, and the references there. As with many other distinctions based on the exact wording of documents, this one, it seems to me, cannot hold for eleventh-century Normandy, the tenses of whose documents seem random and sometimes manifestly illogical. See the similar doubts for other areas of de Fontette, *Recherches*, pp. 80–81; Vigneron, "Vente," pp. 23–24; Clanchy, *Memory*, p. 208.

10. Above, Chapter 6, at n. 72. For another instance, see above, Chapter 7, n. 60: Archbishop John died eight years after William fitz Osbern. See also P. Le Cacheux, "Date," pp. 318–19; Sauvage, *Troarn*, p. 301; Matthew, *Norman Conquest*, p. 50.

11. Above, Chapter 6, at n. 72.

12. Document 115 (p. 99). See also Document 140 (p. 160), where the wording is identical to Document 115, and Document 114 (p. 97), where the wording is similar. For the meaning of "[a]stipulatio," see A. de Boüard, *Manuel*, 2:72–73.

13. A. de Boüard, *Manuel*, 1:271–73; ibid., 2:247–48.

14. Anselm, Epistles, p. 216, no. 89; the passage on the Conqueror's failure of memory is quoted above, Chapter 7, n. 60.

15. Document 85 (p. 462). For other examples of this sort of passage, see below, this chapter, at nn. 54–55.

16. Document 354 (p. 536). Gilbert's charter is not extant.

17. *Inventio*, p. 30. Laporte, ibid., p. 12, dates the *Inventio* to between about 1074 and 1087. See ibid., p. 30, n. 21, for the date of the incident.

18. See above, Chapter 2, at nn. 3–6, and below, Appendix A, Table 1. The story is rejected by Lot, *Etudes*, p. xliii, but accepted by Laporte, "Gérard," pp. 156–57, and Bates, *Normandy*, p. 32.

19. Hariulf, *Chronique*, p. 224.

20. Document 193. The charter which Gervinus brought with him is Document 118.

21. Document 393. On the history of Saint-Ouen's possession of Rots, see Musset, "Actes inédits, VI," p. 121.

22. Document 285 (col. 202). This must have occurred between 1078 and 1087, most probably closer to 1078, because the monks' complaint would probably have been made soon after the death of the abbot whose action they protested. The method of dating used at the beginning of the passage also implies that the complaint was made just after the new abbot was installed.

23. Above, Chapter 4, at n. 267.

24. Above, Chapter 7, at n. 46.

25. Above, Chapter 7, at n. 149. In this instance, the charter concerned could not have been used as proof.

26. Document 733 (f° 30v): "Predicta . . . ecclesia ab antiquis temporibus . . . Rothomagensi ecclesie . . . est concessa sicut in carta annotatur que ab ipsa antiquitate edita in eadem ecclesia adhuc monstrabilis habetur."

27. Document 280 (col. 127). See above, Chapter 5, at nn. 68–69, for the background to this suit.

28. Above, Chapter 4, at nn. 31–32. The other notable example of legal argument, the memorandum of Rainald the chaplain, was apparently prepared in anticipation of a suit; see above, Chapter 2, at and in n. 28.

29. The charter in which the exchange of Montivilliers for Saint-Taurin was recorded (above, Chapter 5, at n. 68) can be dated to 1034 or 1035.

30. Above, Chapter 7, at nn. 46–49.

31. Above, Chapter 7, at and in n. 48.

32. Document 227 (p. 347 and note b). See above, Chapter 4, n. 34, and Chapter 7, n. 49, for the dispute.

33. Discussed below, this chapter, at and in nn. 40–41.

34. Document 9.

35. Document 14 (p. 24).

36. Discussed below, this chapter, at and in nn. 45–46.

37. Document 146.

38. Documents 6 and 485 (p. 431). Prou, "Examen," pp. 230–31, thinks that both versions of the forged charter were done by the canons before 1092; in *Recueil*, pp. ccxxxiii–ccxxxiv, however, he argues that the version without the royal confirmation was done by the canons "peu avant 1092" and the version with the royal confirmation was done by the monks "dès 1092." According to ibid., p. ccxxxiv, "le mode de placage du sceau sur le privilège faux [i.e., the later version] est un indice de l'intervention des moines de Marmoutier." Lemarignier, *Etude*, pp. 187–88, thinks that both were done by the monks, the earlier in 1092, the later between 1092 and 1096; see also Lemarignier, "Pontificat," pp. 737–38. Others more casually attribute one or both to the monks or the canons: Yver, "Autour de l'absence," p. 204, n. 41 (monks); Siguret, "Recherches," pp. 8, 11 (canons). See also below, this chapter, at and in n. 47.

39. The fundamental accounts of this complex affair are Prou, "Examen," pp. 215–32, reprinted with revisions in *Recueil*, pp. ccxix–ccxxxv; and Lemarignier, *Etude*, pp. 181–92. The forged charter is accepted as genuine by du Motey, *Origines*, pp. 125–26, and *Champion*, pp. 22–23; but du Motey cannot be trusted on the subject of the Bellême family. Siguret, "Recherches," pp. 14–15, says that the new castle at Bellême had been built by 1031; ibid., p. 25, suggests a date of 1055 for Hugh de Rocé's gift. On the transfer of the church of Saint-Léonard to Marmoutier, see also Yver, "Autour de l'absence," pp. 204–5 and n. 41, and p. 217, n. 9; Chibnall, "Ecclesiastical Patronage," pp. 105, 117.

40. Document 7. Barret dates the charter "vers 1074." *Inventaire sommaire, Orne*, series H, 2:51–52, dates it to between 1070 and 1073. Round, *Calendar*, p. 429, no. 1190, dates it to between 1072 and 1079, and he is followed by *Regesta*, 1:31, no. 118. The terminal dates which I have given are the accession of Robert to the bishopric of Sées in 1070 and the death of Archbishop John of Rouen in 1079. As John suffered an incapacitating stroke about a year before his death, the *terminus ad quem* is probably 1078. 1070 x 1078 is the date given by Prou, "Examen," p. 229.

Goebel, *Felony*, p. 310 and n. 86, points out that the decision, as recorded in this charter, was "episcopum injuriam fecisse non solum comiti Rogerio, verum etiam regi de quo ipse ecclesiam tenebat." He argues from this and from other evidence that "the control that he [the king-duke] maintained over the use of the power of excommunication in his realm suggests that it had in Normandy a quasi-secular force." This may be why the case was heard in the ducal court rather than in the court of the archbishop. Archbishop John, Roger de Beaumont, "et plures alios barones" judged the case. The second version of the charter, cited in the next note, says that Archbishop John and Roger de Beaumont alone "jussu regis fecerunt judicium" but later lists, among others present, the important barons Robert de Vieuxpont and William de la Ferté-Macé.

41. Document 8 (p. 11). This charter and the forged charter of William I de Bellême are the only two references to a bishop of Sées named Richard who lived in the first quarter of the eleventh century. He did not exist; see Prou, "Examen," pp. 220, 230.

42. See also Prou, "Examen," p. 230. For analogous behavior at Mont-Saint-Michel, see Chibnall, "Charter and Chronicle," p. 8.

43. This version also has the bishop complain to the king rather than Roger de

Montgomery to the archbishop; perhaps the canons (or monks) felt more secure as defendants than as plaintiffs; perhaps they were preparing to deny the archbishop's jurisdiction over them as well as the bishop's, as the forged charter of William de Bellême does (see above, Chapter 10, n. 15).

Prou, "Examen," pp. 229–30, points out that some of the "expressions caractéristiques" of the forgery are found already in the first account of the case; he concludes, however, p. 230, that "s'il y a filiation, c'est de la notice à la charte, et non inversement, puisque la notice ne mentionne pas la charte."

44. Prou, "Examen," p. 231, n. 1, suggests that both this act and Document 15, the confirmation of it by Philip I, "demanderaient aussi à être examinées."

45. Document 16. Prou, "Examen," p. 231, points out that this account quotes directly from the forged charter of William de Bellême.

46. It seems unlikely that the ducal court was meant, given the duke's weakness by 1092 and Robert de Bellême's domination of southern Normandy. Moreover, the witness list of the charter is remarkably local in character for the court of a duke, even a weak one: it consists of the abbot and prior of Saint-Martin de Sées, William de Vivoin, prior of Saint-Léonard, Ralph, a monk of that priory, the cantor and four other clerics, doubtless of the cathedral of Sées, a priest named Herbert and nine laymen: Evanus de Sées, Rainfred and Adelelmus de Sées, Fulcher de Sées, Robert Rufus (du Motey, *Champion*, p. 23, says that all five were burgesses of Sées), Mathelinus d'Essai, Richard de la Rochelle and Robert Quadrel (three vassals of the Bellême family), and Ralph de Rouen (du Motey, *Champion*, p. 23, says that he, too, was a burgess; see also Musset, "A-t-il existé," p. 291).

The court may have been that of the bishop of Sées; du Motey, *Champion*, p. 23, thinks that it was. Its composition, however, suggests that the court was Robert de Bellême's. For other instances in which a suit was brought in the court of the lord whom one of the parties in effect vouched to warranty see above, Chapter 4, n. 34, and Chapter 9, at and in n. 28. No similar case was heard in the court of one of the parties, which again suggests that the court was Robert's, not the bishop's.

47. Prou, "Examen," pp. 222–23, and Lemarignier, *Etude*, pp. 183–87, demonstrate that new subject matter was introduced into the second redaction. Prou, *Recueil*, p. ccxxxiv, suggests that the second version of the forged charter of William de Bellême was done in preparation for the second suit.

48. In the case cited above, this chapter, at n. 17, the claim was made between 944 and 953 to lands which had been lost in or before 911, a minimum interval of thirty-three years and probably much longer. In the case cited above, this chapter, at nn. 19–20, the charter comes from between 1010 and 1017 and the case was heard in 1048, a minimum interval of thirty-one years. In the case cited above, this chapter, at and in n. 22, the case was heard between 1078 and 1087, probably closer to 1078; it is difficult to know to which charter reference is made, but the reference is to the foundation charter and the abbey was founded in or just before 1035, a probable minimum interval of forty-three years. The case cited above, this chapter, at n. 26, was heard in 1083; Archbishop Robert, whose actions gave rise to the case and were later than the charter, was archbishop from 989 to 1037. The minimum interval is therefore forty-six years. In the case cited above, this chapter, at and in nn. 27–29, the charter dates to 1034 or 1035 and the case was heard in 1106, an interval of seventy-one or seventy-two years.

The remaining intervals are more difficult to calculate. Roger de Croismare's claim, in the case referred to above, this chapter, at n. 16, was brought between 1078 and 1096; Roger's father-in-law made the gift recorded in the charter before Roger's wife's birth, perhaps as early as between 1035 and the early 1040s (above, Chapter 4, n. 114). In the case cited above, this chapter, at n. 21, the claim was made at some time between 1049 and 1092, perhaps about 1090. It is not known which charters were meant; but the church of Rots, over which the dispute arose, was given to Saint-Ouen by Richard

II in a charter datable to between 1017 and 1024 (Document 134), and the gift was confirmed by the same duke in a charter datable to between about 1025 and 1026 (Document 144, pp. 171–72). If these are the charters meant, the minimum interval is twenty-three years, and the probable interval is about sixty-five years after the later of Duke Richard's charters.

49. In this case, cited above, Chapter 7, at and in n. 48, it is not known what charter the abbot used; but the witnesses are called "antiqui," and Robert Samson's claim dated back to the time of Roger de Montgomery, who died seven years before the case was heard. Moreover, the abbot proved by his charter and witnesses, in part, "quod Rogerius Comes emerat quicquid habuerant antecessores Roberti Sansonis in ecclesia de Croceyo . . . et Sancto Martino ex dono proprio dederat" (Document 788, f° 180v). The church of Crocy is said to have been given to Troarn in Document 212, which apparently was dated 1059. In the abbreviated form in which the charter survives, Crocy seems first to have been given by Hugh bishop of Bayeux, who died in 1049, and there is no mention of any purchase; but both problems may be the result of the abbreviation. Because the suit between Robert Samson and the abbey was heard in 1101, if Document 212 was the abbot's charter, the interval would have been either forty-two or at least fifty-two years. Sauvage, *Troarn*, p. 167, identifies another of the places concerning which Robert Samson made claims, the land of Osbern du Marais, with the land "quam Osbernus tenet in Sancto Germano" which Bishop Hugh also gave, according to Document 212. Saint-Hippolyte and Giboury, two of the other three places where Robert made claims, are mentioned for the first time, along with Crocy but not Le Marais, in Document 493. If this was the abbot's charter, the interval is reduced to thirty-three years. I have not found any mention earlier than 1101 of Commeaux, the fifth and last place where Robert made claims.

50. Above, this chapter, at n. 32.

51. Document 177 (p. 248). The charter cited, which does indeed list witnesses, is Document 145.

52. Above, Chapter 7, at nn. 50–68.

53. See below, at the next note, for the full quotation.

54. Document 45 (p. 37).

55. Documents 221 and 494 (p. 353).

56. Above, Chapter 2, at n. 11.

57. Above, Chapter 7, at nn. 41, 42, and 46.

58. See also Yver, *Contrats*, pp. 232–33 and p. 233, n. 1.

59. Above, Chapter 7, at nn. 129–48.

60. It should, however, be noted that many of these documents were issued by the duke and that such usual evidence of the importance of witnessing as acts of donation and countergifts are recorded less often when the duke was the alienor or confirmer than when someone else was.

61. Above, Chapter 2, at and in n. 24.

62. Above, this chapter, at nn. 17, 22, and perhaps 20.

63. See also Clanchy, *Memory*, p. 256.

64. Above, Chapter 7, at nn. 129–39.

65. Above, Chapter 7, at and in n. 132.

66. Document 146, on which see above, this chapter, at nn. 33–47. There are twelve signatures.

67. Musset, *Actes*, p. 38, points out that the autograph crosses of Duke William and Duchess Matilda are distinctive and easily recognizable, as does Chaplais, "Charte," p. 94, for William's cross alone. See also Matthew, *Norman Conquest*, p. 50. This, however, does not mean that someone else could not easily enough have imitated their *signa*. See above, Chapter 7, at and in n. 122, on extant "originals" whose signatures are not autograph at all.

68. In addition to the charter from Marmoutier repeatedly cited in this section, see,

for examples, Documents 104 (alleged interpolation into a charter for Fécamp granted in 990), 123, 140 (pp. 161–62: interpolation made between 1058 and 1060 to an act of Mont-Saint-Michel from between 1022 and 1026), 147, 172, 173. In addition to the scholarly studies cited by Fauroux in each of these instances, see, for Documents 104 and 172, Hall and Sweeney, "Unpublished Privilege," esp. pp. 665–67, 670–71. The many forgeries and interpolations which date from the twelfth century and later are not relevant here. For forgeries of papal documents, see above, Chapter 8, at and in n. 163.

69. Above, this chapter, at nn. 3–8.

70. Prou, "Examen," pp. 226–28, in discussing the alleged confirmation of King Philip I, which was forged by the monks of Marmoutier in or shortly after 1092 (above, this chapter, at and in n. 38), to which they transferred a genuine royal seal from some authentic act, maintains that signatures were better security than seals, that the royal signature "présentait plus de garantie qu'un sceau assez facile à transporter d'un document authentique sur un faux." In this opinion, he seems to be alone; for the contrary view, see Colmant, "Actes," p. 53; Sauvage, *Troarn*, p. 301 and n. 5; A. de Boüard, *Manuel*, passim, esp. 1:330; Yver, *Contrats*, pp. 232–34; Guillot, *Comte*, 2:10–11 and n. 26. The royal signature was also much more elaborate than any Norman one, even the duke's. On the relationship between seals and signatures, see also Clanchy, *Memory*, pp. 244–48.

71. See esp. Chaplais, "Charte," pp. 94–95, 100–101. See also Chaplais, "Anglo-Saxon Chancery," pp. 160–61; Haskins, *Norman Institutions*, p. 53; Matthew, *Norman Conquest*, p. 50; Strayer, review of Fauroux, p. 607; Le Patourel, *Norman Empire*, p. 244 and n. 1.

72. On these, see Fauroux, *Recueil*, pp. 45–47, which does not, however, mention Document 178. The evidence for the seal of Document 266 is too slight to warrant its inclusion (see Fauroux, *Recueil*, p. 46 and p. 421, n. 1); the verb *sigillare* in the document itself, p. 424, seems to mean "to sign" rather than "to seal" (see below, this chapter, at n. 79 on this word). For others who accept at least some of these seals as genuine, see Giry, *Manuel*, p. 641 and n. 2; Duhamel, "Diplomatique," p. 32; Yver, "Premières institutions," pp. 332–33; Brown, "Some Observations," pp. 153–55. M. de Boüard, "Duché," p. 17, begs the question. For eleventh-century references not cited by Fauroux to seals of charters which she discusses, see Document 735 (f° 3v), which appears to refer to Document 125; Document 85 (p. 462), which appears to refer to Document 150.

73. Document 210, allegedly sealed by a donor named Landricus Aculeus, is suspect for other reasons than the seal; Brown, "Some Observations," p. 154 and n. 56, argues for its authenticity. Document 96 is the foundation charter of Lonlay, allegedly sealed by William de Bellême; at this date, ca. 1020, the Bellême area cannot yet be considered part of Normandy. Document 298 (p. 116), which refers to the "sugillationem vel, ut ita dicam, sigillationem" of the archbishop of Rouen and all the other Norman bishops except Bayeux may mean their signatures rather than their seals; see below, this chapter, at n. 79.

74. The charter of 1067 is Document 483, the seal of Gerald "miles Christi." Archbishop Maurilius, mentioned as a witness in the charter, died in August 1067; Michael bishop of Avranches became bishop only in 1067. Michael appears in the charter as bishop of Evreux (*Ebroicensis*), rather than Avranches. This is not Pommeraye's error: it appears in the copies of this charter in the thirteenth-century cartulary of Saint-Amand in Arch. Seine-Maritime (no number), f° 259v, and in Arch. Seine-Maritime, 55 H, fonds de Saint-Amand non classé, titres généraux, carton I, cote A 1. The charter is nonetheless accepted as genuine by Round, *Calendar*, p. 25, no. 87; and the error of *Ebroicensis* for *Abrincatensis* seems easy enough to make, especially if in the original the word was abbreviated (misreading *Ebroic.* for *Abrinc.*). The gift was confirmed by William the Conqueror in a charter which correctly identifies Michael: Document 343 (p. 251).

The sample of other genuine seals is so small that its statistical reliability is low. Nevertheless, from the decade of the 1060s on, there is a steady increase in the number of references. For charters mentioning seals and originals known once to have borne seals which are dated to particular years or datable to spans of twenty years or less (each of the latter treated as though it came from the midpoint of the span), the figures are as follows: two in the 1060s, four in the 1070s and again in the 1080s, ten in the 1090s, and eleven between 1100 and 1106. Eight can be assigned to William the Conqueror's reign after 1066 and twenty-one to Robert Curthose's reign. The resulting rates of increase are, for the most part, higher than the rates of increase of extant charters, for which see below, Appendix A, Table 1.

On the seals in Norman documents of William the Conqueror between 1066 and 1087, see Duhamel, "Diplomatique," p. 32; Chaplais, "Charte," pp. 94–95; Musset, *Actes*, pp. 39–41. On the seals of Robert Curthose, see Haskins, *Norman Institutions*, pp. 72–73. On the development of the use of seals in general, see Giry, *Manuel*, pp. 600, 622, 632, 636–38, 640–41, 818; A. de Boüard, *Manuel*, 1:355–57; Fauroux, *Recueil*, p. 46, n. 43. Tessier, *Diplomatique*, p. 129, n. 1, dates the appearance of seigneurial seals to the second half of the eleventh century. Giry, *Manuel*, p. 637, accepts as genuine a seal of Arnulf count of Flanders from 942; ibid., p. 641 and n. 1, accepts as genuine seals of the count of Anjou of about 1010 and 1091. A. de Boüard, *Manuel*, 1:356, n. 6, finds the earliest mention of the seal of a count of Anjou in 1060 and says, "Les chartes comtales scellées ne se multiplient qu'à partir de 1080." Guillot, *Comte*, 2:8, 11–12, however, denies the authenticity of the charter of 1060 (n. 31) and says that the counts of Anjou began to use a seal only in 1085, though the bishop of Angers had one in 1076.

75. For examples, see Fauroux, *Recueil*, pp. 55 and 100, with regard to Document 116; Musset, *Actes*, pp. 40–41. See also A. de Boüard, *Manuel*, 1:292, n. 1.

76. Henry count of Eu: Document 746 (f° 7r). William count of Mortain: Document 802. Robert count of Meulan: Document 352. Viscount Neil de Saint-Sauveur: Document 502 (p. 244). Viscount Odo: Document 49 (pp. 55–56, 58). William archbishop of Rouen: Document 734. Odo bishop of Bayeux: below, this chapter, n. 78. Others: above, this chapter, n. 74; Documents 98 (William de Vernon), 469 (p. 196: Richer de Laigle), 482 (p. 676, editor's comment: Harscutus), 508 (Gilbert Crispin), 796 (Robert de *Peissiaco*), 800 (f° 236r: John de Méautis). The following may also be relevant, although they are difficult to date: Documents 538 (f° 50v: Gilbert de Vascoeuil), 742 (Geoffrey and William Bertram), 818 (Ralph de Mairie). Document 721, where the seal is William de Roumare's, may be from the last third of the eleventh century; the William de Roumare who was head of his family in the first half of the twelfth century was born very late in the eleventh century, but an older man of the same name flourished ca. 1090.

77. The clearest examples are three gifts in Document 49 (pp. 55–56). The account of the first gift ends thus (p. 55): "unde cartam suam predicte abbatie fecerunt et sigillo domini sui Eudonis vicecomitis confirmaverunt. Teste et concedente ipso Eudone vicecomite"; the other two gifts contain substantially the same wording. Another likely example is Document 344 (p. 214), in which Rainald the chaplain gave land, which he held from the king and queen, "eorum concessu et sigillo." On this practice, see A. de Boüard, *Manuel*, 1:357; Besnier, *Coutume*, p. 41.

78. The exception is Document 278 (col. 77), which mentions the seals of the duke and the bishop of Bayeux.

79. For those from La Trinité du Mont, see Documents 61, 70, 178 (p. 249), 265. For others, see Documents 27 (p. 2) and 266 (p. 424).

80. There are twenty-one uses of *firmare* or *confirmare* and eight of *signare* or *assignare*. In the former class also occur: *roborare* and variations (seven times), *auctorizare* (twice), *munire* (twice). In the latter class—connecting seals with writing—also occur: *subscribere*, *inscribere*, and *subnotare*, once each.

81. For example, Document 709: "hanc pro testimonio crucis impressione firmo et sigilli mei privilegio munio."

82. E.g., the preceding note and Document 856, as quoted above, Chapter 6, n. 102.

83. Document 319.

CHAPTER 12

1. Le Patourel, *Norman Empire*, p. 11.

2. For the best recent map of this frontier, see ibid., Map 2. On the linearity and stability of the frontier, see Lemarignier, *Recherches*, Chapters 1 and 2, esp. p. 11; Musset, "Observations sur l'histoire"; Yver, "Premières institutions," pp. 311–12; Bates, *Normandy*, chap. 2, passim, esp. pp. 56–58, 62–64, 85. For the contrary view, see Le Patourel, *Norman Empire*, pp. 5–12; Goebel, *Felony*, pp. 190–92.

3. Musset, "Observations sur l'histoire"; Musset, "Quelques observations"; Yver, "Premières institutions," p. 312; Navel, "Recherches sur les anciennes mesures," pp. 164–66; Yver, comments on Navel; Yver, review of Carabie, p. 102. See also above, Chapter 4, at nn. 172–80, and the references in those notes.

4. Yver, "Caractères originaux de Normandie," pp. 332–33; Yver, "Premières institutions," p. 312; Musset, "Observations sur l'histoire"; Le Patourel, *Norman Empire*, p. 11.

5. Génestal, "Formation et développement," pp. 38–44.

6. For the location of the Conquêts Hue de Gournay, see Le Patourel, *Norman Empire*, Map 2, square F2.

7. Lemarignier, *Recherches*, pp. 19–24, seconded by Chibnall, in OV, 4:182, n.4; Vallez, "Exemple," pp. 352–53.

8. Above, Chapter 3, n. 262.

9. Lemarignier, *Recherches*, pp. 19–24; Yver, "Caractères originaux de l'Ouest," p. 22 and n. 1; Yver, "Développement," p. 195; M. de Boüard, *Guillaume*, pp. 42, 66; M. de Boüard, "Duché," p. 16.

The exact date, some time between 1049 and 1052, of the campaign which led to the incorporation of Domfront into Normandy is uncertain. See, most recently, Bates, *Normandy*, pp. 255–56. It is also by no means clear whether, before this campaign, it was Domfront or Alençon—or neither—which was already considered part of Normandy. See Guillot, *Comte*, 1:70, n. 313; Le Patourel, *Norman Empire*, pp. 10, 17; Bates, *Normandy*, p. 69 and n. 62. For evidence that until the later 1050s the Bellême lordships were still not fully committed to Normandy, see Bates, *Normandy*, pp. 79–80.

10. The implicit assumption of the argument for the *terminus a quo* is that the incorporation of the Passais normand into the duchy was not followed by the extension to it of an already developed Norman custom. To deny that assumption in this context would be to posit that Norman law had crystallized before the middle of the eleventh century. The validity of the assumption is not obvious; but, as I can think of no reliable way of testing it and as I am primarily concerned to determine whether Norman custom had crystallized by the end of the century, I have accepted it. On a priori grounds, it seems unlikely that Norman custom could have crystallized much earlier than the middle of the eleventh century: the duchy was then only a century and a quarter old, its early history had been turbulent, and the developed custom is so thoroughly French in its main lines that a good deal of time must have been needed for the assimilation of French practices.

In "Caractères originaux de Normandie," pp. 310–11, Jean Yver draws the same conclusion as I have drawn from the work of Génestal and Lemarignier, giving 1048 x 1049 and 1078 x 1090 as the boundaries of the period of crystallization of the custom of Normandy. See also Yver, "Premières institutions," p. 312, n. 31. Other scholars are not as precise, but most agree that the second half of the eleventh century is the relevant period; see Haskins, *Norman Institutions*, p. 4; Radin, "Quelles idées"; Brown, *Normans*, p. 75; Chibnall, "Droits"; M. de Boüard, "Etat," p. 147. For the assertion that Norman law crystallized unusually early, see Feuchère, "Essai," p. 101; Carabie, "Nature," p. 125, and the references there in n. 2 to the works of Yver. Besnier, *Coutume*, p. 34, seems to favor a twelfth-century date. Le Patourel, *Norman Empire*, p. 11, thinks that crystallization "was not achieved much before the end of the eleventh century"; see also pp. 114, 264, 275–76. He does not discuss the Conquêts Hue de Gournay.

In "Caractères originaux de l'Ouest," pp. 22–24, Yver applies the same method to the custom of Anjou and concludes that it, too, must have crystallized in the second half of the eleventh century. See also Guillot, "Quelques hypothèses."

11. Above, Chapter 4, at n. 393.

12. Above, Chapter 4, at and in n. 114.

13. Above, Chapter 6, at n. 40.

14. Above, Chapter 2, at and in n. 10. See above, Chapter 2, at nn. 3–13, on the novelty of writing charters in Normandy in the eleventh century.

15. Above, Chapter 7, at n. 124.

16. Document 367: "forisfacturas . . . que secundum humanas leges ab homicidis et furibus quoque capitali sententia convictis more patrio exiguntur." The adjective *patrius* derives both from *pater* and from *patria* and is consequently ambiguous in this context. Haskins, *Norman Institutions*, p. 30, translates the phrase as "ancient custom," which conveys the sense of the passage if it does not correspond to the letter.

17. Document 166 (p. 225). On the meaning of *leuva* ("league"), see Fauroux, *Recueil*, p. 223, n. 3. Yver, "Premières institutions," p. 312, n. 31, notices this very early use of *mos* but thinks that it does not mean that the custom of Normandy had then already developed its characteristic traits.

18. Above, Chapter 5, at nn. 72–75.

19. For *ius alodii*, see above, Chapter 5, at and in n. 47. For *ius beneficiale*, see above, Chapter 5, at and in n. 73, and WJ, p. 101, who, in describing the situation of William I de Bellême about the year 1027, refers to Alençon castle, "quod beneficii tenebat jure." For *ius elemosinae*, see above, Chapter 3, at and in n. 229.

20. WP, p. 64; Document 20 (p. 5). OV, 2:318, also refers to this rule of law, calling it *leges Normannorum* (in contrast to the *Anglica lex*, ibid., p. 314), and specifying that under it the punishments, in the case cited below, this chapter, at n. 27, were disinheritance and perpetual imprisonment. As he was writing in the twelfth century, his language may be anachronistic for the eleventh. The reference in William of Poitiers is too vague to confirm Orderic's accuracy as to the law in the eleventh century, but disinheritance and perpetual imprisonment are precisely what happened to the traitor with whose lands the charter of 1074 is concerned.

21. Above, Chapter 5, after n. 43, and the references in that note.

22. Above, Chapter 6, n. 172.

23. Bates, "Notes"; Bates, *Normandy*, pp. 118–20.

24. Génestal, "Formation et développement," pp. 42–43; Génestal, "Formation du droit," esp. pp. 178–79; Yver, "Caractères originaux de Normandie," p. 323.

25. Yver, "Caractères originaux de Normandie," pp. 311–14.

26. Le Patourel, *Normandy*, p. 21.

27. OV, 2:314–18, on which see also above, this chapter, n. 20.

28. Bates, *Normandy*, pp. xiv–xvii, and the references there. Ibid., p. 58, suggests that in the second quarter of the eleventh century "the duchy turned in on itself, and . . . more intensely 'Norman' attitudes emerged."

29. In "Caractères originaux de Normandie," Yver singles out three particular characteristics of Norman law as clearly evident by the time the first Norman custumals were drawn up, that is, the first half of the thirteenth century. The first (pp. 314–21) is "la très forte empreinte . . . de la structure féodale" (p. 314). My study, however, gives some reason to doubt that a feudal imprint was very strong in the eleventh century. The

second (ibid., pp. 321–24) is the very conservative nature of Norman custom once it had formed and its consequent archaism by comparison with other French customs; on this see also ibid., pp. 331–56. This trait, obviously, would not be found as early as the eleventh century: see also ibid., pp. 351–52. The third (ibid., pp. 324–29) is the very great importance of the descent of property in lineages; but on this matter the surviving documents of the eleventh century do not provide enough information to permit firm conclusions. There are occasional hints that this third trait may already have been characteristic, for example, the stress in the agreement between William Paynel and the abbot of Mont-Saint-Michel (above, Chapter 4, at n. 83) on the rights of William's children only by "this wife." On the other hand, the eleventh century also provides contrary examples, one of them the family of Moulins.

30. Above, Chapter 8, at n. 44.

31. Escheats: above, Chapter 4, at nn. 153–63. Restoration of confiscated possessions: above, Chapter 8, at and in n. 120.

32. The exchange with a provision for reexchange, cited above, Chapter 3, at and in n. 220, is an exception.

33. See especially Tardif, "Etude"; but Tardif overestimates the role of legislation in the formation of eleventh-century Norman law, since, in fact, all the instances of legislation which he cites concern public law. See also Valin, *Duc*, pp. 171–73; Haskins, *Norman Institutions*, p. 276; Génestal, "Histoire," pp. 84–85; Besnier, *Coutume*, pp. 43–46; Goebel, *Felony*, passim; M. de Boüard, "Duché," p. 15; Musset, "Gouvernés," pp. 466–67; Bates, *Normandy*, pp. 22, 163–64. Yver, "Très Ancien Coutumier," is concerned with twelfth-century legislation.

Because most of the known ducal legislation of the eleventh century concerned the truce of God, the following also have much to say on this subject: Yver, "Interdiction"; Prentout, "Etudes," pp. 3–25; M. de Boüard, "Sur les origines"; M. de Boüard, "Nouvelles remarques."

Prentout, "Règne," p. 65, thinks that serfdom was abolished by ducal legislation in the first half of the eleventh century; and the suggestion is also made by Musset, "Quelques observations."

Musset, "Apports scandinaves," p. 566, thinks that the use of the acre in place of older Carolingian measures was "généralisée très tôt, au plus tard dès le début du XIe siècle . . . , sans doute par l'autorité ducale." An agrarian measure seems an unlikely subject for an exercise of ducal authority; moreover, the Scandinavian origin of the term "acre" has been denied by Navel and Guinet (above, Chapter 1, n. 29).

The *Consuetudines et Iusticie* of 1091, which Musset, "Gouvernés," p. 467, cites as an instance of ducal legislation, concern secular matters but are not, properly speaking, legislation; they merely record the results of an inquest into "consuetudines et iusticie quas habet dux Normannie in eadem provincia, et Guillelmus rex qui regnum Anglie adquisivit maxime et viriliter eas suo tempore teneri fecit" (Document 315, p. 281).

34. Tardif, "Etude," passim. See also Steenstrup, "Normandiets Historie," p. 304; Le Patourel, *Norman Empire*, pp. 11, 270 and n. 3.

35. Thorne, "English Feudalism"; Milsom, *Legal Framework*, passim, esp. pp. 120–21, 154–86.

36. Bates, *Normandy*, p. 160. More generally, see S. D. White, "*Pactum*"; Clanchy, "Law and Love."

APPENDIX B

1. Corrected by Arch. Orne, H 2156. On the date, see above, Chapter 11, n. 40.

2. Corrected by Arch. Orne, H 2156. This is a reworked version of Document 7; for the circumstances, see above, Chapter 11, at nn. 33–43.

3. Corrected by Arch. Orne, H 2152.

4. Corrected by Arch. Orne, H 2156.

5. Corrected by Bibliothèque du Chapitre de Bayeux, ms. 193, f° 21r–21v. On the date, see above, Chapter 4, n. 63.

6. On the date, see Haskins, *Norman Institutions*, pp. 66–67, nos. 3–4 and n. 19.

7. The dates of the documents cited from this cartulary are taken from Adigard des Gautries, "Noms des lieux du Calvados," pp. 139–40.

8. Corrected by BN, ms. lat. 5441, vol. 1, p. 199.

9. On the date, see Musset, "Actes inédits, V," p. 13.

10. On this document, see ibid. Cf. the doubts about its authenticity expressed by G. H. White, "Companions," pp. 421–22.

11. Concerning an act which allegedly occurred before 1095, probably several decades before.

12. On the date, see above, Chapter 3, n. 161.

13. Corrected by BN, ms. lat. 12878, f° 235r.

14. This cartulary was compiled in the late eleventh century. Documents for which no other date is given are presumed to come from that period.

15. The date is taken from Adigard des Gautries, "Noms des lieux de l'Eure," 4:53, n. 3.

16. Dated thus by *Regesta*, 1:15, no. 55.

17. See below, Document 718, n. 103.

18. Corrected by Arch. Eure, H supplement (no number), which contains fragments of the original. Beaumont-le-Roger was founded as a college of canons. It became a priory of Bec in 1142.

19. Corrected by Adigard des Gautries, "Noms des lieux de l'Eure," passim. This is a pancart of acts of various dates from the foundation of the abbey to the early twelfth century, in roughly chronological order.

20. On the date of this act, see Barlow, *William Rufus*, p. 281, n. 76. The full witness list is published in Haskins, *Norman Institutions*, p. 68, no. 7.

21. Lemarignier et al., "Monachisme," pp. 93 (with n. 4), 95, note certain problems with the language of this act which suggest that the surviving text was drafted later than the late tenth century.

22. Or 996 x 1025, if the Duke Richard mentioned is Richard II rather than Richard I; see Fauroux, *Recueil*, pp. 76, 116.

23. The first series of events related occurred between 996 and 1007. Other events occurred as much as thirty years later, and the notice was probably written shortly after the latest event mentioned.

24. For the reason for the query, see Fauroux, *Recueil*, p. 145.

25. This is the beginning of a long pancart, the whole of which is Document 484. See below, this appendix, n. 84, for the date.

26. Fauroux, *Recueil*, p. 272, gives the *terminus ad quem* as 1048; but the act was witnessed by *Haduaiardus rex*, i.e., Edward king of England. The charter may be suspect because of the use of Edward's regal title while he was in exile (see the references above, Chapter 8, n. 144). If it is genuine, however, it ought to be from no later than 1041, when Edward returned to England.

27. Also in OV, 2:32–40. On the relationship of Orderic's version to the two versions collated by Fauroux, see OV, 1:65–75.

28. On the authenticity of this charter, see above, Chapter 4, n. 158.

29. On the date, see D. C. Douglas, *William*, p. 69 and nn. 2–3.

30. On the authenticity of this charter, see above, Chapter 4, n. 158.

31. The document incorporates an act of 1049 or earlier.

32. On the date, see above, Chapter 3, n. 161.

33. Maillefer, "Famille," pp. 186–87 and n. 42, suggests that this act and the next two cannot be later than 1060.

34. See the preceding note on the date.

35. See above, n. 33, on the date.

36. On the document and its date, see above, Chapter 7, at and in n. 58.
37. On the date, see above, Chapter 7, at and in n. 58.
38. The signatures were added ca. 1050 x 1066.
39. Although for a non-Norman nunnery, this act was written by "Richardus archidiaconus, apud Bajocas" (p. 437).
40. On the date, see above, Chapter 6, n. 94.
41. The end of the witness list is not published. It can be found in BN, fonds Moreau, vol. 42, f° 89r–89v.
42. Corrected by Arch. Eure, H 262, f° 219r–221v.
43. Corrected by Arch. Orne, *Livre blanc* of Saint-Martin de Sées, f° 81r.
44. On the date, see above, Chapter 8, n. 34.
45. Corrected by Arch. Eure, H 711, f° 97r–99v, no. 286, and f° 114v, no. 345.
46. On this source, see above, Chapter 2, n. 48.
47. See Haskins, *Norman Institutions*, p. 81, n. 57.
48. On the date, see above, Chapter 4, n. 296.
49. Guérard dates this charter to 1033 but gives no reason for doing so (p. 115). That date seems impossible because Maugisus (here Maingisus) was bishop of Avranches only from 1022 to 1025 or 1026. A date of ca. 1025 is consistent with all the names in the charter.
50. On this document, see above, Chapter 2, at n. 49, and Chapter 12, n. 33.
51. Possibly 1089 (Bouvris, "Aux origines," p. 333).
52. Or 1090 x 1096; see *Regesta*, 1:98, no. 384.
53. Dated thus for the same reasons as those given for the date of Document 483, above, Chapter 11, n. 74.
54. This document narrates a series of events which began during the reign of Richard II and culminated at the time when the document was written. On it, see esp. above, Chapter 2, at and in n. 28.
55. Corrected by Arch. Eure, H 438, no. 1, paragraph 18.
56. Corrected by Arch. Eure, H 711, f° 133r, no. 417.
57. Corrected by Arch. Eure, H 711, f° 128v, no. 400.
58. Corrected by Arch. Eure, H 711, f° 100r–100v, no. 289. On the date, see above, Chapter 4, n. 114.
59. Corrected by BN, ms. lat. 12878, f° 161r.
60. On the date, see above, Chapter 6, at and in n. 72.
61. Corrected by Arch. Eure, H 711, f° 115r, no. 347.
62. Corrected by Arch. Eure, H 711, f° 136v, no. 436.
63. Corrected by Arch. Eure, H 711, f° 118r, no. 358.
64. On the date, see above, Chapter 9, n. 23.
65. Corrected by BN, ms. lat. 5441, vol. 1, p. 97.
66. This document and the next are dated by the editor to before 1042 (Le Prévost, *Eure*, 3:382). Both the language of the charters and the names of some of the persons in them suggest a date at least several decades later. The readings of both are corrected by the original, Arch. Eure, H 438, paragraphs 15 and 14, respectively.
67. See the preceding note.
68. On the reliability of this charter, see above, Chapter 6, at and in n. 197.
69. Lemarignier, *Etude*, p. 172, n. 133, tentatively dates this document to shortly before 1092.
70. On the dates of this document and the next two, see Round, *Calendar*, pp. liiii, 396–99 (nos. 1112–15).
71. Concerning a confirmation made in 1096. On the date, see D. C. Douglas, *Domesday Monachorum*, p. 53.
72. This may concern English land.
73. On this act, see Musset, *Actes*, p. 31.
74. On this document and the next, see Musset, *Actes*, pp. 26–28.

75. This act exists in two versions. The shorter one is dated 1082; the longer is a 1080 draft reworked in 1082 or soon thereafter (Musset, *Actes*, pp. 28–30, 80). Where they differ in wording or content, Musset prints them in parallel columns.

76. On this document, see Musset, *Actes*, pp. 32–33.

77. On the relationship of this act and the next, see above, Chapter 6, at and in n. 128; Musset, *Actes*, pp. 30–31.

78. See the preceding note.

79. On this document, see above, Chapter 3, n. 145; Musset, *Actes*, pp. 32–33.

80. On the date, see also above, Chapter 8, n. 50.

81. A roll of forty-nine acts (of which nos. 13 through 24 are lost), called by Le Prévost "Rotulus primus monasterii Sancti Ebrulfi," compiled in the late eleventh century. Documents for which no other date is given are presumed to come from that period.

82. The original is extant with no significant differences (OV, 3:151, n. 2).

83. For the date, see above, Chapter 11, n. 74.

84. The beginning of this act is Document 181. On the date, see Lemarignier et al., "Monachisme," p. 102 and n. 5. For an analysis of the contents, see Gazeau-Goddet, "Aristocration," pp. 90–93.

85. Corrected by Arch. Calvados, H 7750.

86. Corrected by Arch. Calvados, H 7813.

87. Completed by Bibl. Avranches, ms. 210, f° 87r. On the date, see above, Chapter 4, at and in n. 278.

88. Collated with Bibl. Caen, ms. 308, f° 274v–275r, the badly worn original.

89. Original in very bad condition, collated with BN, ms. lat. 10086, f° 44r–44v. Words in brackets are legible only in the cartulary copy.

90. Under this number are collected fragments, much damaged, of a seventeenth-century copy of a cartulary of Conches. Each folio is loose and is accompanied by a nineteenth-century decipherment of what could then be read, itself annotated in two other hands. This copy is collated with Arch. Eure, H 251, a 1680 copy on paper.

91. Each act is a separate paragraph.

92. Charters of this abbey are often difficult to date within narrow limits. Moreover, they often recount series of events which began considerably earlier than the date of the charter.

93. This is a continuation of the second copy in the cartulary of Document 362.

94. Partially published in Fauroux, *Recueil*, p. 286, n. 1.

95. The act describes two mortgages to the abbey. The first is dated, as are many acts of this abbey, "Regnante Willelmo martionis Roberti filio," i.e., William the Conqueror. It also mentions Abbot Ansfrid. The second act is dated, "Illum annum quod [*sic*] bellum fuit inter regem et comitem." That might mean William Rufus and Robert Curthose, respectively, but it seems more likely that the king of France and Duke William are meant. If so, the obvious "bellum" is the battle of Mortemer in 1054. See also Adigard des Gautries, "Noms des lieux de l'Eure," p. 238.

96. For the date of the first transaction recorded in this charter, see above, Chapter 6, n. 16.

97. Collated with BN, ms. lat. 5441, vol. 2, pp. 85–86, and BN, ms. lat. 12878, f° 262r–262v. On the date, see Bouvris, "Notice," pp. 87–88 and n. 11.

98. Collated with the 1754 copy in the same liasse and with BN, ms. lat. 5441, vol. 2, pp. 88–89. The date is taken from Round, *Calendar*, p. 432, no. 1198, and *Inventaire sommaire, Orne, H*, 2:xxvii. Bouvris, "Notice," p. 94, n. 6, says that the date is, instead, "vers 1145."

99. In the first half of this manuscript, the order of the folios became somewhat disarranged after the folios were numbered. The manuscript belongs to the bishopric of Sées. I have used only a microfilm and the modern copy in Arch. Orne, H 938.

100. On this document, see Bouvris, "Date," esp. pp. 127–31.

101. "Multorum spatia annorum" after Document 581.
102. "Multum vero temporis" after the preceding act in the cartulary (f° 35v), which is dated 1094.
103. The witness list is also copied onto f° 41v.
104. Now edited by Bouvris, "Possession," p. 181.
105. Partially published in Haskins, *Norman Institutions*, p. 19, n. 60.
106. On this document and the next two, see Musset, "Huit essais," p. 141. He dates Document 695 to 1082 and Documents 696–97 to shortly before that date.
107. On the date, see above, Chapter 1, n. 5.
108. Partially published in *Inventaire sommaire, Seine-Maritime,* G, 3:255.
109. See above, Chapter 3, n. 88.
110. Completed by BN, ms. lat. 5423, p. 134.
111. On the date, see above, Chapter 4, n. 117.
112. This act, an apparent original, is nearly identical to Document 91. The only differences are the names of the abbey, the abbot and the place given; the presence of a date in Document 91; the presence of one signer in each act who is not in the other; and a few minor changes of wording. Only Document 91 is noticed in either Round's *Calendar* (p. 22, no. 79) or the *Regesta* (1:33, no. 126). Nonetheless, Document 718 is accepted as authentic by Léopold Delisle in BN, ms. fr. n. a. 21815, f° 274r–274v; by *Inventaire sommaire, Seine-Maritime, H,* 4:1, p. 79; and by the compiler of a recent, typed handlist, "Chartes originales antérieures à 1121 conservées dans le département de la Seine-Maritime," made for the Centre de Recherches et d'Applications Linguistiques of the University of Nancy, of which a copy is housed in the Archives départementales de la Seine-Maritime.
113. Partially published by Delisle, *Etudes*, p. 22, n. 102. He dates it to the beginning of the twelfth century; but the copy in BN, fonds Moreau, vol. 40, f° 234r–235r, is dated eleventh century, and Delisle's copy in BN, ms. fr. n. a. 21835, f° 814r, is dated to between about 1050 and about 1060. The handlist referred to in the preceding note dates the act to the twelfth century.
114. Several documents have the same number. The one meant is the middle act of the three-act *vidimus* of Philip IV dated 1313. The donor is William de Roumare.
115. Collated with the original, Musée de la Bénédictine de Fécamp, no. 7, which is in very bad shape.
116. Partially published in Haskins, *Norman Institutions*, p. 32, n. 125.
117. Musset, "Huit essais," pp. 139–41, accepts this act as genuine.
118. On the document and the problem of its date, see above, Chapter 8, at and in n. 105.
119. Bouvris, "Contribution," p. 172, dates this to about the same time as Document 821. I have not seen the edition which is cited ibid., n. 123.
120. Collated with Coll. Mancel, vol. 300, f° 227v, p. 2409, no. 25.
121. Collated with Coll. Mancel, vol. 300, f° 239v, p. 2434, no. 99.
122. Also in BN, ms. lat. 12878, f° 278r–278v; ibid., f° 279r–280r; BN, fonds Baluze, vol. 77, f° 60r; Coll. Mancel, vol. 300, f° 243v–244v, pp. 2440–42, no. 127.
123. For the date and the nature of the source, see above, Chapter 2, at and in n. 52.
124. But see Musset, "Sur les mutations," p. 293.
125. On the document, see above, Chapter 7, n. 77.
126. On the document, see above, Chapter 4, n. 41.
127. Items in this manuscript are numbered twice, in ink and in pencil. Both numbers are given, those in ink first.
128. Partially published in Depoin, *Cartulaire*, p. 3, no. 3.
129. Repeated on f° 283r–283v. Collated with Coll. Mancel, vol. 300, f° 244v–245r (pp. 2442–43), no. 128; BN, ms. lat. 5441, vol. 2, p. 404; BN, fonds Baluze, vol. 77, f° 59r.

130. Bouvris, "Contribution," p. 171, suggests a date of about mid-century.

131. The dates are derived from ibid., p. 160 and n. 55 and p. 173.

132. The late twelfth- or thirteenth-century cartulary of Saint-Etienne de Caen is not extant, but two copies are. One, much the fuller and better, is a nineteenth-century copy now owned by the University of Caen. The other, a careless epitome, was published by Etienne Deville. I have relied primarily on the Caen manuscript, corrected occasionally by the epitome. Acts for which no date is indicated are datable by the witnesses to the late eleventh or early twelfth century.

133. The number is omitted by mistake.

134. This is also copied into BN, ms. lat. 17135, pp. 23–24, and excerpted in Bibl. Caen, ms. 300, f° 79r. I have used all these versions to establish the text.

Bibliography

MANUSCRIPT SOURCES

Archives départementales du Calvados:
F, fonds de Beausse, année 1926: copies by Gaston de Beausse
H 1869: documents from Saint-Etienne de Caen
H 7745: "Chartrier blanc" of Troarn
H 7747: "Liber rubeus" of Troarn
H 7750, 7813, 7858: documents from Troarn
Archives départementales de l'Eure:
H 54, 59, 76, 91: documents from Bec
H 251: documents from Conches
H 262: fragments of a seventeenth-century copy of a cartulary of Conches
H 438: pancart of Lire
H 711: cartulary of Saint-Pierre de Préaux
H 793: "Petit cartulaire" of Saint-Taurin d'Evreux
H supplement, no number: fragments of a pancart of Beaumont-le-Roger
Archives départementales de l'Orne:
"Livre blanc" of Saint-Martin de Sées. Microfilm of the original. H 938: nineteenth-century copy by Louis Duval
H 1972: documents from Troarn
H 2007, 2008, 2009, 2023: documents from Saint-Vigor de Perrières, priory of Marmoutier
H 2150, 2152, 2154, 2156, 2369, 3351: documents concerning the possessions of Marmoutier at Bellême
Archives départementales de la Seine-Maritime (formerly Archives départementales de la Seine-Inférieure):
G 4069, 8739, 8740: documents from the cathedral church of Rouen
7 H 2141: documents from Fécamp
14 H 1: "Bref inventaire des chartes . . . de Saint-Ouen de Rouen" (1615)
14 H 18: "Grand cartulaire" of Saint-Ouen, called "Rotomagum et foresta"
14 H 147, 255, 314, 327, 344, 374: documents from Saint-Ouen
55 H, fonds de Saint-Amand non classé, titres généraux, carton I
55 H, no number: thirteenth-century cartulary of Saint-Amand
Bibliothèque municipale d'Avranches:
ms. 210: cartulary of Mont-Saint-Michel
Bibliothèque municipale de Caen:
ms. 300: Gervase de la Rue, "Noticia monastica Diocesis Bajocensis seu excerpta quaedam ex cartulariis abbatiarum . . . ."
ms. 308

Bibliothèque municipale de Rouen:
ms. 1193 (Y 44): cartulary of the cathedral chapter of Rouen
ms. 1207 (Y 51): cartulary of Fécamp
ms. 1235 (Y 201): "Cartulaire de Normandie"
Bibliothèque nationale, Paris:
Collection Baluze, vol. 77, f° 41–71: "Ex chartulario Normannico Majoris Monasterii Turonensis" (1713)
Collection Cinq-cents de Colbert, vol. 190: "Inventaire générale des titres de l'abbaie du Bec" (1670)
Collection Moreau, vols. 21, 29, 30, 40, 41, 42, 341
Fonds français:
mss. 4899–4902: documents on the dioceses of Bayeux, Coutances, and Avranches
ms. 18953: histories of Saint-Martin de Sées
Fonds français nouvelle acquisition:
ms. 7384: Collection De Camp, vol. 54: "Alençon, Maine et Normandie"
mss. 21806–73: Collection Léopold Delisle
ms. 23056: miscellaneous documents, mostly concerning Montivilliers
Fonds latin:
ms. 1939: manuscript from Fécamp of works by Saint Augustine
ms. 5359: liturgical manuscript from Fécamp
ms. 5423: copies of documents from Saint-Ouen
ms. 5441: copies of documents from Marmoutier
ms. 5650: cartulary of La Trinité de Caen
ms. 10058: copies of documents concerning Saint-Laurent d'Envermeu, priory of Bec (1770)
ms. 10059: copies of documents from Longueville
ms. 10086: "Chartrier rouge" of Troarn
ms. 10087: cartulary of Montebourg
mss. 11055–56: cartulary of Saint-Evroul
ms. 12777: "Miscellanea Monastica"
mss. 12878–79: Edmund Martène, "Histoire de l'abbaye de Marmoutier en Touraine, seconde partie, contenant les titres autentiques tirés des archives de la même abbaye. . . ."
ms. 12880: Edmund Martène, "Preuves de l'histoire de l'abbaye royale de Marmoutier"
ms. 12884: Dom Thibault, copies of documents from Bec
ms. 13905: Jacques Jouvelin, copies of documents from Bec
ms. 17135: miscellaneous copies
ms. 17137: copy of a cartulary of Saint-Sauveur-le-Vicomte
Fonds latin nouvelle acquisition:
ms. 1406: C. Hippeau, copies of documents from Saint-Etienne de Caen
Bibliothèque de l'Université de Caen:
cote 21420: Cartulary of Saint-Etienne de Caen, manuscript copy by H. de Toustain (1853)
Collection Mancel:
vol. 73: "Varia quorumdam prioratum Normanniae chartae. . . ."
vol. 74: "Varia variarum abbatiarum Normanniae chartae. . . ."
vol. 300: C. Duhérissier de Gerville, copies of Norman documents, vol. 5
Musée de la Bénédictine de Fécamp:
various originals from Fécamp

PUBLISHED SOURCES CONSULTED AND SECONDARY WORKS CITED

Abbreviations

AN	*Annales de Normandie*
BSAN	*Bulletin de la Société des antiquaires de Normandie*
BSO	*Bulletin principal de la Société historique et archéologique de l'Orne*
EHR	*English Historical Review*
Mém. Acad. Caen	*Mémoires de l'Académie nationale des sciences, arts et belles-lettres de Caen*
Mém. S.A.N.	*Mémoires de la Société des antiquaires de Normandie*
PBC	*Proceedings of the Battle Conference on Anglo-Norman Studies*, ed. R. Allen Brown (Woodbridge, Suffolk); with vol. 5 the title becomes *Anglo-Norman Studies*
RA	*Revue de l'Avranchin*
RCN	*Revue catholique de Normandie*
RHD	*Revue historique de droit français et étranger*
TRHS	*Transactions of the Royal Historical Society*

Additamenta ad historiam Normannorum. In William of Jumièges, *Gesta Normannorum ducum*, ed. Jean Marx, pp. 335–41. Rouen and Paris, 1914.

Adigard des Gautries, Jean. "Etudes d'onomastiques 'ornaise.' IV. Les noms des personnes attestés à Sées de 1055 environ à 1108." *BSO* 82 (1964): 17–27.

———. "Les noms des lieux du Calvados attestés entre 911 et 1066." *AN* 2 (1952): 209–28; 3 (1953): 22–36, 135–48.

———. "Les noms des lieux de l'Eure attestés entre 911 et 1066." *AN* 4 (1954): 39–59, 237–55; 5 (1955): 15–33.

———. "Les noms des lieux des îles anglo-normandes attestés entre 911 et 1066." *AN* 2 (1952): 27–33.

———. "Les noms des lieux de la Seine-Inférieure attestés entre 911 et 1066." *AN* 6 (1956): 119–34, 233–44; 7 (1957): 135–58; 8 (1958): 299–322; 9 (1959): 151–67.

———. "Les possessions de l'abbaye de Saint-Wandrille dans la région d'Argentan aux XIe, XIIe et XIIIe siècles." *BSO* 74 (1956): 21–37.

Alexander, J. J. G. *Norman Illumination at Mont St Michel 966–1100*. Oxford, 1970.

Allix, E., and Robert Génestal. "Les opérations financières de l'abbaye de Troarn du XIe au XIVe siècle." *Vierteljahrschrift für Sozial- und Wirtschaftsgeschichte* 2 (1904): 616–40.

The Anglo-Saxon Chronicle. Translated by Dorothy Whitelock, David C. Douglas, and Susie I. Tucker. New Brunswick, N.J., 1961.

Anselm. Epistles from Bec. In Franciscus Salesius Schmitt, ed., *S. Anselmi Cantuariensis archiepiscopi opera omnia*. Vol. 3. Edinburgh, 1946.

Appert, J., and P. Bernier. "Essai sur le prieuré et la baronnie de la Ferté-Macé d'après les chartes fertoises de l'abbaye de Saint-Julien-de-Tours." *RCN* 1 (1891–92): 66–78, 165–72, 273–83, 327–32.

Astoul, Charles. "L'histoire du droit privé normand." *BSAN* 37 (1926–27): 53–73.

Aubenas, Roger. "Les châteaux forts des Xe et XIe siècles: contribution à l'étude des origines de la féodalité." *RHD*, 4th ser., 17 (1938): 54-86.

Barlow, Frank. *Edward the Confessor*. Berkeley and Los Angeles, 1970.

———. "The Effects of the Norman Conquest." In C. T. Chevallier, ed., *The Norman Conquest: Its Setting and Impact*, pp. 123–63. New York, 1966.

———. *William Rufus*. Berkeley and Los Angeles, 1983.

Barret, Ph. *Cartulaire de Marmoutier pour le Perche. Documents sur la province du Perche*. 3d ser., 2. Mortagne, 1894.

Bates, David R. "The Character and Career of Odo, Bishop of Bayeux (1049/50–1097)." *Speculum* 50 (1975): 1–20.

———. "The Earliest Norman Writs." *EHR* 100 (1985): 266–84.

———. *Normandy before 1066*. London, 1982.

———. "Notes sur l'aristocratie normande. I. Hugues, évêque de Bayeux (1011 env.–1049). II. Herluin de Conteville et sa famille." *AN* 23 (1973): 7–38.

———. "The Origins of the Justiciarship." *PBC, IV, 1981* (1982): 1–12, 167–71.

Beaunier. *Abbayes et prieurés de l'ancienne France*. Vol. 7, *Province ecclésiastique de Rouen* by J.-M. Besse. Ligugé and Paris, 1914.

Beckerman, John S. "Succession in Normandy, 1087, and in England, 1066: The Role of Testamentary Custom." *Speculum* 47 (1972): 258–60.

Bénet, Armand. "Etude sur la diplomatique des ducs de Normandie." *Positions des thèses des élèves de l'Ecole des Chartes . . . 1881*, pp. 3–4. Paris, 1881.

Berlière, Ursmar. "Le nombre des moines dans les anciens monastères." *Revue bénédictine* 41 (1929): 231–61; 42 (1930): 19–42.

Besnier, Robert. *La coutume de Normandie. Histoire externe*. Paris, 1935.

———. " 'Inquisitiones' et 'requisitiones': le nouveau système de preuves à l'époque des coutumiers normands." *RHD*, 4th ser., 27 (1950): 183–212.

Bessin, Guillaume. *Concilia Rotomagensis Provinciae*. Rouen, 1717.

Bloch, Marc. *Feudal Society*. Translated by L. A. Manyon. Chicago, 1961; French original, Paris, 1939–40.

Boulet-Sautel, Marguerite. "Aperçus sur le système des preuves dans la France coutumière du Moyen Age." In *La Preuve*. Vol. 2, *Moyen Age et temps modernes*, pp. 275–325. Société Jean Bodin, *Recueils*, 17. Brussels, 1965.

Bourrienne, V. *Antiquus cartularius ecclesiae Baiocensis (Livre noir)*. 2 vols. Paris and Rouen, 1902.

———. "Odon de Conteville, évêque de Bayeux. Son rôle au début de la première Croisade." *RCN* 7 (1897–98): 389–405; 8 (1898–99): 20–41, 242–54, 336–45, 507–32; 9 (1899–1900): 420–40, 530–42; 10 (1900–1901): 266–89.

Boussard, Jacques. "Le comté de Mortain au XIe siècle." *Le Moyen Age* 58 (1952): 253–79.

———. "Thomas de Saint-Jean-le-Thomas et l'abbaye du Mont-Saint-Michel (début du XIIe siècle)." In *Droit privé et institutions régionales: études historiques offertes à Jean Yver*, pp. 87–96. Paris, 1976.

Bouvris, Jean-Michel. "Un bref inédit de Robert Courte-Heuse Duc de Normandie, relatif à l'abbaye de Montebourg, au diocèse de Coutances." *Actes du cent cinquième congrès national des sociétés savantes, Caen, 1980, section de philologie*, pp. 125–50. Paris, 1984.

———. "Contribution à une étude de l'institution vicomtale en Normandie au XIe siècle. L'exemple de la partie orientale du duché: les vicomtes de Rouen, de Fécamp et de Lillebonne." In Lucien Musset, Jean-Michel Bouvris, and Jean-Marie Maillefer, *Autour du pouvoir ducal normand, X^e^–XIIe siècles*. Cahiers des Annales de Normandie 17 (1985): 149–74. See also the summary in *AN* 33 (1983): 302–4.

———. "La date de la restauration de l'abbaye d'Almenêches." *BSO* 98 (1979): 113–41.

———. "Aux origines du prieuré de Baupte (Manche): quatre actes inédits du XIe siècle, dont deux actes du duc Robert Courte-Heuse, extraits du cartulaire perdu de l'abbaye de Saint-Etienne de Caen." *AN* 32 (1982): 332–34.

———. "Les plus anciennes chartes du prieuré de Saint-Sulpice près de L'Aigle, dépendance normande de l'abbaye de Saint-Laumer de Blois (XIe–XIIe siècles)." *AN* 31 (1981): 327–30.

———. "Une notice originale inédite du XIe siècle du prieuré de Perrières dépendance de l'abbaye de Marmoutier à l'ancien diocèse de Sées." *BSO* 99 (1980): 87–102.

———. "Une possession de l'abbaye de Saint-Martin de Sées en Cotentin à la fin du XIe siècle: Pirou." *Mélanges de la Société de la Manche*, 12th ser. (1983): 169–82.

Branch, Betty. "The Development of Script in Eleventh and Twelfth Century Manuscripts of the Norman Abbey of Fécamp." Ph.D. dissertation, Duke University, 1974.

Bréard, Charles. *Cartulaires de Saint-Ymer-en-Auge et de Bricquebec*. Rouen and Paris, 1908.

Breese, Lauren Wood. "The Persistence of Scandinavian Connections in Normandy in the Tenth and Eleventh Centuries." *Viator* 8 (1977): 47–61.

Brevis relatio de origine Willelmi Conquestoris. Edited by J. A. Giles. *Scriptores rerum gestarum Willelmi Conquestoris*, pp. 1–23. Caxton Society, vol. 3. 1845.

Brown, R. Allen. *The Normans and the Norman Conquest*. New York, 1968.

———. "Some Observations on Norman and Anglo-Norman Charters." In Diana Greenway et al., eds., *Tradition and Change: Essays in Honour of Marjorie Chibnall*, pp. 145–63. Cambridge, 1985.

Canel, A. "Le combat judiciaire en Normandie." *Mém. S.A.N.* 22 (1856): 575–655.

Carabie, Robert. "La nature du droit de la femme mariée aux conquêts faits dans les bourgages normands." In *Droit privé et institutions régionales: études historiques offertes à Jean Yver*, pp. 125–36. Paris, 1976.

———. *La propriété foncière dans le très ancien droit normand (XIe–XIIIe siècles)*. Vol. 1, *La propriété domaniale*. Caen, 1943.

Le cartulaire du prieuré de Notre-Dame de Longpont de l'Ordre de Cluny au diocèse de Paris. Lyon, 1879.

Castaing-Sicard, Mireille. "Donations toulousaines du Xe au XIIIe siècles." *Annales du Midi* 70 (1958): 27–64.

Chanteux, Henry. "L'abbé Thierry et les églises de Jumièges, du Mont-Saint-Michel et de Bernay." *Bulletin monumental* 98 (1939): 67–72.

———. "Quelques notes sur les vavassories." *RHD*, 4th ser., 35 (1958): 630–31.

Chaplais, Pierre. "The Anglo-Saxon Chancery: From the Diploma to the Writ." *Journal of the Society of Archivists* 3 (1965–69): 160–76.

———. "Une charte originale de Guillaume le Conquérant pour l'abbaye de Fécamp: la donation de Steyning et de Bury (1085)." In *L'abbaye bénédictine de Fécamp: ouvrage scientifique du XIIIe centenaire, 658–1958*. 4 vols. 1:93–104. Fécamp, 1959–63.

———. *Diplomatic Documents Preserved in the Public Record Office*. Vol. 1, *1101–1272*. London, 1964.

———. "English Diplomatic Documents to the End of Edward III's Reign." In D. A. Bullough and R. L. Storey, eds., *The Study of Medieval Records: Essays in Honour of Kathleen Major*, pp. 22–56. Oxford, 1971.

Chesnel, Paul. "Le bel arbre généalogique de la famille du comte de Mortain Robert." *RA* 29 (1936): 230–37.

———. *Le Cotentin et l'Avranchin sous les ducs de Normandie (911–1204)*. Caen, 1912.

———. "Le département de la Manche aux temps des Gaulois, des Romains, des Francs et des Normands. Chapitre V. Invasions et établissement des Normands. Le Cotentin et l'Avranchin aux Xe et XIe siècles." *RA* 24 (1931): 29–60.

———. "De quelques usages féodaux en Normandie sous Guillaume le Conquérant d'après un acte du cartulaire de Mont-Saint-Michel." In *Congrès du millénaire de la Normandie (911–1911). Compte rendu des travaux*. 2 vols. 1:544–48. Rouen, 1912.

———. "Le traité de Saint-Clair-sur-Epte." *RA* 28 (1935): 319–28.

Chevreux, Paul, and Jules Joseph Vernier. *Les Archives de Normandie et de la Seine-Inférieure: état général des fonds; recueil de fac-similés d'écriture du XIe au XVIIIe siècle accompagnés de transcriptions*. Rouen, 1911.

Chevrier, G. "Evolution de la notion de donation dans les chartes de Cluny du IXe à la fin du XIIe siècle." In *A Cluny: congrès scientifique . . . 1949*, pp. 203–9. Dijon, 1950.

———. "Remarques sur la distinction de l'acte à titre onéreux et de l'acte à titre gratuit d'après les chartes de Rouergue au XIIe siècle." *Annales de la Faculté de Droit d'Aix* 42 (1950): 67–79.

Chibnall, Marjorie. *Anglo-Norman England, 1066–1166*. Oxford, 1986.

———. "Charter and Chronicle: The Use of Archive Sources by Norman Historians." In C. N. L. Brooke et al., eds., *Church and Government in the Middle Ages: Essays Presented to C. R. Cheney on his 70th Birthday*, pp. 1–17. Cambridge, 1976.

———. *Charters and Custumals of the Abbey of Holy Trinity Caen*. British Academy, Records of Social and Economic History, n.s., 5. Oxford, 1982.

———. "Les droits d'héritage selon Orderic Vital." *RHD*, 4th ser., 48 (1970): 347.

———. "Ecclesiastical Patronage and the Growth of Feudal Estates at the Time of the Norman Conquest." *AN* 8 (1958): 103–18.

———. "Fécamp and England." In *L'abbaye bénédictine de Fécamp: ouvrage scientifique du XIIIe centenaire, 658–1958*, 4 vols. 1:127–35. Fécamp, 1959–63.

———. "Feudal Society in Orderic Vitalis." *PBC, I, 1978* (1979): 35–48, 199–202.

———. "Military Service in Normandy before 1066." *PBC, V, 1982* (1983): 65–77.

———. "Some Aspects of the Norman Monastic Plantation in England." In *La Normandie bénédictine au temps de Guillaume le Conquérant (XIe siècle)*, pp. 399–415. Lille, 1967.

———. *The World of Orderic Vitalis*. Oxford, 1984.

Chrimes, S. B. *An Introduction to the Administrative History of Mediaeval England*. 1952. 3d ed. Oxford, 1966.

Clanchy, M. T. *From Memory to Written Record*. Cambridge, Mass., 1979.

———. "Law and Love in the Middle Ages." In John Bossy, ed., *Disputes and Settlements: Law and Human Relations in the West*, pp. 47–67. Cambridge, 1984.

Collection des inventaires sommaires des archives départementales antérieures à 1790 publiée sous la direction du ministre de l'instruction publique et des beaux-arts. Paris, 1863–. For the departments of Calvados, Eure, Manche, Orne, and Seine-Maritime.

Colmant, Pierre. "Les actes de l'abbaye de Marmoutier jusque vers le milieu du XIIe siècle." *Positions des thèses des élèves de l'Ecole des Chartes . . . 1907*, pp. 51–56. Mâcon, 1907.

The Complete Peerage of England . . . . Edited by G. E. C[okayne], 13 vols. in 14. London, 1910–59.

Corbett, William John. "The Development of the Duchy of Normandy and the Norman Conquest of England." *Cambridge Medieval History* 5 (1929): 481–520.

———. "England, 1087–1154." *Cambridge Medieval History* 5 (1929): 521–53.

Couppey, L. "L'abbaye de Notre-Dame du Voeu près Cherbourg (Manche). Sa fondation." *RCN* 10 (1900–1901): 41–59, 210–26.

———. "Encore Héauville! Supplément aux notes historiques sur le prieuré conventuel d'Héauville à la Hague." *RCN* 10 (1900–1901): 345–55, 437–43, 516–30; 11 (1901–2): 23–32, 84–90, 168–78.

———. "Notes historiques sur le prieuré conventuel d'Héauville à la Hague." *RCN* 7 (1897–98): 421–52; 8 (1898–99): 42–59, 144–57, 215–27, 359–68; 9 (1899–1900): 120–31, 232–43, 303–25, 469–80.

Cowdrey, H. E. J. "Bishop Ermenfrid of Sion and the Penitential Ordinance following the Battle of Hastings." *Journal of Ecclesiastical History* 20 (1969): 225–42.

Curia Regis Rolls of the Reigns of Richard I and John Preserved in the Public Record Office. 7 vols. London, 1922–35.

David, Charles Wendell. *Robert Curthose Duke of Normandy*. Cambridge, Mass., 1920.

Davis, R. H. C. *The Normans and their Myth*. London, 1976.
———. "William of Jumièges, Robert Curthose and the Norman Succession." *EHR* 95 (1980): 597–606.
———. "William of Poitiers and his History of William the Conqueror." In R. H. C. Davis et al., eds., *The Writing of History in the Middle Ages: Essays Presented to Richard William Southern*, pp. 71–100. Oxford, 1981.
de Bieville, Marc. "Les 'fieffermes,' institution originale du droit normand." *RA* 43 (1966): 186, and *RHD*, 4th ser., 45 (1967): 405–6.
———. "Les fieffermes, mode de gestion du domain normand de la couronne." *RHD*, 4th ser., 41 (1963): 551-52.
de Boüard, Alain. *Manuel de diplomatique française et pontificale*. Vol. 1, *Diplomatique générale*. Paris, 1929. Vol. 2, *L'acte privé*. Paris, 1948.
de Boüard, Michel. "L'apogée de la Normandie ducale." In de Boüard, ed., *Documents de l'histoire de la Normandie*, pp. 99–139. Toulouse, 1972.
———. "Le duché de Normandie." In Ferdinand Lot and Robert Fawtier, eds., *Histoire des institutions françaises au Moyen Age*. Vol. 1, *Institutions seigneuriales*, pp. 1–33. Paris, 1957.
———. "L'état normand: croissance et apogée." In de Boüard, ed., *Histoire de la Normandie*, pp. 131–57. Toulouse, 1970.
———. *Guillaume le Conquérant*. 1958. 2d ed. Paris, 1966.
———. "De la Neustrie carolingienne à la Normandie féodale: continuité ou discontinuité?" *Bulletin of the Institute of Historical Research* 28 (1955): 1–14.
———. "La Normandie ducale: économies et civilisation." In de Boüard, ed., *Histoire de la Normandie*, pp. 159–93. Toulouse, 1970.
———. "Nouvelles remarques sur l'introduction de la trêve de Dieu en Normandie." *RHD*, 4th ser., 38 (1960): 481–82.
———. "Sur les origines de la trêve de Dieu en Normandie." *AN* 9 (1959): 169–89.
———. ed. *Documents de l'histoire de la Normandie*. Toulouse, 1972.
Deck, Suzanne. "Essai sur l'ancienne forêt ducale de Fécamp." *AN* 20 (1970): 67–84.
———. "La formation des villes et des bourgs en Haute-Normandie." *RHD*, 4th ser., 27 (1949): 331–32.
de Farcy, Paul. *Les abbayes de l'évêché de Bayeux*. Vol. 4, *Histoire de l'abbaye de Fontenay*. Laval, 1887.
de Fontette, François Pontenay, *Recherches sur la pratique de la vente immobilière dans la région parisienne au Moyen Age (fin X^e^–début XIVe siècle)*. Paris, 1957.
de Lasteyrie, Robert. "Notice sur un couteau du XIe siècle conservé à la bibliothèque nationale." *Mémoires de la Société de l'histoire de Paris et de l'Ile-de-France* 5 (1878): 308–15.
Delisle, Léopold Victor. "Canons du concile tenu à Lisieux en 1064." *Journal des savants* (1901): 516–21.
———. *Etudes sur la condition de la classe agricole et l'état de l'agriculture en Normandie au Moyen Age*. Evreux, 1851.
———. *Histoire du château et des sires de Saint-Sauveur-le-Vicomte*. Valognes, Paris, and Caen, 1867.
———. "Jugements de l'Echiquier de Normandie au XIIIe siècle." *Notices et extraits des manuscrits de la Bibliothèque impériale et autres bibliothèques* 20 (1862): 238–482. Also separately published as *Recueil des jugements de l'Exchiquier de Normandie au XIIIe siècle*. Paris, 1866.
———. "Lettre de l'abbé Haimon sur la construction de l'église de Saint-Pierre-sur-Dive en 1145." *Bibliothèque de l'Ecole des Chartes* 21 (1860): 113–39.
———. *Littérature latine et histoire du Moyen Age*. Paris, 1890.
———. "Notice sur un traité inédit du douzième siècle intitulé *Miracula Ecclesiae Constantiensis*." *Bibliothèque de l'Ecole des Chartes* 9 (1847–48): 339–52.
——— and Elie Berger. *Recueil des actes de Henri II roi d'Angleterre et duc de*

Normandie concernant les provinces françaises et les affaires de France. 3 vols. Paris, 1909–27.

Denis, Louis J. *Chartes de Saint-Julien de Tours (1002–1227).* Société des archives historiques du Maine, *Archives historiques du Maine* 12. Le Mans, 1912.

Depoin, Joseph. *Cartulaire de l'abbaye de Saint-Martin de Pontoise.* Publications de la Société historique du Vexin. Pontoise, 1895.

Deville, Achille. *Cartulaire de l'abbaye de la Sainte-Trinité du Mont de Rouen.* In Benjamin Guérard, *Cartulaire de l'abbaye de Saint-Bertin*, pp. 403–87. Collection des cartulaires de France 3. Paris, 1840.

Deville, Etienne. *Cartulaire de l'église de la Sainte-Trinité de Beaumont-le-Roger.* Paris, 1912.

______. *Notices sur quelques manuscrits normands conservés à la Bibliothèque Sainte-Geneviève.* Vol. 4, *Analyse d'un ancien cartulaire de l'abbaye de Saint-Etienne de Caen.* Evreux, 1905.

Dhondt, Jan. "Les relations entre la France et la Normandie sous Henri Ier." *Normannia* 12 (1939): 465–86.

Dialogus de scaccario: The Course of the Exchequer, by Richard son of Nigel. Edited by Charles Johnson. London and New York, 1950.

Dieudonné, Adolphe Edmond. "La nummismatique normande. Les monnaies féodales." *BSAN* 36 (1924–25): 337–44.

"Discussione sulla lezione Yver." In *I Normanni e la loro espansione in Europa nell'alto medioevo (Settimane di studio del Centro italiano di studi sull'alto medioevo)*, pp. 589–98. Spoleto, 1969.

Douglas, Audrey W. "Tenure in *elemosina*: Origins and Establishment in Twelfth-Century England." *American Journal of Legal History* 24 (1980): 95–132.

Douglas, David C. *The Domesday Monachorum of Christ Church, Canterbury.* London, 1944.

______. "The Earliest Norman Counts." *EHR* 61 (1946): 129–56.

______. "The First Ducal Charter for Fécamp." In *L'abbaye bénédictine de Fécamp: ouvrage scientifique du XIIIe centenaire, 658–1958.* 4 vols., 1:45–56. Fécamp, 1959–63.

______. "The Norman Conquest and British Historians" (1946). In *Time and the Hour: Some Collected Papers*, pp. 57–76. London, 1977.

______. *William the Conqueror: The Norman Impact upon England.* Berkeley and Los Angeles, 1964.

______ and George W. Greenaway, eds. *English Historical Documents.* Vol. 2, *1042–1189.* London, 1953.

Du Cange, Charles du Fresne. *Glossarium mediae et infimae latinitatis.* New ed. by Léopold Favre. 10 vols. Paris, 1883–87.

Dudo of Saint-Quentin. *De moribus et actis primorum Normanniae ducum.* Edited by Jules Lair. *Mém. S.A.N.*, 23, pt. 2, Paris and Caen, 1865.

Duhamel, Léopold. "De la diplomatique de Guillaume le Conquérant." *Positions des thèses des élèves de l'Ecole des Chartes . . . 1863–1864*, pp. 29–33. Paris, 1864.

du Monstier, Arthur. *Neustria Pia seu de omnibus et singulis abbatiis et prioratibus totius Normanniae. . . .* Rouen, 1663.

du Motey, Henri Regnault, Vicomte. *Le champion de la Normandie: Robert II de Bellême.* Paris, 1923.

______. *Origines de la Normandie et du duché d'Alençon.* Paris, 1920.

Durand of Troarn. "Liber de corpore et sanguine Domini." In J. P. Migne, ed., *Patrologia latina . . . .* Vol. 149, cols. 1375–1423.

Duval, Louis. "De l'état des personnes et des terres dans le diocèse de Séez au XIIe siècle d'après le cartulaire de l'abbaye de Saint-Martin de Séez." *Positions des thèses des élèves de l'Ecole des Chartes . . . 1863–1864*, pp. 35–37. Paris, 1864.

Eadmer. *Vita Sancti Anselmi archiepiscopi Cantuariensis.* Edited and translated by Richard W. Southern. London, 1962.

Engels, L. J. "De obitu Willelmi ducis Normannorum regisque Anglorum: textes, modèles, valeur, origines." In *Mélanges Christine Mohrmann*, pp. 209–55. Utrecht and Anvers, 1973.
Farrer, William, and Charles Travis Clay. *Early Yorkshire Charters*. Vol. 6, *The Paynel Fee*. Yorkshire Archaeological Society Record Series, Extra Series, 3. 1939.
———. ———. Vol. 9, *The Stuteville Fee*. Yorkshire Archaeological Society Record Series, Extra Series, 6. 1949.
Fauroux, Marie. *Recueil des actes des ducs de Normandie (911–1066)*. *Mém. S.A.N.* 36. Caen, 1961.
———. See also Le Roy Ladurie.
Feuchère, Pierre. "Essai sur l'évolution des principautés françaises (X^e^–XIIIe siècles): étude de géographie historique." *Le Moyen Age* 58 (1952): 85–117.
Flament, Pierre. *Répertoire des abbayes et prieurés de l'Orne*. Alençon, 1979.
Foreville, Raymonde. "L'ancien droit, le droit des gens et l'équité chez Guillaume de Poitiers." *RHD*, 4th ser., 27 (1950): 153–54.
———. "Hastings et la couronne d'Angleterre." *Etudes normandes* 59–60 (1966): 35–46.
———. "Aux origines de la renaissance juridique. Concepts juridiques et influences romanisantes chez Guillaume de Poitiers, biographe du Conquérant." *Le Moyen Age* 58 (1952): 43–83.
———. "The Synod of the Province of Rouen in the Eleventh and Twelfth Centuries." In C. N. L. Brooke et al., eds., *Church and Government in the Middle Ages: Essays Presented to C. R. Cheney on his 70th Birthday*, pp. 19–39. Cambridge, 1976.
Fourquin, Guy. "Au seuil du XIVe siècle." In Georges Duby, ed., *Histoire de la France rurale*, 1:553–601. Paris, 1975.
Gallia Christiana in provincias ecclesiasticas distributa. . . . Vol. 11, *De provincia Rotomagensi*. Paris, 1759.
Gazeau-Goddet, Véronique. "L'aristocration autour du Bec au tournant de l'année 1077." *PBC, VII, 1984* (1985): 89–103.
Génestal, Robert. "La formation du droit d'aînesse dans la coutume de Normandie." *Normannia* 1 (1928): 157–79.
———. "La formation et le développement de la coutume de Normandie." In *Travaux de la Semaine d'histoire du droit normand tenue à Guernesey . . . 1927*, pp. 37–55. Caen, 1928.
———. "Les formes du testament dans le droit normand." In *Travaux de la Semaine d'histoire du droit normand tenue à Guernesey . . . 1927*, pp. 221–40. Caen, 1928.
———. "L'histoire du droit public normand." *BSAN* 37 (1926–27): 75–149.
———. "L'interdiction du legs d'immeuble." *RHD*, 4th ser., 7 (1928): 683–84.
———. "Note sur les vicomtés fieffés en Normandie." *Nouvelle RHD* 28 (1904): 766–75.
———. "L'origine et les premiers développements de l'inalienabilité dotale normande." *RHD*, 4th ser., 4 (1925): 566–89.
———. *Le parage normand*. Caen, 1911.
———. *Le rôle des monastères comme établissements de crédit étudié en Normandie du XIe à la fin du XIIIe siècle*. Paris, 1901.
———. *La tenure en bourgage dans les pays régis par la coutume de Normandie*. Paris, 1900.
———. *La tutelle*. Caen, 1930.
———. "La tutelle dans l'ancien droit normand." *RHD*, 4th ser., 3 (1924): 708–12.
Gilbert Crispin. *Vita Sancti Herluini*. Edited by J. Armitage Robinson. In *Gilbert Crispin, Abbot of Westminster*, pp. 87–110. Cambridge, 1911.
Giry, Arthur. *Manuel de diplomatique*. Paris, 1894.
Glanvill. *Tractatus de legibus et consuetudinibus regni Anglie*. Edited and translated by G. D. G. Hall. London, 1965.
Gleason, Sarell Everett. *An Ecclesiastical Barony of the Middle Ages: The Bishopric of*

Bayeux, 1066–1204. Cambridge, Mass., 1936.
Goebel, Julius, Jr. *Felony and Misdemeanor: A Study in the History of English Criminal Procedure*. New York, 1937.
Gonthier, Dominique, and Claire Le Bas. "Analyse socio-économique de quelques recueils de miracles dans la Normandie du XIe au XIIIe siècle." *AN* 24 (1974): 3–36.
Guérard, Benjamin. *Cartulaire de l'abbaye de Saint-Père de Chartres*. 2 vols. Collection des cartulaires de France, 1–2. Paris, 1840.
Guilhiermoz, Paul Emilien. *Essai sur l'origine de la noblesse en France au Moyen Age*. Paris, 1902.
Guillot, Olivier. *Le comte d'Anjou et son entourage au XIe siècle*. 2 vols. Paris, 1972.
———. "Quelques hypothèses de recherche à propos de la naissance, peu après 987, et notamment dans l'ouest du royaume de la France, d'un ordre juridique coutumier." *AN* 27 (1977): 358–59.
Guinet, Louis. *Contribution à l'étude des établissements saxones en Normandie*. Caen, 1967.
Gurevič, A. "Représentations et attitudes à l'égard de la propriété pendant le haut moyen âge." *Annales: Economies, Sociétés, Civilisations* 27 (1972): 523–47.
Gurney, Daniel. *The Record of the House of Gournay*. 4 vols. London, 1848.
Hall, Edwin, and James Ross Sweeney. "The 'Licentia de Nam' of the Abbess of Montivilliers and the Origins of the Port of Harfleur." *Bulletin of the Institute of Historical Research* 52 (1979): 1–8.
———. "An Unpublished Privilege of Innocent III in Favor of Montivilliers." *Speculum* 49 (1974): 662–73.
Halphen, Louis. "Les institutions judiciaires en France au XIe siècle: région angevine." *Revue historique* 77 (1901): 279–307.
Hardouin, Christian. "Clécy (Calvados). I. Les origines; la formation de l'ancienne paroisse. II. Les fiefs et les manoirs." *BSAN* 52 (1952–54): 34–93.
———. "Manses carolingiens et vavassories féodales à Clécy." *BSAN* 53 (1955–56): 361–63.
Hariulf. *Chronique de l'abbaye de Saint-Riquier (Ve siècle–1104)*. Edited by Ferdinand Lot. Collection de textes pour servir à l'étude et à l'enseignement de l'histoire. Paris, 1894.
Haskins, Charles Homer. *Norman Institutions*. 1918. Reprint. New York, 1960.
Henry of Huntingdon. *Historia Anglorum*. Edited by Thomas Arnold. Rolls Series, 1879.
Herval, René. "Un moine de l'an mille: Guillaume de Volpiano, Ier abbé de Fécamp (962–1031)." In *L'abbaye bénédictine de Fécamp: ouvrage scientifique du XIIIe centenaire, 658–1958*. 4 vols., 1:27–44. Fécamp, 1959–63.
Hollister, C. Warren. "The Anglo-Norman Civil War: 1101." *EHR* 88 (1973): 315–34.
———. "The Greater Domesday Tenants-in-Chief." In J. C. Holt, ed., *Domesday Studies*. Woodbridge, Suffolk, forthcoming, 1987.
———. *The Military Organization of Norman England*. Oxford, 1965.
———. "Normandy, France and the Anglo-Norman *Regnum*." *Speculum* 51 (1976): 202–42.
———. "The Strange Death of William Rufus." *Speculum* 48 (1973): 637–53.
Hollyman, K. J. *Le développement du vocabulaire féodal en France pendant le haut Moyen Age (étude sémantique)*. Geneva and Paris, 1957.
Holt, James C. "Feudal Society and the Family in Early Medieval England: I. The Revolution of 1066." *TRHS*, 5th ser., 32 (1982): 193–212.
———. "Feudal Society and the Family in Early Medieval England: II. Notions of Patrimony." *TRHS*, 5th ser., 33 (1983): 193–220.

———. "Feudal Society and the Family in Early Medieval England: IV. The Heiress and the Alien." *TRHS*, 5th ser., 35 (1985): 1–28.
———. "Politics and Property in Early Medieval England." *Past and Present*, no. 57 (November 1972): 3–52.
———. *What's in a Name? Family Nomenclature and the Norman Conquest.* Stenton Lecture, 1981. University of Reading, 1982.
Huisman, Gerda C. "Notes on the Manuscript Tradition of Dudo of St Quentin's *Gesta Normannorum.*" *PBC, VI, 1983* (1984): 122–35.
Inventaire sommaire. See *Collection.*
Inventio et miracula Sancti Wulfranni. Edited by Jean Laporte. *Mélanges de la Société de l'histoire de Normandie* 14, *Documents*, pp. 7–87. Rouen, 1938.
Jaffé, Philipp. *Regesta Pontificum Romanorum ab condita ecclesia ad annum post Christum natum MCXCVIII.* 2d ed. Corrected and augmented by Wilhelm Wattenbach, S. Loewenfeld, F. Kaltenbrunner, and P. Ewald. 2 vols. Leipzig, 1885, 1888.
John, abbot of Fécamp. *Epistolae.* In J. P. Migne, ed., *Patrologia latina. . . .* Vol. 147, cols. 464–76.
Keefe, Thomas K. *Feudal Assessments and the Political Community under Henry II and his Sons.* Berkeley and Los Angeles, 1983.
Keeton, George W. *The Norman Conquest and the Common Law.* London and New York, 1966.
Knowles, David. *The Monastic Order in England.* Cambridge, 1941.
Körner, Sten. *The Battle of Hastings: England and Europe, 1035–1066.* Lund, 1964.
Laffleur de Kermaingant, Pierre Paul. *Cartulaire de l'abbaye de Saint-Michel du Tréport.* Paris, 1880.
Lagouëlle, Henri. *Essai sur la conception juridique de la propriété foncière dans le très ancien droit normand.* Vol. 1, *La conception féodale.* Paris, 1902.
Laporte, Jean. "L'abbaye du Mont Saint-Michel aux Xe et XIe siècles." In *Millénaire monastique du Mont Saint-Michel.* 4 vols., 1:53–80. Paris, 1966–71.
———. "Gérard de Brogne à St-Wandrille et à St-Riquier." *Revue bénédictine* 70 (1960): 142–66.
———. "Les origines du monachisme dans la province de Rouen." *Revue Mabillon* 31 (1941): 1–13, 25–41, 49–68.
La Roque, Gilles-André de. *Histoire généalogique de la maison de Harcourt.* 4 vols. Paris, 1662.
Lauer, Philippe. *Le règne de Louis IV d'Outremer.* Paris, 1900.
Le Cacheux, Marie-Josephe. *Histoire de l'abbaye de Saint-Amand de Rouen, des origines à la fin du XVIe siècle.* Caen, 1937. Republished from *BSAN* 44 (1936): 5–289.
Le Cacheux, Paul. "Une charte de Jumièges concernant l'épreuve par le fer chaud (fin du XIe siècle)." *Mélanges de la Société de l'histoire de Normandie* 11 (1927): 205–16.
———. "La date de la fondation de l'Abbaye Blanche de Mortain." *RCN* 10 (1900–1901): 309–23.
Legras, Henri. *Le bourgage de Caen: tenure à cens et tenure à rente (XIe–XVe siècles).* Paris, 1911.
Le Hardy, Gaston. "Le dernier des ducs normands. Etude de critique historique sur Robert Courte-heuse." *BSAN* 10 (1882): 3–184.
Le Maho, Jacques. "L'apparition des seigneuries châtelaines dans le Grand-Caux à l'époque ducale." *Archéologie médiévale* 6 (1976): 5–148.
Lemarignier, Jean François. "Les actes de droit privé de Saint-Bertin au haut Moyen Age." *Revue internationale des droits de l'antiquité* 4 (1950): 35–72.
———. "Le domaine de Villeberfol et le patrimoine de Marmoutier (XIe siècle)." In

Etudes d'histoire du droit privé offertes à Pierre Petot, pp. 347–62. Paris, 1959.

———. *Etude sur les privilèges d'exemption et de jurisdiction ecclésiastique des abbayes normandes depuis les origines jusqu'en 1140*. Paris, 1937.

———. *Le gouvernement royal aux premiers temps capétiens (987–1108)*. Paris, 1965.

———. "Paix et réforme monastique en Flandre et en Normandie autour de l'année 1023: quelques observations." In *Droit privé et institutions régionales: études historiques offertes à Jean Yver*, pp. 443–69. Paris, 1976.

———. "Political and Monastic Structures in France at the End of the Tenth and the Beginning of the Eleventh Century." In Fredric L. Cheyette, ed., *Lordship and Community in Medieval Europe*, pp. 100–27. New York, 1968.

———. "Le pontificat d'Urbain II (1088–1099) et le développement de l'exemption monastique en Normandie." *RHD*, 4th ser., 13 (1934): 737–38.

———. *Recherches sur l'hommage en marche et les frontières féodales. Travaux et mémoires de l'Université de Lille*. N.s., *Droit et lettres* 24. Lille, 1945.

———, Evelyne Lamon and Véronique Gazeau. "Monachisme et aristocratie autour de Saint-Taurin d'Evreux et du Bec (Xe–XIIe siècles)." In Lucien Musset, ed., *Aspects du monachisme en Normandie (IVe–XVIIIe siècles). Actes du Colloque scientifique de l'"Année des Abbayes Normandes," Caen 18–20 octobre 1979*, pp. 91–108. Paris, 1982.

Lennard, Reginald. *Rural England, 1086–1135: A Study of Social and Agrarian Conditions*. Oxford, 1959.

Léonard, Emile-G. *Histoire de la Normandie*. 3d ed. Completed by Jean Vidalenc. Paris, 1963.

Le Patourel, John. "Geoffrey of Montbray, Bishop of Coutances, 1049–1093." *EHR* 59 (1944): 129–61.

———. *Norman Barons*. 1066 Commemoration Series of the Hastings and Bexhill Branch of the Historical Association, 4. 1966.

———. "The Norman Colonization of Britain." In *I Normanni e la loro espansione in Europa nell'alto medioevo (Settimane di studio del Centro italiano di studi sull'alto medioevo)*, pp. 409–38. Spoleto, 1969.

———. *The Norman Empire*. Oxford, 1976.

———. "The Norman Succession, 996–1135." *EHR* 86 (1971): 225–50.

———. *Normandy and England, 1066–1144*. Reading, 1971.

Lepelley, Georges. "La jeunesse de Guillaume le Conquérant." *Etudes normandes* 59–60 (1966): 57–64.

Le Prévost, Auguste. *Mémoires et notes pour servir à l'histoire du département de l'Eure*. Collected and published by Léopold V. Delisle and Louis Passy. 3 vols. Evreux, 1862–69.

Le Roy Ladurie, Marie. "Rôle des abbayes du Val de Loire dans la colonisation monastique normande (Xe–XIe siècles)." *RHD*, 4th ser., 31 (1953): 322–23.

Levison, Wilhelm. *England and the Continent in the Eighth Century*. Oxford, 1946.

Little, Lester K. "Formules monastiques de malédiction aux IXe et Xe siècles." *Revue Mabillon* 58 (1970–75): 377–99.

———. "La morphologie des malédictions monastiques." *Annales: Economies, Sociétés, Civilisations* 34 (1979): 43–60.

Lot, Ferdinand. *Etudes critiques sur l'abbaye de Saint-Wandrille*. Paris, 1913.

———. *Fidèles ou vassaux?* Paris, 1904.

Lyon, Bryce D. *From Fief to Indenture*. Cambridge, Mass. 1957.

Mabillon, Jean. *Annales Ordinis Sancti Benedicti*. Vol. 5. Paris, 1713.

Maillefer, Jean-Marie. "Une famille aristocratique aux confins de la Normandie: les Géré au XIe siècle." In Lucien Musset, Jean-Michel Bouvris, and Jean-Marie Maillefer, *Autour du pouvoir ducal normand, Xe–XIIe siècles*. Cahiers des Annales de Normandie, 17 (1985): 175–206.

Mansi, Giovanni Domenico. *Sacrorum conciliorum nova et amplissima collectio*. Vols. 19–20. Venice, 1774–75.

Marchegay, Paul. "Chartes normandes de l'abbaye de Saint-Florent près Saumur de 710 à 1200 environ." *Mém. S.A.N.* 30 (1880): 663–711.

Mason, J. F. A. "The Norman Earls of Shrewsbury: Three Notes." *Transactions of the Shropshire Archaeological Society* 57 (1961–64): 152–61.

———. "Roger de Montgomery and his Sons (1067–1102)." *TRHS*, 5th ser., 13 (1963): 1–28.

Matthew, Donald J. A. *The Norman Conquest*. New York, 1966.

———. *The Norman Monasteries and their English Possessions*. Oxford, 1962.

Ménager, Léon-Robert. "Inventaire des familles normandes et franques emigrées en Italie méridionale et en Sicile (XIe–XIIe siècles)." In *Roberto il Guiscardo e suo tempo*, pp. 259–390. Rome, 1975.

Milsom, Stroud Francis Charles. *The Legal Framework of English Feudalism*. Cambridge, 1976.

Mollat, Guillaume. "La restitution des églises privées au patrimoine ecclésiastique en France du IXe au XIe siècle." *RHD*, 4th ser., 27 (1949): 399–423.

Mollat, Michel. "La seigneurie maritime du Mont Saint-Michel." In *Millénaire monastique du Mont Saint-Michel*. 4 vols., 2:73–88. Paris, 1966–71.

Musset, Lucien. "A-t-il existé en Normandie au XIe siècle une aristocratie d'argent? Une enquête sommaire sur l'argent comme moyen d'ascension sociale." *AN* 9 (1959): 285–99.

———. *Les actes de Guillaume le Conquérant et de la reine Mathilde pour les abbayes caennaises. Mém. S.A.N.* 37. Caen, 1967.

———. "Actes inédits du XIe siècle. I. Les plus anciennes chartes du prieuré de Saint-Gabriel (Calvados)." *BSAN* 52 (1952–54): 117–41.

———. "Actes inédits du XIe siècle. II. Une nouvelle charte de Robert le Magnifique pour Fécamp." *BSAN* 52 (1952–54): 142–53.

———. "Actes inédits du XIe siècle. III. Les plus anciennes chartes normandes de l'abbaye de Bourgueil." *BSAN* 54 (1957–58): 15–54.

———. "Actes inédits du XIe siècle. IV. Deux nouvelles chartes normandes de l'abbaye de Bourgueil." *BSAN* 56 (1961–62): 5–11.

———. "Actes inédits du XIe siècle. V. Autour des origines de Saint-Etienne de Fontenay." *BSAN* 56 (1961–62): 11–41.

———. "Actes inédits du XIe siècle. VI. L'abbaye de Saint-Ouen de Rouen et la ville de Caen." *BSAN* 58 (1965–66): 119–26.

———. "Actes inédits du XIe siècle. Un nouveau document sur la fortune de Saint-Martin de Sées." *BSO* 78 (1960): 19–29.

———. "Aperçus sur la colonisation scandinave dans le Nord du Cotentin." *Annuaire des cinq départements de la Normandie* 111 (1953): 34–37.

———. "Aperçus sur la dîme ecclésiastique en Normandie au XIe siècle." *RHD*, 4th ser., 52 (1974): 544–45.

———. "Les apports scandinaves dans le plus ancien droit normand." In *Droit privé et institutions régionales: études historiques offertes à Jean Yver*, pp. 559–75. Paris, 1976.

———. "L'aristocratie normande au XIe siècle." In Philippe Contamine, ed., *La noblesse au Moyen Age (XIe–XVe siècles). Essais à la mémoire de Robert Boutruche*, pp. 71–96. Paris, 1976.

———. "Un aspect de l'esprit médiéval: la 'cacogéographie' des Normands et de la Normandie." *Revue du Moyen Age latin* 2 (1946): 129–38.

———. "Autour des modalités juridiques de l'expansion normande au XIe siècle: le droit d'exil." *RHD*, 4th ser., 51 (1973): 561–62.

———. "Autour de la seigneurie rurale normande. Quelques problèmes d'évolution." *RHD*, 4th ser., 31 (1954): 160–62.

———. "Le cimitière dans la vie paroissiale en Basse-Normandie (XIe–XIIIe siècles)." *Cahiers Léopold Delisle* 12 (1963): 7–27.

———. "Les conditions financières d'une réussite architecturale: les grandes églises romanes de Normandie." In *Mélanges offerts à René Crozet*, 1:307–13. Poitiers, 1966.

———. "La contribution de Fécamp à la reconquête normande de la Basse-Normandie (990–1066)." In *L'abbaye bénédictine de Fécamp: ouvrage scientifique du XIIIe centenaire, 658–1958*. 4 vols., 1:57–66. Fécamp, 1959–63.

———. "Les destins de la propriété monastique durant les invasions normandes (IXe–XIe s.): l'exemple de Jumièges." In *Jumièges: congrès scientifique du XIIIe centenaire, Rouen, 10–12 juin 1954*. 2 vols., 2:49–55. Rouen, 1955.

———. "Les deux âges des Vikings." *Mediaeval Scandinavia* 2 (1969): 187–93.

———. "Une expédition d'une charte de Richard II (1014) pour la cathédrale de Chartres." *BSAN* 55 (1959–60): 476–83.

———. "Foires et marchés en Normandie à l'époque ducale." *AN* 26 (1976): 3–23.

———. "Gouvernés et gouvernants dans le monde scandinave et dans le monde normand (XIe–XIIIe siècles)." In *Gouvernés et gouvernants.* Vol. 2, *Antiquité et haut Moyen Age*, pp. 439–68. Société Jean Bodin, *Recueils*, 23. Brussels, 1968.

———. "Huit essais sur l'autorité ducale en Normandie (XIe–XIIe siècles)." In Lucien Musset, Jean-Michel Bouvris, and Jean-Marie Maillefer, *Autour du pouvoir ducal normand, X^{e}–XIIe siècles*. Cahiers des Annales de Normandie, 17 (1985): 3–148.

———. *Les invasions. Le second assaut contre l'Europe chrétienne (VIIe–XIe siècles)*. Paris, 1965.

———. "Les invasions scandinaves et l'évolution des villes de la France de l'Ouest." *RHD*, 4th ser., 43 (1965): 320–22.

———. "Monachisme d'époque franque et monachisme d'époque ducale en Normandie: le problème de la continuité." In Musset, ed., *Aspects du monachisme en Normandie (IVe–XVIIIe siècles). Actes du Colloque scientifique de l'"Année des Abbayes Normandes," Caen 18–20 octobre 1979*, pp. 55–74. Paris, 1982.

———. "Naissance de la Normandie." In Michel de Boüard, ed., *Histoire de la Normandie*, pp. 75–130. Toulouse, 1970.

———. "Notes sur la gestion économique d'un grand abbé de Fécamp: Jean de Ravenne (1028–1079)." *RHD*, 4th ser., 33 (1955): 159.

———. "Notes sur l'histoire économique de la Normandie pendant les âges obscurs (IXe–XIe siècles)." *RHD*, 4th ser., 30 (1953): 321–22.

———. "Notes pour servir d'introduction à l'histoire foncière de la Normandie: les domaines de l'époque franque et les destinées du régime domanial du IXe au XIe siècle." *BSAN* 49 (1942–45): 7–97.

———. "Notules fécampois." *BSAN* 54 (1957–58): 584–98.

———. "Observations historiques sur un mesure agraire; le bonnier." In Charles-Edmond Perrin, ed., *Mélanges d'histoire du Moyen Age dédiés à la mémoire de Louis Halphen*, pp. 535–41. Paris, 1951.

———. "Observations sur l'histoire et la signification de la frontière normande (X^{e}–XIe siècles)." *RHD*, 4th ser., 41 (1963): 545–46.

———. "Aux origines d'une classe dirigeante: les Tosny, grands barons normands du Xe au XIIIe siècle." *Francia* 5 (1977): 45–80.

———. "Les origines du prieuré de Saint-Fromond: un acte négligé de Richard II." *BSAN* 53 (1955–56): 475–88.

———. "Peuplement en bourgage et bourgs ruraux en Normandie du Xe au XIIIe siècle." *Cahiers de civilisation médiévale* 9 (1966): 177–208.

———. "Les premiers temps de l'abbaye d'Almenèches, des origines au XIIe siècle." In Yves Chaussy, ed., *L'abbaye d'Almenèches-Argentan et Sainte Opportune*, pp. 11–36. Paris, 1970.

———. "Quelques observations sur l'esclavage et le servage dans la Normandie ducale." *AN* 36 (1986): 339.

———. "Recherches sur Bayeux, de l'époque franque au XIIe siècle." *RHD*, 4th ser., 35 (1958): 620–21.

———. "Recherches sur les bourgs et les bourgs ruraux du Bocage normand." *Pays bas-normand* 53 (1960): 86–94.

———. "Recherches sur les communautés de clercs séculiers en Normandie au XIe siècle." *BSAN* 55 (1959–60): 5–38.

———. "Recherches sur la consistance géographique des patrimoines monastiques normands: Iles Britanniques et continent (de l'époque franque au XIIIe siècle)." *AN* 8 (1958): 185–86.

———. "Recherches sur les pèlerins et les pèlerinages en Normandie jusqu'à la première Croisade." *AN* 12 (1962): 127–50.

———. "Réflexions sur l'*alodium* et sa signification dans les textes normands." *RHD*, 4th ser., 47 (1969): 606.

———. "Réflexions sur les moyens de paiement en Normandie aux XIe et XIIe siècles." *AN* 31 (1981): 330–31.

———. "Ruine et reconstruction d'une administration: de la Neustrie franque à la Normandie ducale." *RHD*, 4th ser., 29 (1952): 275.

———. "Sur les mutations de la monnaie normande au XIe siècle: deux documents inédits." *Revue numismatique*, 6th ser., 11 (1969): 291–93.

———. "La tenure en bordage, aspects normands et manceaux." *RHD*, 4th ser., 28 (1950): 140.

———. "Une transformation du régime seigneurial: l'essor des bourgs ruraux normands (XIe–XIIe siècle)." *RHD*, 4th ser., 25 (1948): 169–70.

———. "La vie économique de l'abbaye de Fécamp sous l'abbatiat de Jean de Ravenne (1028–1078)." In *L'abbaye bénédictine de Fécamp: ouvrage scientifique du XIIIe centenaire, 658–1958*. 4 vols., 1:67–79. Fécamp, 1959–63.

Navel, Henri. "A propos de recherches sur les fiefs de la vicomté de Caen." *BSAN* 49 (1942–45): 319–43.

———. "L'enquête de 1133 sur les fiefs de l'évêché de Bayeux." *BSAN* 42 (1934): 5–80.

———. "Monographie de Feuguerolles-sur-Orne (Calvados)." *BSAN* 38 (1928–29): 141–459; 39 (1930–31): 77–282.

———. "Recherches sur les anciennes mesures agraires normandes. Acres, vergées et perches." *BSAN* 40 (1932): 29–183.

———. "Recherches sur les institutions féodales en Normandie (région de Caen)." *BSAN* 51 (1948–51): 5–176.

———. "Les vavassories du Mont-Saint-Michel à Bretteville-sur-Odon et Verson (Calvados)." *BSAN* 45 (1937): 137–65.

Notitia de libertate Beccensis monasterii circa professionem episcopis ab abbatibus faciendam. In M. Bouquet, ed., *Recueil des historiens des Gaules et de la France*. 14:270–77. Paris, 1806.

Novum Glossarium mediae latinitatis ab anno DCCC usque ad annum MCC. Copenhagen, 1957–.

De obitu Willelmi ducis Normannorum. In William of Jumièges, *Gesta Normannorum ducum*, edited by Jean Marx, pp. 145–48. Rouen and Paris, 1914. Also L. J. Engels, ed., "De obitu . . . ." In *Mélanges Christine Mohrmann*, pp. 223–30. Utrecht and Anvers, 1973.

Odegaard, Charles E. "Legalis homo." *Speculum* 15 (1940): 186–93.

Olivier-Martin, François J. M. *Histoire du droit français des origines à la Révolution*. Paris, 1948.

Orderic Vitalis. *The Ecclesiastical History of Orderic Vitalis*. Edited and translated by

Marjorie Chibnall. 6 vols. Oxford, 1969–80.
______. *Historiae ecclesiasticae libri tredecim*. Edited by Auguste Le Prévost with Léopold V. Delisle. 5 vols. Paris, 1838–55.
______. Interpolations to William of Jumièges, *Gesta Normannorum ducum*, edited by Jean Marx, pp. 151–98. Rouen and Paris, 1914.
Painter, Sidney. *Studies in the History of the English Feudal Barony*. Baltimore, 1943.
Perrot, Ernest. *Précis élémentaire d'histoire du droit français public et privé*. 2d ed. Paris, 1935.
Perrot, Serge. "Catalogue des plus ancien actes concernant le temporel français de Saint-Evroult (1050–1214)." *Positions des thèses des élèves de l'Ecole des Chartes . . . 1964*, pp. 101–4. Paris, 1964.
The Peterborough Chronicle, 1070–1154. Edited by Cecily Clark. 2d ed. Oxford, 1970.
Petot, Pierre. "L'hommage servile: essai sur la nature juridique de l'hommage." *RHD*, 4th ser., 6 (1927): 68–107.
______. "Le mariage des vassales." *RHD*, 4th ser., 56 (1978): 29–47.
Pigeon, E.-A. *Le diocèse d'Avranches: sa topographie, ses origines, ses évêques, sa cathédrale, ses églises, ses comtes et ses châteaux*. 2 vols. Coutances, 1888.
Piletta, Françoise. "Les bourgs du sud du pays d'Auge du milieu du XIe au milieu du XIVe siècle." *AN* 30 (1980): 211–30.
Pollock, Frederick, and Frederic William Maitland. *The History of English Law before the Time of Edward I*. 1895. 2d ed., 2 vols. Cambridge, 1898.
Pommeraye, Jean François. *Histoire de l'abbaye de Saint-Amand de Rouen*. Rouen, 1662.
______. *Histoire de l'abbaye royale de Saint-Ouen de Rouen*. Rouen, 1662.
Porée, A. A. "L'abbaye du Bec et ses écoles." *RCN* 1 (1891–92): 407–30, 513–41; 2 (1892–93): 28–50, 129–61.
______. *Histoire de l'abbaye du Bec*. 2 vols. Evreux, 1901.
Powicke, F. Maurice. *The Loss of Normandy, 1189–1204: Studies in the History of the Angevin Empire*. 1913. 2d ed. Manchester, 1961.
Prentout, Henri. *Etude critique sur Dudon de Saint-Quentin et son histoire des premiers ducs normands*. Paris, 1916.
______. "Etudes sur quelques points de l'histoire de Guillaume le Conquérant." *Mém. Acad. Caen*, n.s., 6 (1931): 1–56.
______. "Le règne de Richard II duc de Normandie, 996–1027: son importance dans l'histoire." *Mém. Acad. Caen*, n.s., 5 (1929): 57–104.
Prou, Maurice. "Examen de la charte de fondation de Saint-Léonard de Bellême confirmée par Philippe Ier." In *Mélanges Paul Fabre*, pp. 215–35. Paris, 1902.
______. *Recueil des actes de Philippe Ier*. Paris, 1908.
______ and Alexandre Vidier. *Recueil des chartes de l'abbaye de Saint-Benoît-sur-Loire*. Documents publiés par la Société historique et archéologique du Gâtinais 5. Paris, 1900–1907.
Quivy, Paul, and Joseph Thiron. "Robert de Tombelaine et son commentaire sur le Cantique des Cantiques." In *Millénaire monastique du Mont Saint-Michel*. 4 vols., 2:347–56. Paris, 1966–71.
Rabasse, Maurice. *Du régime des fiefs en Normandie au Moyen Age*. Paris, 1905.
Radin, Max. "Quelles idées sur la nature de la coutume les Normands ont-ils apportées en Angleterre." *RHD*, 4th ser., 6 (1927): 726–27.
Ray, Roger D. "Orderic Vitalis on Henry I: Theocratic Ideology and Didactic Narrative." In George H. Shriver, ed., *Contemporary Reflections on the Medieval Christian Tradition: Essays in Honor of Ray C. Petry*, pp. 119–34. Durham, N.C., 1974.
Recueil des historiens des Gaules et de la France. Vol. 14. Paris, 1806. Vol. 23. Paris, 1876.
The Red Book of the Exchequer. Edited by Hubert Hall. 3 vols. Rolls Series, 1896.

Regesta regum Anglo-Normannorum, 1066–1154. Vol. 1, *Regesta Willelmi Conquestoris et Willelmi Rufi, 1066–1100*. Edited by H. W. C. Davis and R. J. Whitwell. Oxford, 1913. Vol. 2, *Regesta Henrici Primi*. Edited by C. Johnson and H. A. Cronne. Oxford, 1956.
Regnault, R. "La condition des bâtards en droit normand au Moyen Age." *RHD*, 4th ser., 2 (1923): 147–48.
Revised Medieval Latin Word-List from British and Irish Sources. Edited by R. E. Latham. London, 1965.
Rioult de Neuville, Louis, Vicomte. "Les barons d'Orbec." *Mém. S.A.N.* 30 (1880): 712–69.
Robert de Torigny. *Chronique . . . suivie de divers opuscules historiques de cet auteur et de plusieurs religieux. . . .* Edited by Léopold V. Delisle. 2 vols. Rouen, 1872, 1873.
———. Interpolations to William of Jumièges, *Gesta Normannorum ducum*, edited by Jean Marx, pp. 199–334. Rouen and Paris, 1914.
Round, John Horace. *Calendar of Documents Preserved in France Illustrative of the History of Great Britain and Ireland*. Vol. 1, *A.D. 918–1204*. London, 1899.
———. *Feudal England*. London, 1895.
———. *The King's Serjeants and Officers of State*. London, 1891.
Saltman, Avrom. *Theobald, Archbishop of Canterbury*. London, 1956.
Sauvage, René Norbert. *L'abbaye de Saint-Martin de Troarn au diocèse de Bayeux des origines au seizième siècle: histoire et développement économique d'un monastère normand au Moyen Age*. Caen, 1911.
Schieffer, Theodor. *Die päpstlichen Legaten in Frankreich vom Vertrage von Meersen (876) bis zum Schisma von 1130*. Berlin, 1935.
Schnapper, Bernard. "Les baux à vie (X[e] au XVIe siècle)." *RHD*, 4th ser., 35 (1957): 347–75.
Searle, Eleanor. "Fact and Pattern in Heroic History: Dudo of Saint-Quentin." *Viator* 15 (1984): 119–37.
———. "Frankish Rivalries and Norse Warriors." *PBC, VIII, 1985* (1986): 198–213.
———. "Women and the Legitimisation of Succession at the Norman Conquest." *PBC, III, 1980* (1981): 159–70, 226–29.
Senn, Félix. *L'institution des avoueries ecclésiastiques en France*. Paris, 1903.
Sheehan, Michael M. *The Will in Medieval England*. Toronto, 1963.
Siguret, Philippe. "Recherches sur la formation du comté du Perche. Deuxième partie." *BSO* 80 (1962): 3–42.
Société Jersiaise. *Cartulaire des Iles normandes: recueil de documents concernant l'histoire de ces îles. . . .* Jersey, 1918–24.
Stapleton, Thomas. "Letter . . . Accompanying Two Transcripts of Ancient Charters Relating to Property in Normandy." *Archaeologia* 27 (1838): 21–28.
———. "The Pretended Marriage of William de Warren." *Archaeological Journal* 3 (1846): 1–26.
Steenstrup, Johannes. "Normandiets Historie under de syv første hertuger. Avec un résumé en français" (1925). *Mémoires de l'Académie royale des sciences et des lettres de Danemark, Section des lettres*, 7th ser., 5 (1936): 1–319.
Stenton, Frank Merry. *The First Century of English Feudalism*. 1932. 2d ed. Oxford, 1961.
———. "The Scandinavian Colonies in England and Normandy." *TRHS*, 4th ser., 27 (1945): 1–12.
———. *William the Conqueror and the Rule of the Normans*. 1908. Rev. ed. London, 1925.
Strayer, Joseph R. Review of Marie Fauroux's *Recueil*. *Speculum* 37 (1962): 607–10.
Tabuteau, Emily Zack. "Definitions of Feudal Military Obligations in Eleventh-Century Normandy." In Morris S. Arnold et al., eds., *On the Laws and Customs of*

England: Essays in Honor of Samuel E. Thorne*, pp. 18–59. Chapel Hill, 1981.

———. Review of David R. Bates, *Normandy before 1066*. *Speculum* 59 (1984): 610–15.

Tardif, Ernest Joseph. *Coutumiers de Normandie*. Vol. 1, *Le Très Ancien Coutumier de Normandie*. Part I: *Texte latin*. Paris, 1881. Part II: *Textes français et normand*. Rouen and Paris, 1903. Vol. 2, *La Summa de legibus Normannie in curia laicali*. Rouen and Paris, 1896.

———. "Etude sur les sources de l'ancien droit normand et spécialement sur la législation des ducs de Normandie." In *Congrès du millénaire de la Normandie (911–1911). Compte rendu des travaux*. 2 vols., 1:570–619. Rouen, 1912.

Tessier, Georges. *Diplomatique royale française*. Paris, 1962.

Teulet, J. B. A. T. *Layettes du Trésor des Chartes*. Vol. 1. Paris, 1863.

Thompson, Kathleen. "Family and Influence to the South of Normandy in the Eleventh Century: The Lordship of Bellême." *Journal of Medieval History* 11 (1985): 215–26.

Thorne, Samuel E. "English Feudalism and Estates in Land." *Cambridge Law Journal* 6 (1959): 193–209.

———. "Livery of Seisin." *Law Quarterly Review* 52 (1936): 345–64.

Tillman, Helene. *Die päpstlichen Legaten in England bis zur Beendigung der Legation Gualas (1218)*. Bonn, 1926.

Valin, Lucien. *Le duc de Normandie et sa cour (912–1204): étude d'histoire juridique*. Paris, 1909.

Vallez, Anne. "Un exemple de 'paroisses mixtes': les conquests Hue de Gournay et speciautez de Beauvoisis." *RHD*, 4th ser., 48 (1970): 352–53.

van Houts, Elisabeth M. C. "Quelques remarques sur les interpolations attribuées à Orderic Vital dans les *Gesta Normannorum ducum* de Guillaume de Jumièges." *Revue d'histoire des textes* 8 (1978): 213–22.

———. "Scandinavian Influence in Norman Literature of the Eleventh Century." *PBC, VI, 1983* (1984): 107–21.

van Luyn, P. "Les milites dans la France du XIe siècle: examen des sources narratives." *Le Moyen Age* 77 (1971): 5–51, 193–238.

Vaughn, Sally N. *The Abbey of Bec and the Anglo-Norman State*. Woodbridge, Suffolk, 1981.

Vernier, Jules Joseph. *Chartes de l'abbaye de Jumièges (v. 825 à 1204) conservées aux Archives de la Seine-Inférieure*. 2 vols. Paris and Rouen, 1916.

Vigneron, Bernard. "La vente dans le Mâconnais du IXe au XIIIe siècle." *RHD*, 4th ser., 37 (1959): 17–47.

Villers, R. "Aperçus sur la formation de la noblesse en Normandie." *RHD*, 4th ser., 32 (1954): 148–49.

Viollet, Paul. "Les coutumiers de Normandie." In *Histoire littéraire de la France*, 33:41–190. Paris, 1906.

Wace. *Le Roman de Rou*. Edited by A. J. Holden. 3 vols. Paris, 1970–73.

Werner, Karl Ferdinand. "Quelques observations au sujet des débuts du 'duché' de Normandie." In *Droit privé et institutions régionales: études historiques offertes à Jean Yver*, pp. 691–709. Paris, 1976.

White, Geoffrey H. "Companions of the Conqueror." *Genealogists' Magazine* 9 (1940–46): 417–24.

———. "The First House of Bellême." *TRHS*, 4th ser., 22 (1940): 67–99.

White, Stephen D. "*Pactum . . . Legem Vincit et Amor Judicium:* The Settlement of Disputes by Compromise in Eleventh-Century Western France." *American Journal of Legal History* 22 (1978): 281–308.

Wiffen, J. H. *Historical Memoirs of the House of Russell*. 2 vols. London, 1833.

Wightman, Wilfrid Eric. "La famille de Lacy et ses terres normandes." *AN* 11 (1961): 267–77.

———. *The Lacy Family in England and Normandy, 1066–1194*. Oxford, 1966.
William of Jumièges. *Gesta Normannorum ducum*. Edited by Jean Marx. Rouen and Paris, 1914.
William of Malmesbury. *De gestis regum Anglorum libri quinque*. Edited by William Stubbs. 2 vols. Rolls Series, 1887, 1889.
William of Poitiers. *Gesta Guillelmi ducis Normannorum et regis Anglorum*. Edited and translated by Raymonde Foreville. Les classiques de l'histoire de France au Moyen Age 23. Paris, 1952.
Yver, Jean. "Autour de l'absence d'avouerie en Normandie. Notes sur le double thème du développement du pouvoir ducal et de l'application de la réforme grégorienne en Normandie." *BSAN* 57 (1963–64): 189–283.
———. "Une boutade de Guillaume le Conquérant: note sur la genèse de la tenure en aumône." In *Etudes d'histoire du droit canonique dédiées à Gabriel Le Bras*, 1:783–96. Paris, 1965.
———. "Le bref anglo-normand." *Tijdschrift voor Rechtsgeschiedenis* 29 (1961): 313–30.
———. "Les caractères originaux de la Coutume de Normandie." *Mém. Acad. Caen*, n.s., 12 (1952): 307–56.
———. "Les caractères originaux du groupe de coutumes de l'Ouest de la France." *RHD*, 4th ser., 29 (1952): 18–79.
———. "Les châteaux forts en Normandie jusqu'au milieu du XIIe siècle: contribution à l'étude du pouvoir ducal." *BSAN* 53 (1955–56): 28–115.
———. Comments on a paper by Henri Navel, *BSAN* 50 (1946–48): 299–301.
———. *Les contrats dans le très ancien droit normand (XIe–XIIIe siècles)*. Domfront, 1926.
———. "La coutume de Normandie à travers l'oeuvre de R. Génestal." *Normannia* 5 (1932): 201–26.
———. "Le développement du pouvoir ducal en Normandie de l'avènement de Guillaume le Conquérant à la mort d'Henri I (1035–1135)." *Atti del Convegno internazionale di Studi Ruggeriani*, 1:183–204. Palermo, 1955.
———. "Le droit privé des villes de l'Ouest de la France, spécialement des villes normandes." *La ville*. Vol. 3, *Le droit privé*, pp. 133–61. Société Jean Bodin, *Recueils*, 8. Brussels, 1957.
———. "Le droit romain en Normandie (avant 1500)." *Ius Romanum Medii Aevi*, pars V, 4, a (1976): 1-27.
———. *Egalité entre héritiers et exclusion des enfants dotés*. Paris, 1966.
———. "Les institutions féodales en Normandie d'après les recherches du Commandant H. Navel." *RHD*, 4th ser., 31 (1953): 271–77.
———. "L'interdiction de la guerre privée dans le très ancien droit normand." In *Travaux de la Semaine d'histoire du droit normand tenue à Guernesey . . . 1927*, pp. 307–47. Caen, 1928.
———. "Les premières institutions du duché de Normandie." In *I Normanni e la loro espansione in Europa nell'alto medioevo (Settimane di studio del Centro italiano di studi sull'alto medioevo)*, pp. 299–366. Spoleto, 1969.
———. Review of Robert Carabie, *Propriété foncière*. *RHD*, 4th ser., 21 (1943): 102–6.
———. "Le 'Très Ancien Coutumier' de Normandie, miroir de la législation ducale? Contribution à l'étude de l'ordre public normand à la fin du XIIe siècle." *Tijdschrift voor Rechtsgeschiedenis* 39 (1971): 333–74.
Zimmermann, Michel. "Protocoles et préambules dans les documents catalans du Xe au XIIe siècle." *Mélanges de la Casa de Velasquez* 10 (1974): 41–76.

Index